MARKETING STRATEGY

MARKETING
STRATEGY

DR. PETER YANNOPOULOS, PH.D.
Brock University

THOMSON

NELSON

Australia   Canada   Mexico   Singapore   Spain   United Kingdom   United States

Marketing Strategy

by Peter Yannopoulos

Associate Vice President, Editorial Director:
Evelyn Veitch

Executive Editor:
Veronica Visentin

Senior Marketing Manager:
Charmaine Sherlock

Senior Developmental Editor:
Elke Price

Permissions Coordinator:
Terri Rothman

Copy Editor:
Wendy Thomas

Proofreader:
Liba Berry

Indexer:
Andrew Little

Production Coordinator:
Sharon Latta Paterson

Design Director:
Ken Phipps

Interior Design:
Tammy Gay

Cover Design:
Ken Phipps

Cover Image:
Daisuke Morita/Photodisc Red/Getty Images

Compositor:
ICC

Printer:
Transcontinental

Library and Archives Canada Cataloguing in Publication Data

Yannopoulos, Panayotis Peter, 1948–
Marketing strategy / Peter Yannopoulos.

Includes bibliographical references and index.
ISBN 0-17-641488-6

1. Marketing—Textbooks. 2. Marketing—Management—Textbooks. 3. Marketing—Case studies. I. Title.

HF5415.Y35 2005   658.8
C2005-906469-2

To my wife, Pat, and my daughters, Christiana and Natasha

Contents

Chapter 4   Competitive Advantage and Competitive Strategies   70

Chapter 5   Market Segmentation and Target Marketing   90

Chapter 8 Product Strategy   156

Chapter 9 Brand Strategy   184

Chapter 10   Pricing Strategy   210

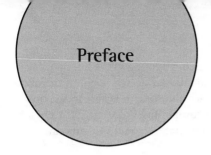

Preface

Marketing Strategy is a highly readable text that provides real solutions to real problems. The focus is on demonstrating strategic marketing decisions that managers working in small or large businesses need to make on a daily basis, instead of merely describing such marketing situations.

The book is well planned and straightforward, with a clear and easy-to-follow writing style. It provides students with the tools necessary to make strategic marketing decisions and it also provides the strategic framework students can use to think about the challenges without getting bogged down in a lot of tactical issues. It builds on concepts taught in other marketing courses but it doesn't dwell on them as it moves on to more strategic concepts.

Intended Audience

This book offers a solid text for capstone or elective marketing courses that focus on strategic issues. These courses are called Marketing Strategy, Strategic Marketing, Strategic Market Planning, Strategic Marketing Management, or Strategic Brand Management. They are taught at the undergraduate or second-year MBA level. The book is aimed at students with a foundation in basic marketing concepts. It builds on this knowledge and focuses on building effective marketing strategies. It also serves the needs of participants in executive development programs who need a practical, hands-on approach to the study of marketing strategy.

Strategic Marketing

Marketing Strategy includes a number of special features and pedagogical aids designed to reinforce the learning process. The set of materials provided to students enables them to master marketing strategy concepts so they can make sound strategic marketing decisions.

Canadian Focus

A unique and welcome feature of this text is its use of small, medium, and large Canadian corporations and well-known global companies operating in Canada in its numerous examples. It is important for students enrolled in marketing strategy courses at Canadian educational institutions to learn about the marketing practices of Canadian companies.

Cutting-Edge Topics

In addition to traditional marketing strategy topics, the text includes cutting-edge concepts such as triple bottom line, marketing convergence, strategic networks, data mining, supply-chain management, and the balanced scorecard. The chapter on customer relationship management is comprehensive and ties the concepts together with a customer value model. It gives practical tools on how to determine customer satisfaction levels and perceived benefits, and how to establish customer relationships. The discussion of Internet marketing is up-to-date and addresses the key issues relating to the Internet. The chapter is more than just a solid base upon which students can strategize about the use of this important marketing tool. It is a chapter in which the student is able to see how various elements of the Internet can be used to gain a competitive advantage. The chapter on defensive and offensive strategies provides several strategies that students can use as part of their firm's marketing strategy.

Cases

Most of the cases were written specifically for this text. The rest of the cases were reviewed carefully and selected personally by the author. The goal was to choose cases that were well written and focused on clear and important strategic marketing concepts. The cases used in this text are a good mix of small and large, manufacturing, services, retail, and high-tech Canadian companies. *See* Case Matrix on p. xxii.

A Real-World Approach

The text presents an excellent balance between theory and application. It reflects the experience of entrepreneurs and marketing managers. References are up-to-date and reflect current trends in marketing strategy. The use of metaphors allows the students to grasp concepts by relating them to familiar cognitive structures. It discusses tactics that are used extensively in the real world. It is filled with relevant examples that illustrate the concepts discussed in the text. Unlike other marketing strategy texts that focus only on large non-Canadian businesses, it uses examples of both Canadian and global small, entrepreneurial firms, as well as large, more established firms.

Key Features of the Text

Learning Objectives   Each chapter begins with a listing of the major topics of the chapter that indicate what the reader is expected to learn from the chapter.

Opening Vignettes   Each chapter begins with an opening vignette, which is a marketing strategy story related to the topics covered in the chapter. The purpose of the opening vignette is to illustrate some of the major concepts and provide students with a real-life perspective on the topic discussed in the chapter.

Strategy in Action Boxes   Strategy in Action boxed features are provided throughout the text to help students relate the material to an actual marketing situation and reinforce learning with practical examples.

Chapter Summaries   The chapter summaries provide point-by-point reviews to facilitate a comprehensive review of the chapter.

Review and Discussion Questions   Each chapter contains several end-of-chapter questions intended for review of the chapter material and to engage the student in all the key concepts of the chapter to reinforce learning. These questions are also useful to instructors as potential exam questions.

Critical Thinking and Application Questions   Critical thinking and application questions are asked at the end of the chapter to engage students in deeper thinking about the chapter material. These questions are useful suggestions to apply the chapter concepts in a practical manner. Their purpose is to get the student involved in the application of the concepts, which leads to a much better understanding of the chapter material. Critical thinking and application questions are useful for debate and discussion, assignments, and quizzes.

Key Terms   Definitions of key terms are provided in the margins to reinforce learning.

Ancillaries

The text is supported by an Instructor's Manual with course planning suggestions, answers to end-of-chapter questions and critical thinking and application questions, teaching notes for cases, and a selection of multiple choice, true/false, and discussion questions.

Acknowledgements

There are numerous individuals to whom I owe a debt of gratitude for their assistance in making this project a reality. In particular, I would like to thank Elke Price, Senior Developmental Editor; Ric Kitowski, Executive Editor; Veronica Visentin, Executive Editor; and Susan Calvert, Director, Editorial Production.

I also wish to thank the following instructors who participated in reviewing the manuscript and its original proposal. They provided encouragement, criticism, ideas, and enthusiasm, all at the right times.

Tammy Kiss
College of the Rockies

Marianne Marando
Seneca College of Applied Arts and Technology

Len Olszewski
St. Clair College

Terrance Power
Royal Roads University

Simon Pierre Segue
Athabasca University

Carolyn Sterenberg
Bissett School of Business, Mount Royal

William J. Wellington
University of Windsor

Brian Wrightson
Northern Alberta Institute of Technology

Angela Zigras
Seneca College

I would like to express my appreciation for the assistance of Dr. Nick Papadopoulos who wrote several cases for this book. I would also like to express my gratitude to the other case writers for generously giving us the right to use their cases.

#	Case Title	Time Period	Country	Manufacture/ Industrial	Service	Consumer Goods	High Tech	Food/ Retail	Social-Ethical Issues/ Non-Profit	Entrepre-neurial	Chapters
1	Spectrum Consulting International	2004	Canada		✓						1
2	Mobile Knowledge Inc.	2005	Canada	✓	✓		✓				2, 5
3	Steinhouse Knitting Mills (Canada) Ltd.	1999	Canada	✓		✓					1, 2, 3, 15
4	WestJet Airlines	2004	Canada		✓	✓					2, 3, 4, 5, 6, 14
5	Green Acres Seed Company	2001	Canada		✓						5, 10, 12
6	The Workabout: Developing & Introducing a New Product	2002	Canada	✓		✓				✓	8
7	Front 54	2003	Canada			✓		✓		✓	5, 7, 9
8	Bombardier Inc.	2004	Canada	✓			✓				8, 14
9	Atlas Chemical Company	2000	Canada		✓						8, 10
10	Hannas Seeds	2001	Canada		✓						11
11	A New Spirit for the New Age	2004	Canada	✓		✓					12
12	Tim Hortons	2004	Canada			✓		✓			3, 4, 5, 6, 7, 9, 15
13	AutoPlus Ltd.	2004	Canada		✓					✓	8, 10, 11, 12
14	Centre for the Arts	2004	Canada		✓				✓		12
15	Organ Transplant Centre	2003	Canada		✓				✓		5, 12
16	Boston Pizza International Inc.	2005	Canada			✓		✓			12
17	Nature-Plus Limited – US Expansion?	1998	Canada	✓		✓					2, 11
18	Research in Motion Ltd.	2005	Canada	✓	✓		✓				11, 13
19	Zeneca Ag Products	2001	Canada		✓						6, 8, 10, 11, 12, 15
20	Wal-Mart	2004	USA			✓		✓			5, 15

About the Author

Peter Yannopoulos is an Associate Professor at the Faculty of Business, Brock University, in St. Catharines, Ontario, where he teaches marketing strategy, marketing research, and management of high-growth organizations. He received his Ph.D. from the University of Toronto in the field of marketing. He is an accomplished researcher, instructor, and consultant to various organizations. He has a solid understanding of the barriers to understanding marketing strategy that many students face. Dr. Yannopoulos has published widely in various academic and professional journals and conference proceedings. His research interests are in the areas of marketing strategy, marketing research, small business marketing, and export marketing.

MARKETING STRATEGY

Chapter One

Strategic Marketing Planning and Market Orientation

The warrior who understands strategy will see many opportunities to win.

Miyamoto Musashi, A Book of Five Rings

Learning Objectives

After studying this chapter, you should be able to:

1. Identify the components of marketing strategy

2. Outline the role of the strategic marketing planning process in formulating and implementing effective marketing strategies

3. Describe the importance of market orientation for using strategic marketing planning effectively in developing sound marketing strategies

4. Explain how globalization, marketing convergence, and triple-bottom-line planning influence marketing strategy formulation

Cora's Strategy Is a Success

How can a newcomer succeed in the overcrowded restaurant industry where it must compete with giants such as McDonald's, Wendy's, and numerous others, each vying to satisfy people's dining-out needs? It seems that Cora's has found a way of doing that. Cora's is a Quebec-based restaurant chain founded by Cora Tsouflidou, a single mother of three from Gaspé, Quebec. Cora opened a snack bar in the city of St. Laurent in 1987, but after a few months converted it into a restaurant specializing in breakfast. The menu initially consisted of traditional breakfast items such as fruits, cheeses, cereals, omelettes, pancakes, and French toast. Based on customers' requests and suggestions, Cora came up with new breakfast and lunch ideas, incorporating many new trends in healthful eating, and added them to her traditional menu.

The superior breakfast and lunch offerings and friendly customer service made Cora's an instant success. The restaurant's reputation soon exceeded its capacity, and in February 1990 Cora's opened its second outlet in Laval, Montreal. The initial success of the first two stores proved the popularity of Cora's concept and led to many more store openings. Cora's soon became the queen of breakfast in Quebec. In April 1994, Cora's opened its first franchise after the company realized that expansion through franchising was the best way to accomplish its growth plans. Franchising would also be the strategy to build a strong image and dominate the Quebec market. Today, Cora's operates 60 outlets employing over 1,500 employees in various provinces across the country. More than 150,000 customers visit Cora's each week.

Cora's vision is to be the leader in breakfast service in an environment that stresses value and excellent service to the customer. Today, Cora's specializes in offering one of the most original and complete menus anywhere. Its menu is so extensive that crepes, for example, are prepared and served in countless ways in batters ranging from white to whole wheat to buckwheat. The decor, atmosphere, and environment are comfortable, friendly, clean, and inviting. Employees pride themselves in being able to offer home-cooked meals to make customers feel as if they were eating at home.

Cora's, as part of its contribution to local communities, established Cora's Foundation to provide help for needy young children. The foundation makes donations to community organizations that work with schools. Cora's group believes that feeding today's needy children contributes to improving their quality of life. The foundation raises money by holding an annual golf tournament that takes place on the first Tuesday of every June.

The decision to offer breakfast and lunch service of superior value draws customers to Cora's in droves. It is not unusual to encounter long lines of customers on weekends waiting patiently for their turn to be served—the restaurants are so busy on weekends that they don't take reservations. The company's success can be attributed to its decision to target the breakfast segment of the restaurant industry and to a strong market orientation that focuses on delighting customers with original and high-quality meals, served in a warm family-style atmosphere. Effectively employing strategic marketing planning concepts enabled Cora's to identify and capitalize on attractive market opportunities, and a strong commitment to customer satisfaction and a superior understanding of customer needs helped the company rise to its current leadership position in the breakfast industry in Canada. Using strategic marketing planning and a strongly held market orientation, Cora's was able to match its resources and capabilities with external opportunities and design effective customer-oriented marketing strategies.[1]

Introduction

Cora's story shows the importance of strategic marketing planning and market orientation to achieve market success. Cora's used many elements of the strategic marketing planning process in developing its marketing strategy by demonstrating a cunning ability to recognize and capitalize on important market opportunities. Cora's success also demonstrated that having strong marketing capabilities is especially crucial as the advent of the 21st century continues to bring new challenges to commercial organizations. Competition continues to intensify, as new competitors emerge, bringing new ways of competing, threatening established competitors, and creating new industries.

Maintaining an advantage in the marketplace has never been more challenging. The increased competition in recent years has led to price pressures and lower barriers to market entry as rivals find new ways of circumventing these barriers. Customers are also becoming more difficult to please, as their expectations of quality and value rise. Rapid imitation and rapid diffusion of innovations have minimized differences among products or services. Competitive advantages such as low cost, new technologies, and higher quality are not sustainable. These high-velocity environments have been called **hypercompetitive**[2] to describe the rapid pace of change that is occurring. Markets become hypercompetitive because of strategic manoeuvring by innovative companies, radical new technologies, low-cost foreign labour, and new forms of competition. Hypercompetition is often the result of escalating price-quality competition, efforts to establish first-mover advantages, and attempts to invade or protect established products or markets.

Hypercompetition is characterized by consistent change and disequilibrium, short product life cycles and new product designs, new technologies, frequent positioning changes by established firms, and dramatic redefinitions of market boundaries. These rapid changes and aggressive moves by innovative competitors who enter markets unexpectedly neutralize the advantages of the large incumbent firms. By using new product designs and manufacturing technologies, nimble firms erode the competitive advantages of incumbent firms and overcome existing barriers to entry. For this reason, most competitive advantages in these environments are unsustainable. As a result, companies must strive to disrupt their own advantages as well as the advantages of competitors. Firms that cling to their current advantages are in danger as rivals erode these advantages.

The ongoing change and associated problems make it extremely challenging to successfully manage today's business organizations. Many firms that were highly successful in the past have found it difficult to survive in today's turbulent market environments. These firms suffered huge market share losses and in an effort to survive have merged with or been acquired by other companies. Well-known companies such as Air Canada, IBM, Kmart, and General Motors have had great difficulty maintaining their market positions, while other firms such as Chrysler and Compaq have been acquired by other companies—in our example, by Daimler and Hewlett-Packard respectively.

On the other hand, many other firms have been able to cope successfully with environmental change and have improved their market position by taking advantage of opportunities and minimizing the threats generated by the external environment. For example, Research in Motion, a Waterloo-based high-technology firm, has been able to capitalize on wireless technology, enabling it to compete successfully against other powerful companies such as Palm and Motorola. Through the development of integrated hardware, software, and services that support multiple wireless networks standards, Research in Motion provides access to time-sensitive information including e-mail, phone, SMS messaging, Internet, and intra-based applications.

In order for firms to succeed in today's fast-changing business environment, they need to develop and implement effective marketing strategies that enable them to cope with environmental changes and satisfy customers with products of superior value. Firms

Hypercompetitive business environments are rapidly changing business environments in which competitive advantages such as low cost, new technologies, and higher-quality products are not sustainable.

need a high degree of market orientation to develop superior marketing strategies. Market-oriented firms are better attuned to their environment and exhibit a higher focus on their consumers and competitors. They are characterized by an externally oriented culture that focuses on providing customers with superior quality and value. Such companies have a better chance of survival in this ever-changing environment, with their keen understanding of markets, ability to respond to attractive emerging opportunities, and the creation of new competitive advantages and customer relationships with loyal customers.

This chapter first defines marketing strategy and discusses its different components. It then provides a framework that will help managers with their strategic marketing planning in order to develop customer-oriented marketing strategies. It then discusses the role of marketing orientation in making strategic planning more effective. Next, it discusses the challenges posed to marketing managers by a number of developments such as globalization, marketing convergence, and triple-bottom-line planning. Finally, it includes an outline of a marketing plan to help readers write their own marketing plans.

Marketing Strategy as a Means of Creating Customer Value

Strategy comes from the Greek word *strategia*, which means "the art of the general." The word *strategy* is used in many different fields. For example, one can talk about legal strategy, election strategy, financial strategy, or marketing strategy. **Marketing strategy** is a plan to satisfy valuable customers in a superior way. Companies succeed when they create value for their customers. Customer value is created when the benefits customers receive from a product exceed the cost they incur to acquire and use the product. Offering superior value leads to higher customer satisfaction and enables the company to retain customers. Firms use their assets and capabilities to offer products and services that are superior to those offered by competitors to targeted customer segments. Customers are satisfied when the product performance exceeds their expectations.

> **Marketing strategy** is a plan to satisfy valuable customers in a superior way.

Designing a marketing strategy involves more than offering a superior product or service to customers, however. In fact, a marketing strategy involves making choices about which customers will be targeted, which positioning strategy will be adopted, which products or brands will be offered, what price levels will be chosen, which channels of distribution will be utilized, and which promotional approach will be used to achieve the marketing objectives of the organization. The components of a marketing strategy are listed in Figure 1.1.

Figure 1.1	The Components of Marketing Strategy

- Market segment strategy
- Positioning strategy
- Product strategy
- Pricing strategy
- Distribution strategy
- Promotion strategy

Determining the marketing strategy involves choosing a certain course of action and rejecting other alternatives after careful consideration. The objective is to focus on those marketing strategies that are more in line with the organizational goals and capabilities. According to Day, "The art of strategy formulation lies in putting together the best arrangements of skills and resources to enhance their combined effectiveness and to ensure that the position being staked out can be attained and defended. If the requisite capabilities cannot be acquired or developed, then management is forced to ask what position can be attained with the available skills and resources."[3]

Failure to implement a carefully selected marketing strategy will lead to lack of strategic direction. All firms, even the largest ones, have limited financial, human, physical, and other resources. Organizations that avoid making hard choices and pursue several courses of action simultaneously will spread their resources thinly over too many markets, and they will be unable to pursue any one of them with adequate resources. Many successful firms start out highly focused on a product or market. Over time, some of these companies introduce too many products or enter too many unrelated markets. As a result, they become unfocused and lose their sense of direction.

At the same time, a balance is needed: successful marketing strategies should not remain static, as this would inhibit innovation and creativity. When the environment changes, the marketing strategy normally has to change to remain relevant and in tune with the new environment. The choice of which marketing strategy to pursue depends on how management interprets trends, events, developments, and the new direction the environment will take. Marketing managers must remain vigilant and maintain a certain degree of flexibility, in case their understanding of the environment proves inaccurate, to quickly make the necessary adjustments to the marketing strategy. Frequent changes, however, cause customers and the organization itself to become confused.[4] Ideally, marketing strategies change only when the firm needs to respond to environmental trends or forces.

The Strategic Marketing Planning Process

The **strategic marketing planning** process provides the framework that integrates the various marketing activities involved in developing and executing the marketing strategy for a product or service.

Firms need to follow a systematic process for developing and implementing marketing strategies. The **strategic marketing planning** process provides the framework that integrates the various marketing activities involved in developing and executing the marketing strategy for a product or service. By embarking on the strategic marketing planning process, a firm is looking to design effective customer-oriented marketing strategies. The outcome of the strategic marketing planning process is the development of an effective and implementable marketing plan (see Appendix 1.1).

Before we proceed with the discussion of the strategic marketing planning process, we need to make a distinction between strategies and tactics. Strategies refer to the overall plan designed to accomplish the firm's objectives. Tactics, on the other hand, are the specific ways in which the strategy is being implemented. This chapter presents an integrated strategic marketing planning process to help marketing managers develop and implement effective marketing strategies. The marketing activities carried out by a firm can be represented as different steps in the strategic marketing planning process, as shown in Figure 1.2. The process is described in the next section.

Corporate Vision, Mission, and Goals

The corporate vision, mission, and goals are used to provide direction and to express what the organization hopes to achieve in its chosen market. They are determined by top management and serve as guidelines in the development of the firm's marketing strategy. Marketing's role is to identify market opportunities that are consistent with the corporate vision and mission and help achieve the goals of the organization.

The **corporate vision** is a mental image of a desirable future state of an organization.

Corporate Vision. The corporate vision is a mental image of a desirable future state of an organization.[5] It reflects management's intentions about where it wants to be in the future and provides a sense of direction. Visions reflect a future state for the company

Figure 1.2 | The Strategic Marketing Planning Process

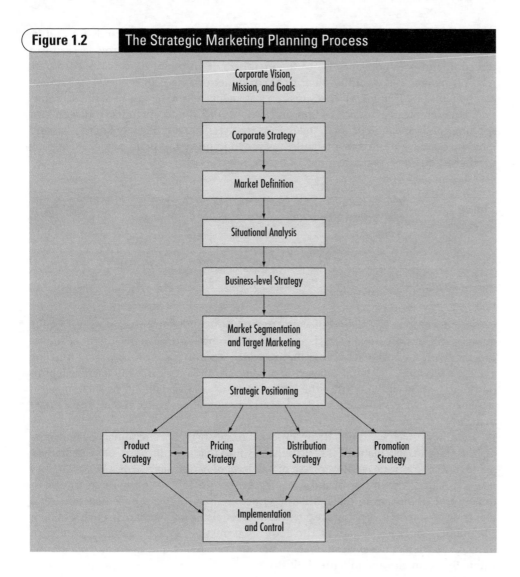

that is better than its current position. As such, visions are more like broad-based goals rather than a way of behaving, which is the essence of mission.[6] Once the vision has been accomplished by reaching the desirable future state, its power to motivate and provide direction is lost. At this point, the company needs to articulate a new vision.

Effective visions must be informed, grounded in reality, shared, and incorporate a strategic intent.[7] **Strategic intent** is a vision to win and implies that a competitive spirit must permeate the entire organization.[8] It is often stated as an ambition to achieve a leadership position in the marketplace. For example, Molson Coors' strategic intent "is to become and remain one of the top performing beer companies in the world."[9] Strategic intent requires firms to set stretch goals, which are highly ambitious aims whose fulfillment extends beyond their current capabilities. These stretch goals can be satisfied only with radical rather than incremental increases in performance. For companies with a strategic intent and stretch goals, strategy is about both the deployment of resources to exploit opportunities in the short term and the development of resources, to take advantage of challenging opportunities in the long term.

Strategic intent is a vision to win and implies that a competitive spirit must permeate the entire organization.

The **corporate mission** identifies what the firm stands for and its operating philosophy.

Corporate Mission. The corporate mission identifies what the firm stands for and its operating philosophy. Corporate missions are important because they provide a sense of direction and common purpose to the members of an organization. The corporate mission statement is a multidimensional consumer-oriented concept that has several components (see Figure 1.3). First, mission statements reflect the values of the organization. For example, the mission of Sporting Life, one of Toronto's premier retail stores for sporting goods and athletic wear, states, "We are a retailer with passion, knowledge, and integrity & are committed to a relentless desire to improve our performance in creating the highest quality experience for all our customers & staff."[10]

Figure 1.3	The Components of Corporate Mission

- It reflects the values of the organization.
- It reflects the true purpose of the business.
- It includes the policies and operational standards of the organization.
- It includes the firm's competitive position and competitive advantage.

Second, corporate missions reflect the true purpose of the business by answering the question of why the company exists and what it is doing to pursue its vision of the future. Together with the corporate vision, they provide direction for the business by focusing attention on doing the things needed to accomplish the mission, while taking steps to pursue the vision of the future—the firm's long-term strategic intent. As such, mission statements provide managers with the necessary guidelines to formulate appropriate marketing strategies.

Some companies assert that their purpose is to satisfy their shareholders by maximizing their wealth. But many of these companies find that maximization of shareholders' wealth fails to motivate employees to a higher level of performance. For this reason, they take a broader view of organizational purpose, by incorporating the interests of customers and employees in their mission. Other companies include in their mission a higher ideal, such as protecting the environment or raising the standards of living in their community. For example, part of The Body Shop mission is "to passionately campaign for the protection of the environment, human and civil rights, and against animal testing within the cosmetics and toiletries industry."[11]

Third, many mission statements include the policies and operational standards that help employees decide what is acceptable behaviour in their organization. Policies and operational standards refer to the company's views on product quality, customer service, supplier selection, and other important operational aspects. These are often reflected in expressions such as "Our customers come first," or "We will not be undersold." Lastly, many mission statements often include the competitive position the firm holds in the business and the competitive advantage that helps it compete effectively. For example, Federal Express's mission is to offer reliable and competitively superior global air-ground transportation. Figure 1.4 shows examples of mission statements of several organizations that incorporate many of these components.

Corporate goals are broad, overall aims set by management.

Corporate Goals. Corporate goals are broad, overall aims set by management. They can take the form of performance indicators such as profitability, market share, or more general aims such as being more market oriented and more responsive to the changing needs of customers. Goals state what is to be achieved in the medium to long term. Once the broad corporate goals are determined, every functional area—finance, production, marketing, and other functions—sets its own specific objectives. Functional objectives are annual targets designed to fulfill the organization's long-term goals.

Figure 1.4 Sample Mission Statements

Bombardier Inc.

Our mission is to be the world's leading manufacturer of planes and trains. We are committed to providing superior value and service to our customers and sustained profitability to our shareholders by investing in our people and products. We lead through innovation and outstanding product safety, efficiency and performance. Our standards are high. We define excellence—and we deliver.

Federal Express

To produce outstanding financial returns by providing totally reliable, competitively superior global air-ground transportation of high priority goods and documents that require rapid, time-sensitive delivery.

PepsiCo

We will be an outstanding company by exceeding customer expectations through empowered people, guided by shared values.

Alcoa

Alcoa is a growing worldwide company dedicated to excellence through quality—creating value for customers, employees, and shareholders through innovation technology and operational expertise. Alcoa will be the best aluminum company in the world and a leader in the industries in which we choose to compete.

Corporate Strategy

Corporate strategy helps provide the means of integrating and utilizing corporate resources in the areas of research and development, human resources, finance, production, marketing, and information technology, to achieve the firm's vision, mission, and goals. The primary focus of corporate strategy is to determine the organization's scope and how to allocate its resources across the various businesses. Some of the questions corporate strategists attempt to answer include the following: What businesses are we in? What businesses should we be in? How should we allocate our scarce resources over our different businesses? For example, Bell Canada's decision in 2004 to acquire Toronto-based Infostream Technologies represented a corporate-level strategy decision to enter the data storage business. Such a decision necessitated the allocation of cash, marketing, and engineering resources to help Infostream maintain its rapid growth.

Market Definition and Situational Analysis

As we saw in the previous section, corporate strategy determines the number of different businesses the firm is going to compete in. Once the corporate strategy is determined and the businesses in which the firm is going to participate are decided, the organization needs to define the strategic and served market(s) in which it is going to compete. Identifying the strategic market—consisting of current and future markets—is essential for setting the parameters for future decisions. The strategic market defines the arena for conducting the situational analysis and the search for environmental opportunities and threats. Once the market is defined, firms can track competitive activity and market trends. The served market is the market in which the organization is currently competing for customers. The process of defining strategic and served markets and the issues associated with them are discussed in Chapter 2.

After defining its market, the firm is able to conduct the situational analysis. This is an important step in developing an effective marketing strategy. An important objective of the situational analysis is to construct the preliminary and final SWOT (strengths, weaknesses, opportunities, and threats), which helps a firm assess the existing strategic fit between a firm's resources and its external environment. The degree of strategic fit determines how much strategic change is required. A close fit will necessitate very little strategic change and vice versa. The process of conducting a situational analysis is discussed in Chapter 3.

Business-Level Strategy

Business-level strategies encompass the company's overall competitive posture, its distinctive competencies, and the competitive strategy it pursues to capitalize on these capabilities. Competitive strategies shape the formulation of the functional area strategies (marketing, finance, production, human resources, and research and development) to carry out the organization's mission, vision, and goals.

Firms with a competitive advantage can achieve top performance in areas that are important to their target customers. Competitive advantages result from superior organizational resources and capabilities. **Resources** are assets owned by the firm such as plants, equipment, capital, brand image, and customer relationships. **Capabilities** are skills, technologies, and knowledge that are embedded in organizational processes and enable the firm's assets to be deployed profitably.

Our understanding of how firms create and sustain competitive advantages can be aided by the so-called resource-based view of the firm. This view asserts that organizations are unique bundles of resources and capabilities that are used to achieve a competitive advantage. Resources that are better than those of competitors can become the basis for competitive advantage. Differences in resource endowments—the resources and capabilities owned by a firm—account for differences in performance.

A firm's unique capabilities need to be matched with an appropriate competitive strategy that reflects how the organization will compete in its market segment. Competitive strategies represent the specific way in which managers leverage the organization's distinctive competencies to offer outstanding value to their customers. Competitive advantage and competitive strategies are discussed in detail in Chapter 4.

Marketing Strategy Development

The situational analysis and assessment of the firm's competitive advantages are followed by the development of marketing strategy. Marketing strategy consists of the target segments, strategic positioning in the segments, and the specification of the marketing mix. Once marketing opportunities have been identified, the firm segments the market into distinct, homogeneous groups. Choosing which customers to serve is one of the most significant decisions a firm must make. Market segmentation and target marketing are discussed in Chapter 5.

Once a firm has selected the segments to target, it needs to find a position for the product in the segment. Correct positioning is essential to the success of the marketing effort. While market segmentation is about who the customer is, positioning entails how the company is going to compete in the chosen segment to offer extraordinary

Resources are assets owned by the firm such as plants, equipment, capital, brand image, and customer relationships.

Capabilities are skills, technologies, and knowledge that are embedded in organizational processes and enable the firm's assets to be deployed profitably.

value to customers and achieve superior performance. Strategic positioning forms the basis from which all aspects of the marketing mix are developed. In order for the firm to reach maximum success in the marketplace, all its marketing mix activities, including product, price, distribution, and promotion, must be consistent with its desired position. Strategic positioning also affects decisions made throughout the organization whether in areas such as research and development, hiring, training, or location selection. Strategic positioning issues are discussed in Chapter 6.

Once the positioning strategy is decided on, a marketing mix tailored to the characteristics of the segment is created. Effective marketing strategy involves designing an optimal combination of marketing mix elements for each product to support its positioning strategy. Decisions need to be made about the products offered, pricing levels established, distribution channels used, and promotional efforts undertaken. The elements of the marketing mix are examined in the following chapters: product strategies are discussed in Chapter 8; brand strategies are explored in Chapter 9; Chapter 10 covers the strategic aspects of pricing; distribution decisions are studied in Chapter 11; Chapter 12 examines issues related to integrated marketing communications, including advertising, personal selling, public relations, and sales promotion strategies; Chapter 13 covers Internet marketing; Chapter 14 discusses defensive and offensive marketing strategies.

Implementation and Control

The discussion of strategic marketing planning up to this point has been about the development of effective marketing strategies. Implementation is the stage at which the marketing strategy is carried out. It is not enough for a firm to simply develop a cohesive marketing plan; effective implementation of the plan is also required. While executing its marketing plan, the firm must put control measures in place to assess the effectiveness of its implementation efforts. Controls are needed to monitor progress and to ensure the company is achieving its marketing objectives. Chapter 15 discusses implementation and control issues.

Competing on the Edge

The strategic marketing planning process discussed in the previous section assumes that marketing managers use the process in a linear fashion by implementing each step before moving to the next. Such an approach is practical only in environments that are either stable or changing in a highly predictable fashion. However, as we discussed in the introduction to this chapter, many industries are characterized by rapid change and are highly unpredictable. This poses the question of how firms should go about formulating their marketing strategies in such hypercompetitive environments. According to two strategy researchers, Shona Brown and Kathleen Eisenhardt, for firms to succeed in such environments they need to use strategies that involve creating a continuous stream of competitive advantages that, if taken together, form a strategic direction.[12] A central aspect of this approach and one that is key to superior performance is the ability to change. Firms that do well are those that have the ability and willingness to change and reinvent themselves constantly over time.

Competing on the edge means taking action, observing what happens, and adopting the course of action that seems to work best. Such an approach to strategy is unpredictable, uncontrollable, and even inefficient but it is necessary given that the linear approach to developing strategies rarely works in fast-changing environments.

Competing on the edge means taking action, observing what happens, and adopting the course of action that seems to work best.

This approach to strategy development assumes that planning is not working very well as the future is too uncertain to forecast with any degree of accuracy. Competing on the edge assumes that industries have no clear boundaries and have no predictable competitors or that trends and patterns cannot be predicted with certainty. Competing on the edge implies that strategy is the result of perpetual organizational change that, in turn, causes a semi-coherent strategic direction to emerge.

Competing on the edge also implies that strategy development in the short term is a very inefficient process. It is about making errors, duplication, and eventually adopting the course of action that works. It is not about a close fit between firm resources and the external environment but using change to continuously reinvent the business through the ongoing search for new competitive advantages.

Deliberate Versus Emergent Strategies

Deliberate strategies are developed following a formal planning approach.

Emergent describes informal, bottom-up strategies that occur as a result of responses to customer requests, manufacturing problems, competitive threats, and technological advances that offer opportunities for creating new products or exploiting new markets.

The concepts of hypercompetition and competing on the edge imply that not all strategies are developed following a rational, deliberate process similar to the one implied by the strategic marketing planning process discussed earlier. According to Mintzberg and McGugh,[13] many strategies are deliberate but there are others that are emergent and not the result of a formal process. **Deliberate** strategies are developed following a formal planning approach. **Emergent** describes informal, bottom-up strategies that occur as a result of responses to customer requests, manufacturing problems, competitive threats, and technological advances that offer opportunities for creating new products or exploiting new markets.

Marketing strategies are often the outcome of both deliberate and emergent strategies. Deliberate strategies are used because they represent the best response to current and anticipated environmental trends and forces. Formal planning of some sort is needed to ensure that the various parts of the strategy fit together. Such formal planning is also needed to ensure that the various strategies of individual functional units or departments are coordinated and consistent with the overall goals and direction of the organization. In addition, during the course of business new strategies emerge that are not the result of a formal process. These emergent strategies are then incorporated into the strategies formulated during the formal planning process.

While it is important for all firms to undergo formal planning exercises on a regular basis, certain difficulties are associated with such approaches. One issue related to the deliberate approach is that top managers are often removed from everyday operations and lack the detailed knowledge of customers, competitors, and other market factors. Very often the strategies developed through a formal planning process are modified to some degree during their implementation.

Emergent strategies pose risks for organizations, too, as they can lead to a less than optimal marketing strategy. Emergent strategies are typically developed in an ad hoc fashion and often reflect the preferences of the managers involved. It is known that managers make decisions and pursue courses of action consistent with their own professional orientation, background, and personal preferences that may or may not be consistent with organizational goals.[14] Therefore, firms that rely exclusively on emergent strategies often introduce changes that are inconsistent with their mission and organizational goals.

Despite their shortcomings, successful emergent strategies can evolve spontaneously from actions of individuals anywhere in the organization. Marketing managers have a responsibility to deal with emergent strategies as they arise and foster those strategies that are consistent with the overarching vision, mission, and goals of the organization. Oftentimes, the emergent strategies are more significant, and have a much greater impact, than the strategies developed through formal planning. Successful organizations are those that effectively implement both deliberate and emergent strategies.

Strategic Marketing Planning in Market-Oriented Firms

In order to succeed in ever-changing, complex marketing environments, firms need to possess a high degree of market orientation. **Market orientation** is the type of organizational environment that encourages the behaviours needed for dealing with fast-changing and unpredictable environments and for the creation of effective marketing strategies. In fact, market orientation has been the cornerstone of marketing thought and practice for the past several decades. Market-oriented firms have excellent strategic marketing planning skills and are characterized by a strong external orientation. Such firms are in tune with customer requirements, competitors' strategies, emerging technologies, and new environmental trends. These qualities enable market-oriented firms to make a more effective use of the strategic planning process and formulate more realistic and implementable marketing strategies.

Market-oriented firms outperform their competitors.[15] Because they are in tune with customer needs they offer top-notch customer value, for which they can charge higher prices. They have loyal customers, which usually means they are more profitable for the firm and are easier to retain. Market-oriented firms can preempt competitors by tapping the best opportunities before them. Market orientation is a three-prong concept encompassing customer orientation, competitor orientation, and interfunctional coordination.[16] Figure 1.5 shows a number of characteristics that firms can use to assess their own market orientation.[17]

> **Market orientation** is the type of organizational environment that encourages the behaviours needed for the creation of superior customer value such as a strong external orientation, especially toward customers and competitors, and a superior interfunctional coordination.

Figure 1.5	Market Orientation Characteristics

Customer orientation

Has an intimate knowledge of customer needs
Strongly committed to customer
Creates excellent value for customer
Has superior market-sensing capabilities
Develops customer relationships with valuable customers
Segments markets and chooses the most attractive segments

Competitor orientation

Knows direct and indirect competitors
Monitors competitor activity
Regularly analyzes competitors' strategies
Benchmarks performance against competitors
Responds rapidly to competitors' actions

Interfunctional coordination

Regularly collects market information
Shares market information among functions
Ensures all functions contribute to meeting customer needs
Sees there is a strong coordination of all functions

Customer Orientation

A firm with a **customer orientation** has an ability to understand and satisfy customers. Market-oriented firms stay close to their customers and ahead of their competitors. They listen to the market and keep improving their products. Such firms know their customers well and emphasize the attributes customers value most. They try not only to satisfy

> **Customer orientation** is an ability to understand and satisfy customers.

customers but to create loyal customers and long-term relationships with their best customers. The best marketing companies demonstrate an ability to understand, attract, and keep valuable customers.[18]

The thorough customer knowledge associated with a higher customer orientation enables firms to develop superior marketing strategies. Customer-driven firms segment their markets and choose the most attractive customers. They have the discipline to focus only on the markets they have decided to serve and not try to be all things to all people. Customer-oriented firms recognize that a segment's profit potential differs for different companies; this potential depends on the segment's inherent attractiveness and how the company's capabilities match the segment requirements.

To achieve a high degree of market orientation, a firm needs a culture that is externally oriented. This external orientation allows firms to anticipate market changes and align the marketing strategy to the market and customer needs. Market-driven organizations have keen market-sensing and market-relating capabilities that give them the market knowledge to create and maintain close relationships with valuable customers. The result is a better alignment of the marketing strategy with the market. In contrast, firms dominated by product-driven cultures are typically unresponsive to customer concerns.

Competitor Orientation

Competitor orientation
describes a firm that wants
to understand its direct
and indirect rivals, their
strategies, objectives,
market position, and
strengths and weaknesses.

Competitor orientation describes a firm that wants to understand its direct and indirect rivals, their strategies, objectives, market position, and strengths and weaknesses. This understanding is a necessary condition for creating value that is better than its competitors'. A firm needs to know who its direct and indirect competitors are. Being aware of both types of competitors is necessary, as many of the threats to a firm may come not from direct competitors, who are readily known, but from indirect rivals and from firms outside the industry. For example, a serious threat to steel companies is not only traditional steel manufacturers but also plastics manufacturers.

Market-oriented firms are paranoid about their competitors and very aggressive in dealing with them. They benchmark their performance against the best of their competitors. Competitor-focused firms use signalling to discourage potential rivals from entering their markets—that is, they counter competitors' moves before rivals become large enough to put up a credible fight. Market-oriented firms continually search for new advantages. Although competitive advantages erode over time, this continual search allows them to maintain their competitive position.

Strategic interdependence
is a situation in which the
outcome of a firm's strategy
depends not only on the
strategy it chooses, but also
on the strategy chosen by
its rivals.

A competitor orientation is necessary because relationships among most competing firms are characterized by a great deal of strategic interdependence. **Strategic interdependence** is a situation in which the outcome of a firm's strategy depends not only on the strategy it chooses, but also on the strategy chosen by its rivals. When a firm makes a move to obtain an advantageous position, rivals often respond quickly with a countermove. The countermove may negate the impact of the initial move, and the firm making the first move could end up worse off. Due to this mutual interdependence, firms that strive to satisfy market needs with appropriate products are frequently frustrated. While a firm may invest in improving the quality of its products or lowering its costs, competitors also may aggressively invest in improving their product quality and costs.

Firms must be aware of the possible moves and countermoves of direct and indirect competitors and adjust their marketing plans to reflect these actions. In thinking about competitor reaction, marketers must ask questions such as the following: If we increase our advertising budget, will competitors also increase their advertising spending? If the firm's strategy involves a price cut, how will competitors react? Will they also cut their price?

The ongoing battle between McDonald's, Burger King, and Wendy's illustrates this process of strategic interaction. In 2001, in response to declining sales, Wendy's began offering certain menu items at rock-bottom prices. McDonald's and Burger King also cut their prices across the board in response to Wendy's low prices and in an effort to increase their sales, which were also sagging. In addition, given the trend toward healthier eating, the two burger giants introduced quality salads as a healthier alternative to beef and french fries. This move brought McDonald's and Burger King closer to the menu offered by Wendy's and to a degree closed the quality gap that existed among the three companies.

Interfunctional Coordination

Interfunctional coordination occurs when different organizational functions coordinate their efforts and resources to create improved customer value. Market orientation requires a good deal of market information.[19] It includes understanding and satisfying current needs, anticipating future customer needs, and taking actions to fulfill them. Also, market-focused companies have a thorough knowledge of how environmental factors such as competition, government regulation, and demographics influence customer needs.

Interfunctional coordination occurs when different organizational functions coordinate their efforts and resources to create improved customer value.

All the information obtained from customers, competitors, and other market players together with environmental trends and changes should be allowed to permeate throughout the organization and reach all those who are involved in the development and marketing of the products and services. Sharing this knowledge with product designers, engineers, manufacturing, service, and field sales personnel enables the different functional areas to work better together and be more effective.

Market orientation requires the participation of practically all organizational functions. Marketing is a business for everyone in the company and not just professional marketing specialists. Marketers, designers, engineers, top managers, and every employee should be involved in marketing. This makes the existence of a strong interfunctional coordination necessary to ensure that all functions work together well.

Major Trends Affecting Marketing Strategy Formulation

As suggested in the introduction to this chapter, the business landscape is currently undergoing a number of dramatic changes that make strategic marketing planning especially challenging. Changes in technologies, consumer tastes and preferences, and competition are occurring faster than ever before. In rapidly changing markets such as computer software and microchips, product life cycles as short as six months are common. Methods of dealing with rapidly changing environments were discussed earlier in the context of hypercompetition and competing on the edge strategies. In addition, marketing managers must deal with several trends that influence their efforts at formulating marketing strategy. These influences include globalization, marketing convergence, and triple bottom line, as shown in Figure 1.6.

Figure 1.6   Major Influences on Marketing Strategy Formulation

Major Influences on Marketing Strategy Formulation

Globalization   Marketing Convergence   Triple Bottom Line

Globalization

The globalization of markets and business activity is a powerful force shaping markets around the world. One of the most important reasons for its emergence is the lessening of barriers to trade in past years, as countries have lowered tariffs, quotas, and other similar trade barriers. For example, the average tariff on manufactured goods has declined from around 40 percent to under 4 percent in the past 50 years.[20] Regulations prohibiting foreign companies from acquiring domestic companies and making a direct investment have been drastically reduced or eliminated. All these changes have created both opportunities and threats for companies, as they are no longer protected by trade barriers.

The rise in the standard of living in many countries around the world allows consumers in those countries to afford products made in other countries. For example, the rise in living standards in China has led to an increase in demand for foreign goods such as cars and foreign foods. Differences in national tastes and preferences have diminished due to more frequent travel and exposure to global media such as CNN, *New York Times*, and *Time* magazine.[21] This homogenization of the world's wants has resulted in the demand for the same standardized products such as chemicals, pharmaceuticals, autos, and steel, causing the emergence of global markets for these products.[22] These markets allow for large economies of scale in production, marketing, and distribution.

In addition, the amount of foreign investment has increased as companies take advantage of lower trade barriers and invest heavily in production facilities in foreign countries. Foreign direct investment allows companies to benefit from differences in the cost and quality of labour and capital, which in turn lets companies lower costs. Global companies such as Nortel, Magna International, and Nestlé have expanded operations into other countries to capitalize on the opportunities provided by lower costs of labour and capital.

Many companies have expanded into foreign countries as a means of maintaining their sales growth rates as their markets at home have become saturated. Still others have turned to foreign producers by outsourcing the manufacturing of the products to offshore suppliers while maintaining the marketing and managerial part of their operations at home.

All these factors have contributed to the globalization of markets and business activities as companies are scrambling to find ways of getting involved in international markets. Also, globalization has resulted in a dramatic increase in the volume of goods and services traded internationally. The implications of globalization for marketers can be summarized as follows:[23]

- Markets have been broadened and they are no longer national but have become global in scope. This change has increased the threat of entry and the competitive intensity in home-country markets, which are coming under attack by foreign competitors seeking growth opportunities. For example, Canadian home improvement centres such as RONA and the Building Box have felt the effect of U.S. home improvement giant Home Depot moving into their territory. It's clear that managers need to take foreign competitors into account when they prepare their marketing plans.
- The greatly concentrated national markets now become parts of highly fragmented global markets. Companies no longer dominate these global markets the same way they did their home markets as they now face strong competition from other countries. The exposure to more competition forces companies to compete hard to maintain their position in global markets. This pressure causes prices and profits to fall, leading companies to restructure or downsize in an effort to lower costs and become more competitive.

- The heightened competitive conditions often lead companies to intensify their innovation efforts in order to gain an advantage over competitors. This challenge has resulted in shorter product development cycles and life cycles.
- Lastly, although globalization has created threats, it has equally created opportunities for companies in markets around the world. For example, investments by North American, European, and Japanese firms have accelerated in China and Eastern European countries as companies try to capitalize on investment opportunities in those regions.

In moving from domestic to international markets, managers need to develop new capabilities and acquire new knowledge. Managers must learn about new cultures and business practices. In formulating their marketing strategies, managers must determine which products and services to offer in the various countries and how much to adjust their marketing mix to the needs and requirements of the local markets.

Marketing Convergence

One of the most significant changes that have occurred in the last decade is the rise of the Internet as an indispensable tool in marketing strategy. The increased importance of the Internet in the formulation of a business's marketing strategy has led to what has been called marketing convergence.[24] **Marketing convergence** is the integration of different technologies, such as television, computers, wireless phones, traditional stores, direct mail, catalogues, and the Internet into one coherent marketing and communication strategy.

E-commerce has also brought about a convergence of the traditional consumer with the new cyber-consumer.[25] Consumers buy products or services from many channels, everywhere from traditional stores to the Internet, as they become comfortable shopping online. They are combining various approaches such as searching offline to purchase online or searching online to purchase from a store. Others research catalogues and buy online or research online but buy over the phone.

These changes pose significant challenges for marketing managers who must understand what these developments mean for marketing strategy. To better satisfy the needs of the increasingly flexible consumer, firms need to merge their own approaches by combining old and new, online and offline strategies. They need to find the best way of integrating interactive media with traditional promotion and selling methods, such as advertising, direct mail, catalogues, and retail stores. The companies that better understand how to deal with these new challenges stand to benefit the most as they find new ways to connect with consumers. Even companies that have built their reputations and business on the old bricks-and-mortar model are combining that strategy with an online presence.

In the era of marketing convergence, it is important to point out that new e-commerce technologies do not replace the old but they converge by existing side by side. Marketing convergence integrates both, e-commerce and the traditional way of doing business, into a holistic view of both consumers and businesses. Most marketers have realized that the Internet is more likely to serve as a valuable tool rather than requiring a total transformation. They employ the Internet as an enhancement to traditional methods of doing business, not as a revolutionary new tool. To these companies, e-commerce is a complement to existing business, not a substitute.[26] However, for online companies such as eBay and Amazon.ca, marketing convergence requires a total transformation of the business, as the Internet is their only way of doing business.

Marketing convergence is the integration of different technologies, such as television, computers, wireless phones, traditional stores, direct mail, catalogues, and the Internet into one coherent marketing and communication strategy.

Triple Bottom Line

A commonly occurring trend among corporations is recent years is an effort to integrate traditional business with environmental and social planning. This approach to running a business is called **triple bottom line,** and it aims to create corporate wealth in a way

Triple bottom line aims to create corporate wealth in a way that minimizes damage to the society and the environment.

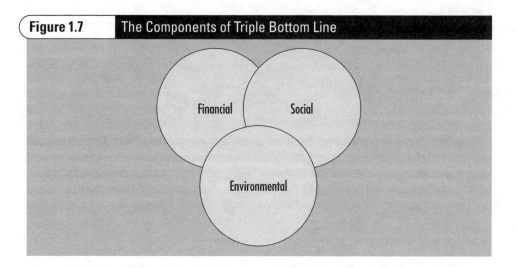

Figure 1.7 The Components of Triple Bottom Line

that minimizes damage to the society and the environment. Triple-bottom-line planning uses three measures of organizational success: financial, social, and environmental performance (see Figure 1.7). Firms that have adopted triple-bottom-line thinking are guided not only by a desire for profit but by the values of environmental integrity and social fairness.

The triple-bottom-line concept warns that emphasizing only the financial "bottom line" falls short in important ways. It stresses that the social and environmental impact of a firm's activities must also be taken into consideration. At the heart of the triple-bottom-line concept is the idea that companies must meet consumer needs for goods and services without destroying social and natural capital. It takes into account that the earth's carrying capacity is at risk, and a more balanced approach is needed to avoid a breakdown of climate or depletion of nature's resources.

The term *triple bottom line* was coined in the mid-1990s by John Elkington, a British environmentalist and chairman of the London-based consultancy company SustainAbility Ltd. Elkington used the term to indicate that corporations have responsibilities to the wider community, not just to their shareholders. The term, however, became widely known with the 1997 publication of Elkington's *Cannibals With Forks: The Triple Bottom Line of 21st Century Business.*[27]

The impetus that led more and more corporations to adopt the triple-bottom-line perspective came from the demand for companies to be more transparent regarding their business activities.[28] Societies around the world are demanding that corporations have greater social responsibility and look beyond return on investment and address other issues such as pollution from car emissions, water pollution from mining activities, and the impact on local communities from closures of local plants or bank branches. Governments also are increasingly becoming interested in triple bottom line, especially in light of increased environmental pollution and major corporate improprieties such as the recent Enron and WorldCom scandals, in which the two companies collapsed amid revelations of billions of dollars' of accounting fraud with company executives inflating earnings and hiding expenses.

Adopting the triple-bottom-line approach requires profound change in organizations. These changes include the following:

- Triple bottom line requires that organizational leaders recognize the limits of conventional strategic planning. It calls for a shift in linear, mechanistic thinking about strategic marketing planning and marketing strategy formulation and adopting innovative ways of competing.

- Triple bottom line requires a more open and vision-driven approach to strategy formulation built on openness, diversity, and the free flow of information.
- Companies need to align their strategies with the broad context of sustainable development. Business strategies must be integrated with environmental and social concerns into a coherent whole in a way that benefits shareholders, society, and the environment.

What are the benefits of adopting the triple-bottom-line approach? Advocates of the triple bottom line argue that addressing social and environmental concerns can help create substantial advantages and enhance long-term competitiveness. The most important benefits are the following:

- *Appeal to consumers.* Socially and environmentally concerned companies are more likely to appeal to customers and therefore be more financially successful. Such companies can make their concerns for such issues a central point in their marketing communication campaigns.
- *Look into the future.* Triple bottom line enables companies to look farther into the future in order to remain sustainable and competitive. By being more attuned to their social and natural environment, organizations may be in a better position to spot opportunities and make appropriate adjustments.[29] For example, companies in industries such as oil exploration conducting extensive research in renewable forms of energy will have a head start if oil becomes obsolete.
- *Encourages innovation.* The adoption of triple bottom line encourages innovation, and it can make a company more productive or competitive by improving its product and processes. For example, ever since Interface Inc., the largest commercial carpet manufacturer in the world, adopted the goal of becoming the world's first sustainable and restorative company by 2020, it has pioneered management and manufacturing processes to help achieve this goal and become a leader in industrial ecology. Interface is pioneering management and manufacturing processes that will achieve this goal and has developed ground-breaking products such as Solenium, a floor covering that can be fully remanufactured back into more Solenium.[30]

Many companies already address social and environmental concerns, taking a socially responsive approach to production by attempting to maintain the integrity of air, water, and the environmental generally. For instance, since 1998 Starbucks has partnered with Conservation International (CI), a nonprofit organization devoted to conserving the earth's living natural heritage, to encourage the use of ecologically sound growing practices that help protect biodiversity and provide economic opportunities for coffee farmers. As part of these ecologically responsible practices, Starbucks is using shade-grown beans in order to reduce the impact of bean growing on rain forests. In another example, Sleeman Breweries recently topped the food and beverage category of the Corporate Social Responsibility rankings published by the *Globe and Mail* for its record on limiting emissions and waste-water discharge.[31]

- In order for firms to succeed in today's fast-changing external environments, they need to develop and implement marketing strategies that allow them to compete more effectively. Strong marketing strategies entail finding superior ways to satisfy customers. A marketing strategy involves making choices about which customers to serve, which positioning strategy to adopt, and which products, price, distribution, and promotional strategies to pursue.

- It is important for firms to focus on a carefully selected marketing strategy instead of pursuing many courses of action. Unfocused companies will spread their resources thinly over many different pursuits and they will fail to become a strong contender.

- Strategic marketing planning is a systematic process that helps firms develop and implement customer-oriented marketing strategies. It provides an integrative framework for the various activities needed to develop marketing strategies.

- Given that many marketing environments are hypercompetitive and fast changing, the strategic marketing planning process is not used in a linear fashion by implementing each step before moving to the next. For firms to succeed in such environments they need to use strategies that involve creating a continuous stream of competitive advantages that if taken together form a strategic direction. A central aspect of this approach and key to a superior performance is the ability to change. Firms that do well are those that have the ability and willingness to change and reinvent themselves constantly over time.

- There are two types of strategies: deliberate and emergent. Deliberate strategies result from a deliberate, planned approach to strategy formulation. Emergent strategies occur from responses to customer requests, manufacturing problems, competitive threats, and technological advances that offer opportunities for creating new products or exploiting new markets.

- Effective strategic marketing planning and marketing strategy formulation require a strong market orientation. Market orientation enables firms to use strategic marketing planning more effectively because it encourages an external orientation and a more thorough analysis of the external environment. Market orientation consists of three main components: a customer orientation, a competitor orientation, and an interfunctional coordination.

- Some of the most significant factors affecting business planning and marketing strategy formulation are the globalization of markets, the rise of the Internet as an important marketing tool leading to the so-called marketing convergence, and the adoption of the triple-bottom-line approach to business management.

Review and Discussion Questions

1. What is marketing strategy? What are the components of marketing strategy? Why do firms need a marketing strategy?

2. Why does marketing strategy formulation involve a number of hard choices among various alternatives? What happens when organizations fail to make these hard choices?

3. Describe the strategic marketing planning process. Why should firms use the strategic marketing planning process in generating and implementing marketing strategies?

4. Discuss the desirable properties of an effective organizational vision. What are the components of an organization's mission statement?

5. Is the strategic marketing planning process applicable in all marketing environments? Explain your answer.

6. Explain the concept of competing on the edge. What is the difference between deliberate and emergent marketing strategies?

7. Briefly explain the dimensions of market orientation. What are the benefits of market orientation?

8. How is an organization's marketing strategy affected by hypercompetition, globalization, marketing convergence, and triple-bottom-line management?

1. The following is the mission statement of Atlantic Marine Underwriters Inc.: "To be the best marine insurance underwriting agency in Canada, providing superior service, diversity of products, financial security for our insureds and offering a competitive product at a fair price while fostering synergies among all of the carriers open to Atlantic Marine Underwriters Inc." Compare this mission statement with the guidelines for writing mission statements discussed in this chapter. How could you improve this mission statement?

2. Talk with a local business owner about his or her company's strategic marketing planning. To what extent does this business owner follow a formal strategic marketing planning process similar to the one discussed in this chapter? How are his or her marketing planning efforts being affected by the nature of the marketing environment in which this firm operates?

3. Large firms have many advantages over smaller companies, including more resources, lower costs due to economies of scale and other cost advantages, and greater purchasing power. Yet many large companies fail to compete effectively against smaller competitors. Why?

4. A high-ranking executive of a medical equipment manufacturer made the following comments regarding her company's approach to marketing: "Our company is a high-technology firm with a strong engineering-driven culture. Listening to customers is a waste of time because they never come up with new product ideas. As a result we gather very little customer information before we introduce a new product." What does this statement say about the market orientation of this medical equipment manufacturer? Do high-technology companies need to be market-driven?

5. Check the websites of Starbucks, General Motors, Sleemans, IBM, Ford, and other companies and look for evidence that these companies are engaged in triple-bottom-line planning.

Notes

1. This information is drawn from various publicly available sources.
2. Richard D'Aveni, *Hypercompetitive Rivalries* (New York: The Free Press, 1995), 1.
3. George S. Day, *Strategic Market Planning* (St. Paul, Minnesota: West Publishing, 1984), 31.
4. George S. Day, *Market Driven Strategy: Strategies for Creating Value* (New York: The Free Press, 1990), 6.
5. Andrew Campbell and Laura L. Nash, *A Sense of Mission* (Reading, Mass.: Addison-Wesley, 1992), 32.
6. Campbell and Nash, 32.
7. Day, 1990, 17.
8. Gary Hamel and C. K. Prahalad, "Strategic Intent," *Harvard Business Review*, (May–June 1989), 63–76.
9. www.molson.com, retrieved on July 10, 2003.
10. www.sportinglife.ca, retrieved on July 10, 2003.
11. www.thebodyshop.ca, retrieved on July 10, 2003.
12. Shona L. Brown and Kathleen M. Eisenhardt, *Competing on the Edge* (Boston: Mass.: Harvard Business School Press, 1998).
13. Henry Mintzberg and Alexandra McGugh, "Strategy Formation in an Adhocracy," *Administrative Science Quarterly* 30 (1985): 160–197.
14. Joseph N. Fry and J. Peter Killing, *Strategic Analysis and Action* (Scarborough, Ontario: Prentice Hall, 1995), 111.
15. Stanley F. Slater and John C. Narver, "The Positive Effect of a Market Orientation on Business Profitability: A Balanced Replication," *Journal of Business Research* 48 (2000): 69–73.
16. John C. Narver and Stanley F. Slater, "The Effect of Market Orientation on Business Profitability," *Journal of Marketing* 54 (October 1990): 20–35.
17. Some of the items on this list are taken from Narver and Slater, 1990, and Slater and Narver, 2000.
18. George S. Day, *The Market Driven Organization: Understanding, Attracting, and Keeping Valuable Customers* (New York: The Free Press, 1999), 5.
19. A. K. Kohli and B. J. Jaworski, "Market Orientation: The Construct, Research Propositions, and Managerial Implications," *Journal of Marketing* 54 (April 1995): 1–18.
20. Charles W. L. Hill and Gareth R. Jones, *Strategic Management Theory*, 6th ed. (Boston, Mass.: Houghton Mifflin Company, 2004), 64.
21. Theodore Levitt, *The Marketing Imagination* (New York: The Free Press, 1983), 24.
22. Levitt, 23.
23. Hill and Jones, 65–67.
24. Yoram Wind, Vijay Mahajan with Robert E. Gunther, *Convergence Marketing* (Upper Saddle River, N.J.: Prentice Hall, 2002), xviii; Susan K. Jones and Ted Spiegel, *Marketing Convergence* (Mason, Ohio: South-Western, 2003), 12–13.
25. Wind, Mahajan, Gunther, xviii.
26. Jones and Spiegel, 32.
27. John Elkington, *Cannibals With Forks: The Triple Bottom Line of 21st Century Business* (Gabriola Island, B.C.: New Society Publishers, 1997).
28. John Elkington, *The Chrysalis Economy* (Oxford: Capstone Publishers, 2001), 172.
29. Bob Willard, *The Sustainability Advantage* (Gabriola Island, B.C.: New Society Publishers, 2002), 139.
30. Paul Hawken, Amory Lovins, and Hunter L. Lovins, *Natural Capitalism* (Boston, Mass.: Little Brown and Co., 1999), 139.
31. David MacFarlane, "Why Now?" *Report on Business, The Globe and Mail*, March 2004, 45.

Appendix 1.1 — Outline of a Marketing Plan

As we noted in Chapter 1, the purpose of the strategic marketing planning process is to help develop an effective marketing plan. Writing an effective marketing plan requires a great deal of information from different sources. The job of the person writing the marketing plan is to assemble all this information into a coherent and actionable document that will guide the marketing manager's activities in the upcoming year. The ultimate purpose of the marketing plan is to help a firm achieve its goals and objectives. This is accomplished by crafting and executing viable marketing strategies.

Since the duration of a marketing strategy is usually longer than one year, it is advisable for firms to create a three-year strategic plan and a series of successive annual marketing plans—including annual budgets—to manage marketing activities during the year. Because a firm's environment may change during the year, it must be prepared to alter its marketing strategy when necessary. For example, if a competitor begins an advertising campaign that threatens to capture market share from the firm, the latter must be prepared to change its advertising plans to respond to the competitive threat.

The Structure of the Marketing Plan

Marketing plans used by business organizations differ depending on the size of the organization, product and market scope, and other factors. Although marketing plans vary from company to company, they all need a number of common elements. In this appendix we present the outline of a typical marketing plan (shown in Figure 1.1A) and a brief discussion of the various components of the marketing plan to illustrate the nature and purpose of each of them.

Figure 1.1A — Outline of a Marketing Plan

I. Executive Summary

II. Situational Analysis
- a. Review of current marketing program
  - A. Target market(s)
  - B. Positioning
  - C. The marketing mix
- b. Internal analysis
  - A. Finance
  - B. Management
  - C. Marketing
  - D. Production
- c. External analysis
- d. Task environment
  - A. Demand
  - B. Industry
  - C. Market segments
- e. General environment
  - A. Competition
  - B. Economy
  - C. Social cultural factors
  - D. Technological factors
  - E. Political factors
- f. SWOT analysis
  - A. Strengths
  - B. Weaknesses
  - C. Opportunities
  - D. Threats
- g. Marketing Objectives

III. Development of the Marketing Program
- A. Target market
- B. Positioning strategy
- C. Marketing mix

IV. Implementation and Control

Executive Summary

The executive summary is a synopsis of the entire marketing plan that communicates the main elements of the situational analysis, the marketing strategy, and its implementation.

The purpose of the executive summary is to provide the reader with an overview of the contents of the marketing plan. Company executives can get a general idea about the contents of the plan quickly before they spend more time reading it in its entirety.

Situational Analysis

This part of the marketing plan involves the following: First, a review of the current marketing program that includes the firm's current target market(s), positioning strategy, and marketing mix (product, price, distribution, and promotion). The purpose of this review is to describe the firm's marketing strategy and identify the areas that are in need of change in next year's marketing plan. Second, an internal analysis is undertaken that involves an evaluation of the firm's internal resources and capabilities of its various functions—finance, management, marketing, and production—and an external analysis of the environment (task and general environment).

The internal and external analyses lead to the development of the SWOT matrix (strengths, weaknesses, opportunities, and threats). The situational analysis is a critical step in formulating the marketing strategy. The purpose of the external and internal analysis is to identify the relevant environmental trends and forces and to assess the organization's resources and capabilities. The final outcome is to identify its strengths, weaknesses, opportunities, and threats. Strengths and weaknesses are derived from the internal analysis while opportunities and threats are identified from the external analysis.

In this section we also discuss the marketing objectives to be achieved by the marketing strategy. Marketing objectives specify a desired outcome to be achieved within a certain period of time. The marketing objectives are determined after the SWOT analysis is completed. Marketing objectives are performance targets that are derived based on a realistic evaluation of the opportunities and threats and the company's strengths and weaknesses identified in the SWOT analysis. Marketing objectives convert overall corporate goals into more specific performance targets. As such, they can be seen as the intermediate steps to be taken to accomplish the organizational goals.

Development of the Marketing Program

This is the most critical part of the marketing plan. In this part we describe the various parts of the firm's marketing strategy for the upcoming year. It involves the target market, the positioning strategy, and the marketing mix. Some of the elements of the marketing strategy such as target market and positioning strategy may remain the same as last year's. The elements of the marketing strategy that need to change will be thoroughly discussed.

The product component will describe the needed product strategies such as quality improvements, modifications, product line extensions, and product deletions. Pricing strategy involves a discussion of the price level, price promotions, discounts, and other pricing actions. Distribution decisions includes the type of distribution strategy, types of middlemen to be employed, distribution intensity, and suggestions for resolving conflict in distribution. Promotion decisions involve the type of advertising, personal selling, promotion and public relations actions needed to implement the marketing strategy.

Implementation and Control

Developing a cohesive marketing strategy is not enough for marketing success. The marketing strategy needs to be implemented. Effective execution of the marketing plan also requires that the firm put in place control measures to assess the effectiveness of its implementation efforts. These controls are required to monitor progress and to ensure the company is achieving its marketing objectives. Controls include financial and non-financial measures such as return on investment, return on sales, sales, market share, customer satisfaction, and others.

Chapter Two

Defining and Assessing Markets

The starting point of strategic market planning is to define your business.

Derek Abell, Founding President of the European School
of Management and Technology

Learning Objectives

After studying this chapter, you should be able to:

1. Define strategic and served markets

2. Use the multidimensional approach for defining strategic and served markets

3. Avoid the problem of marketing myopia

4. Describe the dynamic nature of markets

5. Illustrate the factors that affect market attractiveness

6. Discuss the various methods of defining market structure

7. Describe methods for assessing market potential

Trojan Technologies' Market Definition Is Key to Its Success

Trojan Technologies is a Canadian-based high-technology company based in London, Ontario, that designs, manufactures, and markets a full range of ultraviolet disinfection products for waste-water and clean-water applications. Waste-water disinfection technology is employed for municipal, industrial, and commercial waste-water treatment uses. Clean-water disinfection technology is employed in private drinking water supplies, municipal drinking water treatment plants, industrial product and process water applications, and residential and commercial applications.

Primary customers in the waste-water disinfection side of business include municipalities that have waste-water treatment problems. Residential and commercial customers for clean-water systems include hospitals, rural homes, cottages, restaurants, and nursing homes. Industrial applications include process or pure-water requirements in the food, beverage, cosmetics, electronics, optical, semiconductor, and pharmaceutical industries. Trojan also provides UV technology for the treatment of environmental contaminants.

Trojan Technologies was established in 1977. The company employs approximately 350 employees at its London headquarters. In addition, it has offices in the United States, the United Kingdom, Spain, the Netherlands, Germany, and Norway. An established professional network of dealers and manufacturer representatives in Canada, the United States, South America, the Middle East, and the Pacific Rim complements Trojan's own offices around the world. Today, Trojan is the world leader in UV disinfection systems with installations in over 3,000 municipal facilities in more than 25 countries.

Trojan's mission and broad strategic market definition is to provide lasting solutions to environmental problems, using safe and effective ultraviolet disinfection. The company asserts that UV is an effective way of eliminating disease-causing pathogens found in drinking water and a safe alternative to chemical disinfection. The technology employed in Trojan's products uses high-intensity UV lamps; to achieve the required kill rate, water needing treatment is channelled past the lamps at various speeds depending on the amount of waste contained in the water.

Trojan employs a labour force of highly qualified experts in microbiology, chemistry, and engineering. The company has created a culture of trust, integrity, learning, respect for employees and customers, and a strong sense of constancy of purpose. These values lead to an environment that fosters product innovation and commitment to customer service.

Among Trojan's distinct competencies is excellent customer service, which is possible due to the company's highly trained technicians who make up a strong support network around the world. Combined with the company's advanced technical support centre, these service capabilities allow Trojan to diagnose customers' problems and respond to their calls quickly. Fast, ongoing customer support is an important requirement in this market because of the devastating implications when breakdowns occur at municipal waste-water plants.

The market for UV-based disinfection systems is largely untapped, as only a small percentage of municipal waste-water sites in North America and worldwide have adopted UV disinfection systems. The vast majority of Trojan's revenues comes from its line of waste-water products, which includes the System UV3000 series and System UV4000Plus. These products are primarily used by municipalities for waste water. A small percentage of

(continued)

revenues comes from clean-water products that are used for municipal, residential, and industrial process applications.

UV technology is different from the alternative technology, chlorination, by being environmentally safe and cost-effective. Using UV light technology, Trojan has defined its strategic market in a different way than competitors, who use the traditional chlorine-based waste-water treatment technology. Trojan Technologies is a major threat to competitors who define their strategic markets narrowly using chlorination technology.[1]

Introduction

Defining the market is an important part of the strategic marketing planning process.[2] Before the environmental analysis or other steps in marketing strategy formulation are taken, the market arena needs to be established. The Trojan Technologies story above is an example of how a company defines its market and how this definition differentiates the company from its competitors.

Market-driven organizations need to, first, define the broad strategic market that represents their long-term view of the market. The strategic market includes both the currently targeted segments and those segments where the firm searches for emerging opportunities to exploit and threats to counter. For example, the definition of the strategic market for a producer of premium beer may include all beer segments including regular, light, premium, and imported beers. Such strategic market definition indicates that this company, although it currently competes in the premium market, is interested in pursuing opportunities in the broader beer market.

Once the broad market arena is defined, the served market can be defined as a subset of the strategic market. The served market represents the choices the firm has made about which specific market segments to target within the broad strategic market. Decisions about market segmentation and the direction of the firm's product development efforts are all driven by the choice of the strategic market arena.

Marketing managers usually lack the expertise to fully address the problem of market definition.[3] They encounter difficulty with properly defining their markets because they don't have an overall road map or framework to guide their efforts. Consequently, the resulting market definition is unfocused or is very similar to those of their competitors. Despite the difficulties in defining markets, every firm needs an effective strategic market definition to survive in the long run. Poorly defined markets are a common cause of business failure. An appropriate definition must fit a firm's distinctive capabilities, help avoid powerful competitors, lower costs, satisfy customer needs, and allow the firm to exploit new market trends.

This chapter will describe both strategic and served markets. The multidimensional approach to defining a firm's strategic and served market will also be discussed. Next, the chapter will elaborate on the factors that determine the attractiveness of the strategic and served markets. The various ways that marketers use to find the structure of their markets will be covered in some detail. Lastly, two ways of measuring market potential will be discussed.

Strategic Markets

As we stated earlier, defining the market is a crucial step in the strategic marketing planning process. A market is a flexible concept that can be defined in different ways. Most of the subsequent strategic analysis, including the choice of served markets and market segments, depends on the market definition.

Markets are defined at two levels: the strategic and served market level. The **strategic market** is the broad market and includes both current and potential markets.[4] It includes substitute products and technologies, and emerging or unserved markets. Broadly defined strategic markets allow managers to see beyond current products, customers, and technologies to spot untapped or emerging threats and opportunities, which are not visible to organizations with narrow visions of the market. By spotting these opportunities or threats early, companies can act quickly before competitors do and obtain considerable competitive advantages. The Strategy in Action box below illustrates the role of the strategic market definition in Sobey's expansion into Ontario.[5]

Strategic market is the broad market and includes both current and potential markets.

SOBEY'S

Sobey's is the leading grocery store chain in the Maritimes, where it does about 70 percent of its business. When Loblaws, Canada's leading supermarket chain, entered the market the dynamics of supermarket competition in the Maritimes changed, putting great price pressure on local retailers. Sobey's knew action was needed. Instead of remaining in its local market and facing the predictable onslaught by Loblaws while also watching its margins and profits shrink, Sobey's began its expansion into Ontario by acquiring the Oshawa Group and other smaller grocery chains—in other words, its vision of its strategic market changed from local to national. The acquisitions allowed Sobey's to continue its pattern of growth, and they provided it with a means to go on a cross-parry attack in Ontario—that is, to put some competitive pressure in Loblaws' stronghold in Ontario and offset to a large degree its vulnerability in the Maritime market. Sobey's expansion drive has continued unabated with further acquisitions and store openings, resulting in Sobey's being today one of the largest grocery chains in Canada with more than 1,300 stores in 10 provinces.

What is wrong with narrow strategic market definitions? Narrowly defined strategic markets focus attention on the specific customer group, product, or technology currently sold by the firm. A narrow focus allows firms to readily identify threats and opportunities coming from similar products, but it makes them oblivious to developments in nearby markets such as new technologies and substitute products that may render its existing products obsolete and threaten its current position.[6] If Smith-Corona, the now defunct maker of typewriters, had defined its strategic market not as being in the typewriter business but in word processing, it would have probably been able to see the threats coming from personal computers and make the transition to that business in time. According to Sam Walton, founder of Wal-Mart, Sears' failure to react to Wal-Mart's rapid advance in the 1980s was because it failed to recognize Wal-Mart as a competitor.[7]

A narrow scope could also prevent a firm from identifying promising opportunities that could help increase its sales and profitability. For example, because of their focus on the cola drink market, cola drink manufacturers were late in entering the emerging segments of sports drinks, fruit drinks, non-cola drinks, and fruit juices. However, once they realized these market opportunities, Coca-Cola and PepsiCo purchased juice and other companies (Coke purchased Minute Maid and Pepsi purchased Tropicana and Gatorade) in order not to miss these emerging segments.

Narrowly defining strategic markets is often the reason many industry leaders have failed or survived as marginal competitors. Firms that define their strategic markets narrowly based on pure product definitions are said to suffer from a condition called **marketing myopia**.[8] Marketing myopia prevents companies from spotting threats or opportunities coming from substitutes—products that perform the same functions but differ in technology, raw materials used, or production process.

In order to avoid the problem of marketing myopia, a firm needs to define its strategic market broadly enough to include all potential substitutes for the products it currently sells. For example, Wang Laboratories failed because it defined its business narrowly as a provider of dedicated word-processing machines, instead of word processing. Wang's dominant position was undermined by personal computers that offered word processing as one of its functions; its market evaporated as personal computers became more popular. The much cheaper personal computers made dedicated word processors obsolete and uneconomical. Had Wang defined its market broadly in terms of, let's say, word processing, it might have been able to detect technological and competitive threats

Marketing myopia is a condition that affects companies that define their strategic markets narrowly based on pure product definitions.

gathering in the periphery of its currently served markets.[9] Another example is a major pet food manufacturer that lost market share because of the wrong definition of its strategic market, as explained in the Strategy in Action box.[10]

Strategy in Action — PET FOOD COMPANY

When scientific pet food formulas began to be sold through non-traditional specialty outlets and intermediaries, one major pet food manufacturer began to lose market share—it had entirely missed the emergence of this trend. Managers had been focusing their attention only on sales data that were readily available, and according to that data, the company was maintaining its market share in the mature and non-growing regular pet food category. However, this view was myopic as it failed to look at events that were taking place beyond its served market. As a result, this pet manufacturer was losing market share in a total market that was in fact growing. The company's failure to look at its broader strategic market contributed to overlooking an important marketing opportunity and experiencing a heavy market share loss.

Balance is important, though. While broad strategic market definitions are preferred to narrow ones, if they are too broad they can be counterproductive. Strategic market definitions that are too broad may prevent a firm from obtaining the required in-depth knowledge of the opportunities and threats that occur in its strategic market; firms that define their businesses too broadly may have their resources spread too thinly over too many products or markets and not be able to compete effectively; very broad definitions also may lead companies to diversify into markets that may fit poorly with their existing resources and competences.[11] The example discussed in the Strategy in Action box illustrates the problems of overly broad strategic market definitions.[12]

Strategy in Action — BLUE CIRCLE INDUSTRIES

British-based Blue Circle Industries PLC, one of the world's leading producers of cement, diversified from its core business, cement, into a variety of other businesses that included property management, brick production, waste management, industrial minerals, gas stoves, bathroom furnishings, and lawnmowers. What was the rationale for this diversification drive by Blue Circle? In the words of a retired senior manager, the company expanded into these markets because management believed that its business was not just the cement business but also the supply of building materials—one of which is cement. This type of thinking led management into bricks, cooking appliances, and central heating boilers because these are all products you need when you build your house with Blue Circle's cement. Blue Circle also diversified into the lawnmower manufacturing business because, in management's thinking, people need lawnmowers for their garden, which is after all next to the house they built with Blue Circle's material. This growth strategy led, as one would expect, to disastrous results because the company spread itself too thinly into markets that didn't match its core competencies.

Multidimensional Scope of Strategic Markets

Strategic markets are an inherently flexible concept that can be defined in different ways. They can be defined as broadly as an entire industry or as narrowly as a market segment. The scope of the strategic market can be defined by choices along three dimensions: customer groups, functions or applications, and technologies and competencies.[13] Viewed this way, a strategic market combines both demand and supply approaches. The demand approach is reflected in the customer groups chosen to serve, and it is similar to the traditional definition of markets as consisting of those people who are buying the company's product or service. The supply approach is close to the traditional view of an industry, and it is reflected in the products or services offered, as represented by the functions or applications and technologies or competencies involved in the product.

Customer Groups. Many companies define their markets in terms of the customer group being targeted and those customers that could be targeted in the future. Firms selling to individual consumers can define their target customer group in terms of demographics, geography, and buying behaviour. For example, some companies in the coffee industry, such as Kraft Foods or Procter & Gamble, focus on those customers who buy instant coffee for home consumption. Starbucks, on the other hand, sells gourmet coffee to those customers who enjoy their coffee in a relaxing retail environment. Firms selling to other firms or institutions can use the user industry or firm size as the basis of market definition.

One difficult issue for managers is how to define a market in which the company is dealing with more customers than just end users. This can occur when the company sells its products to other businesses, which, in turn, use the products to manufacture their product. In those cases, the company could either focus on the needs of the immediate customer group or the end user. Usually, it is better to focus on the needs of end users as they determine whether the final product is appropriate, and whether it meets their expectations.

Functions or Applications. Firms often take a supply or industry view when they define their markets. In defining markets from a supply perspective, firms look at markets in terms of functions or applications currently offered or that could be offered to customers. For example, BCE Inc. competes in the markets for long-distance telephone, wireless communications, Internet access, data, and satellite television. Trojan Technologies, as we've discussed in the opening vignette, uses waste-water disinfection technology for designing, manufacturing, and marketing a full range of products for waste-water and clean-water applications by municipal, industrial, and commercial users.

Supply-oriented market definitions can be broader or narrower depending on the individual firm. For example, the B.C.–based manufacturer of surveillance cameras, Extreme CCTV, takes a narrow view of its market by specializing in manufacturing closed-circuit cameras that can see in near pitch darkness or endure extreme environments, such as the mouth of volcanoes. Extreme CCTV's customer list includes the RCMP and the U.S. Enforcement Agency. On the other hand, industry-leading Tyco Fire & Security is more broadly based, as it is involved in security alarm monitoring, fire-suppression systems, video-surveillance systems, emergency breathing apparatuses, anti-theft systems, and fire alarms. Some of its major projects include the fire-suppression system in Berlin's Parliament building, the security system for the World Bank headquarters in Washington, D.C., and the fire-detection and -suppression system for Australia's Sydney Harbour Tunnel.

Technology and Competencies. Another dimension refers to the technology and competencies employed to produce the product so that it has the required functionality or applications. It is common for products and services in the same market to use competing technologies. In the personal computer industry, most computers use the Windows operating system while a small percentage uses Linux. Companies using one of the two operating systems cannot use the other because the two systems are not compatible. Computer language developer Borland International takes a broad view of its market by making its computer language Delphi available in both versions, Windows and Linux. Microsoft, on the other hand, makes its computer languages available only for its Windows operating system.

Core competencies are the distinctive capabilities that characterize and differentiate firms. Hamel and Prahalad suggest that core competencies should be the primary dimension firms use when they define their business.[14] For example, FedEx's core competence could be defined as superior logistics management that enables the company to offer excellent on-time delivery. Knowing the firm's core competencies can lead to the creative expansion of product lines: 3M's core competencies in adhesives, substrates, and advanced materials have led the company to develop numerous new products in areas such as abrasives, sandpapers, adhesives, and tapes.

A key challenge for any company is to build the competencies that will allow it to take advantage of current and future opportunities. Core competencies are more valuable when they allow a company to compete in many markets. For example, Sharp invested hundreds of million of dollars in flat-screen display technology in the early 1990s. This core competence allowed the company to enter various markets, including pocket diaries, laptop computers, video telephones, and LCD projection televisions. On the other hand, a company that fails to develop a core competence will have difficulty participating successfully in many markets.

Markets consist of many segments. Each segment represents a product that performs a distinct function for a distinct customer group, and that uses a distinct technology or competence. The multidimensional market definition can be portrayed graphically, as shown in Figure 2.1. Each combination of the three dimensions is a distinct market segment. Managers can identify a broad array of potential new market opportunities along the three dimensions. A business can expand by entering untapped customer groups, new geographical markets, or introducing new products and new technologies. In addition, the multidimensional market definition allows firms to visually assess the degree of differentiation and overlap with their competitors. The extent of overlap depends on the degree to which competitors have chosen to include similar customer groups, functions and applications, and technologies and core competencies.

Core competencies are the distinctive capabilities that characterize and differentiate firms.

| Figure 2.1 | Multidimensional Strategic Market Definition |

Chapter 2 / Defining and Assessing Markets

Served Markets

Served market is a subset of the strategic market and represents the part of the strategic market where the firm actively competes for customers.

Once the broad strategic market is determined, a company chooses the part of the market it will serve, the specific segments it will emphasize, and the differentiated position it will seek to establish within the segments.[15] The **served market** is the part of the strategic market where the firm actively competes for customers.[16] It reflects the choices of markets and products made by management among the many sub-markets that make up the broad strategic market.

Firms define their served market by selecting from all the available possibilities within the strategic market the kinds of customers they will serve, the products or services they will offer, and the technologies and core competencies to emphasize. For example, if we assume that WestJet's strategic market definition is the entire Canadian air travel market, its served market may be defined as the Canadian discount travel market. Served markets are represented as smaller cubicles inside the larger strategic market cubicles, as shown in Figure 2.2.

Figure 2.2	Served Market as a Subset of the Strategic Market

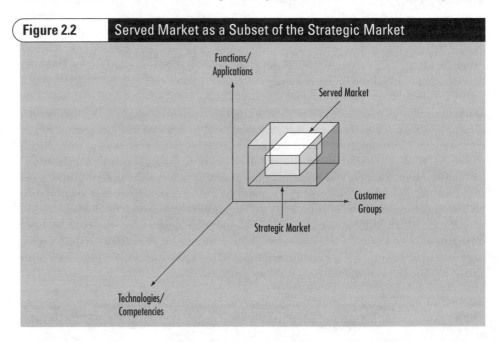

One of the common mistakes marketing managers make is to equate the strategic market with the served market. Strategic markets are made up of many served markets. A key question is whether to try to serve all market segments or a subset of the strategic market. Served markets may be identical to the strategic market, but most often their scope is considerably narrower. For example, within the broad soft drink market, Coca-Cola competes in several served markets with its Coke, Minute-Maid, Fruitopia, and Sprite brands. Still, there are many other segments in the soft drink market, such as carbonated water and apple juice categories, that even as large a company as Coca-Cola does not serve.

The served market is the relevant market for tactical marketing management decisions. Decisions such as assessing market potential, market segmentation, budgeting, product, price, distribution, promotion, and sales force decisions are based on narrow market definitions. For example, how would a manufacturer of a new gourmet coffee that has no additives assess the market potential or develop a marketing strategy for this product if it wanted to distribute it through grocery stores? Basing the assessment on the total coffee market would be a mistake since it consists of various segments with different markets and competitors. Therefore, the relevant market is the non-additive gourmet coffee segment and only those brands that are distributed through grocery stores.

Dynamic Nature of Markets

The purpose of strategy is to choose, among the many possibilities in the strategic market, those that are compatible with the firm's resources and capabilities and difficult for competitors to imitate. Markets are moving targets and are in a perpetual state of flux; new ones emerge all the time. These new markets involve combining new customer groups, products, technologies, and competences. Companies that occupy these new markets often become powerful enough to challenge the incumbents, who may have become complacent because of their past success in their own markets. This challenge often leads to devastating losses of market share by firms that were thought to be invincible, by new and relatively unknown entrants. Xerox's case, described in the Strategy in Action box, is illustrative of the threat posed to an incumbent firm by a new competitor that defined its strategic market in a different way and benefited from the subsequent explosive growth of its chosen segment.

Strategy in Action

XEROX AND CANON

Xerox pioneered and dominated the copying industry for over half a century. At one time Xerox copiers were so dominant that its name was synonymous with copying—many people still use it in speech to mean photocopying. Xerox's strategy was fairly straightforward and successful; it targeted large corporations that had high-speed, high-volume needs and used its direct sales force to distribute its products.

Xerox had been unsuccessfully challenged in the past by IBM and Kodak because they had pursued markets very similar to Xerox's. A new competitor, however, was more successful. Canon chose to adopt a different strategic market definition by targeting small and medium-sized businesses, using quality and price—not speed—to distinguish its copiers from Xerox's. Canon also chose to sell its products through a dealer network rather than lease them as Xerox did. Xerox's and Canon's strategic market definitions are shown in Figure 2.3A.

Canon's strategy of not attacking Xerox directly, but to enter a different product-market cell, proved to be greatly successful. Within a few years, Canon overtook Xerox as the market leader. Canon went from 0 to 35 percent market share in a span of slightly more than 20 years.[17]

Xerox's narrow view of its markets made it oblivious to the emerging low-volume, low-price segment, which Canon exploited to its advantage. This segment later exploded, proving that there was a huge pent-up demand as the market responded to Canon's offering of high-quality, low-priced copiers, and it became the dominant segment in the copier industry. Because of its focus on the high-volume segment, Xerox was late in responding to the threat posed by Canon and lost its dominance in the copier business.[18]

Once Canon consolidated its position in the low end of the copier market, it broadened its view of its strategic market and started invading the high end, threatening Xerox's core market. Xerox finally responded to Canon's threat by moving down-market and produced products similar to Canon's. Eventually, this led to the two companies having virtually identical strategic (and served) market definitions, as shown in Figure 2.3B.

As the Xerox example illustrates, the nature of markets is ever-changing due to factors such as shifting customer needs, moves and countermoves made by competitors, and changing industry conditions. However, the rate of change differs among markets.

A. Strategic Market Definition in the 1960s and 1970s

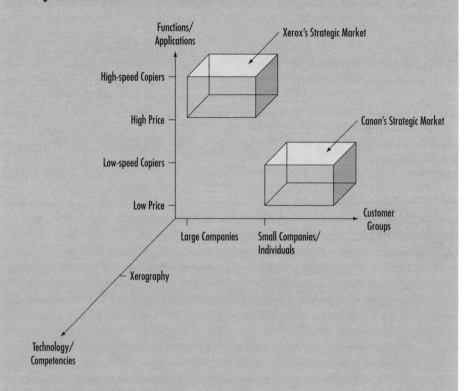

B. Strategic Market Definition in the 1990s and 2000s

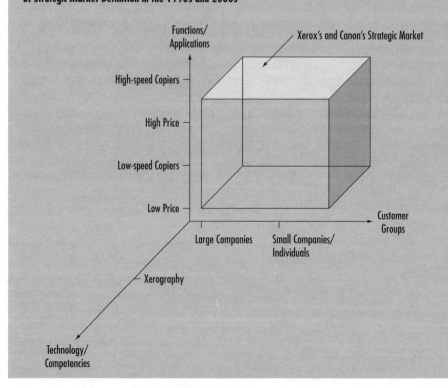

Some markets are characterized by relatively stable boundaries and are well defined. In such markets, competitors and customers are clearly identified. For example, Labatt and Molson are fighting the beer war in Canada, a market that is dominated by these two companies.

In more dynamic markets, however, market boundaries become more difficult to define precisely. The continuous change in market boundaries is often the result of efforts to expand product offerings, technological change, deregulation, globalization, and demanding customers, or channels of distribution.[19] For example, the entry of Grocery Gateway, a Toronto-based online grocery retailer, has expanded the boundaries of the food retailing market in that city.

Frequently, a change in one dimension brings about changes in the other dimensions of the market definition. The introduction of a new product or technology can cause the birth of a new segment. For example, the use of Internet technology in bookselling has led to the emergence of a new segment of online book buyers. Alternatively, the emergence of a new segment may lead to the demand for a new product or technology to satisfy the needs of the segment. For example, the increased importance of the over-65 age group has led to the introduction of a number of services designed for this group, such as cruises for seniors.

For these reasons, established firms need to maintain a broad vision of their markets and continuously search for new positions to occupy within an industry. Failure to do so will allow more agile rivals to exploit these opportunities. The difficulty is that leading companies usually become very adept at competing in their established positions—by lowering costs and improving their operations, products, and services. The better they become at their game, the harder it is for them to compete under different rules. This can make them vulnerable to a new entrant who attacks them by playing a different game. Established firms need to be flexible and prepared to change their strategy and market definition. In addition, companies need to continually question the viability of their current position and constantly search for new opportunities in order to be the first to discover and exploit them.

Assessing Market Attractiveness

Markets differ in their degree of attractiveness. Managers must assess the attractiveness of the market in which they are currently doing business or which they are contemplating entering. The decision whether to remain in or enter a market depends on such an assessment. Market attractiveness is an important determinant of a firm's profitability, as it is common for firms competing in attractive markets to earn above-average returns. The determinants of market attractiveness include both market and industry factors as shown in Figure 2.4 and discussed in the next section.

Market Factors

Several market-related factors determine the attractiveness of a market. These include market size, market growth, profit margins, price elasticity, seasonality, and cyclicality.

Market size

Large markets are attractive because of their higher sales potential and increased revenues. Such markets also present more opportunities for segmentation than smaller ones. However, the attractiveness of a market of a given size differs among firms. A market that is deemed to be large to certain firms may be viewed as small by other firms. For example, the size of most local community newspaper markets may be adequate for

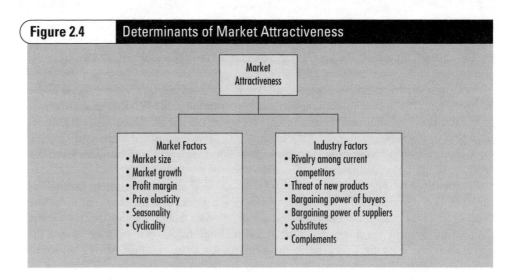

Figure 2.4 Determinants of Market Attractiveness

Market Attractiveness

Market Factors
- Market size
- Market growth
- Profit margin
- Price elasticity
- Seasonality
- Cyclicality

Industry Factors
- Rivalry among current competitors
- Threat of new products
- Bargaining power of buyers
- Bargaining power of suppliers
- Substitutes
- Complements

Majority fallacy occurs when large markets become less attractive because they attract more competition.

locally run community newspapers but too small for the large national newspapers. One problem with large markets is that they attract more competition due to their higher sales potential, making the market less attractive. This situation is often called **majority fallacy.** Many firms, in order to avoid the problem of majority fallacy, enter smaller markets if competitive conditions are less intense in those markets.

Market growth

Market growth is also an important influence on market attractiveness because, even if the market is small, its growth represents a significant opportunity for the organization. The growth rate of a market depends on its stage in the product life cycle and trends in the external environmental forces: economic, political, technological, competitive, social, and cultural. High-growth markets are desirable because they provide higher margins and sustain profits for a long time; however, they may attract more competition. Competing firms in high-growth markets are likely to be more preoccupied with building capacity to meet demand and are less likely to respond to aggressive attacks on their market position. However, contrary to popular opinion, incumbent firms often compete aggressively in attractive high-growth markets, increasing the degree of competitive intensity in the market.

Low-growth markets, on the other hand, are generally less attractive than growth markets because of highly intensive competitive conditions as incumbents attempt to grow at the expense of their rivals. Also, the price sensitivity of customers in mature, slow-growth markets increases as they become more knowledgeable about the product and are less willing to pay a premium.

Profit margin

Profit margin is an important performance indicator for measuring the financial health of the firm. Adequate profit margins are needed to cover operating expenses, interest charges, income taxes; to pay dividends; and to reinvest in retained earnings. Profit margins vary among markets as they are affected by industry and competitive conditions. Firms in industries characterized by price wars suffer from low profit margins. For example, airlines consistently earn lower profits than pharmaceutical firms because of higher price pressures.

Price elasticity

Buyer price elasticity also affects market attractiveness. Price elasticity affects profits because it influences price levels. Highly elastic customers demand lower prices and are constantly looking for price deals. Firms that sell products to markets characterized by low price elasticity, on the other hand, can charge higher prices and are, in general, more profitable. For example, manufacturers of premium, high-priced watches earn higher profit margins because there is less resistance to higher prices than less expensive, low-end watches.

Seasonality and cyclicality

Seasonality and cyclicality also affect market attractiveness. Markets that are characterized by these conditions are less attractive because of lack of sales stability, either throughout the year or over the duration of the business cycle. The lack of sales stability creates problems in production, staffing, and inventory planning. Cyclical industries often experience a high degree of rivalry when they enter periods of slow demand. For example, rivalry in the automobile industry becomes very intensive during periods of recession when many people stop buying cars and carmakers try to entice customers by offering lower prices, rebates, low-interest financing, and other price-related incentives.

Industry Factors

Michael Porter[20] has argued persuasively that the profit potential of an industry depends on the collective strength of five competitive forces: rivalry among existing competitors, threat of entry by firms currently outside the industry, bargaining power of buyers, bargaining power of suppliers, and threat posed by substitute goods and services. The five competitive forces drive the profitability of the industry because they affect the costs, prices charged, and investment required for a firm to maintain its competitive position. The strength of the five forces varies in different industries and changes as the industry evolves. As a result, markets differ in their inherent profitability potential. If the collective strength of these forces is strong, the profit potential of the market will be negatively affected. Porter's Five Forces framework is shown in Figure 2.5.

Rivalry among current competitors

Rivalry is the process of competition among firms in an industry. It is manifested in the form of price competition, product innovation, advertising battles, customer service, warranties, sales promotions, and other tactics. Rivalry takes place because firms are looking for opportunities to improve their competitive position and profitability. High competitive intensity among current competitors often leads to lower prices and higher

Rivalry is the process of competition among firms in an industry, and it is manifested in the form of price competition, product innovation, advertising battles, customer service, warranties, sales promotions, and other tactics.

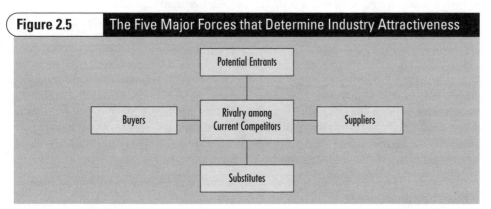

| **Figure 2.5** | The Five Major Forces that Determine Industry Attractiveness |

investment in product development and promotional costs, sales force, and plant capacity. The intensity of rivalry is higher if the following conditions exist:

- *There are many small firms in the industry.* It is likely that one or more firms will try to gain market share by believing that its action will not be detected.
- *High diversity of rivals.* Diverse competitors have difficulty in understanding each other's goals and intentions and reaching an agreement on a set of "rules of the game" for the industry.
- *Slow rate of industry growth.* Firms engage in aggressive marketing behaviour in an attempt to achieve their sales or market share objectives.
- *High fixed or storage costs.* Firms often resort to price-cutting in order to maintain the volume required to cover their high fixed or storage costs.
- *Low product differentiation.* Low product differentiation is associated with weak brand loyalties, creating an incentive for firms to gain market share with price cuts or other price-related incentives.
- *It is easy for customers to switch from one competing product to another.* Low switching costs make it easier for rivals to take sales away from other companies, creating an incentive to compete more aggressively.
- *High exit barriers.* Exit barriers such as highly specialized assets, binding labour agreements, or long-term supplier contracts usually force incumbent firms to stay in the industry and compete even if they lose money.

Threat of new entrants

New entrants often bring substantial new capacity and resources to an industry and need to gain adequate market share to survive. The seriousness of the threat depends on the presence of entry barriers and the expected retaliation of existing competitors. Barriers to entry are obstacles that make entry into an industry difficult. They are advantages that incumbents have over entrants and often take the form of additional costs that must be incurred by new entrants but not by those firms that already exist in the industry. High barriers to entry help keep the number of companies in an industry small and allow incumbents to earn higher profits. For example, the cost of building a wide-bodied airplane is so high that entry into the aircraft manufacturing industry is virtually impossible. Barriers to entry are high when the following conditions prevail:

- *High economies of scale or experience.* The entrant will have to enter either at a large scale and risk the threat of strong retaliation or at a small scale and operate at a cost disadvantage relative to existing firms.
- *High product differentiation.* Entrants will have to spend heavily to overcome existing brand loyalties.
- *High capital requirements.* Entrants must invest large amounts of financial resources in order to compete effectively.
- *High cost of switching suppliers.* It is difficult for new entrants to obtain sales.
- *Blocked access to channels of distribution.* Entrants will have difficulty finding channels of distribution.
- *High expected retaliation.* The expectation of a vigorous reaction may alter the entrant's plans.

Bargaining power of buyers

Buyers with enough bargaining power can affect an industry's profitability by forcing down prices, demanding higher quality, or demanding more service. These buyers play competitors against each other and buy from many suppliers. Buyers have more bargaining power if the following conditions are true:

- *Few buyers.* If a few buyers account for a large portion of industry sales, buyers have more bargaining power.

- *Low switching costs.* Buyers can easily switch to another supplier, enhancing their bargaining power.
- *Lack of importance of product to buyer's product.* The buyer's bargaining power increases as the product is not important to the buyer.
- *Low buyer profitability.* Buyers earning low profits are more price sensitive and bargain harder for price concessions.
- *Credible threat of backward integration.* Buyers who can produce the required inputs through backward integration have more bargaining power.

Bargaining power of suppliers

Suppliers can exert considerable power over companies in the industries they are supplying. Suppliers can affect an industry's profitability by raising their prices, reducing the quality of the goods and services supplied, or reducing the output to a company or the whole industry. Suppliers are more powerful and have more bargaining power if the following conditions are true:

- *Few suppliers.* The more concentrated the supplier group, the greater their bargaining power over the buying industry.
- *Lack of close substitutes.* Absence of substitutes increases the supplier's bargaining power.
- *Importance of supplier's product.* The more crucial the suppliers' product is to the success of the buyer's product, the greater the bargaining power of the supplier.
- *High switching costs.* The more difficult it is for the buyer to switch from one supplier to another the higher the bargaining power of suppliers.
- *Credible threat of forward integration.* If the supplier group has the ability to integrate forward and become buyers of their own products, their bargaining power relative to the buyer increases.

Threat of substitute products

Substitutes are products that are different in their technology, production process, or materials used but can satisfy the same need as another product. The availability of substitutes provides customers with an additional option to choose from when they make purchasing decisions. The existence of close substitutes reduces the profitability of an industry as firms are forced to keep prices lower. Firms frequently fail to identify the substitutes to their products, and this can have serious implications for their long-term survival. Substitutes are a threat to an industry when the following conditions are true:

Substitutes are products that are different in their technology, production process, or materials used but can satisfy the same need as another product.

- *Favourable price performance.* The better the price performance of substitutes relative to products in the industry, the greater the threat posed by them as customers will have an incentive to switch.
- *Low switching costs.* Lack of switching costs makes switching to substitutes easier.
- *High propensity to substitute.* The higher the propensity of buyers to substitute, the higher the threat to products of an industry.

Complements

In addition to Porter's five competitive forces, complements are an additional factor that affects market profitability. **Complements** are products whose presence makes another product more attractive than if it were alone.[21] Lack of proper complements can slow down the sales of a new product, as the product is less attractive without them. Many people may postpone purchasing a new product until suitable complements become available. For example, sales of personal computers took off only when spreadsheets and other software became available. Also, the quantity of gasoline sold depends on the number of cars purchased. The more cars driven, the more attractive the gasoline industry will be.

Complements are products or services whose presence makes another product or service more attractive than if it were alone.

It is in the best interest of a firm to have as many complements as possible. With more complements, the value of a product to customers increases. Also the more attractive or inexpensive the complements are, the more valuable they are for the product. Some companies provide support to their complementors to develop new versions of their products that would require updated versions of their own products. For example, Intel encourages and financially supports various complementors to develop new applications, such as voice recognition and voice processing, because they require a lot of processing power and would mean increased demand for its microprocessors.[22]

If complements don't exist, some businesses create them. For example, electronic game-makers Sega and Nintendo, in addition to hardware, developed games themselves to make their game players more attractive.[23] Drugstores such as Shoppers Drug Mart and Pharma Plus have established walk-in medical clinics within their premises to boost the volume of prescriptions filled in their pharmacy. Sometimes a complement may be worth supporting even if its profitability is low or even negative. Managers need to keep in mind that although the complement's profitability may be low, what is critical is the overall profit and not each business's profits separately. Although a firm may incur losses on the complement, the increased sales of its main product might more than compensate for these losses.

Methods for Defining Markets

How do marketers define their markets? Defining the market scope is not easy, as there are no strict guidelines available. Because there are many ways to define a market and no single criterion, market definition is a clearly subjective process, where each firm can define the market in its own way. One complicating factor is that market boundaries shift continuously because of evolution in competition, customers, and other environmental factors.

Different market definitions lead to different estimates of market potential and market shares. Broad market definitions are associated with higher market potential than narrow ones. Also, broad market definitions lead to lower market shares, while narrow definitions have the opposite effect. There are a number of methods for defining the structure of markets. Some are based on the observed hierarchical structure of the market, while others rely on managerial and customer judgments, consumer purchase, or usage data. These methods are shown in Figure 2.6 and discussed below.

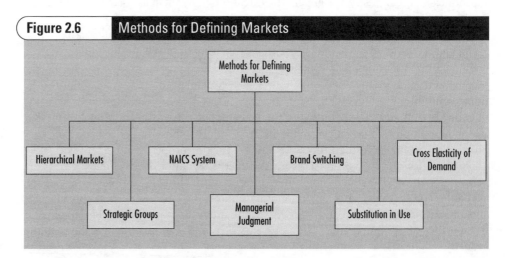

Figure 2.6   Methods for Defining Markets

Hierarchical Markets

One particularly useful way to define markets is to capitalize on the structural properties of markets. Most markets are structured in a hierarchical manner, resembling a tree with its highest branches representing broadly defined markets, and the lowest branches representing those that are narrowly defined. At the highest level of aggregation, a market can be defined by the product offered. One can speak of the soft drink market or the coffee market. The same markets can be defined in more precise terms by narrowing down the scope. For example, the soft drink market can be defined as non-carbonated and carbonated drinks. Similarly, the coffee market can be defined as instant and ground coffee markets.

This hierarchical property can help define a market at different levels. Strategic markets are defined at a broad level and served markets at a more narrow level. A useful approach to structuring a market includes the following: We begin with the highest level of aggregation, which is the **industry** level, which consists of all the products sold by direct and indirect competitors. A **product class** represents all possible ways a customer's need may be met. In the beverage industry example shown in Figure 2.7, coffee is a generic product class within the beverage industry, consisting of all brands of coffee. Soft drinks are another product class within the beverage industry.

An **industry** consists of all the products sold by direct and indirect competitors.

A **product class** represents all possible ways a customer's need may be met.

Figure 2.7	Hierarchical Structure of the Beverage Industry

Each product class consists of different product categories. A **product category** consists of products that satisfy different needs within the broad generic need defined by the product class. Ground and instant coffee are separate product categories in the coffee market. Each product category may consist of two or more **product variants** that satisfy different needs within each product category. Within the instant coffee category, one can find international and domestic coffee variants. Lastly, there are different brands of coffee within each product variant that are usually differentiated on the basis of colour, flavour, quality, features, and price.

A **product category** consists of products that satisfy different needs within the broad generic need defined by the product class.

Product variants satisfy different needs within each product category.

The number of levels of aggregation differs among different industries depending on several factors. First, the greater the breadth and complexity of the generic need to be satisfied, the larger the number of aggregation levels.[24] Second, as a product class matures, more market segments with distinct needs emerge, adding more levels to the hierarchy. Third, as firms strive to come up with new ways to meet market needs, they cause a proliferation in the number of product categories, variants, and brands.

In the beverage example presented in Figure 2.7, any level in the coffee hierarchy could be used for defining the strategic or served market. For example, a coffee company could define its strategic market at the industry level, which is the beverage market; or it could define it at the product class level, which is the coffee market, and so on. The served market also could be defined by making appropriate choices within the boundaries of the strategic market.

Strategic Groups

A **strategic group** is made up of all firms in an industry that have similar resources and strategies.

An industry consists of many firms, some of which are closer competitors than others. A **strategic group** is made up of all those firms in an industry that have similar resources and strategies.[25] Firms within a strategic group employ similar strategies and compete more directly than firms belonging to different strategic groups. For example, Mercedes-Benz and BMW are close competitors because they compete in the luxury car market segment with similar strategies. Mercedes-Benz and Hyundai belong to the automobile industry, but they belong to different strategic groups, because they target different customers with different products and capabilities.

NAICS System

Competitors can be identified by looking for some degree of similarity, such as form, function, materials, production process, physical appearance, or technology. These criteria are the basis of the North American Industry Classification System (NAICS) and are widely accepted because they are easy to implement. The main advantage of NAICS is that it is easily available; the major problem with the system is that competitors frequently include products from entirely different industries. For example, television manufacturers are classified together with radio, stereo, and video game producers. It is debatable that all companies in these industries compete against each other. This type of classification limits the usefulness of NAICS as an accurate method for defining the market structure.

Managerial Judgment

Managers who are experienced in a particular industry can draw up a list of their competitors based on their own direct experience and knowledge of their industry, salesperson reports, or information obtained from suppliers or distributors.[26] When using this method, managers need to be all-inclusive in defining the competitive set because competition can be both direct and indirect. For instance, competitors of a courier company come not only from other courier companies but also from the post office, e-mail, and fax machines. Also, Loblaws' competitors, besides other supermarkets, include Wal-Mart, Canada's largest discount retailer.

Substitution in Use

One way to identify the market structure is to ask customers to list all possible uses or benefits they derive from a product or service. Next, for each use, customers are asked to list other products that provide the same uses or benefits. Alternatively, customers could be asked to identify the brands they take into consideration when they are deciding which products to buy. For example, a restaurant chain may ask its customers what other restaurants they visit or consider visiting when they dine out. The list of restaurants mentioned can then be considered as close competitors.

Substitution in use is a particularly useful method because it has the potential to specifically identify substitute products that are produced by firms outside the company's industry. If the now defunct typewriter company Smith Corona had used the substitution-in-use method, it would have learned that its customers were using or considering using personal computers for their word-processing needs. The availability of such information may have been enough to save the company from bankruptcy by quickly diversifying into personal computers.

Brand Switching

Consumers regularly switch from one brand to another. The probability of brand switching measures the degree of substitutability among brands. Higher probabilities of switching imply a higher likelihood of substitution—and competition—between brands. Marketing researchers can calculate the probability of switching between brands from consumers' past behaviour, usually taken from reports submitted from members of consumer panels. The probability of switching among various brands can then be used to construct brand-switching matrices. An example of a brand-switching matrix is shown in Figure 2.8. The figures represent the probability of switching between brands. For example, the probability of switching between brands A and B is 38 percent and between brands B and A is 36 percent. Since the probability of switching is highest between brands A and B, brand A is a close competitor to brand B.

Figure 2.8	Matrix of Probabilities of Switching Among Brands

		Brand		
		A	B	C
	A	.55	.38	.07
Brand	B	.36	.58	.06
	C	.04	.06	.90

One of the requirements for constructing a brand-switching matrix is that competing brands must be known before brand-switching data are collected.[27] Brand-switching measurements also rely on past consumer behaviour. They indicate what customers have done, not what they will do in the future. As a result, the brand-switching method is useful only for determining the current market structure, not how this structure will look in the future.[28]

Cross-Elasticity of Demand

Cross-elasticity of demand measures the percentage change in one product's sales given a percentage change in another product's price. If the sales of one product decline when the price of another brand drops, the cross-elasticity of demand is termed positive, and the two brands are said to be competitors. This method of defining competitors has a few drawbacks. The competing brands must be known before data are collected, something that may not always be possible. Also, competitors should not react to a price cut with a price cut of their own. If competitors lower their price in response to a price cut, the impact of the original price cut is neutralized, and it distorts the value of the cross-elasticity of demand.

Estimating Market Potential

Once the market has been established, its potential can be determined. Market potential is one of a number of criteria firms use to assess market attractiveness and eliminate markets that have poor sales prospects. **Market potential** is the maximum sale that can be obtained from a market in a given period given a specified marketing effort. Market potential includes the total sales that can be achieved by all firms serving the market. Often actual sales fall short of the market potential because of lack of awareness or because existing production and distribution channels are not capable of meeting the demand for the product. For example, many people might be willing to subscribe to high-speed Internet service but they can't because it is not available in their area. Management's job is to eliminate gaps that prevent a market from achieving its full potential.

Market potential is the maximum sale that can be obtained from a market in a given period given a specified marketing effort.

Methods for Estimating Market Potential

There are different ways for estimating market potential. Two of the most popular methods for estimating market potential are the total market potential and the chain ratio method.

The total market potential method

Many marketing managers use the total market potential method for estimating market potential. The total market potential method calculates market potential using the following formula:

$$S = N \times Q \times P$$

Where:

S = market potential
N = number of potential buyers
Q = average quantity purchased
P = average selling price

For example, if 20 million Canadians go to the movies each year, and the average person goes to the movies 12 times a year and spends $10 per movie, then the market potential for movies is $2.4 billion (20,000,000 × 12 × $10).

In the above example, the most difficult component of the equation to estimate is the total number of people who go to the movies. One reasonable way to calculate this figure is to start with the total population in the country, say, 31 million people. The next step would be to eliminate groups that wouldn't go to the movies. For example, certain people do not go to the movies because they cannot afford the cost of admission tickets. Others do not go to the movies because they rent the movie from video stores when it becomes available. This process of elimination allows us to come up with a reasonable estimate of the number of potential moviegoers.

The chain ratio method

Another method of estimating market potential is the chain ratio method. The chain ratio approach calculates market potential by applying a series of ratios to a base estimate of market demand. For example, how does one estimate the market potential for premium beer? The number of all people of drinking age might be a reasonable estimate. But then not every person of drinking age drinks beer. Also, not everyone who drinks beer prefers premium beer. In addition, not all those who prefer beer are willing or are able to pay the higher price of premium beer.

Figure 2.9	Market Potential for Premium Beer
Total number of people of drinking age	21,000,000
% of people who prefer premium beer	.10
% of people who actually drink premium beer	.50
Total number of people who drink beer	1,050,000
Average amount spent on premium beer	$180
Market potential of premium beer	$189,000,000

As shown in Figure 2.9, if we assume that the total number of people of drinking age is 21 million, 10 percent of them prefer premium beer, and 50 percent of those who prefer premium beer actually drink premium beer, the total number of people who drink premium beer is 1,050,000 (21,000,000 $\times$ .10 $\times$ .50). If premium beer drinkers spend an average amount of $180 per year on premium beer, then the market potential for premium beer is $189 million (1,050,000 $\times$ $180).

- Defining the market is an important part of the strategic market planning process. The choice of the market needs to be made before the environmental analysis and other steps toward the formulation of marketing strategy are taken.

- The strategic market is the broadly defined market where the firm is pursuing current and future opportunities. It includes currently served segments in which the firm might be interested in the future.

- The strategic market is broadly defined and is appropriate for long-term planning and dealing with environmental trends, emerging technologies, and substitute products. Served markets are narrowly defined and are useful for tactical decisions.

- Both the strategic and served markets are defined by choices made along the following three dimensions: customer groups, functions or applications, and technologies and competencies. These dimensions can be portrayed graphically. Combinations of the three dimensions represent distinct market groupings.

- Strategic markets are broadly defined and help draw the boundaries within which the firm pursues its current and future activities. Narrowly defined strategic markets are the reasons why companies frequently fail. Firms that define their strategic markets narrowly suffer from marketing myopia. The served market is a subset of the strategic market definition.

- Markets are not static but are in a perpetual state of flux as new ones constantly emerge. For this reason, marketing managers need to continually search their markets for new positions to occupy.

- The factors that determine market attractiveness include markets factors (market size, market growth, profit margin, price elasticity, seasonality, cyclicality) and industry factors (rivalry among current competitors, threat of new entrants, bargaining power of customers, bargaining power of suppliers, substitutes, and complements).

- Firms can use several methods to determine the structure of markets, including the hierarchical structure of markets, strategic groups, NAICS, managerial judgment, substitution in use, brand switching, and cross-elasticity of demand.

- Once the market is established, management can calculate the potential of the market. Two popular methods for assessing market potential are the total market potential and chain ratio methods.

1. Why is the definition of the strategic market an important part of the strategic marketing planning process?

2. What is the role of strategic markets? Describe the three dimensions marketing managers can use to define their strategic and served markets. Use a diagram to illustrate your answer.

3. Why should strategic markets be defined broadly? What kinds of problems might be associated with narrow strategic market definitions? Why should managers avoid using extremely broad strategic market definitions?

4. Describe served markets. What is the process by which firms arrive at served market definitions? What kinds of decisions are based on served markets?

5. Discuss the implications of the dynamic nature of markets for strategic marketing planning.

6. Discuss the factors that affect market attractiveness.

7. Describe the different methods for defining market structures.

8. Identify and discuss the two methods of estimating market potential.

1. How should a coffee retailer such as Second Cup define its strategic and served market? What about a department store such as The Bay, or a newspaper such as the *Globe and Mail*?

2. Using the methods for defining market structure, identify the market structure of the Canadian soft drink market.

3. Assess the attractiveness of the airline market in Canada.

4. Assume that the number of potential buyers for carbonated water in St. Catharines is 30,000, the average quantity purchased annually per buyer is 20 cases, and the price of each case is $6.95. Using the total market potential method, calculate the market potential for carbonated water in St. Catharines.

5. Assume the total number of wine drinkers in Canada is 8 million. Let's further assume that 80 percent of them prefer imported wine but 70 percent of them actually purchase imported wine. Drinkers of imported wine spend an average $500 per year on imported wine. Using the chain ratio method, calculate the market potential for imported wine in Canada.

Notes

1. John H. Eggers, David C. Shaw, Jim E. Hatch, and Al Mikalachki, *Cases in Entrepreneurship* (Toronto: Prentice Hall, 2001), 29; www.trojanuv.com, retrieved on July 10, 2003.
2. Derek Abell, *Defining the Business: The Starting Point of Strategic Planning* (Englewood Cliffs, N.J.: Prentice Hall, 1980), 1; Derek F. Abell and John Hammond, *Strategic Market Planning* (Englewood Cliffs, N.J.: Prentice Hall, 1979), 389; Constantinos C. Markides, *All the Right Moves* (Boston, Mass.: Harvard Business School Press, 2000), 36.
3. Derek F. Abell, *Managing With Dual Strategies* (New York: The Free Press, 1993), 45.
4. George S. Day, *Strategic Market Planning* (St. Paul, Minn.: West Publishing Company, 1984), 71; Roger J. Best, *Market-Based Management* (Upper Saddle River, N.J.: Prentice Hall, 2004), 59.
5. Lawrence Stevenson, Joseph C. Shlesinger, and Michael R. Pearce, *Power Retail* (Toronto: McGraw-Hill Ryerson, 1999), 99.
6. Gerard J. Tellis and Peter N. Golder, *Will and Vision: How Latecomers Grow to Dominate Markets* (New York: McGraw-Hill, 2002), 20.
7. Quoted in Dorothy Leonard, *Wellsprings of Knowledge* (Boston, Mass.: Harvard Business School Press, 1995), 31.
8. Theodore Levitt, "Marketing Myopia," *Harvard Business Review*, 38 (July–August 1960), 45–56.
9. Tellis and Golder, 20.
10. George S. Day, *The Market Driven Organization: Understanding Attracting, and Keeping Valuable Customers* (New York: The Free Press, 1999), 81.
11. David Aaker, *Strategic Market Management*, 6th ed. (New York: John Wiley, 2001), 41.
12. Markides, 35–36.
13. Abell, 1980, 7; Abell and Hammond, 392.
14. Gary Hamel and C. K. Prahalad, "The Core Competence of the Corporation," *Harvard Business Review* (May–June 1990), 79–91.
15. Day, 1984, 73.
16. John Cady and Robert Buzzell, *Strategic Marketing* (Boston, Mass.: Little, Brown and Company, 1986), 124; Abell and Hammond, 185–186.
17. The Xerox and Canon story is discussed in Constantinos C. Markides, *All The Right Moves: A Guide to Crafting Breakthrough Strategy* (Boston, Mass.: Harvard Business School Press, 2000), 8–10.
18. David T. Kearns and David A. Nadler, *Prophets in the Dark: How Xerox Reinvented Itself and Beat Back the Japanese* (New York: HarperBusiness, 1992), 121.
19. George S. Day, "Assessing Competitive Arenas: Who Are Your Competitors?" in George S. Day, David J. Reibstein, and Robert E. Gunther (eds.), *Wharton on Dynamic Competitive Strategy* (New York: John Wiley, 1997), 24.
20. Michael E. Porter, *Competitive Strategy* (New York: The Free Press, 1980), 3.
21. Luis M. B. Cabral, *Introduction to Industrial Organization* (Cambridge, Mass.: The MIT Press, 2000), 217.
22. Adrian Ryans, Roger More, Donald Barclay, and Terry Deutscher, *Winning Market Leadership: Strategic Market Planning for Technology-Driven Businesses* (Toronto: John Wiley and Sons, 2000), 59.
23. Adam M. Brandenburger and Barry J. Nalebuff, *Co-opetition* (New York: Currency, Doubleday, 1996), 103.
24. Day, 1984, 75.
25. Porter, 129.
26. Donald R. Lehmann and Russell S. Winer, *Analysis for Strategic Market Decisions*, 2nd ed. (Homewood Ill.: Irwin, 1991), 27.
27. Lehmann and Winer, 29.
28. Lehmann and Winer, 29.

Chapter Three

Situational Analysis and Strategic Approaches

Acquire better and more reliable intelligence. Know the enemy, and know yourself; in a hundred battles you will never be in peril.

Sun Tzu, Ancient Chinese General

The function of grand strategy is to discover and exploit the Achilles' Heel of the enemy.

Liddell Hart, Military Strategist

Learning Objectives

After studying this chapter, you should be able to:

1. Discuss the role of situational analysis in the strategy formulation process

2. Outline a process for determining a firm's strengths, weaknesses, opportunities, and threats

3. Construct the preliminary and final SWOT matrix

4. Identify the pitfalls of SWOT analysis

5. Discuss the desirable properties of marketing objectives

6. Identify sources of external and competitive information

7. Conduct a competitor analysis

Challenges Facing the Canadian Banking Industry

The banking industry is a significant component of the Canadian financial system and economy. As of July 2002, Canada had 14 domestic banks, 33 foreign bank subsidiaries, and 20 foreign bank branches. The total assets managed by all these banks was $1.7 trillion. The Canadian banking industry is dominated by the six major domestic banks, which collectively account for over 90 percent of all banking industry assets.

According to figures issued by the International Monetary Fund, Canada has one of the most stable and sound financial systems in the world. However, the Canadian banking system has been challenged by a number of environmental trends and forces in recent years. Following the global economic slowdown and the impact of the September 11, 2001 terrorist attacks, the performance of Canada's major banks in 2001 was down from 16.8 percent return on common equity to 15.2 percent.

The Canadian banking system has undergone major changes over the years. The main function of a bank until the 1950s was to accept deposits and give out commercial loans. Changes in customer needs and the growth in international trade presented banks with the opportunity to offer more services. Revisions to Canada's Bank Act in 1954 and 1967 allowed banks to sell consumer loans and mortgages. Further changes to financial institution legislation in 1987 and major revisions to the Bank Act in 1992 increased competition in Canada's financial system, as these changes permitted banks to operate trust and securities subsidiaries. Banks rushed to acquire most of Canada's largest trust and securities firms.

Canadian banks have also expanded and diversified their operations geographically. After years of pursuing international opportunities, the six major domestic banks are currently present in many locations outside of Canada, including the United States, South America, Asia, and the Caribbean. The significance of foreign operations for Canadian banks is evident from the high percentage of foreign revenues that accounted for 33 percent of total gross revenues in 2001.

Canadian banks are currently facing a number of challenges. Global competition and technology are posing direct threats to the Canadian banking industry. A significant threat for Canadian banks is the increased number of foreign banks operating in Canada. New legislation passed in 1999 permits foreign banks to operate in Canada without having to set up Canadian incorporated subsidiaries. Canadian banks are also experiencing competitive pressures from other financial institutions. Among the new entrants are companies that traditionally operate in non-financial service fields such as Canada's leading grocery chain, Loblaws. New technologies and especially the Internet allow competitors such as ING Direct to operate without having to set up branches. There is some positive news, though. Because interest rates have declined since 2001, banks have seen an increase in net interest income. The lower interest rates created a boom in housing sales and an increase in the number of mortgages. Many homeowners also refinanced their existing mortgages to reduce their debt-services costs.

All these environmental changes present significant challenges to the Canadian banking industry. In an attempt to remain competitive, banks have responded by investing in technology to provide innovative products and services such as online banking to satisfy consumer needs. Many banks have restructured their operations to reduce costs and pursued high-growth niches such as corporate and investment banking and wealth management. While defending their home turf, many Canadian banks are also actively pursuing opportunities in foreign markets as part of their long-term growth strategy.[1]

Introduction

Once the market has been defined, the next step in the strategic marketing planning process is to obtain a good understanding of the business environment in which the firm competes and of its internal capabilities. The Canadian banking industry, discussed in the opening vignette, illustrates how the business environment can create significant challenges for organizations. Effective strategic marketing planning requires a clear understanding of the dynamics of the firm's environment. The firm's external environment largely determines what is possible and what a firm must do to succeed in its chosen market. A major task for management is to examine how internal and external factors affect the firm's ability to achieve its vision, mission, and goals.

Analysis of the current situation is a critical early step in the process of strategy formulation.[2] The purpose of the situational analysis is to identify the relevant environmental trends and forces and to assess the organization's resources and capabilities. The outcome of the situational analysis is a set of conclusions about the external environment and internal resources and capabilities known as strengths, weaknesses, opportunities, and threats, usually referred to by the acronym SWOT.[3]

Analyzing the external and internal environment is an ongoing effort as opposed to just an annual ritual. To be effective, this analysis needs to be systematic and supported by adequate information. Having enough up-to-date information enables managers to quickly assess environmental developments and take appropriate action. Missing out on an important new trend or having an inaccurate assessment of the organization's resources and capabilities may lead to serious strategic error.

SWOT analysis
summarizes a firm's strengths, weaknesses, opportunities, and threats.

SWOT analysis is the most widely known method of situational analysis.[4] It summarizes a firm's strengths, weaknesses, opportunities, and threats. The purpose of the SWOT analysis is to determine an organization's ability to deal with its external environment. This is accomplished by assessing the fit between the internal—a company's marketing strategy with its internal resources and capabilities (strengths and weaknesses)—and the external—outside trends and forces (opportunities and threats).[5] Through a thorough analysis, a firm can discover important strengths that can be used to build its strategy in markets where these strengths will be competitively advantageous. Firms that fail to explore their competitive strengths will often have an inferior performance.

SWOT analysis is commonly used for organizing the numerous pieces of information created by the internal and external analyses. The information gathered through these analyses needs to be organized for marketing decision-making.

The objective of this chapter is to explain how to use situational analysis to deal with changes that take place in a firm's external environment. This chapter will demonstrate how to conduct a thorough analysis of the external environment and identify the trends and forces that affect a firm's ability to carry out its strategy and achieve its objectives. According to the old saying, "You cannot direct the wind but you can adjust your sails," and this applies to the business environment in no small measure. The external analysis together with an internal evaluation of company resources and capabilities helps firms "adjust their sails"—that is, assess the viability of their current strategies and make any needed adjustments. An important goal of the chapter is to construct the preliminary and final SWOT matrices, for summarizing the strengths, weaknesses, opportunities, and threats facing the organization and for developing marketing strategies. In addition, this chapter will discuss the properties of effective marketing objectives. This sequence of activities is illustrated in Figure 3.1. Finally, the topics of collecting external information and competition will be discussed.

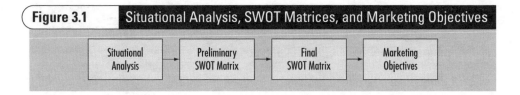

Figure 3.1 Situational Analysis, SWOT Matrices, and Marketing Objectives

Situational Analysis → Preliminary SWOT Matrix → Final SWOT Matrix → Marketing Objectives

Situational Analysis

Situational analysis is an important step in the strategic marketing planning process. It is used to summarize all the important aspects of a firm's internal and external environment. One of the most important benefits managers derive from the situational analysis is information about the current and future state of factors that affect the firm's performance.

Internal Analysis

Marketing strategy reflects actions intended to match an organization's resources and capabilities with the opportunities and threats in its environment. Successful marketing strategies build on the firm's distinctive competencies to provide goods and services that satisfy customers' needs and wants. In order to develop the most effective marketing strategy, marketing managers need to know the areas in which their organization is strong and the areas in which it is weak.

Internal analysis involves an assessment of a firm's resources and capabilities to identify its strengths and weaknesses. **Strengths** are the areas that can be used as sources of competitive advantage. **Weaknesses** are the areas in which the organization is deficient and are sources of competitive disadvantage.[6] Strengths and weaknesses are determined when organizational resources and capabilities are compared to the competition, as shown in Figure 3.2.[7]

Most organizations have the following functions: marketing, management, finance, production, and research and development. Figure 3.3 lists the major functional areas of the organization and examples of resources and capabilities within each function. Each of these functions must be assessed to determine if it represents a strength or a weakness.

> **Situational analysis** is used to summarize all the important aspects of a firm's internal and external environment.

> **Internal analysis** involves an assessment of a firm's resources and capabilities to identify its strengths and weaknesses.

> **Strengths** are the areas that can be used as sources of competitive advantage.

> **Weaknesses** are the areas in which the organization is deficient and are sources of competitive disadvantage.

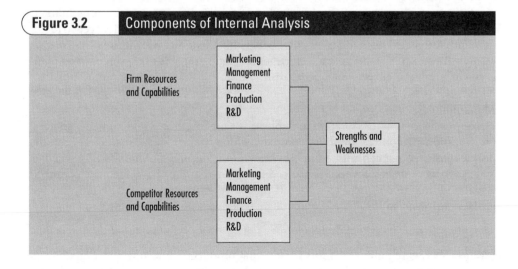

Figure 3.2 Components of Internal Analysis

Firm Resources and Capabilities → Marketing / Management / Finance / Production / R&D

Competitor Resources and Capabilities → Marketing / Management / Finance / Production / R&D

→ Strengths and Weaknesses

Figure 3.3	Examples of Resources and Capabilities

Marketing

Market sensing
Customer relating
Brand equity
Breadth of product line
Market share
Market development skills
Access to channels of distribution
Advertising spending and skills
Effectiveness of sales force

Management

Experience in the business
Quality of company culture
Ability of managers
Effectiveness of strategic planning
Ability to implement plans
Employee training
Employee skills
Use of work teams
Shared organizational goals and
objectives
Effectiveness of systems and control

Production

Access to raw materials
Capacity
Age and location of facilities
Inventory-control procedures
Quality-control procedures
Manufacturing cost
Order handling

Finance

Cash reserves
Financing from parent company
Ability to borrow or raise capital
Debt levels

Research and development

Technological research capabilities
Product design and innovation skills
New product development time
Communication between research and
development and other functions
Patents

A function is a strength or a weakness to the extent that the organization performs this function better or worse than its major competitors. Each of the functional areas is discussed below:

Marketing

Companies succeed when they create highly satisfied customers, and marketing plays an important part in seeing that this happens. As we discussed in Chapter 1, market orientation is a fundamental marketing capability. Market-oriented firms possess strong market-sensing and customer-relating skills.[8] **Market sensing** entails all the activities needed to understand customers' needs and competitor behaviour. **Customer relating** involves creating relationships with valuable customers. Other marketing capabilities include brand management, product management, pricing, distribution, and marketing communications.

Management

The term *management* refers in part to a company's organizational and human resources. Organizational resources are those company-wide variables such as structure, culture, policies, systems, and controls. A firm's human resources consist of the skills, knowledge, and expertise of its employees. Firms need to ensure that they have adequate organizational and human resources to carry out their marketing strategy and accomplish the goals of the organization.

Production

Business success requires that firms have strong production and operation capabilities and excellent quality-control procedures to ensure product quality, low defect rates, and customer satisfaction. A good quality-control system will institute procedures that improve the organization's ability to prevent defects before they occur instead of relying on inspection after the fact. Available productive capacity and modern and conveniently located facilities also provide a firm with competitive advantages. Manufacturing cost is another important aspect of a firm's competitiveness. Low-cost capability—the firm's ability to make products at low production costs—is especially critical to firms that target price-sensitive customers with low prices. Other production and operations capabilities include inventory-control procedures, manufacturing cycle time (the time it takes to produce a product), and order handling.

Finance

Financial resources include cash reserves, financing from a parent company, borrowing ability, ability to raise capital, and debt levels. Firms need to audit their financial resources to determine if they have the necessary capital to support the marketing strategy. Marketing plans often fail because firms overextend themselves and run out of capital before the plan is implemented. Firms that grow rapidly are especially susceptible to financial problems by exhausting their financial resources and finding themselves facing bankruptcy. Cash-flow problems associated with high-growth firms arise because growth requires the firms to expand their facilities, purchase equipment, and increase accounts receivable and inventory levels. All these can cause an otherwise profitable company to become insolvent as it runs into cash-flow problems.

Research and development

An essential part of internal analysis is to examine a firm's research and development capabilities, including technological research, product design, and innovation skills. Research and development skills are especially important for firms that compete on product innovation and are seeking first-mover advantages. Many firms rely on speed as a way to improve their competitive position. Speed entails cutting the lead time from concept to product development, enabling firms to bring new models to market more quickly than competitors. Also, the number of patents in effect is another aspect of a firm's research and development capabilities because it gives a firm a monopoly position for the duration of the patent.

Strengths and Weaknesses

The purpose of internal analysis is to assess the organization's resources and capabilities and draw up a list of strengths and weaknesses. As we already stated previously, strengths are areas in which the firm performs exceptionally well relative to its competitors. Weaknesses, then, are deficiencies or limitations that place a firm at a disadvantage relative to its competition, as they inhibit its ability to implement its marketing strategy and fulfill its objectives.

An objective evaluation of strengths and weaknesses is necessary for a company that wants to grow and compete effectively. The process of identifying strengths and weaknesses, however, is fraught with difficulties. Evidence indicates that few managers agree on the strengths and weaknesses of their organization.[9] The perception of what constitutes strengths and weaknesses is influenced by the manager's position in the organization and type of responsibilities. For example, facilities are of more concern to lower levels while higher levels of managers concentrate on the financial aspects. Also, managers are generally more optimistic about the organization's capabilities and they perceive there are more strengths than weaknesses.[10]

Another common mistake managers make is to define their strengths relative to past performance instead of comparing their performance with that of their competitors; if performance improves, they declare it as a strength; if it deteriorates, it is classified as a weakness. Some managers also compare actual performance against stated organizational goals. Organizational goals should not be used as a criterion in identifying strengths and weaknesses. Thus, strengths should not be internally assessed against past performance or organizational goals. The true test of whether resources and capabilities are strengths or weaknesses is to see how they compare to competitors.

External Analysis

All firms are surrounded by various environmental forces over which they have very little control and which affect the firms' ability to meet their performance objectives. These forces vary from the broadest and most indirect, such as consumer demographics and political and legal developments, to more immediate forces, such as market demand, unmet market needs, suppliers, distributors, and competitors. A firm needs to develop a thorough understanding of these forces and their impact on the organization. The success of a firm's marketing strategy depends largely on how well management understands these forces.

External analysis involves scanning the external environment to identify relevant trends and forces. To be effective, external analysis needs to satisfy the following:

- It should be a creative process instead of just being a simple extrapolation from past trends.
- It must not be an annual ritual but it should be carried out continuously as the environment constantly generates threats and opportunities.
- It needs to be characterized by discipline and direction. Otherwise, it can generate huge amounts of useless output. One way to reduce the amount of worthless data is to confine the external analysis within the boundaries of the strategic market.

Figure 3.4 presents a framework for conducting the external analysis.[11] As can be seen in Figure 3.4, the external environment is made up of two components, the general environment and the task environment. Each of these environmental components is described in the following section.

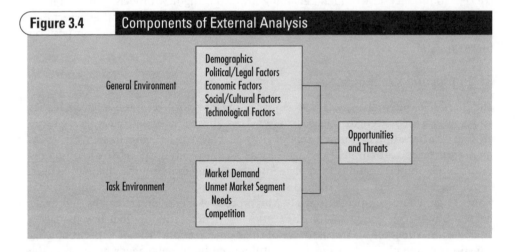

Figure 3.4   Components of External Analysis

The general environment

The **general environment** consists of all broad external factors that have an indirect impact on the organization. Organizations have very little or no control over their general environment. The major components of the general environment are demographic, political and legal, economic, social and cultural, and technological factors.

Demographic Factors. Demographics involve the study of trends in population characteristics. Demographic variables include age, gender, income levels, birth rates, education, and family life cycle. Changes in the demographic profile of the population can have a

---

External analysis involves scanning the external environment to identify relevant trends and forces.

The **general environment** consists of all broad external factors that have an indirect impact on the organization.

Demographics involve the study of trends in population characteristics.

dramatic impact on a firm's market segmentation, product positioning, and new product development. For example, the greying of the Canadian population has led to increases in demand for health care and travel services. New segments emerge or existing segments disappear as the population changes. Modifications in the design of a product may be needed to adapt to the new demographic trends. New distribution channels may be required to reach the new target markets. Existing advertising and promotional strategies may become ineffective and in need of drastic overhaul.

Political and Legal Factors. Changes in the political and legal environment can alter the competitive landscape and affect the performance of firms. Political and legal factors can include new legislation in the areas of regulation, safety and packaging laws, competition laws, taxation, and international trade. Political and legal changes can affect any or all aspects of the marketing mix, as companies have no choice but to comply. Marketing managers need to be aware of how laws, legislation, regulation, and political decisions affect their organization. New regulations or changes to existing regulations can have an impact on the manner in which a firm conducts its business. For example, the deregulation of the Canadian banking industry allowed a number of foreign banks to enter and establish operations in Canada, ending the monopoly of the Canadian banks.

Economic Factors. Economic factors include interest rates, gross national product, exchange rates, unemployment rates, disposable income, and national debt levels. Firms must have an excellent understanding of their economic environment as their ability to carry out their marketing program may be affected by changing economic conditions. Changes in economic factors may mean either opportunities or threats for the organization. For instance, an increase in the exchange rate is a threat to Canadian exporters of Canadian grains since it will make the product more expensive in foreign markets. It will be an opportunity, however, to importers of foreign goods, as it will make them less expensive than those domestically produced.

Social and Cultural Factors. Consumption behaviour is affected by the social and cultural norms of a society, including a society's shared values, traditions, attitudes, and patterns of behaviour. Social and cultural characteristics are not as easy to measure and track as demographic characteristics. Still, marketing managers need to track these trends and assess their implications for their organization, as some of them may be favourable and others not. For example, an increased concern about quality of life, physical fitness, and nutrition and healthier eating are creating both opportunities and threats for companies. The Strategy in Action box illustrates how Pepsi responded to these new trends:[12]

Strategy in Action — PEPSI COLA

The recent trends toward healthier eating and drinking habits and diets with fewer carbohydrates have forced many companies to modify their products to accommodate consumers' new tastes and preferences. Among those companies are PepsiCo, which responded to the new health trends by reducing the fat content in some of its products. It removed all trans fats—the main culprit in clogging arteries—from its Frito-Lay snacks. The company announced that it would introduce Pepsi Edge, a "full-flavoured" cola with 50 percent less sugar, carbohydrates, and calories than regular Pepsi. In responding to the popularity of the Atkins diet, a diet with fewer carbohydrates, the company cut the carbohydrate content of its Doritos Edge and Tostitos Edge products to less than half of the original. By keeping up with recent social trends and making changes in its product lines, Pepsi was hoping to maintain or even increase sales of its products in a fiercely competitive marketplace.

Technological Factors. Advances in technology can have an enormous impact on the competitive environment in which the firm participates. For example, the Internet has changed the nature of competition in many industries by allowing small firms to compete more effectively against much larger rivals. If they are to remain competitive, firms must keep up with the pace of technology. Firms that fail to create new products risk being surpassed by innovative competitors. The introduction of new products or production processes can catapult a competitor into a leading market position. Innovative products can render a firm's current product line obsolete. For this reason, new technological advancements need to be adopted quickly to remain competitive. For example, new technologies such as nanotechnology and biotechnology are creating enormous opportunities for certain firms to capitalize on. The need to be attuned to technological change has increased in recent years as the pace of change continues to rapidly accelerate.

The task environment

The **task environment** consists of forces that are closest to the organization and have a direct and immediate impact on it. They are the forces with which organizations interact directly, including market demand, unmet market needs, and competitive trends.

Market Demand. Marketing success requires a thorough understanding of the demand for a firm's products. Market demand is one of the most important situational variables because it determines to a large extent the market potential for the product. **Market demand** is defined as the number of units people want to purchase over a period of time under certain conditions. Demand for a product is affected by factors such as industry trends, consumer income levels, price of the product, and the price of competing products. The Strategy in Action box describes the impact of industry trends on market demand for a firm's products. [13]

Strategy in Action   BACHMAN INFORMATION SYSTEMS

Bachman Information Systems achieved dramatic growth rates in the early 1990s by marketing its highly successful software designed for mainframe applications. It grew from $13 million in 1990 to $48 million in 1992, ranking 19th among *Inc.* magazine's fastest-growth companies in 1992. However, Bachman failed to see the trend toward PC-based client-server computing that had begun replacing mainframe computers. As a result, sales plummeted in 1993. The company's close ties with IBM, which was a joint developer and stockholder and the leader in the market for mainframe computers, may have also contributed to the poor performance of Bachman by making the company oblivious to the shift to distributed computers that was taking place at that time. IBM was indeed slow in responding to the trend toward distributed computers largely because it had the most to lose by making the switch from mainframes to such computers.

Unmet Segment Needs. An important aspect of external analysis is to identify segments whose needs are not being met by existing companies. Segments with unmet needs represent important opportunities for firms to increase their market share or new entrants to break into new markets. These segments often exist either because firms think they are too small to warrant making an investment, or because they have been neglected or simply overlooked. For example, Bravado! Designs is a company that was created by two young mothers who entered the market for underwear for pregnant women. These two women realized that there was an unmet need for underwear for pregnant women, as none of the existing underwear companies were paying attention to this segment.

Competition. Having a good understanding of competitors, their strengths and weaknesses, market share, strategies, and future goals and objectives is fundamental to developing effective marketing strategies. Firms must be alert to the threat of competitive actions in the marketplace. Competition often determines the success or failure of a firm's marketing strategy. For this reason, marketing managers need a thorough understanding of their competition. Managers need to be aware of all direct and indirect, current and future competitors. Managers also need to be aware of the potential threat from new entrants into their market or from existing competitors expanding into their markets.

Firms must also be alert to the possibility of radically new forms of competition. Firms that fall into the trap of narrowly defining their businesses are particularly susceptible to such events. The emergence of new competitors can be particularly unsettling for firms. While existing competitors can threaten a firm with new and improved products, their competitive actions and underlying goals can be understood through an analysis of their past actions. But in the case of new competitors, a firm does not have the opportunity to analyze actions with the benefit of historical perspective. Consequently, it becomes much more difficult to determine the most appropriate form of response to new competitor threats. More details on competitive analysis and sources of environmental and competitive information will be offered in a subsequent section.

Opportunities and Threats

The ultimate purpose of external analysis is to identify the firm's opportunities and threats that exist outside the organization. Together with strengths and weaknesses, they help managers focus their efforts on developing strategies that take advantage of opportunities using strengths and overcome or minimize weaknesses and threats. The importance of correctly identifying opportunities and threats facing an organization can be demonstrated by Molson's decision to appoint a senior executive to monitor consolidation in the beer industry and assess opportunities and threats as they arise.[14] The merger of Molson with Coors has most likely been the response by the two companies to the recent trend toward greater consolidation in the beer industry.

Opportunities are favourable trends, forces, or changes in the external environment that have the potential to help the firm improve its competitive position if appropriate action is taken. Opportunities may take the form of new technologies, new markets, and new social trends. Also, competitors may present opportunities when they become vulnerable because of high levels of debt or cash problems due to expansion or leveraged buy-out.

Threats are unfavourable trends, changes, or forces that can threaten the firm's competitive position or cause problems if no appropriate action is taken. Threats can take the form of a decline in the firm's market size, changing customer needs and adverse demographic shift, or an increase in the price sensitivity of customers. An example of threat due to changing customer needs is described in the Strategy in Action box:[15]

Opportunities are favourable trends, forces, or changes in the external environment that have the potential to help the firm improve its competitive position if appropriate action is taken.

Threats are unfavourable trends, changes, or forces that can threaten the firm's competitive position or cause problems if no appropriate action is taken.

Strategy in Action — NOKIA

In the early days of the cellular telephone industry, the little Finnish company Nokia overtook leader Motorola by scanning for emerging trends around the world. By observing its customers it was the first company to see the potential of cellular phones as a fashion accessory. In the process, Nokia became the cellular phone industry leader. However, its market share declined in early 2004 from previous levels as the company struggled to sell cellular phones in Europe and

(continued)

North America. While Nokia chose to focus on selling smart phones and regular mobile phones without a flop, customers were buying the clamshell design or flip phones equipped with colour screen and cameras sold by its rivals.

As Nokia was losing market share, its main competitors—Motorola, Samsung, Siemens AG, and Sony-Ericsson—were increasing their market share. According to a report written by analyst Ben Wood of the technology research group Gartner Inc., Nokia's share declined because cellular companies in Western Europe were sourcing more phones from Nokia's competitors. However, a big factor was Nokia's weak product line, especially in the midrange where the company was slow to bring out their own clamshell and flip phones.

A list of potential strengths, weaknesses, opportunities, and threats is shown in Figure 3.5.

Figure 3.5	Potential Strengths, Weaknesses, Opportunities, and Threats

Potential Strengths	Potential Weaknesses
Financial resources	Weak product development skills
High brand awareness	Weak distribution
Superior service	Poor management skills
High market share	Lack of product development skills
Low manufacturing cost	Narrow product focus
Proprietary technology	Inadequate financial resources
Access to distribution	Poor quality-control procedures
Brand reputation	Lack of product awareness
Strong marketing skills	Weak research and development skills

Potential Opportunities	Potential Threats
Weak competitors	Raw materials shortages
Attractive new market segments	Slow industry growth
High growth prospects	Increased competitive entry
High profit potential	New substitute products
High barriers to entry	Increasing bargaining power of buyers
New complements	Increasing bargaining power of suppliers
Low rivalry	Adverse social trends
New technological developments	

Developing the SWOT Matrix

SWOT analysis offers a concise method for organizing information and summarizing the key issues facing the firm. An important aspect of SWOT analysis is that it allows management to obtain a better understanding of the strategic issues that affect the long-term performance of the organization and to formulate strategies to address them.

It must be noted also that SWOT analysis does not provide managers with ready answers but requires them to offer their own insights on how to best address the important issues affecting the organization. SWOT analysis requires that managers interpret and classify the internal and external information using their own industry knowledge and experience.

Construction of the SWOT Matrix

The construction of the SWOT Matrix involves the following steps:

Step 1

The first step in using the SWOT analysis technique is to identify the organization's strengths, weaknesses, opportunities, and threats. This involves gathering and interpreting internal and external information (collected through market research and competitive intelligence activities) and an iterative and consultative process between top management and functional specialists. Once all strengths, weaknesses, opportunities, and threats are identified and ranked in terms of their potential attractiveness or severity, the marketing manager develops an intermediate SWOT matrix such as the one shown in Figure 3.6 for a small premium food products company.

Figure 3.6	An Example of an Intermediate SWOT Matrix
I *Strengths* 1. Well-known brand name 2. Strong marketing skills 3. Superior product quality 4. Large financial resources	**II** *Weaknesses* 1. High cost of operations 2. Narrow product line 3. Concentration in higher-end brands 4. Limited distribution in specialty stores
III *Opportunities* 1. Increased emphasis on family values 2. Growing demand for healthy food 3. Aging population 4. Demand for a low-priced version of the product 5. Growing foreign markets	**IV** *Threats* 1. Declining demand for core product 2. Growing demand for away-from-home eating 3. Growing demand for ready-made food

Step 2

The second step in SWOT analysis is to assess the strategic fit between the internal capabilities and environmental trends and developments. The **strategic fit** reflects how well the firm's competencies match the predicted external environment. The greater the fit, the less the strategic change required. A poor fit would indicate that strategic changes are needed. This should prompt management to seek strategies that achieve a better fit. For example, the SWOT analysis illustrated in Figure 3.6 shows a declining demand for the firm's core product and a growing demand for healthy foods. The declining demand for the firm's core product and rising demand for healthy foods should signal to management that there is a need to develop new products that match the changing requirements of the marketplace.

Strategic fit reflects how well the firm's competencies match the predicted external environment.

Step 3

The final step in SWOT analysis is a proposed list of strategies to exploit the strengths and opportunities and convert or minimize weaknesses and threats. These strategies represent specific opportunities that should be pursued, and they provide the basis for the design of the organization's marketing strategy. Figure 3.7 shows the final SWOT matrix, which includes a list of ranked strengths, weaknesses, opportunities, threats, and possible strategies for the small food manufacturer.[16]

Figure 3.7	An Example of a Final SWOT Matrix

Internal Factors / External Factors	Strengths 1. Well-known brand name 2. Strong marketing skills 3. Superior product quality 4. Large financial resources	Weaknesses 1. High cost of operations 2. Narrow product line 3. Concentration in higher-end brands 4. Limited distribution in specialty stores
Opportunities 1. Increased emphasis on family values 2. Growing demand for healthy food 3. Aging population 4. Demand for a low-priced version of the product 5. Growing foreign markets	I Possible strategies 1. Appeal to older groups with healthier products 2. Establish or acquire family restaurants 3. Establish or acquire restaurants specializing in healthy eating 4. Expand into foreign markets	II Possible strategies 1. Diversify into health-conscious segments using specialty stores 2. Develop low-priced version of the product
Threats 1. Declining demand for core product 2. Growing demand for away-from-home eating 3. Growing demand for ready-made food	III Possible strategies 1. Introduce convenience foods 2. Target older age market segments	IV Possible strategies 1. Emphasize cost reduction 2. Sell the company

The potential strategies listed in the final SWOT matrix are ranked by their ability to provide an extremely good strategic fit between the firm's external environment and its resources and capabilities. Given that firms have limited resources, it is impossible to pursue all strategies listed in the final SWOT matrix, so marketing managers need to rank these strategies and consider pursuing only the most attractive ones. The final SWOT matrix is constructed using the following guidelines:

Quadrant I. Strategies in this quadrant represent the best match between strengths and opportunities. Strategies are generated by considering ways in which the organization can employ its strengths to take advantage of opportunities. Only those strategies that match the organization's strengths with the most significant opportunities are selected. For example, in the final SWOT matrix presented in Figure 3.7, the company could take advantage of its superior product quality, marketing skills, and financial strength to capitalize on the growing demand for healthy food. Also, promising opportunities for which the organization has no strengths to exploit are rejected, and critical capabilities should be further improved to maintain competitive advantage.

Quadrant II. Strategies in this quadrant are designed to help the organization take advantage of opportunities and overcome weaknesses at the same time. For example, an opportunity may exist for a low-priced version of the firm's product, and a weakness is its narrow product line. The firm could invest in developing a low-priced version of its product, thus taking advantage of the opportunity while at the same time overcoming its narrow product-line weakness. Firms could also invest to transform areas of vulnerability into strengths needed to take advantage of opportunities. If management cannot improve its critical weaknesses, it should concede the opportunity to competitors.

Quadrant III. Strategies in this quadrant aim at turning threats into opportunities. For example, a firm whose market position is being challenged by a new technology could eliminate this threat by adopting the new technology. Firms often acquire their competitors instead of developing the technology themselves. Marketing strategies are developed that are intended to neutralize the threats by diversifying into segments where the threat no longer applies. For example, small beer companies facing stiff competition from large breweries avoid direct competition by competing in the premium beer segment.

Quadrant IV. Strategies in this quadrant are designed to avoid threats and minimize the impact of weaknesses. Positions in this quadrant are typically the worst among the four. Most of the strategies generated in this quadrant are defensive in nature, such as improving weaknesses or divesting the business to focus on promising strategies in other quadrants.

Pitfalls of SWOT Analysis

SWOT analysis is one of the most popular tools used by marketers for strategy analysis and formulation. One of its strengths is that it can be applied in many situations such as managing products, product lines, business units, and functional areas. The analysis can be completed relatively quickly as it does not have extensive financial and computational requirements. Despite its wide acceptance and usefulness, SWOT analysis has several limitations. These limitations are discussed next, along with ways of overcoming them.

- SWOT analysis is a general framework for organizing external and internal information. It provides only general recommendations on the basis of broadly based information. For this reason, more specific research may be required to complement the SWOT analysis.
- It is based on subjective interpretation of the information. Some analysts may view an environmental event such as a new technology as an opportunity while others may perceive it as a threat. As we have previously discussed, managers tend to be more optimistic in their evaluation of strengths and opportunities than in their evaluation of threats and weaknesses. Managers also differ in their identification of strengths, weaknesses, opportunities, and threats, depending on their position or type of responsibilities. Such behaviour often results in the firm failing to generate strategies that are built on genuine strengths. In analyzing the internal situation, it is crucial that managers are critical and honest in identifying strengths and weaknesses.
- SWOT analysis demands a tight fit between the organization's resources and marketing strategies. This may cause firms to miss out on more attractive opportunities that require it to stretch its resources. Firms need to allow for a looser fit and should consider setting stretch goals.[17]
- SWOT analysis can result in a long list of strengths and weaknesses, many of which are not affecting the firm's performance. Resources and capabilities are truly labelled

strengths or weaknesses if they lead to a competitive advantage or disadvantage. For example, a firm's manufacturing cost is a strength only if it is lower than the competitors' manufacturing cost, giving it a low-cost advantage.

- A common problem with SWOT analysis is that resources and capabilities are often defined too broadly to be actionable. Only by using detailed definitions can managers truly determine whether a particular competence is a strength or weakness. For example, a firm that claims it has strong manufacturing skills is using a term that is too broad to be practical. This area can be subdivided into various sub-areas, such as low-cost manufacturing, short manufacturing cycle time, and low defect rates. By defining resources more specifically, managers can be more effective in assessing their resources and target those opportunities that correspond to their own strengths.
- Another problem with SWOT analysis is resource mobility. In pursuing new markets, firms must assess the transferability of their resources. Many firms find it difficult to replicate their current success in new markets or new products because resources are industry specific. For example, Philip Morris believed it had strong marketing skills based on its long experience in marketing tobacco products. It used these strengths successfully in the beer market when it acquired Miller Breweries. However, it had a hard time competing against Coca-Cola and Pepsi when it acquired 7-Up. Philip Morris's marketing skills turned out to be weaknesses compared with the specific marketing skills of Coca-Cola and Pepsi that they had developed over many years of competing in that market.[18]
- SWOT analysis must be performed at the appropriate segment level. Some firms perform SWOT analysis for the entire market instead of the appropriate segment. SWOT analysis should be performed for each segment separately because there are usually differences between segments in the area of customers, competitors, and segment requirements. For example, IBM couldn't use its superior mainframe product development and service capabilities in the personal computer segment where low price and mass distribution were key success factors. As a result, it failed to maintain a viable market position and it sold its PC division to China-based Lenovo Group and took a minority interest in its former rival.

Marketing Objectives

Marketing objectives specify a desired outcome to be achieved within a certain period of time.

Once the SWOT analysis is completed and the specific strategy is selected, a firm determines the objectives to be achieved. **Marketing objectives** specify a desired outcome to be achieved within a certain period of time.[19] Marketing objectives are performance targets that are derived from a realistic evaluation of the opportunities and threats and the company's strengths and weaknesses identified in the SWOT analysis. For example, the more attractive the opportunities and the greater the strength of the company, the higher the marketing objectives should be.

Marketing objectives are the targets needed to accomplish the firm's vision, mission, and goals. They translate overall corporate goals into more specific ends. They are normally viewed as the intermediate steps that need to be taken to accomplish the organizational goals. For example, if the organizational goal is to increase market share from 10 percent to 15 percent in five years, the marketing objectives might be to increase market share by 1 percent in each of the next five years. The specific magnitude of the marketing objectives depends on the strengths, weaknesses, opportunities, and threats identified in the SWOT analysis.

Marketers typically use more than one objective, and it is important that they are checked to ensure they are consistent among themselves. Like the marketing strategy, marketing objectives should be evaluated periodically to ensure they are still relevant and consistent with the rest of the marketing plan. Also, the opportunities pursued should be evaluated periodically to ensure they are attractive enough to help the firm achieve its organizational goals. For example, careful assessment of market size is needed from time to time to ensure that the market is still large enough to provide the sales assumed by the objectives. The properties of effective objectives are described below:

- *Measurable and timely*. Effective objectives need to be measurable and timely. They should be set in quantitative terms so management can verify that the objectives have been achieved or can measure the degree of progress made in achieving them. Vague objectives are not helpful for comparing actual performance with desired performance and are also difficult to communicate.
- *Feasible*. Objectives need to be feasible and challenging at the same time. Realistic objectives are those that fit the firm's internal and external environment. Setting unrealistic objectives can be damaging to organizational morale as employees realize that it is very difficult to meet such demands. On the other hand, setting challenging or stretch objectives can help an organization achieve higher than average performance by stretching its resources accordingly.
- *Consistent*. Organizations typically pursue more than one objective. Management must ensure that all objectives are relevant and consistent with each other. But pursuing too many objectives may distract the employees and dilute the effort. Also, setting a lot of objectives can lead to contradictory objectives and it can be difficult to monitor them all.
- *Acceptable to management*. Objectives need to be acceptable to management in order to have a better chance of being achieved. Managers who accept the objectives are more likely to strive to accomplish them. Managers accept objectives more readily when they are part of the process that generates them. Such participation increases their commitment to strategy and acceptance of the accompanying objectives.
- *Understandable*. Managers frequently have trouble understanding objectives and this poor understanding is a frequent reason for failure. Managers fail to understand objectives either because the objective is difficult to understand or the objective has not been communicated clearly in easy-to-comprehend terms. For example, if a company's objective is to increase its market share by 10 percent in five years, employees throughout the organization should be aware of the objective, the rationale for the objective must be clearly explained, and the employees must understand how achieving the objective will help the organization become successful overall.

Collecting External Information

Effective situational analysis requires extensive environmental information. This knowledge is needed to develop strategies that exploit opportunities and avoid threats to outperform the competition. Methods of collecting external information can vary from informal, ad hoc unscientific observations to more formal and systematic approaches. Informal approaches may produce useful information but a more formal and systematic method is needed for optimal results. Formal approaches often take the form of **external information systems** that provide management with the required environmental information.[20] The problem managers often face is not lack of information but too much information. Managers can avoid the problem of information overload by concentrating on those external variables that are significant for their industries. An external information system should contain only relevant and up-to-date information about environmental trends and changes that affect the organization's business. For example,

External information systems are formal approaches that provide management with the required environmental information.

if the company is in the airline business, it should be primarily concerned with economic downturns and the unemployment rate, as these two factors are among the most important determinants of the demand for air travel.

Environmental information can be found in the form of trends, projections, forecasts, statistics, statements by experts, and other sources. Environmental information can be obtained from customers, suppliers, distributors, competitors, employees, trade journals, newspapers, magazines, and business consultants. The Internet can also be an excellent source of environmental information. In using the Internet as a source of competitive information, however, we need to be cautious, as such information is not always reliable.

Competitor Analysis

Producing products that satisfy customers' needs is a necessary but not sufficient condition for marketing success. Many companies offered products that filled unmet market needs but they eventually lost out to powerful competitors that moved in and took the market as soon as they realized the market created by the pioneer was a viable one. For this reason it is very important to be informed about competitors in order to develop proper strategies that avoid those that are stronger than the firm and engage those competitors that are weaker.

In order for marketers to gain a better understanding of their competitors, they need to know their competitors' strengths and weaknesses and their objectives and strategies. The key competitors' strengths and weaknesses should be identified to help the firm gain a better understanding about its competitors' ability to respond to its marketing initiatives. Understanding competitors' objectives and strategy can be also useful competitive information. These aspects of competitor analysis are discussed in more detail below.

Competitor Strengths and Weaknesses

Managers need to know their competitors' strengths and their key vulnerabilities. The success of a marketing strategy or a competitive move will depend on the resources and capabilities of their rivals. A firm would be hesitant to launch an attack against a competitor with comparable or superior resources if the defendant is capable of launching an effective retaliatory attack. The first question to ask is what are the key competitors' strengths and weaknesses? Do competitors have the resources to implement their future strategies? Do competitors have the resources to defend their market position if the firm decides to pursue strategies designed to increase its market share? The following are the main areas in which competitors can be assessed.

Management. The quality of management is a key part of a competitor's evaluation. What is the quality of managerial skills, decision-making, and flexibility? Is management knowledgeable and experienced? Are managers risk takers or risk averse? What is the fit of managerial skills and capabilities with the strategy the competitor is pursuing? What is the competitors' type of leadership? Is it autocratic or participative? Is management willing to delegate authority or do they prefer the top-down, command style of management?

Finance. The financial position of the competitor needs to be assessed, including liquidity ratios, debt to equity, cash flow, profitability, access to capital, and cost efficiency. It is important to know a competitor's major financial constraints. What is the competitor's ability to obtain financing from internal and external sources? Does the competitor have deep pockets? What is its ability to finance its strategy? Can the competitor withstand a price war if the firm lowers its price?

Production. This part of competitor analysis involves evaluating the ability of competitors to compete through their production capabilities. One of the questions that should be asked is what is the efficiency of competitors' manufacturing plants? Are competitors' costs of operations lower or higher than others in the industry? What is the quality of the competitors' products or services? Are competitors burdened with excessive overhead costs?

Marketing. What is the competitors' market orientation? How effective are their product, pricing, distribution, and promotion strategies? What is their ability to listen to the voice of the customer or anticipate customers' needs? Some competitors are internally focused and become so product-centred that they do not see changes in the market. Firms that have been successful in the past are especially vulnerable to this problem. These firms became successful by pursuing a strategy and an approach that was refined over a number of years. This makes them miss important opportunities that can allow more alert competitors to exploit and gain ground against them.

Other firms, especially high-technology ones, believe that customers cannot be a source of innovative ideas and discard them altogether. This leads them to the conclusion that customers should be ignored altogether in the product development process. Other competitors spread their resources too thinly as they pursue every possible market opportunity or customer demand. This leads them to lose focus and dilute the resources of the organization. This lack of strategic focus is sometimes the result of lack of coordination between the different functions of the organization.

Research and Development. How innovative are competitors? Do they spend enough on product innovation? Companies that spend less on research and development are vulnerable to competitors that spend more than they. Are they risk takers or do they pursue risk-averse strategies? Do they prefer first-mover strategies or do they prefer to enter late in the market, waiting for others to prove that there is demand for the innovation? Are competitors late in introducing new models to the market where speed of new product introduction is important?

Competitor Objectives and Strategies

In addition to knowing competitors' strengths and weaknesses, a company needs to find out about their objectives and strategies. What are the key competitors' market share plans? Are competitors prepared to launch a major effort to capture a higher portion of the market? Different competitors in the same industry have different objectives and strategies. For instance, Microsoft and Corel are two companies competing in the application software industry but their objectives and strategies differ greatly. While Microsoft's objective is to maintain its dominance of the software industry by pursuing appropriate strategies, Corel's objective is simply to survive in this very competitive market. Furthermore, competitors assign a different importance and demonstrate a different commitment to their industries. If an industry is a core business to a competitor, it is expected to defend this business vigorously and retaliate against competitors that are perceived to be making threatening moves.

Other questions a firm could ask include the following: What is the competitors' competitive strategy? Cost leadership, differentiation, or focus? How successful are competitors in pursuing their competitive strategy? Maybe they are stuck in the middle, making them vulnerable to a competitor who successfully executes its competitive strategy. Competitors' current and future strategies should be studied as well. A small firm that enters a segment that is of great interest to a large competitor will likely end up in failure when the large competitor decides to move into the segment.

Competitive Intelligence

Competitive intelligence is the process by which organizations gather actionable information on competition and the business environment and apply it to their decision-making and planning processes.

Industrial espionage involves illegal activities such as gaining unauthorized entry into competitors' premises, theft of trade secrets, bribery, coercion, and electronic eavesdropping.

Offensive competitive intelligence needs refers to the need to evaluate the impact of a company move on the industry and its competitors.

Defensive competitive intelligence needs refers to information required to evaluate actions intended to minimize the impact of competitive attack.

Informational competitive intelligence needs refers to information required to help a company better understand its competitive and industry environment, as well as future industry needs.

Obtaining information on competitors and other external factors is an important aspect of environmental analysis. **Competitive intelligence** is the process by which organizations gather actionable information on competition and the business environment and apply it to their decision-making and planning processes. Competitive intelligence activities vary from broad market intelligence such as new technology or market trends to narrow competitor focus such as analyzing a competitor's annual report or reverse-engineering its products.

Competitive intelligence uses publicly available sources to obtain information on competition and the business environment. It is an ethical activity and it is different from **industrial espionage**, which involves illegal activities such as gaining unauthorized entry into competitors' premises, theft of trade secrets, bribery, coercion, and electronic eavesdropping.

There are many ways to get information about one's competitors. In fact there is so much information and so many ways to obtain information about competitors that there is no need for any firm to resort to illegal ways of gathering competitor intelligence. Competitive intelligence involves the following core tasks:[21]

1. **Planning**—Planning involves understanding the user's information needs, knowing resource constraints, collecting data, and creating an analysis plan. The user's information needs may be offensive, defensive, or informational.[22] **Offensive** refers to the need to evaluate the impact of a company move on the industry and its competitors. **Defensive** refers to information needed to evaluate actions intended to minimize the impact of a competitive attack. **Informational** means helping a company to better understand its competitive and industry environment, as well as future industry trends.

2. **Data Collection**—Data collection is the next stage, in which the fieldwork is conducted and the competitive intelligence data collected. Companies use many different ways to collect competitive intelligence. Some marketing companies ask their marketing staff to learn about consumers and competitors by visiting stores, watching TV commercials, or talking with friends and families. Procter & Gamble has a company rule that any employee who travels to another city for either business or pleasure is required to visit at least three stores that carry its own brands and competitive brands. These employees then submit a report in which they analyze their observations. During their visits, they pick up competitive activity such as new product introductions, sales promotions, price reductions, or market-testing of new products.[23] Figure 3.8 lists various commonly used sources of competitive information.

Figure 3.8	Sources of Competitive Intelligence
Competitors' speeches	Books
Competitors' financial reports	Magazine articles
Competitors' ads	Newspaper articles
Competitors' flyers	Online sources
Competitors' publicity releases	Customers
Competitors' brochures	Employees
Using competitors' product	Industry experts
Competitors' mailing lists	Trade associations
Visiting competitors' stores	Trade journals
Government documents	Suppliers
Analysts' reports	

3. **Data Analysis**—During this stage data gathered during the data collection stage are reviewed, tested, and converted into intelligence before they are disseminated for decision-making. The purpose of the analysis is to provide information that helps management better understand the strengths and weaknesses, goals, strategies, and plans of competitors.
4. **Implementation**—Intelligence findings must be organized into a format appropriate for the end user and presented to the decision-makers for implementation. Intelligence can be disseminated in various forms such as reports, special memos, bulletin boards, computerized databases, and newsletters. Since some of the intelligence is time-sensitive, the information should be delivered to management as quickly as possible for timely action.

- Understanding the business environment and internal capabilities is a key step in the strategic marketing planning process. The purpose of the situational analysis is to identify the external trends and changes and the internal capabilities of the firm, and to summarize the most important aspects of the firm's internal and external environment.

- Internal analysis involves an assessment of the firm's performance in its different functions: marketing, management, finance, production, and research and development. External analysis involves scanning the external environment to identify favourable and unfavourable trends and forces.

- SWOT analysis is the best-known method of situation analysis. It is a general framework that summarizes the key issues facing the organization. The purpose of SWOT analysis is to determine the organization's ability to deal with its external environment. This is accomplished through an assessment of the strategic fit between a company's strategy with its internal strengths and weaknesses and external opportunities and threats.

- Once all strengths, weaknesses, opportunities, and threats are summarized and ranked, management develops the preliminary SWOT matrix and the final SWOT matrix. The preliminary SWOT matrix includes the ranked strengths, weaknesses, opportunities, and threats. The final SWOT matrix includes several ranked potential strategies that management can assess to select the most promising ones.

- Managers need information to stay in tune with their environment. Managers should establish an external information system that contains relevant and up-to-date information on environmental trends and changes.

- SWOT analysis is a useful tool for strategic analysis, but it suffers from several pitfalls: lack of specific recommendations, subjective interpretation of information, the requirement for a tight strategic fit between strategy and resources, long lists of strengths and weaknesses not affecting performance, resources and capabilities being defined too broadly to be helpful, asset immobility, and lack of appropriate level of analysis.

- Once the SWOT analysis is completed and the strategy is selected, the firm determines the marketing objectives to be achieved. Marketing objectives are performance targets that are derived based on a realistic valuation of strengths, weaknesses, opportunities, and threats. Effective objectives are measurable and timely, feasible, consistent, acceptable, and understandable.

- Competitor analysis includes competitors' strengths and weaknesses, objectives, and strategies. Competitive intelligence is information about competitors and their business environment. Competitive intelligence includes information on key market trends, evolving market structures, competitors' strengths and weaknesses, and environmental opportunities and threats.

1. Describe why SWOT analysis is an important step in the strategic marketing planning process.

2. Discuss briefly how strengths, weaknesses, opportunities, and threats are determined.

3. Briefly describe the components of the general and task environment.

4. Describe the preliminary and final SWOT matrices.

5. Although SWOT analysis is an important aspect of strategic marketing planning, it suffers from a number of pitfalls. Describe the pitfalls involved in SWOT analysis.

6. How are marketing objectives determined? What are the desirable properties of marketing objectives?

7. Describe the components of competitive analysis.

8. Define competitive intelligence. What are the core tasks involved in competitive intelligence?

1. Referring back to the opening vignette, what other actions might Canadian banks have pursued in light of the environmental changes that occurred in the banking industry?

2. "Failure to properly define a company's strategic market leads to a flawed SWOT analysis." Elaborate on this statement.

3. Why can situational analysis, properly carried out, be a source of competitive advantage for an organization?

4. Why is it important to rank the strengths, weaknesses, opportunities, and threats in terms of their potential attractiveness or severity?

5. When Krispy Kreme, the number two doughnut maker in the United States, opened its first store in Mississauga, Ontario, in December 2001, there were lineups for the company's hot glazed doughnuts. But in April 2005, Krispy Kreme Doughnuts Inc. filed for bankruptcy protection for its Canadian franchise. A major cause of the company's misfortunes was the recent trend away from high-carb foods like pasta and bread. There was also a long-term trend in sustained healthier eating. In the meantime, Krispy Kreme's fad appeal appeared to have waned, and it had increasingly become dependent on selling doughnuts in grocery stores and other retailers. What strategies could Krispy Kreme's management have pursued to be more successful?

Notes

1. This material draws from http://www.fin.gc.ca/toce/2002/bank_e.html, retrieved on February 29, 2004.
2. R. Duane Ireland, Michael A. Hitt, Richard A. Bettis, and Deborah Auld De Porras, "Strategy Formulation Processes: Differences in Perceptions of Strength and Weaknesses Indicators and Environmental Uncertainty by Managerial Level," *Strategic Management Journal* 8 (1987), 469–485.
3. George S. Day, *Market Driven Strategy: Processes for Creating Value* (New York: The Free Press, 1990), 65.
4. Craig S. Fleisher and Babette E. Bensoussan, *Strategic and Competitive Analysis: Methods and Techniques for Analyzing Business Competition* (Upper Saddle River, N.J.: Prentice Hall, 2003), 96.
5. Fleisher and Bensoussan, 92.
6. Mary K. Coulter, *Strategic Management in Action* (Upper Saddle River, N.J.: Prentice Hall, 1998), 141.
7. A similar approach is used in George S. Day, *Strategic Market Planning* (St. Paul: West Publishing Company, 1984), 52.
8. George S. Day, *The Market Driven Organization: Understanding, Attracting, and Keeping Valuable Customers* (New York: The Free Press, 1999), 7.
9. Howard H. Stevenson, "Defining Corporate Strengths and Weaknesses," *Sloan Management Review* (Spring 1976), 51–68.
10. Fleisher and Bensoussan, 98.
11. A similar approach is used in Day, 1984, 52.
12. "The New Pepsi Generation," *Forbes*, April 12, 2004, Vol. 173, No. 7, 56.
13. Michael E. McGrath, *Product Strategy for High Technology Companies*, 2nd ed. (New York: McGraw-Hill, 2001), 7.
14. Keith McArthur, "Molson's assigns strategy executive," *The Globe and Mail*, June 16, 2004, B4.
15. Roma Luciw, "Nokia market share slides as firm hit hard by rivals," *The Globe and Mail*, June 9, 2004, B12.
16. A similar matrix appeared in H. Weihrich, "The TOWS Matrix—A Tool for Situational Analysis," *Long Range Planning* 15(2), 1982, 54–66.
17. Gary Hamel and C. K. Prahalad, "Strategy as Stretch and Leverage," *Harvard Business Review* 71(2), 1993, 75–84.
18. Michael Hay and Peter Williamson, *The Strategy Handbook* (Cambridge, U.K.: Basil Blackwell Ltd., 1991), 252–253.
19. Robert J. Hamper and L. Sue Baugh, *Strategic Market Planning* (Lincolnwood, Ill.: NTC Business Books, 1990), 124.
20. Coulter, 102.
21. Craig S. Fleisher, "An Introduction to Competitive Intelligence," in Craig S. Fleisher and David L. Blenkhorn, eds., *Managing Frontiers in Competitive Intelligence* (Westport, Conn.: Quorum, 2001).
22. J. E. Prescott, "Competitive Intelligence: Its Role and Function Within Organizations," in J. E. Prescott, ed., *Advances in Competitive Intelligence* (Vienna, Va.: Society of Competitive Intelligence Professionals, 1989).
23. Eric Schulz, *The Marketing Game* (Holbrook, Mass.: Adams Media Corporation, 1999), 29.

4

Chapter Four

Competitive Advantage and Competitive Strategies

One of the most common causes of failure is a lack of sufficient capabilities for the firm's aspirations.

John Kay, Business Strategist

Learning Objectives

After studying this chapter, you should be able to:

1. Describe the role of competitive advantage for marketing success

2. Explain how the resource-based view of the firm helps us understand competitive advantage

3. Identify and evaluate distinctive competencies

4. Explain the importance of dynamic competencies in dealing with rapid environmental change

5. Discuss how Porter's generic competitive strategies and the value discipline approach can help a company obtain a competitive advantage

BMW Exploits Its Competitive Advantages

Organizations succeed when they can offer superior value to valuable customers and defend their position from attacks by aggressive competitors. Firms must identify their distinctive competencies, select the markets best suited to these competencies, and develop competitive strategies to maximize the value of these competitive advantages. One of the most common causes of failure is lack of capabilities for the firm's aspirations.[1]

An example of a company that was failing until it found a way to use its competitive advantages is BMW. Before World War II, BMW was Germany's leading manufacturer of aircraft engines. Due to the war and military reparations, BMW's market and capital equipment were in ruins. Air raids had destroyed the Munich plant in 1944, but the Allach plant survived the attacks virtually intact. In mid-1945, BMW received permission from the military authorities to start repairing U.S. army automobiles in Allach. It also started making spare parts for farming machinery and bicycles. However, in October 1945, the U.S. military ordered the dismantling of BMW plants in Munich and Allach, and the machinery removed and shipped as war reparations.

These setbacks were temporary, and BMW rebuilt its plants and started production soon after its plants were dismantled. However, in the late 1940s and 1950s, with a product line ranging from tiny bubble cars to limousines, BMW lacked a clear strategic direction and focus. Some of the products introduced during this period were the BMW Isetta, a bubble car just under three metres long, powered by a 12 or 13 hp BMW motorcycle engine, and the BMW 501, the first car to be completely built in the Munich plant. It was a spacious, curvy, and full-bodied design that earned the nickname "Baroque angel."

By 1959, BMW was facing bankruptcy, and most people thought it would be acquired by Mercedes-Benz. Instead, BMW was acquired by financier Herbert Quandt, who began to radically reorganize the company. Quandt sought to identify BMW's true competencies and the markets in which they would be a competitive advantage. Quandt chose the market for high-performance sedans as the one that would allow BMW to effectively exploit its distinctive competencies—its highly educated and skilled workforce and engineering capabilities.

This new goal was met in 1961 when model 1500 was introduced, establishing BMW's reputation for engineering quality. The BMW 1500 was a compact, high-performance car that brought BMW great success. It was an instant hit with and a symbol for young, affluent European professionals. The BMW 1800 and the BMW 2000 series were launched in 1963 and 1966 respectively, and enhanced BMW's reputation as a maker of high-performance sedans. Quandt is credited with saving the company and contributing to the rise of BMW as a global power in automobiles.

BMW's core competencies include first-rate engineering capabilities and a highly educated and skilled labour force. The company avoids mass-production techniques that rely heavily on robots, or production in Third World countries using cheap labour. Its superior production system and worldwide reputation for top-notch handling and engineering make BMW one of the most successful automobile companies in the world.

BMW's marketing strategy is built around its competitive advantages. The company targets affluent, upwardly mobile automobile buyers who are attracted by the car's fine handling and engineering. Dealers are carefully selected and tightly controlled to maintain its upscale image. Consistent with its high-end image, prices are maintained at premium levels at par with other luxury automobiles. BMW also maintains a tight control over its suppliers to ensure a high quality of input from them. Its advertising and communications

(continued)

are focused on the main positioning theme "The ultimate driving machine," a slogan created by Ammirati & Puris, BMW's first U.S. advertising agency.

BMW succeeded because it understood its core competencies and exploited them by targeting a market in which these competencies were a source of competitive advantage. It then pursued actions that were aimed at maximizing the value of these advantages.[2] A reputation for building high-performance sedans has followed BMW ever since—and it owes its existence to Quandt's decision to reposition BMW as a pre-eminent manufacturer of premium automobiles to match its resources and capabilities.

Introduction

Competitive advantage is a key concept in strategic management. **Competitive advantage** is something that the organization possesses exclusively or does better than the competition. It is whatever sets the organization apart from its competitors. A firm has a competitive advantage when it has better resources and capabilities than its competition does.[3] Advantages must be sustainable, otherwise it is of little use if competitors can replicate the advantage with relative ease.

As the BMW case showed in the opening vignette, a competitive advantage allows a firm to achieve a superior position on attributes that are important to target customers.[4] BMW succeeded only after it identified its distinctive advantages and exploited them in a market in which these competencies were a source of competitive advantage. The challenge for management is to find a position of advantage and maintain superiority in the resources and capabilities that support its competitive advantage. Since most advantages erode over time, companies need to constantly search for new sources of competitive advantage.

All organizations have resources and capabilities to carry out their operations. Organizations differ, however, in their ability to effectively exploit their resources and capabilities. Some organizations are more proficient and successful than others in developing the distinctive competencies that provide them with a sustainable competitive advantage. When Fujio Cho, president of Toyota Motor Company, was asked what was unique about Toyota's remarkable success, his answer was: "The key to the Toyota way and what makes Toyota stand out is not any of the individual elements. But what is important is having all the elements together as a system. It must be practised every day in a very consistent manner—not in spurts."[5] Distinctive competencies enable firms to outperform competitors, take advantage of market opportunities, and neutralize threats in ways that competitors cannot.[6]

Companies succeed when they match their competencies with market and competitive requirements. Important organizational decisions, including market segmentation and positioning, are shaped by the competitive advantages of the organization. Firms should enter segments in which they have competitive advantages—and customers value their offerings more than competing ones. As we saw earlier, BMW was struggling for years until it found a market segment in which it was able to utilize its capabilities. Positioning decisions should also be made in a way that leverages the core capabilities of the company.[7]

Competitive advantages are important because they are why customers prefer one company over another. If the advantage is sustainable, it will be difficult for competitors to emulate it. Competitive advantages enable a company to enjoy higher margins and lower costs, have more satisfied customers, and experience higher sales. For these reasons, firms that have a competitive advantage enjoy higher than average earnings.

The purpose of this chapter is to explain the importance of competitive advantage in formulating effective marketing strategies. The resource-based view of the firm will be discussed first because it helps explain the role of competitive advantage in competitive strategy. The central role of distinctive competencies—and how to identify them will be explained as well. Lastly, Porter's generic strategies and the value disciplines framework will be described to illustrate the role of competitive strategies in obtaining positional advantages.

Competitive advantage is something that the organization possesses exclusively or does better than the competition.

The Resource-Based View of the Firm

The resource-based view of the firm provides us with an understanding of how firms create and sustain competitive advantages. The basic principle of this view is that strategy formulation begins with an assessment of organizational resources and capabilities.

Resources that are superior to competitors' can become the basis for competitive advantage if they are used to take advantage of attractive environmental opportunities.

In the resource-based view, the firm is a bundle of resources and capabilities that are the key to achieving a competitive advantage and above-average returns.[8] As we noted in Chapter 1, resources are assets such as financial and physical possessions, customer relationships, brand image, and corporate culture. Capabilities are the skills and accumulated knowledge that enable a firm to deploy its assets effectively. Although certain resources in different organizations may be identical, it is the firm with the superior capabilities that will give the best performance. Capabilities cannot be easily transferred or imitated because they are deeply embedded in organizational routines and practices.[9] Unlike assets, the more capabilities are used, the better they become.

Different firms possess different resources and capabilities.[10] These differences account for variances in profitability among firms in the same industry. Firms that have superior resources and capabilities have a competitive advantage and are positioned to perform better than their rivals.[11]

In the resource-based view, marketing strategy is essentially a search for, and exploitation of, competitive advantage. All actions taken by a firm are aimed at establishing superiority over competitors. This view coincides with the ancient military writer Sun Tzu's assertion that the art of strategy is the exploitation of relative advantages over opponents. Sun Tzu wrote, "One mark of a great soldier is that he fights on his own terms or fights not at all," and competent strategists are those who "engage in battle only when odds are overwhelmingly in your favour."[12] The well-known military theorist Clausewitz also believed that identifying one's own relative advantages and disadvantages, as well as those of the opponent, is key to success in war.[13]

Distinctive Competencies

Distinctive competencies are those resources and capabilities that are sources of competitive advantages and are critical in helping a firm pursue effective marketing strategies.

According to the resource-based view of the firm, critical issue for all organizations is how to gain and maintain a competitive advantage.[14] It must be noted that not all resources and capabilities of a firm are of equal strategic importance. Some of them may inhibit a firm from pursuing certain strategies, while others may have no impact on its strategy.[15] **Distinctive competencies** are those resources and capabilities that are sources of competitive advantages and are critical in helping a firm pursue effective marketing strategies.[16] Distinctive competencies are unique to an organization and no other firm in the industry does those particular things as well. For example, the industrial services division of Atlas Holdings & Investment Inc., the leading industrial services in the Greater Toronto area, has experienced a high growth rate and above average earnings primarily due to a combination of low-cost and superior technology and human resources.

A firm's core task is to identify, improve, and take advantage of its distinctive competencies.[17] For a resource to be a distinct competence, it must meet the following criteria: (a) it must be valuable, (b) it must be rare, (c) it must be imperfectly imitable, (d) there are no strategically equivalent substitutes, and (e) there are complementary assets.[18] These criteria are shown in Figure 4.1 and described below.

Figure 4.1	Criteria for Distinctive Competencies

- Valuable
- Rare
- Imperfectly imitable
- Lack of strategically equivalent substitutes
- Complementary assets

Valuable Resources

Firms that occupy a strong competitive position in the marketplace have several distinctive capabilities that allow them to outperform the competition. **Valuable resources** are those assets and capabilities that contribute disproportionately to the creation of superior customer value or allow the firm to serve its customers in a cost-effective manner. For example, Toyota's efficient manufacturing process allows the company to produce cars at a lower cost than its competitors.

The value of resources and capabilities depends on how well the resources match market requirements. Firms gain a competitive advantage when they acquire assets specific to market requirements. **Specialized assets** are more valuable than general-purpose assets and provide a firm with strategic advantages. Specialized assets, however, are dedicated to specific tasks and may no longer be suitable when the environment changes. A resource or capability that is valuable in a particular market segment may not have the same value in a different market or at a different time. Even worse, resources that are an advantage in a certain environment can become a core disadvantage in a different environment because of different requirements. The IBM example discussed in the Strategy in Action box illustrates how market changes can render a company's capabilities useless.

> **Strategy in Action**
>
> **IBM**
>
> IBM stumbled in the 1980s because the market evolved in a way that made its capabilities less valuable. This company dominates the mainframe market because it is capable of offering both hardware and software products and its technical support capabilities are very difficult for other companies to match. However, the personal computer market is very different from the mainframe market, and it requires different capabilities. Personal computers are largely a commodity, assembled from standard components, and large firms—unlike the mainframe market—have no special advantages over small firms. Small firms—not just large firms—can build personal computers, and they can be repaired by small local shops in the same way as TV sets or radios.[19] In this new competitive environment, IBM found that its traditional competitive advantages were inadequate. IBM was forced to look for other areas in which it could utilize its competitive advantages. In the process, IBM became the leader in e-business applications, incorporating information technology, hardware, software, and services.

Valuable resources are those assets and capabilities that contribute disproportionately to the creation of superior customer value or allow the firm to serve its customers in a cost-effective manner.

Specialized assets are those resources and capabilities that are dedicated to specific tasks and provide a firm with strategic advantages.

Rare Resources

Rare resources and capabilities are valuable because they are not widely shared by competitors. Resources common to many firms allow competitors to pursue similar strategies, giving no one firm a competitive advantage. Commonly available resources enable firms to achieve competitive parity and may ensure their long-term survival, but they do not lead to a competitive advantage. For this reason, assets that can be purchased are not a source of competitive advantage. On the other hand, inputs that cannot be purchased, such as organizational culture, are more valuable and better sources of competitive advantage. For example, Coke's secret formula is not available to other soft drink companies, and it has been a major factor in Coca-Cola's dominance of the soft drink industry.

Imperfectly Imitable

Across one industry, the firms within that industry will have persistent differences in how well they perform.[20] This suggests that there are barriers to imitation that allow some firms to consistently outperform their rivals. The primary cause of such barriers is **imperfect imitability,** an inability to completely imitate the capabilities of competitors.

Imperfect imitability is an inability to completely imitate the capabilities of competitors.

Causal ambiguity is an isolating mechanism that makes it difficult to understand the link between resources and capabilities and superior performance of a firm.

Imitation is difficult because isolating mechanisms prevent companies from imitating their competitors' distinct competencies. Common isolating mechanisms include barriers to entry such as scarce resources, producer learning, buyer switching costs, channel crowding, and causal ambiguity.[21] **Causal ambiguity** exists when the link between the resources and capabilities and superior performance is not understood by all industry firms. As a result, it is very difficult to figure out why one firm consistently performs better in order to imitate its competitive advantages.[22] For example, some airlines, including Continental Airlines, have tried to imitate the Southwest Airlines' highly effective low-cost strategy with very little success.

What makes it difficult to analyze competitors' capabilities is that they are embedded in processes that span many organizational functions or units. For example, new product development involves several functions, including research and development, marketing, engineering, and manufacturing. The knowledge that makes the capabilities possible is difficult to fully understand because not only is it shared by many individuals, but it exists in implicit or tacit form.[23] This knowledge exists in the following forms:[24] First, it is the accumulated knowledge and skills gained from experience with the product. Second, it exists in operating and information systems, databases, formal routines, and procedures established to solve problems. Third, it is included in management systems comprising recruiting, hiring, training, remuneration, and performance evaluation procedures. Finally, it is knowledge incorporated in the complex social phenomena that include the organizational culture; relationships with customers, suppliers, and distributors; and the collective learning of the organization.[25]

For causal ambiguity to prevent imitation and be a source of competitive advantage, all competing firms must have an incomplete knowledge of the link between a firm's resources and capabilities and its sustained competitive advantage. This link may eventually be understood by either studying the superior performing company's processes or hiring away some of its key personnel. Although it may take some time, actions like these can lead to widespread knowledge of the sources of competitive advantage, and the causal ambiguity will be eliminated.[26] Many successful firms fail to understand exactly the source of their own competitive superiority because of causal ambiguity. As a result, they may not continue investing in the factors that contribute to their great performance.

Lack of Strategically Equivalent Resources

Strategically equivalent resources are used in the place of another resource to implement the same strategy.

Another requirement for a resource to be a source of competitive advantage is that there are no strategically equivalent resources. **Strategically equivalent resources** are used in the place of another resource to implement the same strategy. For strategically equivalent resources to be effective in preventing another firm from gaining a competitive advantage, they need to be widely available and imitable.

An example of a strategically equivalent resource is the following. A firm may have an advantage in developing effective marketing strategies because of a very effective marketing research program that allows it to identify customers' problems or negative environmental trends and make timely adjustments to the company's marketing strategy. Another firm's strategically equivalent resource might be the presence of highly experienced managers who have considerable knowledge of customers' problems and trends. These managers neutralize the advantage of the first firm's marketing research program. If competing firms have access to such experienced managers, then the firm that uses the marketing research program will have difficulty in obtaining a competitive advantage.

Complementary Assets

Complementary assets are related assets used to produce and deliver products and services that are valuable in the production of current products or services.

The strategic value of a firm's assets may be enhanced if it has other strategic assets known as complementary assets. **Complementary assets** are related assets used to produce and deliver products and services that are valuable in the production of current products or services. For example, a firm that has a technological advantage over its competition may fail to exploit this advantage if it lacks appropriate distribution channels or service capabilities. The existence of such complementary assets makes the impact of the combined assets greater than deploying each asset individually—the whole, in effect, being greater than the sum of its parts.[27]

Dynamic Competencies

A fundamental question about competitive advantage is how firms create and sustain these advantages. Environments constantly change, rendering existing resources and capabilities obsolete. Firms that insist on making products or services in a particular way may not survive for too long. They need to constantly update their organizational routines and capabilities. Companies that accumulate a large number of resources and capabilities but lack the ability to redeploy these competencies in new and relevant ways often fail when significant environmental change occurs. For example, the now defunct department store chain Eaton's failed to develop the necessary competencies required to compete in the retail environment of the 1990s and went out of business.

The resource-based view of the firm asserts that firms achieve superior performance when their resources, environment, and strategy are aligned with each other, an occurrence we defined in Chapter 3 as strategic fit. Achieving a strategic fit during periods of limited competition, long product life cycles, and slow technological change is a relatively easy task. However, maintaining a strategic fit in turbulent market environments, where there is rapid technological change, competitive entry, and changing customer needs, is difficult. As markets evolve and new segments are born, customers' requirements change. These changes result in erosion of a firm's competitive advantages.

Because most competitive advantages are temporary, organizations must invest continuously in their resources and capabilities to maintain their advantages and remain competitive.[28] They need to develop the new capabilities to succeed in the new environment. **Dynamic competencies** is the term used to refer to an organization's ability to create new forms of competitive advantage by developing and reconfiguring its resources and capabilities in response to environmental change.[29] This ability to transform an organization's assets is especially important in rapidly changing environments where existing competencies become obsolete at a rapid rate.

Firms with strong dynamic capabilities adapt their competencies and create new sources of competitive advantage that enable them to capitalize on new market opportunities or stave off threats. Such companies constantly survey their markets, benchmark their competitors, and are willing to adopt best practices. Firms with weak dynamic capabilities, on the other hand, will fail to adapt their resources and capabilities to changing environmental demands and lose market share to agile competitors who make timely adjustments.

The dynamic view of competitive advantage recognizes the importance of reconfiguring organizational resources and capabilities to adapt to the demands of changing environments. Organizations can succeed only if they adapt to change.[30] Successful adaptation, in turn, requires a reconfiguration of the sources of competitive advantage so current competencies are reshaped into new capabilities.

A firm's effort to build dynamic capabilities may be hampered by several factors. First, the search for new sources of competitive advantage is dependent on the path chosen and heavily influenced by organizational history. Systems that are successfully set up to deliver a certain product or service are exceedingly difficult to change, and core capabilities may eventually become core rigidities.[31] This makes it difficult for managers to conceive fundamentally new ways of running the organization.

Dynamic competencies refer to an organization's ability to create new forms of competitive advantage by developing and reconfiguring its resources and capabilities in response to environmental charge.

Second, existing assets of a firm are important determinants of its strategic advantage and may stand in the way of meaningful organizational change. For example, complementary assets may be rendered less valuable if the company changes its routines. Consequently, managers may resist such a change because of their reluctance to write off these assets.[32] Finally, the firm's reputation often stands in the way of adopting new practices or ways of doing business. It is often difficult to separate an organization from its current products, assets, and market position. Managers may be leery about establishing new routines and changing a firm's strategic direction.

Competitive Advantage and Competitive Strategy

A firm has a competitive advantage when it outperforms its competition. Positional advantages, such as low cost or outstanding customer value, are the result of distinctive competencies. The ultimate outcome of distinctive competencies, through their impact on positional advantages, is superior performance. These performance outcomes can be seen in the form of higher market share, profitability, customer satisfaction, customer loyalty, and customer retention.

Although distinctive competencies are the primary source of competitive advantage, they are not enough by themselves to lead to a competitive advantage. Firms need a competitive strategy to leverage their distinctive competencies and differentiate themselves from the competition. A firm's **competitive strategy** represents the choice of how it will compete in its chosen market. The purpose of a competitive strategy is to seek a position of competitive advantage such as low cost, operational excellence, higher product quality, and close customer relationships. This position of advantage allows firms to create a defendable position in the industry against competitive forces and enables them to obtain an optimum return on their investment.

Firms can compete in numerous ways. It is possible to summarize the different strategies followed by firms into a small number of generic strategies. One of the earliest attempts was the framework of generic strategies developed by Michael Porter.[33] Porter's framework describes successful companies as seeking positions of low cost or differentiation as a means of attaining a competitive advantage. In a more recent framework, generic strategies are expressed as value propositions: operational excellence, product leadership, and customer intimacy.[34]

A firm's **competitive strategy** represents the choice of how it will compete in its chosen market.

Porter's Generic Strategies

According to Michael Porter,[35] firms earn above-average returns if they possess a sustainable competitive advantage. Although firms may have many competencies, there are two main types of competitive advantage: low cost and differentiation. To be successful, firms must possess one of these competitive advantages.

The combination of the two types of competitive advantage with the choice of competitive scope—broad scope or narrow scope—leads to three generic strategies: cost leadership, differentiation, and focus; focus strategies are further subdivided into cost focus and differentiation focus. Each generic strategy combines the choice of competitive advantage a firm seeks to achieve with the scope of the arena in which the competitive advantage will be applied. These strategies are termed generic because they can be pursued by any type or size of company.[36] Porter's generic strategies are shown in Figure 4.2.

Cost Leadership

Having low-cost operations is especially important in today's business environment, with customers demanding more value for their money. **Cost leadership** involves producing products or services at a lower per unit cost than the competition. The thrust of a

Cost leadership involves producing products or services at a lower per unit cost than the competition.

| Figure 4.2 | Porter's Generic Strategies |

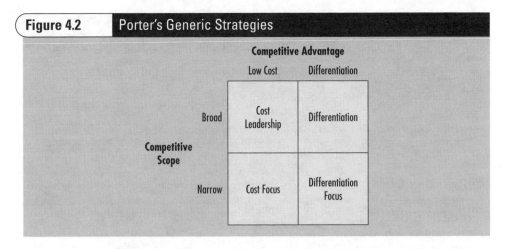

cost leadership strategy is competition based on low cost, not on image or uniqueness. Low-cost companies focus customer attention on pricing, often using slogans like "The lowest price is the law," "Everyday low prices," or "The lowest price in town."

Cost leadership is a powerful source of competitive advantage. The advantage of having the lowest cost is that it allows the firm to underprice the competition, achieve the highest sales volume, and still make the same profit margin as other firms. Low-cost companies can sell their products at a lower price relative to competitors or maintain prices at market levels and earn higher margins than competitors. If competitive conditions intensify, the cost leader can withstand the effects of a price war better than less efficient competitors.

Companies become cost leaders by adopting one or more of the following methods:

Low-cost culture. Companies promote a low-cost culture in which all functional areas strive to become as efficient as possible. Employees are dedicated to cost-cutting and think creatively about cutting costs in all areas where there are inefficiencies.

High volume. Companies pursue high volume to obtain economies of scale and experience, and higher purchasing power that is manifested in obtaining better terms from suppliers.

Reconfiguring the value chain. Changing the value chain and the way the firm designs, manufactures, markets, distributes, and services its products. Some firms use **value engineering** to improve and simplify the product design to reduce the product complexity, number of parts, and manufacturing cost.

Value engineering involves improving and simplifying the product design in order to reduce the product complexity, number of parts, and manufacturing cost.

To be successful in pursuing a cost leadership strategy firms must achieve differentiation parity, or equality, otherwise the cost advantage will be negated (see Figure 4.3). Price-sensitive markets are needed to achieve the large volume required to build market share and lower costs. The fact there are no switching costs will help attract the customers of less efficient rivals. Also, no other company should be pursuing a cost leadership strategy to avoid price wars, as each firm is vying to achieve a higher sales volume to bring costs down.

Cost leadership strategies are not devoid of risks. One of the characteristics of a low-cost company is that the cost structure is deeply embedded in the technology, management systems, organizational structure, plants, and distribution systems. This may make it extremely difficult for the cost leader to respond to market changes. Another risk is that competitors may imitate the cost leader's low-cost strategy or find ways to lower costs even more.

| Figure 4.3 | Requirements for Successful Implementation of Porter's Generic Strategies |

Cost Leadership	Differentiation	Focus
Maintain differentiation parity	Maintain cost parity	Excellent understanding of segment needs
Large price-sensitive market	Basis of differentiation is unique and valuable	The requirements for success in the segment must differ from requirements in other segments
Lack of switching costs	A large number of customers desires unique features of product or service	The segment is of little interest to major competitors
No other competitor is pursuing a cost leadership strategy	Firm possesses the necessary resources and capabilities to pursue differentiation strategy	Firm possesses the necessary resources and capabilities to satisfy segment needs

Differentiation

Differentiation involves achieving a competitive advantage over the competition by creating a product that is better or unique in some meaningful ways.

Differentiation involves achieving a competitive advantage over the competition by creating a product that is better or unique in some meaningful ways. By focusing customers' attention on an improved or unique attribute of the product or service, the firm hopes to gain customer loyalty and benefit from attractive profit margins.

Differentiation allows for higher margins because brand-loyal customers are willing to pay premium prices for products they value and can't get elsewhere. As a result of being ahead of competitors on the basis of perceived customer value, a differentiated firm usually gains market share. The increased market share leads to lower costs through economies of scale and experience. The higher margins and lower costs allow the firm to invest further in product improvements or innovations and increase the value gap from rivals. There are four major methods for differentiating products, as shown in Figure 4.4.

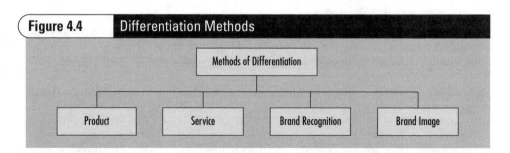

| Figure 4.4 | Differentiation Methods |

Methods of Differentiation

Product | Service | Brand Recognition | Brand Image

Product differentiation

By improving a product's quality, design, performance, technology, reliability, or user friendliness, or by adding special features, a product is differentiated from others in the same market. For example, Kyocera, a company that makes cameras, copiers, printers, mobile phones, ceramic goods, and other electronic products, was able to differentiate its new cellular telephone, Smartphone, from its competitors by incorporating features found out that time only on electronic organizers such as the Palm Pilot. Using a smaller screen than those on other electronic organizers, the phone offered all the functions of the Palm V, including handwriting recognition, infrared beaming, and an address book, allowing the owner to phone or e-mail his or her contacts with a tap of the stylus. Smartphone could also be used as a modem for laptop computers, and even supported a mini-browser for surfing the Web. The Bernard Callebaut case discussed in the Strategy in Action box provides an example of a high-quality product that has developed a strong quality reputation in the Canadian chocolate market.[37]

Strategy in Action

BERNARD CALLEBAUT

Bernard Callebaut, a Belgian chocolate maker, arrived in Canada from Belgium in 1982. By March of the following year, he had established Chocolaterie Bernard Callebaut Canada, manufacturing what is considered to be the highest-quality line of Canadian-made chocolates and chocolate-related products, which include sauces, bars, and ice cream. He has earned many awards and accolades over the years since, the most recognized being those won at three recent annual International Festivals of Chocolate in France.

The chocolate is made from high-quality cocoa beans that are roasted to Callebaut's specifications at the company's factory in Wieze, Belgium. The whipping creams and sweet butters are purchased from Alberta dairies, well known for maintaining high standards of quality control. Other ingredients are imported from countries that specialize in producing those items: hazelnuts from Turkey, almonds from California, walnuts from France, and marzipan and praline from Belgium.

The milk and dark chocolate is also of a high quality and is manufactured specifically for the company. Bernard Callebaut's policy of quality is a simple one: he strives to offer the consumer the freshest, highest-quality chocolate available. Vegetable oils, animal fats, and artificial additives are not used as a method of reducing costs or extending the shelf life of chocolate. The customer pays a premium for the higher quality of Bernard Callebaut chocolate, but the success of the business proves it's been a worthwhile way to differentiate the company from other chocolate makers.

Service differentiation

Firms can differentiate their products by improving the service component of the product and offering higher responsiveness, reliability, maintenance, installation, delivery, and repairs. For example, OnStar is a mobile data service that GM has developed and currently installs in many of its passenger vehicles. GM also sells it to other automakers for use in their vehicles. Vehicles equipped with OnStar receive a range of services that make driving easier and safer. Motorists can have their car doors unlocked when they've locked the keys inside, get roadside assistance, or notify emergency personnel just by pushing a dash-mounted button (or making a phone call if locked out). Other basic services include airbag deployment notification and remote diagnostics and concierge, information, and route support services.

Brand recognition

Many firms differentiate their products by stressing advertising and other promotional methods. Advertising can help create effective brand recognition and convince buyers that the advertised brands are better than competing ones. Procter & Gamble has successfully used advertising and promotion for years to differentiate its products.

Brand image

Another method of differentiation is to establish a distinct brand image or reputation. This is a long-term endeavour as the brand image is developed over a long time. It reflects the company's efforts at improving product quality and service or research and development or some other notable feature. For example, Gucci products are known around the world for their quality and fashionability. Inniskillin, a company that produces Canadian ice wine and other wines, is widely recognized as one of the best makers of ice wines in the world. It has won prestigious awards, helping to establish its reputation and setting it off from its competitors.

The requirements for successful differentiation were listed in Figure 4.3. If cost parity with competitors is not achieved, the advantages of differentiation are lost. If the basis of differentiation is not unique and valuable or not enough people prefer the unique features of the product or service, the differentiation effort will fail. Also, the firm must possess the resources and capabilities required to implement the differentiation strategy.

What are the risks of differentiation? A firm may differentiate its products in ways that are not important to customers. For example, adding features to a product that are not required by the market will add to the cost but will not make the product more desirable to customers. Also, there is always a possibility that market needs will change over time and a successful differentiation strategy will become obsolete. For example, a key differentiating feature of early personal computers was the ease with which a consumer could get information from various manufacturers and suppliers and the service provided after purchase. As the market matured and buyers became more knowledgeable, information and service became less important; computing power and speed were the new factors in being successful. The personal computer manufacturers and retailers who were not aware of the shift from information and service to computing power and speed were surpassed by competitors.

Focus

Focus strategy concentrates on the needs of a single segment that often has special requirements. A focus strategy allows a firm to offer highly specialized products or services that can command a premium price. By knowing their markets well, focusers can stay close to customers and react quickly to their changing requirements. Small firms often pursue a focus strategy because they lack the resources to serve broad markets. Focusing on a niche market allows firms with limited resources to avoid a risky direct confrontation with large firms.

Focus strategy entails achieving a low-cost position, high differentiation, or both. The cost focuser competes with lower costs than the broadly based industry cost leaders. The differentiation focuser can use the same form of differentiation that broad differentiators use; the only difference is that the focuser is specializing in one or a few niches. Regardless of the particular focus strategy chosen, the aim is to serve a particular target segment more efficiently and effectively than broadly based competitors.

What are the requirements of a focus strategy? Firms pursuing such strategies require a thorough understanding of individual segment needs, as shown in Figure 4.3. It is also important that the requirements for success in the segment differ from the requirements in other segments. If success requirements among segments are similar, it will be easy for firms serving adjacent segments to enter the focuser's segment. For example, success requirements in the mass market segment of the wristwatch industry include low cost and mass distribution capabilities. Requirements for success in the super-premium-quality segment include manufacturing of high-precision components, innovation, and a high-end image. These differences make entry of the low-end wristwatch manufacturers into the high end difficult as they lack these requirements for success. Also, the segment must be of little interest to major competitors to ensure that large companies will not target

Focus strategy concentrates on the needs of a single segment that often has special requirements.

the segment. Focusers must possess the resources and capabilities to satisfy segment needs.

The risks of focus strategy include the following. The possibility exists that shifts in buyer needs and preferences may result in segment differences disappearing, allowing broad-based competitors to operate in the segment. Also, focused competitors run the risk of large competitors becoming interested in the segment and investing resources to produce the products or services sold in the segment. Finally, cost focusers may have difficulty lowering their costs significantly due to the small scale of operations.

Stuck in the Middle

According to Michael Porter, for a firm to succeed and outperform its rivals, it must select one of the three generic strategies and pursue that strategy with a single-minded focus and determination. Firms that fail to choose one of these generic strategies are described as being **stuck in the middle**.[38] Companies that are stuck in the middle are unable to compete effectively against their rivals. Their costs are too high to compete effectively with the cost leader or the product is not differentiated enough to compete with differentiated firms.

Porter also asserts that firms cannot successfully pursue more than one generic strategy because each one of these strategies requires different production, marketing, and organizational resources and capabilities; style of leadership; and organizational arrangements. Also, there may be trade-offs between low-cost leadership and differentiation strategies. For instance, differentiation may be not be possible because, for example, having a high market share is normally incompatible with an image of exclusivity. Many types of differentiation are costly to implement because they require high-quality materials, expensive product designs, or extensive customer service and support—and therefore are incompatible with a low-cost strategy.

Some strategy researchers, however, have challenged Porter's assertion by claiming evidence that firms can achieve above-average return by simultaneously pursuing cost leadership and differentiation strategies.[39] These critics argue that companies that successfully pursue a differentiation strategy can introduce cost-reduction programs and drastically lower their costs. Alternatively, cost leaders can use part of their profits to improve the quality of their products and become more differentiated. Technological advancements, including just-in-time inventory systems, flexible manufacturing systems, and computer integrated manufacturing systems, have made it possible for firms to compete on both a low-cost and a differentiation basis. We also know that businesses that improve quality through continuous improvement programs experience reductions in costs as well.

Stuck in the middle are those firms that fail to choose one of Porter's three generic strategies.

Value Disciplines

The role of competitive strategy is to help firms deliver optimum value to the chosen market segments. In the value disciplines approach, generic strategies are expressed by three value propositions: operational excellence, product leadership, and customer intimacy (see Figure 4.5). Each value proposition represents a promise to customers to deliver a certain type of value.

A central aspect of the value disciplines approach is that firms succeed when they specialize in a value discipline because the requirements of customers vary and it is impossible for the same company to be all things to all people.[40] For example, some customers want low prices and convenience. Others want premium products that incorporate the latest in technology. Still others prefer personalized service, trust, and personal relationships. Although firms specialize in one value discipline, they should not

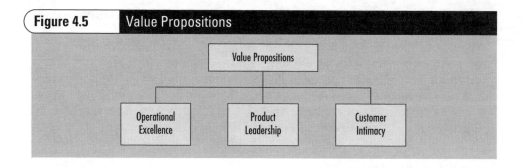

Figure 4.5   Value Propositions

abandon the others in which they have to perform adequately and maintain acceptable standards. If the performance in other dimensions drops, it reduces the contribution of the primary value discipline.

Another reason firms must choose one value discipline is that each discipline differs in the resources and capabilities needed to implement it. To achieve a position of superior customer value, a company requires the resources and capabilities to provide it with the capacity to deliver on its value proposition. As a result, the choice of which value discipline to concentrate on depends on the distinctive competencies of the organization.[41]

Choosing a value discipline shapes every subsequent decision the company makes, including segmentation, positioning, and resources and capabilities to acquire and nurture. In a sense, the chosen value determines what the company is or what it is to become as illustrated by the BIC example in the Strategy in Action box.[42]

Once a company chooses a value model, it needs to excel in the chosen value proposition and offer unmatched value to set itself apart from the competition. The choice of a value discipline forces companies to channel their efforts at building their core competencies and enhance the one core value instead of trying to be all things to all people.[43]

Operational Excellence

Operational excellence is a value proposition that focuses on offering customers the best price and the most convenience.

Operational excellence is a value proposition that focuses on offering the best price and the most convenience. Customers purchase from operationally excellent companies because they value low prices and convenience more than products that incorporate the latest technology or the highest level of services. Companies that pursue this value proposition are not product or service innovators and do not incorporate the latest technology in their products. Neither do they develop close relationships with their customers. Instead they produce products of acceptable quality that they sell at the best price with the least inconvenience.

Operationally excellent companies are industry leaders in price and convenience. They focus their efforts not so much on the product but on price, distribution, and delivery. Core competencies at these companies are characterized by efficiency, consistency, and speed. These companies scrutinize every part of the organization looking for ways to cut costs. They seek new ways to minimize overhead costs, streamline processes, and reduce transaction costs. Processes are standardized, simplified, and centrally planned and controlled. Management systems are tightly integrated. The organizational structure is highly centralized and allows limited employee empowerment.

The ways in which operational excellence strategies are executed are quite similar in most firms that follow this strategy. The Strategy in Action box describes Costco as a prime example of an operationally excellent company.[44]

Strategy in Action
COSTCO

Costco, a membership warehouse club chain headquartered in Issaquah, Washington, focuses on small business owners who are too small to have separate accounts with large manufacturers and distributors to buy their own supplies from them. Costco buyers buy large quantities from suppliers to obtain favourable prices. In turn they make customers purchase in large quantities by requiring that vendors provide special packaging that is larger than most merchants' standards. Some items such as jam may come only in extra-large sizes, or bread is available only in packages of three loaves. The special packaging in combination with the low margins on most highly visible items, as well as the annual membership fee charged to customers, allows Costco to charge low prices.

Costco employees move merchandise around frequently, creating the belief that the item will not be available the next time the customer is in the store and instilling in the customer a sense of urgency about purchasing the merchandise now. This tactic allows Costco to take advantage of manufacturers' promotional deals and to keep prices low. Costco's logistics strategy is one of its competitive advantages. Its outlets are large, bare-boned, and warehouse-like, designed to facilitate quick and efficient unloading and displaying of merchandise. They are also designed to allow overnight reconfiguration to make room for new merchandise.

Product Leadership

Product leadership is a value proposition that involves producing state-of-the-art products using the latest technology. For product leaders such as Gillette and Research in Motion, innovation is fundamental to the firm's business strategy. Customers buying from product leaders are primarily interested in the latest trends, fashions, or technology. They consider product performance as the most important component of value. Price also plays a role, but product matters most.

Product leaders excel at technology and product development. Core processes for product leaders include innovation, product development, and market development. Product leadership thrives in an organizational culture that encourages creativity and the generation and dissemination of new ideas. Effective product leaders create an environment that

Product leadership is a value proposition that involves producing state-of-the-art products using the latest technology.

encourages and rewards experimentation with new ideas, innovation, and risk-taking. Ideas may come from anywhere outside or inside the company. Product leaders ensure that no new product idea is blocked or discarded before it is considered.

Product leaders engage in continuous innovation and are the first ones to introduce truly new products. Speed in new product development is essential in all the stages of developing new products: screening ideas, research and development, engineering, manufacturing, and commercialization. This makes it difficult for competitors with slower product development times to compete effectively. The Strategy in Action box describes Canon as an example of a product leader company.[45]

Strategy in Action

CANON

Canon, a company that produces a variety of consumers products including cameras, printers, and office equipment, strives to be in the forefront of technological developments. Canon's new product technology strategy is to create previously unexplored technologies and new markets. Its technological achievements include the world's first bubble jet printer, the world's first compact fax machine, the world's first autofocus SLR camera, and the world's first eye-controlled autofocus camera.

Canon achieved its admirable innovation record by creating an environment that encourages innovative thinking and a highly efficient product development program. The company has an executive committee that sets its future strategic thrust, including its strategy, organizational goals, and a broad outline of technology directions. These strategic directions are communicated to middle managers in research and development. They, in turn, interpret these strategic directions and translate them into technological goals that can be acted on through specific applications and technology targets. They also create the environment to achieve these targets by hiring appropriate personnel and providing incentives to encourage innovative thinking.

Customer Intimacy

Customer intimacy is a value proposition that involves offering products or services to customers to solve their problems with specific applications to their needs and personalized service.

Customer intimacy is a value proposition that involves offering solutions, not just a product or service, to customer problems. Companies that follow this strategy combine specific applications to customers' needs and personalized service and aim at building long-term relationships with their customers. They segment their markets and then tailor their products or services to meet the exact needs of those chosen segments.

Customers of these companies buy products that meet their unique requirements. These customers prefer personalized service and personal attention. Their desire to purchase exactly what they need is so strong that they are willing to pay a premium for the product and even experience a degree of inconvenience in acquiring such a product.

Customer intimacy requires detailed customer knowledge and operational flexibility to fulfill the diverse customer needs and to customize the product to special requests. Proper production facilities are needed that allow producing and delivering different types of products or service. For this reason, many customer intimacy firms carry a large variety of their product to better meet the diverse needs of their customers. First-rate service and customer relationship management are among the most important core processes for such companies.

The organizational structure of customer intimacy firms requires delegating decision-making to frontline employees who are close to customers. Empowering frontline employees allows companies to be more effective in developing customer relationships; the close proximity of these employees to customers and their superior knowledge of their needs provide customers with solutions quickly. The Strategy in Action box describes a chain of retails stores that specialize in customer intimacy.[46]

HARRY ROSEN

Harry Rosen is a clothing retailer selling high-end men's clothing. The main thrust of Harry Rosen's strategy is to provide personal solutions to customers' clothing problems and develop close relationships with them. Sales associates at Harry Rosen act as a personal shopper for their customers. They keep an eye out for specific items they believe the customer could be looking for in the future and advise them of their arrival by phone, fax, or e-mail. Appointments are made at convenient times for the customer, even outside the store's business hours. Harry Rosen employees will visit customers at home to take an inventory of their closet and provide suggestions on changes to their existing wardrobe. A tailor is also usually on hand to suggest needed changes.

Harry Rosen also provides complimentary maintenance and repairs to the original owner for the lifetime of the garment. If the garment requires alterations due to weight gain or loss, Harry Rosen will make the necessary adjustments free of charge. For customers who need a button replaced, a seam fixed, or other minor repairs, Harry Rosen will provide these services as soon as possible, on-site and free of charge.

- Competitive advantage and distinctive competencies enable firms to compete successfully in their chosen markets. All organizational and marketing decisions including market segmentation, positioning, and marketing mix management are driven by the distinctive capabilities and advantages of the organization.

- The resource-based view of the firm helps explain how firms create and sustain competitive advantages. The firm is viewed as a bundle of resources and capabilities. Superior resources and capabilities are the key to achieving a competitive advantage. Differences in resources and capabilities account for differences in performance among firms.

- Distinctive competencies are the resources and capabilities that are critical in helping a firm implement its strategy. Resources and capabilities are distinctive competencies if they are valuable, rare, and imperfectly imitable, and if there are no strategically equivalent substitutes, and if complementary assets exist.

- Most competitive advantages are not sustainable. Competitors imitate successful strategies, new market segments with different requirements constantly emerge, and new competitors enter existing markets. Firms that possess dynamic capabilities are in a better position to deal with changes in their environment.

- Distinctive competencies need to be matched with an appropriate competitive strategy that reflects how the organization will compete in its chosen market. Competitive strategies represent the specific way in which managers leverage the organization's distinctive competencies to offer their customers superior value. The purpose of strategy is to seek a position of competitive advantage.

- Firms compete in numerous ways. One of the earlier attempts to summarize the many ways of competing is Porter's generic strategies framework. According to Porter there are three mutually exclusive ways in which a firm can obtain a competitive advantage: cost leadership, differentiation, and focus. Companies that fail to follow one of these strategies are stuck in the middle and earn below-average earnings. Research and experience have shown that firms can successfully pursue more than one strategy at the same time.

- The value disciplines approach is a more recently proposed generic strategies framework. In this conceptualization, generic strategies are expressed as value propositions. The value disciplines are operational excellence, product leadership, and customer intimacy. Companies succeed when they choose one value discipline and perform adequately in the others.

Review and Discussion Questions

1. Define competitive advantage. Discuss the importance of competitive advantage for marketing success.

2. Discuss the importance of competitive advantage in shaping important organizational decisions.

3. Describe the relationship between distinctive competencies and competitive advantage.

4. Why is the resource-based view of the firm useful for understanding competitive advantage? Identify and discuss three important principles or elements of the resource-based view of the firm.

5. What is the relationship between "resources and capabilities" and "distinctive competencies"? Discuss the criteria that resources and capabilities must meet to be considered

distinctive competencies and sources of competitive advantage.

6. Describe dynamic competencies. How do dynamic competencies differ from conventional competencies?

7. Discuss the relationship between competitive advantage and competitive strategy.

8. Discuss Porter's three generic strategies. What are the requirements and risks of each strategy? Can organizations follow more than one generic strategy?

9. Discuss the value disciplines approach to competitive strategies. Compare and contrast the three value propositions. Compare the value disciplines approach with Porter's generic strategies.

1. Referring back to the opening vignette, identify the factors that led to BMW's emergence as a major automobile company.

2. Some companies such as Coca-Cola and Gillette have maintained their market leadership for decades. On the other hand, leading companies such as General Motors and Kmart have been losing market share or have even gone bankrupt. Using the concepts of resource-based view and dynamic competencies, explain the performance of these firms.

3. Automaker Toyota is considered one of the best manufacturing companies in the world. Other car companies have studied its manufacturing system but they have failed to copy it successfully. What, in your opinion, are the reasons for anyone else being unable to completely imitate Toyota's manufacturing system?

4. The Canadian beer industry is dominated by Molson Coors and Labatts, which together account for over 85 percent of the Canadian beer market. Yet there are numerous microbreweries that, individually, account for a tiny part of Canada's beer production. Despite their small size and lack of resources compared with the industry giants, these microbreweries not only survive but, in many cases, do very well. What, in your opinion, accounts for the existence of microbreweries, and what are the risks that such firms are subject to?

5. Bombardier, Zellers, and Second Cup are three highly visible Canadian companies. What in your opinion is the value proposition of each of these companies?

Notes

1. John Kay, *Why Firms Succeed* (Oxford University Press: New York, 1995), 3.
2. This section draws from Kay, 5–6.
3. Jay Barney, "Firm Resources and Sustained Competitive Advantage," *Journal of Management*, Vol. 17, No. 1, 1991, 99–120; Margaret A. Peteraf, "The Cornerstones of Competitive Advantage," *Strategic Management Journal*, Vol. 14, 1993, 179–191.
4. George S. Day, *Market Driven Strategy: Processes for Creating Value* (New York: The Free Press, 1990), 9.
5. Jeffrey K. Liker, *The Toyota Way: 14 Management Principles From the World's Greatest Manufacturer* (New York: McGraw-Hill, 2004), xv.
6. J. T. Mahoney and J. R. Pandear, "The Resource-Based View Within the Conversation of Strategic Management," *Strategic Management Journal*, Vol. 13, 1992, 363–380.
7. Leonard Lodish, Howard Lee Morgan, and Amy Kallianpur, *Entrepreneurial Marketing* (New York: Wiley, 2001), 4.
8. Barney, 1991.
9. I. Dierckx and K. Cool, "Asset Stock Accumulation and Sustainability of Competitive Advantage," *Management Science*, 35 (December 1989), 1504–11.
10. David J. Collis and Cynthia A. Montgomery, "Competing on Resources: Strategy in the 1990s," *Harvard Business Review*, (July–August 1995), 118–128.
11. Collis and Montgomery.
12. Sun Tzu, *The Art of War*, Translated by Samuel B. Griffith (Oxford University Press: New York, 1971).
13. Carl von Clausewitz, *On War*, Edited with an introduction by Anatol Rapoport (Harmondsworth: Penguin, 1968). This edition is based on the J. J. Graham translation.
14. Jay Barney, "Strategic Factor Analysis: Expectations, Luck, and Business Strategy," *Management Science*, 32, 1986, 1231–41.
15. Barney, 1991.
16. Barney, 1986.
17. Richard P. Rumelt, Dan Schendel and David Teece, "Strategic Management and Economics," *Strategic Management Journal*, 12 (Winter 1991), 5–30.
18. Barney, 1991.
19. Kay, 11.
20. Rumelt, Schendel, and Teece, 1991.
21. M. A. Peteraf, "The Cornerstones of Competitive Advantage: A Resource-Based View," *Strategic Management Journal*, Vol. 14, 1993, 179–191.
22. R. Reed and R. J. DeFillipi, "Causal Ambiguity, Barriers of Innovation, and Sustainable Competitive Advantage," *Academy of Management Review*, 15(1), 1990, 88–102.
23. Andrew Bartness and Keith Ceny, "Building Competitive Advantage Through a Global Network of Capabilities," *California Management Review*, (Winter 1993), 78–103.
24. Dorothy Leonard-Barton, "Core Capabilities and Core Rigidities: A Paradox in Managing New Product Development," *Strategic Management Journal*, 13 (Summer), 111–125.
25. C. K. Prahalad and Gary Hamel, "The Core Competence of the Corporation," *Harvard Business Review*, (May–June 1990), 79–91; Barney 1991.
26. S. Lippman and R. Rumelt, "Uncertain Imitability: An Analysis of Interfirm Differences in Efficiency Under Competition," *Bell Journal of Economics*, 13, 1992, 418–438.
27. Raphael Amit and Paul J. H. Schoemaker, "Strategic Assets and Organizational Rent," *Strategic Management Journal*, 14, (1993), 33–46.
28. Collis and Montgomery, 1995.
29. David J. Teece, Gary Pisano, and Amy Shuen, "Dynamic Capabilities and Strategic Management," *Strategic Management Journal*, Vol. 18:7, (1997), 509–533.
30. R. Henderson, and K. B. Clark, "Architectural Innovation: The Reconfiguration of Existing Product Technologies and the Failure of Established Firms," *Administrative Science Quarterly*, 35, (March 1990), 9–30.
31. Dorothy Leonard, *Wellsprings of Knowledge* (Boston, Mass.: Harvard Business School Press, 1995), 34.
32. D. Besanko, D. Dranove, M. Shanley, and S. Schaeffer, *Economics of Strategy*, 3rd ed. (New York: Wiley, 2004), 467.
33. Michael E. Porter, *Competitive Strategy* (New York: The Free Press, 1980), 35.
34. Michael Treacy and Fred Wiersema, "Customer Intimacy and Other Value Disciplines," *Harvard Business Review*, (January–February 1993), 84–93.
35. Michael E. Porter, *Competitive Advantage* (New York: The Free Press, 1985), 11.
36. J. David Hunger and Thomas L. Wheelen, *Essentials of Strategic Management*, 2nd ed. (New Jersey: Prentice Hall, 2001), 82.
37. www.bernardcallebaut.com, retrieved on April 19, 2005.
38. Porter, 1980, 41.
39. W. W. Hill, "Differentiation Versus Low Cost or Differentiation and Low Cost," *Academy of Management Review*, 13(8), 1988, 401–412.
40. Michael Treacy and Fred Wiersema, *The Discipline of Market Leaders* (New York: Addison-Wesley, 1995), xiv.
41. Treacy and Wiersema, 1995, xvi.
42. Brian Sternthal and Alice M. Tybout, "Segmentation and Marketing," in Dawn Iacobucci, ed., *Kellogg on Marketing* (New York: Wiley, 2001), 25–26.
43. Treacy and Wiersema, 1995, 26.
44. Evan M. Dudik, *Strategic Renaissance* (New York: Amacom, 2000), 25–28.
45. New Product Development at Canon, *Harvard Business School Case*, 9-396-247, March 25, 1996.
46. www.harryrosen.com/services/e_index.html, retrieved on July 8, 2003.

Chapter Five

Market Segmentation and Target Marketing

There is no higher and simpler law of strategy than that of keeping one's forces concentrated.

Carl von Clausewitz, Military Theorist

Learning Objectives

After studying this chapter, you should be able to:

1. Explain the reasons why market segmentation is a core organizational process

2. Distinguish the various segmentation bases

3. Describe how to segment consumer and business markets

4. Outline how to segment markets for new and existing products

5. Explain how to discover new market segments

6. Evaluate market segments

7. Outline the four target marketing strategies

8. Describe the sequenced entry strategy

Starbucks Uses Market Segmentation Successfully

In 1987, when Starbucks was established, coffee consumption was on the decline. Yet, although the overall coffee market was shrinking, the gourmet coffee segment was growing. It had started to grow in the 1960s, when coffee drinkers started to react against poorer quality. U.S. coffee companies had started to use lower-quality beans to reduce costs, and the practice of storing roasted beans for too long caused coffee quality to deteriorate even more. These developments caused a lot of people to turn to higher-quality gourmet coffee. The shift started the trend of differentiation in the coffee market, as shops opened all over the United States to satisfy the growing demand for higher-quality gourmet coffee.

When Howard Schultz acquired Starbucks in 1987 from its original owners, the specialty coffee retail market was made up of many established firms, but none dominated the market. Instead of following the example of the two largest U.S. national chains of specialty coffee shops, Gloria Jean's Coffee and Barney's Coffees and Teas that offered flavoured coffees, Starbucks offered full-bodied dark-roasted beans. By shunning the flavoured coffee segment, Starbucks failed to tap into the fastest growing segment of the specialty coffee market, but it avoided competing head-to-head with Gloria Jean's and Barney's. Schultz understood that he could not participate in this market because he lacked the resources to compete effectively against the much larger competitors; he was happy to just enter a small, growing market niche.

Gourmet coffee drinkers are described as young urban professionals, 25 to 40 years of age, with a higher level of education, and earning more than $55,000 a year. Starbucks segmented the gourmet coffee market even further by focusing on the segment, known as the sophisticates segment. Sophisticates eat out more often than other segments, experiment with new foods, are health conscious, and like to travel. Starbucks also addressed the changing lifestyles and underlying needs of the sophisticates, to whom bars and pubs have become less acceptable meeting places. Starbucks' offer of an elegant coffee bar was viewed as a viable alternative to the neighbourhood pub as a late-night hangout for young adults.

Starbucks' vision is to become the premier purveyor of gourmet coffee in the world. Schultz built on Starbucks' distinct competence of purchasing high-quality beans and greatly improved roasting techniques and added the ambience of Italian coffee shops. This gourmet coffee chain differentiates itself from the competition with an outstanding product and an exciting retail atmosphere. The company also uses stringent quality control by applying high standards of purchasing, roasting, and fresh delivery of coffee.

The company provides an attractive work environment where people are expected to treat each other with respect. An additional effort is made to buy, sell, and use environmentally friendly products. In response to complaints regarding the treatment of farmers in the coffee-producing countries, Starbucks has vowed to protect the way of life of coffee farmers by supporting social, economic, and environmental issues that are crucial to maintaining their traditional lifestyle.

Today, Starbucks is the leading retailer of gourmet coffee in the world, with more than 6,500 retail locations in about 25 countries throughout North America, Latin America, Europe, the Middle East, and the Pacific Rim. Starbucks operates in a variety of locations, including office buildings, shopping centres, airport terminals, and supermarkets.

The company uses its coffee shops as distribution outlets for other Starbucks products and takes advantage of the Starbucks name to diversify into other goods such as coffee

(continued)

beans, pastries, and other food items and beverages as well as mugs, coffeemakers, coffee grinders, and storage containers. The company also sells its beans to restaurants, businesses, airlines, hotels, and through catalogues and the Web. Starbucks coffee and Starbucks ice cream are sold in a variety of flavours through grocery stores. Its super-premium ice creams are sold through a joint venture partnership with Dreyers. A recent addition to its product line is the "ice shaken refreshments" product line, which includes fresh brewed coffee and traditional black and herbal teas sweetened and shaken with ice.

Starbucks is successful because customers are attracted to the high quality of its coffee and the Starbucks experience. The company managed to exploit the trend to gourmet coffee and build on its competitive advantages of purchasing and roasting methods. Credit should also be given to Schultz's decision to avoid the larger flavoured coffee segment and focus on the smaller but less competitive gourmet coffee segment. Judging by its performance to date, Starbucks is a company that exploited the concept of market segmentation successfully.[1]

Introduction

Managers choose within the previously defined strategic markets the specific segments they will serve and the differentiated positioning they will claim for their products in the selected segments. The choice of the segments to serve defines the scope of the served market, as discussed in Chapter 2. As the Starbucks example illustrates in the opening vignette, market segmentation is a key factor in marketing success. Starbucks was able to carve the coffee market into different segments and pursue the segment that was most appropriate for the company. Although the concept of market segmentation has been practised since people began trading goods, it was only in the 1950s—with the publication of a seminal article by Wendell Smith—that it became a key concept for organizing and planning a firm's marketing activities.[2] Today, many firms recognize the central role of market segmentation and spend a significant part of their marketing planning time and resources segmenting markets and identifying the most promising segments.

Market segmentation assumes that customers are different and that most, if not all, markets are made up of smaller groups of customers that are similar in some respects. **Market segmentation** is the process of dividing the market into specific groups of customers with similar needs, purchasing behaviours, and identifying characteristics.[3] Once the market is segmented, the important segments are chosen and their requirements are assessed. Managers use several criteria to help select the segments that are most attractive to their firms.

Once markets are segmented and target segments are selected, marketing managers must decide on a positioning strategy. Market segmentation and positioning form the basis from which all aspects of the marketing mix as well as core organizational activities are developed. Therefore, managers need to design an effective marketing mix and allocate resources to implement the positioning strategy and satisfy the unique segment needs better than the competition. Strategic positioning issues will be discussed in Chapter 6.

The concept of segmentation is simple, but the actual segmentation process can be quite complex. Dividing the market into meaningful, profitable segments is one of the most difficult and important marketing tasks. The main difficulty is that there are numerous ways to segment a market but there are no established procedures to guide the segmentation effort or evaluate the various segments that result from such an effort. This is sometimes the reason that some marketers avoid using segmentation or use it in a rather superficial manner.

Many market segmentation approaches are intuitive and rely on the practitioner's experience and knowledge of the market. Other firms conduct marketing research designed to discover the demographic, geographic, and behavioural characteristics of buyers. Marketing researchers often use various advanced segmentation techniques, such as cluster analysis, factor analysis, multidimensional scaling, and perceptual mapping. These techniques allow marketers to look at their markets in more ways, more depth, and from different angles.

This chapter provides an understanding of the relationship between distinctive competencies and market segmentation and how to segment for new and existing products. Additional topics include discovering new market segments, evaluating market segments, and a discussion of the different target marketing strategies and of the sequenced entry strategy.

> **Market segmentation** is the process of dividing the market into specific groups of customers with similar needs, purchasing behaviours, and identifying characteristics.

Market Segmentation as a Core Organizational Process

Market orientation requires firms to be adept practitioners of market segmentation. Having superior segmentation skills is a source of a sustainable competitive advantage. First, market segmentation helps management obtain a deeper understanding of customers and directs firms to develop a different marketing strategy for each segment. This understanding is then used in the design of the marketing strategy. For example, Home Depot has been successful, in large part, because it understands the needs of the do-it-yourself market for a wide range of merchandise selection, low prices, and good service. Home Depot uses this information to deliver outstanding value for the customer and to create loyal customers.

Second, the premise of segmentation is that firms cannot achieve superiority in all markets with the same product. Firms that cover several markets with the same product become vulnerable to focused opponents that target specific niches with specialized products. Market segmentation helps firms avoid the "all things to all people" syndrome by targeting only carefully selected segments. The targeted segments receive the investment and resources required for the firm to compete effectively.

Third, segmenting and targeting certain segments help minimize competition as the firm avoids competing with companies outside its selected segments. In a sense market segmentation levels the playing field and allows small companies to survive alongside large firms. If it were not for market segmentation, smaller companies would find it extremely difficult to compete effectively against firms with much larger resources. For example, the Premium Beer Company is a highly successful beer importer that focuses on the imported premium beer segment. By targeting this segment, the company avoids a direct confrontation with market leaders Molson Coors and Labatts.

Finally, when sales are stagnant, firms can look for new segments in their market that have growth potential. Market segmentation helps firms find new segments for corporate growth, as the firm finds consumers who have needs that may not be completely addressed by existing suppliers. Finding a new segment with growth potential can help put a firm on a growth path and even revitalize a struggling business.

Selecting a Segmentation Basis

Market segmentation begins with the choice of a basis for segmentation. Different segmentation efforts normally require different segmentation bases. The use of the same segmentation basis for all marketing problems, and the view that there is a single best way of segmenting a market, could result in faulty marketing decisions.[4] Also, following conventional wisdom in segmenting markets typically leads to imitative strategies and causes firms to miss emerging opportunities. Many promising segments are overlooked because of such segmentation practices. Effective market segmentation requires creative thinking and looking at markets from a fresh perspective. Indeed, successful segmentation efforts are often those that involve a great deal of creativity and insight in finding innovative, meaningful, and useful ways to segment markets.

Identification bases reflect relatively permanent descriptions of individual customers that can be used to classify them in distinct groups.

Response profile bases classify customers according to their needs, the benefits they seek from products in the category, and their buying behaviour patterns.

There are numerous ways to describe market segments. Bases used to segment markets may be broadly classified as identification bases and response profile bases.[5] **Identification bases** reflect relatively permanent descriptions of individual customers that can be used to classify them in distinct groups. **Response profile bases** classify customers according to their needs, the benefits they seek from products in the category, and their buying behaviour patterns. Marketers use combinations of these bases to segment their markets.

Segmenting Consumer Markets

Figure 5.1 shows a number of common identification and response profile bases for segmenting consumer markets. Identification bases are discussed first, followed by a description of response profile bases.

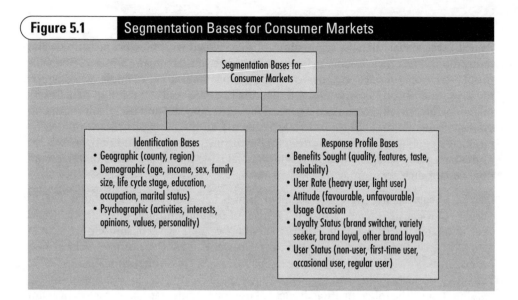

Figure 5.1 Segmentation Bases for Consumer Markets

Segmentation Bases for Consumer Markets

Identification Bases
- Geographic (county, region)
- Demographic (age, income, sex, family size, life cycle stage, education, occupation, marital status)
- Psychographic (activities, interests, opinions, values, personality)

Response Profile Bases
- Benefits Sought (quality, features, taste, reliability)
- User Rate (heavy user, light user)
- Attitude (favourable, unfavourable)
- Usage Occasion
- Loyalty Status (brand switcher, variety seeker, brand loyal, other brand loyal)
- User Status (non-user, first-time user, occasional user, regular user)

Identification bases for segmenting consumer markets

Geographic Segmentation. Geographic segmentation involves dividing the market into groups of customers according to their geographic area. Geographic segmentation is often used because consumers' needs and behaviour patterns often differ from one geographic area to another. Food companies frequently modify their products to better meet the food preferences of local populations. For example, when McDonald's opened its restaurants in India, it respected the religious beliefs of many Indians when it did not use beef or pork in food served there. Instead, the company created two products similar to the Big Mac with mutton and chicken patties and called them Maharaja Mac and Chicken Maharaja Mac.[6]

> Geographic segmentation involves dividing the market into groups of customers according to their geographic area.

Demographic Segmentation. Demographic segmentation is the most frequently used segmentation basis. It includes age, income, sex, family size, family life cycle, education level, occupation, and marital status. For example, Le Chateau targets young women and men who prefer dressy and modern fashions. Using demographic bases is a popular type of segmentation because it describes characteristics of a customer that enable firms to infer consumer consumption preferences and what products they want. Also, demographic data are widely available from government sources, such as the census of the population. Most media outlets use demographic data to describe their viewers, listeners, or readers. One disadvantage of demographics is that, like all other identification bases, it provides no guidelines as to what product features to offer or how to differentiate the product.

> Demographic segmentation includes age, income, sex, family size, family life cycle, education level, occupation, and marital status.

Psychographic Segmentation. Psychographic segmentation involves using consumer lifestyle and psychological information to segment markets. This information typically includes a person's activities, interests, opinions, values, and personality. Marketers often use psychographic information to describe market segments because demographics alone are often not enough to discriminate among consumers. Psychographic information enriches the description of the segment and offers additional insight into the segment behaviour. For example, Roots, one of Canada's leading clothing and lifestyle brands, emphasizes an athletic lifestyle and a strong team spirit expressed through a wide variety of clothing, leather goods, and accessories, as well as through its sponsorship of various athletic events, including the Olympic Games. The company has also outfitted several national sports teams.

> Psychographic segmentation involves using consumer lifestyle and psychological information to segment markets.

Benefit segmentation is concerned with how people's needs and motivations affect their buying behaviour.

Benefit Segmentation. **Benefit segmentation** is concerned with how people's needs and motivations affect their buying behaviour. This type of segmentation uses the benefits people seek from products as a means of segmenting markets. For example, Volvo targets those upscale car buyers who desire a high-quality, safe, and durable car. Benefit segmentation is generally recognized as one of the most powerful and useful approaches to market segmentation because it defines segments on the basis of benefits offered by products—people's primary motivation for buying the product.[7] In addition, knowledge of the benefits people desire from products is valuable for product design, differentiation, and product positioning.

User rate segmentation is based on the principle that a small number of users are often responsible for most of the consumption in a category.

User Rate Segmentation. **User rate segmentation** is based on the principle that a small number of users are often responsible for most of the consumption in a category. It has been estimated that in many situations, including beer and wine consumption, less than 10 or 15 percent of households account for the overwhelming majority of volume and profits.[8] This principle is especially true in business-to-business marketing, because most industries are highly concentrated with a small number of firms dominating an industry.[9] But despite the inherent attractiveness of user rate segmentation, marketers may not target the segment because its popularity attracts competition. Also, the company's products may not be designed for the use of the heavy user. For example, certain machine tools are designed for the amateur user and they are not suitable for professional users who make up the heavy user segment.[10]

Attitude segmentation employs consumer attitude toward a specific product or category as a basis of classification.

Attitude Segmentation. **Attitude segmentation** employs consumer attitude toward a specific product or category as a basis of classification. Segmenting by attitudes can be especially useful for developing advertising campaigns, as they provide clues about how customers feel about the product in relation to their needs and consumption patterns. A company may target customers who hold a negative attitude toward its product because they have incomplete or inaccurate knowledge. In such cases, firms may use informative advertising, testimonials, or endorsements to challenge beliefs held by buyers, dispel any misconceptions, and properly inform customers. For example, a tutoring school used advertising to inform prospective customers that its service is not only for poor students, but also for good students who want to further improve their performance.

Usage occasion segmentation groups consumers on the basis of the occasion or reason they use a product.

Usage Occasion Segmentation. **Usage occasion segmentation** groups consumers on the basis of the occasion or reason they use a product. For example, the reasons people go to a restaurant might include breakfast, business luncheon, birthday party, dinner, or a night out with friends. Usage occasion can be an effective segmentation strategy for selecting target segments and increasing brand sales, as the Band-Aid example discussed in the Strategy in Action box illustrates.[11]

Strategy in Action

BAND-AID

Two products dominated the adhesive bandage category during the 60s, 70s, and 80s: Band-Aid, produced by Johnson and Johnson, and Curad, manufactured by Colgate-Palmolive. The market also included several smaller competitors such as 3M and KidCare. There was very little innovation in this industry during those years. Each competitor held its own share, as people saw no reason to switch from one brand to another.

Suddenly, in the mid-90s, Band-Aid broke with convention and, through innovation, introduced an entire array of new products specifically designed to be used on certain occasions by customers. There were antiseptic Band-Aids to be used as antimicrobial agents, special Band-Aid strips shaped for finger and knuckle cuts, sport Band-Aids, Band-Aids containing aloe vera and vitamin E for skin problems, waterproof Band-Aids, clear Band-Aids, brightly coloured Band-Aids, and Band-Aids featuring Mickey Mouse and other Disney characters. But Colgate-Palmolive failed to follow Band-Aid's innovation efforts. As a result of this innovation activity and the skilful use of occasion segmentation, Band-Aid turned a tight race for market share into a dominant position with 75 percent of the category shelf space.

Loyalty Status Segmentation. **Loyalty status segmentation** divides customers into brand switchers, variety seekers, brand loyals, and other brand loyals. Brand switchers prefer to buy brands that offer low prices, coupons, or other promotional incentives. Variety seekers are customers who prefer to buy different brands instead of being loyal to one brand. Brand loyals prefer to buy the same brand and are not willing to switch even if they are offered special incentives. Other brand loyals are those customers who are loyal to other brands. Loyal customers are typically targeted first as they are worth more than non-loyal ones. Companies design frequency and loyalty programs to reward loyal customers and maintain their loyalty. Examples of such programs include Air Canada's Aeroplan, Zellers' Club Z points, and Air Miles. Similarly, firms may design special marketing programs directed at brand switchers, variety seekers, or other brand loyals.

> **Loyalty status segmentation** divides customers into brand switchers, variety seekers, brand loyals, and other brand loyals.

User Status Segmentation. **User status segmentation** classifies customers into non-users, first-time users, occasional users, and regular users. Non-users include customers who do not use the category or those who use the category but not the firm's brand. Marketers must investigate the reasons customers do not buy their products before they introduce marketing programs for non-users. Some of the non-users are simply not aware of the product. Other non-users may have tried the product but didn't like it. It may be very difficult to persuade those who hold unfavourable attitudes to buy the product. Companies have a better chance to persuade non-customers who are not currently buying the product but are favourably predisposed toward it. Companies can target first-time or occasional users with special programs to convert them into regular customers or they can appeal to regular users with special incentives such as frequent-patron programs to retain them as customers.

> **User status segmentation** classifies customers into non-users, first-time users, occasional users, and regular users.

Segmenting Business Markets

The major bases that marketers use to segment business markets are similar to those used to segment consumer markets. There are important differences, however, as both consumers and businesses have market needs but the factors that contribute to these needs differ in important ways. These differences are reflected in the detailed bases and the labels used to identify these bases. Figure 5.2 lists the major identification and response profile bases for segmenting business markets.

Identification bases for segmenting business markets

Organizational Geographic Segmentation. **Organizational geographic segmentation** much like consumer markets, involves segmenting a market on the basis of geographic location. Geographic bases include global regions, countries, provinces or states, counties, and cities. A company may segment its market by regions such as Europe or Asia. Geographic segmentation is normally needed as companies must identify the geographic region in which they are going to focus their marketing efforts. But geographic segmentation is often necessary because some industries, such as textile manufacturers and watch manufacturers, are concentrated in particular geographic regions.

> **Organizational geographic segmentation**, much like consumer markets, involves segmenting on the basis of geographic location.

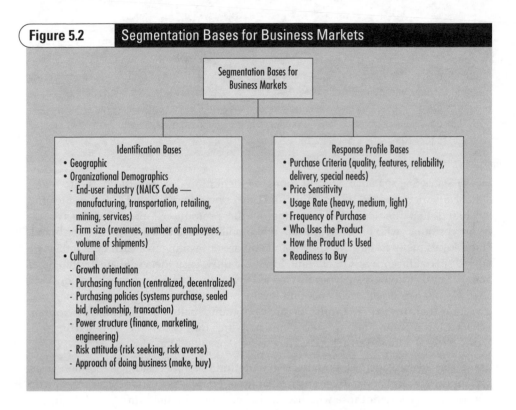

Figure 5.2 Segmentation Bases for Business Markets

Segmentation Bases for Business Markets

Identification Bases
- Geographic
- Organizational Demographics
  - End-user industry (NAICS Code — manufacturing, transportation, retailing, mining, services)
  - Firm size (revenues, number of employees, volume of shipments)
- Cultural
  - Growth orientation
  - Purchasing function (centralized, decentralized)
  - Purchasing policies (systems purchase, sealed bid, relationship, transaction)
  - Power structure (finance, marketing, engineering)
  - Risk attitude (risk seeking, risk averse)
  - Approach of doing business (make, buy)

Response Profile Bases
- Purchase Criteria (quality, features, reliability, delivery, special needs)
- Price Sensitivity
- Usage Rate (heavy, medium, light)
- Frequency of Purchase
- Who Uses the Product
- How the Product Is Used
- Readiness to Buy

Organizational demographics include the relevant North American Industrial Classification System (NAICS) Code, revenues, number of employees, and volume of shipments.

Organizational Demographics. **Organizational demographics** often reflect the type of economic activity represented by the relevant North American Industrial Classification System (NAICS) Code. Examples of economic activity include manufacturing, transportation, retail trade, and mining. Other organizational demographics include size measured by revenues, number of employees, and volume of shipments. For example, Varian is an Internet provider that provides high-speed Internet services to small businesses in Canada. But large size is not always associated with purchasing large quantities of products as large customers may be buying from several suppliers. Also, relying on a few large customers may be risky, as losing even one large customer could lead to a drastic drop in sales.

Organizational cultural segmentation includes growth orientation, company purchasing policies, power structure, risk attitude, and approach to doing business.

Organizational Cultural Segmentation. **Organizational cultural segmentation** can also be useful for segmenting business markets. Among the most important cultural differences for firms is their growth orientation. Some firms are more growth oriented, while others are more concerned with cost-cutting or defending their existing business. The purchasing function—centralized or decentralized—is another way to segment business markets. A company's purchasing policies—systems purchases, sealed bids, close relationships with suppliers, or simple arm's length transactions—can also be used for segmentation purposes.

The power structure that prevails in the organization is commonly reflected in one function dominating the organization. In some organizations finance may be the most powerful function while in others it could be marketing or engineering. Instead of appealing to all functions, marketers should appeal to managers who have real decision-making power. Other aspects of organizational culture include attitude toward risk. Some firms are more risk seeking than others and are willing to invest in higher-risk projects. Firms also differ in their approach to doing business—some firms make the components or parts they use; others buy them from independent suppliers.

Response profile bases for segmenting business markets

Response profile bases provide useful ways for segmenting business markets. A commonly used response profile basis for segmenting business markets is purchase criteria such as quality, price, reliability, and delivery. Additional response profile bases include price sensitivity, usage rate, purchase frequency, who uses the product within the organization, how the product is used, and readiness to buy. All these variables influence the needs and buying behaviour of business customers and can be useful bases for market segmentation purposes. The Strategy in Action box describes how Quality Printing Inc., a company on the east coast, used special needs and end-user industry-based segmentation to grow successfully when company sales were stagnant and its long-term prospects were poor.

Segmenting for New and Existing Products

There are numerous ways to segment markets, making market segmentation a creative process. Marketers need to experiment with different segmentation bases until they are satisfied with the segmentation result. Trying different bases minimizes their chances of missing a useful way to segment the market.

Effective market segmentation combines identification and response profile bases, as shown in Figure 5.3. Identification or profile response bases alone are not enough to adequately describe segments, however. For example, a demographic description of a segment may be incomplete, as consumers with similar demographic characteristics could seek different product benefits or prefer a different lifestyle from one another. Alternatively, when a response profile basis such as benefits sought, loyalty, or user status is selected first, a more complete segment profile should be developed using geographic, demographic, and psychographic variables to provide a more detailed description of the segments.

The next section discusses two commonly encountered market segmentation situations: segmentation for new products and segmentation for existing products.

Figure 5.3 | Combining Identification and Response Profile Bases

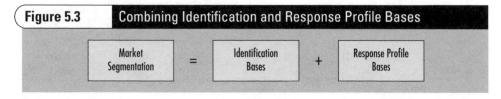

Market Segmentation = Identification Bases + Response Profile Bases

Segmenting for New Products

When segmenting a market for a new product, the marketing analyst may proceed in one of the following two ways. He or she may, first, segment the market with one or more identification bases, such as demographic or psychographic—and then describe the resulting segments with one or more response profile bases. For example, a retailer of high-quality clothing could define his or her market as young, high-income, socially active female professionals who are looking for high-quality fashionable clothing and are relatively price insensitive.

Alternatively, the marketing manager may start with response profile bases and then describe the segment using identification bases. For example, a perfume manufacturer who developed a new high-quality premium perfume could target fashion-conscious, upwardly mobile, high-income females looking for an alternative to existing perfumes.

Segmenting for Existing Products

How should marketing managers segment the market for an existing product? A good way to segment an existing market is to divide the market between current customers and all other customers. Current customers are usually an attractive segment to target for several reasons. Current customers are likely to have a favourable attitude toward the firm's product. Also, retaining current users is less expensive than finding new users. For these reasons, increasing retention of existing customers has a large impact on company profits.[12]

Once the current user market is fully penetrated, a firm may target other segments such as variety seekers and competitors' customers. The latter may be a difficult segment to attract if people have established strong loyalties to the firm's competitors. Also, competitors may retaliate if their core segments are attacked. If competitors' customers are not an attractive opportunity, the firm may pursue customers who are not currently users of the category.

Creativity in Market Segmentation

Markets are in a constant state of flux. New segments emerge and old ones disappear all the time. One reason for these changes is shifts in consumer preferences, demographics, and new social and cultural trends. These changes cause shifts in the important attributes consumers use to evaluate products and often make previously insignificant segments more appealing. For example, car buyers' preference for luxury changed to a preference for fuel-efficient automobiles during the oil crisis in the 1970s, and then shifted to safety and comfort in the 1980s and 1990s, causing a proliferation of minivans and sports utility vehicles. In the early part of the new century, an increase in gasoline prices caused a reduction in demand for large passenger cars and a spurt in more fuel-efficient vehicles such as those powered by a combination of gasoline and batteries.

New segments often emerge after they have been overlooked for a while, only to be discovered by inquisitive competitors. Companies frequently find out about the existence of market segments through personal experience and knowledge of the market, marketing research, or just luck.[13]

It is important for marketing managers to segment their markets in unique and creative ways. Creative segmentation can help firms discover promising segments whose needs have been overlooked or underserved by other companies. Competitors find it more difficult to respond to a creative segmentation of a market than to copy a new product, a new advertising campaign, or a price cut. New and unusual market segmentations are difficult to imitate because they require changes in all areas of the business's operations.[14]

A good way of discovering new segments is to ask the questions "What customer needs is our product satisfying? What customer needs are not currently satisfied that our company is able to satisfy?" These questions may help a firm think of customers who are not currently buying the firm's products. For example, Starbucks fulfilled the need of people for gourmet coffee, something that none of the major coffee companies were doing. The Strategy in Action box describes how one company discovered a new market segment in the market for frozen treats for dogs.[15]

One of the reasons some firms experience high growth rates is that they reach an untapped customer segment. Canon's dramatic growth in the copier business was due, in large part, to discovering the untapped segment of small businesses and individuals that was witnessing explosive growth rates in the 1970s. Xerox lost the market leadership mainly because it let a competitor discover this segment. By the time Xerox realized the existence of this segment, it was too late, as it was already dominated by Canon. For this reason, firms must be prepared to experiment with unorthodox ways of segmenting and re-segmenting their markets, in the hope of discovering unexploited segment opportunities.

Evaluating Segment Attractiveness

Once segments are defined, marketers must select the most attractive among them. A potential problem of market segmentation is that it may result in too many segments because of the numerous ways a market can be divided. A good rule of thumb for marketers to keep in mind is that the purpose of market segmentation is to find a small number of segments that are attractive enough to warrant an investment. How do firms find the most attractive segments? Firms can use several criteria to evaluate the attractiveness of market segments, as shown in Figure 5.4.

- Size and growth
- Profitability
- Accessibility
- Corporate vision, mission, and goals
- Competitive intensity
- Distinctive competencies

Size and Growth

The segment must be of sufficient size to generate enough sales to satisfy the objectives of the firm and to justify the investment in the segment. Because developing a separate marketing strategy for each segment is costly, a segment must be large enough to support its own marketing strategy.[16] But it is not sufficient to find segments that promise large volume. Current and future growth is an important consideration, as growing segments are normally more attractive than stagnant or declining ones. Reitmans, a women's clothing chain, owes its success largely to targeting a fast-growing segment—plus-sized women—as described in the Strategy in Action box:[17]

Strategy in Action

REITMANS

Reitmans, a Montreal-based women's wear chain with about 850 stores across the country, sells clothes mostly under the banners of Reitmans, Smart Set/Dalmys, Penningtons, Addition Elle, and Thyme Maternity. Despite encountering ferocious competition in its market segment in 2004, Reitmans was looking ahead to another successful year. The company's first-quarter profits more than tripled to $13 million from $4.1 million for the three months ended on May 1, 2004, while sales rose to $193.4 million from $177.8 million for the same period. Reitmans' success can be partly attributed to its targeting a fast-growing segment–plus-sized women. Reitmans seems to be the only company that takes this segment seriously as other Canadian retailers are largely neglecting this group. Although independent market research shows that nearly one-third of Canadian women wear size 14 or above, women's wear stores devote only 5 percent of floor space to that category. It seems that Reitmans' focus on market segments that are neglected by its rivals along with its excellent customer service and resulting customer satisfaction is paying handsome dividends for the company.

Profitability

Current and expected profitability should also be considered in evaluating segments. Segments with prospects for higher profitability are, not surprisingly, more attractive targets. Some segments are more profitable because firms can charge higher prices because of low competitive intensity or because customers are not price sensitive. The cost of distribution or serving the segment also affects its profitability. It may be too expensive to serve certain segments because customers buy in small quantities, causing high ordering and delivery costs. Firms should evaluate segments with regard to their profitability and target the most profitable ones.

Accessibility

Once an attractive segment has been identified, the firm should confirm that it is easily accessible through channels of distribution and marketing communication. New and relatively unknown firms often face the problem of lack of suitable distribution or adequate promotion due to lack of financial resources. The availability of Internet has mitigated this problem somewhat. In some cases, the Internet may become the cornerstone of the firm's marketing strategy, as is the case of eBay and E*Trade, the Internet securities trader.

Corporate Vision, Mission, and Goals

The segment should be consistent with the company's vision, mission, and goals. Some firms enter small niches not to earn profits but to use these niches as a base to enter more profitable segments later. Other firms use the profits from the niche to fund other initiatives. Some companies invest only in markets they can dominate or in which they can be a strong contender. For example, the strategic goal of General Electric is to participate in markets in which it can be either number one or number two. Adherence to this goal caused General Electric to withdraw from certain markets, such as the small appliances market, and concentrate on markets it could dominate, such as aircraft engines and financial services.

Competitive Intensity

Companies should not enter segments that are well defended by powerful rivals. For example, Jetsgo entered the Canadian airline market, which was dominated by Air Canada and WestJet and failed miserably. Firms that enter a segment using a frontal attack require overwhelming resources in the form of first-rate technology, financial resources, productive capacity, and advertising budget.

Distinctive Competencies

Market segmentation decisions are also driven by the distinctive competencies of the firm.[18] A firm is more likely to succeed if it has the competencies to meet the requirements of targeted segments in a superior way. For example, segments that require a large investment in R&D and advertising spending would probably be out of reach for a small undercapitalized start-up, but probably not so for a much larger company. A useful question to ask when looking for the right segment is "Given our capabilities, which customer needs can we satisfy?"

Segment Interrelationships

Segments are often related in important ways.[19] Because of these interrelationships, companies competing in more than one segment are often presented with many opportunities to share activities and obtain an advantage over single-segment competitors. For example, firms can use the same manufacturing facilities to make products designed for different segments. Because segment interrelationships can involve both benefits and costs, segment interrelationships result in a competitive advantage if the benefits of sharing activities exceed costs.

Segment interrelationships have several other advantages. They may lead to greater economies of scale or scope, yielding a cost advantage relative to single-segment competitors. They may also lead to greater capacity utilization, in turn leading to further cost reductions and increasing revenues. For example, when Canadian banks began selling various types of insurance, they were able to better utilize their existing human resources. Segment interrelationships may also lead to increased differentiation by using the same well-known name on all company products regardless of the segment targeted, increasing product recognition and acceptance. For example, McCain Foods uses the same brand name across its different products, providing it with a source of differentiation.

Sharing an activity such as segment interrelationships is likely to raise costs. And indeed, segment interrelationships often lead to increased costs as a result of coordination, compromise, and inflexibility in servicing segments that share common activities. **Coordination costs** result from the increased complexity of serving various segments with the same activities. For example, serving different buyer groups with the same sales force is much more complex than if each buyer group is served with its own specialized sales force. Although using the same sales force in different segments can lead to decreased overall selling costs, the resulting increases in complexity cause increases in selling cost.

Compromise costs result from an activity having to be performed in the same manner for all segments, which may not be optimal for any of the segments involved. For example, using the same sales force to sell two different product lines will force salespeople to pay less attention to each of the two products, and they will be less knowledgeable than a dedicated sales force would be. Lastly, sharing activities in various segments often results in costs due to **inflexibility**—an inability to modify the firm's strategy in the various segments. Such inflexibility often leads to suboptimal strategies as sharing activities makes it difficult to respond to environmental threats. Responding to threats in one segment by modifying the shared activity may reduce the value of the activity to other segments.

Interrelationships among some segments are often stronger than others as they are more closely allied. Firms may be able to share certain activities across some segments and another set of activities across another group of segments. Consequently, segment interrelationships often define the segments served, as firms enter segments characterized by strong interrelationships; a firm that serves a certain segment will most likely enter other segments where there are strong positive interrelationships. For example, cable TV providers Rogers Communications and Shaw Communications entered the high-speed Internet segment to exploit strong interrelationships with its existing cable business. These interrelationships included the existence of a customer base and the availability of technology. On the other hand, the high costs of coordination, compromise, or inflexibility force firms to either avoid these segments or serve them with customized marketing strategies.

The Segment Attractiveness–Company Capabilities Matrix

The criteria discussed in the previous section may be conveniently summarized graphically in the Segment Attractiveness–Company Capabilities Matrix, shown in Figure 5.5. This matrix classifies segments on the basis of segment attractiveness and the company's capabilities relative to segment needs and the capabilities of competitors in the segment. Market attractiveness is a composite score of the segment size, growth, profitability, accessibility, and competitive intensity in the segment. Each of the four quadrants is discussed below:

- *Superior Company Capabilities, Low Segment Attractiveness:* Segments in this quadrant have very little potential and they do not represent attractive opportunities. Before these segments are discarded, management should look to see if there are attractive niches to target within these segments.
- *Superior Company Capabilities, High Segment Attractiveness:* Segments in this quadrant are the most attractive segments and should be selected as target markets, as they represent the best potential among the four categories.

Coordination costs result from the increased complexity of serving various segments with the same activities.

Compromise costs result from an activity having to be performed in the same manner for all segments, which may not be optimal for any of the segments involved.

Inflexibility costs result from an inability to modify the firm's strategy in the various segments.

Figure 5.5 | Segment Attractiveness–Company Capabilities Matrix

		Segment Attractiveness	
		Low	High
Company Capabilities	Superior	Look for attractive niche or discard segment	Most attractive segment; high priority
	Inferior	Least attractive segment; discard segment	Build capabilities or discard segment

- *Inferior Company Capabilities, Low Segment Attractiveness:* These segments should be avoided, as they are the least attractive ones. Management should look at other quadrants to find attractive segment opportunities.
- *Inferior Company Capabilities, High Segment Attractiveness:* Firms in this quadrant should try to develop the capabilities needed to serve the segment. If the investment required to develop the resources and capabilities to serve these segments adequately is excessive, the firm should look at other attractive segments that it can serve more readily.

Target Marketing Strategies

Once the market is segmented and the segment's potential is assessed, the firm selects the most attractive segments and designs appropriate marketing strategies for these segments. Everyone in the organization should be encouraged to contribute ideas about segments the company might enter. Frontline employees especially are close to customers and know which customer needs are not met, or why potential customers are not buying the firm's products. These employees should be given some flexibility in testing new ideas and trying to sell to new segments. However, the responsibility for deciding which customers to serve should lie with the top management.

In selecting segments, firms make decisions along the three dimensions that make up strategic markets. For example, marketing managers may target one group or several groups of customers. Focusing on a few segments allows firms to narrow the scope of their served market to a portion of the total market in which they have the best chances of success. If the choice is to target different customer groups, the manager must decide whether to treat the various groups similarly or develop separate marketing strategies for each customer group. Some companies produce a broad product line while others specialize in a narrower product line. Some firms may also choose to use several technologies while others employ single technologies.

Some firms enter new segments and expand their product line by adding new products. The addition of a new product or service or offering a full product line benefits customers who prefer a "systems solution"—a total package. When a firm sells to many groups, customers can benefit from network effects and lower prices resulting from cost efficiencies due to segment interrelationships. Other firms redefine their served markets by abandoning certain segments and concentrating on those segments that they see as having a greater potential. By narrowing the scope of the served market, firms hope to achieve greater focus in servicing the remaining segments. This focus enables a firm to develop a better degree of specialization in understanding and serving the needs of the chosen segments.[20] It also allows firms to devote more resources to meet the needs of the segments and be a stronger competitor.

Some of the segments currently served by firms may be unprofitable. There is an opportunity cost in serving a segment. Investing in poor segments leaves fewer funds to invest in more attractive segments. One way to increase profitability, though seemingly counter-intuitive, is to reduce the number of customers the company serves. Existing accounts should be examined to determine their profitability. When a full analysis is performed, it may be discovered that some customers are unprofitable. In these cases, management must investigate why these customers are unprofitable and take the necessary action. For example, some firms try to work out an agreement with customers to place larger orders on a less frequent basis, in order to reduce transaction costs. If customers are unwilling to change their purchasing behaviour, the company should look for ways to terminate them.

In selecting segments, firms adopt the following target marketing strategies: undifferentiated, single-segment, multiple-segment, and mass customization. These target marketing strategies are shown in Figure 5.6 and are described in the next section.

Figure 5.6 Target Marketing Strategies

Undifferentiated Strategy

An **undifferentiated strategy** or mass marketing strategy treats the entire market as one segment and offers a standardized product to this market.

An **undifferentiated strategy** treats the entire market as one segment and offers a standardized product to this market. This strategy is also referred to as a mass marketing strategy. For example, some cable companies such as Rogers Communications offered for years high-speed Internet service using a mass marketing strategy without regard to segments. This strategy generally relies on a low-cost position to achieve a competitive advantage through lower prices.

Firms pursue an undifferentiated strategy for the following reasons. First, they may fail to recognize that the market consists of different segments. Second, an undifferentiated strategy is more cost efficient since it avoids the high costs associated with segmentation. Segmentation is normally more costly than mass marketing because it requires tailoring the product to each segment's specific needs. An undifferentiated strategy is associated with lower costs because it involves a standardized product and experience and scale economies in production, advertising, and purchasing. Third, companies sometimes treat all segments the same because the market is too small to justify different treatment of each segment. As the market grows larger, it becomes economically viable to develop different marketing strategies for different market segments. Lastly, the existence of positive segment interrelationships often leads firms to combine segments and serve them with shared activities.

A major risk of an undifferentiated strategy is that it makes the firm vulnerable to attacks by rivals who segment the market and target specific customer groups with specialized products. For example, Henry Ford used an undifferentiated strategy for years to lower production costs and keep prices low. This strategy was successful until General Motors came along with a differentiated strategy that treated segments differently, and it was able to dominate the automobile market.

Another risk exists when companies try to accommodate different segments with the same product, but the segments have conflicting goals. In this case, the sales of the product may be negatively affected. For example, some resorts in the Caribbean cater to both tourists from other countries such as Canada, the United States, and Europe, and local families, which get special deals on weekends. This creates a problem, as the desire of the foreign tourists for a quiet vacation is interrupted by the large noisy crowds that pack the resort on weekends.

Single-Segment Strategy

A **single-segment strategy** focuses on only one segment of the market. Firms using the single-segment strategy pursue the chosen segment aggressively and serve customer needs in the segment well. For example, Research in Motion is a high-tech company based in Waterloo, Ontario, that follows a single-segment strategy: it competes in the mobile communications market with a single product, BlackBerry, which allows people to send e-mails and make phone calls using a proprietary wireless communication technology.

> A **single-segment strategy** focuses on only one segment of the market.

Most successful start-ups begin by serving local markets or offering customized products to customers with specialized needs.[21] By focusing on these segments, small firms avoid competition from large, well-established competitors. A company such as CanJet Airlines is an example of a firm that started with very little capital compared with its established competitors and moved into niches—in this case, discount air travel—that did not interest its much larger competitor, Air Canada. In many cases, these small, undercapitalized entrants help transform these niches into large mass markets.[22]

One risk associated with the single-segment strategy is that, if the large firms in the industry become interested in the segment, the small firms in the segment may be easily wiped out. Firms that pursue a single-segment strategy are not a threat to large companies if they confine their activities in the segment. They can become a threat, however, if they decide to invade neighbouring segments. For this reason, large companies should monitor smaller single-segment firms to ensure they are not evolving into a major threat. Single-segment firms, on the other hand, need to keep a low profile to avoid a powerful retaliation by their larger competitors, while continuing to improve their business and focus on dominating the niche.

Multiple-Segment Strategy

A **multiple-segment strategy** targets more than one segment with a marketing program tailored to the needs of each segment. For example, Nissan competes in several segments of the automobile market with its various Infiniti and Nissan models, which target specific segments of the passenger car, sports utility, and truck market.

> A **multiple-segment strategy** targets more than one segment with a marketing program tailored to the needs of each segment.

Many companies that compete in the high end of the market use their brand recognition to enter low-end segments. Although it can be an excellent opportunity to expand sales, firms moving to the low end of the market need to be aware of the potential to tarnish their image. Companies that already compete in the low end often extend their product lines and enter the middle or high end of the market. However, companies moving up-market frequently face resistance by consumers who associate the company with low-end, inexpensive products.

The advantages and disadvantages of multiple-segment strategies are the reverse of those of undifferentiated strategies. The major advantage is that multiple-segment companies tailor their products to meet the needs of selected segments, increasing customer satisfaction and loyalty. The major disadvantage is that such strategies are normally associated with higher costs owing to offering a differentiated product and lower scale economies.

Mass-Customization Strategy

Mass customization treats individual consumers as single segments and provides them with offerings tailored to their needs.

Most marketers pursue an undifferentiated, single-, or multiple-segment strategy. In recent years, however, many marketers have begun to apply mass-customization techniques. **Mass customization** treats individual consumers as single segments and provides them with offerings tailored to their needs. Mass customization looks at target segments of one. For example, Dell Computer practises mass customization by allowing customers to customize the personal computers they purchase from the company.

Companies have shunned mass customization for years because it was uneconomical to produce products in small quantities. Mass customization has become feasible in recent years because of advances in computer technology and manufacturing techniques, which have made small batch production possible at a reasonable cost. Mass customization is considered an integral part of relationship marketing, which considers the creation of close relationships with valuable customers a critical aspect of marketing success. Mass customization will be further examined along with other relationship marketing concepts such as data mining, customer retention, loyalty, and customer share in Chapter 7.

Sequenced-Entry Strategy

A **sequenced-entry strategy** is a long-term entry strategy that involves entering a market on a small scale and gradually expanding into adjacent segments.

How do firms time their entry into chosen segments? Many firms, instead of entering all segments at once, follow a sequenced-entry strategy. A **sequenced-entry strategy** is a long-term entry strategy that involves a firm entering a market on a small scale, consolidating its position, gathering strength, and establishing the niche as a launching pad from which to invade adjacent segments.[23] For example, when Gatorade was introduced in Canada, its sales were confined to Ontario for the first year of operation, with the intention of expanding into other provinces in the future.

The premise of a sequenced strategy is that entering a market on a narrow front usually is not viewed as a threatening move by large competitors. The failure to perceive the entrant as a threat allows the entrant to build a viable position before it gets noticed by larger competitors. In addition, by limiting the scope of entry, the amount of investment put at risk is reduced. By proceeding with slow and deliberate steps, the firm has the time to study the market and competition carefully, correct any initial errors, and fine-tune its marketing strategy at a very low cost. A full-blown entry, on the other hand, could cause huge losses if errors were discovered after the entry had occurred. Figure 5.7 shows the sequenced-entry strategy followed by Canadian discount airline WestJet in expanding from its initial base in western Canada into central and eastern Canada.

Figure 5.7 — WestJet's Sequenced-Entry Strategy

	Western Canada	Central Canada	Eastern Canada
Discount Segment	————————————————————————→		
Full-fare Segment			
Charter Segment			
Year	1996	2000	2005

There are advantages and disadvantages to the sequenced-entry strategy. One of the advantages, as we discussed earlier, is that it minimizes the risk of retaliation by competitors. Also, the firm avoids the risks of a high-growth strategy, including running out of cash because of increases in accounts receivable; increases in debt for building capacity, purchasing equipment, or working capital; and reduction in service levels. As such this entry strategy is suited for firms that prefer to expand by taking small and gradual steps to avoid risking the bigger losses associated with full-blown introductions in case demand for the product fails to materialize. Disadvantages include the possibility of the firm's failure to preempt and dominate the market before competitors enter and get established. Also, given the limited scope of operations and resources invested in the business, the entrant is an easy target in case incumbents decide to retaliate.

- Market segmentation is a core organizational process because it helps firms (1) acquire a deeper understanding of customer needs, (2) avoid being all things to all people, (3) minimize competition, and (4) find new growth opportunities.

- Although there are numerous ways to segment markets, segmentation bases may be classified into two broad groups: identification and response profile bases. Identification bases are relatively permanent descriptors of customers. Response profile bases classify people according to their needs and behaviour toward products.

- Identification bases in consumer markets include geographic, demographic, and psychographic bases. The major response profile bases include benefits sought by customers, user rate, attitudes, usage occasion, and loyalty status.

- Identification bases in business markets include geographic, organizational, demographic, and cultural bases. Response profile bases include purchase criteria, price sensitivity, usage rate, frequency of purchase, who uses the product, how the product is used, and readiness to buy.

- Effective segmentation combines both identification and response profile bases. A market for a new product can be segmented with the use of one or more identification bases, followed by one or more response profile bases. Alternatively, marketing managers could start with one or more response profile bases and then describe the segments using one or more identification bases. Markets for existing products may be segmented by focusing on current customers, who are described with identification and response profile bases. Once the current customer segment is fully penetrated, the marketer can target other segments such as competitors' customers, non-users, or overlooked segments.

- Markets continuously change. New segments are born and old ones disappear all the time. Marketers often find new segments through market knowledge, marketing research, or luck.

- Once segments are formed, managers need to evaluate them and select the most attractive ones. Criteria for segment evaluation include size and growth; profitability; accessibility; consistency with corporate mission, vision, and goals; competitive intensity; and distinctive competencies.

- In evaluating segments, marketing managers should examine possible interrelationships between segments. Although there are benefits from segment interrelationships such as economies of scale, increasing capacity utilization, and differentiation, there are also costs such as coordination, compromise, and inflexibility.

- Once the segments are evaluated, the manager chooses the ones on which to focus his or her efforts and the timing of entry into these segments. There are four target marketing strategies: undifferentiated (or mass strategy), single-segment strategy, multiple-segment strategy, and mass customization.

- In choosing a segment entry strategy, many firms follow a sequenced-entry strategy by entering a single segment first and then gradually expanding into adjacent segments.

Review and Discussion Questions

1. While the concept of market segmentation is simple, the implementation of segmentation can be quite complex. Why?

2. Why is market segmentation a core organizational process? Discuss the benefits of market segmentation.

3. Discuss the major identification and response profile bases for segmenting consumer and business markets. What are the similarities and differences between bases used for consumer and business segmentation?

4. Effective market segmentation requires the use of both identification and response profile bases. Why?

5. What is the role of creativity in market segmentation? Why do marketers need to look at a market in novel ways? Why do competitors find it more difficult to respond to creative and unusual ways of segmenting markets?

6. Describe the criteria used by marketers to evaluate market segments.

7. Give examples of benefits and costs involved in segment interrelationships. How do segment interrelationships affect the choice of segments?

8. Describe the segment attractiveness–ability to serve the segment matrix. What are the marketing strategy implications of this matrix?

9. Describe the various target marketing strategies. What are the advantages and disadvantages of each strategy?

10. Discuss the sequenced-entry strategy. What are the advantages and disadvantages of the sequenced-entry strategy?

1. Referring back to the opening vignette, outline how Starbucks' use of market segmentation helped the company compete successfully against much larger competitors.

2. Assume that your company has developed a low-fat substitute for margarine and other higher-fat products. Using the guidelines described in this chapter, outline an approach for segmenting this market.

3. Using the guideline described in this chapter, how would the management of Home Depot segment its market? Which segment(s) should be selected first, and which one(s) should be targeted subsequently?

4. Contrast the segmentation strategies of Wal-Mart and Zellers. Are they the same? Are they different? Why?

5. Choose a market you are familiar with. Identify the major current market segments. Then analyze the market in creative ways to see if you can come up with new attractive segments that have been overlooked or neglected.

6. While other fast food burger chains were introducing low-fat healthy offerings such as salads and yogurt, Toronto-based Harvey's decided to buck the trend and introduce "The Big Harv," a six-ounce hamburger aimed directly at those men who prefer beef over healthier choices. Despite widespread skepticism by industry observers about the soundness of Harvey's market segmentation strategy, the company feels confident about the success of its strategy. Under what conditions will Harvey's new market segmentation strategy succeed?

Notes

1. This section draws from Robert J. Thomas, *New Product Success Stories* (New York: Wiley, 1995), 19–30.
2. Wendell Smith, "Product Differentiation and Market Segmentation as Alternative Marketing Strategies," *Journal of Marketing* 21 (July 1955), 3–8.
3. Smith.
4. Yoram Wind, "Issues and Advances in Segmentation Research," *Journal of Marketing Research* 15 (August 1978), 317–337.
5. A similar classification has also been used in George S. Day, *Market-Driven Strategy: Processes for Creating Value* (New York: The Free Press, 1990), 101, and Adrian Ryans, Roger More, Donald Barclay, and Terry Deutscher, *Winning Market Leadership* (Toronto: Wiley, 2000), 47.
6. http://www.mcdonalds.com/countries/india/, retrieved on July 9, 2003.
7. Peter Yannopoulos and Ronald Rotenberg, "Benefit Segmentation of the Near-Home Tourism Market: The Case of Upper New York State," *Journal of Travel and Tourism Marketing* 8(2), 1999, 41–55.
8. Garth Hallberg, *All Consumers Are Not Created Equal* (New York: Wiley, 1995), 4.
9. Peter Yannopoulos, *The Size Distribution of Firms in Canada: A Stochastic Model With Implications for Strategic Planning and Public Policy*, Unpublished Ph.D. dissertation, 1984, p. 19.
10. James H. Myers, *Segmentation and Positioning for Strategic Marketing Decisions* (Chicago, Ill.: American Marketing Association, 1996), 21.
11. Eric Schulz, *The Marketing Game* (Holbrook, Mass.: Adams Media Corporation, 1999), 94.
12. Brian Sternthal and Alice M. Tybout, "Segmentation and Marketing," in Dawn Iacobucci (ed.), *Kellogg on Marketing* (New York: Wiley, 2001), 5.
13. John Cady and Robert Buzzell, *Strategic Marketing* (Boston: Little, Brown and Company, 1986), 129.
14. Derek F. Abell, *Managing With Dual Strategies* (New York: The Free Press, 1993), 50.
15. Dana Flavelle, "Ice cream maker caters to cool dogs," *Toronto Star*, April 21, 2004, E1.
16. David Aaker, *Strategic Market Management*, 6th ed. (New York: Wiley, 2001), 41.
17. Donald McKenzie, "Reitmans sees strong year despite fierce competition," *Toronto Star*, June 10, 2004, D4.
18. Leonard Lodish, Howard Lee Morgan, and Amy Kallianpur, *Entrepreneurial Marketing* (New York: Wiley, 2001), 2.
19. Michael E. Porter, *Competitive Advantage: Creating and Sustaining Superior Performance* (New York: The Free Press, 1985), 258.
20. Cady and Buzzell, 127.
21. Amar Bhide, *The Origin and Evolution of New Businesses* (New York: Oxford University Press, 2000), 40.
22. Bhide, 42.
23. Michael E. Porter, *Competitive Strategy* (New York: The Free Press, 1980), 356.

Chapter Six

Strategic Positioning

At the heart of every good marketing strategy there is a good positioning strategy.

Regis McKenna, Marketing Strategist

Learning Objectives

After studying this chapter, you should be able to:

1. Explain the meaning of strategic positioning

2. Describe the difference between strategic positioning and operational efficiency

3. Describe how strategic positioning affects organizational and marketing mix activities

4. Distinguish between tangible attribute and intangible attribute positioning

5. Outline the strategic positioning process

6. Describe several positioning strategies

7. Understand the most common positioning errors

8. Discuss how to reposition competitors

Canadian Tire Changes Its Positioning Strategy

Canadian Tire, which started in 1922 as a retailer of tires, batteries, and a homemade brand of antifreeze, has over the years greatly expanded the range of markets it sells into. Today it operates more than 1,000 stores and gas bars in Canada. The 449 stores known collectively as Canadian Tire Retail are operated by associate dealers across Canada and offer products and services in three specialty categories: automotive, sports and leisure, and home products. Another arm, Canadian Tire Financial Services, offers financial products and services and other value-added services to Canadian Tire customers. PartSource, owned by Canadian Tire, is an automotive parts specialty chain with 33 stores targeting professional automotive installers and serious do-it-yourselfers. Another business, Canadian Tire Petroleum, is the country's largest independent gasoline retailer with more than 200 gas bars. Canadian Tire also owns Mark's Work Wearhouse, a retailer of work-related apparel that operates 300 stores in Canada.

Canadian Tire's package of location, price, service, and merchandise assortment distinguishes the company from its competition. Location has been its key differentiating factor. Eighty-five percent of the Canadian population lives within a 15-minute drive of a local Canadian Tire store, but a visit to the store is not always necessary—products can also be ordered online and through catalogues. By having highly efficient operations, Canadian Tire has been able to offer customers very competitive prices and good value. The "three stores under one roof" approach enables Canadian Tire to offer customers a wide assortment of merchandise.

Canadian Tire's positioning as "Still the right place," which began in the mid-90s, changed to "Let's get started" in the early 2000s. This new positioning theme was part of a marketing campaign designed to portray Canadian Tire as the right place to start something new, whether it is a hobby or a project.

A key aspect of Canadian Tire's new positioning was to solidify its reputation as one of Canada's leading retailers of hard goods like radios, TVs, coffee makers, tires, and bicycles. Canadian Tire also wanted to enhance its image as a retailer of new and innovative products, by introducing new product lines and products available exclusively at its stores. In order to further differentiate itself from its competition, including Home Depot, Wal-Mart, and Zellers, Canadian Tire planned to open new format stores that were larger and brighter, and with different interior and exterior designs from existing stores. The product assortment carried in the new format stores included services such as equipment rentals, home delivery, and gift registries.

Canadian Tire's new positioning was promoted through a variety of communications media, including radio and TV ads, in-store signage, and catalogues. Advertisements were presented against a musical background of country rock and showed highly satisfied customers using products purchased at Canadian Tire.

How well Canadian Tire's new positioning will work is too early to tell. Despite fierce competition, Canadian Tire had sales of $1.5 billion in the third quarter of 2002, an increase of 7.6 percent over the same quarter of 2001. Revenues for the previous nine months of 2002 were $4.2 billion, up by 6.8 percent from the same period in 2001. Canadian Tire's goal was to reach combined sales of $9 billion by 2005 for its Canadian Tire, Canadian Tire Petroleum, PartSource Stores, and Mark's Work Wearhouse. The new marketing and positioning strategy implemented by Canadian Tire is expected to make a significant contribution toward achieving this goal.[1]

Introduction

As discussed in the opening vignette, managers of companies such as Canadian Tire find it necessary to reposition their firm in an effort to appeal to the changing needs of the marketplace. Strategic positioning is an important part of a firm's marketing strategy. Once the market is segmented and target markets are selected, firms need to decide their brand's positioning in the target markets. Market segmentation and the choice of target market influence the positioning decision. If segmentation helps to answer the question of which customers to target, positioning answers the question of how the firm competes in the selected segments.

Effective positioning requires managers to have a keen understanding of customers' needs and perceptions of competing products. This information is valuable in helping marketers decide on the most effective positioning for a brand. Without a solid understanding of customer needs, managers will find it difficult to develop sound positioning strategies.

Success in the marketplace largely depends on how the product is perceived by targeted customers. Positioning is a method of creating a distinctive and desirable image in the minds of potential customers. This image informs customers of the function of the product or service, how the product differs from others, and why they should prefer it to competing products. If the firm fails to establish a unique image in the minds of customers, the positioning will not have been successful and the identity will not be distinct. When a product does not have distinctive positioning, it commonly will not have top-of-mind awareness and is excluded from the **evoked set**—the group of products that come to mind when a consumer is considering a purchase.[2]

> **Evoked set** describes the set of products that come to mind when a consumer is considering a purchase.

> **Unique selling proposition** is a concept used in advertising that focuses on a single benefit distinguishing the product or company from the competition.

The importance of positioning brands was recognized at least as early as the 1950s, when advertising executive Rosser Reeve advised advertisers to focus only on a single benefit, which he called the **unique selling proposition**.[3] The prosperity of the 1960s led to a huge increase in the number of brands, which made the advertising job of attracting people's attention even more difficult. The term *positioning* was coined by two advertising executives, Al Ries and Jack Trout, who called marketers' attention to the problem of the proper positioning of their brands.

This chapter explores the concept of strategic positioning. It explains the meaning and relevance of strategic positioning for the organization. The differences between positioning and operational effectiveness and tangible attributes and intangible attributes positioning are explained. The strategic positioning process and the criteria for selecting benefits or attributes are also discussed. Finally, various approaches to strategic positioning are described, and how to carry out repositioning of a product or a firm's competitors.

Defining Strategic Positioning

> **Strategic positioning** expresses the long-term strategy of the organization and reflects the core identity and related associations of the brand.

Strategic positioning expresses the long-term strategy of the organization. It reflects the core identity and related associations of the brand.[4] At the same time, positioning represents the perception or image that the market forms about a firm's product. Strategic positioning is based on the idea that, in order to compete successfully in the marketplace against other strong brands, each product must establish its own distinct positioning in the market.

Strategic positioning is derived from the value proposition offered for the target market. Should the company be known as the cost leader, quality leader, or technological leader? Tim Hortons has become one of North America's largest coffee and baked goods chains by being positioned as always having fresh, high-quality products. Strategic positioning starts with the customer. Customers view products in relation to other competing products. Successful positioning is the result of occupying a unique position in the minds of customers. Companies that achieve such a position own an important benefit or attribute. For example, FedEx owns the attribute of on-time delivery in the highly competitive overnight courier market.

Positioning a product is relatively easy when a firm competes in a segment that has few or no competitors or when the brand is clearly superior to other brands. The positioning task becomes especially difficult in highly crowded and competitive markets, where brands have few real differences. However, even such markets provide many positioning opportunities that allow creative companies to break through the advertising clutter and marketplace noise and attain a distinct position. Volvo, for example, has successfully positioned its cars in the highly competitive automobile market by claiming outstanding performance, a sleek design, and safety, the latter a key attribute to many car buyers.

Some companies regard positioning as manipulation of consumers' minds. They decide on a certain positioning such as being perceived as the industry's low price leader or highest-quality firm. Next they create a slogan that summarizes the desired positioning. Finally, they spend heavily on advertising and promotion to create a widespread awareness of the company's desired image. For such an approach to work, a large advertising and promotional budget is required to create the necessary awareness for the product. Even then, there is no guarantee that the heavy promotional spending will cause the positioning effort to succeed. Establishing a strong positioning requires more than advertising or promotion. What is needed is a comprehensive marketing program involving appropriate product, price, distribution, and advertising actions.[5]

The position chosen has far-reaching implications for the organization. Strategic positioning drives all organizational activities such as research and development, production, and human resource decisions.[6] It also affects everything the organization does or stands for: policies, procedures, hiring, training, and facilities. The organizational culture, values, and capabilities must be consistent with the strategic positioning. For example, Tim Hortons' positioning is based on the three Fs: fresh, fast, and friendly. The company's hiring, training, facilities, and the products sold in its stores must be consistent with the company's positioning. In order to properly implement its positioning, Tim Hortons needs to hire and train friendly people, its products must be always fresh, and the design of its facilities must allow orders to be filled in a speedy manner.

The company's decisions about its marketing mix also play an important role in implementing a company's positioning strategy. All marketing mix activities must align with the positioning: the product offers the benefits promised, the price matches the value implied by the positioning, the product is distributed through appropriate channels, and the benefits are communicated to customers. For example, companies that emphasize top quality and service must ensure that their products incorporate a first-class design, that manufacturing is free of defects, and that employees with appropriate skills are hired. Second Cup charges higher prices than other coffee shops to emphasize its outstanding quality. PepsiCo's advertisements reinforce its positioning as the choice of young consumers of soft drinks by using youthful pop stars such as Britney Spears and Shakira. The relationship between strategic positioning and organizational activities is shown in Figure 6.1.

Strategic Positioning Versus Operational Effectiveness

According to Michael Porter,[7] some managers reject strategic positioning in favour of operational effectiveness. These managers view positioning as too static in the face of rapidly changing technologies and shifting markets. In their opinion, firms operating in these environments must remain flexible and nimble in order to be able to rapidly respond to changing market conditions. Furthermore, they believe, competitors quickly imitate a rival's positioning, rendering any competitive advantages temporary.

Figure 6.1 Alignment of Strategic Positioning and Organizational Activities

Operational effectiveness entails performing activities similar to a competitor's better than the competitor.

Operational effectiveness, which is preferred by these managers, entails performing activities that are similar to a competitor's better than the competitor. It often involves benchmarking competitors and investing heavily to improve operations and make the firm leaner and more flexible. This approach is often reflected in programs such as continuous improvement, empowerment, and teamwork, which are designed to lower costs, increase quality, and eliminate waste. Differences in operational effectiveness among firms are reflected in the relative cost position of these firms.

However, focusing only on operational effectiveness and ignoring strategic positioning can be a serious mistake. Operational improvements, although necessary to maintain a firm's competitiveness, often fail to provide a sustainable advantage. One problem is that best practices are quickly imitated. Rivals copy new technologies and management and manufacturing techniques. In addition, benchmarking leads to a convergence of strategies and competitors looking increasingly alike, causing destructive wars of attrition.

Strategic positioning is about being different; it requires performing different activities from those performed by competing firms, or performing the same activities differently, to deliver a unique and meaningful value to customers. One aim is to establish a difference that the firm can continue to deliver. For firms that fail to differentiate their activities, positioning becomes an empty slogan.

Further, effective positioning involves trade-offs with other positioning approaches—in other words, a company cannot pursue two positioning strategies simultaneously. Such trade-offs protect companies from competitors who attempt to reposition themselves or straddle positions.[8] **Straddling** occurs when a company seeks to broaden its positioning by adding new positions. For example, in facing stiff competition from low-fare airlines such as WestJet and Jetsgo, Air Canada could not straddle positions and operate as a full- and low-fare air carrier at the same time. To meet the competition, Air Canada was forced to establish a different airline, Tango, a low-cost subsidiary. The Strategy in Action box illustrates the concept of differentiating activities to achieve a firm's strategic positioning.[9]

Straddling occurs when a company seeks to broaden its positioning by adding new positions.

Strategy in Action

IKEA

Ikea, the Swedish furniture retailer, targets young furniture buyers who want style at low prices. Ikea turns this marketing idea into a powerful strategic positioning concept by performing certain activities different from its rivals. Conventional furniture stores display in their showrooms samples of only a fraction of the available styles. They also provide books containing large numbers of additional product styles for customers to choose from. Shoppers are accompanied by a salesperson who shows them the various choices and answer questions. When a customer makes a selection, an order is placed to a third-party manufacturer and the furniture is delivered in several weeks.

Ikea approaches its business differently. It uses in-store displays and a self-service approach without salespeople escorting customers in the store. Ikea relies on third-party manufacturers but it designs the low-cost, ready-to-assemble furniture it has become known for. It displays every product it sells in room-like settings. Customers pick up and carry the furniture themselves from an adjacent warehouse. By selling to customers who are willing to trade off service for lower prices and by performing many activities differently than traditional furniture retailers, Ikea has been able to develop a successful strategic positioning that is different from its rivals' but difficult to imitate as it would require significant changes in their business model.

Types of Strategic Positioning

There are two types of positioning: tangible attribute and intangible attribute positioning.

Tangible Attribute Positioning

Tangible attribute positioning involves positioning a brand based on objective, observable characteristics, such as length, price, weight, and horsepower. Procter & Gamble commonly relies on physical differentiation by positioning its products on real attribute differences. For example, Crest toothpaste claims that it fights cavities, while Head and Shoulders Shampoo is designed to prevent recurrence of the flaking and itching associated with dandruff.

> **Tangible attribute positioning** involves positioning a brand based on objective, observable characteristics, such as length, price, weight, and horsepower.

Intangible Attribute Positioning

Intangible attribute positioning entails positioning brands on intangible characteristics, such as perceived quality, image, and emotions. This type of positioning, like tangible attribute positioning, can be an effective way to position a product, especially when the product has no clear advantages over the competition. An example of an intangible attribute positioning strategy is Pepsi-Cola's "Choice of a New Generation" advertising campaign, in which it successfully positioned Pepsi for young cola drinkers. By implying that Coke drinkers are older, this campaign was instrumental in portraying Coke as an old, tired brand.

> **Intangible attribute positioning** entails positioning brands on intangible characteristics, such as perceived quality, image, and emotions.

Intangible attribute positioning is especially important for products that have few real differences from their competitors. In these cases, companies attempt to create differences between their brand and rival brands using celebrity endorsers, humour, cartoons, images, emotions, guilt, and other subjective differences. Although these points of difference may be meaningless from a rational viewpoint, they often become effective means of establishing a distinct and favourable positioning in the customer's mind. Empirical research has established that meaningless differentiation can be an effective way to market a product.[10]

The two types of positioning are not in conflict with each other. In fact, the most successful positioning strategies combine tangible and intangible attribute positioning. Using both approaches allows marketers to greatly increase the effectiveness of the positioning strategy.

The Strategic Positioning Process

All that is known about the targeted segment, competitors, customers, and the firm's product comes down to a simple, clear, concise point of difference. This point of difference should be distinct and defensible and built on a competitive advantage. For example, IBM is positioned as the company that provides "peak performance on demand." Marketers developing their firm's positioning strategy should follow a structured process such as the one shown in Figure 6.2.

Figure 6.2	The Strategic Positioning Process

Step 1: Identify direct and indirect competitors.
Step 2: Identify determinant attributes or benefits.
Step 3: Determine customer perceptions.
Step 4: Select a positioning strategy.
Step 5: Implement the positioning strategy.

Step 1. Identify Direct and Indirect Competitors

Effective positioning requires that a firm's placement in the market be distinct from all competitors. In order to establish the right positioning for a brand, the marketer needs to undertake research to figure out the structure of the market as it exists in the minds of customers. The ultimate purpose of the research is finding gaps in the market that could be filled with the right product.

A critical element in making positioning decisions is the firm's competition. The competitors the firm is going to consider need to be carefully selected. It is important not to leave out any important competitors, as that would provide a narrow view of the market structure. A narrow strategic market definition leads firms to focus on their immediate competitors, rather than direct and indirect competitors, all of whom should be included. For example, retailers should not regard their competitors being only those with a similar retail format, but they should include any retailers competing in the same category by serving the same customers, regardless of whether they are department stores, mass merchandisers, or supermarkets. A good place to begin the task of competitor identification is to refer to the strategic market definition discussed in Chapter 2.

Step 2. Identify Determinant Attributes or Benefits

The next step is to identify the product attributes or benefits that motivate consumer choice. The determinant attributes or benefits are often dictated by the competitive strategy or value proposition of the organization. In choosing the most effective benefits to position its products, a company needs to follow the guidelines outlined below:

1. *The Benefit or Attribute Is Unique.* The first requirement for successful positioning is that the brand is distinct from competing brands. Only distinct brands have a chance to break through the clutter of congested markets and be noticed by customers. A positioning strategy that is not based on unique attributes implies that attributes are claimed by one or more competitors; this can lead to ongoing battles among rival firms for supremacy and domination of the attribute. This explains the ongoing wars between Coca-Cola and Pepsi-Cola, as both companies compete on the same attribute, quenching thirst.
2. *The Benefit or Attribute Is Important to the Market.* Being unique is not enough for positioning, as the point of difference must be important to the market. Successful positioning requires differentiating the brand from other brands in the category on the basis of attributes or benefits that are important to the target market; these are called

determinant attributes. Determinant attributes are those attributes that determine choice. Firms need to perform well on the determinant attributes. Focusing positioning on attributes other than those desired by customers will lead to inferior performance.

The overriding principle here is that more is not better—firms should claim superiority on a limited number of benefits. The fewer claims a firm makes, the more focused its message, and the more effective its positioning strategy. Claiming superiority on too many benefits can create credibility problems or confuse customers. When a product is positioned on several benefits, management must ensure that the benefits are consistent with each other.[11] For example, medicines that are advertised as being effective and good tasting will likely undermine their credibility with potential customers. The success of Buckley's cough syrup is commonly attributed to its "bad taste" advertising campaign with the tagline "It tastes awful. And it works."

A distinction must also be made between determinant and salient attributes. As explained previously, determinant attributes are those that determine choice. **Salient attributes** are important attributes that do not determine choice and, therefore, play a less significant role in purchasing decisions than determinant attributes. Lack of proper understanding of the differences between determinant and salient attributes may lead marketers to incorrect positioning decisions. The example of Procter & Gamble's Citrus Hill Orange Juice discussed in the Strategy in Action box illustrates the problems of building positioning on salient, not determinant, benefits.[12]

> **Determinant attributes** reflect core consumer requirements that are used to form the basis of the positioning strategy.

> **Salient attributes** are important attributes that do not determine choice and, therefore, play a less significant role in purchasing decisions than determinant attributes.

Strategy in Action — PROCTER & GAMBLE

Procter & Gamble's Citrus Hill Orange Juice brand was a distant third behind Tropicana and Minute Maid in the orange juice category. Accustomed to brand leadership in each of its categories, P&G made repeated efforts to improve its market position in this category. The company's consumer research had revealed that consumers wanted great-tasting orange juice. Armed with this knowledge, Procter & Gamble's product development team improved Citrus Hill's taste to the point that it won every blind taste test against all competitors, including front-runners Tropicana and Minute Maid. Citrus Hill was positioned, through its advertising campaign, as the product with the best taste among orange juice brands. Yet Citrus Hill kept failing to improve its market position and it was withdrawn from the market.

After much thinking and introspection, the brand management group realized that although taste was the most important attribute to customers, it wasn't a differentiating factor for them. Customers assumed that all orange juice brands were equal in taste. Brand managers also realized that freshness was the product benefit most consumers used to choose among orange juice brands. Most consumers believed that freshly squeezed orange juice was a better juice than that made from concentrate. Although Citrus Hill was made from concentrate, the processing and freezing methods it used made it more nutritious than many fresh-picked brands. On the other hand, the category leader Tropicana, which claimed to be fresh-picked and not from concentrate, was perfectly positioned to meet the consumers' needs in the category.

3. *Claims Can Be Supported by Resources and Capabilities.* Developing effective positioning strategies requires that the company has the resources and capabilities to deliver on the positioning promise. For instance, Volvo positions its cars as safe and backs this promise with research on safety and by constantly adding new safety features. In an effort to reinforce its positioning as a safe vehicle, Volvo has expanded its head-curtain protection system by adding a second inflator and a third element to

the curtain bag on each side of the car, to protect the side-window area in case of a side-impact collision or a rollover.[13]

Step 3. Determine Customers' Perceptions

Perceptual maps are visual representations of consumers' perceptions of a brand or an organization in two or more dimensions.

The third step in positioning involves determining current perceptions of brands by customers. A useful method for establishing the positioning of a brand or an organization is perceptual mapping. **Perceptual maps** are visual representations of consumers' perceptions of a brand or an organization in two or more dimensions. The dimensions used in perceptual mapping should be related to the evaluative criteria consumers use in choosing brands in the category. These maps allow managers to assess the product's current positioning and to evaluate how well it performs on the determinant attributes. The maps also help management understand how customers perceive competing products and assess how their products are positioned vis-à-vis their rivals. In addition, they can help managers monitor how the positioning of their brands changes over time.

Figure 6.3 is a perceptual map of several nonprescription pain relievers with two important attributes used by consumers to evaluate such products: effectiveness and gentleness. This perceptual map was developed using information from consumers about their current perceptions of different brands in the market. The perceptual map shows that Tylenol is perceived to be the gentlest product followed by Nuprin and Advil. Tylenol is perceived more effective than other products such as Nuprin, Advil, Bayer, Anacin, and private-label aspirin. However, it is perceived less effective than Excedrin. Excedrin is perceived as the most effective nonprescription pain reliever but it scores low on gentleness. For a company that is developing a new over-the-counter pain reliever, the information gleaned from this perceptual map would be of great help in positioning the new product.

Step 4. Select a Positioning Strategy

The next step is to make a decision about how the product should be positioned in light of customers' perception of brands in step three. If the product's current positioning is

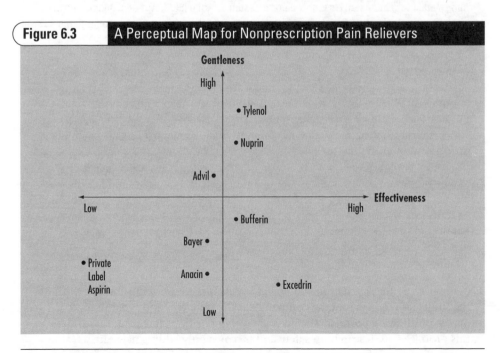

Figure 6.3 — A Perceptual Map for Nonprescription Pain Relievers

SOURCE: Carl McDaniel Jr. and Roger Gates, *Contemporary Marketing Research*, 3rd ed. (St. Paul, Minn.: West Publishing Company, 1996), 680. Reprinted with permission of Carl McDaniel, Ph.D., The University of Texas at Arlington.

viewed as a desirable one, then no change is needed and the company should continue its current product positioning efforts. But if the firm is not satisfied with its product's current positioning, it should begin efforts to reposition it. In the example given in Figure 6.3, management of Excedrin might decide to reposition its product on the gentleness dimension, since that is an important attribute to consumers.

Besides perceptual mapping, companies use other ways to determine their positioning strategy. For example, the product's competitive ranking may determine the choice of positioning. Large companies usually claim the benefit associated with the category.[14] For example, Wal-Mart claims lowest prices and unmatched convenience; Chrysler minivans claim the best customer value. Small firms compete in market niches where they commonly position their products on the basis of the main category benefits and an associated benefit to distinguish them from the industry leaders. For example, Dreft, a detergent that is specially formulated for cleaning baby clothes, is positioned on the main category benefit that it cleans clothes well but also that it does not contain harsh chemicals, enabling it to leave clothes soft and comfortable, and it is specially designed to rinse out thoroughly, leaving clothes virtually residue free, a feature that appeals to mothers with small babies.

Step 5. Implement the Positioning Strategy

Establishing category membership is the first task in implementing strategic positioning.[15] **Category membership** identifies the benefits consumers could expect to receive from the product and the product's competitors. Establishing category membership is especially important for new products for which category membership is not obvious to potential customers. For example, Apple failed to establish a category membership for its Newton electronic organizer, and potential customers thought of it as a small personal computer with electronic organizer features. As a result, Newton failed and it was withdrawn from the market. However, the same mistake wasn't made by palmOne when it subsequently introduced its Palm Pilot personal digital assistant, which became wildly successful. The difference between the Newton electronic organizer and the Palm Pilot was that the former was loaded with numerous features that gave the impression of a small personal computer with electronic organizer features, while the latter was perceived as a true electronic organizer and it established a new category for itself.

Category membership can be established by asserting that the brand has the features or provides the benefits that are common to brands in the category. For example, a new ready-to-eat cereal could claim that it has all the benefits associated with cereals. The category also may be established by promoting the occasion the product is used for. For example, Gatorade tells endurance athletes or teams to eat its Energy Bar when they need a boost of energy before, during, and after exercise and competition.

The next critical step in the implementation of the positioning strategy is to successfully establish the superiority of the product over the competition. Companies must give targeted customers reasons they should prefer them to other products. As we discussed earlier in the chapter, successful positioning is built on only the determinant attributes that are the most important and unique differentiating attributes. Unfortunately, marketers often don't know these attributes. Lack of such knowledge causes marketers to undertake random promotional acts involving promotion, advertising, coupons, price reductions and giveaways, and trying different things to find out what works and what doesn't.

Implementing a positioning strategy requires close cooperation between all organizational functions. As we discussed earlier in the chapter, each organizational function contributes to the firm's positioning. Successful companies should not rest on their laurels but they need to work hard to maintain their positioning. For example, even after it became the world's largest company, Wal-Mart continued to seek ways to reduce costs and improve the shopping experience. On the other hand, Tim Hortons' recent change of strategy—reheating previously frozen products instead of cooking them on-site—may

Category membership identifies the benefits consumers could expect to receive from the product and the product's competitors.

have a negative impact on its performance, as its positioning strategy calls for selling fresh products. It is not known how much Tim Hortons is saving by using this new policy. However, its doughnuts are now smaller and most customers believe they don't taste as good as before.[16]

Companies should not change their positioning strategy frequently. Once the positioning strategy is determined, the firm should make every effort to excel and consistently promote this positioning. A firm's image needs to be consistent because inconsistency confuses customers and potential customers. For this reason, once a successful positioning is found, the firm should adhere to it unless conditions change, in which case repositioning may be necessary. For example, Burger King lost market share against other burger rivals because it confused consumers with inconsistent advertising messages. In an effort to increase sales, Burger King employed different advertising agencies, which, in turn, tried different advertising approaches, leading to consumer confusion rather than reinforcing a consistent advertising message.

The Positioning Statement

The **positioning statement** is a general summary of all targeting and positioning decisions.

It is useful to include the details of the strategic positioning in a brief statement that serves as a quick reference. The **positioning statement** is a general summary of all targeting and positioning decisions. It is used as an internal document that is available to all those who need to know the particulars of the strategic positioning of the company, including advertising agencies, sales force, and design personnel. The positioning statement is the basis of all public communication, which includes packaging, pricing, advertising, promotion, and public relations.

The positioning statement should be short, specific, and concise. Some managers write broad positioning statements to avoid making hard choices about the target market or the key benefit. This allows them to hedge their bets but as the marketing saying goes, a product that stands for everything stands for nothing. Catchall phrases are ineffective, and they should be avoided. A positioning statement is made up of the components shown in Figure 6.4.

Figure 6.4	Components of a Positioning Statement

- Product category
- Target customers
- Product benefits
- How product performs benefits

Product Category. A positioning statement should specify the product's category. Establishing the category is especially important for new products. If the company does not specify a category for the product, the market will establish one. Sometimes customers may be aware of the broad industry but they are not aware of the specific category. For example, car drivers may know that Mitsubishi manufactures automobiles but are not certain of their price range.

Target Customers. A positioning statement should make a specific reference to target customers. The choice of the customer group should be clarified during the target marketing stage when the company determines the target market. Companies need to include the target customers in order to ensure that when the positioning message is delivered, it is clear who the recipient of the message is.

Product Benefits. Customers purchase products because of the benefits offered by them. A positioning statement must link the purchase of the product with a desirable consequence for the customer. For example, Sleeman Brewery, a maker of premium beer, promises potential customers a premium craft beer made of all-natural ingredients. The claims made in positioning statements need to be unique, compelling, and believable. Failure to clearly state a compelling consumer benefit is a frequent cause of marketing failure. For this reason, advertising campaigns that promise no benefits to the customers and merely differentiate the product from its competition typically fail to accomplish their objectives.

How Product Performs Benefits. A positioning statement should include an explanation of how the product performs the benefits it provides. The reason customers should prefer the product must be believable to them. Providing customers with information about the sources of competitive advantage increases the credibility of the product's claim.

A firm's communication efforts should incorporate, ideally, all four components of the positioning statement. The Strategy in Action box about Tylenol illustrates a positioning statement that incorporates all four components.

Strategy in Action

TYLENOL'S POSITIONING STATEMENT

To all arthritis sufferers who want fast and effective relief from pain, no other over-the-counter arthritis pain reliever has been proven to work better or faster on arthritis pain than Tylenol Arthritis Pain. Tylenol Arthritis Pain works best because it contains acetaminophen, which is the preferred first-line drug therapy for the pain of osteoarthritis, the most common form of arthritis. An additional benefit of Tylenol Arthritis Pain is that it is aspirin free and it is unlikely to cause gastric irritation often associated with aspirin and other nonprescription drugs. With Tylenol Arthritis Pain you will be relieved of your arthritis pain and you will be able to go on with your daily activities.

Positioning Strategies

Successful positioning strategies are based on the competitive strategy or the value proposition of the organization. The determinant attributes also play a central role in the specific form of the positioning strategy. In practice, marketers use a variety of approaches to implement their positioning strategy. Although these approaches differ, their common objective is to persuade potential buyers that the firm's products are the most qualified to meet their needs. This section discusses some of the most common positioning strategies.

1. *Product attribute or benefit.* **Product attribute** or **benefit** positioning involves selecting a unique, highly desirable attribute or benefit that differentiates the product from its competition and positioning the product on that attribute or benefit. For example, QuickTax, a leading income tax preparation software, is positioned as an easy-to-use and accurate program. The attribute or benefit should reflect the determinant attributes or unique selling proposition, which is the single most important reason a customer buys the brand. It needs to be stressed that attributes and benefits are not the same; benefits are derived from attributes. When it is not clear how an attribute benefits consumers, it is preferable to position the product on the benefit derived from the product. For example, the benefits to buyers of a computer program that is written using the Java computer language (an attribute) may not be apparent. However, if the product is positioned on the basis of power and portability (benefits), these benefits are more readily apparent to customers.

2. *Price-Quality.* **Price-quality positioning** entails positioning an offering on the basis of the relationship between quality and price. High quality at a fair price indicates value. Experienced marketers know that a low price may be used to portray a brand

Product attribute or **benefit positioning** involves positioning a product on a unique, highly desirable benefit or attribute that differentiates the product from its competition.

Price-quality positioning entails positioning an offering on the basis of the relationship between quality and price.

as inexpensive, affordable, and good value, while a high price may be a signal of higher quality to customers who find it difficult to judge the quality of a brand. For example, No Frills Supermarkets use low prices to signal value, while Ferrari and Lamborghini automobiles use high prices to signal higher quality, status, and prestige. The Strategy in Action box about Chanel's introduction of its No. 5 fragrance in the Asian market is illustrative of the relationship between price and quality.

Strategy in Action — CHANEL

The perceived relationship between price and quality can be used to stimulate sales and profits, a lesson Chanel learned when entering the Asian marketplace. The company introduced its popular No. 5 fragrance at a significantly lower price than in the North American market in an attempt to stimulate trial use. To the company's surprise, sales of the product were well below expectations. The company undertook research to investigate its poor performance and found that consumers were leery of purchasing the product for fear that it was counterfeit. In the mind of consumers, the price truly was "too good to be true." In response, Chanel increased the price of the fragrance to match the prices offered in the North American market, and sales immediately skyrocketed.

Technical innovator positioning is used by companies with a reputation for innovativeness and creativity.

3. *Technical innovator.* **Technical innovator positioning** is used by companies with a reputation for innovativeness and creativity. This positioning strategy puts emphasis on technological leadership. Positioning a company as a technical innovator can be a more enduring way to position a company, in relation to other approaches, such as having the lowest prices or special features, which can quickly become obsolete as competitors imitate such strategies. The Strategy in Action box discusses Gillette, a company that is positioned as an innovative company and derives a large percentage of its sales from recently introduced products.

Strategy in Action — GILLETTE

Gillette positions itself as an innovator in technology and marketing, and uses the slogan "Innovation is Gillette" to reinforce its image as an innovator and to differentiate itself from its competition. Gillette supports its image as an innovator by constantly challenging itself to develop new products. Gillette claims that it introduces more than 20 new products annually. In 1999, for example, 40 percent of the company's sales came from products introduced in the previous five years. Among these new products were the Gillette Mach3 razor, the Duracell Ultra line of premium alkaline batteries, the Oral-B 3D plaque remover, and the premium Oral-B CrossAction toothbrush.

Use or **application positioning** involves positioning a product or service according to the manner in which it is used by consumers.

Product class positioning portrays products as being associated with a particular product class or category.

4. *Use or application.* **Use** or **application positioning** involves positioning a product or service according to the manner in which it is used by consumers. Firms using this positioning strategy state the use or application of the brand. For example, Arm & Hammer stresses different applications for its baking soda, such as an odour-killer for refrigerators, a deodorizer, and a toothpaste.
5. *Product class.* Firms using the **product class positioning** approach portray their products as being associated with a particular product class or category. For example,

the Mazda Miata is positioned as an affordable sporty convertible. When this positioning strategy is used successfully, it enables a brand to dominate the category as customers may come to associate the brand with the entire product class or category. An example of a company that managed to have its brand become synonymous with the product class is Kleenex, which has become the common term for facial tissues. This gives Kleenex an absolute advantage in brand recognition and preference.

6. *Hometown favourite.* **Hometown favourite positioning** emphasizes that a product is made locally or domestically. For example, a product may be promoted as "Made in Canada" to appeal to a sense of patriotism among Canadian consumers. Molson used such an approach in its "Rant" advertising campaign for its flagship brand, Molson Canadian. The Rant featured Joe, a Canadian who is proud of what makes him different from Americans. A company may also position itself as a local player in order to gain business. This strategy can be particularly effective in smaller communities, where residents may feel a desire to support local merchants in order to stabilize the local economy.

> **Hometown favourite positioning** emphasizes that a product is made locally or domestically.

7. *Product user.* **Product user positioning** involves associating the brand with the group of consumers who use it. Specifically, positioning by product user addresses a particular customer chosen by age, income, other demographics, or other characteristics. For example, Revlon introduced its Charlie cosmetics line as fitting the lifestyle profile of the liberated woman, and Bell's Sympatico Internet service has been positioned as "High speed Internet for Canadians."

> **Product user positioning** involves associating the brand with the group of consumers who use it.

8. *Competitor.* **Competitor positioning** involves comparing the product with another brand, usually the leader, and claiming to be better on attributes such as price, value, quality, performance, or other features. For example, Pepsi attacked Coke by claiming Pepsi has better taste. Firms using competitive positioning sometimes compare their products not with a specific competitor but with the market in general. This way, they minimize the potential of a lawsuit by any specific competitor. To avoid legal difficulties, a firm using competitive positioning must be able to substantiate any claims it makes against competitors.

> **Competitor positioning** involves comparing the product with another brand, usually the leader, and claiming to be better on attributes such as price, value, quality, performance, or other features.

9. *Brand dominance.* **Brand dominance positioning** is used only by firms with the highest market share. Atlas Van Lines is the largest moving company in Canada. Not surprisingly, Atlas Van Lines' positioning slogan is "Canada's largest coast to coast moving company." Automobile manufacturers whose models outsell their competitors are positioned as best-selling cars in their category. The implication of the dominance positioning strategy is that the firm is the market leader because it has the best product.

> **Brand dominance positioning** is used only by firms with the highest market share.

10. *Experience or originality.* Firms that have been in business longer than competitors may choose to position themselves on the basis of their heritage, experience, or stressing the length of time they have been in the business, a strategy called **experience or originality positioning.** The rationale for this strategy is that customers favour companies that have been in business for a long time or give preference to those businesses that were the first to introduce a new product or service. For example, Points, a paralegal company, stresses that it is the original paralegal services company.

> **Experience or originality positioning** is used by firms that have been in business longer than competitors.

Positioning Errors and Repositioning

An ineffective positioning strategy can put the entire marketing strategy at risk. Organizations must assess the effectiveness of their positioning strategy periodically and reposition themselves if their positioning becomes ineffective. Repositioning becomes necessary when market conditions change, firms see an opportunity to position the product in a new or different segment, or their current positioning is incorrect.

Companies may commit the following positioning errors:[17]

Underpositioning. Customers remember the companies that have distinct products. Underpositioning occurs when consumers do not have a strong image of the company and do not consider it when making a purchasing decision. This positioning error occurs when the company has made an inadequate effort to implement and communicate the positioning strategy. Products also lack a strong image when market needs change, and the product is no longer considered by buyers when they make purchasing decisions.

Confused positioning. Confused positioning leads to the company lacking a true identity so customers do not know what to expect from the company. This positioning problem occurs when the company has not settled on a specific positioning strategy and it tries to be all things to all people. Frequent changes in advertising messages create a confusing image in the minds of customers, something that often happens when a new advertising agency is hired.

Doubtful positioning. When customers do not believe in the claims made for the product, doubtful positioning is the problem. Reasons for the lack of credibility include exaggerated product benefits, too many benefit claims, poor previous experience with the product, or negative word-of-mouth publicity.

Faulty positioning. Faulty positioning occurs when positioning is based on a benefit that is not important to customers or when the benefit is important but it is also claimed by a stronger competitor, forcing the firm to engage in a frontal attack against a much bigger opponent.

Repositioning an existing product is not easy. Intel successfully repositioned itself from a semiconductor manufacturer—an industry that was getting too crowded—to making microprocessors for personal computers. While some repositioning efforts like Intel's were successful, many others were unsuccessful. For example, Sears tried to move to a more upscale positioning in the 1970s. This repositioning effort failed as it alienated its traditional customer base of middle-class consumers, and Sears was forced to return to its traditional positioning.

In trying to reposition a firm or product, management must consider its existing image as well as the new image it wishes to establish. Reconciling the two images may be difficult or impossible. Many repositioning efforts are hampered by an existing negative image that must be overcome before a new positioning can be created. Before the new perception is created, the new market in which the repositioning will take place must be extensively studied. In fact, poor repositioning efforts may make things worse than they previously were. This can happen if the new positioning is not viable due to intensive competition or lack of sufficient market demand. Marketers also need to be aware that sales may temporarily fall during the repositioning effort as the company goes through its image change. The Strategy in Action box describes McDonald's as an example of a company that repositioned itself in response to environmental changes.

Strategy in Action

McDONALD'S

After years of uninterrupted growth in sales and profits, McDonald's lost money for the first time in recent years. As a result of poor sales, the chain had to close a number of poorly performing stores. The reason for McDonald's lacklustre performance was, largely, its failure to recognize recent societal trends toward healthier food. While other hamburger companies such as Wendy's and Burger King had made adjustments in their menu to accommodate such trends, McDonald's was late in responding to these environmental changes. As soon as McDonald's recognized these changes, it began a massive effort at repositioning itself as a health-conscious restaurant. The company backed its claim as a champion of healthy food by unveiling new menu items that included salads and related products such as exercise booklets and pedometers. It even hired Oprah Winfrey's personal trainer, Bob Greene, to help promote the $4.99 (U.S.) "Go Active Meal."

Competitor Repositioning

Mark Fields, Mazda's U.S. president, once stated that one of the reasons for his company's poor performance was that it had let its competitors define his company, instead of his company defining itself. Through a series of advertising campaigns by Mazda and its competitors, Mazda had come to be viewed in the minds of the car buying public as a maker of impractical sports cars. Companies reposition their competitors to make their brands more desirable. A competitor can be repositioned directly or indirectly. Beck's beer's repositioning of its competitor Lowenbrau, discussed in the Strategy in Action box, is an example of direct repositioning.[18]

Strategy in Action — BECK'S

Beck's beer was the most popular beer in Germany, but lagged behind Lowenbrau in sales in the United States. At some point, Beck's decided to attack Lowenbrau and looked for a way to reposition its German competitor. Beck's repositioning of Lowenbrau was achieved with the following statement in its advertising material: "You've tasted the German beer that's the most popular in America. Now taste the German beer that's the most popular in Germany."

Beck's repositioning of its competitor was successful because it informed American beer drinkers that Beck's was the most popular beer in Germany, a fact of which they were unaware. Since Beck's is a more popular beer in its home country, the implication was that it must be better than other beers, including Lowenbrau. This new piece of information helped boost the reputation of Beck's as a better-tasting beer than Lowenbrau and helped increase its sales in the United States

A company can reposition a competitor indirectly without making a specific direct reference to this competitor. The Strategy in Action box illustrates how Pepsi managed to reposition and paint a negative image of its main rival, Coke, over a number of years with its advertising and marketing actions.[19]

Strategy in Action — PEPSI

Pepsi, through a number of actions over the years, managed to establish an unfavourable image for Coca-Cola. For example, when Pepsi used larger bottles than Coke, it gave customers the impression that Coke was too expensive and that Pepsi was of better value. Its highly successful commercials, "You've got a lot to live and Pepsi's got a lot to give," implied that Pepsi helps people enjoy life. Pepsi's "Choice of a new generation" campaign helped solidify Pepsi's image as a soft drink that appeals to the young and those who feel young. With these actions, Pepsi directly and indirectly helped position Coke as too expensive, as having an inferior value, and as a brand that appeals primarily to older people.

- Strategic positioning is an important aspect of a firm's marketing strategy. It requires a thorough knowledge of customers' needs and customers' perceptions of competing products. The purpose of positioning is to establish a distinct and desirable image in the minds of potential customers. It reflects the long-term strategy and identity of the organization. Positioning is derived from the competitive strategy and the value proposition of the organization.

- Many managers pursue operational efficiency programs in an attempt to increase profitability. Ignoring strategic positioning can be a serious mistake, as operational excellence is a necessary but not sufficient condition for organizational success.

- The choice of strategic positioning drives all organizational activities such as research and development, production, human resource decisions, and marketing mix activities.

- There are two types of strategic positioning: tangible and intangible attribute positioning. Tangible attribute positioning is based on objective and observable characteristics; intangible attribute positioning relies on intangible characteristics, including image and emotions.

- The strategic positioning process involves identifying direct and indirect competitors, identifying determinant attributes, determining customer perceptions, selecting a positioning strategy, and implementing the positioning strategy.

- The criteria for choosing benefits or attributes are uniqueness, importance, and existence of enough resources and capabilities to support the positioning strategy.

- Implementing the positioning strategy includes establishing category membership and superiority over competitors on the determinant attributes. Implementing a positioning strategy requires close cooperation between all organizational functions.

- The positioning statement includes the product category, the target market, the benefits offered by the product, and an explanation of how the product performs the benefit(s) it provides.

- In practice, firms implement their positioning strategy in many ways, including product attribute or benefit, price and quality, technical innovator, use or application, product class, hometown favourite, product user, competitor positioning, brand dominance, and experience or originality positioning.

- The most common positioning errors are underpositioning, confused positioning, doubtful positioning, and faulty positioning. Firms may have to reposition their products or services for a number of reasons, including incorrect positioning.

- Companies can reposition their competitors through direct and indirect positioning actions.

1. Define strategic positioning. What is the difference between strategic positioning and operational effectiveness?

2. The choice of positioning has far-reaching implications for the organization. Discuss how strategic positioning affects the marketing mix and other organizational aspects.

3. Describe tangible and intangible attribute positioning. Can marketers use both types to position their products or services or do they need to choose one or the other?

4. Briefly identify and describe the steps in the strategic positioning process.

5. What is the difference between determinant and salient attributes?

6. How many benefits or attributes should a firm choose to claim superiority over competitors?

7. Describe the components of a positioning statement.

8. Discuss the various strategic positioning approaches.

9. Discuss the difficulties involved in repositioning a firm's offering.

10. Describe the major positioning errors. What are the causes of these errors and what can the firm do to correct them?

11. How many different ways are there to reposition a competitor?

1. Referring back to the opening vignette, what, in your opinion, are the factors that led to the change in Canadian Tire's positioning strategy?

2. Identify the positioning strategies of three companies based on their advertisements, websites, and other information. Evaluate the effectiveness of these positioning strategies based on the criteria set out in this chapter.

3. Perform the previous exercise for the category leader and another non-leading brand in the category. Compare the effectiveness of the positioning effort of the two companies.

4. Watch a television commercial. Write a positioning statement on the basis of the commercial. Does the commercial include the product category, a clear target market, a clearly stated consumer benefit, and an explanation of how the product performs the benefits it provides?

5. In the summer of 2004, Sony announced the launch of a Walkman digital player dubbed the Network Walkman NW-HD1. Sony said its new digital music player would take direct aim at Apple's market-leading iPod brand. The 20-gigabyte device would sell at $400 and store 13,000 songs compared with iPod, which sold at $499 and stored 10,000 songs. The NW-HD1 battery will last 30 hours at least, three times longer than iPod's. How should Sony position its new brand?

6. Health Care Inc., a manufacturer of various hair care products, has developed a specialized shampoo for people with severely damaged hair. Health Care is taking a tangible attribute positioning approach by promoting product attributes such as its ability to restore the health of people's hair, its ingredients, and its competitive price. Discuss how taking both a tangible and intangible attribute positioning approach could help make Health Care's positioning efforts more effective.

Notes

1. This section draws from "Starting from Its Strength, Canadian Tire," *Marketing Magazine*, December 16/23, 2003, 7.
2. Robert C Lewis and Richard E. Chambers, *Marketing Leadership in Hospitality* (New York: Wiley, 2000), 322.
3. James H. Myers, *Segmentation and Positioning for Strategic Marketing Decisions* (Chicago: American Marketing Association, 1996), 168.
4. David A. Aaker, *Managing Brand Equity* (New York: The Free Press, 1991), 194.
5. Regis McKenna, *Relationship Marketing* (Reading, Mass.: Addison-Wesley, 1991), 47.
6. Aaker, 193.
7. This section draws from Michael E. Porter, "What Is Strategy," *Harvard Business Review* (November-December), 1996, 61–78.
8. Porter.
9. Porter.
10. Gregory S. Carpenter, Rashi Glazer, and Kent Nakamoto, "Meaningful Brands From Meaningless Differentiation: The Dependence on Irrelevant Attributes," *Journal of Marketing Research*, Vol. XXXI (August 1994), 339–350.
11. Allice M. Tybout and Brian Sternthal, "Brand Positioning," in Dawn Iacobucci (ed.), *Kellogg on Marketing* (New York: Wiley, 2001), 37.
12. Eric Schulz, *The Marketing Game* (Holbrook, Mass.: Adams Media Corporation, 1999), 35–37.
13. *Toronto Star*, November 2, 2002.
14. Tybout and Sternthal, 36.
15. Tybout and Sternthal, 33.
16. David Menzies, "Water-down brands," *Marketing Magazine*, April 19, 11.
17. Graham J. Hooley, John A. Saunders, and Nigel F. Piercy, *Marketing Strategy and Competitive Positioning*, 2nd ed. (London: Prentice Hall Europe, 1998), 205.
18. Jack Trout and Al Ries, "Positioning Cuts Through Chaos in the Marketplace," *Advertising Age*, May 1, 1972, reprinted in Ben M. Enis, Keith K. Cox, and Michael P. Mokwa, *Marketing Classics* (New Jersey: Prentice Hall, 1990).
19. Sergio Zyman, *The End of Marketing As We Know It* (New York: HarperBusiness, 1999), 88.

Chapter Seven

Strategic Networks and Customer Relationship Management

The cost of making the first sale is generally considered to be 5 to 10 times more than the cost of making additional sales.

Tom Duncan and Sandra Moriarty, Driving Brand Value

Learning Objectives

After studying this chapter, you should be able to:

1. Describe the reasons firms form strategic networks, types of strategic networks, and the reasons strategic networks fail

2. Explain the differences between transaction and relationship management

3. Learn the relationship between customer value, customer satisfaction, and customer retention

4. Explain the concept of customer net worth

5. Describe the major customer relationship programs

6. Review strategies for improving customer relationship programs

Jones Soda Creates Relationships with Distributors and Customers

Jones Soda Inc. is a small and unconventional Canadian beverage company that recently moved its headquarters from Vancouver to Seattle, Washington. The company began operations in 1987, under the name Urban Juice and Soda Company Ltd., as a beverage distributor of such brands as Thomas Kemper Soda, Arizona Iced Tea, and Just Pik't Juices. But in 1995, Jones Soda decided to capitalize on its knowledge and experience over the years as a beverage distributor and started to produce its own brands.

The company's product line includes premium carbonated soft drinks under the Jones Soda brand, Jones Naturals noncarbonated juices and teas, and Jones Energy WhoopAss brands. Its soft drinks have names such as Blue Bubblegum, Fufu Berry, and Bug Juice. The firm has even painted its offices in orange and blue to match the colours of its product line. The popularity of Jones Soda bottles is so high that some discontinued labels have become collectibles selling on eBay for up to $10 (U.S.).

Jones Soda has formed several partnerships with its distributors to gain access to new markets and increase its market share in the premium soda category. In 2002, it partnered with Panera Bread, one of the fastest-growing retail food chains in the United States, to create a customized bottled beverage program exclusively for the food chain. In April 2004, Jones Soda signed an exclusive partnership with Zumiez Inc., which sells cutting-edge clothing and skates, snow, and surf gear to young people with active lifestyles. Under the terms of the agreement, Jones Soda products would be sold in more than 120 Zumiez retail stores.

Jones Soda's promotional activities include sponsorships for extreme athletes and it also sponsors the teenaged motivational speaker and cancer survivor Josh Sundquist, covering the cost of his equipment and his travel expenses. His sweatshirt is emblazoned with Jones Soda's logo and the message that Jones Soda is cool.

Jones Soda Inc. has established an emotional connection with young, hip consumers who consider Jones Soda as much an attitude as a drink. Jones Soda, with its unconventional marketing strategy, has managed to earn the loyalty of young and often rebellious consumers. In the process, Jones Soda has increased revenues from $2.4 million (U.S.) in 1997 to $19.6 million (U.S.) in 2000.

The strategy of Jones Soda's CEO and president, Peter Van Stolk, is based on creating a brand that people could relate to. He uses an approach he calls "grounding the brand," which involves forging an emotional connection with his target market of 12- to 24-year-old consumers. To achieve his objective, Van Stolk placed his products where his customers like to buy them, using what he calls an "alternative distribution strategy," selling his products in tattoo and piercing parlours, dance clubs, fashion stores, and skate, surf, and snowboarding shops. Recently Jones Soda has gained distribution in more conventional outlets that include convenience and food stores and chain stores such as Safeway, Albertson's, and 7-Eleven.

Van Stolk also utilizes advances in labelling technology that make it possible to provide consumers with their own custom-labelled soft drink. Jones offers consumers a "create-your-own" label option for birthdays, weddings, and other occasions. While the name Jones Soda always appears on the label, consumers can add their own words and pictures. For example, a customer whose birthday is coming up can order his or her face

(continued)

on a case of 12 bottles of Jones Soda. These tactics have helped Jones Soda to develop strong relationships with its customers. In addition, it helps keep the product current and fresh.

According to Van Stolk, the concept behind Jones Soda is working because it allows customers to speak directly to Jones Soda. By encouraging consumers to personalize the product and get involved with the process, Jones Soda creates fiercely loyal customers. The company claims that it has created a cult following among customers, employees, and shareholders.[1]

Introduction

As discussed in the opening vignette, Jones Soda's success depends on creating relationships with distributors and customers. Aligning with its distributors—Panera Bread and Zumiez—allows Jones Soda to gain access to new markets and increase its market share. Also, establishing an emotional connection with customers creates very loyal customers.

In recent years, managers have realized the importance of developing long-term, mutually supportive relationships with valuable customers—end users and distributors. This approach has been extended by embracing suppliers and even competitors. In some cases, the relationship takes the form of a formal partnership or strategic network. A **strategic network** is created by cooperative and collaborative actions intended to establish, maintain, and enhance mutually advantageous long-term relationships with important industry stakeholders, such as customers, suppliers, distributors, competitors, and other organizations. Because of advances in manufacturing technologies and quality-control techniques, differences in quality among products and services have been minimized, so when customers perceive virtually identical products, prices, delivery, or convenience, the differentiating factor becomes how the customer is treated and feels about the organization. Marketers have realized that developing genuine relationships with their customers and other important industry players can be an effective method of competing with their rivals.

The central goal of a business is to gain and maintain a competitive advantage. However, in today's global marketing environment it is very difficult for any individual firm to attain this goal without collaborating with other organizations. Rapid technological advances demand considerable development resources.[2] In many industries, technological requirements far surpass the capabilities of a single organization. For this reason, forming strategic networks with other organizations has become necessary.

Technological and other demands require firms to form strategic networks. Such networks enable firms to build on the capabilities of their partners to compete more effectively in the marketplace. Even companies that possess the required capabilities often enter into networks to speed up the development process. Firms need partners to obtain the funds for competing or to spread the risks of developing and marketing new products. Cooperative relationships help firms to acquire resources and technology, access new markets, lower costs, improve quality, and build strong brands.

Many firms try to offer their customers a total experience. However, it is not possible for any one organization to possess the resources and capabilities required for such an experience. For example, Air Canada can't fly to every country in the world or support its customers in all the airports it flies into. Through Star Alliance, a network of several airlines including Air Canada, Lufthansa, and United Airlines, Air Canada passengers can make reservations with partner airlines, use partners' airport lounges and services, and earn frequent flyer miles.

In addition to forming networks with other organizations, marketing managers have realized that developing long-term relationships with valuable customers can increase the firm's profitability. The transaction approach to marketing—choosing a market segment and a positioning strategy, and developing an effective marketing mix—is no longer enough for long-term marketing success. Marketers are increasingly recognizing that developing long-term relationships with customers based on superior value and customer satisfaction is the most effective way of competing in today's marketplace. Many marketers know that it is more expensive to find a new customer than to retain one. The longer the relationship between the firm and the customer, the more profit the customer can generate for the firm. For this reason companies such as Marriott hotels have partnered with large corporate customers to offer special rates and other benefits.

> A **strategic network** is created by cooperative and collaborative actions intended to establish, maintain, and enhance mutually advantageous long-term relationships with important industry stakeholders, such as customers, suppliers, distributors, competitors, and other organizations.

Creating relationships with valuable customers increases marketing productivity and customer satisfaction. Companies benefit from higher profits from retaining customers. As customers enter a relationship with a company and the company learns about their needs, requirements, and tastes, customers will be reluctant to end the relationship and start all over with another supplier. The benefits of relationship marketing may even have a more significant impact on profits than economies of scale, market share, and other competitive advantages.[3]

This chapter begins with a discussion of strategic networks and the reasons firms enter such arrangements. It then focuses on efforts by firms to build relationships with valuable customers. Next, the concepts of customer value, customer satisfaction, and customer retention are explained. The last part of this chapter outlines the major customer relationship programs and several strategies for enhancing the effectiveness of customer relationship programs.

Strategic Networks

The model of individual firms competing against each other in an impersonal marketplace is inadequate in a world in which firms are embedded in networks of social, professional, and exchange or buying and selling relationships.[4] Such networks are built on relationships between a firm and other organizations—suppliers, customers, competitors, or other entities. These networks are strategically significant and long-lasting for the firms involved and include strategic alliances, joint ventures, long-term buyer partnerships, and other similar arrangements. Strategic networks provide a firm with access to resources, information, markets, channels of distribution, and technologies. They allow firms to achieve their strategic objectives, share risks, and outsource organizational functions.

In the last few years there has been a rapid proliferation of strategic networks. In fact, strategic networks have become central to the corporate strategy of many organizations. Companies such as IBM, Starbucks, Federal Express, and Bell Canada are relying on strategic networks to execute their strategy. In Japan, cooperation is common among companies in the form of *keiretsu*—corporate networks of interlocking affiliates. Networks exist everywhere between producers and their suppliers, distributors, customers; between rival firms; and between totally unrelated firms.

As we defined it earlier, a strategic network is an agreement between firms that involves cooperation between participant firms or between firms and customers. Strategic networks are, essentially, relationships between separate companies that involve joint contribution and sharing of technological, manufacturing, distribution, and marketing capabilities.[5] This approach to marketing, also called **network marketing,** takes into account all relationships in a market; it is a holistic view of marketing. The Bell Canada–Microsoft partnership discussed in the Strategy in Action box is an illustration of the type of cooperative relationships that are becoming increasingly common in today's markets.[6]

Network marketing takes into account all relationships in a market; it is a holistic view of marketing.

BELL CANADA AND MICROSOFT

In June 2004, Bell Canada and Microsoft Canada Corporation introduced their co-branded website and additional Internet services in an attempt to establish the "most complete" online experience and capitalize on each other's core competencies. The Bell-Microsoft site, called Sympatico.MSN.ca, is available to all Internet users. It includes services such as mapping, video games, and content for children. The novelty in this co-branding effort was the introduction of a premium package for Bell Internet customers. The package costs $4.95 a month and is offered on top of the standard monthly $44.95 high-speed connection. It provides an array of services, including a junk e-mail filter, large storage space, and programs to share digital photos. The Bell-Microsoft initiative was soon followed by two other companies, Rogers and Yahoo! Inc., which were expected to unveil their own co-branding agreement for a co-branded website and similar services and similar Internet tools.

Reasons for Forming Strategic Networks

There are many reasons for forming strategic networks. Globalization forces firms to make a priority of exploiting business opportunities across nations, and strategic networks help firms use one another's resources and capabilities to meet this goal. For example, General Motors entered into a strategic alliance with Toyota in order for GM to learn the latter's manufacturing system.[7] The reasons firms form strategic networks are summarized in Figure 7.1.

Figure 7.1	Reasons for Forming Strategic Networks

- Rapid technological advances
- Defend against powerful entrants
- Learn new skills
- Expand into new markets
- Share risks

Rapid technological advances demand considerable development capabilities. Designing, producing, and selling many of today's highly complex products such as hybrid car engines or wireless communications products demand skills that are not possessed by a single company. Many pharmaceutical and chemical companies have formed strategic alliances with universities because they have found it extremely difficult to innovate successfully on their own in areas such as biogenetics and bioengineering. Also, Philips and Sony used an alliance that pooled their patents to develop the compact disc, which they licensed as an open standard.[8]

In cases where governments opened local markets to foreign firms, the local firms had to form networks to defend themselves against powerful entrants that had tremendous resources such as the latest technology or powerful brands. For example, Gradiente, a leading Brazilian electronics firm, allied with Nintendo and JVC to manufacture and market products under the names of the three companies separately. The alliance helped Nintendo and JVC build volume rapidly in the all-important Brazilian market and gave Gradiente the technology it needed to compete successfully in its market.

Some companies use strategic networks to learn new skills. Electronics manufacturer Samsung has acquired various skills and technologies through numerous joint ventures and licensing agreements that helped the company build a world-class company between 1953 and 1995. In one of those alliances, Samsung and Corning established a joint venture in 1973 to make CRT (cathode ray tube) glass for the Korean electronics market. Samsung needed a technology partner to get into the electronics components and materials market, and Corning wanted to enter Asian markets. The alliance between the two companies has not only continued until today, but it has expanded in other markets and countries.

Some companies form alliances with their competitors. For example, General Motors, Ford, and DaimlerChrysler have formed Covisint, an electronic data interchange system designed to form a single global business-to-business supplier exchange. The purpose of Covisint is to integrate and enhance collaboration among companies and their suppliers to lower costs and increase efficiency in the entire automobile industry. When partners are competitors, they will have many opportunities for inter-partner learning and there will be important consequences for these firms.[9]

Firms acquire new capabilities more easily when they already have a competence base that is similar to the competence base they seek.[10] Firms in the same industry typically share a common competence base because they use similar technologies, serve similar customers, and sell similar products. For this reason, many firms use partnerships as a means of acquiring new skills from partners in those areas where they have deficiencies. Learning is highest when partners contribute resources and skills to the alliance. For firms to have an opportunity to learn from each other, partners should have different resources and capabilities.

Companies form joint ventures or other types of agreements to enter new markets. For example, Starbucks has formed alliances with book retailer Chapters and with complementary producers such as PepsiCo and Dreyer's Ice Cream in an effort to reach new customers. For some companies it can be a way to leverage a partner's distribution network or low-cost manufacturing capabilities as was the case of Daimler-Benz's acquisition of Chrysler.

Networks are typically used between businesses when risks are high.[11] Some companies enter long-term agreements with their suppliers to shift some of the risk and capital investment to the suppliers. For example, Bombardier has formed a long-term partnership with Mitsubishi, which manufactures the wings for Bombardier's Global Express business jet. Sharing the risk is often why oil exploration companies team up.

Companies participating in strategic networks share risks and rewards. When many partners are involved in a risky venture, the exposure of each partner is reduced. Companies often form alliances to hedge their bets when there are competing technologies whose outcome is uncertain. In such situations, it is advisable that firms invest with several other firms with the desired technology to avoid missing out on the eventual winner. Using this strategy, a company reduces its exposure to failure in any one project, while its chances of succeeding somewhere are increased. For example, Microsoft has invested in a number of companies offering competing technologies in the impending convergence between television and the personal computer. In order to hedge its bets, Microsoft invested in AT&T to support high-speed Internet access over telephone lines, in Nextel Communications to develop wireless Internet access, and in Cousat to promote access over cable systems. Microsoft's rationale was that it is likely that one or more of these alliances would bear out results while others would not. But no matter what happened, Microsoft would be on the winning side.[12]

Types of Strategic Networks

Some firms view forming relationships from a narrow perspective. For example, customer retention is a narrow approach to relationship marketing that uses various tactics for keeping customers. Other narrow approaches include one-to-one or individual marketing that integrates database knowledge with a strategy of long-term customer retention and growth.[13]

A broad view of relationship strategy holds that a firm should establish, develop, and maintain successful relationships with customers, various partners, and even competitors.[14] This broader view looks at relationships from a more strategic view and holds that marketing's role is not just selling products to customers but establishing relationships with important industry stakeholders such as customers, suppliers, distributors, and

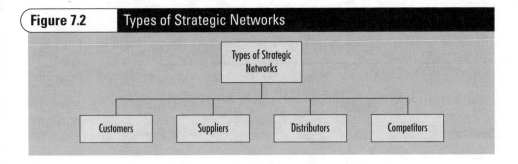

Figure 7.2 Types of Strategic Networks

competitors.[15] Strategic networks come in many forms, from simple joint ventures to complex consortia and co-development efforts.[16] Most types of partnership agreements involve customers, suppliers, distributors, and competitors (see Figure 7.2).

1. *Customers*. Creating relationships with selected end users and offering higher customer value increases customer satisfaction, loyalty, and retention, and leads to higher profits. Higher customer retention leads to higher profits, as the cost of attracting new customers to replace lost customers is reduced. Also, highly satisfied customers are a free form of positive word-of-mouth advertising. In an attempt to develop formal long-term relationships with customers and ensure repeat business, some hotels create preferred customer programs such as "executive service plans" that include priority reservation and upgraded rooms for frequent customers. The rest of this chapter focuses on issues related to building long-term customer relationships.

2. *Suppliers*. Firms often establish partnerships with companies that provide them with needed components or technologies. For example, Toyota works closely with its suppliers in developing new products. Toyota established a partnership with Matsushita Electric to develop a battery to be used in its hybrid Prius vehicle. A benefit of long-term relationships with suppliers is that instead of playing them off against one another, these relationships lower transaction costs, leading to higher profits. Supplier relationships are briefly covered in Chapter 11, as part of the discussion of supply chain management.

3. *Distributors*. Companies that cultivate long-term relationships with distributors benefit as their products receive a greater effort or a more prominent display at the point of sale. Developing smooth relationships with distributors can, at times, be difficult, due to conflict that can arise between distributors and the manufacturer or among distributors themselves. Conflict can seriously jeopardize the firm's market performance, as intermediaries may not perform as expected. Manufacturers must take proper action to reduce channel conflict, and members of a channel need to realize that their common goal is customer satisfaction. The Strategy in Action box describes how Cott Corporation has successfully teamed up with Wal-Mart, the world's largest retailer:[17]

Strategy in Action

COTT CORPORATION

Cott Corporation, the world's largest private-label beverage supplier, has developed a close relationship with Wal-Mart, which accounts for 40 percent of Cott's annual sales. The Canadian-based Cott makes all of Wal-Mart's private-label pop in Canada, the United States, and Mexico. In order to solidify its relationship with Wal-Mart and other distributors, Cott implemented a "customer-centric"

(continued)

approach by aligning Cott's marketing and quality-control experts with those of its clients. Cott's close relationship with Wal-Mart is especially advantageous for the company because of Wal-Mart's rapid expansion overseas, especially in Europe and Asia. This represents a tremendous growth opportunity if Wal-Mart introduces private-label beverages in those markets. Cott's ability to produce large amounts of beverages gives it a competitive edge over its rivals. Cott also has a chance to land more key accounts in the United States as several large retail chains, including Winn-Dixie Stores Inc. and Target Corp., are considering introducing private-label beverages in their stores.

4. *Competitors.* Firms can compete and cooperate simultaneously. For example, Eastman Kodak and Fuji Photo Film allied with a number of other companies by pouring $1 billion into a ten-year research program to reinvent the modern camera. Networks among rivals are meant often to enhance the competitive advantage of all alliance members. For example, in the face of rising product development costs, six of the largest semiconductor manufacturers formed a strategic alliance to develop technology for the most common type of memory chip used in personal computers. The group included Intel Corporation, Micron Technology (U.S.A.), NEC, Samsung Electronics, Hyundai Electronics, and Infenion Technologies AG, a unit of Siemens. The goal was to develop high-performance advanced DRAM technology. Each member of the alliance would provide a design team to the project, which would be overseen by a senior technology committee.[18]

Reasons Strategic Networks Fail

In a study of alliances involving Canadian firms, approximately two-thirds were reported to have been successful.[19] Many strategic alliances had to be terminated or required restructuring, however. Among the reasons for failure of networks are weak support from senior management, unclear strategies, poor partner selection, and clashing corporate values and goals. Other difficulties stem from different ownership, structure, and management styles. For example, state-owned companies can be frustrating partners because there is no single decision-maker. Also, a common reason for failure of networks is differences in the size or resources of the partners. For example, among alliances established in India in the mid-1990s, foreign companies were typically 30 times the size of the local firms. Large differences in the size of the partners invariably leads to failure of networks because the larger partner typically dominates the smaller partner.

Building Successful Customer Relationships

The balance of this chapter focuses on efforts by organizations to build successful relationships with valuable customers. Building customer relationships has increased in importance as marketers recognize it as a source of sustainable competitive advantage. This renewed emphasis is also the result of increased competition and consumer demand for better service and greater attention to individual customer needs. Marketers have realized that the traditional approach to marketing that views the customer as a passive target has several shortcomings.[20] Having a good product and a good price may not be enough to compete effectively. The softer side of the interaction with the customer is important as well.

As more companies strive to retain their customers, they are abandoning the traditional approach to marketing, where a sale is seen as a discrete transaction, and are adopting relationship marketing. Relationship marketing goes beyond the view of marketing as a function primarily responsible for developing, selling, and delivering products. The major focus of relationship marketing is on developing and maintaining long-term customer relationships instead of short-term transactions. For example, public radio and television broadcasters create membership clubs for donors and offer them free program guides. Airlines offer frequent flyer programs and create clubs for high-mileage customers.

In a relationship marketing environment, customers and product quality are the responsibility of all functions, not just marketing or quality-control specialists. Companies establish frequent contact with customers and emphasize customer service. Employees are trained for customer retention and know the cost of customer defections; performance measures include customer retention, loyalty, and satisfaction. Relationship marketing requires a culture that recognizes the benefits of long-term customer retention and complete customer satisfaction. Companies that embrace relationship marketing treat their customers with respect and offer them high-quality products and services.

Customer relationship programs begin with deciding which customers the firm will build relationships with. Customers differ in their needs and their potential value to a company. The most profitable customers are those who remain loyal to a company for a long time. Marketers divide their customers into groups ranging from the most profitable to the least profitable ones. The most profitable groups are then considered for developing close relationships while the least profitable ones are dropped from further consideration. This selection process is also needed because most firms lack either the resources or commitment to establish relationship marketing programs with all customer groups.[21] Once a company successfully implements its initial relationship marketing program and gains experience, it can expand the program to include more customers or programs.

Relationship marketing is **customer-centric** (focusing on creating customer value) instead of **product-centric** (emphasizing product features). Being customer-centric is consistent with a market orientation. It enables firms to be close to their customers and gain a better understanding of their needs. Customer loyalty is earned by consistently delivering superior customer value. The main differences between transaction and relationship marketing are listed in Figure 7.3.

The **customer-centric** approach to marketing focuses on creating customer value.

The **product-centric** approach to marketing emphasizes product features.

Figure 7.3	Transaction Marketing Versus Relationship Marketing
Transaction Marketing	**Relationship Marketing**
Focus on one-time transactions	Focus on long-term relationships
Customers are marketing's responsibility	Customers are the responsibility of all functions
Emphasis on short term	Emphasis on long term
Product-centric—emphasis on product features	Customer-centric—emphasis on customer value
Sporadic customer contact	Frequent customer contact
Little knowledge of most valuable customers	Know most valuable customers
Little emphasis on customer service	A lot of emphasis on customer service
Little employee training for customer retention	A lot of employee training for customer retention
Lack of knowledge of cost of customer defections	Know cost of customer defections
Lack of knowledge of lifetime value of customers	Know lifetime value of customers
Negotiations are adversarial	Close collaboration with key customer accounts
Performance is measured in financial terms such as profits, market share, and ROI	Performance measures includes customer retention, satisfaction, and loyalty

Customer Value, Satisfaction, and Retention

Customer value, satisfaction, and retention are key aspects of relationship marketing. Firms build long-term relationships when they offer outstanding value to customers. Value creates satisfied customers and higher rates of customer retention. The end result is first-rate market performance.

Firms need to continually try to create and maintain an outstanding value for buyers. As competitors strive to reduce the customer value gap, firms need to implement new sources of value for their customers. Opportunities for creating value for the buyer exist at any point in the buyer's value chain. Also, any individual or function in the selling firm can contribute to the creation of customer value.

Customer value depends on the quality of four Ps: product, processes, performance, and people.[22] The better the firm performs on these dimensions, the higher the value of the product. The definitions of the four determinants of customer value are provided in Figure 7.4.

Figure 7.4	The Four Ps of Customer Value

Product is the core product or service offered to customers. For example, the product can be a television set or a meal at an upscale restaurant. The more closely the product meets customer requirements, the greater the value to customers.

Processes are the system and support activities required to make the product available to customers or to perform the service. Processes include scheduling, staffing, training, delivery, ordering, and billing. The quality of these processes is a major determinant of the value created for customers.

Performance is the ability of the product to live up to its promises. Performance includes reliability, durability, and performing to specifications. If a product or service fails to perform according to expectations, the value received from the product is reduced.

People refers to frontline employees who come in contact with customers. People can be sales representatives, store personnel, repairpersons, receptionists, or anyone who interacts with the customer. As the quality of the interaction increases, the value created for customers increases too. Lack of qualified personnel can reduce the value of the product or service to customers.

A customer is satisfied when the performance of the product exceeds his or her expectations. A product that provides superior customer value is more likely to satisfy customers than products of inferior value. When customers are satisfied with the products they use, they are more likely to be loyal to these products. **Loyalty** is repeat purchase accompanied by a favourable attitude toward the product. Loyal customers are desirable because they are more profitable than non-loyal ones. They are less price sensitive, so companies can charge premium prices. They are less predisposed to switching when they are offered attractive incentives by competitors. Also, they are willing to wait if a firm is late with the introduction of a new product, even if competitors have already introduced their own products.

Customer value, satisfaction, and retention are closely related to organizational performance. Higher customer value and satisfaction lead to higher retention, which in turn leads to higher revenues and lower costs, and greater profitability and market share. They also affect profitability indirectly as satisfied customers normally require fewer product

Loyalty is repeat purchase accompanied by a favourable attitude toward the product.

repairs, warranties, and returns. Higher customer retention also affects profits, as revenues from repeat customers increase and the cost of finding new customers to replace lost customers is reduced. Higher customer satisfaction also leads to a more desirable product image. The relationship between customer value, satisfaction, retention, and performance is depicted in Figure 7.5.

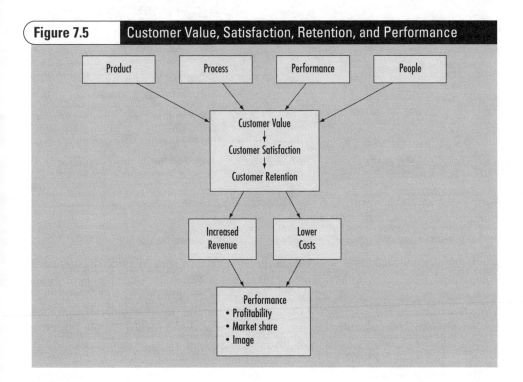

Figure 7.5   Customer Value, Satisfaction, Retention, and Performance

Customer Value

Customer relationships are built when the organization focuses on customer satisfaction, and satisfaction is created when the organization is offering top value to its customers. **Customer value** is defined as the difference between the benefits customers receive from a product and the cost incurred by customers to acquire it.

In determining customer value, we need to identify the important attributes that create value for customers. Customers are satisfied and are loyal to those products that perform best on the attributes that are most important to them. Equally, products that perform poorly on the most important attributes are the least profitable.

As we noted in Chapter 6, every market segment has key attributes that determine consumer choice. In the casual restaurant market, key attributes may include food quality, service quality, value for money, and location. Restaurants that perform well on these attributes offer high customer value. Marketers use different methods to identify the key attributes, including in-depth customer research and the managers' own experience with the industry.

To gain a better understanding of customer value, the customer value equation needs to be specified. The **customer value equation** is a diagnostic tool for managing customer value where customer value equals perceived benefits minus perceived life cycle costs. Perceived benefits include attributes such as performance, quality, convenience, value for money, and features. Perceived life cycle costs include the purchase price, set-up costs, operating costs, maintenance costs, financing costs, and disposal costs. Firms maximize

Customer value is defined as the difference between the benefits customers receive from a product and the cost incurred by customers to acquire it.

The **customer value equation** is a diagnostic tool for managing customer value where customer value equals perceived benefits minus perceived life cycle costs.

Figure 7.6	Customer Value Analysis							
Customer Value Attributes	Importance Weights	Firm A		Firm B		Firm C		
		Rating	W × R	Rating	W × R	Rating	W × R	
Handling	25	9	225	7	175	8	200	
Traction	20	9	180	8	160	7	140	
Rolling resistance	15	8	120	7	105	9	135	
Noise levels	15	7	105	8	120	6	90	
Resistance to punctures	10	7	70	8	80	7	70	
Treadwear rate	10	8	80	9	90	7	70	
Appearance	5	7	35	8	40	8	40	
Total	100		815		770		745	
Performance score:			815		770		745	
Relative performance score:			1.00		0.94		0.91	

customer value by increasing perceived benefits, decreasing perceived life cycle costs, or both.

Perceived customer value = Perceived benefits − Perceived life cycle costs

Customer value analysis may include comparing the firm's offering with that of major competitors. The important attributes are identified and customers rate competitors on each attribute. Attributes are usually weighted, as different attributes vary in their importance to customers. Next, the overall performance score and the relative performance for each competitor are computed. Figure 7.6 provides a hypothetical example from the automobile tire industry. In this example, Firm A received a higher performance score, implying that it offers a higher perceived value than Firms B and C.

The information needed to construct the customer value analysis table is obtained as follows:

Step 1: Identify segments. Markets consist of segments with different needs. Different segments are characterized by customers that have different needs.

Step 2: Customers and non-customers are asked what attributes are most important when they make purchasing decisions. It is preferable not to provide respondents with a list of attributes but let them mention freely the attributes that are most important to them.

Step 3: Ask respondents to assign an importance weight to each attribute. These importance weights are often obtained by asking respondents to distribute 100 points among the attributes identified in step 2.

Step 4: Customers are then asked to rate each competitor on a performance scale of 1 to 10. Ask non-customers to rate competitors as well.

Step 5: Each performance score is then multiplied by its corresponding weight and all results are added to get an overall performance score.

Step 6: The relative performance score is calculated by dividing the performance score of our firm by the performance score of competitors.

Customer Satisfaction

Customer satisfaction exists when the product's performance exceeds the customer's expectations. The key to retaining customers and a rewarding long-term financial performance is complete customer satisfaction. There is a large difference between just satisfied

Customer satisfaction exists when the product's performance exceeds the customer's expectations.

and completely satisfied customers.[23] Completely satisfied customers are much more loyal than merely satisfied customers and are six times more likely to repurchase products than merely satisfied customers.[24] Therefore, only completely satisfied customers are truly satisfied customers.

Dissatisfied customers, on the other hand, can have a serious negative impact on a firm. Studies show that out of 100 dissatisfied customers, only 4 will complain to the organization. Also, of the 96 percent of dissatisfied customers who do not complain, 92 percent will switch to a competitor. Furthermore, each dissatisfied customer will tell 8 to 10 other people of his or her negative experience.[25] Many dissatisfied customers do not complain because it requires too much effort for a small payoff, the experience can be very unpleasant, they don't know how to complain, or they believe the company won't do anything if they do complain.[26]

The impact of such statistics can be enormous on firms that create dissatisfied customers. For example, assume that a company has a total of 400,000 customers. If 10 percent of these customers were dissatisfied, the company would have 40,000 dissatisfied customers. According to the statistics sited above, 35,328 customers, would switch to the competition each year. (This number does not include the number of customers who complained and would actually switch to the competition.) This company would have to attract 35,328 new customers each year to maintain its market share (see Figure 7.7).

Figure 7.7	Number of Customers Who Would Switch
Total number of customers	400,000
Number of dissatisfied customers (10%)	40,000
Number of dissatisfied customers who do not complain (.96 × 40,000)	38,400
Number of customers who would switch (.92 × 38,400)	35,328

Customer satisfaction is more important in markets in which competitive intensity is high. However, in the long term, even in markets with little competition, companies that fail to completely satisfy customers are vulnerable. People often buy products because of inertia, high switching costs, or lack of viable alternatives. When these barriers cease to exist, customers who are not completely satisfied will defect to the competition.

Measuring customer satisfaction and loyalty is a top priority. Measurement should be unbiased and consistent to produce objective and accurate results. Ideally, an independent agency should obtain the data to ensure little interference with the process. Furthermore, the measurement procedures must be consistent to allow a valid comparison with previous measurements and to monitor trends in satisfaction.

The measurement of satisfaction must be made at the right level to provide management with the detailed information needed to make appropriate decisions. High-level measures of satisfaction are useful, but it is equally important to measure satisfaction with specific benefits or attributes.[27] For example, measuring satisfaction with the overall quality of product is important, but it is vital to measure the individual components of product quality such as reliability, ease of use, and durability.

The strategic satisfaction matrix

The strategic satisfaction matrix helps managers establish priorities for performance improvement based on consumers' measures of attribute importance and satisfaction with actual performance (see Figure 7.8). It enables a company to see where it has a competitive advantage and where it needs to improve. If the company performs poorly on an important attribute, it needs to focus on improving this attribute if it hopes to succeed in

Figure 7.8 — The Strategic Satisfaction Matrix

		Importance	
		Low	**High**
Satisfaction with Performance / High		*Possible Overkill* Maintain or reduce investment or change target market	*Competitive Advantage* Maintain or improve performance
Satisfaction with Performance / Low		*Low Priority* Do not waste resources	*Competitive Vulnerability* Focus improvements here

SOURCE: Adapted from Michael D. Johnson and Anders Gustafsson, *Improving Customer Satisfaction, Loyalty, and Profit: An Integrated Measurement and Management System* (San Francisco: Jossey-Bass, 2000). © 2000 Jossey-Bass. Reprinted with permission of John Wiley & Sons Inc.

the segment. Attempting to excel on an unimportant attribute wastes resources and leads to inferior customer value. The strategic prescriptions of the strategic satisfaction matrix are the following:

- *High Importance–Low Satisfaction.* Firms in this quadrant are at a competitive disadvantage. Investments in this area are the most cost effective and they should receive top priority. Improvements here can have the greatest impact on customer satisfaction and loyalty.
- *High Importance–High Satisfaction.* Firms in this quadrant reflect a competitive advantage. Firms should maintain or even improve performance.
- *Low Importance–High Satisfaction.* Resources are usually wasted here and demonstrate a displaced priority on attributes that are not important to customers. Firms should maintain or reduce investments to divert funds to more important areas. Alternatively, a firm might seek a different target market where its strengths will be more appreciated.
- *Low Importance–Low Satisfaction.* This includes attributes that are not important and the firm's performance is weak. The firm should not spend any more resources in this area, as they would be wasted given the low importance of the attributes to customers.

The strategic satisfaction matrix is constructed for each customer segment, as customer requirements and attribute importance vary among segments. For example, in air travel, being on time is more important to business travellers than to economy travellers, who prefer low prices. Also, some of the less important factors may become more important in the future. Nutritious food, for example, has become much more important for fast food customers in recent years. This has forced McDonald's to introduce healthier and more nutritious items in its menu to maintain its market share.

Customer Retention

The purpose of having fully satisfied customers is to retain them. Customer retention is desirable because it is more expensive to find new customers than retain existing customers. It generally costs between five and ten times more to find a new customer than to retain an existing one. Finding new customers is more expensive because of high recruiting costs, including advertising, credit search, personal selling, product samples, administrative, and other up-front costs.

It is crucial that the company attracts the right customers. Firms should avoid investing resources on customers who are prone to defect to competitors. Unattractive customers are typically those customers who require a disproportionate share of the firm's resources to serve, are difficult to satisfy, and switch to the competition at the first opportunity.

Sales and profits increase the longer a customer stays with a company.[28] As newly acquired customers use the product and are relatively satisfied, they may use more of it. Marketing expenses decrease as accounts get older. Loyal customers are also likely to purchase additional products or services as they become familiar and comfortable with the company.

The additional profits generated by retained customers vary by industry. For example, while profits per customer stop increasing after the fourth year in the auto services business, they keep increasing long after that time in the industrial distribution business.[29]

It is important for marketers to know the cost of attracting a customer and the defection rate to calculate the investment required to retain customers. For example, according to a 1995 Digital Equipment Corporation report, the combined marketing and advertising cost of attracting a cellular telephone subscriber is $279 to $400 (U.S.). Assuming a 30 percent defection rate in the cellular industry and an average cost for each new telephone subscriber of $340, a 100,000-subscriber base costs $10.2 million (U.S.) to maintain.[30]

Marketers should also calculate the customer's net worth. The customer's net worth equals the net present value of all projected profit streams from this customer. The following example illustrates how the net present value is calculated. Assume that a customer lives in an area for five years; if a supermarket earns from this customer $500, $700, $900, $1,000, and $1,200 respectively during these five years, using a discount rate of 5 percent, his or her net worth is $3,651 (see Figure 7.9).

Figure 7.9   Calculation of a Customer's Net Worth

Year	Earnings
1st year	$500
2nd year	$700
3rd year	$900
4th year	$1000
5th year	$1200

$$\text{Net worth} = \frac{\text{Earnings}_1}{(1+k)^1} + \frac{\text{Earnings}_2}{(1+k)^2} + \frac{\text{Earnings}_3}{(1+k)^3} + \frac{\text{Earnings}_4}{(1+k)^4} + \frac{\text{Earnings}_5}{(1+k)^5}$$

$$= \frac{\$500}{(1+5)^1} + \frac{\$700}{(1+5)^2} + \frac{\$900}{(1+5)^3} + \frac{\$1000}{(1+5)^4} + \frac{\$1200}{(1+5)^5}$$

$$= \$3,651$$

Although its impact differs from industry to industry, the longer a customer is retained the higher the profits.[31] For example, increasing retention rates by 5 percent increases profits from 25 percent to 85 percent.[32] When a company increases its retention rate, the cost of serving customers falls and profits increase considerably. By being more profitable, the company can pay employees better, which in turn enhances employee commitment and productivity. The increased employee satisfaction causes them to stay longer with the company and this decreases training costs. This also leads to better customer service, which further boosts customer loyalty. Loyal customers are likely to refer the company to their friends and relatives and speak favourably of its products and services. Referrals from friends and relatives are powerful endorsements for a company's offerings and a source of free and highly credible advertising.

Customer Share

Customer share focuses on increasing the amount obtained from an individual customer.

Customer retention is closely associated with the concept of customer share. Retaining customers longer provides companies with opportunities to sell them more of their products, increasing the value of the customer to the company. **Customer share** focuses on increasing the amount obtained from an individual customer. Marketers increase their customer share by exploiting cross-selling opportunities with existing customers. Cross-selling opportunities enable firms to increase the sales of one product with another product. Banks sell additional financial services such as mutual funds or mortgage insurance to existing accounts. Manufacturers may place crossruff coupons in the package of popular products such as cereals as an incentive to motivate customers to try a slow-selling or a newly introduced product. Telephone companies such as Bell Canada train their telephone operators to promote their various services to current customers. For example, if the customer is not currently using the call display service, this service is mentioned to the customer and, by offering an incentive such as a month's free subscription, the customer is urged to subscribe to the service.

Companies often introduce new products or acquire other companies because of the cross-selling opportunities they provide. For example, Rogers Communications, a sports and broadcasting company, owns a number of companies strategically positioned to provide cross-selling opportunities. Rogers owns the Toronto Blue Jays, a Major League baseball team; a Blue Jays digital TV channel; Sportsnet, a sports TV channel; Rogers Wireless, a cellular telephone company; FAN 590, a sports radio station; Rogers Video, a chain of video stores; and Rogers Cable, a cable company. The cross-selling opportunities for Rogers Communications appear to be numerous. For example, viewers can watch Blue Jays games on Sportsnet and talk about the Blue Jays game on FAN 590 using Rogers Wireless cellular phones.

Major Customer Relationship Programs

Marketing managers can choose from several programs to help them build relationships with customers. The major customer relationship programs are mass customization programs, loyalty programs, and partnering programs (see Figure 7.10).

Figure 7.10 Major Customer Relationship Programs

Major Customer Relationship Programs

Mass Customization | Loyalty Programs | Partnering Programs

Mass Customization Programs

Mass customization or one-to-one marketing is aimed at satisfying each customer's needs individually in a cost-effective way.[33] It is a strategy that applies to any industry with customers that prefer products tailored to their needs. In addition to consumer markets, mass customization techniques have been applied successfully in business-to-business marketing in the form of key account management programs. Such programs involve the appointment of teams that analyze customers' needs and implement customized programs intended to meet these needs in a way that satisfies both parties. These types of programs are now gaining widespread application in consumer marketing as well.

Mass customization often involves a learning relationship in which the producer learns about the customer's needs. This relationship is improved as the interaction between the two parties continues and the producer learns more about consumers and translates this knowledge into better-tailored products.[34] Both parties gain from learning relationships. Customers gain because they don't have to teach their suppliers every time they purchase from them. If they switched to a new supplier they would have to educate this new supplier about their needs and requirements, something that is very time consuming. Producers also win because, by understanding their customers' needs better than the competitors do, they can obtain their loyalty and retain them.

As the term might suggest, mass customization combines mass production with customization. The idea of mass customization is to use technology to tailor products to the requirements of individual customers. Recent advances in computer and information technology, such as CAD/CAM and flexible manufacturing techniques, have made it possible to economically tailor a product to the needs of many segments.[35]

Advances in laser technology make it possible to custom fit products to human physical requirements. For example, laser technology has made it possible to custom fit bicycles and jeans to individual buyer specifications—shoppers at Levi's flagship store in London's Regent Street can order customized jeans with the help of laser technology. Details are fed into a computer, and the jeans arrive three weeks later with a personalized bar code to make reordering easy. The Strategy in Action box describes how the National Bicycle Industrial Company has used mass customization successfully.[36]

Strategy in Action

NATIONAL BICYCLE INDUSTRIAL COMPANY, LTD.

In 1986, the National Bicycle Industrial Company, a subsidiary of Matsushita, became one of the first Japanese companies to use mass customization techniques in the production and marketing of bicycles. While demand for conventional sport bicycles for average users was falling, demand for customized sports bicycles for serious users was increasing. Mitsure Omoto, the newly appointed president of National Bicycle Industrial Company, Ltd. decided to tap into this increasing demand and introduced computers into the production system to enable the production of made-to-order products. Because production costs and speed of delivery were important for profitability, Omoto knew he had to reduce production costs and order-to-delivery cycle time. In fact, the high cost and low profitability of customized production of sports bicycles had bedevilled the companies that were involved in craftsmanship-oriented production by skilled workers. By incorporating computers into the production system, Omoto reduced the cost of customized production. The problem of accurate measurement was also

(continued)

solved by developing a tool that was called a fitting scale and looked very much like a bicycle without wheels or a bicycle mock-up. Customers would walk into a Panasonic Ordering System, which were stores selling customized bicycles, and sit on a fitting scale. A staff member would then identify the most comfortable riding position for the customer by adjusting the fitting scale and record the length of the customer's legs, reach, and shoulders. Customers would also choose a colour for the bicycle and a logo to be printed on the bicycle's top bar or frame. Each order was faxed directly to the factory and the data in the order form were entered in the factory's CAM host computer and a UPC bar code was generated from the data and sent to the production line. The information included in the bar code was used to guide production of each bicycle part until the bicycle was completed. The mass customization strategy allowed the National Bicycle Industrial Company to crack open a new market segment and also provided it with a powerful way to differentiate its products.

One of the disadvantages of mass customization is that some customers may not be willing to pay the extra cost associated with the mass customized product. Also, some customers may not feel it is worth waiting for the product to be manufactured or assembled when they have the ability to buy something off the rack.

Loyalty Programs

Loyalty programs are intended to retain customers and enhance customer loyalty through special incentives that can increase customer value.

Loyalty programs are intended to retain customers and enhance customer loyalty through special incentives that increase customer value. Loyalty programs include memberships programs whereby customers are rewarded for their membership and loyalty. Rewards include discounts, free items, preferred customer programs, special sourcing arrangements, and continuous replenishment programs. For example, Air Canada's Aeroplan members collect Aeroplan Miles, which can be used at Air Canada and other affiliated airlines and at hundreds of hotel, car rental, retail, and telecommunications partners.

Many companies are reevaluating the merit of loyalty programs for two reasons. First, loyalty programs that reward customers with points do not constitute a relationship.[37] They are simply rewards offered to customers for purchasing their products. Second, the cost of administering such programs is very high. Some frequent buyer programs have become so expensive that many companies cannot afford them but maintain them because competitors have similar programs. A way of getting around the high cost of loyalty programs is to tap into an existing program, as Shoppers Drug Mart did, described in the Strategy in Action box.[38]

Strategy in Action — OPTIMUM LOYALTY PROGRAM

In 2000, Shoppers Drug Mart, Canada's largest drugstore chain, launched its Optimum card and soon established it as one of the most successful loyalty programs in Canada with over eight million members. All purchases are automatically registered on a mainframe computer. This allows Shoppers Drug Mart to accumulate information about the customer's shopping habits, frequency of visits, average dollar spent per visit, and items purchased.

At the 2003 Canadian Marketing Awards, Shoppers won in the category for Sales Promotion: Trade and Employee Incentive for its 2002 launch of the Shoppers Optimum Vendor Marketing Program. This new program is making Shoppers' Optimum database available to its vendors. The program enables Shoppers Drug Mart vendors, including packaged goods and pharmaceutical companies, to latch onto Optimum and have essentially their own loyalty program without spending millions of dollars in setting up and maintaining their own. By mining the massive database to extract specific information about customers, such as allergy sufferers, new mothers, or customers who purchase toothpaste, the program enables its vendors to customize their marketing programs. Such programs are very difficult for individual marketers to create because they require a large investment and are expensive to maintain. An advantage to Shoppers is that it can pay off the cost of its Optimum program by increasing store sales and charging its partners for using it.

In one such application of the program, Montreal-based L'Oréal Canada used Optimum to launch its Couleur Exterte hair colouring in April 2004. L'Oréal also developed an interactive, game-like direct mail piece, which was sent to women who had Optimum cards and who were chosen based on their ages and purchasing habits; they were offered Optimum points they could apply to the purchase of the product. Shoppers also supported the program with large point-of-purchase billboards. L'Oréal was able to monitor the results and impact of the program because the database is linked to real sales data. L'Oréal could also track the number of people who purchased the product by monitoring the number of points awarded. The program was considered a success as it showed better results than other programs the company had used in the past.

Partnering Programs

Partnering programs involve collaborative relationships between companies to better meet end-user needs.[39] Popular partnering programs are co-branding and affinity partnering. **Co-branding** involves two companies combining their resources and capabilities to offer joint products to their customers. For example, the Bank of Montreal and MasterCard have entered into a co-branding arrangement to jointly market their financial services.

In the case of **affinity partnering programs**, marketers try to use customers' membership in one group to cross-sell other products and services. Affinity partnering programs often involve logistics partnering and cooperative marketing efforts, where the producer and the middleman cooperate to manage inventory and supply logistics and engage in joint marketing efforts. In business-to-business situations, partnering programs involve co-design, co-development, and co-marketing efforts.[40]

Using Data Mining Technology

As we noted earlier in this chapter, many marketers have realized the advantages of relationship marketing and treating each customer as an individual. However, effective relationship marketing and one-to-one programs require the use of sophisticated databases. Recent advances in information technology have satisfied this requirement. Developments in data storage and database technology have resulted in the creation of databases with large amounts of data. These databases contain personal customer information and purchase-related data. This information can be used to generate mailing lists of customers with specific characteristics and identify market segments. **Data mining** is the process of discovering useful knowledge from data stored in corporate databases by sorting through large quantities of data to find patterns and relationships.[41] The firm hopes to find valuable information in these patterns that may be used to improve the

Partnering programs involve collaborative relationships between companies to better meet end-user needs.

Co-branding involves two companies combining their resources and capabilities to offer joint products to their customers.

Affinity partnering programs are programs in which marketers use customer membership in one group to cross-sell other products and services.

Data mining is the process of discovering useful knowledge from data stored in corporate databases by sorting through large quantities of data to find patterns and relationships.

decision-making of the organization, solve customer problems, target individual customers, or introduce new products.

Data mining is a sub-field of artificial intelligence. It integrates statistics, machine learning, artificial intelligence, pattern recognition, database technology, neural networks, and other related disciplines.[42] It consists of computer programs that sift through databases looking to discover patterns or regularities in the data. Effective data mining programs employ algorithms that enable them to deal with these problems and produce useful information.

Many of the tasks performed by data mining used to be carried out by trained statisticians or contracted out to outside companies in the past. As a result, marketing campaigns were slow in adopting database techniques, putting firms at a competitive disadvantage.[43] Data mining eliminates this problem because it can be used by non-statisticians—and this speeds up the implementation of marketing campaigns.

Data mining may be used for solving various marketing problems. Some of the most profitable uses of data mining are in customer acquisition, customer retention, and cross-selling:[44]

1. *Customer acquisition.* Direct mail marketers use data mining to increase responses to direct mail campaigns and facilitate the task of customer acquisition. Data mining enables direct mail marketers to build models to improve their direct mail campaigns. Such models predict those customers who are more likely to buy the product. By screening and targeting only those customers who meet certain qualifying criteria, direct marketers can save large amounts of money.
2. *Customer retention.* Why do some customers remain loyal while others leave? How can we predict those valuable customers who are likely to defect to the competition? Data mining may be used to model loyal and defecting customers on the basis of billing histories, length of subscription, and demographic information. The objective is to identify the most profitable customers within the customer base and predict which of the profitable customers are likely to defect in the near future. Such information can be used to develop customer retention programs such as offering incentives to stop valuable customers from defecting.
3. *Cross-selling.* What types of customers are buying certain products? Which products can be sold together? Data mining can help provide direction when looking for products to use for cross-selling purposes. It can help marketers understand which customers are more likely to purchase new products and which products are usually purchased together. Profiles of customers who purchase more than one product may also be developed on the basis of data mining information.

Data Warehouses

Data warehouse is a type of data architecture with a single site containing data from different sources and organized in a way that facilitates decision-making.

Data mining requires that data are stored in a format that allows easy access for data analysis. Data can be stored in different types of databases, and one type is a **data warehouse**—a data architecture with a single site containing data from different sources and organized in a way that facilitates decision-making. Data warehouses are valuable because they bring together into a single place the bits of information that exists in various places in the organization.

The task of integrating the different databases is complicated because, in most real business situations, the data are stored in various databases in different departments or different locations. The task of data mining is even more complicated because each database may use different kinds of record keeping, over different time periods, or different aggregation formats.[45] For example, a company may have sales data stored in databases located in three different places. The data may be organized by address, sales amount, and product type. A data warehouse is typically modelled as a multidimensional data cube.[46] In such multidimensional database structures, each dimension represents an attribute such as age, occupation, amount spent in the store, or city.

Because the data are stored in various forms in different places, they need to go through a laborious process of integration, being cleaned up, and aggregation before they can become useful for analysis and decision-making. Data warehousing technology incorporates data cleaning, integration, and online analytical processing (OLAP) capabilities. Online analytical processing capabilities include data analyses techniques such as summarization, consolidation, aggregation, and the ability to view the information from different angles.[47] In addition to OLAP techniques, users need additional statistical tools that include cluster, classification, and trend analysis. These capabilities are offered by general purpose statistical packages such as SPSS and SAS.

Increasing the Effectiveness of Customer Relationship Programs

When customer relationship programs are successful, companies will increase their revenues and profits. However, moving from a transaction-based to a relationship-based type of marketing is not easy. It requires a different way of thinking about customers and a redefinition of the concept of marketing. Getting managers and other employees in the organization to think in terms of customer relationships is often a difficult task, and the majority of customer relationship programs do not succeed. According to Gartner Group, a research and advisory firm, 55 percent of all customer relationship programs fail to produce results. A survey of 451 senior executives showed that one out of every five respondents reported that customer relationship initiatives not only failed to help companies but also hurt customer relationships.[48]

The ultimate test of a customer relationship program is whether it leads to increased customer value, satisfaction, and loyalty.[49] The following are ways that may help firms make their relationship marketing efforts more effective.

Commitment from Top Management

In order for a customer relationship program to succeed, management must fully support the program and invest the resources to implement it. Customer loyalty expert Frederick Reichheld found in his research that top company executives help greatly in making customer relationship programs succeed.[50] Many companies attempt to introduce customer retention programs but they fail to commit the time and resources to bring about the changes required to implement such programs. For example, many customer relationship programs flounder because they are introduced before aligning the operating processes, such as order taking, order processing, inventory, production, and accounting and information systems, that are necessary for implementing customer relationships.[51]

Target the Right Customers

Many customer relationship programs fail because companies establish relationships with the wrong customers. Some companies incorrectly target those customers that are the easiest to attract or are the most profitable in the short term. Price promotions, free samples, or coupons frequently attract those customers who are looking for a deal and very seldom remain loyal to one company. People who purchase because of a price promotion are less loyal than people who buy because of a referral.[52] Firms should avoid investing resources attracting those customers who don't stay loyal to one company regardless of the value they receive.

Communicate with Customers

Communicating with customers can help customer relationship programs succeed by establishing trust and avoiding the potential for misunderstanding. Creating trust helps build loyalty. Companies that are successful with their relationship marketing communicate constantly with their customers to inform them about prices, delivery, and order status. Customers are turned off by surprises such as hidden costs or unexpected delays.

Establish Common Bonding with Customers

Firms involved in relationship marketing need to establish a common bonding between the company and its customers.[53] Bonding, which can be established through personal interaction between buyers and sellers, can include offering an outstanding service, being responsive to customers' needs, staying close to customers and listening to his or her voice, treating customers right, and following up the sale by asking customers if they are satisfied with the product. In large consumer markets, given the size of the market, establishing bonding through social interaction may be too costly. In these cases, bonding is established through product guarantees, customer reward programs, and superior product quality.

Establish a Customer Retention Culture

Customer relationship programs can be sustained only if organizations make a conscious effort to build a culture that supports and rewards customer acquisition, satisfaction, and retention.[54] A culture of customer retention exists when managers and other employees consider the impact of their marketing actions on customer relationships. Everyone in the organization must be committed to retaining customers. Employees at all levels must realize that building customer loyalty and customer relationships is the way to long-term organizational success. The transition to a culture of customer retention requires hiring the right kinds of employees and training them in the importance of keeping customers. Employees need to understand the lifetime value of customers and the cost of customer defections. Also, encouraging the right employee motivations through rewards, remuneration, and other incentives is important for increasing retention rates.

Retain Employees

Employee retention is important for retaining customers. Companies need to initiate policies designed to create a loyal and efficient labour force. The longer employees stay with a company, the more knowledgeable they become and the more productive and valuable they are. Employees who stay longer with a company get to know customers better and have the opportunity to earn their trust.

Monitor Customer Relationship Program Performance

Relationship marketing programs need a periodic evaluation to ensure they produce the expected results and so corrective action can be taken in areas in which performance is failing. Managing conflicts in relationships is critical to ensure proper implementation of customer relationship programs. Proper and timely monitoring is required to identify areas where the relationship is failing; management will then be able to see that required action is taken. Such performance evaluation requires the use of appropriate measures. Quantitative measures such as market share or return on investment are too broad-based and reflect the impact of many other activities besides customer relationships. Measures such as customer retention rates or customer satisfaction are more suitable for monitoring relationship marketing performance.

- A strategic network is defined as cooperative and collaborative actions intended to establish, maintain, and enhance mutually advantageous long-term relationships with important industry stakeholders, such as customers, suppliers, distributors, competitors, and other organizations.

- Firms form strategic networks for the following reasons: rapid technological advances, defence against powerful entrants, need to learn new skills, expansion into new markets, and risk sharing.

- Transaction marketing differs from relationship marketing in several important ways. The major focus of relationship marketing is on developing and maintaining long-term relationships with customers instead of short-term discrete transactions. Relationship marketing is customer-centric and is the responsibility of the entire organization. It stresses customer retention, satisfaction and loyalty, and close collaboration with valuable customers.

- Customer value, satisfaction, and retention are key concepts of relationship marketing. Superior customer value creates satisfied customers who are easier to retain. Customer value depends on the quality of the product, processes, performance, and people. Loyalty is shown by repeat purchases associated with a favourable attitude toward the product. Customers remain loyal only when they are completely satisfied.

- Marketers can use the customer value equation and the customer value analysis methodology to manage customer value. The customer value equation defines perceived value as the difference between perceived benefits and perceived life cycle costs.

- Major customer relationship programs include mass customization, loyalty programs, and partnering programs.

- Strategies for improving customer relationship programs include commitment from top management, targeting the right customers, communicating with customers, establishing common bonding with customers, creating a customer retention culture, retaining employees, and monitoring relationship marketing performance.

Review and Discussion Questions

1. What are the major reasons firms form strategic networks? What are the different types of strategic networks? Why do strategic networks fail?

2. List five major differences between transaction marketing and relationship marketing. Why is relationship marketing potentially more effective than transaction marketing?

3. Discuss the relationship between customer value, customer satisfaction, customer retention, and organizational performance.

4. Briefly describe the four Ps of relationship marketing.

5. Discuss the customer value equation. Provide an example to illustrate your answer.

6. Describe the strategic satisfaction matrix. What is the usefulness of the matrix to marketers?

7. What is customer share? Discuss two ways to increase customer share. Why might customer share be more profitable than brand share?

8. What is mass customization? What makes mass customization possible?

9. Describe loyalty programs. How do they work?

10. Discuss partnering programs. What are the different types of partnering programs?

11. Describe the methods for making customer relationship management programs more effective.

1. Referring back to the opening vignette, what other actions might Jones Soda have undertaken to improve its customer relationship management efforts?

2. Forming strategic networks is a major part of the strategy of many companies. Scan the business press to find examples of companies that have formed strategic networks and the reasons they formed these networks.

3. Many firms purchase customer relationship management software designed to help organizations with their relationship management efforts. Yet most of these companies express their dissatisfaction with such programs. In your opinion, what are the reasons

for the failure of these programs to live up to expectations?

4. Give examples of companies that have successfully mass customized their products.

5. Assume that the net yearly earnings from an average customer for a gasoline station is $500. Also assume that this customer stays in the area for six years. Calculate this customer's net worth for this gasoline station assuming a discount rate of 6 percent.

6. How can a hardware store use data mining to improve its relationship marketing efforts?

Notes

1. This section draws from Beverly Cramp, "Reinventing Cool," *Profit Magazine*, December/January 2002, 41–47; and http://www.jonessoda.com, retrieved on July 17, 2003.
2. Desiree Blankerbury Holm, Kent Ericson, and Jan Johanson, "Creating Value Through Mutual Commitment to Business Network Relationships," *Strategic Management Journal* 20 (1999), 467–486.
3. Frederick F. Reichheld and W. Earl Sasser Jr., "Zero Defections: Quality Comes to Services," *Harvard Business Review* (September–October, 1990), 105–111.
4. Ranjay Gulati, Nitin Nohria, and Akbar Zaheer, "Strategic Networks," *Strategic Management Journal* 21 (2000), 203–215.
5. James D. Bamford, Benjamin Gomes-Casseres, and Michael S. Robinson, *Mastering Alliance Strategy* (San Francisco: Jossey-Bass, 2003), 20.
6. Dave Ebner, "Bell and Microsoft introduce co-branded website services," *The Globe and Mail*, Thursday, June 10, 2004, B3.
7. Jeffrey K. Liker, *The Toyota Way* (New York: McGraw-Hill, 2004), 74.
8. Bamford, Gomes-Casseres, and Robinson, 21.
9. Gary Hamel, "Competition for Competence and Inter-partner Learning Within International Strategic Alliances," *Strategic Management Journal*, Summer Special Issue, 12, 1991, 83–103.
10. W. M. Cohen and D. A. Levinthal, "Absorptive Capacity: A New Perspective on Learning and Innovation," *Administrative Science Quarterly* 35, 1990, 128–152.
11. Bamford, Gomes-Casseres, and Robinson, 21.
12. Bamford, Gomes-Casseres, and Robinson, 39.
13. Don Peppers and Martha Rogers, *The One to One Future* (New York: Currency/Doubleday, 1993), 7.
14. L. L. Berry, "Relationship Marketing," in L. L. Berry, G. L. Shostack, and G. D. Upah (eds.), *Emerging Perspectives on Services Marketing* (Chicago: American Marketing Association, 1983), 25–38.
15. Regis McKenna, *Relationship Marketing: Successful Strategies for the Age of the Customer* (Reading, Mass.: Addison-Wesley, 1991), 1.
16. Bamford, Gomes-Casseres, and Robinson, 37.
17. Richard Bloom, "With a fresh new CEO and a Wal-Mart deal, soft-drink firm looks ready to take on the world," *The Globe and Mail*, April 17, 2004, B3.
18. Refik Culpan, *Global Business Alliances* (Westport, Conn.: Quorum Books, 2002), 48.
19. Sunder Magun, "The Development of Strategic Alliances in Canadian Industries: A Micro Analysis," Working paper No. 13, Industry Canada, October 1996, 27.
20. James G. Barnes, *Secrets of Customer Relationship Management* (New York: McGraw-Hill, 2001), 5.
21. Atul Parvatiyar and Jagdish N. Sheth, "The Domain and Conceptual Foundations of Relationship Marketing," in Jagdish N. Sheth and Atul Parvatiyar (eds.), *Handbook of Relationship Marketing* (Thousand Oaks, Calif.: Sage Publications, 2000), 3–38.
22. Barnes, 15.
23. Thomas O. Jones and W. Earl Sasser Jr. "Why Satisfied Customers Defect," *Harvard Business Review* (November–December 1995), 88–99.
24. Jones and Sasser.
25. TARP, "Consumer Complaint Handling in America: Final Report," White House Office of Consumer Affairs, Washington, DC, 1979; TARP, "Consumer Complaint Handling in America: An Update Study," White House Office of Consumer Affairs, Washington, DC, 1986.
26. James L. Heskett, W. Earl Sasser Jr., and Leonard A. Schlesinger, *The Service Profit Chain* (New York: The Free Press, 1997), 180.
27. Jones and Sasser.
28. Reichheld and Sasser.
29. Reichheld and Sasser.
30. Robert Groth, *Data Mining: Building Competitive Advantage* (Upper Saddle River, N.J.: Prentice Hall PTR, 2000).
31. Reichheld and Sasser.
32. Reichheld and Sasser.
33. Peppers and Rogers, 5.
34. B. Joseph Pine II, Don Peppers, and Martha Rogers, "Do You Want to Keep Your Customers Forever?" *Harvard Business Review* (March–April 1995), 103–114.
35. Pine, Peppers, and Rogers.
36. Johny K. Johansson and Ikujiro Nonaka, *Relentless: The Japanese Way of Marketing* (New York: HarperBusiness, 1996), 42–43.
37. Barnes, 5.
38. Chris Daniels, "Vendor Bender," *Marketing Magazine*, April 5–12, 2004, 15.
39. Parvatiyar and Sheth.
40. W. Mitchell and K. Singh, "Survival of Businesses Using Collaborative Relationships to Commercialize Complex Goods," *Strategic Management Journal* 17, 1996, 169–195.
41. Groth, 3.
42. Jiawei Han and Micheline Kamber, *Data Mining: Concepts and Techniques* (San Francisco: Morgan Kaufmann Publishers, 2001), 9.
43. Groth, 8.
44. Groth, 6.
45. Ian H. Witten and Eiber Frank, *Data Mining: Practical Machine Learning Tools and Techniques with Java Implementations* (San Francisco: Morgan Kaufmann, 2000), 48.
46. Han and Kamber, 13.
47. Han and Kamber, 13.
48. Darrell K. Rigby, Frederick F. Reichheld, and Phil Schefter, "Avoid the Four Perils of CRM," *Harvard Business Review* (February 2002), 101–109.
49. Rigby, Reichheld, and Schefter.
50. Frederick F. Reichheld, "Lead for Loyalty," *Harvard Business Review* (July–August 2001), 76–84.
51. Rigby, Reichheld, and Schefter.
52. Frederick F. Reichheld, "Loyalty-Based Management," *Harvard Business Review* (March–April, 1993), 64–73.
53. Parvatiyar and Sheth.
54. Reichheld and Sasser.

Chapter Eight

Product Strategy

In the factory we make chemicals, but in the drugstore we sell hope.

Charles Revson, Founder of Revlon Cosmetics

Learning Objectives

After studying this chapter, you should be able to:

1. Distinguish between the two new-product development approaches

2. Describe the classification of new products

3. Outline the elements of new product strategy

4. Describe the first-mover and late-mover strategies

5. Explain the stage-gate system for new product development

6. Describe how marketing strategies change over the product's life cycle

7. Identify the different product line strategies

8. Explain the differences between physical products and services and the implications of such differences for the marketing of services

Toyota's Successful New-Product Development Strategy

In the early 1990s, Toyota was a very successful company. It was running at full capacity and financially it was performing better than ever. Despite the company's enormous success, Toyota chairman Fiji Toyoda had begun to wonder whether his company could continue to thrive without radically altering its product development strategy. Toyota's product development strategy, which was designed to make minor modifications to existing models, hadn't changed for decades. In response to these concerns, Toyota initiated the Global 21 (G21) project, the precursor to the hybrid Prius car.

In the beginning, the G21 project's mandate was not about developing a hybrid vehicle. Instead, it sought to find ways to minimize car size and fuel consumption and at the same time maximize interior space. The target fuel consumption was initially set at 20 kilometres per litre, which was 50 percent better than the fuel consumption of the Corolla. This target was subsequently increased to 100 percent of the current fuel economy, as the 50 percent improvement was considered not adequate for a 21st-century automobile.

Given that the Prius group's mandate was to develop a small and efficient car, and since natural resources and the environment were to be crucial issues of the 21st century, the team decided to proceed with the hybrid engine, which combines an electric engine with a gas engine. Hybrid technology joins fuel economy with low-level emissions in a practical way, combining the best features of the two types of engines. Electric cars are fuel efficient and produce almost no emissions but are not considered convenient or practical. They require battery-charging stations to recharge the batteries, as electric vehicles can travel only a short distance before their battery requires recharging, and they require huge batteries to accomplish their task. In hybrid vehicles, the batteries are recharged when the gas engine is running.

Electric motors are more efficient at rapid acceleration than gas engines, but gas engines are quite efficient once the vehicle reaches a certain rpm level. The engine switches from electric to gas depending on road conditions. In more advanced hybrid vehicles, computers determine which engine will be employed based on speed, road conditions, number of passengers, and other variables.

In making a decision on the hybrid technology, the Prius team thoroughly examined 80 hybrid engines before it zeroed in on its final choice. Once the choice of the hybrid engine was made, the period of concept development and research into alternative technologies was over. The team now had a clear direction and was able to proceed toward building the first mass-production hybrid vehicle in the world. As the new vehicle was developed, it would require an appropriate design, product technologies, and a new manufacturing system.

The team set a production target date for the end of 1998 or early 1999, at the latest. But at the request of the new Toyota president Hiroshi Okuda, it was moved to an earlier date, December 1997, to speed up the introduction of the new vehicle. The target date, less than two years away, put a lot of pressure on the Prius team. In addition to developing the new engine technology, Toyota needed to come up with an entirely new manufacturing process, prepare a new marketing plan, and have a service organization in place to service the new vehicle.

In July 1996, the product development team unveiled a clay model of the Prius, which was approved two months later, in September. This left 15 months for developing and commercializing Prius. At that time, the standard new-product development process time in the United States was five to six years. Toyota was already on an 18-month development cycle

(continued)

for variations of an existing model. Considering that the breakthrough Prius was on a 15-month development cycle, it was a truly challenging objective. Although it was facing a tight deadline, the team refused to take shortcuts by using an existing model such as Camry, even though its large size could easily house the larger engine and electric motor. In the opinion of Takeshi Uchiyamada, the project's chief engineer, trying the hybrid system on an existing car would force the team to make too many compromises in design, size, and cost.

Despite numerous problems encountered during this period, Prius was launched in the Japanese market in October 1997, two months ahead of the scheduled target date. Prius dominates the world hybrid market with 80 percent market share, and worldwide sales continued to grow, reaching 120,000 in early 2003. The trend toward higher gas prices has made a lot of car buyers shun high-fuel-consumption sports utility vehicles and turn to much more fuel-efficient vehicles such as Prius as well as smaller vehicles.

The Prius experience has benefited Toyota in several ways. It developed several hybrid technologies and it now sells hybrid engine components to other manufacturers. It also has developed important innovations in product development that are now used in the product development of its other vehicles. Also, Toyota is now working on other hybrid cars, including a hybrid version of Lexus RX330.[1]

Introduction

The development of Prius shows the importance of product innovation for organizational success. Had Toyota continued to rely on its existing and highly successful products in the early 1990s, it would have never made such a dramatic change in its product development strategy. As the Prius example illustrates, the economic viability of firms depends on their ability to design, produce, and market products that meet current and future customer needs. Firms need strong products to compete successfully. Making products that meet or exceed customer needs, with the right features and quality and service levels, is key to market success.

As we have discussed in earlier chapters, a firm must decide which products to introduce and how to differentiate them from competitors' products to achieve a top position in the marketplace. In addition to introducing new products, companies need to continually improve their existing products. When marketing their products, firms should not think about those products in a physical sense but about the benefits the products offer to their customers. Looking at products this way allows a firm to identify the real reasons people buy its products and therefore to market them more effectively. For example, if a supermarket sees itself not as selling grocery products but as offering a unique shopping experience, it should invest resources in creating an environment that distinguishes it from the competition.

Developing and managing products are two of the most challenging aspects of marketing. Existing products become obsolete as new technologies emerge, competitors introduce improved products, and market requirements change. In recent years, the pace of new product development has accelerated, putting more pressure on firms to reduce the new-product development cycle time. At the same time, the failure rate of new products is high due to problems in marketing, design, technology, and other areas.

Developing superior products and attracting and retaining valuable customers require effective product strategies. This chapter begins with a discussion of new-product development issues, the elements of new product strategy, a classification of new products, the stage-gate new-product development process, market entry strategies, and the product life cycle. Next, we describe the product line strategies: product line trade-up, trade-down, and product line extension. The last section outlines the differences between physical products and services and their marketing strategy implications.

New Product Development

Markets undergo continuous change because of shifts in customer needs and tastes, technologies, and competitive offerings. At the same time, companies strive to develop new products to keep pace with these changes. Successful product development requires a solid understanding of the benefits customers are seeking from products and the attributes that produce these benefits.

New products must fit the organizational vision, goals, distinctive competencies, and value proposition. Companies following an operational excellence strategy reduce costs and produce standardized products. Firms excelling in product leadership emphasize continuous innovation and rapid product development; they standardize only those product aspects that are not important to customers and customize in areas that are important to customers. Firms pursuing customer intimacy strategies focus on customer applications.[2]

Companies adopt the following approaches to new product development. Some companies employ the **technology-push** approach, in which the company owns a technology and seeks markets in which to apply it. For example, W. L. Gore Associates applies its proprietary Gore-Tex technology in a variety of products including fabric outerwear,

The **technology-push** approach is used by companies that own a technology and seek markets in which to apply it.

The **market-pull** approach to product development involves first identifying a market need opportunity and then developing appropriate products to satisfy the market need.

dental floss, artificial veins for vascular surgery, and high-performance electric cables.[3] Other companies employ the **market-pull** approach to product development in which they first identify a market opportunity and then develop appropriate products to satisfy the market need. For example, pharmaceutical companies spend millions of dollars in an attempt to develop drugs to treat difficult medical conditions.

Classification of New Products

The degree of newness varies among new products. Some new products differ radically from existing products while others are minor modifications. The newness of a product is important because it determines, in large part, the product's competitiveness and risk. For example, radically new products have greater profit potential than minor modifications of existing products, but their introduction is much riskier because of uncertainties that will be discussed later in this chapter. The consulting firm Booz, Allen, and Hamilton (1982) has classified new products into the following six categories:[4]

New-to-the-world products. These products are radically different from existing products and create entirely new industries. Companies that introduce such products are pioneers in that industry. Examples of new-to-the-world products include fax machines, cellular telephones, and personal computers. These products often destroy existing industries and create new industries. For example, the establishment of the electronic calculator industry meant the end of the slide rule industry.

New product lines. New products allow a firm's entry into an established category— products are new to the firm but not to the world. Examples are Sympatico's entry into the high-speed Internet market and *National Post*'s late arrival into the Canadian newspaper industry.

Additions to existing product lines. New items are added to an existing line of products. These products are commonly called line extensions and are intended to fill gaps in the product line. Examples include Honda's introduction of its Pilot minivan, which complemented its car offerings and Hewlett Packard's DeskJet 1350 all-in-one printer, which was added to its line of printers to meet the needs of those who needed a printer, a scanner, and a copier together.

Improvements in existing products. New generations of existing products or enhancements to the performance of existing products represents another category of new products. For example, Intel's Pentium 4 processor uses a new technology that allows different parts of a software program to operate in parallel so software runs faster and multitasks are performed more effectively.

Repositioning. Products that appeal to new segments or that change consumer perceptions of existing products are considered new products. For example, Arm & Hammer baking soda has been repositioned over the years as a dental care product, odour control for kitty litter, and a refrigerator deodorant.

Cost reductions. New products are also considered to be those that offer equivalent value to existing products but at a lower price. Examples include AMD microprocessors, which perform similar functions to Intel's but sell at a lower price, or private labels such as Shoppers Drug Mart's Life brand or Canadian Tire's Motomaster line of products.

New product strategy guides new product activities and reflects the value proposition, positioning, and distinctive competencies of the organization.

New Product Strategy

Effective new product development requires a **new product strategy** to guide new product activities. The new product strategy reflects the value proposition, positioning, and distinctive competencies of the organization. A major objective of a new product strategy is to help manage the new-product development process in an effective manner. A new product strategy entails the following:

- *New product objectives.* A new product strategy sets the new product objectives such as degree of newness, percentage of sales from new products, and criteria to measure the success of the new product. Innovative companies such as 3M and Canon require that a certain percentage of sales comes from new products. This type of guideline forces managers to constantly look for new products to achieve such a balance. The absence of such a policy might lead managers to focus on existing products and avoid new products.
- *Area of search for new products.* The new product strategy specifies the appropriate area of search for new products; this decision is heavily influenced by the strategic and served market definition and core competencies of the organization. Most innovations take place within the boundaries of existing product lines—new flavours, sizes, or colours—and are intended to fill gaps in those lines. Companies that strive to avoid marketing myopia are searching for product opportunities within the broader scope of strategic markets. As we discussed in the opening vignette, Toyota developed its Prius model after it decided to look beyond its existing range of cars and technologies.
- *Behaviour of team members.* The new product strategy spells out ways to help bring together the various team members and increase team effectiveness.[5] New-product development teams consist of employees with diverse backgrounds—design, engineering, marketing, or purchasing—and agendas. In order for all these people to work effectively as a team, they must be provided with guidelines that govern their behaviour as members of the team. Such guidelines might include reporting relationships, degree of empowerment, team structure, and individual and team responsibilities.
- *Speed of new product introduction.* Speed to market has become an important part of a firm's business and new product strategy. Firms strive to increase the rate of innovation and bring new products to the market faster than competitors. For example, it takes Toyota under 12 months to design a new car, while other car manufacturers require two to three years.[6] Speed in introducing new products provides a firm with several advantages, such as reducing the cost of new product development and preempting the competition. A new product strategy should specify organizational policies intended to help improve the speed of new product introduction.

  Companies can increase their rate of innovation and speed of new product introductions in several ways. They can change the organizational structure to make new product development more effective. IBM, for instance, was able to design and market its IBM PC product in much less time after it created a new organizational unit dedicated to development of its personal computer. Many companies employ cross-functional teams to speed up the new-product development process, cut costs, and reduce the number of defects. The use of targeted investment in R&D and product design can reduce new-product development time. Entering into alliances with other companies through R&D joint ventures, forming mergers with companies that can provide the skills needed to quickly complete projects, or technology licensing to avoid having to develop their own technology are additional ways firms can speed up new product development.
- *Timing of entry.* Many firms develop policies with regard to the timing of entry into the market. Being first into a market is one possible entry strategy. An alternative approach is to enter the market late with a better or less expensive product. Many marketers believe that being first to enter a market is a sure path to obtaining a competitive advantage. While there are enduring competitive advantages associated with early entry, these advantages are not universal.[7] Many companies entered late into a market with a superior product and took away the market leadership from the pioneers.[8] These options will be further discussed in a later section.

The Stage-Gate New-Product Development System

The importance of the new-product development process has led firms to develop various approaches to help better manage the process. One such approach is the stage-gate system for managing the development of new products from idea generation to commercialization.[9] The **stage-gate** process acts as a framework that adds focus to the new-product development effort. It enables firms to eliminate non-viable ideas quickly and inexpensively before they reach production and commercialization, where the cost is much higher.

The **stage-gate** process acts as a framework that adds focus to the new-product development effort.

The stage-gate system requires that the product development process is divided into several stages or activities. An appropriate number of formal "go/no go" decision points are then built into the process to control entry into the subsequent stage. The number of gates used in a stage-gate system varies in different firms. A stage-gate process is presented in Figure 8.1.

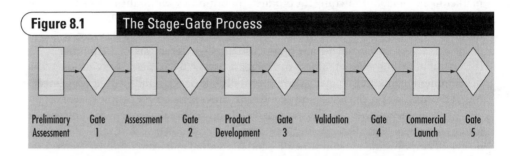

| Figure 8.1 | The Stage-Gate Process |

Preliminary Assessment — Gate 1 — Assessment — Gate 2 — Product Development — Gate 3 — Validation — Gate 4 — Commercial Launch — Gate 5

A stage-gate system helps product developers focus on the tasks that need to be performed. Each new product idea must pass through a series of gates on its way to launch. Between each gate, various analyses and product development activities are carried out. When these tasks are completed, a management review is conducted. If management feels that the work is satisfactory, the next stage is normally authorized. But if management feels that the work performed at the stage is not sufficient to justify a go decision, product developers will normally be told to go back and continue the work until it is deemed satisfactory. Otherwise, the new-product development effort will be cancelled. The objective is to eliminate early in the process, and before a large investment is made, those ideas that lack commercial value, while retaining viable projects.

Stage-gate processes have been criticized for being too slow. However, the speed of a stage-gate process depends on how it is implemented. A fast stage-gate system requires that the time spent at the gates is as short as possible and that there is no idle time between stages. In order to make the process more flexible and speed it up, some firms allow work to begin in one stage before the work in the previous stage has been completed.[10] Also, a simultaneous engineering approach is adopted where the various functions work together. Companies adopting such an approach set up a cross-disciplinary team consisting of marketing, design, manufacturing, and other functions.

Gate 1: Idea generation and preliminary assessment

The objective of this stage is to generate as many new ideas as possible. The search for new ideas is normally guided by the organization's strategic goals, core competencies, value proposition, and new product strategy. There are many sources of new product ideas, inside and outside the organization, including customers, employees, competitors, suppliers, channel members, and consulting firms that specialize in generating new product ideas.

Once a large number of ideas have been generated, management must eliminate the ideas that are not commercially viable or do not fit certain organizational criteria. Dropping bad ideas early on saves money, as the cost of evaluating ideas is much higher in subsequent stages. Firms commonly evaluate new product ideas on the basis of product, manufacturing, market, technological, financial, and organizational criteria. Companies will reject an idea for any one of several reasons: it might have a low market potential, the company lacks the technology to build the product, or the anticipated return on investment is low.

Gate 2: Assessment

Ideas that survive the initial screening process will be subjected to another, more rigorous assessment. In this stage, a product concept is developed and consumer reactions to the proposed product are obtained. **Concept development** involves establishing a concrete concept by determining the target customers, the primary product benefit, features, performance, price, and the occasions at which the product will be used.

Once the concept is developed, it is tested by obtaining feedback from potential customers. The purpose of concept testing is to assess consumer interest in the proposed product before large resources are committed to developing the product. Information obtained from concept testing helps clarify potential users' understanding of the new product's benefits, whether the concept fills a need, how the product could be improved, and whether there is interest in the product.

Once the concept test is carried out, management conducts a detailed business analysis. Business analysis includes forecasted revenues, profits, budgets, costs, and cash flows, as well as a preliminary marketing plan that covers the target market, major competitors, product positioning, and a marketing program. Other aspects of business analysis include a technical part that contains product design details, technical feasibility, product specifications, and a manufacturing plan.

> **Concept development** involves establishing a concrete concept by determining the target customers, the primary product benefit, features, performance, price, and the occasions at which the product will be used.

Gate 3: Product development

The next stage involves the development of a prototype or a working model. Most organizational functions, including design, engineering, production, and marketing, participate in developing the prototype. In addition to the prototype, firms put together an appropriate package that includes a suitable name and a marketing strategy.

Before market testing begins, companies test the prototype to ensure that it achieves its performance specifications.[11] During this pilot program, the product is produced in small quantities and tested under conditions resembling the real-life circumstances. The objective of prototype testing is to discover any flaws in the design before full production begins. Computer simulation programs provide a way to save time and reduce costs by conducting simulated rather than laboratory testing.

Gate 4: Validation

Validation normally consists of a market test that allows marketers to evaluate the new product under real-world conditions. The product is introduced in carefully selected markets and its sales behaviour is observed. Market tests provide marketers with valuable information about the product's potential, allow the testing of different marketing strategies, and discover ways of improving the marketing mix. The major benefit of market testing is that it allows companies to test new products on a limited basis before they are introduced on a larger scale.

Many marketers eschew market testing because of its high cost, its slowness, and the possibility of tipping off competitors about the company's new product plans. Competitors are known to have stolen ideas from products that are being market-tested and introduce their

> **Validation** normally consists of a market test that allows marketers to evaluate the new product under real-world conditions.

Chapter 8 / Product Strategy

own products before the market test is over. Competitors have also been known to interfere with market tests by not allowing the company to properly carry out the market test or obtain reliable information about the new product. The companies that avoid market tests instead may conduct **simulated market tests**—tests carried out in simulated supermarkets or retail environments. Simulated market tests overcome many of the problems associated with real market tests but they introduce an element of artificiality into the process.

Simulated market tests are tests carried out in simulated supermarkets or retail environments.

Gate 5: Commercial launch

If the outcome of market testing is favourable, the product is commercialized. **Commercialization** involves full-scale production, distribution, and an all-out marketing effort. It is the most expensive stage of the stage-gate new-product development process. During commercialization, responsibility for the product shifts from the new-product development team to manufacturing and marketing. The goal of manufacturing is to optimize the manufacturing process, meet the forecast volume, and achieve the product quality required to ensure customer satisfaction. The marketing task is to meet the sales and profit targets set for the new product.

Commercialization involves full-scale production, distribution, and an all-out marketing effort.

It is advisable for a company to conduct a post-implementation review to assess how the launch is proceeding and make the necessary adjustments in its marketing strategy. Since it is impossible for management to know all the details of strategy implementation beforehand, it must monitor its actions closely and make all necessary changes in its program. Any marketing, product design, or manufacturing flaws found should be quickly corrected.

The commercialization of a new product signals the beginning of the product life cycle. The next section discusses the timing of market entry strategies followed by marketing strategies commonly used during the different stages of the product life cycle.

Market Entry Strategies

The timing of entry into a market can be a very important decision and it can have a significant impact on a firm's success in that market. For example, Sony is a company that thrives on innovation. It has been a pioneer in its introduction of innovations such as the Trinitron technology, the beta technology, and the Walkman. But while Sony is the industry innovator and pioneer, some of its competitors, such as Sanyo, are followers who simply wait for Sony and other companies to come up with the new product ideas. Sony is a company that embraces the first-mover strategy. Sanyo, on the other hand, follows a late-mover strategy.

First-Mover Strategy

First-mover strategies involve being first to a market with a new product. Such strategies often enable companies to obtain significant advantages over their competitors. Industry pioneers such as Coke and Tide have been leaders for many years. Being first to a market is especially important when there are significant first-mover advantages. The following are the most significant first-mover advantages:

Barriers to Entry. Some of the potential advantages of a first-mover strategy include raising significant barriers to entry for late entrants in the form of economies of scale, proprietary technology and learning effects, and brand loyalties. These barriers can slow down the rate of imitation and entry by potential rivals, allowing the first mover to earn substantial profits as a temporary monopolist.

Switching Costs. Early entrants earn their highest returns when they move into markets with significant switching costs. Although some consumers prefer to use different products, most consumers would rather avoid these switching costs and stick to existing products unless the additional benefits from the new brand exceed these switching costs.[12]

Consumer Search Costs. Early entrants have an advantage because when consumers buy a new product, they need to acquire information to properly evaluate the new product, a procedure that can be costly for them as they re-evaluate their consumption patterns. Late entrants incur switching costs in their efforts to establish a viable market position. Another barrier for late entrants is that some consumers may dislike sampling new brands.

Buyer Uncertainty. First movers also benefit most when consumers are uncertain regarding product quality and do not feel they will gain much from a long and time-consuming search for information. Schmalensee (1982) argued that risk-averse buyers usually establish a stable preference pattern after they try a product and are satisfied with it, and they may be reluctant to try a new and unproven product.[13] Risk-averse consumers, especially, may even be willing to pay a premium for the pioneer brand. The tendency to stay with a brand usually is greater for low-priced products where the rewards to finding a superior brand are not great.

Image and Reputation. First movers may establish a reputation as the market leader and pioneer and create loyal customers. Late entrants must convince customers to try an unknown brand. This can give a first mover a significant competitive advantage over late entrants.

First Choice of Market Segments and Position. First movers have an opportunity to pick the best market position by being the first to offer the attributes most important to the market. They can obtain a patent and become the industry standard by selling the first product associated with the industry. As a result, late entrants will be forced to compete in less attractive segments with inferior positioning strategies.

Preempt Scarce Resources. First movers can preempt scarce resources such as advertising media, locations, land, raw materials, skilled personnel, distribution channels, and shelf space. For instance, it may be difficult for latecomers to find uncluttered advertising media and appropriate channels of distribution. Also, first movers can build relationships with distributors, retailers, wholesalers, and agents. The story of iPod described in the Strategy in Action box illustrates how a first mover can establish itself as a market leader and reap the benefits for years to come.[14]

Strategy in Action

APPLE'S iPod

Spurred by the soaring sales of its iPod digital music player, Apple Computer's profit in the second quarter of 2004 more than tripled and revenue jumped nearly 30 percent. For the three months ended on March 27, 2004, Apple posted a profit of $46 million (U.S.), while a year earlier the company had earned a profit of $14 million (U.S.). With strong iPod sales expected to continue, the trend toward higher profits at Apple was predicted to continue as well. It is interesting to note that Apple sold more iPods—807,000—than computers—749,000—during the quarter. These results highlighted Apple's shift from a computer company to a broader digital entertainment and lifestyle company. Steve Jobs, Apple's chief operating officer, had been moving the company toward a broader portfolio of digital products since the iPod was released in 2001.

The latest results were evidence of how successful Apple's first-mover strategy was with respect to the iPod, as the latter was very successful and was the company's main engine of growth. While iPod sales were rising in a spectacular fashion, the company's

(continued)

---

computer sales grew just 5 percent from a year earlier, compared with a 15 percent increase for the personal computer industry as a whole. In fact, there was anecdotal evidence that the iPod was even helping its personal computer sales. In other words, the iPod was the source of the near-term growth in revenues and profits for Apple.

Apple's first-mover strategy for the iPod was aided by the company being able to develop the device in just six months—faster than any major product in the company's history. The iPod was created by a 35-member team of designers led by Tony Fadell, an engineer who had worked at an Apple spinoff, General Magic, at Philips Electronics, and briefly at RealNetworks. The product development team employed a version of a microprocessor that was used in cellphones and relied on software licensed from Pixo, a cellphone software developer founded by Paul Mercer, another former Apple employee. The rapid new-product development cycle helped Apple enter the market quickly and establish the iPod as the indisputable market leader.

But being a first mover does not guarantee a sustainable competitive advantage. This strategy involves certain risks and, in some cases, can have large resource requirements, as the pioneer has to do the research and development and incur substantial product and market development costs. In certain cases, such as the development of the Boeing 747 aircraft, a company is required to "bet the firm" with regard to investment requirements. In case the product fails, the losses can be so high that the firm cannot continue and has to shut down operations. Market development is also one of the greatest challenges facing a first mover as markets frequently take very long to take off and require large amounts of money to be spent to educate the market. All these activities are very costly and may bankrupt a company with limited resources or weaken it to the point that it is vulnerable to powerful second movers who may move quickly and take over the market. The Strategy in Action box discusses how EMI, a company with an outstanding technology and product, failed to profit from its first-rate technology.[15]

Strategy in Action — EMI

Originally, EMI was a record company that promoted the early Beatles. But it later moved into the medical field, pioneering CAT scanners. After investing heavily in R&D, market development, and educating the markets for years on the use of these machines, it lost its leadership position to companies with greater resources such as General Electric and other companies who leapfrogged EMI with technologically superior products. Eventually, EMI was forced to withdraw from the market, and eight years after it had introduced its pioneering product, EMI was acquired by General Electric for a bargain-basement price. The major reasons given for EMI's demise were the overwhelming R&D costs, lack of complementary assets such as market knowledge and service support, and fierce competition from powerful imitators.

The fear of competitive imitation is always present when a firm pioneers a product, as was illustrated with EMI. In fact, first-mover advantages in many markets erode over time as the leaders' skills and products are imitated or replaced with new ones to serve the markets. In these instances, competitors with larger resources enter the industry and overwhelm the start-up with an imitative but better product. For this reason, as first-mover advantages erode, first movers need to undertake new initiatives that will give them new advantages to maintain their market leadership.

Late-Mover Strategy

A first-mover strategy has many advantages for the firm that decides to be first in a market with a pioneering product but, as we have seen, many risks are associated with such a strategy. Late movers avoid many of the risks and costs incurred by the first mover, giving rise to what has been called **free-rider effects**. Free-rider effects enable late movers to enter the new market at a low risk as it already been developed, been established, and proven its viability, and with minimal product development costs. Because of the lower risk and potential advantages many companies adopt a late-mover strategy. A study of imitation practices showed that 60 percent of successful patented innovations were imitated within four years and the imitators' development costs were 35 percent less than innovators'.[16] In the case of unpatented innovation, imitation is more rampant as another study found that about 65 percent of new products were copied in a year or less. The late-mover advantages are discussed next.[17]

> **Free-rider effects** are late-entrant benefits such as avoiding the high cost of product and market development that help offset the advantages of early entrants.

Let the First Mover Enter First and Test the Waters. The late mover can learn from the innovator's mistakes and can move in with a product better suited to the needs of the market. Pioneers can incur substantial costs in the form of developing the product, educating customers and generating customer awareness, gaining regulatory approval, and building infrastructures. Late entrants avoid the expenses of product development and can profit from the pioneer's investment in buyer education. For example, while it took Matsushita and Sony researchers over ten years to develop the videotape recorder, once it was on the market it took JVC less than six months to come up with its own version of the Betamax technology.[18]

Let First Movers Face the Uncertainty. Pioneers face the uncertainty about the final form of technology and the size of the market opportunity, and the possibility that it can take years to grow to a viable size. Pioneers face greater uncertainty and consumer resistance toward adopting their product than products introduced later. These uncertainties involve some degree of risk and that makes an early entry less attractive. For instance, Time Inc. left the teletext market a few years ago because of the uncertainty regarding market acceptance.

Avoid Being Locked into an Obsolete Product Design. As the initial product design can change, the late mover avoids the risk of being locked into an obsolete product and the associated sunk costs in R&D, manufacturing, distribution, and plants. That was the fate of Sony when the Betamax technology it pioneered was supplanted by VHS technology, causing it to incur huge write-offs in investments made over several years.

Marketing Strategies During the Different Stages of the Product Life Cycle

The product life cycle is a basic concept in marketing. It assumes that a product goes through various stages during its lifetime, much like living organisms. The product life cycle is assumed to exhibit an S-shaped sales behaviour as shown in Figure 8.2. It consists of the following stages: introduction, growth, shakeout, maturity, and decline. The length of the product life cycle varies among brands; some brands have lived over 100 years (Ivory soap) while others' life cycle is as short as a few months (IBM PC Junior).

The length of the product life cycle varies for different firms. Some products display a short life cycle. For example, the minivan category grew very quickly in the mid-1980s and reached its maturity stage in a very short period of time. Other products go through a very long life cycle that can last for decades. For example, the microwave oven market lingered in the introduction stage for many years before it reached its growth stage. Product life cycles often exhibit one or more recycles. These recycles are caused by increases in

Figure 8.2 | The Idealized Product Life Cycle

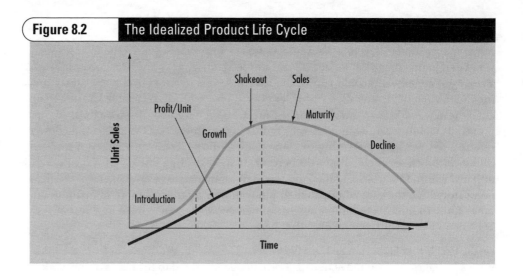

popularity of the product among additional groups or improvements in technologies that revitalize the product.[19]

The product life cycle results from the interaction among market, technological, and competitive forces.[20] It is extremely difficult to forecast the outcome of the interplay among these forces. This makes the prediction of the precise form of the product life cycle—and when a stage ends and another one begins—virtually impossible.

Although it is difficult to predict a product's specific life cycle, the product life cycle provides a useful framework for the analysis and planning of marketing strategies. Each stage requires different marketing strategies and tactics. The product life cycle also provides a means to align diverse organizational functions and give a focus to the firms' decisions so that they reinforce rather than detract from the attainment of organizational goals.[21] The marketing strategies that can be employed in each product life stage are described next.

Introduction Stage

The introduction stage begins when the product enters the marketplace. During this period, the product appeals to everyone, as the market is too small to warrant treating it as consisting of separate segments. Distinct segments do not emerge until much later on. Buying patterns are characterized by experimental purchases and pilot tests, especially for highly complex and innovative products. The new product is underutilized as consumers are not aware of its full range of applications.

At this stage, competition is minimal as competitors are carefully evaluating the attractiveness of the market. Firms experience low sales growth and high costs because of the small scale of production, which does not allow for economies of scale, and high promotional expenses relative to sales. As a result, companies typically experience losses in this period. Emerging markets are characterized by **market, competitive,** and **technological** uncertainties:

Market uncertainty is the concern that the expected demand for the product may not materialize.

Competitive uncertainty is the lack of knowledge about how existing competitors will react to the firm's entry.

Technological uncertainty results from design difficulties and the existence of alternative technologies that may make the firm's technology obsolete.

1. *Market uncertainty.* The concern that the expected demand for the product may not materialize.
2. *Competitive uncertainty.* Lack of knowledge about how existing competitors will react to the firm's entry.
3. *Technological uncertainty.* Possibilities of design difficulties and the existence of alternative technologies that may make the firm's technology obsolete.

New products often fail because of technical problems such as a faulty product design. Pioneers who focus on the wrong technical solution may be overtaken by competing technologies as happened to Sony's beta technology, which lost out to VHS technology. These uncertainties are a major reason that many new products fail in the introductory stage and never reach the growth stage. Companies competing in emerging markets need to accomplish the following:

- *Decide on an entry strategy.* As we noted earlier in this chapter, firms choose to enter a new market either as a first mover or a late mover. As we've seen in an earlier section, pioneers have the opportunity to preempt a new market, obtain economies of scale, raise switching costs, preempt scarce resources, and create loyal customers. On the other hand, late entrants avoid the high cost of product and market development that help offset the advantages of the early entrants.[22] First movers are frequently leapfrogged by late entrants who benefit from observing and improving on the pioneer's product.

- *Choose a pricing strategy.* Firms choose between penetration pricing (low price), price skimming (high price), and parity pricing. Price skimming is consistent with the absence of potential competition, superior products, and price-insensitive consumers. On the other hand, penetration pricing is called for when competitive imitation is likely or consumers are highly price sensitive. Parity pricing is chosen when conditions do not favour any of the other two approaches. These new-product pricing strategies will be further discussed in Chapter 10.

- *Establish distribution.* It is important that the firm find appropriate channels of distribution. Market-leading companies such as Procter & Gamble normally have little difficulty establishing distribution for their product. However, small and relatively unknown companies typically have a hard time finding intermediaries for their new products. Channels of distribution represent a significant barrier to entry and a common reason for new product failure.

- *Design a promotional strategy.* In emerging markets, promotional expenditures are a high percentage of sales. Market leaders spend large amounts on promotion—advertising, point-of-sale displays, coupons, and free samples. Smaller firms lacking large promotional budgets rely more on direct sales, publicity, word of mouth, online selling, and trade incentives.

A major marketing goal of companies competing in emerging markets is to create awareness, educate potential customers about the product, and obtain trial by potential users by identifying early adopters and convincing them to try the product. It is important to retain customers who have tried the product. The product's survival depends on repeat customers. It is at this point that relationship marketing becomes crucial to help retain valuable customers. Unfortunately, because companies fail to practise relationship marketing, some products sell well to first-time buyers but they fail to obtain repeat sales.

The time a product stays in the introductory stage varies depending on the product. Some products spend a lot of time, while others are adopted very quickly. Continued uncertainties prolong the duration of these markets. Until the various uncertainties are resolved, competitors are reluctant to invest in new markets. The length of the introduction stage also depends on the **diffusion rate,** the speed with which the product spreads through the target market. The diffusion rate depends on the perceived advantage of the new product relative to existing alternatives, perceived risk felt by prospective buyers, and other factors that affect adoption such as lack of awareness and product availability.

Diffusion rate is the speed with which the product spreads through the target market.

Growth Stage

Products that survive the introductory stage begin to grow at a rapid rate as the product starts to penetrate the bulk of the target market. New customers enter the market, and customers who tried and liked the product purchase it again. As the market grows, market segments emerge, enabling firms to tailor their products or services to better serve the needs of these segments. The high growth rate attracts competitors who rush to the market to share in the success of the early entrants. Having survived the emerging stage, the product proves that there is a market demand.

Growing markets are characterized by less uncertainty. As customers gain experience with the new product, their uncertainty is reduced and growth becomes self-sustained. If there are competing designs in the introduction stage, the product with the most desirable design emerges in this next stage, reducing technical uncertainty.[23] Standardization is necessary for moving to large-scale production with the concomitant reduction in unit cost gained from economies of scale. Evidence of wider acceptance is the impetus needed to spur further investment and buyer adoption. The adoption of commonly accepted standards has been largely responsible for the explosion in growth rates of a wide range of industries such as the Internet, television, and telecommunications.

Companies competing in growth markets need to accomplish the following:

- *Determine value proposition.* Customers at this stage are becoming more experienced, and their requirements often change from information and service to valuing price and convenience. Segments also emerge with different needs. Firms need to determine their value proposition—operational excellence, product leadership, or customer intimacy—based on customers' requirements and the firms' resources and capabilities.
- *Raise barriers to entry.* Manufacturing and distribution are becoming important at this stage. Companies should strive to raise barriers to competitor entry, including blocking access to distribution and switching costs.
- *Create brand loyalty and favourable attitudes.* In growth markets, the objective of marketing strategy is to create brand loyalty, nurture customer relationships, and gain market share. Promotion needs to be geared toward building selective demand, promoting the product's benefits, and developing favourable attitudes toward the product.
- *Do not lose customer focus.* A common problem in the growth stage is the loss of customer focus due to more pressing internal concerns, such as building volume, reducing costs, and meeting production schedules. Even if the product is successful, a preoccupation with operational concerns may place the future of the company—no matter how successful—in jeopardy.[24] This is why many new products fail at this stage. For example, People Express was a highly successful discount airline in the early 1980s that experienced a phenomenal growth rate. The company became a victim of its own success, however, because the quality of its service declined as the company attempted to maintain its high rates of growth. As a result, customers became highly dissatisfied, sales dropped precipitously, and People Express had to be sold to a competitor to avoid bankruptcy.
- *Improve product and operations.* If the product is successful, there is a potential for complacency to set in. For this reason, the growth stage is the time to improve the product or service and fine-tune operations. Profits must be reinvested to improve the competitive position. Successful companies continue conducting customer research to discover flaws in their marketing strategy and to quickly correct them.
- *Fine-tune prices and expand distribution.* The behaviour of prices depends on the cost behaviour, volume increases, and the popularity of the product. Prices typically decline during the growth period but if demand exceeds supply, prices may even increase during this period. Some growing businesses raise prices, believing that customers will not resist such increases. This can be a serious mistake because it can alienate customers and cause the business to fail. As the market expands, management must seek ways to expand distribution and find new ways of reaching its markets.

Shakeout Stage

The great increase in sales during the growth stage attracts a large number of companies. But the high-growth period ends as product sales begin to reach their market potential. As we will discuss further in Chapter 10, the shakeout period, which occurs at the end of the growth stage, is characterized by a reduction in industry prices.[25] Prices are often reduced by market leaders looking to weed out weaker competitors or fill up excess production capacity. As a result of the lower prices, weaker competitors are forced to exit the industry.

Management must begin planning for the shakeout period and for the inevitable maturity stage long before this stage occurs. This may involve differentiating the product by adding new features and appealing to specific market segments with distinct marketing programs or by decreasing costs and streamlining operations. Many efficiencies result from redesigning work or using a different organization structure. Finally, some firms try to lower costs by increasing their scale of production and thus benefit from economies of scale and experience. In many cases engineers redesign the product through value-engineering methods that lower the cost of production. The firms that survive the shakeout are either the most differentiated or the ones with a low cost structure.

Companies competing in shakeout markets need to accomplish the following:

- *Rationalize product lines.* During shakeout, firms need to rationalize their product lines by eliminating weak-performing items.
- *Lower prices.* Prices must be adjusted downward to reflect the drastically lower new prices as the previously held pricing structure no longer exists. Low-cost firms enjoy the highest profit margins, but less efficient competitors experience a squeeze on their profits. Those who can no longer cover their high costs leave the market.

Maturity Stage

Most products are in mature markets. These markets are characterized by stability in buying patterns and a growth rate that approaches the rate of population growth of the target market. The product is established in the marketplace and enjoys a high degree of awareness. There is great stability in the market, the competition, and the technology. The benefits people seek from products typically change from earlier stages as customers become more knowledgeable than in earlier stages.

The number of competitors stabilizes in this stage. The less efficient competitors have left the market during the shakeout period that occurred at the end of the growth period. Prices and promotion expenditures remain stable during the maturity stage. But in some cases prices continue to drop as costs decline and competition increases, as differences among competing products disappear through imitation, leading to **product commoditization.** Advertising for differentiated products remains high while imitative products rely more on sales promotions.

Mature markets often contain unexplored or overlooked market segments or new ones open up. Sales sometimes increase during this stage because of changing customer needs or demographic shifts. For example, demand for golf facilities has increased in recent years because of increases in the number of retired people who have more leisure time. Technological changes frequently occur during the maturity stage. For instance, high-definition TV and digital technology are reshaping the television and camera industries. Marketers need to focus on the following tasks during the maturity stage:

- *Appeal to selected segments.* Mature markets consist of segments with specific needs. The focus of the marketing strategy in this stage is to appeal to selected segments with highly targeted marketing programs.
- *Differentiate product and reduce costs.* Marketers must seek ways to further differentiate their products. However, it is difficult to physically differentiate the product in the

Product commoditization is the process by which differences among competing products disappear through imitation.

maturity stage. Therefore, companies should use other ways such as service, recognition, image, availability, and distribution to differentiate their products.

- *Find new ways of increasing sales.* Companies in mature markets must pursue new ways of increasing revenues. For example, the piano industry was declining by 10 percent annually in the late 1980s, when Yamaha, the market leader, revamped its piano product line by adding digital and optical capabilities. These technologies allowed piano owners to reproduce recorded performances on their pianos with great accuracy. The result was a renewed interest in pianos and a revitalization of the industry.[26] Figure 8.3 lists several ways of increasing product sales in mature markets.

Figure 8.3	Ways of Increasing Sales in Mature Markets

- Promote new uses or applications to existing product users
- Encourage customers to increase their usage of the product
- Promote more frequent use of the product
- Promote the product for use on different occasions
- Reach market segments whose needs are ignored or underserved
- Broaden the customer base by converting non-users
- Attract users of competitors' brands
- Expand product line by adding new items, sizes, or flavours
- Enhance product appeal by improving quality and service or adding new features
- Replace product with superior new products

Decline Stage

Eventually, most products enter the decline stage. A product enters this stage when sales decrease from previous levels. The length of the decline stage may be short as in dedicated word processors or long as in cigarettes. Sales decline for primarily three reasons:

1. *Changes in tastes and preferences.* Changes in tastes and preferences make the product less attractive. Demand for coffee fell in the 1960s until the emergence of specialty coffee, a change that partly stemmed the overall coffee decline.
2. *Product substitution.* Substitution of one product for another slows down the sales of a product. For example, station wagons were replaced by minivans and sports utility vehicles in the 1980s and 1990s.
3. *Demographic changes.* Demographic changes can decrease product sales. For example, demand for baby products in industrialized countries has declined because of the lower birth rates.

In declining markets, competitors begin to exit the industry. Prices may fall if management wants to clear excess inventory or rise if there are loyal customers. Investment in product research and development is discontinued. Promotional spending is reduced and the number of distributors is drastically reduced.

The firm must decide the timing of its exit from a declining market. Some declining markets are more attractive than others, depending on the rate of decline. A declining market is more attractive when the decline is slow and predictable, when there are one or more pockets of demand, when products are differentiated, and when barriers to exit are low.[27] If a declining market meets these conditions, a firm could stay on to harvest the market and extract any profits left in the product before it too leaves the market. A remaining company could pursue an aggressive harvesting strategy if market conditions are deteriorating rapidly or a mild harvesting strategy if the rate of decline is slow.

Product Line Strategies

Product line strategies involve actions taken by a firm to extend the product line up or down, or to fill gaps in the product line (see Figure 8.4). Firms adopt such strategies in response to environmental opportunities and strategic considerations. In pursuing such product line strategies firms must be aware not only of their advantages but of the risks inherent in these strategies.

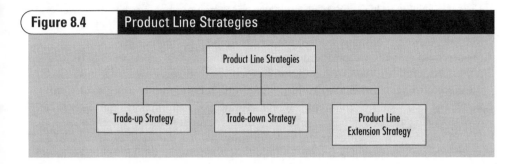

Figure 8.4   Product Line Strategies

One common risk to all firms pursuing these strategies is deviating from their core focus and reaching too far beyond their area of expertise, in effect spreading themselves too thin.[28] For example, Secure Computing Corp., a security firm, tried to service both ends of the market, the low-end segment that demanded inexpensive security services and the high end that needed expensive specialized services. By trying to do many different things, the company spread itself too thin and it wasn't focused enough. As a result, Secure Computing fell on hard times, and it was forced to restructure and focus on the few things it could do well. The narrower focus helped the company improve its performance considerably. Product line strategies and their advantages and risks are discussed below.

Trade-Up Strategy

A **trade-up strategy** is employed by a low-end company that introduces products to the high end of the market. For example, Honda, after being a manufacturer of small cars for a number of years, gradually introduced higher-end brands under the Acura name. Toyota also entered the high end of the car market with its highly successful Lexus brand. Many other companies have made similar moves.

Entering the high end entails a different marketing strategy than the one employed in the low end. First, it requires premium or prestige pricing. The promotion of the product will also need to be different than the low-end product with more image and less of the mass advertising and appeal used for the low-end products. The high-end product should utilize separate channels of distribution and use higher levels of service consistent with the higher image of the brand. There are several reasons why a firm would extend upward its product line:

- *Lack of growth opportunities.* Firms frequently experience a lack of growth opportunities in current markets. For example, Wal-Mart has recently introduced higher-priced merchandise because of lack of expansion opportunities in its traditional segment.
- *Prestige.* Firms often expand up-market to add prestige to their product line. It is likely that Ford acquired Jaguar, Volvo, and Aston Martin to add some prestigious, high-performance nameplates to its product line.
- *To become a full-line competitor.* Some companies extend their product line upward to become a full-line competitor. Being a full-line competitor is important in markets in which distributors or customers prefer to purchase a complete line of products.

A **trade-up strategy** is employed by a low-end company that introduces products to the high end of the market.

Risks of Trade-Up Strategy. There is no guarantee that an attempt by a firm to expand its product line upward will be successful. A trade-up strategy is subject to the following risks:

- *Great competitive intensity in high end.* The level of competitive intensity at the high-end segment may be great. If the high-end segment is dominated by powerful competitors, the up-market move may fail.
- *High-end competitors may counteract.* High-end competitors may counteract by entering the low-end segments in a cross-parry attempt to retaliate against the firm's move up-market.
- *Lack of credibility in high end.* High-end customers may not believe that the lower-end company can actually produce high-quality products. Lack of credibility has proven to be the downfall of many trade-up attempts in the past, including Sears' unsuccessful effort to become a more upscale retailer and Levi's effort to become a manufacturer of business wear and more expensive clothing. One way to overcome the credibility problem is to introduce the new high-end product using a different name and market it in a different way. For instance, Nissan introduced its luxury car division using a different name, Infiniti, to differentiate it from its other models.
- *Lack of resources.* In moving up, the low-end company may lack the resources and capabilities to adequately serve the high-end segment. Serving the needs of high-end segments commonly requires superior engineering skills, higher-quality products, and higher service capabilities. Lexus's entry into the luxury segment was, in large part, successful because Toyota had the resources and capabilities to produce a high-quality car at a lower cost than its competitors and support it with a service level that has become legendary in the car business.
- *Alienation of existing customers.* Retailers who trade up run the risk of alienating existing customers. For example, people who patronize low-end stores may not appreciate it when these stores begin to carry upscale merchandise. The Strategy in Action box describes Wal-Mart's decision to carry higher-priced merchandise as an example of the potential risks of such a move.

Strategy in Action

WAL-MART

Wal-Mart recently began selling upscale merchandise to more affluent shoppers who are looking for bargains. The reason for trading up is probably that Wal-Mart ran out of locations and it had to trade up in order to stay on its growth path. Many of its new stores are in well-off suburbs and include large grocery sections with gourmet desserts and fresh herbs, electronic sections with expensive big-screen televisions and digital cameras, and housewares sections that feature gourmet cookware. Also, in the grocery section, Kraft marshmallow spread shares the same space with Nutella, an imported chocolate-hazelnut purée.

According to industry experts, Wal-Mart's new strategy carries risks as it could alienate its traditional price-conscious customer base if it replaces too many private-label items with high-priced merchandise designed to appeal to higher-income shoppers. Many traditional shoppers may not feel at home when they look at premium-priced merchandise such as Godiva chocolate that is beyond their budget.[29]

A **trade-down strategy** is employed when a high-end company brings lower priced versions of its products to the mass-market segment of the market.

Trade-Down Strategy

A **trade-down strategy** is employed when a high-end company brings lower-priced versions of its products to the mass market segment of the market. For example, Mercedes-Benz, which traditionally has been producing high-end luxury cars, has recently introduced cars at lower prices. Firms trade down for a variety of reasons:

- *Limited growth opportunities in high end.* Premium-product firms are faced with limited growth opportunities due to highly competitive conditions or other reasons in the high end of the market. For example, Mercedes-Benz came under pressure by Toyota and Nissan when they introduced their high-end models Lexus and Infiniti respectively. Mercedes-Benz responded by reducing its bloated cost structure and introducing more models at the low end of the market.
- *To become a full-line competitor.* Some firms enter the low end of the market to become full-line competitors and benefit from the advantages of selling a full line. These advantages include satisfying customers demanding entire systems, economies of scale or scope associated with a longer product line, and satisfying those distributors who prefer to deal with companies that sell a full line of products.
- *Blocking or fighting brand.* Firms often employ the trade-down strategy as a blocking brand to obstruct access to the low end by competitors or as a fighting brand to confront a competitive entry at the low end.
- *Advertise as starting at a low price.* The low-end product gives a firm the ability to advertise its product line as starting at a low price.
- *Attract first-time buyers.* Some firms introduce entry-level models to attract young customers who cannot afford the more expensive models, hoping that they will remain loyal and will purchase higher-priced models as their incomes increase in the future. This strategy has been followed by BMW for years, and it has been adopted more recently by Mercedes and other companies.

Risks of Trade-Down Strategy. What are the risks of a trade-down strategy? Similar to a trade-up strategy, a trade-down strategy is associated with the following risks:

- *Tarnish image.* The low-end brand may tarnish or dilute the image of the higher-priced line. This is probably the single most important reason that many high-end companies do not venture into the low-end segment of their markets. A few years ago, Pierre Cardin began to license its brand name to a variety of manufacturers of inexpensive products. Although Pierre Cardin's revenues from royalties increased substantially, the value of the brand was cheapened and lost its prestigious and up-scale reputation.
- *Cannibalization of sales of high-end product.* There must be a distinct value difference between the different brands to prevent the low-end product from cannibalizing the sales of the higher-end product. **Cannibalization** occurs when the addition of a new product reduces the sales of one or more existing products. To achieve such a distinction in value, the low-end product should be marketed using different pricing, distribution, sales organization, and advertising strategies. For instance, Rollerblade, in addition to its premium-priced Rollerblade models, markets a different brand name called Blade Runner to bring lower-priced skates to the mass market. By giving the lower-priced skates a different brand name and marketing it in a different way, Rollerblade is able to uphold its high-quality image while covering the mass market with an inexpensive product.
- *Inconsistency in quality.* The low-end brand's quality must be consistent with the high-end brand's quality. That is, although prices are different, the low-end product must meet the same high standards of quality as the high-end product. Otherwise, the entire product line may be hurt from any inconsistencies in quality between the high- and low-end products. For example, any low-end Black & Decker product is clearly a Black & Decker product in quality and image, although there is a difference in the price between the low-end and high-end products. This preserves the company's reputation for high-quality equipment.

Cannibalization occurs when the addition of a new product reduces the sales of one or more existing products.

Product Line Extension Strategy

The **product line extension strategy** entails adding new products to serve customers' needs better, provide customers with more choices and options, and other reasons. For example, Procter & Gamble added Ultra Tide to its detergent product line to offer its customers more choice. Retailers often expand their product line to adapt to trends or serve local customers' needs more effectively, as the Indigo Books and Music company example described in the Strategy in Action box illustrates:[30]

Strategy in Action

INDIGO BOOKS AND MUSIC INC.

Heather Reisman, chief executive officer of Indigo Books and Music Inc., the company that owns Indigo, Chapters and Coles bookstores, has plans to convert the country's leading bookseller into a "cultural department store" rather than just a bookstore that sells other merchandise. As part of this plan, the company hired Eric Berthold, vice-president of the furnishings, housewares, and apparel retailer Caban, to help Indigo expand its assortment of "lifestyle" merchandise.

Indigo is planning to add more gift and non-book merchandise. The new merchandise will help fill stores that are too big for their location, according to Reisman. The new merchandise would be added to stores according to customers' needs. For example, two of its stores in Montreal and Toronto recently began selling Greek titles. Also, stores near universities will carry different things than stores in suburban locations. The new merchandise will be available mainly in Chapters and Indigo stores. However, limited offerings will be found in smaller mall-based Coles bookstores. The company's new $17-million software system will be an important part of Indigo's new strategy. This advanced information system will enable the company to assess store-by-store demand depending on the surrounding community's tastes and preferences and to make changes to merchandise carried by the store.

Product line extensions commonly use the same name as any well-known brand marketed by the same company. This way the new product benefits from the name recognition of the existing product and its introductory advertising costs are much lower. For example, when Advil introduced its Advil Migraine brand it was instantly recognized and benefited from Advil's wide brand recognition and reputation. Firms introduce line extensions for several reasons:

- *Strengthen product line.* Firms with weak product lines introduce or acquire products from other companies to reinforce them. For example, Bermuda-based Bacardi Ltd., the producer and marketer of a number of internationally known spirits including its Bacardi trademark brand, the world's top-selling spirit brand, acquired Grey Goose vodka, the top-selling premium vodka brand in the United States. The acquisition was expected to complement Bacardi's vodka line of spirits and make it a serious player in the vodka category.[31]
- *Lower costs.* As new items are added to the product line, overall costs decline due to economies of scale and scope. Economies of scale are obtained in areas such as production, advertising, and management. Economies of scope result from using the same component, such as a product platform, as an input to the production of two or more products and from improving the use of resources, including productive capacity and sales force personnel.

- *Enhance perceived value.* The perceived value of a company's product line may be enhanced by offering customers more variety. Many customers prefer variety instead of being loyal to a specific brand. By offering a variety of different breakfast cereals, Kellogg's has a good chance of retaining those customers who prefer to switch to different cereals. Product variety is especially important for customers who want to buy the whole range of products from one supplier. For example, airlines prefer to buy from one aircraft manufacturer because they save in maintenance, parts, and training. These savings are estimated at 10 to 20 percent of the aircraft's cost.[32]
- *Fill market gaps or preempt shelf space.* Some manufacturers introduce line extensions to fill out gaps in the market or to occupy and preempt more shelf space. Procter & Gamble has been a prime practitioner of this strategy, introducing multiple versions of its brands to prevent other companies from entering the market or gain access to retail shelf space.

Risks of Product Line Extensions. What are the risks of product line extensions? Managers attempting to extend their product lines need to be aware of the following risks:

- *Overextension.* A brand may suffer from overextension if it is used in too many line extensions. It is important that the original brand name does not lose its specific meaning as more items are added to the product line.
- *Cannibalization.* Cannibalization is another risk associated with product line extensions. Marketers must ensure that new line extensions target specific market segments and have a clear position in the product space to avoid interfering with other items in the product line. Cannibalization sometimes is intentional, as when firms replace existing products with improved versions. Also, cannibalization is beneficial when the new product replaces lower-margin products. However, careful analysis is needed to study the impact of cannibalization.

Marketing Services

Services have become an important part of modern economies. As demand for services has increased over the years, the percentage of services as a component of our national economy continues to grow. Recent socioeconomic trends such as an increase in individual incomes and demand for health, financial, and other services are responsible for the increase in the importance of services. Many of today's customers demand more than a good product. They expect solutions and a total experience from products they purchase. Offering a total experience often implies that the offering includes a substantial service component. These trends increase the demand for services.

Competitive reasons also account for the increased demand for services. Adding value through services can provide a firm with a competitive advantage. As markets mature and physical goods become low-margin, commodity businesses, manufacturing firms are adding various services to their products in order to add value and differentiate their offering from competing products. Some companies, instead of selling just physical products, sell a total experience. For example, many telecommunications companies regard their physical product as only a part of the total solution to a customer's communications needs and regard what they are selling to include logistics, delivery, order processing, billing, installation, and maintenance.[33]

Differences Between Products and Services

Services are different from products. A product is an object or a good, while a service is a performance or an effort. Marketing a performance is different from marketing a physical product. For example, marketing a product such as bottled water is different from

Figure 8.5   Service Characteristics and Marketing Challenges

Service Characteristic	Marketing Challenge
Intangibility	No storage
	No patents
	Difficult to communicate
	Difficult to price
	Customers can't take possession
Service heterogeneity	Difficult to standardize
	Quality control is difficult
Simultaneous production and consumption	Lack of mass production
	Consumer presence
	Other customers affect outcome
	Difficult to distribute
	Frontline employees important for service delivery
Perishability	Services cannot be inventoried
	Difficult to match demand and supply

marketing services such as banking. Banking services require trained personnel, convenient location, and quality of services. The marketing challenges associated with services are shown in Figure 8.5.

Services are more intangible than physical products. Although services often include physical products such as cars in car rental businesses, the service performance is intangible. This intangibility makes services difficult to evaluate. Also, services are inherently more heterogeneous than physical goods. A major reason for service heterogeneity is that most services are labour intensive, and it is difficult to standardize human work.

In many cases, the production of services coincides with its consumption. Whereas physical goods are produced in a factory separate from the customer, services are produced in a way that directly involves the customer. Because they are present, service customers are actively involved in the service production process and interact with the employees and physical resources.[34] Often customers are actively involved in helping to perform the service either by performing the service themselves as in self-serve gasoline stations or cooperating with service providers in hospitals, dental offices, or hair salons. Additionally, the people who use the particular service help define the nature of the experience themselves. For example, the quality of people who patronize a seaside resort help define the quality of the service people derive from the resort. If visitors to the resort are rowdy, the quality of the resort goes down.

Because a service is a performance rather than a tangible item, and it is produced and consumed at the same time, it is perishable and cannot be inventoried. So, unless the service is consumed while it is produced, it is wasted. For example, if the seats in an airplane are not filled, they cannot be stored in inventory, and the performance, measured by such categories as fuel consumption, equipment depreciation, and labour effort, is wasted. Therefore, productive capacity must be fully utilized. Additionally, when demand exceeds supply, the firm cannot meet it because it has no products in inventory. The firm must find ways to match demand levels with available capacity.

Manufacturing firms can hold inventories of their products as a hedge against fluctuations in demand. This allows them to operate their plants at constant levels and avoid costly interruptions in production. The inability to hold inventories poses significant challenges for service firms. For example, a rental car business will lose potential income if its vehicles sit idle on the company parking lot. Service firms also lose income when demand exceeds the productive capacity of the firm. For example, if an airplane fills up, passengers will purchase tickets from another airline.

Lack of inventories is especially a problem when there are wide fluctuations in demand as often happens in the airline, restaurant, and lodging industries. The problem of fluctuating demand can be solved through supply and demand management strategies. Service firms can smooth out fluctuations by offering special discounts or adding extra value to the product that encourage customers to change their plans during periods of low demand. During periods of high demand, a firm may ask customers to perform certain tasks normally performed by company personnel. For example, fast food restaurants rely on customers to pick up their trays during busy times. Supply management may involve adjusting the capacity of the service provider. Banquet halls adjust the room capacity based on the number of guests. Railroad companies add extra cars depending on demand conditions. Airlines fly aircraft more hours a day. Other companies use part-time employees during periods of high demand.

Many of the principles and tools used by managers of physical products apply to the marketing of services. But the differences between products and services create additional problems for service firms. Service managers need to address these concerns when designing their marketing mix. The rest of the chapter discusses several marketing mix strategies taking into account the unique characteristics of services.

Product Strategies for Services

Services consist of a core service and a cluster of supplemental services.[35] For example, the core service of an airline is the safe transportation of passengers by air between destinations. To remain in business, every airline has to offer safe air transportation, otherwise it will be driven into bankruptcy. The real determinant attributes in choosing among airlines include supplemental services, such as on-time arrival, frequent flyer programs, meals, and cities served. These services allow firms to differentiate themselves from the competition subject to industry standards. While large airlines such as Air Canada and American Airlines offer a range of amenities, discount airlines such as CanJet and WestJet offer fewer services in return for lower fares.

Because of their nature, services can be tailored to the needs of individual customers. For example, financial planners provide clients with a portfolio tailored to their specific requirements. But customization results in higher costs than standardization does. Service providers have to consider the trade-off between customization and standardization. In resolving the dilemma between adding value and keeping costs low, the firm needs to be aware of the criteria consumers use when making a choice, as some buyers might prefer lower prices while others may opt for the higher value offered by the customized services. Although it is difficult to standardize most services, some services are highly standardized. Examples include movie theatres, Internet banking, and museums. In some cases, standardization even results in greater speed, consistency, and savings, increasing customer value and satisfaction.

Service intangibility is another concern for service firms. Marketers can get around the intangibility issue by creating a tangible representation of the service. Educational institutions hand out diplomas as tangible proxies of their service. A credit card is also a tangible representation of the line of credit granted by the issuing financial institution. By issuing credit cards, these companies make it more convenient for customers to access this line of credit.

Technology has become an integral part of the service offering. Many companies use technologies to improve their service. For example, many companies use the Internet to provide customers with relevant information. Airport authorities install automated ticket checking machines to speed up the check-in process, making the process more convenient. Self-serve gasoline stations give customers quick-pay options.

The perishability of services also makes quality control for services challenging. Physical goods can be inspected for conformance to specifications after they are made but before they are sold to customers. This cannot be done with services. Because services are produced and consumed simultaneously, such inspection can take place only while the service is being performed. Since inspection after the service is provided is not possible, flaws in the service must be corrected before the service is provided again but it is best to ensure that the service is right the first time.

Marketers need to recognize that customers affect the atmosphere of high-contact service businesses and thus need to target appropriate segments of the population. For example, a restaurant that is trying to build up a clientele of middle-aged business executives should not target young, informally dressed customers.[36] Front 54 is a popular bar in St. Catharines, Ontario, that attracted mainly students from nearby Brock University. However, its sales began to decline when thug-like customers started patronizing the establishment. A service firm should try to discourage incompatible customers from visiting the premises. In other cases it should physically separate the different groups of customers. For example, hotels place convention attendees on a separate floor of the hotel.

Pricing of Services

Pricing services is not an easy task because of the difficulty of determining and allocating overhead costs. For this reason, service firms must have cost accounting systems that ensure the tasks of determining and allocating these costs are done properly. Service organizations try to match demand and supply to achieve maximum use of their productive capacity by charging appropriate prices. For example, airlines price their tickets high during the high season and charge lower prices during the off-season to increase demand. One concern with such pricing practice is that charging high prices when demand is high may lead to charges of gouging. Also, firms are reluctant to lower prices in case it suggests a deterioration of quality. For example, Honda Canada refused to lower its prices during a recent economic downturn in order to maintain its reputation for quality.

Service companies that lower prices to boost lagging demand must have capacity available to meet the expected increase in demand. For example, when Sprint Canada reduced long-distance telephone rates, it ran out of capacity because of increased demand, and it had to raise prices again. Firms that reduce prices to stimulate demand during non-peak times must understand the nature of consumer demand before such action is undertaken. For example, charging lower public transit rates during non-rush hour may not lead to increased demand for transit services if public transit riders cannot alter their work schedule to take advantage of the lower rates.

Distribution of Services

Because customers can't take possession of services, services must be sold directly to them in convenient locations where they expect to find them. Consequently, intermediaries play a less important role in services than physical goods. Also, mass production and distribution of services is very difficult. However, a service business can achieve wide distribution by opening outlets to increase customer convenience and reach large numbers of customers.

Because services are intangible, it is not always clear what the service is or what it does for the customer. People's satisfaction with services will be influenced by the nature of their interaction with service personnel, the quality of the service facilities, and the type of other customers using the same service. Factors such as location and schedule convenience as well as timely delivery of service are important determinants of service quality in cases in which the customer has to be physically present for the transaction. In these cases, the process of service delivery is very important. In cases where the customer doesn't visit the premises of the service firm, the process of service delivery is less important (although the outcome is). For example, financial services such as stock investing may be performed without the customer having to meet the stock broker in person.

Managers of service firms should look for opportunities to improve the delivery of their service through more convenient forms of delivery. Many service firms are using technology such as ATM machines or the Internet to improve the quality of their services and increase customer satisfaction. For example, many universities offer courses online for those students who cannot physically attend classes. Some service providers can package their services into a physical product. For example, some physical fitness instructors package their instructions on videotapes.

The service must be delivered in an efficient and timely manner so that receiving the service should not take longer than expected by consumers. Even when the service does not require the presence of the customer, such as dry cleaning, preparation of accounting statements, or repairing a car, the service should be performed in an expeditious way.

While manufacturers use physical distribution channels, service providers combine the service production facilities, distribution, and consumption into a simple entity. Service firms manage frontline personnel and the consumption behaviour of customers to ensure that other users of the service are not annoyed by their behaviour. For example, noisy hotel guests would disturb those guests who prefer quiet surroundings. For this reason, hotel managers either try to appeal to one group of customers but not the other or find ways to separate the two groups.

Promotion of Services

The promotional strategies discussed in the previous sections can be used not only for products but for services as well. For example, advertising can be used to inform prospective buyers about the service or any price reductions. But there are important differences between advertising products and advertising services. For example, since services cannot be inventoried, service promotion can help marketers influence demand to match available capacity. Unlike physical products, service firms benefit from buildings in prominent locations, store fronts, window displays, and company trucks emblazoned with the company's name and colour that help create awareness for the business.

In addition to selling the product to customers, advertising can target employees to encourage them to deliver higher-quality service. In fact, service firms could use their own employees in their promotion.[37] To counteract the intangible nature of service, firms should provide tangible representations of the service by showing their employees, physical facilities, or equipment. For example, commercial airlines often feature flight crews and airplanes in an effort to make their service more tangible. Some service businesses use animals as physical symbols. For example, Merrill Lynch uses the logo of a bull while Lloyd's of London uses a black horse. Service companies could also use tangible metaphors to make intangible claims easier to understand. For example, the Co-operators Insurance Company claims to be "a better place for you" while Allianz Insurance promotes itself as "the power behind the promise."[38]

Promotions for services can be implemented more rapidly than for physical goods. Manufacturing firms need to ship additional merchandise to meet the anticipated increase in demand. Service firms, on the other hand, can use several supply-management methods to match the demand with the supply. These could include the use of part-time employees, customer participation when demand is high, and peak-time efficiency routines such as servicing vehicles when demand is slow.

- Marketing success depends on a firm's ability to design, produce, and market products that meet customers' needs at a profit.

- New products are essential for maintaining a firm's competitive position. Companies rely on technology-push and market-pull approaches to product development. New products are developed because, among other reasons, they provide firms with a competitive advantage and help meet consumer needs.

- Effective new product development requires a new product strategy to guide its activities. A new product strategy involves the following: it sets the new-product development objectives; it specifies an appropriate area of search for new products; it spells out ways to help bring together the various team members and increase team effectiveness; it specifies organizational policies to improve the speed of new product development; and it decides the timing of entry into the market (first mover vs. late entrant).

- The stage-gate process acts as a framework that adds focus to the new-product development effort. The stage-gate system enables firms to eliminate non-viable new product ideas quickly and inexpensively before they reach production and commercialization, where the cost is much higher. This process requires that the product development process is divided into several stages or activities, including idea generation and preliminary assessment, assessment, product development, validation, and commercial launch.

- Market entry strategies include first-mover and late-mover strategies.

- The product life cycle is a basic concept in marketing. It consists of five stages: introduction, growth, shakeout, maturity, and decline. Companies need to change their marketing strategies over the product's life cycle.

- Product line strategies include trade-up, trade-down, and product-line extensions. Each strategy has its specific advantages and risks. One common risk is that firms may deviate too much from the core areas of expertise, spreading themselves too thinly.

- The main differences between physical products and services are intangibility, service heterogeneity, simultaneous production and consumption, and perishability. These differences give rise to certain marketing problems that need to be taken into consideration when developing marketing strategies for services.

Review and Discussion Questions

1. Describe the two approaches to new product development.

2. Describe the classification of new products.

3. Why do firms need a new product strategy? What are the elements of a new product strategy?

4. Briefly describe the stage-gate process of new product development.

5. Describe concept testing.

6. What are the advantages and disadvantages of first-mover and late-mover strategy?

7. Describe the marketing strategies appropriate for the introduction, growth, shakeout, maturity, and declining markets.

8. Describe the trade-up, trade-down, and product line extension strategies. Discuss the reasons companies are using these strategies and the potential risks involved when employing these strategies.

9. Discuss the characteristics of services and the marketing challenges caused by these characteristics.

1. Referring back to the opening vignette, what would have happened if Toyota hadn't changed its product innovation strategy?

2. Harper Manufacturers is a small company that makes premium-quality bicycles for high-income bicycle enthusiasts. Over the years, Harper has acquired a reputation for making one of the highest-quality bicycles on the market. James Conan, its marketing director, has lately been pushing the idea of making a low-priced version of their highly successful product for the masses. Is this a good idea? If no, why? If yes, how would you market this low-priced product?

3. Several manufacturers of luxury automobiles, including Mercedes-Benz and BMW, have introduced low-priced versions of their products in recent years. What are the risks of such a strategy? Would you recommend that these companies bring into the market even lower versions of their products?

4. Sears attempted to move up several years ago and become a high-end retailer. This effort failed, and the company was forced to withdraw to its previous position. Using your knowledge of product line strategies described in this chapter, discuss alternative strategies Sears could use to achieve its objective of moving up-market. How would you implement your recommended strategies?

5. Contact a local manufacturer and analyze his or her new-product development strategy. Does this manufacturer have a new product strategy? Is a system similar to the stage-gate new-product development system being used?

Notes

1. This case draws from Jeffery K. Liker, *The Toyota Way: 14 Management Principles from the World's Greatest Manufacturer* (New York: McGraw-Hill, 2004).
2. Dipak Jain, "Managing New Product Development for Strategic Advantage," in Dawn Iacobucci (ed.), *Kellogg on Marketing* (New York: Wiley, 2001), 130–147.
3. Karl T. Ulrich and Steven D. Eppinger, *Product Design and Development* (New York: McGraw-Hill, 1995), 21.
4. Booz, Allen and Hamilton, Inc., *New Product Management for the 1980s, Phase I* (New York: Booz, Allen and Hamilton, Inc. 1981), cited in Alexander Hiam and Charles D. Schewe, *The Portable MBA in Marketing* (New York: Wiley, 1992), 243.
5. C. Merle Crawford, *New Products Management* (Homewood, Ill.: Irwin, 1991), 45.
6. Liker, 5.
7. Roger A. Kerin, P. Rajan Varadarajan, and Robert A. Peterson, "First-Mover Advantage: A Synthesis, Conceptual Framework, and Research Propositions," *Journal of Marketing* 56 (October 1992), 33–52.
8. Gerard J. Tellis and Peter N. Golder, *Will and Vision* (New York: McGraw-Hill, 2002), 41.
9. Robert G. Cooper, "Stage-Gate System: A New Tool for Managing New Products," *Business Horizons,* May–June 1990, 44–54.
10. Milton D. Rosenau Jr., "Choosing a Development Process That Is Right for Your Company," in Milton D. Rosenau Jr., (ed.), *PDMA Handbook of New Product Development,* (New York: Wiley, 1996), 87.
11. Stephen R. Rosenthal, *Effective Product Design and Development* (Homewood, Ill.: Business One Irwin, 1992), 26.
12. Paul Geroski, Richard Gilbert, and Alexis Jacquemin, *Barriers to Entry and Strategic Competition* (New York: Harwood Academic Publishers, 1990).
13. R. Schmalensee, "Product Differentiation Advantages of Pioneering Brands," *American Economic Review* 72 (June, 1982), 159–180.
14. Pui-Wing Tam, "Popularity of iPod amplifies Apple profit," *The Globe and Mail,* April 15, 2004, B9.
15. David J. Teece, "Profiting from Technological Innovation: Implications for Integrating Collaboration, Licensing and Public Policy," in David J. Teece (ed.), *The Competitive Challenge: Strategies for Industrial Innovation and Renewal* (Cambridge, Mass.: Ballinger Publishing Company, 1987), 185–219.
16. Edwin Mansfield, Mark Schwartz, and Samuel Wagner, "Imitation Costs and Patents: An Empirical Study," *Economic Journal* 91 (December 1981), 907–918.
17. Peter F. Drucker, *Innovation and Entrepreneurship* (New York: Harper & Row Publishers, 1985).
18. Johny K. Johansson and Ikujiro Nonaka, Relentless: *The Japanese Way of Marketing* (New York: HarperBusiness, 1996), 73.
19. William L. Moore and Edgar A. Pessemier, *Product Planning and Management* (New York: McGraw-Hill, 1993), 49.
20. Mary Lambkin and George S. Day, "Evolutionary Processes in Competitive Markets: Beyond the Product Life Cycle," *Journal of Marketing* 53 (July 1989), 4–20.
21. Laura M. Birou, Stanley E. Fawcett, and Gregory M. Magnan, "The Product Life Cycle: A Tool for Functional Strategic Alignment," *International Journal of Purchasing and Materials,* Spring 1998, 37–51.
22. Steven P. Schnaars, *Managing Imitation Strategies: How Late Entrants Seize Markets from Pioneers* (New York: The Free Press, 1994), 15.
23. William J. Abernathy and James M. Utterback, "Patterns of Industrial Innovation," *Technology Review* 80 (1978), 41–47.
24. Alexander Hiam and Charles D. Schewe, *The Portable MBA in Marketing* (New York: Wiley, 1992), 255.
25. George S. Day, "Strategies for Surviving a Shakeout," *Harvard Business Review,* (March–April, 1997), 92–102.
26. Kenichi Ohmae, *The Borderless World: Power and Strategy in the Interlinked Economy* (New York: HarperBusiness, 1990), 38–40.
27. Kathryn Rudy Harrigan, Strategies for Joint Ventures (Lexington, Mass.: Lexington Books, 1985).
28. Michael Porter, "What Is Strategy?" *Harvard Business Review* (November–December 1996), 61–78.
29. Constance L. Hays, "Enriched by Working Class, Wal-Mart Eyes BMW Crowd," *New York Times,* February 24, 2002.
30. Dana Flavelle, "Next chapter Indigo: More gifts," *Toronto Star,* June 9, 2004, E1.
31. Jane Sutton, "Bacardi reaches deal to buy Grey Goose," *The Globe and Mail,* June 21, 2004, p. B8.
32. Joseph P. Guiltinan, "A Strategic Framework for Assessing Product Line Additions," *Journal of Product Innovation Management* 10 (1993), 136–147.
33. Anders Gustafsson and Michael D. Johnson, *Competing in a Service Economy: How to Create a Competitive Advantage Through Service Development and Innovation* (San Francisco: Jossey-Bass, 2003), 3.
34. Gustafsson and Johnson, 4.
35. Christopher H. Lovelock, *Services Marketing,* 2nd ed. (Englewood Cliffs, N.J.: Prentice Hall, 1991), 18.
36. Lovelock, 121.
37. William R. George and Leonard L. Berry, "Guidelines for the Advertising of Services," *Business Horizons* (July–August), 1981.
38. George and Berry.

Chapter Nine

Brand Strategy

Manufacturers make products; consumers buy brands.

Jean-Noël Kapferer, Brand Strategist

Learning Objectives

After studying this chapter, you should be able to:

1. Distinguish between the different types of brands

2. Explain the importance of brands for consumers and companies

3. Describe the meaning of brand equity

4. Measure the value of brands

5. Understand the strategic roles of brands

6. Describe the barriers to successful brand building

7. Discuss how to build strong brands

8. Explain the desired characteristics of effective brand names

Cavendish Farms' Brand Building Activities

Cavendish Farms is the second-largest french fry brand in Canada, trailing market leader McCain and outpacing private-label brands. Historically, Cavendish Farms has been a market follower with a value-price position. Communication with customers consisted mostly of free-standing inserts (FSIs) and occasional in-store activities.

With the changing Canadian retail landscape, due to consolidation and the growth of private-label brands, it was clear Cavendish Farms needed to do something to support and grow the brand for the future. To achieve these objectives, the management of Cavendish Farms decided to undertake new product-innovation and brand-building activities. The first step was to find out what the brand stood for. A series of consumer focus groups were conducted in collaboration with Michelle Massie Marketing of Toronto. The cities selected for this research were Halifax, Montreal, and Toronto, reflecting the focus of Cavendish Farms' market in Ontario and east. The results turned up a few pleasant surprises. French fries have a far greater emotional connection than initially presumed. They're not just a fast, simple, and appealing side dish to serve at home. Comments from respondents in all groups made it clear that "eating fries contributes to feelings of nostalgia, joy, fun, contentment, comfort, being together as a family and showing your family you care about them."

Even better news was that there was already considerable strength behind the Cavendish Farms brand. Both users and non-users saw Cavendish as a potato specialist with products that are "natural, wholesome, and fun." The name itself conjures up images of "a farm where people are active and friendly and where potatoes are grown and harvested." Cavendish Farms consumers rated taste, followed by golden appetizing colour and consistent quality, as the main reasons they prefer the brand.

Meanwhile, back in the R&D lab in New Annan, P.E.I., Cavendish researchers had reformulated their regular french fry and now had a product with both enhanced taste and colour. In blind taste tests, the new product scored overwhelmingly well on both counts. The challenge was to get the consumer to try it. Cavendish Farms enlisted the help of Cossette Communication-Marketing, which had produced successful television spots for Cavendish's sister company Irving Tissue and its Majesta and Royale brands.

Scott Armstrong, national group account director with Cossette's Toronto office, explains, "While we knew we had a foundation of some strength in the Cavendish brand from which to build, there was also the perception that Cavendish Farms was a little too 'laid back, down home' and therefore not seen as being extremely innovative. Our mandate was to break through the clutter with innovation and creativity and change that perception with increased product trial."

Two creative concepts were tested with focus groups conducted by Cossette's Impact Research and it became clear that the ad called "Sample Lady" met the strategy on all counts—it was entertaining, clearly delivering the message of great taste, and encouraging non-users to try the Cavendish product. The ad starts with a father and son in a grocery store. The father agrees to let his son try one french fry from the sample lady. They like the taste so much, they come back for more but the lady won't give them another sample. The father then goes through a series of increasingly desperate moves in order to get more fries. He even turns off the store lights. Once the power is back on, we see both the father and son with their mouths full of french fries.

The 30-second spot ran from February to June, took a summer hiatus when french fry sales are traditionally soft, and was back on air in the fall. The "Sample Lady" concept provided a natural bridge to conduct an in-store sampling program in all regions within

(continued)

the first month of the spot airing. It quickly became clear that the ad was noticed and extremely well liked. Post-wave research—research carried out after the communication program ended—conducted by Ipsos-ASI showed that brand awareness, usage, and purchase intent all showed significant increases. Cavendish Farms market share also showed gains and sales growth exceeded targets. These results made clear to management that its efforts to build a strong brand were successful as evidenced by the increased awareness and market share of its brand.[1]

Introduction

As we've seen in the opening vignette, Cavendish Farms' brand-building activities developed a strong brand that helped the company achieve its sales growth objectives. A key goal of any marketing program is to build and maintain strong brands. Companies that own well-recognized and highly regarded brands perform well in the marketplace. Brands are among a firm's most valuable assets because they link products to desirable associations such as quality, trust, or prestige. Brands represent important long-term relationships between consumers and products. They are also valuable because many people prefer to buy brands that they like and trust. Because people cannot normally evaluate a product before they buy and actually use it, they place their faith in the brands that they trust most.

Branding has had a long history in commerce and trade. It has been used since ancient times on products such as bricks to identify the producer and distinguish one good from another. Trademarks were used in medieval Europe by guilds to provide legal protection to the producer and assure the customer of the quality of the product.

The presence of brand names influences people's choice, demonstrating the power of brands.[2] In many product categories there are only minor differences between brands. For example, blind taste tests of beer brands show no significant differences in taste. When the tests were repeated with brand names present, there were significant differences in preferences.

Brand names are used to identify products or services and differentiate them from the competition.[3] Strong brands reduce the importance of pricing by focusing on attributes, features, and other product aspects. Therefore, strong brands are more than commodities as they link their products with a unique and desirable image. The difference between a branded and an unbranded product is the perceptions and feelings of consumers about the product, its name, and the company that owns the brand.[4]

Branding is an important strategic decision. While traditionally branding was viewed as simply naming products, today it is considered an important determinant of market success. This type of thinking about the role of branding is due, in large part, to the realization that brands are a source of competitive advantage and their value, in many cases, can far exceed the value of the physical and financial assets of the organization.

A brand is built over a long time. Developing strong brands may take years and, once developed, they require a continuous effort to maintain them. Building and maintaining a strong brand requires maintaining consistency in positioning and all aspects of the marketing mix strategy—product, price, distribution, and promotion.[5] Strong brands compete on product quality and features, not on price. Companies selling strong brands base their price on the value of the brand and avoid price-based promotions. They know not only that a low price can suggest low quality but that price promotions erode brand loyalty and focus customers' attention on price and away from product attributes.

Strong brands have amazing staying power. Ivory soap, Tide detergent, and Goodyear tires have remained category leaders for decades. Brands that failed to evolve over the years by making the necessary changes—in light of market changes—have lost their dominance or market leadership. Such brands include Eaton's, Kmart, Xerox, and Polaroid. No matter how strong a brand is, it needs constant nurturing and careful management.

The Strategy in Action box offers an example of brand mismanagement by the company that owns the Cardhu distillery:[6]

The purpose of brand strategy is to build powerful brands. Powerful brands dominate their category. Examples of powerful brands are Coke (refreshing), Volvo (safety), Gillette with Sensor (closest shave), Colgate (healthiest teeth), and Tide (exceptional cleaning). In this chapter we explain the nature of brands and the importance of brands for consumers and companies. The meaning of the components of brand equity will also be discussed. A number of different methods to measure the value of brands will be examined. Next, the strategic role of brands will be looked at. The barriers to successful brand building and several guidelines for building strong brands will be discussed. Lastly, the desired characteristics of effective brand names will be covered.

What Is a Brand?

A **brand** is a name, symbol, sign, logo, trademark, or design that is used to identify products, differentiate them from competitors, and protect consumers and companies from counterfeit products or imitators. Successful brands offer more than the product's basic attributes, as shown in Figure 9.1. They include the product category (Canada Dry is a soft drink), physical attributes (Hummers are large automobiles), features (personal computers have flat monitors), intangible attributes (prestige, status, fun, heritage), symbols (Green Giant, BMW emblem, McDonald's arches), and other characteristics.

Brands have higher value than commodities. **Commodities** are products that are perceived as lacking any meaningful differences, such as grain, potatoes, and aluminum. The value of a commodity equals the sum of the product's components. Brands are more valuable than commodities because they incorporate intangible attributes, such as reputation, trust, image, and styling not found in commodities. However, commodities can be turned into brands. For example, Evian water, although it is based on natural spring water, has become a strong brand sold around the world with the help of advertising that informs people about the quality of the brand, packaging, and high bottling standards.

Strong brands require more than just putting a name on the product that simply identifies the product or a product line. Brand names are assets that stand for a specific set of benefits, values, and meaning for customers. They signal a certain level of quality that customers should expect to receive from a product. These attributes help differentiate a product from its competition. For example, Rolex is not just a watch to its owners but a status symbol, and it invokes images of engineering excellence and premium quality.

A **brand** is a name, symbol, sign, logo, trademark, or design that is used to identify products, differentiate them from competitors, and protect consumers and companies from counterfeit products or imitators.

Commodities are products that are perceived as lacking any meaningful differences, such as grain, potatoes, and aluminum.

Figure 9.1 | Components of Brands

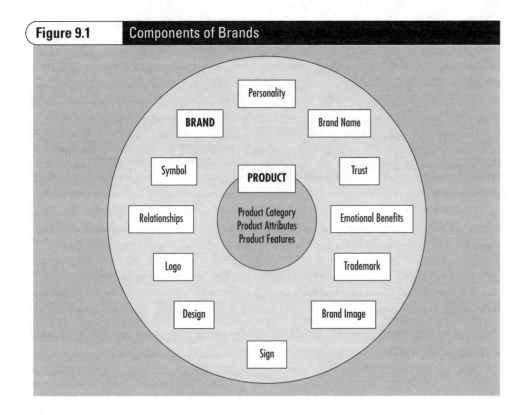

Brand names convey information about the brand. They are also used as devices to help consumers retrieve information stored in their long-term memory about the brand. This stored information is the result of repeated advertising campaigns that link the product with desirable benefits and establish a well-defined image in the minds of customers. As a result, strong brands, such as The Bay and Labatt's Blue, do not need to bombard consumers with large quantities of information. In some cases the brand is so strong that the mere sight of a brand symbol associated with the brand, such as the Nike swoosh or McDonald's golden arches, is enough to remind people of the brand and its benefits.

Consumers often associate brands with a certain personality. For example, Nike means individualism, Kodak is a sincere brand, whereas Marlboro is considered rugged. Coke is perceived as real and authentic, and Pepsi is thought of as young, exciting, and spirited.[7] Brands may become symbols of relationships between products and customers. Such relationships draw people back to the brand time and time again. The Strategy in Action box describes how people protested as if they had lost a valuable friend when Coca-Cola introduced its new Coke in the mid-1980s.[8]

Strategy in Action

COKE

In 1985, Coke replaced its traditional formula with the new and improved version, which it called New Coke. Coke drinkers worldwide were outraged. Some 8,000 complaints were coming in every day to the head office of the Coca-Cola Company. People hated the new taste and demanded their old Coke back. According to reports, in rural Alabama a minister led his Sunday congregation in prayer for the local Coke bottler's soul. Another Coke drinker wrote to the company, "My dearest

(continued)

Coke: You have betrayed me. We went out just last week, as we had so often, and when we kissed I knew our love affair was over. . . . I remember walks across campus with you discussing life and love and all that matters. . . . I remember the southern summer nights we shared with breezes leaving beads of water hanging delicately from your body. . . . But last week, I tasted betrayal on your lips: you had the smooth, seductive sweet taste of a lie. . . ."

On July 10 that same year, the Coca-Cola Company held a press conference and announced that Coke drinkers would be getting their favourite "original" cola back (now called Coke Classic). The New Coke had lasted only three months—June sales of the New Coke dropped off the map.

The reaction of loyal Coke drinkers is testament to the tremendous value of the Coke brand. Although many people prefer sweeter colas, they buy Coke because of the relationship they have developed over the years with the brand. Also, Coca-Cola has done well by capitalizing on the worldwide recognition of its brand. Part of Coca-Cola's growth over the years has come from introducing line extensions of its flagship brand, Coke. It introduced Diet Coke in 1982, Diet Coke with lemon in 2001, and Vanilla Coke in May 2002, and more recently Diet Vanilla Coke.

Types of Brands

Functional brands focus primarily on the physical features of the product. They help consumers fulfill functional needs such as health, safety, or food.

Brands may be classified into functional, image, and experiential brands[9] (see Figure 9.2). **Functional brands** focus primarily on the physical features of the product. They help consumers fulfill functional needs such as health, safety, or food. Examples of functional brands include computers, laundry detergents, and over-the-counter drugs. Functional brands are commonly differentiated from the competition on the basis of performance or price. For example, Tylenol is the market leader in the over-the-counter pain-killer market and competes on the basis of excellent performance. On the other hand, Dollar Stores compete by striving to offer consumers the lowest prices possible without pretending to excel in quality or in-store service. In managing functional brands, firms should invest resources in improving product performance or make the product less expensive.

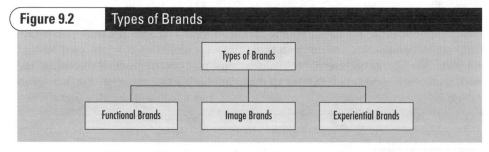

Figure 9.2 — Types of Brands

Types of Brands

Functional Brands   Image Brands   Experiential Brands

Image brands strive to create a distinct image for the product and achieve an emotional connection with consumers.

Experiential brands focus on the interaction between consumers and brands and emphasize the feelings experienced by people when they consume the brand.

Image brands strive to create a distinct image for the product. Image is the manner in which consumers perceive a brand. Successful image brands achieve an emotional connection with consumers. Image building is particularly useful when there are no significant differences between brands in the same category. Also, many products such as clothing, perfume, and premium automobiles that are highly visible to other people are purchased primarily for their symbolic value. These brands enable consumers to communicate a certain image, feelings, or status about themselves.

Experiential brands focus on the interaction between consumers and brands. They emphasize the feelings experienced by people when they consume the brand. They invoke memorable events to customers and offer a larger experience than the specific benefits or image offered by other brands. Experiential brands include Club Med resorts, Starbucks, and Walt Disney World. Families take their children to Disney World for a shared experience that will last for a long time.

Many marketers of functional and image brands attempt to increase the experiential content of their brands. Restaurants try to turn customers' visits into a memorable experience by creating a pleasant environment and offering an exceptional service that customers will remember for a long time. Coca-Cola has invested in an experiential marketing program that involves experience-based activities such as a Coca-Cola Experience section at Atlanta's Turner Field baseball stadium where spectators can drink Coca-Cola products and watch the game. The Strategy in Action box describes the introduction of Acura RL, which was marketed as an experiential brand.[10]

Strategy in Action

ACURA

Acura, Honda's luxury division, has always had a reputation for reliability, luxury features, and superior quality combined with a price that provides value other automobile manufacturers find hard to beat. But it seems that RL, Acura's most recent entry into the crowded luxury segment, is changing the company's pricing and brand strategy. Traditionally Acura used value-pricing, charging lower prices than its competitors, but its new 2005 model was priced at $69,500, making it more expensive than the comparable versions of its major competitors, the Mercedes-Benz E-Class, BMW 5 series, and Audi A6.

Acura's brand strategy has been changing too. The company markets the RL as the ultimate experiential luxury car. According to Acura, luxury car buyers are fragmented into two distinct groups, traditionalists and experientialists. Traditionalists are those who prefer solid, old standards of prestige such as luxury leather, wood, and chrome. Experientialists, on the other hand, favour a more modern interpretation of luxury based more on experience than on status symbols. They buy luxury cars because of their performance, not their image. These buyers seek innovative brands such as Acura instead of the traditional luxury alternatives because, in their thinking, these new brands are loaded with those features that enhance the driving experience.

The company supports its experiential branding strategy with many items found in traditional luxury cars such as high-quality leather, wood, and heated and cooled seats to more innovative high-tech features such as a "blue-lit electroluminescent gauge" with dials that seem to float in space. Other features used to enhance the driving experience include electric blue mood lighting for night use and features such as a 10-speaker DVD-audio Bose sound system, Bluetooth integration for phone and personal organizer, and DVD-based navigation with voice commands.

The Importance of Brands for Consumers

Brands are important to consumers. They help consumers form expectations about the future performance of the brand based on past performance.[11] Brands assume special meaning for consumers. For this reason, brands may be looked at differently by the same individuals or organizations. People often use brands to communicate to others who they are, and they can play a significant role when consumers are choosing products. Brands are important to consumers for the following three reasons:

1. *Shorthand device.* Brands are shorthand devices that simplify decision-making.[12] Consumers use brands to decide about which ones to purchase because brand

Financial risk involves the concern that the product may not be worth the price.

Functional risk involves the concern that the product may not work properly.

Physical risk involves concern that the product may not be safe.

Social risk involves the concern that peers may not approve of the choice.

Psychological risk involves the risk that the buyer will not feel good about the purchase.

names contain large amounts of information about the brand. For instance, buyers of such highly complex products as cameras or camcorders use brand names as a source of valuable information about these products. This minimizes the need for information search and evaluation by consumers. This is an important property of brands in a world in which buyers are faced with an increasing number of brands but less time to choose among them.

2. *Enhance perceived value.* The strength of the brand affects its perceived value. Customers experience a greater perceived value when they purchase well-known brands even if the brand is similar to other lesser-known brands. Consequently, strong brands provide customers with more confidence in their purchasing decisions.

3. *Reduce risk.* Purchasing products involves a degree of risk for customers. Perceived risk includes **financial risk** (is it worth the price?); **functional risk** (will it work properly?); **physical risk** (is it safe?); **social risk** (will peers approve of the choice?); and **psychological risk** (will the buyer feel good about the purchase?).[13] People purchase well-known brands as a means of reducing perceived risk.[14] For example, brands that symbolize prestige and status provide customers with psychological benefits that reduce the social and psychological risk related to purchasing the wrong product.[15] The risk-reducing ability of brands is especially important in decisions involving substantial risk such as the purchase of high-priced consumer products.

The Importance of Brands for Companies

A firm's most valuable assets are often not tangible assets such as plants, equipment, and building, but intangible assets such as marketing and financial skills and the value of brands. Some companies such as Motorola (the maker of cellular telephones), Sara Lee Corporation (Sara Lee food products, Hanes underwear, Kiwi shoe polish, Hillshire Farm products), Baskin-Robbins (ice cream), and Calvin Klein (jeans, underwear, fragrances) have a few tangible assets and outsource most of the manufacturing of their products while they concentrate on the task of managing their brands.[16] Brands are important to firms for the following reasons:

1. *Product differentiation.* Strong brands differentiate the firm's product from competing products. This provides firms with a competitive advantage that is difficult for rivals to overcome. For example, Apple iPod is such a strong name in portable music players that it is difficult for its competitors to successfully challenge it. Branding also allows companies to differentiate products that consumers perceive as similar to other products in the category. For example, over the years through appropriate branding efforts many categories that seem difficult to differentiate, such as water, soap, chickens, and salt, have become differentiated.[17]

2. *Credibility.* Brands provide credibility through a commitment to building and maintaining a set of desirable associations that persist over a long period of time. This creates satisfaction that earns the loyalty of customers. Brand loyalty, in turn, helps attract and retain customers, provide sales stability, and ensure long-run profits. Firms with loyal customers are less vulnerable to competitors' actions and price competition. Loyal customers are less likely to switch when the price of their favourite brand increases.[18] Brand loyalty also creates a barrier to entry, as it is difficult for other firms to enter the market and successfully challenge the firm.

3. *Adding value.* Branding adds value to a product. For example, heavily branded products such as perfumes and cosmetics command a much higher price than similar unbranded products. Nike has created a strong brand, and as a result it charges higher prices than less-known brands. Branded products are routinely priced at 30 to 50 percent higher than unbranded products.

4. *Source of future revenues.* Strong brands guarantee future revenues and make demand for a firm's product more predictable. For this reason, strong brands command a premium over the book value of the company's tangible assets that appear on a balance sheet. Nestlé purchased Rowntree, the maker of chocolate products Rolo, Kit-Kat, Quality Street, and After Eight, in April of 1988 for $5.3 billion, more than five times its book value.[19] The large premiums paid for these brands are justified on the basis of the high profits that can be earned from these products. In addition, companies prefer to acquire well-known brands and pay a premium for them because it is extremely difficult to build strong brands, given the high cost of advertising in recent years and the large number of competing brands.

5. *Enhancing effectiveness of marketing activities.* Strong brands increase the effectiveness of marketing activities. For example, advertising is more effective if consumers are already familiar with the brand and have favourable attitudes toward it. Consumers are more likely to notice an advertisement if they are familiar with the brand. Also, well-known brands are less vulnerable to confusion from competitive advertisements.[20] Additionally, strong brands help manufacturers deal with the growing power of retailers and gain greater trade cooperation and support. A brand that has a strong consumer following is likely to receive greater trade cooperation and more favourable treatment as distributors are more receptive to brands produced by manufacturers with a reputation for building strong brands.

6. *Legal protection.* Branding serves as a means of legal protection of the brand from counterfeit products through trademark registration. Firms typically defend their brands rigorously against competitors who use similar brand names or packaging. For example, McDonald's takes legal action against any fast food company that uses brand names sounding similar to its Big Mac. The Strategy in Action box describes Microcell's efforts to protect its brand from rivals.[21]

Strategy in Action   MICROCELL

In March of 2004, Microcell Telecommunications, owner of the Fido cellular phone brand, filed an injunction against Telus, Bell Mobility, and Rogers Wireless to prohibit them from using its trademarks and brand identity. Microcell's contention was that Fido's competitors featured dogs in their ads. Microcell objected to such practice because it had used dogs in its ads to promote its Fido brand since the brand was established. According to Alain Rheaume, president of Microcell, the action was taken to protect its Fido brand, one of its most valuable assets. In his view, Fido's competitors' activities were damaging to its brand as they were copying one of his company's most valuable symbols.

7. *Capitalizing on the strength of the brand.* Firms often capitalize on the strength of their brands and introduce new brands using the name of a well-known brand. For example, Harley-Davidson, the U.S. motorcycle manufacturer, extends its name to a variety of merchandise such as toys, motorcycle accessories, gifts, and Motorclothes merchandise.[22] Successful brand names such as Gucci and Pierre Cardin are also licensed to third-party manufacturers for use on their products such as luggage, perfumes, accessories, and clothing.

Brand Equity

Brand equity is a set of assets linked to the product or service that add to its value.

Successful branding requires an understanding of the concept of brand equity. **Brand equity** is a set of assets linked to the product or service that add to its value.[23] These assets are brand awareness, brand loyalty, perceived quality, brand associations, and other proprietary assets such as patents, trademarks, channel relationships, customer relationships, and trust, as shown in Figure 9.3.[24] Brand equity represents the incremental value of a brand or business over and above the value of its physical assets.

Figure 9.3	Elements of Brand Equity

- Brand awareness
- Brand loyalty
- Perceived quality
- Brand associations
- Other proprietary assets

Brand awareness represents the strength of the brand's presence in buyers' memory and reflects the consumers' ability to recognize or recall the brand within the category.

Brand awareness represents the strength of the brand's presence in buyers' memory and reflects the consumers' ability to recognize or recall the brand within the category.[25] Brand awareness is an asset because widely recognized brands are preferred over less-known brands. People prefer the brands they are familiar with and perceive them as superior to less recognized brands. This is especially true in the case of low-involvement (low-risk or low-importance) products where consumers choose products on the basis of brand awareness without prior formation of brand attitudes.[26]

Aided awareness measures people's ability to recognize the brand name when they are presented with the brand, or when the name of the brand is mentioned, or some other type of cue is given.

There are two types of awareness. **Aided awareness** measures people's ability to recognize the brand name when they are presented with the brand, or when the name of the brand is mentioned, or some other type of cue is given. **Unaided awareness** measures the ability to retrieve the brand from memory without cues or other aids. A special type of unaided awareness is **top-of-mind awareness,** which measures whether the brand is the first one that comes to mind when the product category is mentioned.

Unaided awareness measures the ability to retrieve the brand from memory without cues or other aids.

Moving from aided awareness to unaided awareness represents a higher degree of awareness and it is more difficult to attain. This however does not mean that unaided awareness should always be the aim of a brand's strategy. The decision of which type of consumer awareness to attempt to achieve depends on the particular situation. Aided awareness is useful for decisions made at the point of purchase, as in the case of purchasing grocery products.[27] Even if unaided awareness is low, if the customer recognizes the brand in the store, the brand will have a large advantage over unrecognized brands.[28] Unaided awareness is important in situations in which the buyer must remember the brand name and make a decision prior to the point of purchase. Thus, a firm may not always be justified in making a large investment in obtaining high levels of top-of-mind awareness or unaided awareness. In these cases, if the level of aided awareness is adequate, management may be better off to increase distribution and the size of its sales force or take some other action rather than increasing awareness.

Top-of-mind awareness measures whether the brand is the first one that comes to mind when the product category is mentioned.

Brand loyalty is the degree to which consumers feel attached to a brand.

Brand loyalty is the degree to which consumers feel attached to a brand. Strong brands have loyal customers—repeat customers with a favourable attitude toward the brand. Loyal customers are valuable customers because they ensure future sales and profits and protect the company from competitive challenges. These customers are willing to pay a premium for their favourite brand. Brand-loyal consumers are not willing to substitute their favourite brand with another brand when the former is not available.

Brand loyalty creates a switching cost and shields the brand from competitors. The higher the brand loyalty, the lower the vulnerability of the brand to competitors' actions.

Truly loyal customers are committed customers who are proud to be owners of the brand, and they feel that the brand is a very important part of their lives. They recommend the brand to others. Brand-loyal customers sometimes become **product evangelists** by actively promoting the brand to others. Products or services that have enjoyed a strong following include Harley-Davidson motorcycles, Beetle automobiles of the 1960s, and Apple Macintosh computers in the 1980s.

Product evangelists are those customers who actively promote the product to others.

Perceived quality is a subjective rather than an objective assessment of the quality of a product. Products with a high perceived quality are not necessarily better than other products. People form their opinion of a brand's quality from previous experience with the brand, its design and packaging, public reports, and opinions of others. Perceived quality is an asset because many people buy brands on the basis of the brand's reputation. If a brand has a reputation for superior quality, buyers will prefer it. A brand's perceived quality affects purchasing decisions, especially of buyers who lack the time or motivation to collect information to thoroughly evaluate the brand.

Perceived quality is a subjective rather than an objective assessment of the quality of a product.

Brand associations are any attributes or symbols consumers link to a brand. Brand associations summarize numerous facts about the product. They reflect the meaning of the brand for consumers, differentiate it from competing brands, and influence consumers' choice. Associations are often the result of successful positioning efforts that link the product to desirable benefits or consequences. For example, WestJet Airlines is associated with low air fares. If such associations are important to customers and are not shared by other airlines, they can be a source of competitive advantage to WestJet.[29]

Brand associations are any attributes or symbols consumers link to a brand.

Brands linked to desirable associations often make it very difficult for rivals to compete effectively against them. For example, although Intel faces strong competition from AMD, it maintains its strong market leadership by being associated as the only microprocessor of choice for most personal computer buyers—something that has been reinforced by its highly successful "Intel Inside" campaign. Also, it would be very difficult for any laundry detergent to attack Tide head-on by claiming that it washes clothes better. Such attacks often fail because they lack the credibility needed to convince buyers that they are indeed superior to the market leader on this attribute.

Other proprietary assets include trademarks, patents, logos, and packaging. Unlike other brand equity assets that represent consumer perceptions and attitudes or knowledge of brands, proprietary assets represent ways of legally protecting the brand or other non-consumer–related assets. Trademarks protect brands from competitors who might attempt to exploit the brand's popularity by using similar-sounding names or symbols. For this reason, companies protect their brands by registering their names, logos, and even their packaging. As we noted earlier in the chapter, companies often defend their trademarks by taking legal action against any company that uses identical or similar-sounding names that might confuse customers.

Other proprietary assets include trademarks, patents, logos, and channel relationships.

Finally, patents are legal means intended to prevent other firms from imitating a product. A patent gives an inventor the exclusive right to make use of or sell his or her invention for a number of years. Although in some cases companies find ways to get around them, patents are valuable because they protect companies from unauthorized use of their technologies.

Measuring the Value of Brands

Companies have long recognized that brand names are valuable to companies. However, it is only recently that serious attempts have been made to estimate their value.[30] Measuring the value of a brand can be required for various reasons. For instance, any investment in building the brand needs to be justified by measuring the impact of the increased spending on the value of the brand; also, companies acquiring brands need to know their value in order to calculate their purchase price. There are several ways to measure the value of a brand:

1. *The Historical Costs Method.* A brand is an asset whose value has increased over the years from investing in the brand. The brand value may be measured by adding all the costs related to building the brand, such as product development and advertising costs. However, there are several issues associated with the historical method of measuring brand value. It is difficult to measure the impact of brand investment on the long-term performance of the brand.[31] Determining the length of time over which costs will be considered represents a major challenge. Some brands such as Dove and Tide go back a long time while others are more recent entries. How does one decide how far back to go to determine the brand's value? Another issue is to decide which costs should be included. It is difficult to establish a direct cause and effect relationship between the various costs and the value of the brand. Furthermore, advertising works with a lagged effect, and it is difficult to trace its effects on the value of the brand.

2. *The Replacement Costs Method.* The replacement costs method looks at the cost of building a comparable brand. It uses the cost to replace the brand weighed by the probability of success in replacing the brand. For example, if it costs $50 million to launch a new product and the probability of success is 25 percent, then the expected cost of establishing an equivalent brand name is $200 million.

   One problem with this method is the difficulty in re-creating an existing brand. Some of today's great brands were born in an era when advertising spending was low and these brands built their reputation over time through a combination of continuous improvement in quality and innovation and consistent positioning. Heavy competition, numerous new product introductions, and high advertising costs make attainment of the market share of market leaders difficult. It is for this reason that companies spend large amounts on acquiring well-known existing brands rather than developing new ones from scratch.[32] For example, Philip Morris paid almost $12.9 billion (U.S.) for Kraft, an amount almost 600 percent over Kraft's book value of its balance sheet assets.[33]

3. *The Price Premium Method.* Strong brands command a price premium. This is due to the loyalty and strong brand recognition effects discussed earlier. The value of the brand may be measured by estimating the price premium that buyers pay for the brand. This price premium is equal to the price charged for the product less the price of unbranded products.

   The price premium can be measured in several ways. One way would be to ask buyers what they would pay for the product with the name and without the name. The difference would represent the value of the brand name. Another way to measure the price premium would be to use conjoint analysis, an advanced multivariate statistical technique, which is a much more reliable and sensitive method.[34] Conjoint analysis involves presenting a series of simple questions that are then analyzed to determine the price premium that buyers are willing to pay for a brand. Consumers may be asked a question such as "Would you prefer Advil at $4, Tylenol at $3.5 or Aspirin at $3?" If Tylenol is chosen, the question is repeated with Tylenol at $4. Next, if Aspirin is selected, the question is repeated with Advil at $3. After this process is repeated a number of times, a relative price for each brand emerges. Differences in these relative prices represent the price premium that buyers would be willing to pay for each brand.

   There are certain problems with the price premium method. One difficulty is that it may be difficult to find appropriate unbranded products. Also, some brands do not command a price premium over other brands but they still have high brand equity. For example, Molson Canadian does not sell at a premium over other beers but it would be difficult to deny that it has brand equity.

4. *The Customer Preference Method.* Another method to estimate the value of a brand is to obtain measures of intent to purchase the product with and without the brand name. If, for example, 35 percent of consumers prefer a product without the brand name but this number increases to 65 when the name is attached to the product, the difference represents the value of the brand. In this case the value of the brand is equivalent to 30 percent of sales.

5. *The Financial Market Value Method.* The financial market value method uses stock market prices to establish the value of a brand. This approach measures brand value as the difference between the firm's market value and the book value of its tangible assets (cash, inventories, accounts receivable, and buildings and equipment). The difference represents the value of the firm's brand equity. One difficulty with this method is that the stock price may be overvalued or undervalued depending on stock market perceptions of the brand.

6. *The Earnings Method.* The earnings method focuses on earnings as a means of measuring brand equity. The earnings method is used by the Interbrand Group of London and is based on average annual after-tax profits less average expected earnings for an equivalent unbranded product and adjusted by a subjective factor that measures brand strength. This factor is based on the brand's performance along several dimensions: its ability to influence the market, its ability to survive based on brand loyalty, the degree to which it is affected by changes in technology and fashion, its ability to expand into other geographically different markets, the corporate support given to the brand, and the degree of legal protection of the brand. The following example illustrates the use of the earnings method.

Average after-tax profits	$550 million
Expected earnings for an equivalent unbranded product	−55 million
Earnings attributed to the brand	$495 million
Brand strength factor	X 12
Estimated value of brand	$5.9 billion

Figure 9.4 shows the annual *BusinessWeek* ranking of the 10 most valuable brands in the world based on Interbrand's brand valuation methodology. Only brands with values greater than $1 billion (U.S.), global in nature (derive over one-third of their sales from outside their home countries), and having distribution throughout Europe, Asia, and North and South America are included. One problem with the earnings method is that the historical data may produce biased estimates because they may not accurately reflect

Figure 9.4 The World's Most Valuable Brands

Rank 2005	Brand Value $Millions (U.S.)	Rank 2005	Brand Value $Millions (U.S.)
Coca-Cola	67,525	Nokia	26,452
Microsoft	59,941	Disney	26,441
IBM	53,376	McDonald's	26,014
GE	46,996	Toyota	24,837
Intel	35,588	Marlboro	21,189

SOURCE: Robert Berner and David Kiley, "Global Brands," *BusinessWeek* (August 1, 2005), 90.

future earnings. Another problem is the use of subjective judgments in estimating the brand strength factor. It is known that human judgment is frequently subject to error.

Strategic Roles of Brands

Brands play different roles within a firm's brand portfolio. Some brand names are used on other brands to reduce introduction costs and lower the risk of new product failure. Other brands are co-branded and are used in conjunction with brands of other organizations. Some provide support and credibility to other brands in the organization. Some companies license their brands to be used on products of other companies.

Brand Extensions

Brand extensions involve using a well-known brand name in one product category to introduce a new brand that belongs to a different product category.

A **brand extension** involves using a well-known brand name to introduce a new brand that belongs to a different product category. The high failure rates of new products, rising advertising costs, and increasing competition for shelf space in retail outlets makes the introduction of new brands risky and expensive.[35] Brand extensions have become popular because they help reduce the cost of new product introduction and increase the chances of success.[36] Almost half of all new packaged goods are brand extensions.[37] Examples of brand extensions include Yamaha pianos, Honda lawn mowers, and Harley-Davidson clothing. The Strategy in Action box details how Ralph Lauren grew its business through a series of successful mixtures of brand extension and non-brand extension.

> ### Strategy in Action — RALPH LAUREN
>
> Ralph Lauren started his company in 1967, with the introduction of a line of men's wear that included wide-collar shirts and wide-lapel suits. This line was produced with fine fabrics to create a distinctive, innovative, but classic and refined look. In 1971, Ralph Lauren introduced a line of women's clothes with an image of understated elegance and femininity. He also introduced a line of sportswear called Polo University Club for college students and young professional men just starting to build their work wardrobes. In 1978, Ralph Lauren introduced two fragrances, Polo for Men and Polo for Women. In 1983, a collection of home furnishings was introduced, to which he later added furniture for a particular lifestyle. This was followed by a line called Safari, one for men and one for women in 1989. In 1994, he introduced Polo Sport, again with a line for men and women, and a new line of women's clothes. In 1996, a Polo line of clothing was introduced for men and women. In recent years, Ralph Lauren has added Purple Label, a line of high-priced men's suits, a line of clothing for infants and toddlers, and a Ralph Lauren line of underwear, Intimate Appeal, for men and women.

It is known that consumers use perceptions of a parent brand to evaluate new products introduced under the same name.[38] Companies take advantage of these perceptions to leverage their equity by introducing new products using parent brand names.[39] The attractiveness of a brand extension increases when the parent brand and the extension category share the same association or the extension product class is very similar to the parent brand class.[40]

Brand extensions capitalize on existing brands' image and popularity. The new brand obtains instant recognition and early acceptance because it uses the name of a brand that is widely recognized. Virgin Group is a company that uses brand extensions successfully. Virgin has extended its name from record stores to airlines, bridal supplies stores, soft drinks, and financial services, among other businesses. A common characteristic of these products is that they all use the Virgin brand name. In another example, when Tylenol introduces a new brand, it gains instant recognition due to the widespread awareness of the Tylenol name.

The ideal brand extension would be one where the new brand actually helps the parent brand by reinforcing its image and enhancing its name recognition. In some cases it is even possible for the brand extension to help revive the stagnant sales of the existing brand if the two brands can use the same promotion so that economies of scale in promotion can be obtained or the extensive promotion of the brand extension spills over to the parent brand.

If the old product has a well-known name, the cost of the introduction of the new product is much lower than usual due to lower advertising and promotion costs. It has been estimated that the cost of introducing a product under a new name is three times the cost of a brand extension.[41] New products are also associated with a high degree of risk and they frequently fail as a result. Because of the instant recognition and early acceptance, brand extensions enjoy a lower risk of market rejection than non-brand extensions. However, the influence of the parent brand on buyers' assessment of the brand extension diminishes after the initial trial; the core brand has very little impact on the long-term repeat purchases of the extension.

Risks of Brand Extensions. What are the risks of brand extensions? Managers involved in brand extension initiatives need to be aware of the following risks:

- *Inferiority of new brand.* The new brand needs to offer superior customer value with regard to quality, uniqueness, features, or other benefits. Otherwise, the new brand will likely fail regardless of the reputation of the existing brand. If a brand extension fails, it can cause long-term damage to the parent brand that may be difficult to reverse.[42] For example, Continental Airlines attempted to imitate Southwest's success and introduced its own low-budget no-frills airline, Continental Lite. The airline continued to operate its original full-service airline under the original Continental name. When Continental Lite was withdrawn because of poor sales, many consumers became aware of the two brands and Continental's name was negatively affected by the failure.[43]
- *Differences in image.* Another risk is that the image of the existing brand may not fit the image of the new brand. This is usually no problem if the original brand does not have an image that is too individual or special. In the case of Tylenol discussed earlier, it is clear that all its products have a similar image as they are all over-the-counter health care products. But when Harley-Davidson failed in its introduction of Harley-Davidson cigarettes, the effort likely failed because the image of a high-performance motorcycle company did not fit that of a cigarette company.
- *Dilution.* A serious risk with brand extension strategies is that the core brand values may be diluted—the brand loses its core meaning—if the brand name is used on too many products. This dilution has happened to Pierre Cardin, for example, because the name has been used in brand extensions in many different product categories. In order to avoid this problem, firms need to avoid overextending their brand names.

Co-Branding

Co-branding occurs when two or more brands form one product or are marketed together in some way.[44] Co-branding is a form of strategic alliance. For example, SAS International Hotels (SIH) of Brussels entered into a strategic alliance with Radisson Hotels and formed a co-brand called Radisson SAS. The rationale was that SIH wanted

Co-branding occurs when two or more brands form one product or are marketed together in some way.

exposure outside Europe, and Radisson Hotels wanted exposure in Europe. Radisson SAS has the rights in Europe, the Middle East, and North Africa while Radisson has the rest of the world. The increased economies of scale and marketing exposure have enabled the two companies to increase their marketing clout and enhanced the overall value of each brand.

Co-branding is usually carried out between manufacturers or service providers. But co-branding agreements may also be made between suppliers and manufacturers. The "Intel Inside" campaign is an example of a successful co-branding strategy between Intel, the dominant microchip manufacturer, and personal computer manufacturers. Co-branding agreements may also be made between products of the same companies. For example, Crest toothpaste has co-branded with Scope mouthwash, both Procter & Gamble products. Co-branding provides firms with the following advantages:

- *Increased strength of combined product.* The combined brand is stronger than if the two brands were to be marketed individually. It enhances the perceived quality and strength of a brand, leading to higher sales and profits. Rogers Communications Inc. signed a long-term strategic alliance with AT&T Canada, which also included a co-branding agreement. The strategic alliance allowed Rogers to make its service available throughout Canada and the United States.
- *Credibility.* In a similar way to brand extensions, co-branding can also increase the credibility of a product by joining it with another well-known product.
- *Lower introduction cost.* Co-branding can reduce the cost of product introduction as teaming with a well-known brand can help reduce advertising and promotional costs. It can also reduce the risk of product failure by piggybacking on the reputation of a popular brand.

Risks of Co-Branding. Brands entering co-branding agreements need to be aware of certain risks that are inherent in these agreements. These risks include the following:

- *Dilution.* A brand's image may be diluted if it is involved in co-branding agreements with too many unrelated brands.
- *Confusion.* Too many co-branding agreements may also cause confusion among customers.
- *Overexposure.* There is a risk of overexposure if one or more brands are involved in too many co-branding agreements.
- *Lack of fit.* There may be lack of fit between the partner brands. For co-branding to work, there needs to be a logical fit between the two brands so that the combined effect is greater than each brand separately.
- *Loss of control.* Firms may lose control over the firm's marketing strategy, which may lead to initiatives that could be detrimental to the brand. Firms should avoid aligning with another product if there is a concern that it will lead to loss of control over the brand's strategic direction.

Endorser Brands

Endorser brands are established brands that endorse other products.

An **endorser brand** is an established brand that endorses another product. Such an endorsement provides instant credibility and support to the endorsed product. The endorser brand assures customers that the endorsed brand will deliver the promised benefits. Well-known corporate names are often used as endorser brands because they can lend credibility and reassure buyers about the quality of the endorsed brand. Endorser brands typically provide ongoing support to the endorsed brand. However, they are sometimes used to provide initial support and credibility to new brands and are dropped from the name when the driver brand becomes strong enough to support itself. An example of an endorser brand is Marriott, which endorses the company's various hotel chains—Courtyard, Renaissance, Residence Inn, Fairfield, Spring Hill, and Town-place Suites—that each appeals to a different segment.

In addition to conventional endorser brands, companies employ two variants of endorser brands—token endorsers and shadow endorsers.[45] **Token endorsers** are parent brands that avoid providing a strong endorsement to another brand. Companies use token endorsers when the associations linked to a sub-brand are different from the associations linked to an endorser brand, or the endorser brand is involved in a large number of markets. Token endorsers often use their company's logo or statements such as "a Bell Canada company" to endorse other brands or companies. **Shadow endorsers** are brands that are not linked visibly to a sub-brand but many consumers know about the relationship. For example, many people know that Acura is a subsidiary of Honda. This provides assurance to Acura buyers that Honda's reputation and financial resources are behind the brand. At the same time, Acura avoids a too close association with Honda that would reduce Acura's upscale appeal.

Sub-brands

Sub-brands are brands related to the parent brand but reflect the specific association or personality of a specific brand. Sub-brands are used to distinguish a specific model from other models within a product line. They also modify or extend the associations of the parent brand. For example, Ford Explorer carries the association linked to Ford, but it also adds more associations to reflect the specific model it represents. This way, a Ford Explorer is linked to different associations than a Ford Taurus.

Sub-brands are linked to a parent brand in order to benefit from it. Such a connection provides the sub-brand with the support and credibility that is essential, especially if the brand is new and unknown. One common reason for introducing sub-brands is to extend a parent brand into a new segment. For example, Air Canada introduced its Air Canada Tango sub-brand in order to enter the airline industry discount segment that is dominated by WestJet. By introducing the Tango brand, Air Canada hoped to stop the further expansion of WestJet and allow Air Canada to participate in the growing discount air-travel segment. Sub-brands are also used to change the image of a parent brand by adding certain associations. For example, Acura's high-priced sports car, NSX, adds an element of high performance and luxury to the Acura line.

Sub-brands can be descriptors, drivers, or both. **Descriptors** are sub-brands that communicate some aspect of the brand such as benefits, attributes, function, or product class. For example, in Heinz ketchup, "ketchup" is a descriptor brand. **Drivers** are non-descriptive sub-brands that represent the value, the position, and the benefits that customers will receive from the brand. For example, in the name Ford Focus, Focus is the driver brand because it carries all the associations and benefits consumers expect to receive from the brand.

Licenced Brands

Firms that have strong brands could profit from them by licensing their brand name, logo, or other trademark to other firms. **Brand licensing** involves agreements among firms whereby a firm pays another so it can use the name, logo, character, or trademark of the other brand to market its own product or merchandise. Licensing, in essence, means a firm is renting another brand to help the sales of its own brand.

Entertainment licensing, a particular type of licensing, has become very popular recently. It has been used with some of the most successful movies, such as *The Lion King*, *Jurassic Park*, and *Star Wars*. Other well-known examples of brand licensing include Porsche sunglasses and Hershey Chocolate Milk, and designer labels such as Tommy Hilfiger, Ralph Lauren, and Calvin Klein.

Token endorsers are parent brands that avoid providing a strong endorsement to another brand.

Shadow endorsers are brands that are not linked visibly to a sub-brand but many consumers know about the relationship.

Sub-brands are brands related to the parent brand but reflect the specific association or personality of a specific brand.

Descriptors are sub-brands that communicate some aspect of the brand such as benefits, attributes, function, or product class.

Drivers are non-descriptive sub-brands that represent the value, position, and the benefits that customers will receive from the brand.

Brand licensing involves agreements among firms whereby a firm pays another so it can use the name, logo, character, or trademark of the other brand to market its own product or merchandise.

Risks of Licensing. Brand licensing has grown in recent years as companies try to capitalize on the popularity of their brands. However, there are risks associated with licensing:

Overexposure. A brand that signs a large number of licensing agreements may suffer from overexposure and become ineffective as a result.

Confusion. Consumers may become confused and the brand can lose its meaning if it is used by too many diverse brands and especially by brands that have very little relation to the company's brand.

Short life. Obtaining the rights to a brand may turn out to be a fad and short-lived—although it may be very popular at the time of the agreement.

Tarnishing of brand image. Careless licensing may tarnish the image of a brand if the licensee brand fails to meet the performance expectations of buyers.

Barriers to Successful Brand Building

Building strong brands is a difficult task. Managers striving to strengthen their brands face several problems that make brand building a challenging endeavour. Barriers to successful brand building include the following:[46]

1. *Pressure to compete on price.* Managers face an enormous pressure to lower prices. Such pressures come from competitors, powerful intermediaries, price-sensitive consumers, slow-growth markets, and overcapacity. Every year, a large number of new products are introduced into the Canadian economy. These entrants represent a tremendous challenge for incumbent brands as they fight to gain shelf space and market share. Retailers are increasingly becoming larger and more powerful and are making demands on manufacturers to lower their prices to them. These competitive pressures coupled with low growth rates and underutilized capacity lead to heightened rivalry as firms strive to increase market share by shaving prices.
2. *Fragmented markets and media.* It is important that there is consistency and tight coordination of the various media and marketing messages. When the number of media is small, achieving consistency in marketing communication is easier. However, the proliferation of mass media and the resulting media fragmentation makes such a task more difficult. Media coordination is especially difficult when different individuals or organizations are in charge of different promotional activities. Lack of close coordination of these activities may harm the brand as they may result in inconsistent messages sent out to target customers.
3. *Complex brand strategies and relationships.* Brands are no longer stand-alone entities but are linked to each other through complex interrelationships. This is the result of companies pursuing growth strategies involving line and brand extensions and large arrays of sub-brands, endorser brands, and corporate brands. The complexity in the relationship among different brands makes brand management difficult. The performance of one brand affects the performance of another linked brand. While a strong brand may have a favourable impact on a linked brand, a weak brand that fails to meet expectations will be harmful to its linked brands. For this reason, efforts at building a strong brand may fail if related brands perform poorly.
4. *Changing strategies.* Building strong brands requires a consistent image for long periods of time. However, there are internal pressures to change the strategy—with negative consequences for the company. Firms often lose focus and enter new markets or introduce new products. Such moves can be harmful to the brand as they siphon resources away from the core brand into the new brands or markets. However, management should not remain committed to a strategy rendered obsolete by environmental changes. Management must be vigilant to opportunities and threats in the

environment and bring about changes in its strategy to maintain the relevance of its brand. Many well-known brands such as Ivory and Gillette Sensor have, over the years, maintained their strategic leadership by making changes to the brand features and packaging, but maintaining the brand's core identity and associations.

5. *Bias against innovation.* Established firms often fall victim to companies that enter the market with innovative products. This usually happens because organizations prefer the status quo over change and fail to make the necessary investment in product innovation. Change can be risky, disruptive, and costly. Introducing radically new technologies makes existing technologies obsolete and reduces return on investment. This is why radical change usually comes from small firms that have little to lose and much to gain from introducing disruptive technologies. As a result, market leaders are vulnerable to aggressive competitors who do not hesitate to pursue risky opportunities. An example of a company that failed to innovate is Sears, which failed to see the advent of discount retailing that had been underway since the early 1960s, causing the company to lose a large part of its brand equity.[47]

6. *Insufficient investment.* Firms often fail to make the necessary investment in maintaining brand equity because of complacency, fear of cannibalization, or pressure to invest in new businesses. Many managers do not see the necessity of preserving brand equity through continuing support and nurturing. Reducing investment on the brand inevitably leads to its decline. This problem is common among firms that seek growth through diversification while neglecting core businesses. For example, while Wal-Mart was sticking to its core business, Kmart moved away from discounting by acquiring Office Max, Sports Authority, and Borders bookstore. These moves were, in large part, responsible for Kmart's filing for bankruptcy protection in 2002.[48]

7. *Short-term mentality.* Many Canadian and U.S. firms suffer from a short-term orientation. Too much emphasis on short-term performance can reduce the long-term value of a brand.[49] The causes of such a short-term orientation include stock market pressures and performance evaluation of managers who are evaluated on the basis of short-term results. This shortsightedness forces managers to adopt measures such as reducing research and development or employee training, moves that boost the stock's short-term earnings and stock price but are harmful to the brand. Also, frequent short-term price-oriented promotions (price-offs, coupons, and price packs) that are not consistent with the brand's image are harmful to the brand. Frequent price promotions cheapen the brand's image, causing permanent damage. In contrast, the use of advertising increases brand differentiation and insulates the brand from future competition.[50]

Building Strong Brands

Building and maintaining strong brands is an important marketing task. To develop a successful brand is to build and maintain the assets that make up brand equity: brand awareness, brand loyalty, perceived quality, brand associations, and other proprietary assets. However, brand building is difficult and risky and requires patience and vision for the long term.[51] One challenging issue facing managers trying to build their brands is that it is difficult to demonstrate the value of brand-building efforts. Achieving a better understanding between such brand-building activities and their impact on brand performance can help managers justify these activities. The need to justify brand-building activities is especially important in the case of advertising that involves large amounts of spending and acts with a time lag on sales.[52]

Building strong brands requires firms to follow certain guidelines, as shown in Figure 9.5. First, developing strong brands requires management to take a long-term view of the brand's profitability. It also requires a substantial initial and ongoing investment,

Figure 9.5	Guidelines for Building Strong Brands

- Take a long-term view of the brand's profitability
- Link the brand with unique, strong, favourable, and consistent associations
- Engage in continuous product improvement and innovation
- Integrate marketing activities
- Adapt to consumer and market changes

which commonly leads to lower profits in the short term. However, the payoff from building brand equity can last for a long time.

Second, at the core of effective brand building is linking the brand with unique, strong, favourable, and consistent associations that reflect the brand's positioning and distinguish it from rival brands. Branding efforts succeed when consumers are convinced that there are meaningful differences among products in the category. For example, the "Intel Inside" branding campaign tries to convince computer purchasers that Intel microprocessors deliver the highest level of performance. The creation of perceived differences among products through branding increases the value of brands, a situation that can translate into increased profits for the firm.[53] For example, Aspirin commands a price premium over competing brands because consumers are convinced that it has fast and safe pain-killing properties. Also, it is very important that there is consistency in the brand's image over time. Frequent changes to a brand's image can be detrimental to its performance.

Third, brands derive part of their strength from strong product performance. Branding is more effective when the product has outstanding quality or features that distinguish it from rival products. Companies such as Nokia, palmOne, and Research in Motion have maintained strong market positions through continuous innovation that produces strong products. Brand building requires continuous improvement and innovation with a relentless focus on the key benefits that the brand claims to own. Powerful brands avoid using price decreases, rebates, or other types of price promotions. These practices tend to direct consumers' attention to price and away from non-price attributes such as quality, image, or features. When this happens, brands start to resemble commodities, firms compete on price, consumers become more price sensitive, and profits erode.

Fourth, a strong brand is the result of integrated marketing activities—using all elements of the marketing mix in a coherent manner.[54] It is important that each part of the marketing mix reinforces the desired associations and positioning. The brand needs to meet the needs of the target market and the brand name, the price, channels of distribution, and promotion (message appeal, execution, media choice) must be consistent with the desirable image and perceptions of the target market.[55] Inconsistencies among the various elements of the marketing mix will reduce brand equity.[56]

Many firms believe that putting a prominent name on the product or service is sufficient to create a strong brand to set them apart from the competition. Others attempt to set themselves off through advertising and other forms of promotion such as events or sport sponsorships, publicity, and supporting social causes, and it is true that these activities are indispensable tools for enhancing awareness and building a brand's image. But branding is more than naming a product, or running a clever advertisement, or having the right product design. Products whose entire marketing mix is neglected often become a little more than a commodity with very little brand equity.

Finally, brands succeed when they create a clear and desired position in the minds of customers.[57] Powerful brands remain faithful to their identity. But it is possible for well-known brands to lose their strength if they are not properly maintained through quality improvements and adaptation to consumers and market trends.[58] Brands need to adapt to changes in technology, customers, and market trends. An example of a strong Canadian brand is McCain Foods, which is described in the Strategy in Action box.

McCAIN FOODS

Since it was established in 1957, McCain Foods has become a global leader among food processors. McCain is, currently, the world's largest processor of french fries as it makes almost one-third of the french-fried potatoes produced internationally. The company is also known for appetizers, desserts, pizzas, vegetables, entrées, oven meals, and other frozen foods around the world. McCain sells hundred of products through retail stores and food service operations such as restaurants and catering companies. Today the company has more than 55 production facilities on six continents and its 2004 net sales reached $5.8 billion.

Through its efforts over the years, McCain has managed to build a strong brand that ensures the continuous success of the company. McCain's success is built, largely, on top technology and state-of-the-art agronomy. McCain Research Farms are dedicated to refining the practice of agriculture and sharing new knowledge with growers. The company employs more than 100 agronomists and potato specialists around the world who help local growers produce potatoes and vegetables of appropriate quality and to ensure dependability of supply.

McCain positions itself as the world's largest producer of frozen french fries and the manufacturer of other quality food products in more than 110 countries. The company's growth drivers are innovation, product quality, customer value, low-cost manufacturing, and continuous improvement. McCain continually improves its manufacturing operations, develops new methods and equipment, and enhances product quality. Also, the company encourages team work, risk-taking, and entrepreneurship through autonomous hands-on local management. Finally, the company promotes its products through an integrated marketing communications mix that includes a well-trained sales force, extensive prime-time television advertising on national networks, and a variety of sales promotions. All these activities have helped McCain build a strong brand that is well known in Canada and many countries around the world.

Naming Brands

The choice of the name is an important aspect of the branding process. The initial choice of the brand name, logos, and symbols is important for the success of the brand-building efforts. Choosing appropriate names can help enhance brand awareness and link the brand with favourable associations. In some cases, brand names even become synonymous with the product category as in the case of Xerox, Kleenex, and Band-Aid.[59] Figure 9.6 lists the desired characteristics of effective brand names.

Figure 9.6	Desired Characteristics of Effective Brand Names

- Name is simple, easy to pronounce, spell, and understand
- Name is distinctive
- Name suggests product benefits or attributes
- Name projects a distinctive quality
- Name can be legally protected
- Name is easy to translate into other languages
- Name uses letters that invoke favourable buyer feelings

Effective brand names should be simple and easy to pronounce, spell, and understand. Some of the most popular brand names are one- or two-syllable words. Examples include Tide, Advil, and Crest. On the other hand, a name such as United Consolidated Industries Inc. would be quite difficult to pronounce in other languages. The name also should be distinctive to reduce confusion with competing brands and attract potential consumers' attention. Choosing familiar words helps increase brand recall, but choosing an unusual or distinctive word may facilitate brand recognition. Examples of distinctive and somewhat unfamiliar names include Xerox and specialty bakery Kinnikinnick Foods.

The name should suggest some of the product's features, benefits, or attributes. For example, Gillette Shaving Foam expresses the product's features attributes, while NBG does not. Using a name that does not reflect the nature of the product makes the introduction of the product more difficult and more expensive as the company needs to spend heavily to inform potential customers about the product's benefits and functions.

The name should also project a distinctive quality such as Infiniti, Clarica, and Lexus. In addition, management must ensure that the name can be legally protected. The name should be easy to use in other languages—Nortel and Canon are good examples. But names that have specific meanings in other languages should be avoided—the automobile name Nova would be inappropriate for Spanish-speaking countries because it means "doesn't go"—so some careful research should be undertaken. Lastly, brand names should invoke favourable buyer feelings. A study of consumer attitudes toward letters of the alphabet found that A, B, S, and M produced the most favourable feelings, while Q, X, Z, F, and U produced the worst feelings.[60]

- Building strong brands is a key goal of any marketing program. A brand is a name, symbol, sign, logo, trademark, or design that is used for brand identification purposes, to differentiate the product and protect consumers and companies from illegal product imitation. Products may be classified into functional, image, and experiential brands.

- Brands are important for consumers because they are shorthand devices that simplify purchasing decisions. Consumers rely on brands as a source of information about products. Strong brands are perceived as having higher value. They also reduce the perceived risk felt by consumers when they purchase certain brands.

- Brands are important to firms for the following reasons: they differentiate their brands from competition, provide credibility to their brands, and add value to their other brands; they are a source of future earnings; they enhance the effectiveness of marketing activities, enable firms to charge a premium, create loyal customers, increase the effectiveness of advertising, are a means of legal protection, and can capitalize on the strength of the brand.

- Brand equity is a set of assets linked to a product or service that add to its value. Brand equity includes name awareness, brand loyalty, perceived quality, brand associations and other proprietary assets such as patents, trademarks, channel relationships, customer relationships, and trust.

- The value of a brand may be measured using the following methods: historical costs, replacement costs, price premium, customer preference, financial market value, and earnings.

- The strategic roles of brands include brand extension, co-branding, endorser brands, sub-branding, and licensed brands.

- The barriers to building successful brands include pressure to compete on price, fragmented markets and media, complex brand strategies and relationships, changing strategies, bias against innovation, insufficient investment, and short-term mentality.

- Building strong brands involves taking a long-term view of the brand's profitability; linking the brand with unique, strong, favourable, and consistent associations; engaging in continuous product improvement and innovation; integrating marketing activities; and adapting to consumer and market changes.

- The choice of an appropriate brand name is important for brand success. The desired characteristics of a strong brand name include the following: the name is simple, easy to pronounce, spell, and understand; it is distinctive; it suggests the product benefits or attributes; it projects a distinctive quality; it can be legally protected; it is easy to translate into other languages; and it uses letters that invoke favourable buyer feelings.

1. What is a brand? How is a brand different from a product?

2. Compare and contrast functional, image, and experiential brands.

3. Discuss the importance of brands for consumers.

4. Discuss the importance of brands for companies.

5. Define brand equity. What are the components of brand equity?

6. Describe brand awareness. What are the two types of awareness? Why is brand awareness an asset for organizations?

7. What are brand associations? Why are brand associations considered important brand assets?

8. Compare and contrast the different methods for measuring brand value.

9. Define brand extensions. Discuss the advantages and risks of brand extensions.

10. Discuss co-branding. Describe the advantages and risks of co-branding.

11. Describe endorser brands. Discuss the two variants of endorser brands.

12. Describe sub-brands. Why do companies use sub-brands? Discuss the different types of sub-brands.

13. Discuss licensed brands. What are the advantages and risks of brand licensing?

14. Discuss the barriers to successful brand building. What can a brand manager do to overcome these barriers?

15. Discuss the guidelines for building strong brands.

16. What are the desired characteristics of effective brand names?

Critical Thinking and Application Questions

1. Referring back to the opening vignette, what other actions might Cavendish Farms have undertaken to further strengthen its brand?

2. When BMW owners proudly turn the ignition keys in their "ultimate driving machines," they are receiving more than a highly engineered car with excellent performance. What else do BMW buyers receive in addition to the above attributes?

3. Many companies approach branding as getting the right design, naming products, or getting the right promotion. Explain why such approaches may fail to build strong brands. How do companies build strong brands?

4. Talk with a local business owner about his or her company's branding practices. In your opinion, to what extent does this business owner follow the guidelines for building strong brands discussed in this chapter? Which of the barriers to building strong brands are preventing this business from building a strong brand?

5. Brands such as Coke and Microsoft are worth billions of dollars. Brands succeed in the long run only if they offer added value over and above their basic product characteristics. Find a product that meets this criterion and one that doesn't. Comment on the marketing success of each product.

Notes

1. Steven Buckler, "How a humorous TV spot for Cavendish Farms staked an emotional bond with consumers," *Marketing Magazine,* February 16, 2004, 16.
2. Leslie de Chernatony and Malcolm McDonald, *Creating Powerful Brands* (Oxford: Butterworth-Heinemann, 1998), 57.
3. Steven A. Sinclair and Kevin E. Sewad, "Effectiveness of Branding a Commodity Product," *Industrial Marketing Management* 17 (1988), 23–33.
4. Kevin Lane Keller, *Strategic Brand Management,* 2nd ed. (Upper Saddle River, N.J.: Prentice Hall, 2003), 4.
5. Kevin Lane Keller, "Conceptualizing, Measuring, and Managing Customer-Based Brand Equity," *Journal of Marketing* 57 (January 1993), 1–33.
6. David Menzies, "Water-down brands," *Marketing Magazine,* April 19, 2004, 11.
7. Joseph T. Plummer, "How Personality Makes a Difference," *Journal of Advertising Research* 24 (December/January 1985), 27–31.
8. Blair Matthews, "Most Consumers Hated New Coke," *Online Soda Pop Dreams Magazine,* 1999, www.pww.on.ca/newcokw.htm, retrieved on September 21, 2003; Edward Hore, "Coke Trademark Always the Real Thing," *The Lawyers Weekly,* November 7, 1997, www.hazzardandhore.com/lw971107.htm, retrieved on September 21, 2003.
9. Alice M. Tybout and Gregory S. Carpenter, "Creating and Managing Brands," in Dawn Iacobucci (ed.) *Kellogg on Marketing* (New York: Wiley, 2001), 74–102.
10. Laurance Yap, "Acura RL buyers lured by performance, not image," *Toronto Star,* April, 23, 2005, G31.
11. Keller, 2003, 9.
12. Jacob Jacoby, Jerry C. Olson, and Rafael Haddock, "Price, Brand Name, and Product Composition Characteristics as Determinants of Perceived Quality," *Journal of Consumer Research* 3, No. 4 (1971), 209–216.
13. Pierre Berthon, James M. Hulbert, and Leyland F. Pitt, "Brand Management Prognostications," *Sloan Management Review* 40 (Winter 1999), 53–65.
14. Ted Roselius, "Consumer Ranking of Risk Reduction Methods," *Journal of Marketing* 35 (January 1971), 56–61.
15. Berthon, Hulbert, and Pitt.
16. Kerry Dolan and Robyn Meredith, "Ghost Cars, Ghost Brands," *Forbes,* April 30, 2001, 106–112.
17. Theodore Levitt, "Marketing Success Through Differentiation of Everything," *Harvard Business Review* (January–February 1980), 83–91.
18. Lakshman Krishnamurthi and S. P. Raj, "An Empirical Analysis of the Relationship Between Brand Loyalty and Consumer Price Elasticity," *Marketing Science* 10 (Spring 1991), 172–183.
19. Fiona Gilmor, *Brand Warriors* (London: HarperCollinsBusiness, 1997), 2.
20. Robert J. Kent and Chris T. Allen, "Competitive Interference Effects in Consumer Memory for Advertising: The Role of Brand Familiarity," *Journal of Marketing* 58 (July 1994), 97–107.
21. "Microcell sues rivals to protect Fido," *Marketing Magazine,* March 1, 2004, 2.
22. Rajendra K. Srivastava and Allan D. Shocker, "Brand Equity: A Perspective on Its Meaning and Measurement," Report #91-124, Marketing Science Institute (Cambridge, Mass.: Marketing Science Institute, 1991).
23. David A. Aaker, *Managing Brand Equity* (New York: The Free Press, 1991), 15.
24. Aaker, 1991, 16.
25. John R. Rossiter and Larry Percy, *Advertising Communications and Promotion Management,* 2nd ed. (Boston: McGraw-Hill, 1997), 113.
26. James R. Bettman and C. Whan Park, "Effects of Prior Knowledge and Experience and Phase of Choice Process on Consumer Decision Processes: A Protocol Analysis," *Journal of Consumer Research* 7 (December 1980), 234–248.
27. Larry Percy, John R. Rossiter, and Richard Elliott, *Strategic Advertising Management* (New York: Oxford University Press, 2001), 134.
28. Jean-Noël Kapferer, *Strategic Brand Management* (New York: The Free Press, 1992), 89.
29. Myers, James H. and Mark I. Alpert, "Determinant Buying Attitudes: Meaning and Measurement," *Journal of Marketing* 32 (October 1968), 13–20.
30. Peter H. Farquhar, "Managing Brand Equity," *Marketing Research* 1 (September 1989), 24–33.
31. Carol J. Simon and Mary W. Sullivan, "The Measurement and Determinants of Brand Equity: A Financial Approach," *Marketing Science* 12, No. 1 (Winter 1993), 28–52.
32. Kapferer, 281.
33. Tom Duncan and Sandra Moriarty, *Driving Brand Value* (New York: McGraw-Hill, 1997), 4.
34. David A. Aaker, "Measuring Brand Equity Across Products and Markets," *California Management Review* 38, No. 3 (Spring 1996), 102–120.
35. Aaker, 1991, 208.
36. Vanita Swaminathan, Richard J. Fox, and Srinivas K. Reddy, "The Impact of Brand Extension Introduction on Choice," *Journal of Marketing* 65 (October 2001) 1–15; E. Tauber, "Brand Leverage: Strategy for Growth in a Cost-Control World," *Journal of Advertising Research* 26 (August–September 1988), 26–30; Srinivas K. Reddy, Susan L. Holak, and Subodh Bhat, "To Extend or Not to Extend: Success Determinants of Line Extensions," *Journal of Marketing Research* 31 (May 1994), 243–262.
37. Tauber.
38. David A. Aaker and Kevin Lane Keller, "Consumer Evaluations of Brand Extensions," *Journal of Marketing* 54 (January 1990) 27–41.
39. Zeynep Gurhan-Canli and Durairaj Maheswaran, "The Effects of Extension on Brand Name Dilution and Enhancement," *Journal of Marketing Research* 35 (November 1998), 464–473.
40. C. Whan Park, Bernard J. Jaworski, and Deborah J. MacInnis, "Strategic Brand Concept-Image Management," *Journal of Marketing* 50 (October 1986), 135–145.

41. Tauber.
42. Aaker, 1991, 208.
43. de Chernatony and McDonald, 97
44. Akshay R. Rao, Lu Qu, and Robert W. Ruckert, "Signaling Unobservable Product Quality Through a Brand Ally," *Journal of Marketing Research* 36 (May 1999), 258–268.
45. David A. Aaker and Erich Joachimsthaler, *Brand Leadership* (New York: The Free Press, 2000), 108–112.
46. David A. Aaker, *Building Strong Brands* (New York: The Free Press, 1996), 26.
47. Clayton Christensen, *The Innovator's Dilemma* (Boston: Harvard Business School Press, 1997), x.
48. Robert Slater, The Wal-Mart Decade (New York: Portfolio, 2003), 57.
49. Simon and Sullivan.
50. William Boulding, Eunkyu Lee, and Richard Staelin, "Mastering the Mix: Do Advertising, Promotion, and Sales Force Activities Lead to Differentiation?" *Journal of Marketing Research* 31 (May 1994), 159–172.
51. Scott M. Davis, *Brand Asset Management: Driving Profitable Growth Through Your Brands* (San Francisco: Jossey-Bass, 2000), 37.
52. Aaker, 1991, 15.
53. Keller, 2003, 8.
54. de Chernatony and McDonald, 16.
55. Kapferer, 53.
56. Lauranne Buchanan, Carolyn J. Simmons, and Barbara A. Bickart, "Brand Equity Dilution: Retailer Display and Context Brand Effect," *Journal of Marketing Research* 36 (August 1999), 345–355.
57. Kapferer, 40.
58. de Chernatony and McDonald, 366.
59. Noel Capon and James M. Hulbert, *Marketing Management* (Upper Saddle River, N.J.: Prentice Hall, 2001), 275.
60. Naseem Javed, *Naming for Power: Creating Successful Names for the Business World* (New York: Linkbridge Publishing, 1993), 60.

Chapter Ten

Pricing Strategy

Strategic pricing involves finding a balance between the customer's desire to obtain good value and the firm's need to cover costs and earn profits.

Thomas T. Nagle and Reed K. Holden, The Strategy and Tactics of Pricing

Learning Objectives

After studying this chapter, you should be able to:

1. Describe the factors that affect the price set by a company

2. Explain the role of the experience curve in pricing

3. Discuss several pricing strategies for new products, existing products, and product lines

4. Understand how to respond to competitors' prices

5. Outline the various price customization methods

6. Conduct a price-profitability analysis

Fast Eddie's Capitalizes on Its Low-Price Strategy

Fast Eddie's is a chain of drive-through take-out restaurants that offers two service windows (called double-drive-through), a limited menu, and no seating inside for customers. The company opened its first store in Brantford, Ontario, in 1987 and currently has stores in several other cities in southern Ontario, including Hamilton, Waterloo, and London. The two service windows operate simultaneously, one on each side of the restaurant, rather than only one as used by other fast food restaurants. In addition, there are two windows at the front of the restaurant for walk-up customers. Although there were several double-drive-through restaurants in the United States, Fast Eddie's was the first to begin operations in Canada.

"We invented discount fast food in Canada," said Mike Gorski, owner/founder of Fast Eddie's. Fast Eddie's is using discount prices as a means of positioning itself as a low-priced alternative to other hamburger restaurants. The chain has developed a low-cost business model that allows it to operate at lower prices than much larger hamburger chains. The restaurants operate in small buildings and that in combination with no in-store services and the greater customer through-put per square foot of space results in lower costs and prices.

The philosophy of high quality, fast service, and low prices is the cornerstone of Fast Eddie's commitment to "Ultimate Customer Value." Its menu consists of high-quality burgers, specialty fries, and gourmet shakes. Fast Eddie's fries come in five different flavours trademarked under the name CrazyFrys. Its milkshakes are described as "gourmet style," come in several different flavours, and are called "WildShakes." The chain also offers chicken burgers, soft drinks, and specialty burgers called Sliders. Fast Eddie's has developed its proprietary "Speedy System" designed to prepare and sell its products in the most efficient possible way. Efficiency is enhanced through its specially designed "Brain-Training Program," which allows the company to eliminate wasted time and effort in preparing and serving customers.

In order to keep costs down, Fast Eddie's tries to keep advertising and promotion costs low. In fact, the company relies on its low prices as one of its major promotional tools. Promotion expenditures average 2 percent of sales and they include spending on local radio and local newspapers. Consistent with its low-cost positioning, Fast Eddie's newspaper advertisements stress low prices and include cents-off coupons. The company's promotional mix also includes cents-off coupons with orders, T-shirts, and hats. Furthermore, low-priced hamburgers are promoted on certain days.

In addition to low prices, Fast Eddie's offers greater convenience with locations in fast food strips such as high-traffic roads near other fast food restaurants and shopping centres. The two service lines greatly reduce waiting times during periods of high demand, adding to the company's claim of excellent convenience. Demand is highest during lunch and dinner, and on Fridays and Saturdays. As a result, demand management and personnel scheduling are important to keep operations running smoothly and at maximum efficiency.

Fast Eddie's lower prices, fast service, high quality, and superior value have placed the company in an advantageous position relative to its competitors. Capitalizing on its lower-cost format, quality, and superior execution, Fast Eddie's has grown from a single outlet in 1987 to ten very profitable stores through a combination of corporate-owned and franchised stores. Fast Eddie's is poised to increase the number of its stores in the coming years.

Introduction

The opening vignette shows that price is an important aspect of a firm's marketing strategy. Firms rely on prices to stimulate demand and win markets from their rivals. Prices reflect the competitive environment and the firm's interaction with its rivals. Management must ensure that its pricing policies and actions are consistent among themselves and with the rest of the marketing mix.

Price makes a statement about a product and helps achieve a desired position in the minds of customers. For instance, a high price positions a product as premium whereas a low price positions a product as an affordable product for budget-conscious consumers. Pricing is also a means of differentiating a product. For example, Fast Eddie's offers "everyday low prices" to differentiate itself from its rivals.

It is important for firms to offer their products at the right price. Charging a price that is higher than customers are willing to pay could lead to lost sales as potential buyers turn to more reasonably priced products. If the price is lower than the market is willing to pay, the firm may be unnecessarily giving up margins and earning lower profits.

Price can be an important tool for gaining a strategic advantage. For example, Wal-Mart has become the world's largest retailer by using low prices as a competitive weapon. Low-cost firms have tremendous advantages, as they can use their low-cost position to undercut their competitors or withstand the ravages of a price war. During a price war, it is the low-cost firms that have a better chance of survival. Also, having a low-cost, low-price structure is a powerful way to dissuade competitors from engaging in price-cutting.

Proper price management can provide a firm with competitive advantages as well. Firms should avoid overly complex prices that tend to confuse customers. Many consumers avoid products that involve a substantial cognitive effort to decipher their true price. For example, airfares have become so complex that it is virtually impossible for air travellers to know what the true airfares are at a particular time. Simplifying the pricing structure can actually help increase sales and market share. In fact, some customers may be willing to pay a higher price for greatly simplified prices.

Competition continually puts pressure on profit margins. This happens because competitors always strive to imitate their competitors' best practices, eroding any advantages held by their rivals. Firms need to monitor their supply environment to find cheaper sources of supply in order to keep costs low and price their products competitively. By finding cheaper sources of supply, firms can make products that might previously have been economically unfeasible to produce. Profit margins can also be improved through creative product designs, convenient distribution, effective advertising, and reducing product defects.

This chapter first discusses the strategic factors that influence the price set by a company. Then the role of the experience curve in pricing is illustrated. Several strategies for new products, existing products, and product lines and pricing strategies companies use to respond to competitors' prices are discussed next. Then the various price customization methods are covered. Finally, several break-even analyses sales, break-even market share, safety margin, and break-even sales change techniques are described.

Strategic Influences on Price

Pricing decisions are influenced by several factors. An important consideration is how potential customers will respond to the price of the product. That will depend to a large degree on the perceived value of the product to customers. The cost of the product will help determine the minimum price that can be charged for the product. Competition also affects prices because it reduces management's flexibility in charging prices. The marketing strategy affects pricing decisions because prices must be consistent with the rest of the marketing mix. Pricing objectives affect price because, depending on the specific pricing objectives, prices will be set high or low. Managers of products that are part of a product line are constrained in their pricing decision by other products in the product line.

Pricing is a balancing act between customers' perceived value, the cost of producing the product, prices of competing products, marketing strategy, pricing objectives, and whether the product is part of a product line. For example, if the cost of producing the product goes up because of increases in the cost of materials and other inputs, the company may have difficulty raising the price and passing the cost on to customers. The ability to increase prices depends on the value of the product to customers. If consumers value a product highly, it may be possible to increase its prices. On the other hand, if perceived value is low, increasing a firm's price and passing cost increases on to consumers would not be feasible. The ability to increase prices will also depend on how competitors will react to the increase in the cost of inputs. If competitors keep prices at current levels, the firm will have to keep its prices at similar levels. The major factors influencing price are discussed in the next section (see Figure 10.1).

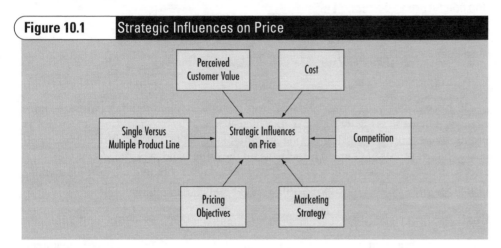

Figure 10.1 Strategic Influences on Price

Perceived Customer Value

Price represents the economic sacrifice a customer makes to obtain a product or service.[1] Effective pricing starts with customers and how they respond to price levels and changes in these price levels. An important task for managers is to find out the value of the product to customers. People purchase products only if the perceived value of the product exceeds its price. When customers are presented with several alternatives, they prefer the product that offers the highest value.

Prices are affected by what potential customers are willing to pay for the product or service. Merely covering the cost of producing the product and adding a profit margin does not necessarily mean that customers will purchase the product. The value customers assign to a brand determines the price they are willing to pay for a product. If the price is set at a level higher than the price customers are willing to pay, they will not purchase the product. On the other hand, if the price is set lower than the price customers are willing to pay, the company is not retrieving the full value of its product.

The perceived value of a product to customers is reflected in the price elasticity of demand. **Price elasticity of demand** is the percentage change in quantity demanded (Q) relative to a percentage change in price (P). It measures the impact of a change in price on product sales, assuming that all other variables that affect the demand of the product remain unchanged. The more valuable the product, the less important price is to customers and the less responsive they are to price changes. This indicates a lower price

Price elasticity of demand is the percentage change in quantity demanded (Q) relative to a percentage change in price (P).

elasticity of demand. On the other hand, the less valuable the product, the more empha-sis customers put on its price and the higher the price elasticity of demand. The price elasticity of demand can be expressed using equation (1):

$$E = -\frac{\Delta Q/Q}{\Delta P/P} \qquad (1)$$

When the percentage change in quantity demanded exceeds the percentage change in price (E > 1), demand is said to be **elastic.** Conversely, if the percentage change in quantity demanded is less than the percentage change in price (E < 1), demand is described as **inelastic. Unitary demand** exists when the percentage changes in quantity demanded and price are equal (E = 1).

The price elasticity of demand can be calculated with the aid of an example as follows. Assume that for a company that makes cordless telephones, when price was $100 the company sold 500,000 units. When the price was $108, quantity sold was 400,000 units. We can calculate the price elasticity of demand at the point where P = $100 and Q = 500,000 by using equation (1):

$$E = -\frac{(500,000 - 400,000)/500,000}{(100-108)/100}$$

$$= -2.5$$

The price elasticity of demand is useful in estimating the change in sales when the price changes. If demand is highly elastic, a price increase could lead to a loss in sales and lower profits, while a price reduction can be a profitable move as it could increase sales and lead to higher profits. If demand is inelastic, on the other hand, a price increase will cause sales to decline and it may lower profits. These price-sales-profit interrelationships will be further explored in the price-profitability analysis section at the end of this chapter.

Cost

Costs are an important influence on prices. Effective pricing requires an accurate knowl-edge of the costs—both fixed and variable—involved in producing and marketing a product. The ability to make a profit depends on whether the firm can charge a price that covers variable and fixed costs and also provides an acceptable profit margin.

Costs do not determine price but may affect the pricing strategy.[2] Costs do not affect prices because setting a price on the basis of cost only may lead to a price that is either too high or too low compared to the value consumers attach to the product. However, costs affect the pricing strategy because high-cost producers are forced to charge higher prices while low-cost firms may charge a lower price, attract more buyers, and sell more. This is what Dell was planning to accomplish in its printer business as the Strategy in Action box illustrates:[3]

Elastic demand exists when the percentage change in quantity demanded exceeds the percentage change in price.

Inelastic demand exists when the percentage change in quantity demanded is less than the percentage change in price.

Unitary demand exists when the percentage changes in quantity demanded and price are equal.

Strategy in Action — DELL COMPUTER

In June 2004, Dell Computer, the low-cost leader in personal computers, announced plans to lower the high prices consumers paid for printer cartridges. This was a direct attack on Dell's arch rival, Hewlett-Packard. According to Kevin Rollins, chief operating officer of Dell, "Customers pay high prices for ink because Hewlett-Packard is 'stuck in the middle' in the personal computer business.

Hewlett-Packard is neither the innovative leader in technology that IBM has historically been nor are they the low-cost producer. So they are stuck in the interim where they don't make a whole lot of money other than on their printing business, where they have to cost-subsidize: They break even or lose money on PCs and make all their money on ink."

After just one year into the printing business, Dell was planning to lower the price of ink. Existing printer manufacturers had designed their products to work only with ink made by the same company. According to Rollins, "It's going to take a little while. We have to get an installed base of ink-jet printers and laser printers. Then we can start to impact the price of consumables." Dell wants to bring the "Dell Effect" to the printer business as it did to the personal computer business. That would mean selling better products for continually declining prices, forcing the entire industry to respond by following the same pricing strategy.

Costs also affect profit. The cost of producing the product determines the floor, or lowest price, that can be charged to remain in business. A firm must cover its fixed or indirect costs such as rent and salaries and direct costs such as materials, supplies, and sales force commissions. If a firm is not capable of charging a price that exceeds the cost of producing the product, the firm will be forced to exit the market.

Pricing managers also need to know how costs behave at different levels of quantities involved. If economies of scale are present, the product's unit cost declines as scale increases. It is also useful to estimate the effect of accumulated knowledge or learning on costs. The relationship between costs and prices over time will be discussed in some detail in the next section.

Competition

Competitors also affect the price level firms can charge. Sometimes, competition is referred to as the price regulator. If prices of competing products are lower, then company prices will have to be lower. The larger the number of competitors and the more diverse they are, the higher the competitive intensity and the lower prices are in that industry. In industries with a small number of firms, strategic interdependence among firms is a basic aspect of a firm's pricing strategy. In these cases, assuming that products are not differentiated, the demand for a firm's products depends on the price of competing firms. For example, when a car company, such as Ford or GM, decides what the prices of its new car models will be, it has to take into account what other car companies are planning to charge.[4]

Customers use the prices of competing products as a reference to make sure they get the best value from the products they purchase. Some companies practise **reference pricing** by providing consumers with a point of comparison for judging the attractiveness of the price of their products. Reference prices include the price of competitive products, the normal nonsale price of the product, the manufacturer's suggested retail price, or an average market-selling price. This technique allows consumers to compare prices quickly, provided they trust that the price comparison provided by the company is accurate.

Reference pricing refers to the practice of providing consumers with a point of comparison for judging the attractiveness of the price of a firm's products.

A firm also needs to know how competitors react when it changes prices. A firm that cuts its price hoping to increase its sales and market share will probably face stiff opposition from rivals who are prepared to match or even beat the firm's price. This could lead to a price war. The result may be that all firms are worse off than before the price change was made.

Marketing Strategy

A firm's pricing strategy must be consistent with the firm's marketing strategy. Ideally, the pricing strategy should reinforce the positioning, product, distribution, and promotion strategies. The strategic positioning of the product should be reflected in its price. If the firm wishes to position its product as a high-end premium product, the price should be high, thus reflecting the positioning strategy. For example, Rolls-Royce charges high prices to reflect its products' desirable image as exclusive, super-premium products. Starbucks charges a higher price than other coffee shops to reflect its quality and image. If a company charges a higher price, the price must be justified by some degree of product superiority in the form of higher quality, service, image, or innovative feature. On the other hand, if the product is intended to be a value brand with an affordable price, a low price should reflect that strategy. Zellers' everyday low pricing policy is intended to reinforce its image of affordable value.

Pricing Objectives

The strategic pricing objectives of the firm are an important determinant of price. Firms have different pricing objectives such as sales, market share, profit, responding to competitors, industry stability, and survival. If the objective is to increase market share or sales, a firm would price more aggressively and seek price-sensitive segments that are receptive to lower prices. For example, McDonald's has aggressively lowered its prices in recent years in an attempt to gain market share in the stagnant fast food market. Firms with market share or sales objectives use price as a promotional tool and a means to improve their competitive position.

If the primary objective is profitability, prices are usually set higher, and the firm should target segments willing to pay higher prices. Sometimes, firms have an objective to match the price of a competitor and not be undersold. In these cases, a firm is prepared to match or beat a competitor's price by a certain amount. Other times, large firms may punish smaller competitors who try to gain market share through price-cutting, by setting their prices at such low levels that the smaller rivals hardly make any money. Firms sometimes price cooperatively, especially after a price war in order to bring about stability in the market. Start-ups or companies that have fallen on hard times frequently adopt survival as their pricing strategy. In these cases, firms will charge any price to ensure their survival. This may entail charging prices below costs to keep the company going, with hopes that when better times arrive, the firm will be able to raise its price to profitable levels.

Single- Versus Multiple-Product Line

Pricing decisions must account for the effects of a single product's price on the rest of the product line. For instance, introducing a cheese-flavoured chip will likely affect the sales of an existing naturally flavoured chip. Introducing a new product at a premium price may also give the rest of the items in the product line a high-price image. On the other hand, introducing a new product at a low price may make the rest of the product line appear cheap in the eyes of potential customers. For example, premium car companies avoid introducing models at very low prices as this may tarnish the image of the product line. For these reasons, firms need to take into account the existence of interrelationships among items in the product line when they set prices.

Cost and Price Dynamics

A phenomenon that affects a firm's pricing is cost dynamics. Marketing and other business researchers have observed that manufacturing costs fall with cumulative experience. This phenomenon was first observed in the 1930s, when the number of labour hours

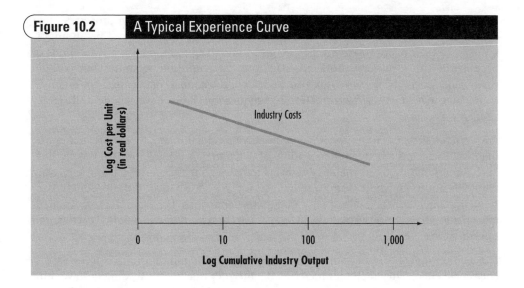

Figure 10.2 — A Typical Experience Curve

Log Cost per Unit (in real dollars)

Industry Costs

0   10   100   1,000

Log Cumulative Industry Output

required to produce an airplane substantially declined as production accumulated.[5] Initially, it was thought that only the labour portion of manufacturing costs decreased with cumulative production. But later on it was demonstrated by the Boston Consulting Group that total costs declined with cumulative output. This relationship between total unit costs and cumulative production became known as the **experience curve.** Figure 10.2 shows the behaviour of industry costs as cumulative volume increases (an experience curve when plotted on a log-log scale appears as a straight line).

Firms have the greatest opportunity to establish a leadership position very early in the industry's life when cost declines at a much faster rate than at later stages. Taking advantage of such cost reduction opportunities will help a firm to build a cost advantage and become an industry price leader. Developing aggressive expansion plans can be facilitated by a high market growth rate. It is relatively easier to increase market share when the market is growing, as additional sales need not be taken from competitors—a move that is normally resisted. In low- or no-growth markets, on the other hand, substantial sales and market share gains are very difficult, as attempts to make such gains are usually countered by competitors.

The **experience curve** represents the relationship between total unit costs and cumulative production.

Sources of the Experience Curve Effect

The effects of the experience curve on cost reduction reflect the impact of a variety of factors. Many firms strive to find better ways to organize work via improved methods and work specialization. Companies are constantly experimenting with new ways to organize their workforce. Management introduces new technologies in an effort to make production more efficient. Cost reduction from experience effects come mainly from learning, technological advances, product redesign and standardization, and economies of scale.

Learning. Learning reflects the improvements that take place in the workplace as a result of practice or application of new methods. Labour efficiency improves as workers repeat a particular task, they become more knowledgeable, and they bring about improvements that increase workplace efficiency. Equipment is used more productively as workers become more familiar with their operation. Learning also includes operational innovations whereby workers figure out how to procure, manufacture, process orders, distribute, and service goods more efficiently. Redesign of work such as using a different organizational structure or greater specialization can also result in greater efficiency.

Chapter 10 / Pricing Strategy

Technological advances. Technological advances such as new production processes often contribute to cost reductions. Process innovation and improvements can be an important source of cost improvement. For example, replacing traditional batch methods of production with continuous-flow manufacturing can contribute to appreciable cost declines. Changes in the resource mix also contribute substantial cost savings. For example, companies that substituted automation techniques for labour have experienced significant cost reductions.

Product redesign and standardization. As cumulative production of a product increases, the manufacturer gains a better understanding of the materials needed to make the product. Such understanding often enables engineers to redesign the product by using less costly materials and even improving, in many cases, the performance of the product. Also, standardizing products can lead to dramatic cost reductions. For example, an auto manufacturer can lower costs by making fewer types of chassis, engines, seats, body styles, and transmissions.

Economies of scale. Economies of scale represent another significant source of the experience curve effect. They represent increases in efficiency due to size, leading to lower unit costs. As the firm increases cumulative output, it obtains economies of scale, which, in turn, lead to lower costs. A larger scale is typically associated with increased purchasing power, as increases in purchasing volume lead to better deals and lower unit prices. This also helps decrease costs, adding to the experience curve effect.

Costs, Prices, and the Product Life Cycle

The experience curve concept is of strategic importance in the planning of prices and other aspects of business planning. It has been observed that as industry costs decline, prices decline as well. In many industries the behaviour of costs and prices varies depending on the stage of the product life cycle. This pattern is illustrated in Figure 10.3, which shows a typical pattern of behaviour of industry costs and prices during the various stages of a product's life cycle.

Introduction stage. In the introduction stage costs exceed prices. Prices are set at levels lower than costs in expectation of lower costs in the future and to expand the market

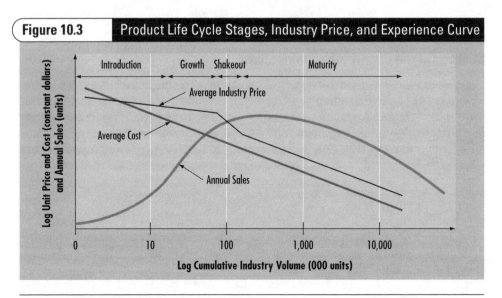

Figure 10.3 Product Life Cycle Stages, Industry Price, and Experience Curve

SOURCE: From *Analysis for Strategic Market Decisions*, 1st edition by George S. Day. © 1986. Reprinted with permission of South-Western, a division of Thomson Learning: www.thomsonrights.com.

through lower prices. The period of negative margins ends as sales take off, an event that signals the beginning of the growth stage.

Growth stage. As demand rises rapidly during the growth stage, outstripping supply, costs decline but price levels remain almost unchanged. In the growth stage the industry leader maintains a price umbrella over less efficient competitors, trading future market share for current profits. These profits are needed to finance the investment in working capital, capacity, and marketing activities.

The prospect of rising profit margins and rapid growth, however, attracts a large number of new entrants. Although the new entrants have higher costs than the market leaders, they are able to survive because the price umbrella is high enough to cover their costs and they can operate profitably. In addition, the recent entrants are motivated by their narrower margins to pursue aggressive marketing actions to increase their market share to lower their costs.

Shakeout stage. The number of entrants attracted to the industry by the high growth and profit prospects can be quite staggering. For example, there were over 200 personal computer companies during the high growth period of this new technology. However, as the period of high growth ends, the market leader abruptly lowers prices much faster than the rate of cost decline. The most important reasons for the significantly lower prices include the following: (1) the market leader attempts to gain or regain market share lost to late market entrants; (2) late entrants added to industry capacity cause a high degree of excess capacity, putting a downward pressure on prices; and (3) aggressive late entrants cut prices in an attempt to buy market share. As a result of the drastically lower prices, marginal competitors are forced to leave the market. This was the case at the end of the growth period of the personal computer industry, when IBM, the market leader, lowered the price of its PC, causing a dramatic shakeout in the industry, leading to the exit of many marginal competitors.

Maturity and decline stages. In the maturity stage, the industry returns to stability and prices begin to decline in parallel with costs while maintaining constant margins.[6] But as the industry progresses into the decline stage, the behaviour of the experience curve and prices becomes quite unpredictable. Although costs can very well continue to decline, in some cases they may actually increase. For example, a manufacturer of industrial gases found that the cost curve for its bottled oxygen not only stopped decreasing but began to increase slightly. In the meantime, the cost of its other oxygen products continued to fall. After careful analysis, management realized that despite a decline in industry sales none of their competitors had dropped out. As a result, all competitors suffered from the excess capacity and higher production costs.[7]

Pricing Implications of the Experience Curve

An important implication of the experience curve is that important cost and pricing advantages can be achieved by pursuing a strategy of accumulating experience faster than competitors do. The location of competitors on the experience curve is determined by their respective accumulated experience or cumulative output. Consequently, competitors with the greatest cumulative output will have the lowest relative total unit costs and highest profit, whereas smaller firms face a significant cost disadvantage. Firms can use their cost advantages to lower their prices and drive competitors out of business.

To illustrate this idea, let us consider an industry with three competitors—A, B, and C. Competitor A is farthest down the experience curve, followed by B and C as shown in Figure 10.4. As a result of their location on the experience curve, A has a significant cost advantage over B and C. Also, while A earns a good profit, B barely makes a profit, and C incurs a loss.

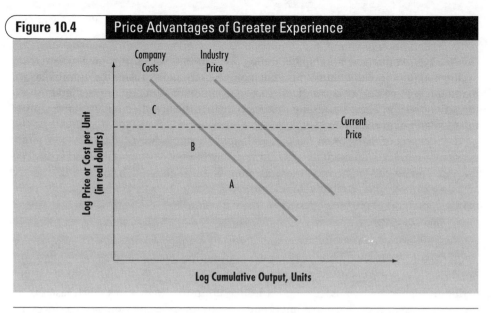

Figure 10.4 | Price Advantages of Greater Experience

SOURCE: Adapted from Derek F. Abell and John S. Hammond, *Strategic Marketing Planning: Problems and Analytical Approaches* (Englewood Cliffs, New Jersey: Prentice-Hall, 1979), 117.

Dominant firms such as A have two options. They can pursue an aggressive strategy of lower prices that could drive out inefficient rivals such as firm C. There is an incentive for firms with the lowest cost to reduce their price. This will make it difficult for less efficient firms to stay in the market. Also, the efficient firm can benefit from the share of exiting businesses and gain experience more rapidly. In addition, the low price may encourage more consumers to enter the market, providing the firm with an opportunity to obtain greater economies of scale. Some firms even lower prices in anticipation of lower unit costs and prices in the future. Such pricing tactics are especially appropriate when there are strong experience effects, which are expected to continue in the future, and when consumers are price sensitive.[8]

However, if firm A chose to maintain a high margin or reduce prices more slowly than costs decline, the resulting price umbrella would allow smaller competitors to remain in the industry. This may not be a wise move for the market leader because it could encourage the smaller firms to gain market share to drive costs down and be in a position to compete more effectively with firm A.

As for the rest of competitors, their costs must keep up with the market leader if they are to maintain their profit margins. Smaller competitors have no other choice but to continue to grow at least as fast as the market leader and pursue cost reductions as effectively as the market leader. If their costs decline more slowly, either because they are growing more slowly or are pursuing cost reductions less aggressively, their profit margins will eventually become too low or negative, forcing them to leave the market. In such a case, a better course of action for a smaller firm may be to find a distinct market segment that it can dominate and where it can build a viable cost position.

Pricing New Products

The pricing problem begins when a product is first introduced to the market. The initial price is the result of the interplay of such factors as the firm's pricing objectives, marketing strategy, positioning, competition, price sensitivity, and costs. There are three choices when pricing a new product. The first choice involves charging a low initial price designed to penetrate the market and capture a high market share before competitors enter the market. The second choice involves charging a high initial price to skim the market. Firms usually choose between these two pricing approaches, depending on the presence of strategic factors such as market, product, pricing, cost, and competitive conditions. If circumstances do not favour choosing one or the other new product pricing strategy, firms charge a price comparable to the price charged by competitors. These pricing strategies are discussed below.

Penetration Pricing

Penetration pricing is the exact opposite of price skimming. It is also known as pricing below the competition, or market share pricing. Penetration pricing involves setting a price below the normal, long-range market price of the product. Firms using penetration pricing sacrifice profit margins in order to gain market share. Many firms have been very successful using penetration pricing, including E*Trade, Schwab, and CanJet Airlines. Penetration pricing is appropriate under the conditions listed in Figure 10.5.

Penetration pricing involves setting a price below the normal, long-range market price of the product.

Figure 10.5	Strategic Factors Influencing the Choice Between Penetration Pricing and Price Skimming	
Penetration Pricing	**Strategic Factors**	**Price Skimming**
	Market factors	
Large	Market size	Small
Elastic	Elasticity of demand	Inelastic
	Product factors	
Low	Product differentiation	High
Long	Product life span	Short
No	Product protected by a patent	Yes
	Price factors	
Yes	High price will attract competition	No
No	Customers use higher prices as an indicator of higher quality	Yes
	Cost factors	
No	Substantial margins are required to recover product development and other costs	Yes
Yes	Substantial cost reductions are expected due to economies of scale and experience effects	No
	Competitive factors	
Yes	A good chance that competitors will enter market shortly with a similar product	No

If a firm introduces a new product at a low price, hoping to raise it afterward, it may experience difficulty as customers become accustomed to the low price and may resist

Chapter 10 / Pricing Strategy

future price increases. The firm needs to make it clear to customers that any low introductory prices are not permanent, and prices will increase in the future. For this reason, instead of introducing the product at a low price, many firms offer temporary price reductions in other forms such as coupons or rebates. It should also be noted that firms that enter a market using penetration pricing run the risk of triggering a price war as the Strategy in Action box illustrates.[9]

Strategy in Action — WESTJET AIRLINES

In June 2004, WestJet Airlines Ltd. announced that it would begin scheduled transborder service into the United States using a very aggressive pricing policy. According to chief executive officer Clive Beddoe, the objective of such a low price was to present an "Oh-my-gosh" fare. At the time of the announcement, WestJet unveiled introductory, one-way base fares ranging from $72 to $102 for flights to five U.S. cities starting in the fall of 2004—Los Angeles, San Francisco, Phoenix, Fort Lauderdale, and Orlando. Regular base fares would range from $142 one way for a Toronto to Los Angeles flight, for example, to $242 for Calgary to Orlando or Fort Lauderdale. WestJet hoped that the low fares would encourage people who wouldn't otherwise fly, and it would also take passengers away from rival Air Canada, whose operating costs were estimated to be almost double the costs of WestJet's. WestJet enjoyed lower costs relative to larger airlines because it operated fewer planes, employed fewer people, and "cherry-picked" by serving only the most profitable routes. WestJet had developed a low-cost culture, and it seized every opportunity to cut costs and make the airline more efficient. WestJet's entry into the transborder market with a low-price policy was certain to cause a price war as Air Canada announced that it would match WestJet's low fares.

Price Skimming

Price skimming is the practice of setting the initial price of a product at the highest level customers are willing to pay.

Sequential price skimming is the practice of setting a high initial price but as the top of the market becomes saturated and costs decline, the initial price is gradually reduced.

Price skimming is the practice of setting the initial price of a product at the highest level customers are willing to pay. The objective of price skimming is to get the greatest possible revenue from the least sensitive buyers. Although such a pricing strategy limits the number of potential buyers, it allows the firm to charge high margins and recoup its investments much sooner than if it set a lower price. For example, Toyota Prius is currently selling at higher prices to capitalize on the lack of competition and recoup the high initial research and development costs.

A common variant of price skimming is **sequential price skimming,** which is the practice of setting a high initial price, but as the top of the market becomes saturated and costs decline, the initial price is gradually reduced. By lowering its price, the firm makes the product available to a larger segment of the market that would not otherwise buy the product. Also, the lower price may discourage some competitors from entering the industry since they would be earning lower profits. In some cases the firm is forced to lower its initially high prices as competitors introduce their own versions of the product and the firm loses its monopoly power. For example, manufacturers of high-definition television introduced their products at high prices to recoup the high development costs. Prices of such products have started to decline as costs are declining and competitive pressures for lower prices continue to mount. Price skimming is appropriate under the conditions listed in Figure 10.5.

Parity Pricing

Parity pricing is the practice of setting a price equal to the economic value of the product. Parity pricing minimizes the role of price as a competitive tool to gain market share or earn higher margins. Firms that use parity pricing rely on other elements of their marketing program to achieve their marketing objectives. Parity prices are not necessarily equal or similar to competitors' prices. They may be higher or lower, depending on the product's relative quality. For example, if the relative quality of a product is higher than the relative quality of competing products, a parity price should be higher to reflect the quality difference.

Parity pricing is typically used when conditions do not favour a penetration or skimming pricing. For example, when demand is elastic but existing competitors will not allow a rival to undercut current industry prices. In this case, managers should avoid using penetration pricing because of fear of competitive retaliation and lower profits. Parity pricing can also be used when a firm has no significant quality or cost advantages over competitors. Companies often use parity prices on successful new products because it increases demand for other company products. For example, auto companies introducing highly popular models often avoid charging high prices to draw more people into their showrooms, hoping that sales of other models will increase.[10]

> **Parity pricing** is the practice of setting a price equal to the economic value of the product.

Pricing Existing Products

The initial pricing strategy—skimming, penetration, or parity—establishes the general level at which a firm expects to sell its product. However, the actual price customers pay for an existing product is seldom the same as the general price established initially. The general price level is usually adjusted to reflect market demand and competitive, promotional, and other industry or company-specific conditions. The most commonly used pricing strategies for existing products are discussed next.

Value Pricing

Value pricing is a market-driven approach to setting prices. It requires a good knowledge of customers' needs and benefits offered by competing products. Companies employing value pricing examine the value of their products relative to competitors' offerings. In **value pricing**, the final price a company charges for its product reflects the value of the product to customers. For this reason, the effective use of value-based pricing requires extensive customer and competitive analysis.

> **Value pricing** is the practice of setting a price that reflects the value of the product to customers.

Value pricing is intended to capture more of the value of the product to customers. Managers must find the price that maximizes profitability in the long run.[11] Maximizing sales is not always associated with maximum profitability. For example, retailers such as Holt Renfrew could gain market share if they lowered their prices but it is doubtful that they would increase their profits. A decision to lower prices may help a firm achieve its sales objectives but at the expense of profitability.

The process of determining value-based prices is shown in Figure 10.6. It involves finding a market segment for the product, determining the needs of the customers in the segment,

Figure 10.6	Value Pricing
1. Determine target price based on consumer, competitive, and other factors
2. Subtract desired channel intermediary markup
3. Subtract desired manufacturer margin
4. Determine target cost to be recouped
5. Produce product

and estimating the value of the product. The selected segment's characteristics, competitors' offerings, and other factors such as marketing strategy, desired positioning, pricing objectives, and products offered in the product line will help the firm determine a target price for the product. Once the target price is determined, the channel intermediary markups and the manufacturer's margins are deducted from the target price to produce the target cost. The product will then be produced only if the company believes that it can meet the target cost. The development and pricing of Miata is a classic example of value pricing: [12]

Strategy in Action — MIATA

Miata was introduced in 1989 to fill a void in the car market that was left when most of the great small sports cars of the time such as MGB, Triumph, and Fiat Spider had been discontinued. The only four-cylinder, front-engine, classic two-seater for sale in North America at the time was the Alfa Romeo Spider Veloce. Although the lack of an affordable true sports car was obvious to all automobile companies, only Mazda decided to do something about it and introduced its small sports car, Miata.

The Miata was designed by Marc Jordan, a designer with Mazda's California design studio, and Bob Hall, an automotive journalist, who had been hired by Mazda in 1981 to work as product planner on the Miata development team. Miata was designed in Mazda's California studio, but the engineering was done in Japan, and the car has always been built in that country.

Introduced in the summer of 1989 as an early 1990 model, the Miata looked like an early 1960s Lotus Elan with a base price of $13,000. Mazda sold 35,944 Miatas during the 1990 model year in the United States. The company could easily have sold three times as many cars at sticker prices or more in that first year had it made enough of them. With its smaller size, simple drivetrain, outstanding handling, and unpretentious character, Miata had a wide appeal that made it a huge success throughout the world.

Mazda, in determining the features and price of its Miata model, studied the type of sports car that buyers desired, the price they were willing to pay, and what competitors were offering. The company's research showed that there was a need for a low-priced sports car, since such a car was not offered by other automobile companies at the time. This led Mazda management to position its Miata model as a true sports car at an affordable price. The value-based approach that Mazda followed in setting the Miata's price, combined with the offering of a true sports car to the market, is believed to be responsible for its successful introduction and the subsequent sales performance of this model.

Cost-Plus Pricing

Cost-plus pricing is a method of setting the price of a product on the basis of its full unit cost and adding a desired margin.

Cost-plus is the most common pricing method. Companies use cost-based pricing because it is simple and easy to administer. Cost-plus pricing is based on cost data that are considered hard data and relatively easily obtainable. Cost-based methods give the impression of fairness as prices are determined on the basis of cost calculations, and a desired margin is added on price.

As shown in Figure 10.7, cost-plus pricing starts with a product that the company thinks customers need. The company invests money to provide the product with features and services that will make the product more attractive to potential customers. Once the product is ready, all fixed and variable costs are added to come up with a full unit cost figure. Then a desired margin is added that determines the manufacturer's selling price. Markups are usually based on individual experiences, but they are sometimes standard in the industry, or they represent the amount of profits the firm needs to make from the

Figure 10.7	Cost-Plus Pricing

1. Produce product with appropriate features and service level
2. Compute full unit cost
3. Add desired manufacturer margin
4. Add desired channel intermediary margin
5. Retail price

product.[13] Finally, distributors add their own markup to determine the final price of the product to customers.

The major advantage of cost-plus pricing is its simplicity and the ease of administering it. The major disadvantages of cost-based methods are the lack of customer and competitor considerations in determining the price, which may cause a firm to charge prices that are either too high or too low. Another problem is that it is not possible to know the unit cost of a product before determining the price. One reason for this problem is that price affects the volume of the product, which in turn affects unit cost.[14] A third disadvantage is that the sales forecast may not be realized. If actual sales are less than expected, the full unit cost will be higher and the profit margin will be lower than originally estimated. Often, firms react to lower margins by raising prices to maintain profit margins. Unfortunately, this may result in even lower sales.

Prestige Pricing

Prestige pricing involves setting prices at the highest possible level. High prices communicate an image of high quality, exclusivity, and prestige. For example, Harry Rosen, the upscale retailer of high-quality men's clothing, charges prices that are higher than the average prices of other retail stores. In the automotive industry, Porsche sells some of its models at prices well over $200,000.

Prices reflect not only the cost of the product or service to a customer but are used as signals of product or service quality.[15] In many product categories, consumers associate high prices with high quality. In studies in which price was the only perceived difference between products, customers' perceptions of product quality was determined by price.[16] Anderson and Simester report that in an experiment they conducted they found that raising the price of an item from $34 to $39 increased demand by a third.[17] Buyers associate high price with high quality under the following conditions:

- It is easier for consumers to obtain information about price than about quality.
- Buyers are looking for a product of high quality so they risk paying the high price without the product necessarily being of higher quality than cheaper brands.
- Consumers believe that in the particular product category, the relationship between high price and high quality is true. Buyers who usually associate high prices with high quality are frequently new consumers who are not aware of the quality of the various brands but consider quality to be important.[18]

> **Prestige pricing** involves setting prices at the highest possible level to communicate an image of high quality, exclusivity, and prestige.

Everyday Low Pricing

Everyday low pricing is the practice of selling merchandise at the same low prices all year round, instead of the sawtooth pattern of alternating price increases and decreases. Firms that adopt everyday low pricing cut prices permanently by 20 to 40 percent, depending on price levels and promotional discounts offered under the previous pricing regime. Under this type of pricing, other forms of trade and consumer promotions, such as rebates and coupons, are abandoned and advertising spending is reduced. Offering everyday low prices is appropriate for markets in which customers prefer to shop at stores that have

> **Everyday low pricing** is the practice of selling merchandise at the same low prices all year round, instead of the sawtooth pattern of alternating price increases and decreases.

consistently low prices. No-Frills Supermarkets attract shoppers by consistently offering low prices. General Motors switched to value pricing by offering low, no-haggle prices to attract customers who dislike shopping at dealerships where prices are determined through haggling. Everyday low pricing offers the following advantages:

1. *Price credibility.* Many consumers are frustrated with commonly used pricing practices because it is often difficult to ascertain the true prices of products. Everyday low pricing establishes greater price credibility in the eyes of customers by having more consistency in prices than the high-low pricing alternative. This pricing method helps build brand loyalty by maintaining consistency in pricing and often helps fend off the challenge of private labels and other low-priced products.

2. *Lower transaction costs.* Everyday low pricing also reduces customer transaction costs as customers are assured of low prices and do not search elsewhere.[19] In essence, everyday low pricing is a low price guarantee, since it takes away the consumers' perceived risk of paying too much. It is costly for consumers to continually monitor all current prices. Many consumers avoid searching for low prices and they base their decisions on the reputation created by past pricing practices by the firm. For example, if there is a gasoline station that has a reputation for always charging the lowest prices, car owners looking for low prices are more likely to patronize that station.

3. *Problems with traditional pricing methods.* Manufacturers are also frustrated with traditional pricing methods. Many of the discounts manufacturers offer customers are absorbed by distributors and are not passed on to customers. There are also problems with forward buying and diversion. **Forward buying** occurs when retailers order more products at discounted prices than they plan to sell. Therefore, when prices increase in future periods, the retailer generates larger profits. **Diversion** means that distributors sell the discounted goods in areas not designated for receiving the discount. For example, if a manufacturer reduces the price of its product in Ontario, distributors may buy large quantities in Ontario at the lower prices and sell the goods in another province at regular prices.

The use of everyday low pricing has met with mixed success. Some retailers including Toys R Us, Wal-Mart, and Home Depot have used it successfully while others, such as Sears, have moved away from it. A disadvantage of everyday low pricing is that shoppers will purchase from rivals when rivals offer special deals on their products. For this reason, companies that have successfully implemented everyday low pricing have found that some type of price discounts is also needed from time to time. As a result, even dedicated practitioners of everyday low pricing have modified their pricing strategy by offering a combination of everyday low prices and sales promotions. Other retailers have used **limited everyday low pricing**, instead of having everyday low prices across the board. For example, The Bay, the leading Canadian department store chain, has used this strategy to increase sales. The "Bay Value Program" started with 120 items sold at everyday low prices with the objective of raising this number to about 300 items by the end of the program's first year.[20]

Randomized Pricing

Randomized pricing involves maintaining a high regular price and discounting this price on a random basis.[21] A firm using randomized pricing varies its price weekly, daily, or even hourly. This pricing strategy benefits the firm because it makes it difficult for consumers to know, or discover, which firm charges the lowest price on any given day. As well, randomized pricing makes it difficult for companies to predict competitors' prices and this reduces their ability to undercut each other's prices.

Randomized pricing is used by diverse companies, including airlines, department stores, services, supermarkets, and specialty stores. In the airline industry, for instance,

Forward buying occurs when retailers order more products at discounted prices than they plan to sell.

Diversion means that distributors sell the discounted goods in areas not designated for receiving the discount.

Limited everyday low pricing involves lowering the prices of a limited number of items instead of having everyday low prices across the board.

Randomized pricing involves maintaining a high regular price and discounting this price on a random basis.

airfares change frequently and randomly. By randomizing their prices, airlines make it difficult for rival airlines and customers to learn from experience and predict airfares. Another example of randomized pricing is the advertised weekly sales or specials in local newspapers. These advertised prices vary weekly, making it difficult for competitors to know which items to place on special to undercut the firm's prices.

Promotional Pricing

Promotional pricing involves using lower prices for promotional reasons. Price cuts are frequently used to promote product sales. The impact of a price cut on competing brands is not symmetric since in every market there are price tiers. For example, in the automobile industry, there are high-priced, medium-priced, and low-priced cars. It has been found empirically that a price cut draws market share from competitors in the same price tier, as well as lower-priced tiers but rarely from the tiers above.[22] Since a price reduction affects brands differently, the response to the price cut should differ depending on the brand's price tier. For example, if a brand from a lower price tier cuts its price, a higher-tier brand should not respond, since it is highly unlikely that it will be affected by the price cut.

> **Promotional pricing** involves using lower prices for promotional reasons.

Product Line Pricing

Pricing products that are part of a product line is more complicated than pricing single products. For example, setting a high price for a product in a product line may cause all products in the line to be perceived as too expensive. Also, charging too low a price on a product that is part of a product line may make the entire line appear low priced and inexpensive. If the products in a product line are complementary, their prices should be determined simultaneously, as the price of one product may affect the demand of another product. This section discusses the specific pricing strategies used by firms to deal with issues related to setting prices for a product line.

Cross-Subsidization Pricing

Cross-subsidization pricing is employed when profits from one or more profitable products are used to cover losses by other products, support an offensive attack against competitors, or penetrate key markets. Cross-subsidization is intended to exploit complementarities among products or support a weak product with profits made by stronger products. Cross-subsidization is used in the following circumstances:

> **Cross-subsidization pricing** is employed when profits from one or more profitable products are used to cover losses by other products, support an offensive attack against competitors, or penetrate key markets.

1. *Pricing complements.* If a firm's products are complements, it may find it advantageous to sell one of the products at cost or even below cost and charge a relatively high price for the other product. For example, manufacturers of computer printers and ink cartridges charge a low price on the printers and a high price on the ink cartridges. This strategy increases the sale of the printers and, consequently, the demand for the much more profitable ink cartridges. The higher profit from the ink cartridges subsidizes the lower profit from the printers, but the overall profit could very well be higher than if the printers had been priced at normal levels. The success of such cross-subsidization strategies depends on whether the buyer of the discounted item also buys the most expensive item from the same company.
2. *Cover low profits or losses.* Cross-subsidization often takes place when a firm covers the low profits or losses by one product with profits from other products. An example of this form of cross-subsidization occurs when a firm introduces a promising new product that is initially unprofitable. In this case, profits from established products are channelled to the new product, with the hope that the new product will become profitable and self-sufficient.

3. *Multiple market competition.* Firms that compete on multiple markets may also use cross-subsidization pricing. A firm may attack competitors with a low price to gain market share from them. The low margins or losses earned on one product are offset by the higher margins earned by products competing in other, less competitive markets. Many global companies have used this strategy to gain market share against domestic firms. Domestic companies are at a disadvantage when they face multi-country competitors with cross-subsidization capabilities. The latter usually operate in many markets in which they enjoy high profits and use these profits to dominate other markets. Often these global competitors lower their prices to steal domestic companies' customers and cover the lower margins with profits earned in other markets.

4. *Defend core brands.* Market leaders also use cross-subsidization to defend their core brands, if they are threatened by smaller companies. Since they own more resources and have a greater variety of brands, they will lower the price of one of these brands to underprice the smaller competitor and once the smaller rival exits the market, the market leader can increase prices again. The Laker Airways example discussed in the Strategy in Action box explains how some companies have used this strategy.[23]

Strategy in Action — LAKER AIRWAYS

Laker Airways, an upstart airline company, took on the major airlines head-on a few years ago when it introduced its skytrain "no-frills" operation in the highly profitable transatlantic route. The airline drastically reduced services normally offered by major airlines. Also, it had a very lean operation as it had only a few airplanes and a small ground staff. As a result of its lower operating expenses, lower overhead and no-frills operation, Laker Airways was able to offer much lower fares than its major competitors. It cut transatlantic passenger fares by half. Thus, a London to New York flight cost the passenger $135, half of what was charged by the giant airlines. Laker's pricing strategy proved highly successful for a period of time. The lower cost of flying attracted a large number of travellers who preferred to pay the much lower fares than fly with the other airlines at a higher cost. But Laker's success was hurting the larger competitors, which began to sustain substantial losses. As a result, the major airlines reacted to the threat by lowering fares on this route while they used profits from other routes to subsidize losses on that route. Laker could not sustain similar losses as it had no other sources of revenues and was forced to exit from the industry.

Price Bundling

Price bundling is the practice of selling two or more products or services together as a package deal at a single "bundle price."

Price bundling is the practice of selling two or more products or services together as a package deal at a single "bundle price." For example, travel agencies sell all-inclusive packages that include airfare, hotel, and meals at a single "all-inclusive" price instead of charging for each item separately.

Companies use price bundling to help increase overall sales of the company's products, as many consumers respond to the lower overall price and buy the bundle. It can build sales of a new product by bundling an existing popular brand with a new brand. Software developers frequently introduce new products by bundling the new products with existing products. Bundling can create barriers to entry and reduce competition by making it harder for smaller companies to compete. For example, Microsoft Office has bundled its Excel spreadsheet with the Microsoft Word processing program and its Microsoft PowerPoint presentation program at one overall low price, making it hard for smaller companies to compete effectively. Finally, consumers can benefit from bundling as they may pay a lower price. For example, vacationers who buy all-inclusive packages that include airfare, hotel accommodation, and meals usually pay a lower overall price than if they paid separately.

There are two types of bundling strategies:

1. *Pure bundling.* **Pure bundling** is the practice of selling two or more products at an overall price lower than the total price a customer would have paid if he or she had bought the products separately. With a pure bundling strategy, buyers can buy the items only as a bundle but not separately. For example, most airlines bundle together airfare and in-flight meals.
2. *Mixed bundling.* **Mixed bundling** allows the customer to buy the different items separately at regular prices or as a bundle at a lower total price as in a pure bundling strategy. For example, sellers of software programs may sell the software and technical support as a bundle or sell the software and technical support separately.

In general, a mixed bundling strategy is more profitable than pure bundling strategies. Consumers often perceive mixed bundling as being of higher value than pure bundling. Pure bundling is not appropriate when buyers do not derive any benefits from the bundled products or if they feel forced to purchase products they do not need. Companies that offer strictly bundled products are also vulnerable to attacks by smaller, focused competitors who offer unbundled products. For example, in the automotive aftermarket, third-party firms focus their efforts on profitable areas such as brakes and mufflers, leaving other maintenance tasks requiring greater investments in facilities and training to the automobile dealers.

> **Pure bundling** is the practice of selling two or more products at an overall price lower than the total price customers would have paid if they had purchased the products separately.

> **Mixed bundling** allows customers to buy the different items separately at regular prices or as a bundle at a lower total price as in a pure bundling strategy.

Two-Part Pricing

Firms using **two-part pricing** charge a fixed amount for the right to purchase the goods or services, plus a per-unit charge for each unit purchased. By charging a usage fee, consumers can vary the amounts they purchase according to their individual demands for the products. This is the pricing strategy used by sports clubs, health clubs, and other membership clubs. For example, golf courses and health clubs typically charge a fixed initiation fee and a variable amount to use the facilities. With membership clubs, such as Costco, members pay a membership fee for the right to buy at low cost.

> **Two-part pricing** involves charging a fixed amount for the right to purchase the goods or services, plus a per-unit charge for each unit purchased.

Two-part pricing can be more profitable than charging a price for each unit sold. By charging a fixed fee up-front, a firm is able to cover part of its expenses and enhance its profits. Often, most, if not all, profits are derived from the initial, fixed amount. Warehouse clubs like Costco and Sam's Club make a good chunk of their profits from membership fees.

Another rationale for the use of two-part pricing is the following. Let's assume that management of a golf club charged a single price that included the initiation fee and the use of facilities. Such a pricing scheme would penalize the heavy user who would have to pay the initiation fee every time he or she used the facilities. This would likely create a disincentive for heavy users to use the golf club facilities. If a two-part pricing were used instead, the price to the heavy user would be lower than the light user, as the initiation fee would be paid only once and would be spread over more units. By charging an initiation fee and a usage fee the golf club overcomes this problem and helps maximize sales.

Responding to Competitors' Prices

Many firms establish pricing policies that dictate how to respond to competitors' prices. Companies in oligopolistic industries follow the price level established by the market leader. Many firms have a policy of matching or beating competitors' prices. Others have mechanisms in place that trigger an automatic response to competitors' price changes.

Chapter 10 / Pricing Strategy

Follow-the-Leader Pricing

Follow-the-leader pricing is used by most firms, especially smaller ones that seldom set their prices independently of competitors. Instead, these firms follow the price established by the market leader. This pricing strategy is usually adopted by firms in oligopolistic industries, where a small number of firms account for most of the production in that industry. The reason firms follow this pricing approach is that they recognize their mutual interdependence and that cooperation is better than confrontation.

Follow-the-leader pricing is essentially a me-too pricing policy designed to avoid pricing confrontations with market leaders. Its main advantage is that it contributes to industry stability and avoids price wars. Its drawback is that it deprives a firm of the opportunity to use price as a valuable tool to establish a unique image in the customers' mind.

Sometimes smaller firms are able to avoid the market leader's reaction and follow an independent pricing policy. The reaction of market leaders depends on how they view the smaller firm. If they view the small firm as a non-threatening competitor, they may permit a price differential to exist. Otherwise, competitors may view a smaller price-cutter as a direct threat and respond with a price reduction of their own.

Price Matching

Price matching is a pricing technique used widely in retail markets where stores promise that they will not be undersold, but that they will match or beat a competitor's lower advertised price. For example, Future Shop promises to beat its competitors' prices by 10 percent. Price matching is a form of price guarantee to consumers that they will not miss out on a deal provided by a competitor's low price.

Price matching appeals to customers because it assures them of low prices. However, if all firms in the market announce a price-matching policy, they may end up with a higher overall price, since the guarantee weakens the incentive for competitors to undercut each other's prices. If a firm lowers its price, it triggers a price war as rivals match the lower price, leaving everybody worse off. In this sense, it seems that price-matching policies are a form of warning to competitors, implying that if they cut their price, the price cut will be matched. Many firms have apparently realized that price matching can, in effect, lead to higher prices and, for this reason, have adopted it.

Price matching can be a successful pricing strategy for some firms such as Future Shop because they have a cost advantage relative to smaller rivals. However, when price matching, especially in the form of a price-beating guarantee, leads to a price war, it may be unsustainable in the long run, since it can cut deeply into profits. This happened to Zellers in the mid-90s when the company responded to Wal-Mart's entry into Canada by matching its prices. This pricing soon led Zellers to drastically lower levels of profitability, forcing the company to seek other ways to restore its previous profitability. For price matching to be a viable pricing strategy, the firm needs to have a low cost structure, preferably the lowest in the industry. If its costs are higher than its competitors' costs, the firm may encounter trouble with such a pricing policy.

Trigger Pricing

Firms that have participated in an industry for a long time frequently make tacit agreements to pricing strategies that maximize the collective profits of all industry rivals. **Tacit collusion** occurs when firms agree on prices indirectly based on their understanding of how their rivals will react to their prices. This understanding has been acquired after observing the rivals' actions over a period of time. For example, if a firm lowers its price to gain market share, and every time its competitors respond by reducing their prices, the firm learns that cutting prices is futile and this results in tacit collusion. On the other hand, if other firms fail to respond to a rival's price cut, tacit collusion does not occur.[24]

Trigger pricing can be used to enforce tacit collusive arrangements. Trigger pricing strategies are based on tacit agreements that everybody will charge a high industry price. If one firm cheats and charges a low price, the other firms will retaliate and punish the cheater by charging the low price. In a sense, when a firm cheats, it pulls the trigger that causes its rivals to lower their prices. Trigger pricing is based on the premise that the losses from being punished far exceed the benefits of cheating in one period. Such pricing strategies are applicable in repeated games—that is, in markets where there are repeat purchases and firms are given a chance to respond to competitors' pricing actions. Trigger strategies are not valid in short-lived, one-period situations because by the time the trigger comes into effect, the game is over.

To use the trigger strategy, a firm needs an effective system to monitor rivals' prices in order to launch a timely response. For this reason, trigger strategies are not always feasible and firms may use other pricing strategies, such as price matching, which do not require a monitoring system.

> **Trigger pricing** is based on tacit agreements that everybody will charge a high industry price.

Price Customization Strategies

Instead of charging the same price to all customers, a firm can increase its revenues by charging different prices for the same product. **Price customization** essentially involves the adaptation of price to differences in price sensitivities among segments. For example, airlines charge higher fares when demand for air travel is higher and people are less sensitive to higher fares, such as during the Christmas holidays or the summer high season. Also, hotel rates in Las Vegas are much higher on weekends because demand is much higher then than on weekdays. Common price customization practices include the following:

1. *Price Customization by Customer.* Demand often varies widely among different demographic and other types of customer groups. In these cases, a firm can gain by charging consumers different prices, depending on their price sensitivities. Some popular pricing schemes include youth fares charged by airlines and lower prices for children at movie theatres.
2. *Price Customization by Time.* Many firms are in markets characterized by wide fluctuations in demand; periods of high demand are followed by periods of low demand. Price customization by time, also called **peak-load pricing,** involves charging a lower price during the non-peak period and raising the price during the peak period. Peak-load pricing is commonly used by public utilities, telephone companies, and private-sector companies, such as airlines and holiday resorts.
3. *Price Customization by Location.* Location is another way of segmenting markets for pricing purposes. Firms can charge different prices in different regions or countries, depending on demand conditions. For example, people attending hockey games or live performances frequently pay higher ticket prices for seats closer to the ice rink or stage.

> **Price customization** involves the adaptation of price to differences in demand elasticities among segments.

> **Peak-load pricing** involves charging a lower price during the non-peak period and raising the price during the peak period.

Price customization works under certain conditions.[25] First, the firm must be able to divide the market into segments with different price sensitivities. If price sensitivities are the same, it is pointless to segment the market, as the firm would maximize its profits by charging the same price in all segments. Second, people must not be able to transfer between segments. For example, if a price discount applies to a certain age group like seniors, other age groups must be prevented from taking advantage of such discounts. Finally, the different prices must be perceived as being fair by customers. For example, people do not normally complain that children pay lower prices at movie theatres. But most individuals would complain if some adults were paying a lower price.

Price-Profitability Analysis

Once a price level is decided on, pricing managers should assess the profit implications of that price. One useful technique for evaluating the profit potential and the associated risk of a pricing decision is break-even analysis. The break-even point, safety margin, break-even market share, and the sales change required to break even following a price change are useful concepts that can aid a firm in its pricing analysis.

Break-even Unit Sales

Break-even analysis shows the level of production at which revenue equals total cost.

Break-even analysis shows the level of production at which revenue equals total cost. If a firm produces above the break-even point, it will make a profit. If a firm produces below the break-even point, it will lose money. Lower break-even points are preferred to higher break-even points. Assuming that variable and fixed costs are known, a firm can evaluate the impact of different price levels on its break-even point. At a given variable and fixed cost, a higher price lowers the break-even point. On the other hand, a lower price raises the break-even point.

The following is an example of break-even analysis. Let's assume that the variable cost is $2 per unit, the fixed cost is $9,000, the expected company sales are 1,500 units, and the size of the market is 5,000 units. What is the break-even point if price is set at $10 per unit? Based on these figures, the break-even point in units is calculated using the following formula:

$$\text{Break-even (units)} = \frac{\text{Fixed cost}}{\text{Price} - \text{Variable cost}}$$

The break-even point is:

$$\text{Break-even (units)} = \frac{\$9,000}{\$10 - \$8}$$
$$= 1,125 \text{ units}$$

Break-even Market Share

The **break-even market share** is the market share a firm needs to achieve before it starts making a profit.

The **break-even market share** is the market share a firm needs to achieve before it starts making a profit. An actual market share lower than the break-even market share suggests that the firm will lose money. The break-even market share is calculated as follows:

$$\text{Break-even market share} = \left[\frac{\text{Break-even unit sales}}{\text{Market size}} \right] \times 100$$
$$= \left[\frac{1,125}{5,000} \right] \times 100$$
$$= 22.5\%$$

Since the break-even market share is 22.5 percent, the firm would have to achieve a market share of 22.5 percent before it starts making a profit.

Safety Margin

Safety margin is a measure of safety or cushion that shows the proportion of sales that can decline (or need to increase) before the break-even point is reached.

The **safety margin** is a measure of safety or cushion that shows the proportion of sales that can decline (or need to increase) before the break-even point is reached. The safety margin can be expressed either in terms of dollar sales or as a percentage. The percentage point varies between 0 percent and 100 percent and the higher the margin of safety, the better. The safety margin percentage is calculated as follows:

$$\text{Safety margin} = \left[\frac{\text{Expected company sales} - \text{Break-even unit sales}}{\text{Expected company sales}} \right] \times 100$$

$$= \left[\frac{1,500 - 1,125}{1,500} \right] \times 100$$

$$= 25\%$$

The safety margin of 25 percent suggests that actual sales would have to fall short of expected sales by more than 25 percent before the firm would experience a loss.

Break-even Sales Change

Firms change their prices for a variety of reasons. They may raise prices if they believe that their price is low relative to the perceived value of their product and profits will increase if the price is raised. Firms may lower prices if they believe that prices are too high and a lower price will stimulate demand and lead to increased profits. Prices are often lowered for promotional reasons. Price is also used to preempt or reduce the effectiveness of competitors' marketing strategies. If a new competitor is preparing to enter a firm's territory, the incumbent could launch a preemptive strike by lowering prices. Such a move could result in customers stockpiling merchandise, thus removing them from the market for a period of time and making the life of the new entrant, at least initially, miserable.

Marketing managers often assume that an increase or decrease in price will cause revenue and profits to increase. However, this is not always true as the price decrease could lead to an overall profit reduction if the increase in sales is not sufficient to offset the decrease in price. Equally, a price increase may lead to a decrease in profits if the decline in revenues more than offsets the impact of the price increase.

When a firm is considering a price change to boost its profits, it could predict the impact of the price change on profit by calculating the sales change required to break even after the price change is implemented. The **break-even sales change** is the amount of additional sales the firm needs to maintain profits at levels prior to the price change following a price reduction. Or in the case of a price increase, the amount of sales reduction the firm can experience before it starts losing money. The break-even sales change technique may be illustrated with the help of an example.

Break-even sales change is the amount of sales change required to maintain profits at levels prior to the price change.

Let's assume that the price is $8, the contribution margin (price minus variable cost) is $4, and the expected company sales are 1,500 units. What is the break-even sales change of a price reduction of $1? The break-even sales change can be calculated with the following formula:[26]

$$\% \text{ Break-even sales change} = \left[\frac{-\text{Price change}}{\text{Contribution margin} + \text{Price change}} \right] \times 100$$

$$\% \text{ Break-even sales change} = \left[\frac{-(-\$1)}{\$4 + (-\$1)} \right] \times 100$$

$$= 33.3\%$$

and

Break-even sales change $= 0.333 \times 1,500 = 500$ units

Based on the results obtained here we can draw the following conclusions:

- If actual sales increase by 500 units, the price cut would be neither profitable nor unprofitable.
- If actual sales increase by more than 500 units, the price cut would be profitable.
- If actual sales increase by less than 500 units, the price cut would be unprofitable.

Chapter 10 / Pricing Strategy

- Price is an important aspect of a firm's marketing mix strategy. It is the only activity that earns a firm revenues while all others cost money. Price to customers is the monetary value they assign to the product. Firms often use price to stimulate demand and position or differentiate the product.

- It is important for firms to offer their products at the right price. If price is too high, consumers may switch to other more appropriately priced products. If prices are too low, the firm may unnecessarily give up margins and leave money on the table.

- Price can be a source of competitive advantage. Firms that can make their products at a low cost can charge lower prices and undercut their competitors. Firms should avoid using complex prices, as they tend to confuse customers. They should also avoid disguising prices, making frequent price changes or bundling products with other unwanted products. Firms could exploit competitors' weaknesses in their pricing practices.

- In setting prices, firms need to analyze their customers and competitors to determine the desired positioning of their products. A firm's final price is determined by the perceived customer value, cost structure, competition, marketing strategy, pricing objectives, and whether the product is part of a product line.

- It has been observed that total costs decline with cumulative production. Cost reductions from experience effects come mainly from learning, technological advances, product redesign and standardization, and economies of scale effects.

- During the product's life cycle, prices initially decline more slowly than costs, leading to the massive entry of firms into the industry. Prices fall precipitously during the shakeout stage, causing marginal firms to exit. At the end of the shakeout stage, the industry enters a period of stability in which prices and costs fall in parallel, maintaining constant profit margins.

- Firms with lower costs due to higher cumulative output can exploit their cost advantages by lowering prices—driving smaller competitors out of business. Smaller rivals must either lower their costs or exit the industry and look for viable market segments.

- There are three main pricing strategies for a new product: skimming, penetration, and parity pricing. Existing product strategies include value pricing, cost-plus pricing, everyday low pricing, randomized pricing, and promotional pricing. Pricing for a product line includes cross-subsidization, price bundling, and two-part pricing. Competitors' response prices include follow-the-leader pricing, price matching, and trigger pricing.

- Price customization involves the adaptation of price to differences in demand elasticities between segments. Price customization allows a firm to maximize its profits by charging prices closer to what consumers are willing to pay. Firms can use price customization by customer, time, and location.

- Price-profitability analysis involves break-even, safety margin, break-even market share, and break-even sales change analysis

Review and Discussion Questions

1. Discuss the role of price as a source of competitive advantage.

2. Discuss the factors that affect price levels.

3. Discuss the behaviour of costs and prices over the different stages of the product's life cycle.

4. Describe how a firm can exploit cost differences due to experience in its pricing.

5. What pricing strategy should the manufacturer of a new low-fat food replacement product adopt, assuming that the market for this product is large and price elastic, and competitors are working on their own version of the product to be introduced soon?

6. What are the advantages of everyday low pricing strategy? Are there any risks associated with everyday low pricing?

7. Why do firms use the cross-subsidization approach to setting prices? What kind of interrelationships need to exist between a firm's products for cross-subsidization to work?

8. What are the differences between price matching and trigger pricing?

9. What are the conditions facilitating price customization? How would you use price customization if you owned a restaurant and your morning business was slow?

10. Assume that price = $8, variable cost = $1.50, fixed cost = $2,300, expected sales = 1,200 units and market size = 4,500. Calculate the break-even point, safety margin, and break-even market share. Comment on the significance of your findings.

11. Assume that price = $7, contribution margin = $3, price reduction = $1.00, expected sales = 3,000 units, and price elasticity of demand = -1.80. Calculate the break-even sales change. Will the price move be profitable?

1. Euro Beauty Products Inc., a manufacturer of quality personal-care products has just introduced a new spray deodorant especially for "her"—its unique fragrance intended to give "her" the freshness she loves. Euro Beauty follows a price-skimming strategy with its new spray deodorant to benefit from a large contribution margin and recoup research and development costs. This seems justified by the product's superior performance and low price sensitivity of the targeted segments. Also, the price skimming is intended to create a prestigious image for this new product and enhance the appeal of its other personal-care brands. Because the sales of the new product were far below expectations, management of Euro Beauty Products began using a promotional pricing strategy that involved reducing the price of the product in an effort to boost sales, bringing the price closer to the price of lower-quality products. Was the price reduction a good move on the part of management of Euro Beauty products? What else might you have done to help the sales of this new product?

2. John Smith is the proud owner of a new casual sit-down restaurant located in downtown Vancouver. John has been trying to use different pricing techniques to boost the sagging restaurant business without much success. Given your understanding of price customization techniques, advise Mr. Smith how he could use the different types of price customization to increase his restaurant sales.

3. A jewellery manufacturer produces two versions of earrings. Both products are essentially the same. The only difference is that one version is a slightly fancier version of the other. The simpler one sells for $19.95 and the fancier one for $24.95. The $19.95 version sells better than the $24.95 one. The company introduces an even fancier version that sells for $35.95. The best-selling version now becomes the $24.95 one. Why?

4. "While everyday low prices is the greatest common denominator, they have to be part of a larger package of benefits." Comment on this statement.

5. In the summer of 2004, Sony announced the launch of a Walkman digital player dubbed the Network Walkman NW-HD1. Sony said its new digital music player would take direct aim at Apple's market-leading iPod brand. The 20-gigabyte device would sell at $400 and store 13,000 songs, compared with iPod, which was sold at $499 and stored 10,000 songs. The battery of NW-HD1 will last 30 hours, at least three time longer than iPod's. What pricing strategy is being used by Sony? What pricing reaction should Sony expect from Apple?

Notes

1. Robert J. Dolan and Hermann Simon, *Power Pricing* (The Free Press: New York, 1996), 24.
2. Thomas T. Nagle and Reed K. Holden, *The Strategy and Tactics of Pricing*, 3rd ed. (Upper Saddle River, N.J.: Prentice Hall, 2002), 15.
3. Rachel Ross, "Dell sees ink as key to success in printers." *Toronto Star*, June 3, 2004, D1
4. Luis M. B. Cabral, *Introduction to Industrial Organization* (Cambridge, Mass.: MIT Press, 2000), 49.
5. Louis E. Yelle, "The Learning Curve: Historical Review and Comprehensive Survey," *Decision Sciences* 10 (1979), 302–328.
6. Gerard J. Tellis, "Beyond the Many Faces of Price: An Integration of Pricing Strategies," *Journal of Marketing* 50 (October 1986), 146–160.
7. George S. Day, *Analysis for Strategic Market Decisions* (St. Paul, Minn.: West Publishing Company, 1986), 46.
8. George S. Day, "A Strategic Perspective on Strategic Planning," in Ben M. Enis, Keith K. Cox, and Michael P. Mokwa, (eds.), *Marketing Classics*, 8th ed., (Upper Saddle River, N.J.: Prentice Hall, 1990), 346–366.
9. John Partridge, "Ultra-low fares launch WestJet service to U.S." *The Globe and Mail*, June 17, 2004, B8.
10. Nagle and Holden, 174.
11. Nagle and Holden, 8.
12. www.edmunds.com/reviews/generations/articles/96932/article.html, retrieved on April 23, 2005.
13. Dolan and Simon, 37.
14. Nagle and Holden, 3.
15. Kent B. Monroe, *Pricing*, 3rd ed. (New York: McGraw-Hill, 1990), 159.
16. Valarie A. Zeinthaml, "Consumer Perceptions of Price, Quality, and Value: A Means-End Model and Synthesis of Evidence," *Journal of Marketing* 52 (July 1988), 2–22; Akshay R. Rao and Kent B. Monroe, "The Effect of Price, Brand Name, and Store Name on Buyers' Perceptions of Product Quality: An Integrative Review," *Journal of Marketing Research* 26 (August 1989), 351–357.
17. Eric Anderson and Duncan Simester, "Mind Your Pricing Cues," *Harvard Business Review* (September, 2003), 96–103.
18. Tellis.
19. Daniel F. Spulber, *The Market Makers* (New York: McGraw-Hill, 1998), 39.
20. Hollie Shaw, "Bay Steps Up Value Battle With Sears," *Financial Post*, October 18, 2001, FP3.
21. Michael R. Baye, *Managerial Economics and Business Strategy*, 3rd ed. (Boston: McGraw-Hill, 2000), 430–432; Tellis.
22. R. C. Blattberg and K. J. Wisniewski, "Price-Induced Patterns of Competition," *Marketing Science* 8 (Fall 1989), 291–309.
23. Leslie de Chernatony and Malcolm McDonald, *Creating Powerful Brands* (Oxford: Butterworth-Heinemann, 1998), 58.
24. Baye, 373–374.
25. Dolan and Simon, 116.
26. Nagle and Holden, 38.

Chapter Eleven

Distribution and Supply Chain Management

The marketing channel is a key strategic asset.

Anne T. Coughlan, Erin Anderson, Louis W. Stern, Adel I. El-Ansary, Marketing Channels

Learning Objectives

After studying this chapter, you should be able to:

1. Understand the strategic advantages of channels of distribution

2. Describe the main channel of distribution methods

3. Outline the various aspects of channel of distribution strategy

4. Explain how to manage channel of distribution change

Harlequin's Successful Distribution Strategy

Harlequin, with headquarters in Toronto, Ontario, is the world's largest publisher of romance fiction. The company, now owned by Torstar, which publishes *The Toronto Star*, provides more than 80 percent of Torstar's annual operating profits. But in 1949, Harlequin Books was headquartered in Winnipeg, Manitoba, where it published pocketbook reprints. Some of the famous authors on its list of reprints were Agatha Christie and Somerset Maugham. In 1958, the company was purchased by Richard and Mary Bonnycastle of Winnipeg who changed the name to Harlequin Enterprises and moved the company headquarters to Toronto. Soon afterward, Mary Bonnycastle recognized the growing popularity of romance fiction and since 1964 Harlequin has focused exclusively on romance books.

In 1971, the Bonnycastles turned the company over to their son, Richard, who hired W. Lawrence Heisey, a Harvard Business School graduate with several years' experience with Procter & Gamble. In addition to conducting an aggressive advertising and sales promotions campaign to increase awareness and sales, Heisey also expanded distribution using outlets not generally used in the retail sales of books. When the company was founded, the book industry relied heavily on bookstores to generate sales. Harlequin decided to place its products in supermarkets, department stores, and drugstores, where they would be readily available to its target market of middle-aged women. The new distribution strategy was so successful that the company realized growth rates in excess of 25 percent throughout the 1970s. Today, many other publishers have recognized the potential of using supermarkets for book distribution, but not before Harlequin had firmly established itself as the dominant player.

These moves helped Harlequin dominate the romance publishing market in the mid-1970s. Its success, however, encouraged a number of competitors to enter the market and challenge Harlequin. Simon & Schuster launched its own Silhouette romance series and gained about 30 percent market share. The entry of Dell Books and Bantam Books caused more erosion in Harlequin's market share and profits.

To stop further decline in Harlequin's market share, Torstar hired Brian Hickey, director of strategic planning at S. C. Johnson and Son, a company that manufactures consumer chemical products, including home cleaners, bug sprays, and plastic bags. Under Hickey's leadership, Harlequin introduced more sophisticated stories to go along with women's changing sexual attitudes in the 1980s and added new series. These changes reestablished Harlequin as the leading company in the romantic fiction industry. Harlequin purchased Silhouette in 1984 and redeployed Simon & Schuster as its distribution agent in the United States. It also expanded worldwide by establishing direct mail-order houses in various European countries and Australia.

In its continued effort to find new ways of reaching romance book readers, Harlequin Enterprises launched www.romance.net in 1996. This website initially provided information about Harlequin authors and enabled book buyers to purchase its books online. This site gradually evolved into eHarlequin.com, the successor of romance.net that was launched in 2000 to provide romance fiction readers with a place where they could escape the daily pressures of life and interact with like-minded romance readers. eHarlequin.com offers romance novels for online sale, community-building discussion groups, online book serials, newsletters, and interactive contests.

Today, Harlequin operates in several countries, including North America, Europe, and Australia. Harlequin books are distributed in North America indirectly through retail channels and directly through the reader service program and over the Internet. In overseas

(continued)

markets, Harlequin books are sold primarily through retail outlets and direct mail operations in several countries (United Kingdom, Sweden, the Netherlands, Italy, France, and Australia).

In 2002, Harlequin sold 146 million books in 27 languages in 94 international markets. In the same year, two of Harlequin's most popular series authors became *New York Times* best-sellers for the first time. More than 50 million women read Harlequin books worldwide. Approximately one in every six mass-marketed paperbacks sold in North America is a Harlequin or Silhouette book.[1]

Introduction

It seems inherently obvious that a company ought to distribute its products through channels that are frequented by its target consumers. But a company can gain a decided advantage if it can find new distribution outlets that attract a similar segment of the market, but where competitors do not have a presence. Often this means thinking beyond the conventional channels of distribution used by an industry. Harlequin Enterprises, publishers of the highly successful Harlequin Romance books, provides a remarkable example of the success that can be achieved using this strategy.

Strong distribution is indispensable for first-class market performance. Channels of distribution are needed to complement a quality product and reinforce a market position. A distribution channel is made up of market intermediaries that facilitate the flow of goods and services to customers together with support services needed to make the sale more convenient to buyers. A channel of distribution is more than a pipeline as it adds value to the product by performing certain activities dictated by consumer requirements and the marketing strategy of the manufacturer. Channel members perform functions such as reducing waiting time, financing, storage, location convenience, creating assortments for one-stop shopping, education, and after-sale service.

Channels of distribution affect all other elements of the marketing mix.[2] Products are affected by distribution decisions. For example, consumer electronics firms sell full-featured versions of their products through higher-end electronics stores and stripped-down versions through mass merchandisers and discount stores. Prices are affected as firms charge higher or lower prices depending on whether they sell their products through high-markup or low-markup retailers. Promotion is also affected by the decision to sell directly to customers or use resellers. Firms selling directly to customers advertise their products to final consumers, while companies that sell through resellers promote their products to them as well as to the final consumer.

Distribution strategies are based on deciding on the most efficient and effective way to distribute a firm's products. Firms need to devise a distribution strategy that will place products in those channels most frequented by the targeted segments. Some firms distribute their products directly to their customers using their own sales force, mail, phone, and online means. Other firms use third-party intermediaries such as wholesalers, distributors, retailers, agents, and brokers.

Today's consumers demand more choices in products and services, and their expectations of a firm's performance has increased as well. But very few companies can meet these expectations alone, so they turn to trading partners. As a result, many firms have adopted supply chain management methods in their channel strategies. Supply chain systems consist of the organizations, activities, structures, and processes that work together to provide exceptional value for customers. This chapter discusses the concept of supply chain management, and the strategic importance and advantages and disadvantages of channels of distribution. Next, different channels of distribution strategies are explained. Finally, issues related to channels of distribution management are described.

Channels of Distribution and Supply Chain Management

Most of the important issues in developing a channel strategy concern channel architecture—that is, how to design the most effective and efficient channel of distribution—or managing a channel and improving channel performance and cooperation. Today, many firms, unlike traditional businesses, take a supply chain view of their channels of distribution. **Supply chain management** encompasses all activities involved in the creation of finished goods from raw materials to the delivery and consumption of the finished goods. The supply chain approach views channels of distribution as part

Supply chain management encompasses all activities involved in the creation of finished goods from raw materials to the delivery and consumption of the finished goods.

of a system whose members are concerned about the performance of the entire chain instead of their individual sales or profit performance. In the traditional channel, each member is concerned primarily with achieving its own sales objectives. But in a supply chain, the major concern is to achieve outstanding customer satisfaction and to maximize the performance of the entire chain.

Traditionally, members of supply chains were mainly concerned about adding value for their immediate customers and not for the output of the entire chain.[3] Today, businesses that have adopted supply chain management methods expect their suppliers to perform important activities in a network of interconnected companies whose objectives are to maximize value for customers. The components of a supply chain management system include procurement, manufacturing, distribution, and customer service (see Figure 11.1).

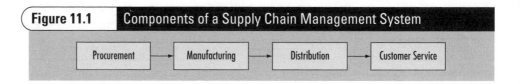

| Figure 11.1 | Components of a Supply Chain Management System |

Procurement → Manufacturing → Distribution → Customer Service

Supply chain management is becoming popular with more and more businesses because it can eliminate waste from the system and help better manage the manufacturing and movement of goods and information among suppliers, manufacturers, and customers. Supply chain management has the potential to improve inventory management, transportation systems, distribution networks, and customer service. The Strategy in Action box illustrates how supply chain management helped Heineken improve its performance.[4]

Strategy in Action

HEINEKEN

In the early 1990s, Heineken, the Dutch beer manufacturer, was facing serious logistical problems. Its shipment of beer to North America from the Netherlands, from order to delivery, was taking approximately three months. This long delivery time was hurting both sales and customer satisfaction. The main reason for this inefficient process was Heineken's antiquated supply chain and customer communication system. In 1996, the company's North American subsidiary developed a web-based supply chain system connecting Heineken with its 450 suppliers and distributors. Using the web, this system provided trade promotion capabilities that allowed Heineken to work with its customers on promotional events. It also enabled the company to place orders in real time at the Heineken brewery in the Netherlands. The changes in Heineken's supply chain led to dramatic improvements in a number of performance indicators for Heineken. The order lead time was reduced from three months to eight days. Its forecasting accuracy improved 15 percent, inventory levels decreased 62 percent, and sales efficiency improved 20 percent. In 2003, Heineken's sales increased 10 percent and net profits grew by 11.2 percent.

Recent developments in information technology have enabled companies to develop supply chain management software that allows companies to plan, implement, optimize, and control their supply chains effectively. For example, orders for raw materials or finished goods are automatically transmitted over the Internet as soon as inventory reaches a certain level. These new technologies help establish communication between members of the supply chain and facilitate the adoption of supply chain management methods. The adoption of supply chain management has also been aided by an increased understanding by managers that cooperation among firms in a supply chain can be beneficial to all participating firms.

Strategic Advantages of Channels of Distribution

Distribution decisions are among the most significant supply chain management decisions made by a firm. Channels of distribution take a long time to build and unlike other elements of marketing mix can be very difficult to change.[5] Building a channel of distribution commits manufacturers to relatively long-term, complex relationships with intermediaries. Long-term commitments are required to motivate channel intermediaries to put adequate effort behind a manufacturer's products. On the other hand, firms that decide to distribute their products directly to the customer through their own efforts will need to build their own sales force using appropriate recruitment, hiring, training, and motivating mechanisms. Setting up a sales force is a high fixed-cost strategy and it represents a large resource commitment to a firm.

Effective channels of distribution are critical for competitive success. Channels are a key external resource that can generate sales for many years into the future, and they should be nurtured like a firm's own resources and assets. Having a better product may not be sufficient to achieve market success if the firm lacks distribution and the product is not available to the target market. Given that products, prices, and advertising can be imitated by rivals, distribution is one of the areas where companies can obtain a competitive advantage. Also, it is very difficult and it takes a long time to develop channels of distribution. For this reason, it is often easier to maintain a sustainable competitive advantage in distribution than in the areas of product, price, and promotion. Channels of distribution offer firms the following strategic advantages (see Figure 11.2).

Figure 11.2	Strategic Advantages of Channels of Distribution

- Increase market coverage
- Help build a desirable image
- Act as barriers to entry
- Increase profitability
- Improve customer satisfaction
- Exploit competitor weaknesses

Increase market coverage. Channels can help a firm increase its market coverage and provide it with new growth opportunities. Leading market share companies, such as Matshushita in consumer electronics, Kao in packaged household goods, Shiseido in cosmetics, and Toyota in autos, are invariably companies that enjoy outstanding distribution coverage.[6] Adding a new channel—agent, distributor, broker, wholesaler, or retailer—can provide access to entirely new markets and increase sales. For instance, in recent years the Internet has provided firms with a new channel for making their products available to additional customers, especially customers who might not have known of their existence or been able to purchase from them. Also, firms with a broader distribution coverage than competitors enjoy more exposure as more potential customers become aware of the firm's products and have a better chance of purchasing their products.

Help build a desirable image. Channels can help a firm build a desired brand image and reinforce its positioning strategy. The intermediaries that a firm chooses to distribute its product and the way the product is displayed in the store send a powerful message to consumers. Proper distribution and display reinforce the firm's positioning strategy and can help increase the sales of the product. For this reason, it is important for marketers to find the distribution that matches and enhances the brand's image. For example, brands distributed through high-end retailers like Holt Renfrew and Harry Rosen benefit from this association and acquire a premium image. On the other hand, low-end brands distributed through discount retailers acquire an image of an inexpensive or affordable product.

Act as barriers to entry. Channels of distribution are important barriers to entry. They can provide a powerful entry barrier that helps protect incumbents from potential entrants. If existing firms tie up all logical channels of distribution in a market, it becomes difficult for newcomers to enter the market and establish operations. For example, Procter & Gamble's clout with its distributors is a powerful competitive weapon that is difficult for newcomers to overcome. A small firm that develops a new grocery product usually has difficulty finding space on overcrowded supermarket shelves.

Increase profitability. Channel efficiency is an important determinant of a firm's profitability. Channel of distribution and sales force activities are often the largest component of a firm's operating costs. The cost of distribution can be as high as 50 percent of the price of the product. Reducing distribution costs can lower a firm's overall costs by a significant percentage, giving it a cost advantage. For instance, Internet-based companies such as Amazon.com have an advantage over competitors who use traditional methods of distributing their products.

Improve customer satisfaction. Distributors differ in the quality of service and satisfaction they provide to customers. An effective intermediary can help a firm deliver the product with the quality level required and expected by the target market. It can provide the after-sales service such as prompt delivery, installation, training, repair, returns, and technical support required by the market. Firms that use distributors that excel in these areas have an advantage over other companies.

Exploit competitors' weaknesses. Finding channels of distribution that can provide the level of service required by a firm can give a firm a competitive advantage over firms that use inefficient and lethargic channels of distribution. Strong channels can help exploit weaknesses in competitors' distribution. Such weaknesses should be analyzed very closely as they can provide excellent opportunities. Competitors may not be using all the important channels of distribution or they might be missing one or more important channels. They may be missing important market segments because they do not use intermediaries that would help them reach those segments. There could also be problems in the form of conflict between a competitor and its distributors. These problems in competitors' channel strategy should be spotted and exploited.

Channel of Distribution Methods

When manufacturers design a distribution system, they may choose one or more methods from various distribution possibilities. Distribution methods include going directly to customers through the manufacturer's own sales force; using its own corporate stores;

using independent channels of distribution such as wholesalers, agents, brokers, distributors, and retailers; piggybacking; using e-commerce; and using multiple channels. The various distribution methods are shown in Figure 11.3.

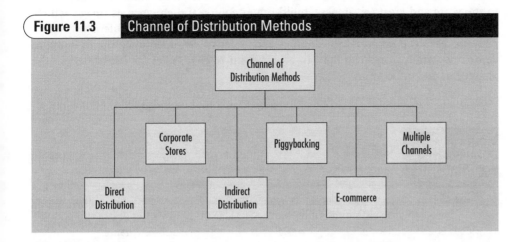

Figure 11.3 Channel of Distribution Methods

Direct Distribution

Direct distribution occurs when firms use their own sales force and resources to distribute their products to customers. Due to the high cost of maintaining a sales force, mainly large firms use this strategy. Small firms often lack the resources and market knowledge required to implement such a strategy. According to one study of industrial products, direct channels are preferable when product information needs are high, product customization is common, product quality assurance is important, purchase lot size is important, and logistics are important.[7]

Firms use direct distribution because it has certain advantages. Company sales representatives are likely to be better trained and more aggressive. The use of a firm's own sales force allows it to control the distribution of the product, service, and price and have direct access to consumers. This enables the firm to market its products more effectively and obtain firsthand consumer and other types of market information. It also allows for better communication and customer interaction, as the firm is in close contact with its customers. As a result, the firm can develop a closer relationship with customers and respond more quickly to customers' requests for information, to provide service, or to resolve complaints.

Direct distribution occurs when firms use their own sales force and resources to distribute their products to customers.

Corporate Stores

Some firms choose to open their own retail outlets instead of using outside channel intermediaries. The manufacturer sets channel objectives such as buying, storage, order handling, inventory control, service levels, and pricing, and expects that they will be met by the corporate-owned stores. Companies that own their own stores include manufacturers such as Levi Strauss, Nike, and Apple; service companies such as Walt Disney; and fashion and accessory designers such as Donna Karan, Giorgio Armani, and Liz Claiborne.

Many manufacturers open their own stores because they are unhappy with what they see as the excessive power of traditional retailers.[8] Corporate stores enable companies to have better control over the distribution of their products and the selling process and build closer relationships with their customers. In addition, company stores allow manufacturers to present their products in ways independent retailers cannot, or are not willing to do. Most manufacturers use company-owned stores as market test grounds for evaluating new products, prices, and promotions. Also, there is evidence that in some cases the role of company stores is less to generate sales and more to showcase and create awareness, build brand equity, and enhance its image, which, in turn, can help increase the sales of the brand.[9] One possible problem with company stores is the potential for conflict with existing retailers, since the opening of company-owned stores can lead to a reduction in their sales, as illustrated in the Strategy in Action box.[10]

Strategy in Action

GEOX SPA

In early 2004, Geox SpA, a fast-growing high-end Italian shoe manufacturer, was making plans to enter the Canadian shoe market with about 15 flagship stores and mini-boutiques within existing retailers in Toronto, Montreal, and Vancouver. Geox SpA was also expanding into the United States by opening its flagship store in New York City and with plans for more store openings in the United States.

Geox SpA's strategy of opening its own stores is part of a trend by certain manufacturers to promote their brands, using their stores as a showcase for their products. According to Gino Stinziani, vice-president of North American operations at Geox SpA, "The retail strategy is really to help us promote the brand and expose the brand so that we can be successful with our current independent retail base."

Geox SpA is known for its patented technology that is designed to fight sweaty feet. Geox shoes are a blend of Italian design and technology that uses air holes and a plastic membrane that lets in air but keeps out water. Geox's unique technology allows the company to differentiate its products from the rest of the highly competitive $4.6-billion (Cdn) shoe market that includes traditional shoe manufacturers such as Bata and more recent entries like Canadian Tire.

The company's ventilating technology is not the only differentiating factor. It has a greater focus on marketing than other shoe makers, spending 20 percent of its revenues in advertising in the first year and cutting back to 10 percent in subsequent years—about twice the spending of its rivals. The company's products were already being distributed through a number of Canadian stores such as Brown's Feet and Foot Shoppe. The company was also in talks with Harry Rosen to set up a separate Geox boutique inside their stores. Geox was also looking for merchants to establish franchises in small Canadian markets.

One of Geox's concerns was that retailers carrying its shoes might not be thrilled if they found out that their supplier was setting up its own shops. Despite such concerns, Geox was planning to go ahead and establish its own stores, which it hopes will generate 40 percent of its sales, with the rest coming from independent retailers.

Indirect Distribution

Indirect distribution involves distributing products using channel intermediaries.

Indirect distribution involves distributing products using channel intermediaries. Firms employing this strategy use a variety of distributors to make the product available to their target markets. These intermediaries include merchants that take title and resell the merchandise such as distributors, wholesalers, retailers, and dealers. Intermediaries also include third parties such as sales agents and brokers that prospect for customers and frequently negotiate prices and conditions of sale but do not take title to the goods.

The indirect channel strategy is less expensive than using direct channels. The firm requires a smaller sales force, as the bulk of channel activities are carried out by intermediaries. A disadvantage of indirect distribution is loss of control over channel activities. Intermediaries may try to meet their own objectives, which are often at variance with the objectives of the manufacturer. In general, they are more interested in building relationships with customers than advancing the manufacturer's interests. As a result, firms that rely on intermediaries are often disappointed with their sales effort and lower service levels. However, even though the concern over losing control over channel activities is a strong one, many companies choose the indirect channel approach because of the high cost of owning their own direct sales force.

Although indirect distribution is normally less costly than direct distribution, there are some circumstances in which it can be costly. A firm can experience high transaction costs such as haggling over contract details, writing and enforcing contracts, monitoring performance, paying high commissions, and dealing with uncooperative behaviour—for example, refusing to fill out sales reports or perform channel support activities. If these costs become too high, the firm may find it preferable to switch to a direct channel strategy.[11] Relying on intermediaries is also risky as intermediaries can be disloyal to manufacturers and switch to a competitor if they are offered a better deal. An example of such a situation is illustrated by the VIP Industries story discussed in the Strategy in Action box.[12]

Strategy in Action

VIP INDUSTRIES

VIP Industries is the world's second-largest producer of moulded luggage, just behind Samsonite. In an effort to break into the U.K. market, VIP contracted with a local distributor to help it. The distributor was able to gain access to the U.K. market for VIP by establishing a specialty luggage department in Debenham's 75 stores; Debenham's is a national chain of department stores in Great Britain. VIP spent large amounts to train Debenham's sales staff, and as a result, VIP's sales reached 60 percent of Debenham's hard luggage sales. Debenham's success, however, was short-lived as VIP's distributor was offered exclusive rights to Samsonite's revolutionary Oyster II model. The distributor accepted Samsonite's offer and dropped VIP immediately. VIP, having made no investment in its own sales and marketing capabilities, was left out in the cold and lost its access to its market.

Piggybacking

Piggybacking occurs when a manufacturer uses another manufacturer's distribution facilities. For example, Palmolive's salespeople have been used to distribute Alpen and Wilkinson's Sword Blades. In India, Eveready used its sales force to distribute birth control products on behalf of the Indian government. This type of activity usually happens during non-peak times when demand on the sales force is at its lowest. Sometimes two firms enter into an agreement that involves making use of each other's distribution.

Piggybacking occurs when a manufacturer uses another manufacturer's distribution facilities or sales force.

Reciprocal piggybacking occurs when two firms enter into a cross-distribution agreement that involves making use of each other's sales force or distribution.

In this instance, in an exchange called **reciprocal piggybacking**, both firms make their products available through the other's distribution channels. Reciprocal piggybacking is a method used by companies that sell in two or more territories where one company has a strong distribution in a territory where the other is weak, but has weak distribution in the other territory in which its partner is strong. It can also occur when two firms, operating in different regions, have a small volume of sales in each other's area. The small volume of sales may not justify establishing a new distribution channel, but, by entering into a cross-distribution agreement, both firms are able to reduce the costs associated with serving new regions.

Firms often merge or acquire other companies to take advantage of each other's distribution facilities and exploit cross-distribution opportunities. The merger of Citicorp, one of the world's biggest banks, and Traveler Group, a large insurance, mutual funds, and investment banking firm, allowed each company to cross-sell their products and take advantage of the distribution channels of each organization. Travelers' distribution system consisted of 10,300 Salomon Smith Barney brokers, 80,000 Primerica Financial Services insurance brokers, and 100,000 Travelers insurance agents. Citicorp's distribution network was spread in many countries all over the world.[14]

E-commerce

E-commerce involves customers placing orders via the Internet and receiving the goods by mail or courier service.

E-commerce involves customers placing orders via the Internet and receiving the goods by mail or courier service. This method of distribution is usually associated with Dell Computer, Chapters.ca, and Amazon.com, but a great many other manufacturers and retailers use e-commerce as a distribution method, and the number is growing all the time. The increased availability of personal computers and access to the Internet, and the possibility of operating with limited resources, have contributed to the popularity of e-commerce and the Internet as a critical component of a firm's channel of distribution.

The Internet is an important channel of distribution for many manufacturers because it has the potential to open up large markets that may not be possible to tap otherwise. Amazon.com, the online virtual bookseller, is a well-known Internet success story. Amazon.com has reached $2 billion (U.S.) in revenues by relying almost exclusively on Internet sales. Dell Computer is another example of a company that has successfully used the Internet to its advantage, and in the process it has become the largest personal computer company in the world.

The advantages of e-commerce to the buyer include the convenience and comfort of ordering through the Internet and the lower cost due to the absence of channel intermediaries. Disadvantages of e-commerce include handling and shipping costs and dependability of delivery. However, recent advances in shipping technology have significantly reduced these concerns.

Other problems associated with e-commerce include communicating about complex products, especially new products with which buyers are not familiar. Buyers may be concerned that the delivered product will be below expectations, as they do not experience the product firsthand when making their purchase decision. Also, existing resellers' sales may be negatively affected when suppliers sell directly to consumers through the Internet, causing a strain in manufacturer-reseller relationships.[15] For example, Spanish Iberia Airlines ran into strong opposition from travel agents when it tried to move its corporate business to electronic ticketing—that is, airline reservations could be made over the Internet, cutting out the travel agents. Iberia resolved the problem by requiring customers to obtain e-tickets only for travel close to the time of departure, but allowed them a choice of paper ticket or e-tickets for bookings well in advance of the departure date.[16]

Multiple Channels

Most firms use multiple channel systems to take their products to their target market and maximize their market coverage. Multiple channels become necessary because most markets are fragmented and consist of different market segments with unique requirements. Customized channels are therefore needed to meet each segment's requirements. Also, adding new channels increases market penetration and company revenues, and helps prevent entry by competitors.

Companies using a multiple channel strategy utilize different distributors to make their products available to many segments. For example, suppliers of motor parts may distribute directly to washing machine manufacturers, use wholesalers to supply appliance repair companies, and serve final consumers through hardware stores and catalogues. As another example, Procter & Gamble sells directly to large hotel chains through its own sales force and to individual consumers indirectly through supermarkets and other retailers.

Multiple channels are frequently the result of a sequential distribution strategy.[17] **Sequential distribution** entails making a product that has initially limited distribution gradually available to more customers by adding new channels of distribution. For example, a company that produces premium-quality peanut butter and sells it initially through specialty stores might make it more widely available through supermarkets and convenience stores. Movies are also known to follow a sequential distribution strategy by making movies available to theatres initially and to video stores subsequently.

A potential problem that can occur when a firm adds a new channel of distribution is **interchannel conflict**.[18] An example of interchannel conflict is, as explained earlier, the case when a firm sells its product through the Internet or its own stores at lower prices and through retailers at higher prices. Such a situation will put retailers at a disadvantage as Internet prices are lower and the practice runs the risk of alienating them. Multi-channel conflicts are often created when manufacturers such as Hewlett-Packard, Toshiba, and Sharp aggressively pursue category killers such as Best Buy and Future Shop to which they give better prices and delivery terms. Adding these intermediaries angers independent retailers; first, because of added competition, and second, because the latter receive inferior terms.[19] Also, in business-to-business multiple channels, conflict is often created over allocation of accounts. Intermediaries who get the least profitable accounts complain about companies that receive the most lucrative ones.

The consequences of using multiple channels must be evaluated and managed carefully to avoid the disruptive impact of channel conflict. The channel designer needs to consider the potential for conflict and possible lack of support when using too many channels against using too few channels, which could lead to inadequate market coverage. In some cases the solution to the problem of conflict may be to give exclusive rights to each distributor.[20]

> **Sequential distribution** entails making a product that has initially limited distribution gradually available to more customers by adding new channels of distribution.

> **Interchannel conflict** is a problem that can occur when a firm adds new channels of distribution.

Channel Strategy

A channel of distribution strategy succeeds when it creates value for customers. A channel of distribution adds value to products marketed through it in the form of service outputs. **Service outputs** are consumer benefits that include location convenience, assortments, one-stop shopping, comparison shopping, financing, technical advice, delivery, and bulk breaking. For example, supermarkets create assortments of grocery products that enable customers to engage in one-stop shopping. Consumers purchase the product and these service outputs.

> **Service outputs** are consumer benefits that include location convenience, assortments, one-stop shopping, comparison shopping, financing, technical advice, delivery, and bulk breaking.

Consumers have different requirements regarding these service outputs. For example, a consumer who purchases a personal computer over the Internet has different service needs than someone who buys at a retailer such as Future Shop. Those who purchase over the Internet need less service and more delivery. Those who buy in stores usually need to see the computer and probably have less confidence than those who purchase online. Service is more important for these people. A good understanding of consumer requirements can help a channel manager design channels to maximize product sales.

Channel strategy determines how channel activities will be performed to achieve overall business objectives. The most common channel activities are breaking bulk and creating assortments of related products, making products or services available and accessible to customers, providing service quality, and responding speedily. An important aspect of channel design involves breaking the market into segments and creating customized channels for each segment. Also, firms need to decide between either selling directly to customers with their own sales force, company-owned stores, or the Internet or using independent resellers to perform distribution activities.

Channel design and management include decisions about consumer analysis, channel objectives, channel length, channel intensity strategy, intermediary selection, channel relationships, and channel change. An effective channel design is one that meets key target market requirements in a cost-efficient way and allows the company to retain adequate control over channel activities.[21]

Consumer Analysis

Consistent with a market orientation philosophy, channel strategy formulation begins with identifying the channel service requirements of each customer segment.[22] Consumers differ in the importance they assign to channel service requirements, depending on their needs and shopping behaviour. Some buyers prefer to buy products from stores while others are comfortable buying them over the Internet. Certain buyers prefer to buy with a minimum of shopping effort while others are willing to accept some inconvenience and look around for the best price. Many buyers prefer to buy only from well-established, reputable dealers while others buy from outlets that offer the lowest prices. Still others prefer to buy only after extensive shopping to compare prices and product attributes. For example, hotel chains purchasing soap bars differ in their shopping behaviour from female heads of households. Hotel chains buy in bulk and expect prompt delivery. Female household heads buy small quantities, are less price sensitive, and expect soap bars to be available in supermarkets, convenience stores, and other retail outlets. The existence of the two segments requires the use of two distinct channels of distribution, one using the firm's sales force to serve hotel chains and the other using independent retailers for individual consumers.

Differences among consumers make it difficult to serve all segments with the same channel. To attain full market coverage, products must be available through several channels. For example, photo finishing may be sold through mail order with limited interaction, one-hour express service with personal interaction, and do-it-yourself scanning and enlargement specialty shops.[23] The channel manager's job is to determine the channel service requirements of each customer segment through marketing research and other ways. Once the buying characteristics of the final consumers are determined, the channel designer can decide the type of intermediary that best matches these characteristics.

A primary objective of consumer analysis is to determine the specific objectives to be achieved by intermediaries. These objectives are derived on the basis of the buying requirements of target segment members. Channel objectives include product delivery within a certain number of hours from taking the order, service level requirements, credit provision to other resellers or customers, inventory and other space requirements, and product return allowance. The chosen objectives are then used to determine the length of the channel and its intensity, and to select intermediaries that are most suitable to meet these objectives.

Channel Length

The next step in developing a channel strategy is to design an appropriate channel to meet the channel objectives. The first step in this direction is to determine the length of the channel. This addresses the question of whether intermediaries should be used or whether the firm must rely on its own sales efforts. **Channel length** is the number of different levels of intermediaries involved in the channel. The length of the distribution channel varies from company to company. Some companies use direct channels while others develop longer channels involving various levels of intermediaries. For example, a producer of premium coffee may sell its product through company-owned coffee shops or through independent retailers such as supermarkets or specialty food retailers. The decision whether to use direct or indirect channels of distribution depends on market, product, company, and channel factors, as shown in Figure 11.4.

Channel length is the number of different levels of intermediaries involved in the channel.

Figure 11.4	Factors Affecting the Choice Between Direct and Indirect Distribution	
Direct distribution	Factor	Indirect distribution
Market Factors		
Small	Number of customers	Large
Large	Order size	Small
No	One-stop-shopping preference	Yes
Product Factors		
High	Perishability	Low
Large	Product weight	Small
High	Product complexity	Low
High	Product unit value	Low
High	Product customization	Low
Yes	Special effort or equipment required	No
Company Factors		
Yes	Channel control is required	No
Yes	Aggressive promotion/sales effort is required	No
Large	Company financial resources	Limited
Extensive	Management industry experience	Limited
Channel Factors		
High	Cost of using intermediaries	Low
Incompatible	Channel and manufacturer image and strategy	Compatible
Limited	Availability of qualified distributors	High

Market factors. The nature of the market, such as its location, size, and distribution, affects the channel choice. If the market is small and concentrated, it calls for a more direct channel system. However, if the market is large and widely dispersed, a longer channel is often required. For example, consumer goods manufacturers rely on retailers, wholesalers, and other types of intermediaries. On the other hand, businesses selling to other businesses often prefer the direct route because the number of their customers is much smaller than consumer markets.

How customers purchase the product also affects the type of distribution to be used. For example, if buyers purchase a product in small quantities, there is usually a need for large numbers of intermediaries to perform the bulk-breaking operations for end users.[24] Also if demand for product variety and one-stop shopping is high, the manufacturer should use intermediaries unless it can provide the required assortment itself. For example, a manufacturer of noodle soup would be well advised to distribute its products through retailers rather than their own retail stores or catalogues because most people prefer to buy their groceries in a one-stop-shopping trip. This has also been confirmed in a study of business-to-business products, which found that intermediaries are preferred when a broad assortment is essential, availability is critical, and after-sales service is important.[25]

Product factors. The type of product also influences the length of the channel. For high-priced products for which the customer feels high risk when purchasing the product, firms rely on their own sales force. Perishable, technically complex, or bulky products that require special effort or equipment are normally sold directly to the market. On the other hand, low-priced products whose purchase involves low risk, as is the case in buying grocery products, are sold indirectly through retail stores. Nonperishable, everyday products that do not require special effort or equipment are sold through intermediaries. Products that are highly customized are distributed directly while products that are highly standardized are distributed indirectly through intermediaries.

Company factors. The issue of channel control is an important one for many companies. It is very important for intermediaries to comply with channel policies, procedures, and the terms of the contract.[26] Therefore, channel decisions depend on how much channel control is required by the company. Also, firms use their own sales force if they desire an aggressive promotion and sales effort that they cannot get from intermediaries.

Similarly, the resources and capabilities of the firm affect channel length. If a firm is large or it has a lot of resources, it may hire additional salespeople and make the necessary investments to allow it to go directly to the market. However, if the manufacturer lacks the capabilities to satisfy the service requirements of target segments or the necessary product line depth required by end users, the attractiveness of the direct distribution method diminishes. For this reason, small firms often go to the market indirectly. Lastly, an important requirement for implementing a direct channel strategy is that the firm has intimate knowledge of and is very experienced in the industry.

Channel factors. A distribution system serves many purposes, including offering target segments convenience, service, bulk-breaking, and selection. The decision to use intermediaries depends heavily on their ability to meet these goals. These goals can be better served if distributors have a positive attitude toward a manufacturer's policies and products and if the cost of using intermediaries is reasonable.

Also, the availability of qualified distributors affects the decision whether to use channel intermediaries or go directly to the market. Many qualified intermediaries are not available or not willing to sell the firm's products because of exclusive arrangements with another manufacturer. Or the distributor's image and strategy are incompatible with the manufacturer's. Using unqualified distributors may hurt the product's image. For this reason, marketers of premium products stop selling through retailers who used their products as loss leaders, a practice that is anathema for a company that sells such products.

Channel Intensity

The next step in developing a channel strategy is selecting distribution intensity. **Channel intensity** is the number of outlets that will be used for distributing the manufacturer's offering at each level in its trading area. That is, if the manufacturer decided to employ wholesalers and retailers, it must decide the appropriate number of wholesalers and retailers. There are three strategic options for distribution measured by the degree of channel intensity: intensive, selective, and exclusive distribution.

Channel intensity is the number of outlets that will be used for distributing the manufacturer's offering at each level in its trading area.

1. *Intensive distribution.* **Intensive distribution** entails having the product available at every possible outlet. This distribution strategy is especially suited for convenience goods—frequently purchased consumer products that customers prefer to buy with a minimum of shopping effort. Companies use intensive distribution to maximize the sales potential of their products. Companies following this strategy attempt to maximize the number of outlets carrying their products and establish more points of distribution. The rationale is that the greater the number of outlets carrying the product, the more customers will buy the product. In addition to a higher sales volume, it creates higher customer awareness and impulse buying.

Intensive distribution entails having the product available at every possible outlet.

    One of the risks of intensive distribution is that as the manufacturer adds new distributors, it creates conflict between the manufacturer and the original resellers who experience more competition from other resellers.[27] The increased competition between distributors of the product often leads to lower margins and a reduced reseller effort. This would especially be a problem if there is little consumer awareness and the manufacturer relies on dealer support.[28] A company that successfully used the intensive distribution strategy is Coca-Cola, as described in the Strategy in Action box.

Strategy in Action   COCA-COLA

Coca-Cola followed a strategy of intensive distribution in the 1990s with great success. As part of this strategy in the United States, the company introduced vending machines in various national parks locations and inside office buildings. It also placed coolers at the checkout at Target and Blockbuster video stores, and installed all-you-can-drink fountain dispensers at McDonald's and other fast food restaurants. Coca-Cola employees worked together with retailers to find new and better ways to offer Coca-Cola products to the public. Grocery stores were one venue where this new approach was tried. Coolers full of single-serve Coca-Cola products, a Coca-Cola vending machine and a Coca-Cola fountain dispenser were soon installed in grocery stores, in addition to the products that were available in the soft drink aisle. Following this method of distribution, Coca-Cola achieved double-digit annual growth even with a product as old and mature as Coke.

2. *Selective distribution.* As we argued in the previous section, the potential conflict between the desire for more exclusive distribution by the retailer and more intensive distribution by the manufacturer frequently creates problems for the manufacturer who needs to come up with creative solutions. **Selective distribution** is an intermediate position between intensive and exclusive distribution. Manufacturers using this distribution strategy are highly selective in their choice of intermediaries and place a limit on the number of intermediaries that carry their products within a trade area. This type of distribution is especially suited for shopping goods—products that consumers purchase after they spend some time shopping around comparing prices, styles, and other features. For example, manufacturers of durable goods such as

Selective distribution is an intermediate position between intensive and exclusive distribution.

appliances and consumer electronics, or high-priced premium products, often limit distribution to a very small number of outlets.

By restricting coverage, selective distribution enhances the image of the product, achieves greater control of pricing and selling practices, and motivates the distributor to aggressively promote the product. Manufacturers often choose a selective distribution system to allow their distributors to obtain a large part of the market and not compete with other distributors. The higher sales volume and unit margins will motivate the retailers to work hard to develop the market. Selective distribution allows the manufacturer to provide intermediaries with sufficient coverage but at the same time it is restrictive enough to keep them motivated.

Exclusive distribution is defined as selling a product only through a single outlet in a particular area.

3. *Exclusive distribution.* **Exclusive distribution** is defined as selling a product only through a single outlet in a particular area. Exclusive distribution encourages more aggressive selling effort by intermediaries and provides greater control of intermediaries. Firms that sell specialty goods—products for which consumers feel a strong loyalty—typically use exclusive distribution. Restricting market coverage can be a disadvantage as the success of the product depends on the performance of a single intermediary.[29]

Companies that position their brands as premium products limit distribution intensity and use retailers with a strong image and a reputation for excellent service. Since relatively few retailers are likely to meet the high standards set by manufacturers of high-quality premium products, distribution is selective or exclusive. For instance, manufacturers of fashion products often use selective or exclusive distribution strategies that might include high-end, upscale boutiques or department stores. By limiting distribution to a few or just one prestigious outlet, manufacturers are trying to maintain the high-fashion image of their products and better control over retail prices and service quality.

In following exclusivity as a distribution strategy, the brand's image should be matched with the consumer perceptions of the retailer. For example, Ralph Lauren markets Polo as an upscale and elite brand and it has followed an exclusive distribution strategy of selling primarily through dedicated Polo shops and high-end clothiers. Its target market is fashion-conscious consumers with annual household incomes over $100,000. Polo's channel strategy matches the personality of the Polo brand and has worked well over the years.

Selection of Channel Partners

Once the channel intensity level is determined, the manufacturer must select those intermediaries that are best qualified to achieve the firm's channel objectives at each level. According to the supply chain view, the goal is to create channels where all members work together to improve efficiencies and product quality in order to offer superior value to customers.[30] At the wholesale level, the firm needs to decide whether to use wholesalers, agents, brokers, or other distributors. At the retail level, the firm needs to decide which retailers to use, including specialty stores, mass merchandisers, and department stores.

Channel gaps are differences between ideal and actual channels.

Demand-side gaps exist when the actual channel either undersupplies or oversupplies the service output.

Supply-side gaps exist when the total cost of performing the required channel services is too high.

Before intermediaries are selected, the channel manager needs to perform a channel gap analysis.[31] **Channel gaps** are differences between ideal and actual channels. **Demand-side gaps** exist when the actual channel either undersupplies or oversupplies the service output. If a service output is undersupplied, the customer will be dissatisfied because his or her service requirements are not met completely. If the service output is oversupplied, the channel will probably be adding to the cost of service unnecessarily, leading to higher prices, lower margins, and loss of market share.

Supply-side gaps exist when the total cost of performing the required channel services is too high. These gaps exist when the cost of performing one or more channel tasks are performed at high costs. A firm must devise strategies to close these channel gaps, but correcting the problems may be difficult and costly. For this reason, it is very important from the beginning to design channels that have as few potential problems as possible to avoid having to fix these problems later.

Once channel gaps are identified, the channel planner needs to choose specific intermediaries within the particular channel type. For example, if it has been decided to use specialty stores, a decision must be made about which specific specialty stores to use. This decision is made on the basis of cost, control, performance, reputation, experience, and image. For instance, if a pharmaceutical company decides to market its new high-quality lotion through retailers, possible options include beauty salons and the beauty section of carefully selected department stores that match the intended image and positioning of the new product.

Managing Channel Relationships

Effective supply chain management requires collaboration and the seamless integration of the activities of key players.[32] Collaboration means the supply chain participants are working together sharing data, technologies, and processes to customize value for the whole supply chain. Such cooperation enables members of the supply chain to better forecast market demand and inventory needs, understand customer requirements better, and serve market needs in an outstanding way.[33] But achieving a close coordination and smooth relationship among channel members is very difficult. Many supply chains become highly complex, with a large number of participants and product flow paths. In such situations, collaboration among supply chain participants can be very difficult.

A successful supply chain collaboration requires the strategic alignment of the various participants in the chain. **Strategic channel alignment** implies that the goals and strategies are consistent across all supply chain participants.[34] When strategies are aligned, all members recognize that a benefit to another participant is also a benefit to itself.

> **Strategic channel alignment** implies that the goals and strategies are consistent across all supply chain participants.

Supply chain collaboration often falls short in practice because participants do not act with the greater good of the supply chain in mind. Conflict is inherent in channels of distribution as the manufacturer adds more channel intermediaries or the manufacturer decides to distribute the products itself. This can be a serious problem as other channel members could view these actions as unacceptable and may stop supporting the product. Another source of conflict between the manufacturer and distributors is poor intermediary performance. Manufacturers know that channel partners often fail to perform as expected. That failure can be a serious problem as the manufacturer who uses intermediaries relies on them for sales and profits. If intermediaries do not perform as expected, a firm will not achieve its profit and sales objectives.

A requirement for successful channel relationships is a change in how channel members view themselves and other channel members. Channel members need to see themselves as an important factor in contributing to the goal of satisfying customers better than competitors. Channel members also need to work together to make the channel more efficient by reducing waste and costs.

Methods for managing supply chain relationships

Firms can use a variety of ways to obtain cooperation and performance from its distributors to ensure they will put a greater effort behind their products.

Clarify the role of each channel member. Managers can reduce conflict in the channel by clarifying the role of each channel member in a way that resolves the conflict. For example, if the manufacturer serves different market segments, the role of each channel partner must be consistent with the market segment it serves. A company that uses the

Internet to sell its products could explain to channel members that the Internet reaches a different market segment and it does not interfere with their own customers. The more familiar each channel partner is with the role of other partners, the higher the likelihood of a smooth relationship between them.

Increase channel power. Power also plays a significant role in reducing conflict and achieving cooperation in supply chains. **Channel power** is the ability to influence another channel member's behaviour. Firms with channel power may punish their channel partners by slowing down deliveries, refusing to promote a manufacturer's brands, or providing other channel members with market information. Companies exert power over channels of distribution if their products are highly profitable or account for a considerable percentage of an intermediary's sales. Products that are easy to sell, have high inventory turns, move through the channel faster, and generate cash and profits more easily provide manufacturers with more channel power.[35]

Firms derive power by rewarding distributors with various benefits such as exclusive territories, marketing and management support, and cash compensation. Manufacturers with strong brands exert power over other channel members. These companies usually obtain better channel performance because intermediaries tend to promote products that sell well.

An example of channel power is the blocking shelf strategy. **Blocking shelf** strategies involve blocking a section of the retailer's shelf, then determining the way the products are to be displayed on the shelf. By using a blocking strategy, companies directly control the placement of their products, instead of leaving it to the discretion of retailers or competitors. A well-executed blocking strategy calls attention to the product and increases sales by making it easy for consumers to find the product. A blocking shelf strategy can be used only if the firm can convince retailers to display its products in a block section on the shelf. Top brands with a lot of power over retailers like Coke, Pepsi, and Maxwell House use blocking strategies.

A variant of the blocking shelf strategy is the **power-of-one strategy,** a term coined by PepsiCo for its strategy of placing Pepsi drinks next to its Frito-Lay chips on store shelves. This strategy requires that the company owns two or more complementary brands, and one brand is a best seller, giving the company the ability to persuade retailers to place the two brands side by side on the shelf. For example, Frito-Lay has a high market share but Pepsi-Cola's market share is low. By leveraging its influence because of Frito-Lay, Pepsi-Cola is allowed to place its soft drinks next to the high-performing chips. By using this strategy, Pepsi increased the odds that when shoppers buy pop and chips, the pop is Pepsi.

Create a vertical marketing system. Manufacturers increase channel cooperation and performance through vertical marketing systems, that is, developing a long-term, binding relationship with resellers through investment or legal agreements.

Increase advertising to the final consumer. Advertising to the final consumer and creating brand awareness and recognition can be a good way to motivate resellers, as customers normally prefer products that they are familiar with. This, in turn, forces resellers to make the product available to their customers.

Grant exclusive distribution. Giving intermediaries exclusive distribution rights often increases their motivation to sell a firm's products.

Offer incentives. Manufacturers can motivate intermediaries with a variety of trade incentives, such as offering higher discounts and promotional allowances, better return policies, and special trade promotions, and increasing the level of service to the intermediaries. Other incentives include sales contests, free tickets to a baseball game, paying for marketing research conducted by a retailer, or financial assistance. The Strategy in Action box below provides an example of a successful attempt to increase channel of distribution performance by applying some of the methods discussed here.[36]

Channel power is the ability to influence another channel member's behaviour.

Blocking shelf strategies involve blocking a section of the shelf, then determining the way the products are to be displayed on the shelf.

Power-of-one strategy is a term coined by PepsiCo for its strategy of placing Pepsi drinks next to its Frito-Lay chips on store shelves.

J. E. EKORNES

J. E. Ekornes is a Norwegian manufacturer of home furniture. Until 1993, Ekornes' relations with its retailers were very adversarial. Ekornes would use any retailer that wished to carry its product line. This sale mentality led to overdistribution, resulting in retailers not trusting Ekornes and Ekornes not providing sales support for its products. Due to the lack of retailer support, Ekornes's sales were far below expectations.

In 1993, Ekornes decided to change its approach to distribution in an attempt to increase the sales performance of its brands. Ekornes instituted a new distribution strategy, with the following changes. First, it drastically reduced the number of distributors. For example, in France where it had 450 distributors, the number was reduced to 150; in Sweden, the number of distributors was cut in half. Ekornes retained those retailers that were not only competent but matched its image and shared the same strategy and customer service philosophy. Further, distributors were given exclusive sales rights in their territories. Ekornes also used computerized software to figure out the optimal territory size, involving the retailers in this research and decision.

Second, it increased retailers' margins to ensure that they made enough profits to locally advertise their product line. Third, visits were arranged for retailers to Ekornes's innovative factory in Norway to increase their knowledge of the quality of the company's products. Finally, Ekornes changed the role of its sales force from selling to providing marketing assistance to retailers. In order to facilitate this change, it switched from a sales commission to a fixed salary and a bonus dependent on the quality of the marketing assistance to retailers.

The changes made by Ekornes led to dramatic sales increases. The reduction in the number of retailers and the switch to exclusive territories increased overall sales. The remaining retailers agreed to sales goals that more than made up for the lost sales due to the reduction in the number of retailers. Retailers dropped competing lines and increased local advertising of Ekornes's products. As a result, in France alone, sales tripled over the first three years after the change was made and the increase continued at a 50 percent annual rate afterward.

Managing Channel Change

Channel arrangements are not static—they change over time. Like other elements of the marketing mix, channels of distribution need to change in response to changing market conditions. Distribution members must constantly evaluate the performance of their channels and make adjustments to increase their effectiveness. These changes are made in response to new market opportunities, such as reaching a new segment or geographic region, reacting to competitive pressure, adapting to market changes, or gaining more control over channel activities.

As markets mature, several things happen. First, firms often change their distribution strategy from a selective to a more intensive one. This, to a large extent, is necessitated by a shift in customer preference from more education in early stages to more convenience or lower prices as they gain experience with the product. As profit margins fall, manufacturers seek higher sales volume and turn to intensive distribution. Second, mature markets splinter into many diverse segments, each with its own distinct requirements, buying behaviour, and channel preferences. As a result of this splintering, we are witnessing a proliferation of marketing channels, as firms in the same market may use a variety of channels of distribution, including direct, indirect, and multiple channels.

Customized distribution involves adapting products to meet the diverse needs of shoppers in the different distribution channels.

Other firms, such as Sony (see the Strategy in Action box), respond with **customized distribution** that involves adapting products to meet the diverse needs of shoppers in the different distribution channels.

Backhauling is a distribution strategy used by retailers such as Wal-Mart to speed up delivery, save on shipping costs, and allow the retailer to lower prices.

Cross-docking is a distribution strategy that can lead to large savings for the retailers that employ it.

Companies constantly attempt to create new distribution systems to reduce costs and improve channel efficiency. Two such recent developments are backhauling and cross-docking. **Backhauling** is a distribution strategy used by retailers such as Wal-Mart to speed up delivery, save on shipping costs, and allow the retailer to lower prices. This strategy requires that suppliers operate warehouses or factories within a retailer's territories. When a retailer's truck drives by one of these warehouses, rather than returning empty to the retailer's warehouse to pick up its next load, it stops and picks up merchandise for delivery to the warehouse. Wal-Mart's fleet of more than 2,000 trucks is estimated to backhaul on 60 percent of their trips, resulting in huge savings for Wal-Mart, lowering its cost structure relative to competitors, and reducing its prices.

Cross-docking is a distribution strategy that can lead to large savings for the retailers that employ it. Like backhauling, cross-docking was also first implemented by Wal-Mart and works as follows. All store orders are gathered and filled by suppliers in full truckloads. The packing of products on incoming shipments is such that they can be easily sorted at intermediate warehouses or for outgoing shipments based on final destination. Retailers using cross-docking transfer merchandise directly from their suppliers' trucks to their own vehicles, which are bound for their stores instead of placing merchandise from vendors' trucks into their warehouses. This has the effect of reducing handling costs, and the amount of inventory carried by the retailer as merchandise is delivered directly to the stores instead of sitting in the retailer's warehouses. Cross-docking is possible through the integration of various technologies, including network management, bar-code technology, inventory control, and systems modelling.

Channel change can have devastating consequences for a company, as the Levi's example discussed in the Strategy in Action box illustrates.[37]

fashion-conscious consumers changed Levi's fortunes forever. Levi's jeans fell out of favour with young consumers because they weren't sold through GAP, Banana Republic, and the other stores aimed at teens. Levi's jeans had acquired an image of being appropriate for older consumers because they were sold in department stores, which were the stores where the parents of young consumers shopped. The big winners were brands like Calvin Klein and Guess and various private-label products that were considered cool and more fashionable mainly because they were sold in these trendy stores. As a result of this strategic mistake, Levi's suffered a big decline in its market share from 70 percent in the 1970s to around 20 percent in the late 1990s, despite its best efforts to reestablish a fashionable image with teenagers.

Companies that fail to deal with channel change will experience a decline in their market share and an erosion of their profits. Managers must take a proactive approach to channel change by monitoring their channel environment in order to identify changes in time and make the necessary adjustments in their firm's distribution strategy. At the same time, channel managers should be constantly looking for ways to improve the existing channel arrangements to make the system more cost efficient and more effective in serving customers.

Chapter Summary

- Strong distribution is necessary for superior market performance. A channel of distribution consists of several intermediaries that facilitate the flow of goods and services together with support services. A distribution strategy is based on the most efficient and effective way to distribute a firm's product.

- Channel strategy encompasses all activities associated with the creation of raw materials to the delivery and consumption of the finished goods. Channel management aims to manage the flow of information, materials, and money between the various paths in the most efficient way. It views channels of distribution as part of a supply chain management system whose members are concerned about the performance of the entire chain instead of their individual sales or profit performance.

- Channels are important because they are a key external resource that can generate profits and sales for many years to come and they affect every other element of the marketing mix. It takes a long time to build a channel of distribution. Manufacturers are committed to complex, long-term relationships with intermediaries. Also, channel members send a powerful message to customers about the desired product image. The strategic advantages of channels of distribution include the following: increase market coverage, help build a desirable image, erect barriers to entry, increase profitability, improve customer satisfaction, and exploit competitor weaknesses.

- Channel of distribution methods include direct distribution, corporate stores, indirect distribution, piggybacking e-commerce, and multiple channels.

- Channel strategy includes consumer analysis, channel length (direct, indirect), channel intensity (intensive, selective, exclusive), selection of channel partners, managing channel relationships, and managing channel change.

Review and Discussion Questions

1. Why are firms adopting the supply chain management approach to managing their channels? What are the benefits of such an approach?

2. Discuss the strategic importance of distribution.

3. Describe the various channels of distribution methods.

4. Discuss sequential distribution.

5. What is the role of consumer analysis in channel design?

6. Compare and contrast the three channel intensity strategies.

7. The channel manager of a company selling USB flash drives is trying to maximize the number of channels through which he is distributing the company's products. What are the benefits and risks of such an approach?

8. Discuss why it is important to recognize the sources of channel conflict and take immediate action to remove them. Describe the methods marketers can use for managing channel relationships.

9. Discuss the customized, backhauling, and cross-docking distribution strategies.

10. Why do managers need to keep track of changes going on in their channels of distribution? How can managers manage such change?

1. You are the marketing manager of a manufacturer of a new line of specialty coffee using wholesalers and a variety of retailers, including supermarkets and convenience stores. However, the growth objectives of your company are not being met as sales are growing only at the rate of growth of the target market. Discuss several alternative channels of distribution that could be used to increase the sales of the new product.

2. The channel manager of a manufacturer of water filters is trying to target both industrial and individual customers with the same channel of distribution. Is this a good idea?

3. Procter & Gamble uses a dual distribution method to sell its products. Specifically, it employs a direct distribution that relies on its own sale force to sell to its business customers and an indirect distribution involving retailers to sell to individual customers. What is the logic behind Procter & Gamble's distribution strategy?

4. Many firms are reluctant to sell their products directly to the public, through their own stores or over the Internet. What is the cause of that reluctance?

Notes

1. Drawn from Mel James, "Harlequin Romances, Marketing Pulp Fiction Fizzles," http://collections.ic.gc.ca, retrieved on October 5, 2003; http://www.torstar.com, retrieved on October 5, 2003.
2. Hirotaka J. Takeuchi, "Strategic Issues in Distribution," in Robert J. Dolan, ed., *Strategic Marketing Management* (Boston: *Harvard Business Review,* 1991), 323.
3. Kevin P. McKormack, William C. Johnson, with William T. Walker, *Supply Chain Networks and Business Process Orientation* (New York: St. Lucie Press, 2003), 1.
4. Peter Koudal and Todd Lavieri, "Profits in the Balance—When Costs and Customer and Supplier Relationships Are Balanced Evenly, Profitability Increases," *Optimize* 1 (June), 81–89.
5. Louis W. Stern and Frederick D. Sturdivant, "Customer-Driven Distribution Systems," in Dolan, 338.
6. Johny K. Johansson and Ikujiro Nonaka, *Relentless: The Japanese Way of Marketing* (New York: HarperBusiness, 1996), 143.
7. V. Kasturi, A. J. Menezes, and E. P. Maier, "Channel Selection for New Industrial Products: A Framework, Method, and Applications," *Journal of Marketing* 56, (July 1992), 69–82.
8. Nirmalya Kumar, "The Power of Trust in Manufacturer-Retailer Relationships," *Harvard Business Review* (November–December 1996), 92–106.
9. Kevin Lane Keller, *Strategic Brand Management* (Upper Saddle River, N.J.: Prentice Hall, 1998), 200.
10. Marina Strauss, "Italian shoe maker looks for toehold in Canada," *The Globe and Mail,* April 19, 2004, B5.
11. George S. Day, *Market-Driven Strategy* (New York: The Free Press, 1990), 248.
12. Christopher A. Bartlett and Sumantha Ghoshal, "Going Global: Lessons from Late Movers," *Harvard Business Review* (March–April 2000), 132–142.
13. James A. Nanus and James C. Anderson, "Rethinking Distribution," *Harvard Business Review* (July–August 1996), 112–120.
14. Anne T. Couchlan and Louis W. Stern, "Marketing Channel Design and Management," in Dawn Iacobucci, ed., *Kellogg on Marketing* (New York: Wiley, 2001), 249.
15. Jonathan D. Hibbard, Nirmalya Kumar, and Louis W. Stern, "Examining the Impact of Destructive Acts in Marketing Channel Relationships," *Journal of Marketing Research* 38 (February 2001), 45–61.
16. Yoram Wind, Vijay Mahajan with Robert E. Gunther, *Convergence Marketing* (Upper Saddle River, N.J.: Prentice Hall, 2002), 133.
17. Donald R. Lehman and Charles B. Weinberg, "Sales Through Sequential Distribution Channels: An Application to Movies and Videos," *Journal of Marketing* (July 2000), 18–33.
18. Rowland T. Moriarty and Ursula Moran, "Managing Hybrid Marketing Systems," *Harvard Business Review* (November–December, 1990), 146–155.
19. Kumar.
20. Anne T. Coughlan, Erin Anderson, Louis W. Stern, and Adel I. El-Ansary, *Marketing Channels,* 6th ed. (Upper Saddle River, N.J.: Prentice Hall, 2001), 123.
21. Day, 1990, 220.
22. Kenneth Rolnicki, *Managing Channels of Distribution* (New York: American Marketing Association, 1998), 17.
23. Steven Wheeler and Evan Hirsh, *Channel Champions* (San Francisco: Jossey-Bass Publishers, 1999), 84.
24. Coughlan, Anderson, Stern, and El-Ansary, 60.
25. Kasturi, Menezes, and Maier, 1992.
26. Kumar.
27. Day, 1990, 225.
28. Coughlan, Anderson, Stern, and El-Ansary, 120.
29. John Burnett, *Introducing Marketing* (New York: Wiley, 2002), 271.
30. Lisa Harrington, "How to Join the Supply Chain Revolution," *Inbound Logistics* (November 1995), 21.
31. Coughlan, Anderson, Stern, and El-Ansary, 35.
32. Denis R. Towill, "The Seamless Supply Chain: The Predator's Strategic Advantage," *International Journal of Technology Management* 13, No. 1 (1997), 37–56.
33. McKormack, Johnson, with Walker, 9.
34. Sanjay Srikanth, "7 Imperatives for Successful Collaboration," *Supply Chain Management Review* 9, No. 1, 30–37.
35. Rolnicki, 148.
36. Kumar.
37. Eric Schulz, *The Marketing Game* (Holbrook, Mass.: Adams Media Corporation, 1999), 127.

Chapter Twelve

Integrated Marketing Communications

He who whispers in a well

Of the goods he wants to sell

Will not make as many dollars

As one who turns around and hollers.

Anonymous merchant

Learning Objectives

After studying this chapter, you should be able to:

1. Develop an integrated marketing communications plan

2. Craft effective advertising strategies

3. Describe how to manage the company's sales force

4. Discuss the various sales promotions methods

5. Describe the various public relations methods

Allstream's Successful Integrated Marketing Communications Campaign

Allstream is a large communications company that offers services to deal with problems of connectivity, infrastructure management, and information technology. Allstream works closely with customers to design tailored solutions that meet their needs and help them compete more effectively.

Allstream is a division of Manitoba Telecom Services Inc. (MTS), Canada's third-largest communications provider. MTS has an extensive broadband fibre-optic network spanning more than 18,800 kilometres and provides international connections through partnerships and interconnection agreements with other international service providers.

The launch of Allstream on June 18, 2003, was one of the most publicized corporate launches in the Canadian telecommunications industry. Since the launch, Allstream has successfully positioned itself as a leading national communications service provider for businesses in North America.

Working in partnership with Publicis Canada, a full-service advertising company, Allstream developed a fully integrated communications program that targeted all its key stakeholders, including employees and customers. The company implemented the communications program in two phases. In phase one, the initial campaign focused on name awareness—the introduction of Allstream and its association with AT&T Canada. This campaign was designed to quickly establish Allstream as a strong, growing, long-term player in the Canadian telecommunications industry. In phase two, the campaign focused on the brand promise. It featured customers' success stories and new product introductions that demonstrated Allstream's capabilities and established its credibility.

Allstream's integrated marketing communications campaign used national and regional newspapers and magazines, radio spots, and electronic outdoor boards. The campaign tag line "There is more to networks" was meant to show that the company "is not just about bits and bytes," but that it understands the value its customers create for their customers and the business solutions Allstream creates as a result of this understanding.

Allstream's employees were engaged at each phase of the campaign and were provided with an overview of the company's communications objectives and the implications of its brand and its promise. This knowledge would enable them to act as ambassadors of the new brand.

Once the brand was introduced to the marketplace, the company communications objective became one of retaining the customers. The company achieved this objective with a variety of communications methods, including billing inserts, special articles in its customer newsletters, and a special support section on its website.[1]

Introduction

As the Allstream case in the opening vignette illustrates, integrated marketing communications is an integral part of marketing strategy and essential to firms' success. Promotion can be a powerful source of competitive advantage. Companies such as Molson Coors and Canadian Tire spend millions of dollars on advertising and other forms of promotion to increase or maintain their market share. Advertising helps firms to differentiate their products from the competitions' and to charge higher prices than equivalent products. Advertising can also help a firm gain market share against competitors.

Promotion is part of a firm's marketing plan and must fit within the organization's overall marketing strategy. As such, promotion strategies should not be developed independently of the other elements of the marketing mix. If the product has a premium image, its price, distribution, and promotion should reinforce that image. For instance, if Rolex were to reduce the price of its watches drastically or advertise in mass circulation print media, it would diminish the image of its products and alienate its target market. If, on the other hand, the product is an economical, low-priced product, the marketing mix should reflect the product's low quality and price.

This chapter examines issues related to developing an integrated marketing communications plan. It discusses how to craft effective advertising strategies and looks into personal selling and sales force management, sales promotion methods, and public relations issues.

Integrated Marketing Communications

The primary functions of promotion are to communicate information to consumers about product features, convince them of the products' benefits, motivate them to buy the advertisers' product, and to remind them periodically about the product in order to maintain the product's share of top-of-mind awareness. The major communication objectives of a new product are to create awareness, inform potential customers about the benefits of the product, and motivate them to purchase the product. On the other hand, the major goal of promotion of well-known existing brands is to remind customers about the brands and sustain their market position.

The **promotion mix** includes advertising, personal selling, sales promotion, and public relations. **Integrated marketing communications** is the coordinated use of all promotion elements to communicate a consistent and unified message about a product in a cost-effective way.[2] The core advertising theme must be consistent with the position taken in personal selling (brochures, catalogues, and presentations), public relations material, and sales promotion. For example, Ikea Canada established a new marketing department in an effort to develop a Canadian-based marketing communications strategy. An external communication manager was responsible for advertising, public relations, Internet, direct marketing, catalogues, and research and planning.[3] These moves represent an effort to ensure that all elements of the promotion mix speak with a consistent voice and send a consistent message to consumers.

The **promotion mix** includes advertising, personal selling, public relations, and sales promotion.

Integrated marketing communications is the coordinated use of all promotional elements to communicate a consistent and unified message about a product in a cost-effective way.

Designing an Integrated Marketing Communications Plan

Establishing an integrated marketing communications plan involves several tasks. These include identifying the target audience, establishing the communication objectives, setting the communications budget, and determining the communications mix.

Identifying the Target Audience

The first task for a promotion manager is to identify the target audience. Market segmentation often determines the segments that will be the focus of the firm's marketing effort. A company may focus on current customers as the primary communications target. In other cases, the target audience may be competitors' customers or people who do not use the product category. For example, Telus targeted Fido's subscribers with newspaper ads encouraging them to switch their cellphone service. A few years ago, BMW Canada aimed its advertising campaign at the buyers of Honda Accord and Toyota Camry, arguing that they could have a BMW by paying a slightly higher price than they would pay for these automobiles. As part of determining the target audience, marketing managers must choose between a defensive and an offensive promotion strategy, as explained in the following section:

Defensive promotion strategy. **Defensive promotion strategy** calls for promoting in geographic markets where the product is already distributed or where sales have been good, instead of promoting in those markets where sales have been poor.[4] The logic of the defensive promotion strategy is that if sales are good in an area, money should be spent there because demand is tried and true, rather than going after markets where demand is unknown and risks are greater. This strategy makes good sense, especially when sales in the good markets have not been fully exploited. However, a firm using this strategy risks missing out on markets that, although currently underperforming, have good future sales potential, and in which adequate advertising spending could help increase sales.

Offensive promotion strategy. **Offensive promotion strategy** calls for promoting in markets where a brand's sales have been low. Such markets frequently require an increase in promotional spending to raise the level of awareness and increase the degree of brand recognition. Promoting in markets where sales have been low can be an opportunity but it can present risks as well. Before a firm increases promotional spending in a market where sales are low, it should first find out if increasing advertising in this market will increase sales. Sometimes, the product is not selling well because of insufficient distribution, because the market is price sensitive and considers the price of the product too high, or because the product may need to be modified in some way to fit the requirements of the market.

Defensive promotion strategy calls for advertising in geographic markets where the product is already distributed or where sales have been good, instead of advertising in those markets where sales have been poor.

Offensive promotion strategy involves advertising in markets where a brand's sales have been low.

Establishing the Communications Objectives

Managers must decide what they want to accomplish with their marketing communications effort. Communications objectives entail the type of response sought from the target audience. They must be as meaningful as possible because they provide the foundation for all other promotion decisions and the benchmark against which promotional results will be measured.[5] All marketing communications must satisfy one or more communication objectives. The ultimate purpose of marketing communications is to increase sales.

Marketing communications must be both informative and persuasive to motivate people to buy the advertiser's product. Consumers pay attention to messages that offer them information that is interesting or useful to them, otherwise they ignore them. Successful marketing communications link the product with a relevant message that reinforces the brand's positioning strategy.[6]

Marketing communications are also used to remind customers about the firm's products. Since people often forget about products they were aware of in the past, they need to be reminded from time to time—especially at the time they are making purchasing decisions. Even the most loyal customers must be reminded of the features that make the product a good value and that the product has offered them excellent value over the years.

Companies such as Nortel and The Bay enjoy high levels of awareness but they need to sustain customers' interest in their products. For this reason, marketers must schedule their marketing communications in appropriate ways to remind customers about their products.

Setting the Communications Budget

There are several considerations involved in setting a marketing communications budget. For example, spending a large advertising budget could serve as a signal that the product is of high quality.[7] Consumers would infer that the company spends a lot of money on advertising because the quality of its products is high and is confident that consumers will purchase the product as long as they are informed about it. Producers of low-quality products, on the other hand, would be unwilling to advertise their products. Other considerations in setting the communications budget include sales levels, desire for using rules of thumb to simplify the administration of the budget-setting process, competitive factors, and availability of funds. As a result, firms use various methods for setting their communications budget.

Percentage of sales is a method of setting the communications budget as a percentage of current or forecasted sales.

Percentage of sales is the most popular method for setting a communications budget. It involves setting the communications budget as a percentage of current or forecasted sales. According to the consulting firm Accenture, about 80 percent of corporations determine their advertising budget as a percentage of expected sales. The advantages of the percentage of sales method include simplifying decision-making by using a simple rule of thumb instead of complicated calculations that may require considerable time and money for data collection and analysis. The use of this method also helps firms avoid engaging in expensive promotion wars. However, although this method appears sound on the surface, it has a logical flaw. It assumes that promotion is the result of sales. In this case, how does a low-share firm increase its sales and market share in order to gain ground on its competitors? Also, if the economy is in a downturn and product sales are low, how is the company going to make its way out of an economic downturn when its advertising spending is low?[8] The following Strategy in Action box illustrates the difficulties associated with the percentage of sales method.[9]

Strategy in Action
KMART AND E*TRADE

Early in 2001, when Kmart's revenues took a hit, its CEO, Chuck Conaway, decided to reduce the company's marketing communications budget. At the time it looked like a smart way to save money. However, as a result of the reduced promotional budget, Kmart lost far more in sales than it had saved in marketing costs and yielded more ground to arch rivals Wal-Mart and Target. Conaway admitted his mistake and announced that he would increase Kmart's marketing communications budget.

Another company, E*Trade, an online broker, approached the task of setting its communications budget in a different way. After having an excellent year in 2000, E*Trade watched revenues drop precipitously between the first and second quarters of 2001, from $550 million to $516 million. Faced with an even dimmer third quarter, E*Trade scrapped its marketing communications budgeting rules and increased its spending in a number of areas. As a result, it signed up 66,000 new customers in the third quarter, up 17 percent from the previous year.

Competitive parity entails spending the same percentage of sales on advertising as the major competitors.

Another method for setting a communications budget is **competitive parity**. Firms using this method spend the same percentage of sales on promotion as their major competitors. The advantages of this method include simplicity and minimizing the chances of a promotion war. However, it deprives the firm from pursuing an independent marketing communications policy tailored to its unique competitive situation and objectives. Companies using this method essentially let competitors determine their promotional budget.

Companies using the **all-you can-afford** method spend whatever funds are available for promotion. Organizations using this method do not have the funds to implement any of the other methods or they may limit their communications spending in certain years because they feel pressured to show satisfactory profits.[10] Many firms using this method view promotion as an expense rather than a productive investment that will benefit the product. This method can result in wild fluctuations in promotional spending depending on the availability of funds. It also fails to take into account the firm's promotional objectives and competitive situation. Like the previous methods for setting the communications budget, this method fails to determine promotion spending on the basis of the firm's marketing objectives and market conditions.

All-you can-afford entails spending whatever funds are available for promotion.

The **objective-and-task** method first determines the communications objectives that need to be achieved and then determines the task needed to satisfy the objective. For example, if, after careful analysis, a firm thinks that the awareness level of its product is low, it could create a communications plan designed to raise awareness by a certain percentage and determine an appropriate budget to achieve this objective. Unlike the other methods, the objective-and-task method shows how promotion affects sales.[11] But this method is not easy to implement and it may require a great deal of effort and time. It is often difficult to develop good communications objectives and to determine the costs and activities required to achieve the objectives. For this reason, it is not one of the most commonly used methods for setting a communications budget.

Objective-and-task requires first to determine the advertising objective that needs to be achieved and then to determine the task needed to satisfy the objective.

Determining the Communications Mix

In designing an effective marketing communications mix, managers must decide which aspects of communications to emphasize in their promotional efforts: advertising, personal selling, sales promotions, or public relations. In making marketing communications decisions, marketing managers should make strategic use of communications tools. They should not think of advertising rather than personal selling or sales promotion but decide whether their communications objectives and market and competitive conditions necessitate emphasizing advertising, personal selling, or sales promotions. Each communications tool has its own special characteristics that make it more or less appropriate given the firm's communications objectives and market conditions. In this section we first discuss the factors that determine the choice between advertising and personal selling, followed by a discussion of the factors that determine the choice between advertising and sales promotion.

Choosing between advertising and personal selling

One of the most important promotion mix decisions for marketing managers is the choice between advertising and personal selling. In choosing between advertising and personal selling, marketers need to take into account the target audience and other factors, as shown in Figure 12.1.

A firm's choice between advertising and personal selling is often dictated by whether a firm follows a pull or a push communication strategy. A **pull strategy** entails directing the communication effort to the final consumer. The objective of a pull strategy is to build awareness and increase brand recognition. If it is successful, a pull strategy influences customers to seek out the firm's products or services, pulling the product through the channel. This in turn forces distributors to carry the products in order to satisfy the customers who demand the promoted products.

A **pull strategy** entails directing the communication effort to the final consumer.

A **push strategy** relies on a sales force to work closely with distributors and offers them incentives to motivate them to make the products available to customers and put a greater effort and support behind the products.

A firm using a **push strategy,** on the other hand, relies on its sales force to work closely with distributors and offer them incentives to motivate them to make the products available to customers and put a greater effort and support behind the products. A firm using a push strategy does little or no advertising but relies on intermediaries to "push" the product toward the customer. Some of the ways to gain channel cooperation and support include better distributor margins, point-of-sale support, and co-op advertising. Push strategies are usually pursued by small firms because of their small advertising budgets. For a small firm to follow a pull strategy would be an ineffective use of its funds as it wouldn't be able to spend the required funds to reach the required level of frequency and awareness.

Choosing between advertising and sales promotions

Advertising and sales promotions are important tools for achieving a firm's marketing communications objectives. Both communications tools must be closely coordinated in order to provide a consistent image for the brand. One important decision for marketing managers is which of these two promotion tools to emphasize. The degree of emphasis on advertising or sales promotions is determined to a large extent by the stage in the product life cycle, the degree of brand differentiation, and loyalty toward the brand (see Figure 12.2).

Figure 12.2	Relative Roles of Advertising and Sales Promotion	
Product Life Cycle Stage	**Advertising**	**Sales Promotions**
Introduction	High	High
Growth/Shakeout		
Differentiated brand	High	Low
Imitative brand	Low	High
Maturity		
High brand loyalty	High	Low
Low brand loyalty	Low	High
Decline	Discontinued	Low

SOURCE: Adapted from Larry Percy, John R. Rossiter, and Richard Elliott, *Strategic Advertising Management* (New York: Oxford University Press, 2001), p. 264. By permission of Oxford University Press.

The introduction stage occurs when the company needs to generate awareness and interest in its product. During this stage, advertising and sales promotion spending are typically high. A high level of advertising spending is necessary to create brand awareness and inform potential buyers about the benefits of the product. A high level of promotion spending is also needed to generate brand trials for the newly introduced product. The introduction of Kellogg Canada's Nutri-Grain Mini Granola Bar, described in the Strategy in Action box, illustrates the use of advertising and sales promotion in introducing a new product.[12]

Strategy in Action — KELLOGG CANADA

Kellogg Canada introduced its first granola bar in 1981 and in 2003 took another step into the Canadian granola market when it introduced its Nutri-Grain Mini Granola Bar. The new mini granola bar was differentiated from other products by its small size and by pairing the tiny bite-size bar with another new product extension, Rice Krispies Squares with Cadbury chocolate. The company ran a television spot featuring a small man—a "mini" man—going to excruciating lengths to explain that nothing in the new minis is mini with the tag line "They're mini if you're not." Kellogg's advertising drive was accompanied by a direct mail sampling campaign to 500,000 homes in Canada. Each package included a high-value coupon. According to Charles Perez, director of marketing of adult brands at Kellogg Canada, "We know we need to get these products in people's mouths, that once they taste them it will increase trial and then result in a strong repeat." The mini granola came in three flavours—chocolate chip, mixed berry, and oatmeal raisin—and was aimed mainly at women, although the company felt that the product would be received well by men too.

In the growth and shakeout stages of a product's life cycle, the relative emphasis depends on whether the product is differentiated or is an imitative product. If the product is differentiated, advertising is emphasized to communicate the product's uniqueness or superiority and to strengthen the brand's image and differentiation. In the case of imitative brands, they require low advertising spending as they can capitalize on spending by competing firms to maintain interest in the product category. Such brands, however, require a heavy emphasis on sales promotions to induce trial and switching as a means of increasing sales. These brands need to compete on the basis of price as they lack any significant advantages over competing products.

In the maturity stage, the relative emphasis on advertising or promotion also differs, but in this case, it is on the basis of the degree of loyalty toward the brand. Brands commanding a high degree of loyalty should emphasize advertising to maintain their strong image and loyalty. Managers of brands with a low degree of loyalty need to spend heavily on promotion to encourage potential buyers to purchase their brands.

Advertising in the decline stage is typically discontinued as the product is being phased out. Sales promotions are reduced considerably and are typically directed at intermediaries to maintain distribution for the product until unsold inventory is entirely cleared.

Crafting Advertising Strategies

Crafting an effective advertising strategy is essential for meeting a firm's communications objectives. **Advertising** is the term used to describe messages about products or services paid for by an identified sponsor and carried by mass media. The purpose of advertising is to sell, or help sell, a company's product or service. Advertising provides information

Advertising is the term used to describe messages about products or services paid for by an identified sponsor and carried by mass media.

and is designed to create a positive feeling or attitude toward a product that will motivate people to purchase it. It further attempts to associate a brand with a desirable experience—a benefit that the brand provides better than competing brands.

Advertising is an effective way to increase product differentiation by informing customers about product characteristics or by creating perceived or subjective product differences. By conveying information, advertising informs customers about differences between brands and in this way it enhances product differentiation. Even if advertising conveys very few differences between a product and its rivals, it can still increase the degree of perceived product differentiation and decrease price competition through better brand recognition. For example, Tylenol and several of its lower-priced competitors contain the same ingredient, acetaminophen. However, Tylenol, by spending heavily on advertising, has managed to differentiate itself from its competitors.

A firm's advertising strategy must be consistent with the firm's integrated marketing communications framework. Elements of a firm's advertising strategy include designing an appropriate message, establishing a media plan, and evaluating advertising effectiveness. Before these aspects are discussed, we will look at the role advertising plays in affecting the target audience's response.

Assessing the role of advertising in target audience response

A useful way of assessing the role advertising plays in affecting the target audience's response is to conceptualize the impact of advertising on several behavioural steps through which potential customers must pass before they purchase the brand. Successful messages require a positive response at each step. These steps are presented as elements of the **target audience response equation,** shown below:

Target audience response equation includes all the behavioural steps through which potential customers must pass before they purchase the brand.

$$TAR = A \times C \times R \times I \times P \times B$$

Where:

TAR = percentage of target audience that will purchase the brand
 A = percentage of target audience that is aware of the message
 C = percentage of those who are aware of and correctly comprehend the message
 R = percentage of those who comprehend the message and actually retain it
 I = percentage of those who have retained the message and are interested in the brand
 P = percentage of those who are interested in the brand and intend to purchase it
 B = percentage of those who intend to purchase the brand and actually do buy it

The target audience response equation presented above demonstrates that the number of people who purchase the brand depends on several factors. The target audience must first become aware of the brand being advertised. For this to happen, audience members must attend to the message. After the audience becomes aware of the message, it must comprehend correctly the message and retain the arguments contained in the message. Next, those who retained the message must develop an interest in the brand, develop an intention to buy the brand, and eventually buy the brand.

Assuming that the percentage of people who respond positively to each of the steps in the equation is 60 percent, the overall percentage of people who will purchase the product is 4.7 percent (.60 × .60 × .60 × .60 × .60 × .60 = 4.7). The above example illustrates that in order for advertising to be successful, all behavioural steps must be completed. For example, if a marketing communications campaign fails to create awareness in the target audience, none of the communication effects that follow are possible. In the above example, 40 percent of the target audience will not be reached with the marketing communication and will therefore not have the opportunity to comprehend, retain, develop an interest,

Poor Response	Marketing Problem	Underlying Cause
Low awareness	Marketing communications	Insufficient reach Insufficient frequency Incorrect media mix Incorrect media scheduling
Poor comprehension	Marketing communications	Insufficient frequency Poor ad copy Poor message execution
Low retention	Marketing communications Product	Insufficient frequency Insufficient consumer benefits
Low interest	Product positioning	Product lacks desirable benefits Lack of product need
Low intention to purchase	Price Transaction costs	High price High switching costs
Low purchase level	Distribution In-store placement	Inadequate distribution Lack of in-store visibility

SOURCE: Roger J. Best, *Market-Based Management*, 3rd Edition, © 2003, p. 248. Adapted by permission of Pearson Education, Inc., Upper Saddle River, NJ.

form an intention to buy, or purchase the brand. Figure 12.3 shows various causes of low levels of response in each of the factors included in the equation.

Marketers can play an active role in helping potential customers go through the various stages to ensure that customers purchase the product. Using informative, persuasive, and reminder messages through appropriate media, marketers can provide potential customers with the information they need to favourably evaluate their brands and convince them that they meet their needs. The Strategy in Action box illustrates how advertising helped a Quebec drugstore chain increase consumer awareness and company sales.[13]

Strategy in Action

FAMILIPRIX

Familiprix, a drugstore chain comprising about 250 small independently owned pharmacies, was not well known in Quebec only a few years ago. In fact, consumers confused it with the similar-sounding Pharmaprix and Uniprix drugstore chains in the province. In late 2002, Familiprix launched a series of entertaining and innovative 15-second television commercials. The ads showed a number of people just as they were falling sick and a Familiprix pharmacist, played by Quebec actor Sylvain Marcel, sympathizing with them and ready to help out. Surveys conducted by the company after a few months showed that more than half of Quebeckers could name Familiprix, up from 19 percent in 2001. The chain's drug sales jumped 33 percent in the first six months of 2003. The commercials also won the Lion d'argent at the Cannes International Advertising Festival, and the Grand Prix at the Canadian Advertising Success Stories (Cassies) in 2003. The success of the commercials and the subsequent rise in the chain's fortune have been credited with pharmacists, who are in short supply in Quebec, clamouring to join Familiprix.

Message Design

Message design is a crucial aspect of a firm's advertising strategy. Effective advertising must attract and hold the viewer's attention and communicate a positive benefit bestowed by the brand. It must encourage reading and processing the advertisement. The effectiveness of an advertising strategy depends on the quality of the advertising message. An effective message should meet the following criteria:

1. *Directed at a specific segment*. Advertising for a product should not be generically directed at all market segments. It should be focused, targeting a specific segment with an appropriate message for the advertised product. For this reason, identifying a firm's best prospects is central to any marketing and advertising strategy.
2. *Believable*. Advertising messages need to be believable to be effective. Unless the audience believes the message, it will probably be lost, as people will likely disregard it as lacking credibility. Making claims that the market finds hard to believe can render the advertising effort ineffective. For example, some commercials show cars being driven on steep and winding mountain roads and other situations in which it is difficult to drive. This creates credibility problems. It is very important to create ads that present situations consumers can imagine themselves part of.
3. *Desirable*. Desirability is an essential element of an advertising message. Effective advertisements need to give people reasons for desiring and buying the product. Successful advertisements sell the advantages of the product and exploit key differences between the firm's product and competitors' products. For example, BMW's perceived advantage of "driveability" is consistent with its advertising claim as "The Ultimate Driving Experience."
4. *Unique*. Uniqueness is also an essential element of an effective advertising message. Messages that do not promote some type of uniqueness usually have difficulty attracting the attention of hard-to-please audiences and breaking through the advertising clutter created by competing brands. Brands that imitate a competitor's successful ad fail to establish their own identity in the marketplace, confuse consumers, and achieve poor brand recall.
5. *Consistent*. An advertising message needs to be characterized by consistency and continuity over time and across media. Constantly changing the direction and focus of the advertising effort is usually harmful to the long-term image of the product because it confuses consumers about what the product stands for. If a firm uses different media, it should make sure that all media are closely coordinated and they all send the same message to their audiences.

Media Plan

The success of commercial products depends on satisfactory levels of consumer awareness and interest toward a firm's products. However, consumers' awareness and interest toward products decline over time unless they are reinforced. An important aspect of an advertising campaign is to maintain these factors at satisfactory levels by keeping the message in front of customers. The media plan specifies how the advertising budget will be spent to achieve these and other relevant advertising objectives.[14] The media plan includes determining the media mix, media scheduling, and reach and frequency, which are discussed next.

Media mix

The media mix refers to the choice of media to be used, such as television, radio, newspapers, magazines, billboards, bus shelter posters, stadium displays, and the Internet. Marketers have also found creative ways to deliver their messages such as on CDs, videocassettes, telemarketing, supermarket cart ads, and others. Choosing the right media mix is necessary for advertising success. The Strategy in Action box illustrates how finding the right media mix can lead to superb advertising performance:[15]

Media scheduling

Once the media mix is chosen, the advertising manager needs to establish a scheduling plan—when the advertisement will be run. Effective scheduling ensures that an advertisement is run at the most favourable times. Several media scheduling strategies are shown in Figure 12.4.

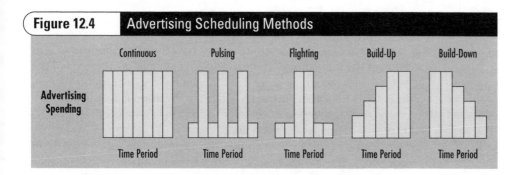

Figure 12.4 Advertising Scheduling Methods

Continuous | Pulsing | Flighting | Build-Up | Build-Down

Advertising Spending

Time Period

Continuous scheduling. **Continuous scheduling** involves running ads at a constant level throughout the selling period. For example, the firm advertises every week, month, or season, following whatever schedule has been chosen. Continuous advertising is appropriate for products with large promotion budgets, year-round buying patterns, short purchase cycle, impulse buying, and weak brand loyalty. An important problem with continuous advertising is that very few companies can afford to maintain constant advertising spending at a sufficient level. Continuous advertising also suffers from copy wearout due to overexposure—people become tired of watching the same ads year round. Due to these problems, advertisers often use other types of scheduling, such as pulsing or flighting.

Continuous scheduling involves running ads at a constant level throughout the selling period.

Pulsing scheduling. **Pulsing scheduling** is similar to continuous advertising except that ads are run every other period instead of every period. It is an effective way to reinforce the communications message, reduce copy wear-out, and keep advertising costs at reasonable levels. For example, a firm could run an advertisement every other week instead of every week. During the week it is run, it builds up awareness, which decreases the following week, and it increases again the subsequent week when the advertisement is run.

Pulsing scheduling is similar to continuous advertising except that ads are run every other period instead of every period.

This way, the firm maintains awareness at satisfactory levels, reduces advertising costs, and keeps copy wear-out at low levels by avoiding overexposure.

Flighting scheduling. **Flighting**—also called heavy-up scheduling—is used for products that are not purchased year round but only during certain periods of the year. Such seasonal products normally use extensive advertising during the heavy buying season and very little or no advertising during the rest of the year. For example, winter resorts advertise only during the winter season. For flighting scheduling to work, it is important to synchronize the timing of the advertising campaign with the time customers actually make their buying decisions. Flighting strategy makes a firm's advertising strategy more effective by spending the advertising budget when it has the most powerful impact. It also helps prevent copy wear-out as advertising is heavily concentrated in a short period of time. Some advertisers combine the flighting with the pulsing approach. These companies use pulsing advertising to maintain a minimum level of awareness throughout the year and flighting advertising for maximum impact before and during the time of heavy demand.

Build-up and build-down scheduling. Two variations of the flighting approach are build-up and build-down scheduling. Companies using the **build-up** method start small as the season approaches and gradually build up their advertising spending until it reaches its highest level at the peak of the selling season. The **build-down** approach starts with a large amount of advertising spending and gradually decreases advertising spending after the peak sales period until it becomes zero during the off-season period. This method is often used with the introduction of a new product to create high levels of awareness and it is gradually reduced afterward.[16]

Reach and frequency

In order for an advertising campaign to succeed, as we have seen in an earlier section, a number of things must occur.[17] Potential customers must have the opportunity to hear or see the message through the right choice of media, notice the message, understand the message, and be persuaded to act in the desired manner by linking the product to a desirable association. For this to happen, it normally takes a few times for a person to see or read an ad before the message is understood and the product is associated with the desired feeling that may lead to purchasing the brand.

Reach or coverage is the percentage of an audience's members that are exposed to an advertisement. **Frequency** is the average number of times the members of the audience were exposed to an ad over the broadcast period. The objective of an advertising campaign is to achieve optimal levels of reach and frequency. Firms optimize their media strategy with regard to reach and frequency by achieving a minimum effective frequency. **Minimum effective frequency** is the level of frequency at which advertising will begin to have a positive impact on the target audience.

The ideal media plan enables a company to reach everyone in the target audience enough times to ensure a favourable response to the message. But since firms have a fixed advertising budget, reach and frequency are inversely related. For example, one may increase reach by selecting different television programs for placing ads. This increases reach but not frequency. As reach increases, frequency remains low since there is less money to spend on achieving a higher repetition of the ad. One mistake some managers make is to try to increase reach without a sufficient level of frequency. A useful rule of thumb is to reach fewer people but with enough frequency to ensure a successful communication effort; this plan is preferable to reaching a larger audience but with a frequency so low that is not enough to elicit a positive audience response.

There is a point at which efforts to increase reach become less effective. As a commercial is repeated over time, its reach grows more slowly if the same program is used every time and the number of new people exposed to the telecast begins to diminish. Eventually the commercial will end up reaching the same people over and over, as most potential audience members have been reached. This results in increases in frequency rather than reach.

To achieve a maximum reach, firms must utilize different media to ensure that as many potential members of the target audience as possible are reached. Reach may be increased using the following techniques.[18] The **multiple content program technique** involves placing the ad during programs whose content changes during the broadcasting of the program or from one week to another. For example, programs that show movies or documentaries increase reach, as different people watch different movies. Programs such as soap operas or TV series increase frequency, as they draw similar audiences when they are broadcasted.

The **scatter technique** entails firms placing the commercial in different programs and time periods to maximize exposure. For example, a company may advertise during various programs such as *Marketplace* and *Hockey Night in Canada*. The scatter technique ensures that different people are exposed to the commercial. This allows the advertiser to reach more people than if the same program and time period were used. Finally, the **roadblock technique** involves firms placing the commercial in different media during the same time. The roadblock method also ensures reaching different people and maximizing reach.

The **multiple content program technique** involves placing the ad during programs whose content changes during the broadcasting of the program or from one week to another.

The **scatter technique** entails firms placing the commercial in different programs and time periods to maximize exposure.

The **roadblock technique** involves firms placing the commercial in different media during the same time.

Frequency required to achieve the minimum effective frequency

One of the most important decisions for media planners is to decide how much frequency will achieve the minimum effective frequency needed to accomplish the firm's advertising objectives. This question is not easy to answer *a priori*. Media planners often conduct test marketing or study previous advertising campaigns to establish a quantitative relationship between frequency and communication response. But even if research is undertaken to show how much frequency is needed to accomplish a communications objective, it is very difficult to establish a clear relationship between the two variables. Currently, advertisers disagree about how many times an advertisement has to be repeated to have the intended impact on the audience. Estimates of the optimum frequency vary from one to as many as ten or even more repetitions.[19]

Since the level of frequency required for advertising to have an impact has not been resolved by the theoretical studies done so far, media planners have to make subjective decisions about how much frequency is needed. The factors that influence the choice between a high and low frequency are listed in Figure 12.5.

Figure 12.5	Factors Influencing the Choice Between High and Low Frequency	
High Frequency	**Factor**	**Low Frequency**
High	Degree of ad clutter in the chosen media	Low
Limited	Medium ability to hold audience interest	Extensive
High	Message complexity	Low
Low	Brand loyalty	High
Low	Audience involvement	High
Strong	Competition	Weak
Short	Purchase cycle	Long

Measuring Advertising Effectiveness

Measuring the effectiveness of an advertising campaign is an important step in the promotional planning process. As managers spend significant sums of money promoting their products and services, they want to know whether these expenditures achieve their company's communication goals. Measuring advertising effectiveness enables marketing managers to evaluate the performance of specific campaign elements and decide whether changes are needed.

Measuring the effectiveness of advertising allows marketing managers to avoid costly mistakes. However, many managers do not undertake this assessment often because of the high cost associated with such activities measured both in money and time. Many managers prefer to spend their time and financial resources on copy development and additional media time or space than on measuring and testing their ads.[20] However, running the wrong campaign can lead to the waste of a firm's financial resources and it may even harm instead of helping sales.[21] For instance, by buying more media time when the advertising message is ineffective is a poor management decision, as illustrated in the Strategy in Action box.[22]

Strategy in Action

BEER MANUFACTURER

After a leading beer manufacturer observed that sales for a new brand of beer fell short of expectations, it decided that more media time was what the company needed. As a result, management purchased all the television time available in the market for a three-month period as long it matched the demographics of its target market. However, at the end of the three-month period, sales hadn't improved at all. After the product had been abandoned, the company conducted a final analysis of the product, and it discovered that the problem was not in the media but rather in the message, as no reason to buy the product was communicated to potential customers.

Marketers have developed several approaches for measuring advertising effectiveness. These methods include pre-testing and post-testing research methods, which are discussed in the next section.

Pre-testing research

Pre-tests are measures taken prior to the launch of the promotional program. Pre-testing enables advertisers to determine which advertisements are more effective before the advertising campaign even begins. Any problems with the ad can be identified early on and corrected before a large amount of money is spent on developing and running the ad. For example, research might have discovered that the well-known "I am Canadian" commercial, although it was a particularly popular commercial with the general population, failed to appeal to Molson's core market of males 18 to 25 years of age, and it didn't result in a significant increase in beer sales for Molson.

Focus groups are used to elicit participants' response to an advertisement. Focus groups may be used to consider the advantages and disadvantages of alternative ads, and participants can suggest additional ideas or improvements. Respondents may also be asked to evaluate the ad using a rating scale. Pre-testing may take place at various points during the ad development. Various ad concepts may be evaluated early on, or layouts of the ad campaign, including copy, headlines, slogan, or story boards, may be tested.

In recent years, devices that track eye movement have been used to determine what respondents saw and the point the eye focused on. Measures that reflect physiological arousal are also employed to assess emotional response to an ad. Among the measures used are skin resistance, facial expressions, muscle movement, and voice pitch.[23]

Post-testing research

Post-testing research is used to determine if the advertisement has met the communications objectives of the organization. Firms use different types of post-tests depending on their objectives. Such tests include ad recognition, brand awareness, changing attitudes toward the product, number of inquiries generated about the product, or number of "hits" in Internet advertising. Sales are not commonly used as a measure of advertising effectiveness because many other factors affect sales. Sales are influenced by the economy, competitors, dealer activity, prices, and other factors. Despite these drawbacks, many companies use sales figures to assess the effectiveness of an advertisement by keeping or discontinuing a product depending on sales performance. The various post-testing methods are discussed next.

Ad recall or recognition. A common advertising objective is to create awareness about the product and get people to remember the name or key attributes of brands. For this reason, many post-tests are designed to evaluate ad recall or recognition. Ad recall or recognition measure whether respondents can recall or recognize the advertisement as one they have seen before. Such measures are evidence that people processed the ad. If large numbers of respondents remember an ad or the brand advertised in the ad, it is an indication that the campaign had an impact on its intended audience.

Ad recall is conducted during or after the ad campaign. There are different ways to measure ad recall. A method called the day-after-recall (DAR) measure of television commercials involves telephoning 150 to 300 viewers the day after a television advertisement appears. Respondents are asked if they can recall any commercials from the previous day for a particular brand. If the answer is yes, they are then asked if they recall anything about the commercial such as what it said, what the main idea was, the story line, the plot, and sales message. These respondents could also be asked how many times they have seen, heard, or read the advertisements. This allows advertising researchers to measure actual advertising frequency and compare it with the targeted frequency in the media plan.

A common ad recognition test involves showing or playing a number of ads and asking respondents if they have seen or heard these ads before. For example, in printed-ad recognition tests, copies of a magazine are given to regular readers who are asked to read it in a normal manner. These readers are then asked the next day questions such as whether they remember seeing a particular ad, what the ad said about the brand, and so on.[24]

Brand recall. Brand recall tests can take the form of unaided and aided recall. **Unaided recall** involves asking participants if they remember the brand or company advertised in a certain commercial by giving no clue as to the brand or company that was advertised. For instance, if the commercial was about Boston Pizza restaurant, respondents could be asked the following question: "Which restaurants do you remember seeing in that commercial?" **Aided recall** involves asking people if they remember a specific brand or company in a certain commercial. For example, if people do not include Boston Pizza in their responses, researchers could ask, "Do you remember seeing Boston Pizza in that commercial?"

Number of inquiries generated about a product. The number of inquiries made about a product is often used to assess the effectiveness of an advertising campaign. This method is common in evaluating the success of direct mail campaigns. It can also be used to assess

Unaided recall involves asking participants if they remember the brand or company advertised in a certain commercial by giving no clue as to the brand or company that was advertised.

Aided recall involves asking people if they remember a specific brand or company in a certain commercial.

advertising campaigns. For example, many business-to-business marketers advertise in trade magazines that reach those prospects mostly interested in their products. Many of these advertisers include a coupon to be redeemed or a phone number to call for additional information. The effectiveness of these campaigns is determined based on the number of coupons redeemed or calls made.

Number of hits. One of the advantages of using the Internet as an advertising medium is that the number of "hits" or visitors can be recorded. The number of "hits" indicates how successful the website is in attracting visitors to the site. One difficulty with using the number of "hits" as a measure of the popularity of a website is that such a number cannot be taken to represent visitors' attitudes toward the site.

Personal Selling

Personal selling involves a person-to-person meeting among buyers and sellers. It is a personal, interactive form of communication, unlike forms of communication that do not allow interaction between buyers and sellers. Having an effective sales force is crucial for all organizations, especially those involved in business-to-business marketing.

Personal selling decisions must be consistent with the other promotion elements in a well-integrated communications mix strategy. Sales force decisions also need to be consistent with the positioning and value proposition of the organization. The question management needs to ask is, given its positioning and value proposition, what can a sales force contribute to make the firm's positioning and value proposition more effective. For example, Internet-based companies such as Chapters.ca do not use salespeople. But business-to-business organizations, such as Infostream Technologies, which sells data storage equipment, rely almost exclusively on their sales force to sell their products.

A sales force may fulfill a number of different roles. Salespeople generate revenues and help satisfy customers by providing superlative service. They create awareness and influence customers' perceptions of their products. Salespeople may find leads and qualify their needs to see if they can be considered good prospects. Sales representatives can be sales consultants to their customers or they may act as problem solvers to customers by recommending appropriate products and finding solutions to their problems.

Salespersons may negotiate prices with customers. They can also close the sale by asking for the order. Completing the sale is an important market activity and should not be viewed as the end of the selling process but the beginning of a relationship with the customer. Sales representatives help build relationships with valuable customers.[25] They follow up after the sale is made and ensure that the customers' expectations have been exceeded. Finally, salespeople are vital in gathering information about market changes and competitive activity in the marketplace.

Many salespeople are order takers with the responsibility of writing up orders, checking invoices for accuracy, and ensuring timely order processing. Examples of order-taking positions include cashiers at McDonald's or wait staff at restaurants. Order getters, on the other hand, look for new customers and try to find solutions to customers' problems by analyzing the problem. The salesperson tries to generate sales that might not be forthcoming without their efforts. Such people includes telemarketers and salespeople calling on potential customers. Salespersons may be involved in "missionary work," such as building goodwill with customers by ensuring that they are satisfied with the service they receive from the company's salespeople and other channel intermediaries. For example, pharmaceutical companies employ missionary salespersons who visit doctors to help with any problems they encounter with the drugs they prescribe. Company engineers or scientists may also support regular sales personnel by serving as technical specialists to customers.

Sales Force Management

Sales management includes setting sales force objectives, structuring the sales force, and determining its size; it also includes recruiting, training, developing, and compensating the sales force, as well as organizing the activities of the sales force and directing, evaluating, and controlling its performance.

Setting sales force objectives

A company's overall marketing plan is translated into sales plans that specify goals for specific regions or territories and how they will be achieved. In addition to the overall sales plans, sales managers and salespeople normally set specific objectives to be achieved by a salesperson.[26] Sales objectives should be mutually agreed upon after a mutual understanding of performance standards and the way they were determined. Such performance standards and sales objectives are determined after sales tasks, such as prospecting, qualifying, order taking, order getting, or sales support are decided. Since organizational and individual salesperson objectives often differ, management needs to close such gaps through its training and compensation packages.

Sales objectives must be motivational, measurable, realistic, and understandable. An example of a sales objective might be to increase the number of accounts by 50 in the coming year. Other examples of sales objectives include sales calls made per month, unit sales per sales call, and sales calls on new accounts. Once the sales objectives are determined, sales managers can structure the sales force and calculate the number of salespeople needed to accomplish these objectives.

Structuring the sales force

There are four main methods for structuring a sales force: territorial, product, market, and complex structures.

Territorial structure. Sales managers often structure their sales force by assigning their salespeople to certain geographical territories. In this structure, salespeople are completely responsible for all the company's products and for meeting the sales objectives of the unit—division, region, district, or branch.[27] In addition, they provide services and solutions to customers' problems, and build goodwill with customers.

An advantage of the territorial structure is the clear assignment of responsibilities. This structure also minimizes travel time and costs compared with other sales force structures. Small companies that have one target market find that a territorially structured organization is usually appropriate. One disadvantage of such a structure is the difficulty in creating territories that are approximately equal in the sales potential of the territory, the number of customers in the territory, and the physical size of the territory. Also, when the company is not specialized by product line, especially when it sells many technically complex products, salespersons have great difficulty performing their job effectively.

Product structure. In large multi-product companies, the sales force is often structured by division or by product line. This type of organization lets the sales force specialize by product line, allowing the salesperson to give proper attention to the products. As salespersons become more experienced, they acquire the knowledge and skills to make effective sales presentations. This ability is especially important for highly complex products that require in-depth detailed technical knowledge.

A product structure is appropriate when the products are technical or complex in nature, or the products are relatively simple but completely different products are sold to the same markets.[28] However, although this type of structure addresses the problem of sales force specialization, it creates another problem when customers have to deal with two or more salespeople from the same supplier.

Market structure. This method of sales force organization is used by companies that have several distinct markets. Each market becomes a focus of the company's effort. Many companies are switching to market structure because of its advantages over other methods. One of these advantages is that by specializing by market, salespersons can become very knowledgeable about the market they service. For example, IBM may use some salespeople to sell to large customers such as the big banks and different salespeople to sell to smaller customers. Although this method allows salespeople to specialize by markets or major customers, its major disadvantages are that it increases travel time and costs and it suffers from lack of specialization by product line.

Complex structure. Each of the sales force structures discussed so far have certain advantages but suffer one or more disadvantages. In practice, in an attempt to retain the advantages of a sales force structure method and address its problems, companies use combinations of these methods. Some companies selling several product lines often combine territorial with product structure. For example, companies such as Trojan Technologies, which sells waste-water treatment systems made up of several product lines to municipal authorities, are organized by products within large geographical regions.

Other companies may structure their sales force by customer type within geographical territories. Still others may use telemarketing to identify certain prospects and then assign external sales representatives to call on the most promising prospects. In even more complex structures, some sales representatives may handle large retail accounts, others may be geographically organized to cover small accounts, and others may service certain sectors such as the government, hotels, or restaurants.

Sales force size

In addition to choosing the sales force structure, companies must also decide its size. The sales force size is normally determined by the size of the target market, the role of personal selling in the promotion mix, and the sales objectives of the firm. Companies have in general reduced the size of their sales force in the past few years. The main reasons for such reduction are the greater use of the Internet as a selling tool and greater reliance on supply chains and outsourcing of many selling tasks. There are three methods for determining the size of the sales force: the sales potential method, the workload method, and the incremental method.[29]

1. *The sales potential method.* The size of the sales force is calculated by simply dividing the sales volume expected from the accounts or territory by the average amount of sales each person is expected to make. For example, if the sales potential is $10 million and the average amount of sales per salesperson is $1 million, then the company would need 10 full-time sales representatives.
2. *The workload method.* This method classifies accounts according to their sales and importance. Larger accounts are called on more often than smaller accounts. The size of the sales force is established by following these steps:
   i. Customers are grouped according to their size or importance.
   ii. The average number of calls required for each group is determined.
   iii. The number of customers is multiplied by the corresponding frequency of calls to arrive at the required number of sales calls that must be made during the year.
   iv. The size of the sales force is determined by dividing the total number of sales calls by the average number of calls a salesperson can make in a year.

   For example, let us assume a company has 800 A accounts, 1,200 B accounts, and 1,400 C accounts. Further assume that A accounts require 24 calls, B accounts require 12 calls, and C accounts require 6 calls a year. The total number of sales calls required to be made in a year is 42,000. If a sales representative can make an average of 1,000 sales calls a year, the company would need 42 full-time sales representatives.

3. *The incremental method.* Firms using this method hire additional salespeople as long as the additional salesperson's contribution to profits is positive and greater than any other investment opportunity. In order to make such decisions, the company must determine the incremental revenues and incremental costs associated with each additional salesperson. For example, if hiring an additional salesperson cost a company $300,000, this person contributed $200,000 to the company's profits, and this profit exceeded the return from alternative investments available to the company, the company should hire this extra person.

Recruitment

Recruitment includes the task of finding and attracting qualified applicants for vacant sales positions. Effective recruitment involves a thorough job analysis—with details of selling activities—and preparation of a list of qualifications candidates need to perform these activities.[30] The details of job analysis are used by sales managers to develop a detailed job description. A job description includes the job's details and duties and the responsibilities of the salesperson, such as selling, sales support, travelling, and prospecting.

It is important that companies hire the right salespeople, for the success of the company depends on the effectiveness of its sales force. Sales managers should therefore determine the requirements of the sales position, for they know that the requirements for an order getter are different from those of sales support personnel or order takers. Getting the right person for the position will reduce employee turnover and keep costs under control—hiring and training salespeople cost organizations substantial sums of money. Hiring the wrong person can be a drain on the company's resources and sales manager's time. In some cases, once salespeople are trained, they leave the organization to obtain a job with another organization that offers a higher salary, commission, or bonus.

Recruitment should be consistent with the company's integrated marketing communication strategy. Companies that want to create long-term relationships with customers are striving to reduce turnover among their salespeople. They spend considerable time interviewing, testing, and screening applicants to ensure the best possible match between the applicant's qualifications and the requirements of the job. The company's goal is to select the type of salesperson who will perform the job well and remain with the company to avoid the high cost of hiring new personnel.[31]

Training and developing the sales force

Training and developing the sales force is an important aspect of sales management for all firms, large or small. Salespeople who have been recruited and hired must be trained in the various aspects of the job. Organizations spend considerable amounts of money training employees on product knowledge, competition, selling skills, policies and procedures, customer knowledge, time, and territory management.

Training programs vary among companies. Some companies put recruits through an intensive training program before they send them out in the field. Other companies send the new recruit out in the field with a senior salesperson for on-the-job training. Still other organizations have no training program at all and send their new salespeople out on their own without training.

Training programs also differ depending on whether they are designed for new recruits or experienced salespeople. Training for experienced salespeople focuses more on new products, new selling techniques, changes in the company's business strategy and competitive conditions, and emerging environmental trends. Many successful sales organizations view sales force training as an ongoing process. Salespeople take refresher courses, they learn new selling techniques, or they learn about the new company products.

Certain large companies such as Procter & Gamble and IBM maintain a sales training department that offers training or retraining programs to the company's subsidiaries around the world. Sales training programs are usually conducted in centralized training facilities by professional trainers or in the field by senior sales personnel and by consulting firms. Training facilities include classrooms, closed-circuit television, videotapes, and facilities for housing trainees during the training period.[32]

A large part of salespeople training is self-directed using online methods. Lower cost and flexibility are advantages of online training. Private consulting firms also offer sales training programs tailored to the client's special needs and taught by experienced professional trainers.

Compensating the sales force

Firms must design an attractive compensation package to help attract and retain good-quality salespeople. Firms also need to motivate their salespeople if they want them to achieve maximum performance. A sales reward system is the most important means of motivating a sales force. Management's job is to design a compensation plan that meets the needs of the company and the salesperson. Many factors go into the development of an effective compensation package.

Firms should always design their reward system after the sales force objectives have been established. Examples of sales force objectives include attaining a certain sales volume, introduction of new products, market penetration, and exploiting the territory's potential. Once sales force objectives are determined, management should establish the compensation package for its sales representatives. Rewards and promotions should be tied directly to the salesperson's performance relative to sales force objectives. The compensation package should also be compared to the compensation package of its competitors. For example, if the compensation is lower than the industry average, salespeople may quit to join the competition. For this reason, salaries and other components of compensation should be set taking into account what other sales representatives earn in the industry. There are three basic compensation plans: straight salary, straight commission, and a combination of salary and commission.

Straight salary. Straight salary entails paying the salesperson a specific dollar amount regardless of the sales volume achieved. Straight salary is appropriate when a large part of the salesperson's job involves non-selling activities such as missionary work or extensive presale and after-sale services. This method is also appropriate in selling environments that are not high pressure, as the salesperson is less likely to use high-pressure tactics in order to load customers with merchandise.[33] The advantages of the straight salary method are its simplicity and the ease of administration. It provides the salesperson with a sense of security because it guarantees a constant stream of income. One disadvantage of straight salary is the lack of monetary incentives to compensate a first-rate performance. Another drawback is that under such a plan, newly hired sales employees receive almost the same compensation as experienced salespeople.[34]

Straight commission. Straight commission involves paying a salesperson an amount proportional to the sales volume he or she achieves. That is, the more the person sells, the more he or she earns. Straight commission is appropriate when very little non-selling work is involved or the company lacks the financial resources to pay its sales force a salary. An advantage of this compensation method is that it motivates the salesperson to sell more in order to receive higher compensation. A disadvantage of the straight commission method is the lack of steady income and the uncertainty and insecurity such a compensation system entails for the salesperson. This uncertainty results in high turnover and high recruiting and training costs.[35]

Combination salary and commission. Most companies use a combination of salary and commission. Combination methods involve paying a portion of a salesperson's compensation in the form of a guaranteed salary and the balance as commission. This arrangement provides the salesperson with a constant stream of income to cover living expenses during periods in which the person is not producing sales, but also differentiates between excellent and poor performers. The proportion of the commission is about 25 to 50 percent of salary to motivate salespeople to increase their performance.

Sales force evaluation and control

An important part of sales management is to evaluate the performance of salespeople and to take corrective action if needed. Such evaluation can determine the areas where a salesperson requires improvement and point out the effectiveness of various aspects of sales management such as sales force training, compensation, and structure. Performance evaluation is also needed for decisions on raising salaries and giving promotions. The evaluation should be conducted on a regular basis at least once a year. It is normally conducted by the salesperson's immediate supervisor.

The evaluation of salespeople's performance must be accompanied by a system of control. Control involves comparing a company's actual performance with predetermined sales objectives or performance standards. Performance standards are commonly based on the sales performance of other employees or the salesperson's previous performance. Control also involves taking corrective actions to improve sales performance. Such actions may include changing the compensation method, training programs, or the sales force structure.

Sales Promotions

Sales promotions are marketing incentives designed to stimulate customers or the trade to buy a firm's products. While advertising is mostly used for long-term marketing purposes, sales promotions serve short-term objectives. Some of the short-run objectives include encouraging consumers to try a product, encouraging repeat buying, and rewarding loyal customers. Sales promotions have become popular because most product categories are mature, and products can increase their sales only by taking market share from competing brands.[36] Sales promotion techniques include trade promotions, retail promotions, and consumer promotions.

> **Sales promotions** are marketing incentives designed to stimulate customers or the trade to buy a firm's products.

1. *Trade promotions.* **Trade promotions** are incentives to retailers and other distributors. They include display allowances, case allowances, trade coupons, price discounts, free goods, and co-op advertising.

> **Trade promotions** are incentives to retailers and other distributors.

2. *Retailer promotions.* **Retailer promotions** are incentives offered to customers by retailers to encourage them to patronize their stores. They include point-of-purchase displays, retailer coupons, and price discounts. Manufacturers and retailers often launch cooperative promotions, which combine their efforts into one joint sales promotion.

> **Retailer promotions** are incentives offered to customers by retailers to encourage them to patronize their stores.

3. *Consumer promotions.* **Consumer promotions** include free samples, point-of-purchase displays, cents-off coupons, bonus packs, rebates or refunds, price discounts, quantity discounts, premiums, contests, sweepstakes, in-store demonstrations, and specials.

> **Consumer promotions** include free samples, point-of-purchase displays, cents-off coupons, bonus packs, rebates or refunds, price discounts, quantity discounts, premiums, contests, sweepstakes, in-store demonstrations, and specials.

Sales promotions must be consistent with the rest of the marketing communications mix and the brand image and positioning. Sales promotions are part of integrated marketing communications and should be coordinated with other promotional methods. For example, sales promotions are often used to support or reinforce the effectiveness of advertising. Advertising, on the other hand, is sometimes used to draw attention to a sales promotion campaign.

Sales promotion incentives fall into two major categories: merchandise or service incentives and money incentives.[37] Merchandise or service promotions include all incentives that are not monetary and are external to the product or service such as premiums or gifts. They may also include increased quantities of the product or service, normally at the same price, to provide an incentive to purchase the product—an example would be bonus packs in which the company offers 20 percent more of the product at the regular price. Money incentives include price reductions and cents-off coupons.

Advantages and Disadvantages of Sales Promotions

Sales promotions have become popular because they benefit companies by creating an urgency for consumers to buy the product, rewarding customers who remain loyal to the same brand, and encouraging repeat buying as consumers try to take advantage of the sales incentives. Sales promotions also encourage buyers of other brands to switch to the company's brand to take advantage of the lower price.

Sales promotions can also be an effective way to break customer loyalty to competing brands. By enticing customers loyal to competing brands to try its own brand, a firm hopes to reduce the loyalty to the competing brand and create an interest in its own brand. Finally, firms may offer sales promotions to counteract competitive activity. For example, if a competitor launches a coupon campaign that threatens to take market share away, a firm may respond by launching its own sales promotion campaign to offset the effects of the rival's sales promotion.

Although sales promotions can be an effective way to increase sales and market share, they suffer from a number of limitations. They achieve only short-term objectives as their impact ends once the promotion is over. Firms that have long-term communication objectives, such as a certain image or positioning, should use other promotional methods, such as advertising. Sales promotions increase price sensitivity because they focus attention on price, making buyers more price sensitive, detracting from a quality image as the emphasis on price amplifies its importance, and making it difficult for the company to build an image of quality. Sales promotions also decrease brand loyalty. The increased use of sales promotions has been blamed for the decline in loyalty to well-known brands.

Forward buying entails buying larger quantities than required for current consumption. The extra quantity bought is consumed after the sales promotion is over.

Diversion entails buying goods sold in one area and selling them in another area where the product is not promoted.

Sales promotions frequently lead to consumers engaging in **forward buying,** which entails buying larger quantities than required for current consumption. The consumers use the extra quantity after the sales promotion is over. In these cases, sales promotions are increasing current sales at the expense of future sales as consumers stock up. Another problem of sales promotions is **diversion,** which is the practice of buying goods sold in one area and selling them in another area where the product is not promoted. Both forward buying and diversion defeat the purpose of the sales promotion, which is to increase product sales in a certain area for a given period of time.

Sales promotions often invite competitive retaliation. For example, as soon as an airline reduces its airfares, other airlines immediately retaliate by matching the price cut. The result is usually an expensive price war. Also, sales promotions are subject to diminishing returns. As sales promotions are used over and over, they become less effective as their novelty wears off. For example, the impact of coupons has diminished over the years as more companies use them and consumers have learned to ignore them.

Because of the limitations of sales promotions, firms such as Procter & Gamble stopped using sales promotions and adopted everyday low-price strategies. As another example, Victoria's Secret used to have 40 to 50 sales promotions each week. When Victoria's Secret stopped running these sales promotions and focused on emphasizing the value of its brand, its sales and profitability increased considerably.[38]

Evaluating Sales Promotion Effectiveness

It is relatively easy to measure the effectiveness of sales promotion methods compared to advertising effectiveness. A common sales promotion evaluation technique is to compare sales or market share before and after a promotion. Any sales increase is then attributed to the impact of the sales promotion campaign, everything else being equal. For example, if the market share of a product is 10 percent and it stabilizes at 12 percent after the sales promotion campaign, assuming there are no alternative explanations, the market share increase may be attributed to the sales promotion program.

Also, scanner data, where scanners are available, provides marketers with the information they need to evaluate the effectiveness of their sales promotion methods, on almost a real-time basis. As the use of scanners becomes more widespread, marketers will be provided with the information they need to test their promotional strategies in more markets.[39]

Public Relations

Public relations have become an important part of integrated marketing communications. **Public relations** is concerned with building a favourable long-term image for the organization through a variety of activities such as financial support of social causes, corporate publications, and efforts aimed at gaining publicity. Another important job of public relations is to build favourable relationships between the organization and the various stakeholders, including stock market analysts, the government, and investors.

A large part of public relations is encouraging the various mass media to write about the firm's accomplishments. Many companies have realized that public relations can help raise awareness for the organization, improve the organization's image, and develop positive relationships with customers. For this purpose, they have created public relations departments that coordinate all publicity efforts made by the organization. The rest of this section discusses publicity, which is an important part of public relations, and the various methods businesses use to obtain favourable publicity for their products or services.

Public relations is concerned with building a favourable long-term image for the organization through a variety of activities such as financial support of social causes, corporate publications, and other events.

Publicity

Publicity is part of public relations and it seeks to obtain favourable press coverage for the organization. It is made up of unpaid messages having no identified sponsor that are usually run on mass media outlets. It includes information about a product that the media consider sufficiently newsworthy to report for free. Unlike advertising, publicity involves a third party such as a news editor or reporter who determines whether and how to present the message.

Publicity is part of public relations and it seeks to obtain favourable press coverage for the organization.

Publicity is more effective than advertising because it is more credible since it is initiated by an independent source such as a journalist or an editor and not by an advertiser with an intention to sell the product.[40] According to some estimates, editorial coverage of a product has three times more credibility than a similar message in a paid advertisement.[41] Consumers are inundated with an increasing number of television, radio, magazine, and newspaper ads; e-mail; and billboards. Publicity can be an effective way to break through this advertising clutter.

Publicity is often carefully orchestrated, such as in the case of automobile shows held in various places around the world. Most major media attend these shows and write extensively about the new automobiles showcased in these fairs. One of the limitations of publicity is that the organization has no control over the message. Also, although publicity is free in the sense that the media carrying the story are not being paid by the company, it may involve costs in the form of salaries paid to public relations personnel or fees for publicity agents. Firms gain publicity through the following methods:

- *Press releases.* Press releases are short statements that provide factual information about the product. For example, some software companies gain publicity by preparing a press release and sending it to software magazines hoping that it will be published. Effective press releases are written in a way that the media can easily incorporate into a news story. Press releases are often accompanied by CDs, videotapes, films, and photographs.

- *Press conferences.* Press conferences are typically used to make an announcement about the company's activities. In such cases, mass media are notified that a press conference will be held for the purpose of making a statement and they are invited to attend.

- *Event marketing.* Managers often try to link a product to an issue or event of interest or concern to consumers. Such activity is called **event marketing** or **social cause marketing** and, for many companies, it is becoming an integral part of their marketing strategy. To be successful these events should fit the marketing strategy of the brand.[42] Like all other promotional activities, sponsorship activities must take into account the target market and other elements of the marketing mix. Effective sponsorships require that the team, events, or athlete involved have values that match those of the brand or the company.

Event marketing or **social cause marketing** involves trying to link a product to an issue or event of interest or concern to consumers.

Event marketing helps keep companies or their products before the public eye. Sponsoring events allows businesses to receive favourable publicity because they support worthwhile social causes. Examples of such involvement include the Molson Local Hero Program, a community-based program in which Molson provides funds to volunteers who refurbish sports and recreational facilities in their neighbourhoods and communities. Other examples of event marketing are Bell Canada's support of the Canadian Opera Company or the Mr. Christie Book Awards, which were established in 1990 to encourage the publishing of high-quality Canadian children's books and to stimulate children's desire to read.

Sponsorship marketing has become an important element in the marketing mix for many companies. According to the Chicago-based IEG Sponsorship Report, sponsorship spending in North America was likely to reach $10.5 billion (Cdn) in 2004. Marketers favour sponsorship because it provides them with an opportunity to connect with their targeted consumers and differentiate their products from the competition. Sponsorships are also a means of aligning brands with entertainment passions or lifestyle choices and they enable companies to connect with consumers in an engaging way.

Sponsorships provide companies with exposure and co-branding opportunities, such as Molson's sponsorship of Toronto Rock, a national lacrosse league team. Molson achieves its goal of reaching its target market, young males, by promoting its products during all Rock home games and leveraging its business relationships with restaurants and bars through programs such as Molson Rock Bashes and Best Seats in the House events.[43] Some firms even launch advertising campaigns to increase the public's awareness of their company's corporate citizen activities, as illustrated in the Strategy in Action box.[44]

Strategy in Action

TELUS

Telus was recently involved in an advertising campaign to increase the public's awareness of its corporate citizen activities. According to Shawn Thomas, vice-president communications, Telus invests millions every year in sponsorship and community involvement. In 2004, Telus contributed cash and support, together equivalent to $10 million, to charities and non-profit organizations across Canada. It also made a five-year, $10-million investment in the Royal Conservatory of Music. According to Thomas, "The whole focus is to help establish, to unprecedented levels, top-of-mind recognition and awareness of how good a corporate citizen Telus is. It's always nice when you are able to talk about all the good things we do in the community. You do it because it's the right thing to do, but you also do it because it's very good for business. Every indicator will show that customers like and want to do business with companies that are seen as good corporate citizens."

- *Other forms of gaining publicity.* In addition to press releases, organizations often seek media interviews with company spokespersons in an effort to generate favourable publicity for the organization. Other forms of publicity include company annual reports, newsletters, catalogues, company magazines, and other publications.

- Promotion is an integral part of a marketing strategy and is essential to the success of a firm. The promotion mix includes advertising, personal selling, sales promotions, and public relations.

- Integrated marketing communications is a coordinated use of all elements of the promotion mix to communicate a consistent and unified message about a product in a cost-effective way. Each promotion tool has its own special characteristics that make it more or less appropriate given the firm's communications objectives and market conditions.

- Important tasks in integrated marketing communications include identifying the target audience, establishing the communication objectives, setting the communication budget, and determining the communications mix.

- There are four main methods of setting a promotion budget: percentage of sales, competitive parity, all-you-can-afford, and the objective-and-task method.

- Message design is a crucial aspect of a firm's advertising strategy. An effective message should meet the following criteria: be directed at a specific segment, be believable, promote something desirable and unique, and be consistent over time and across media.

- The media plan includes determining the media mix, media scheduling, and reach and frequency.

- There are several media scheduling strategies: continuous, pulsing, flighting, build-up and build-down scheduling.

- Effectiveness of advertising can be measured through pre-test and post-test measures.

- Sales force management includes setting sales objectives, structuring the sales force; determining the sales force size; and recruiting, training, developing, compensating, evaluating, and controlling the sales force.

- Sales promotions are marketing incentives designed to stimulate customers or the trade to buy a firm's products. They serve short-term objectives such as encouraging consumers to try the product, stimulating interest, and rewarding customers or distributors to provide the product with greater support.

- Sales promotions include trade promotions, retailer promotions, and consumer promotions. Sales promotions may be also classified as merchandise- or service-related or money-related incentives.

- Public relations is the systematic planning, preparation, and distribution of information intended to manage the publicity the organization receives in the mass media. Publicity is part of public relations and seeks to obtain favourable press coverage for the organization.

- Public relations includes press releases, press conferences, event or social causes marketing, and other forms of gaining publicity such as media interviews, company annual reports, newsletters, catalogues, and company magazines and other publications.

Review and Discussion Questions

1. Explain what an integrated communications strategy is.

2. Discuss the tasks involved in establishing an integrated marketing communications plan.

3. A crucial question for marketing managers is to determine where to promote their products. Explain the defensive and offensive promotion strategies. What are the benefits and risks associated with each strategy?

4. Identify the four communications budget-setting methods. What are the main advantages and disadvantages of each method? Which communications budget-setting method is the best?

5. Explain the factors that affect the choice between advertising and personal selling.

6. Explain the factors that determine the choice between advertising and sales promotions.

7. Identify and discuss the criteria for evaluating advertising messages.

8. Describe the various advertising scheduling strategies. Identify several factors that influence advertising scheduling decisions.

9. Define reach and frequency. How are reach and frequency related, given a fixed advertising budget? Identify three strategies to increase reach. How much frequency is required for an advertisement to achieve minimum effective frequency?

10. Describe the methods used to evaluate advertising effectiveness.

11. Discuss the four methods for structuring a sales force.

12. Describe the three methods for determining sales force size.

13. What are the benefits and drawbacks of sales promotion techniques?

14. Discuss the role of public relations in the promotional mix. Describe various public relations methods.

1. The financial vice-president of a major corporation with a large number of products was against the use of advertising by his company. This financial vice-president used to say, "We waste money on advertising. It has no effect on sales." To support his claim he had graphed the company's advertising expenditures and sales for past years and, in fact, it did appear that there was no relationship between them. The marketing vice-president, however, was not convinced that advertising had no impact on sales. His own experience was that proper use of advertising does affect sales. Assuming that the marketing vice-president is right, what might he mean by proper use of advertising?

2. Assume that you are the advertising manager in charge of a frequently purchased consumer product that has the following characteristics: year-round buying pattern, limited budget, short purchase cycle, weak brand loyalty, and impulse buying. Outline an appropriate media scheduling strategy for this product.

3. The marketing manager of a medium-sized beer manufacturer based in Vancouver, B.C., is concerned about his company's advertising strategy. His company allocates its advertising budget to each of its products based on their sales and other considerations such as competitors' advertising spending, segment growth prospects, and the strategic importance of the segment to the company. Given this method of allocating the advertising budget, some products receive a rather small amount of advertising funds leading to unsatisfying response to advertising efforts. Assuming that the company is not willing to change the method of allocating its advertising budget, what else could this company do to provide promotional support to its products?

4. John's Fish and Chips, located in the west end of Montreal, claimed in its radio ads that it is the nation's best and finest fish and chips restaurant. On the basis of the criteria for evaluating messages discussed in this chapter, evaluate John's Fish and Chips' advertising claims.

Notes

1. John McLeod, "More Than Bits and Bytes," *Marketing Magazine*, November 3, 2003, 19.
2. P. R. Smith, *Marketing Communications: An Integrated Approach* (London: Kogan Page Limited, 1993), 21.
3. Michell Warren, "IKEA Builds New Canadian Strategy," *Marketing Magazine*, March 8, 2004, 3.
4. Jack Z. Sissors and Lincoln Bumba, *Advertising Media Planning*, 5th ed. (Lincolnwood, Ill.: NTC Business Books, 1996), 207.
5. Charles H. Patti and Charles F. Frazer, *Advertising: A Decision-Making Approach* (Hinsdale, Ill.: The Dryden Press, 1988), 236–239.
6. Eric Schulz, *The Marketing Game* (Holbrook, Mass.: Adams Media Corporation, 1999), 157.
7. Luis M. B. Cabral, *Introduction to Industrial Organization* (Cambridge: The MIT Press, 2000), 226.
8. John Gaffney, "The Buzz Must Go On," *Business 2.0*, February 2002, 49.
9. Gaffney.
10. James F. Engel, Martin R. Warshaw, and Thomas C. Kinnear, *Promotional Strategy*, 7th ed. (Homewood, Ill.: Irwin, 1991), 272.
11. Keith J. Tuckwell, *Advertising in Action*, 3rd ed. (Scarborough, Ont.: Prentice Hall, 1995), 317.
12. Lesley Young, "Kellogg's granola line gets mini bars," *Marketing Magazine*, November 10, 2003, 3.
13. Konrad Yakabuski, "No free lunch for Coutou at home," *Globe and Mail*, April 14, 2004, B2.
14. Tuckwell, 323.
15. Norma Ramage, "Frisky business: Calgary tabloid's stock is on the rise with advertisers," *Marketing Magazine*, May 3, 2004, p. 8.
16. Tuckwell, 343.
17. Larry Percy, John R. Rossiter, and Richard Elliott, *Strategic Advertising Management* (New York: Oxford University Press, 2001), 5.
18. Sissors and Bumba, 1996, 129.
19. Sissors and Bumba, 1996, 135.
20. George E. Belch and Michael A. Belch, *Introduction to Advertising and Promotion Management* (Homewood, Ill.: Irwin, 1990), 605.
21. Belch and Belch, 607.
22. Belch and Belch, 607.
23. David A. Aaker, V. Kumar, and George S. Day, *Marketing Research*, 6th ed. (New York: Wiley, 1998), 693.
24. Aaker, Kumar, and Day, 687.
25. Charles M. Futrell, *Sales Management*, 5th ed. (Fort Worth: Dryden, 1998), 106.
26. R. LaForge and D. Cravens, "Steps in the Selling-Effort Deployment," *Industrial Marketing Management* 11, 1982, pp. 183–194.
27. Charles M. Futrell, *Sales Management*, 3rd ed. (Chicago: The Dryden Press, 1991), 79.
28. Futrell, 1991, 81.
29. Ronald R. Still, Edward W. Cundiff, and Norman A. P. Govoni, *Sales Management: Decisions, Strategies, and Cases*, 9th ed. (Englewood Cliffs, N.J.: Prentice Hall, 1981), 63–68.
30. Frank G. Bingham Jr., *Business Marketing Management* (Lincolnwood, Ill.: NTC Business Books, 1998), 408.
31. Bingham, 409.
32. Bingham, 417.
33. Futrell, 509.
34. Futrell, 509.
35. Futrell, 513.
36. Don E. Schultz, William A. Robinson, and Lisa A. Petrison, *Sales Promotion Essentials*, 2nd ed. (Lincolnwood, Ill.: NTC Business Books, 1993), 3.
37. Dan Ailloni-Charas, *Promotion: A Guide to Effective Promotional Planning, Strategies, and Executions* (New York: Wiley, 1984), 47.
38. David A. Aaker and Erich Joachimsthaler, *Brand Leadership* (New York: The Free Press, 2000), 15.
39. Aaker, Kumar, and Day, 696.
40. Smith, 279.
41. Smith, 279.
42. Jim Button, "Events That Build Brands," *Marketing Magazine*, October 6/13, 2003, 32.
43. Chad Richardson, "A Piece of the Rock," *Marketing Magazine*, February 23, 2004, 19.
44. Eve Lazarus, "Thomas tells the Telus story," *Marketing Magazine*, February 23, 2004, 6.

Chapter Thirteen
Internet Marketing

Some businesspeople do not understand that Internet-based commerce is based on the same fundamental principles that have governed business for thousands of years.

Caroline Howard, Winning the Net Game

Learning Objectives

After studying this chapter, you should be able to:

1. Discuss the strategic advantages of the Internet

2. Describe who the Internet users are

3. Explain the role of the Internet in formulating marketing strategy

4. Discuss forming Internet customer relationships

5. Describe the various Internet marketing mix strategies

Schwab Is the Big Winner in Online Stock Trading

In 1971, Charles Schwab established a brokerage firm to provide individual stock market investors with low prices and quick and efficient execution of their orders. By 1981, Schwab was the leader in the discount brokerage industry with 29 offices, 160,000 clients, and $40 million (U.S.) in revenues. Schwab's successful entry into the low-commission (discount brokerage) segment signalled the birth of the discount brokerage industry.

In the late 1990s, online stock trading became a growth industry as individual investors used their own computers to trade stocks and pay lower commissions on their trades. Among the first firms to enter the online stock trading market was K. Aufhauer & Co. in 1994; Aufhauer was acquired by Ameritrade in 1995. Competition quickly took off. Cowbard, a stock brokerage firm, also introduced Internet-based stock trading in the same year while E*Trade entered in early 1996 by offering stock trades for $14.95 (U.S.). E*Trade, prior to introducing Internet-based stock trading, had offered online investing services through America Online and CompuServe since 1992. In 1997, Ameritrade began to offer stock trades for the low price of $8 (U.S.).

Brokerage firms regarded the coming of the Internet as a serious threat. Moving into online trading posed considerable risks for existing brokerage firms, as it would mean they would experience a large reduction in revenues due to much lower commission rates on Internet trading. But Charles Schwab saw it as an opportunity as he realized that the Internet represented the future of the discount brokerage industry. Schwab also understood that the Internet would enable his company to expand the service it could offer its customers and at a much lower cost than through existing brokerage channels. In the meantime, Schwab's traditional competitors continued to focus on existing methods of servicing their customers and avoided responding to the Internet challenge.

Even before Internet technology existed, Schwab had made investments in information technology to improve its customer service. For example, in the 1970s, Schwab purchased an IBM mainframe to automate trading and reporting. Additional investments in technology had made it possible for Schwab to accept automated trades via personal computers and push-button telephones. Schwab's constant interest in technology led him to the Internet, which he saw as a way to improve service to his customers and lower the cost of trades.

Schwab's entry into online stock trading began in January 1996 through a group established within Schwab, called e.Schwab. Using the online service, customers could open accounts that would be handled over the Internet. Within the first two weeks, 25,000 customers signed up, and by the end of 1997 Schwab had 1.2 million online accounts with more than half representing pre-existing customers. Schwab had more than three times as many accounts as its next closest competitor, ahead of online stock trading pioneers Ameritrade and E*Trade. Schwab's online brokerage charged $29.95 (U.S.) a trade—its traditional brokerage unit charged $65 (U.S.) a trade.

In January 1998, Charles Schwab began charging the same price of $29.95 per trade across the board. As a result of the lower price, 500,000 new online accounts were opened in five months. The lower price also caused revenues to decline by 3 percent and pretax profit was reduced by 16 percent or $125 million in the first quarter of 1998 relative to the fourth quarter of 1997. However, revenues and profits quickly rebounded, as annual revenue and pretax profit increased by 19 and 29 percent respectively for the year. On December 28, 1998, Merrill Lynch with $1.5 trillion (U.S.) of assets under management was surpassed by Schwab, which, with $600 billion of assets under management, exceeded

(continued)

Merrill Lynch's market capitalization. Schwab's market capitalization was $25.5 billion (U.S.) while Merrill Lynch's was $25.4 billion (U.S.). At the beginning of 2000, Schwab was the number one online brokerage firm with a 22 percent market share and $350 billion (U.S.) in assets from online investors. Its customer assets totalled $725 billion (U.S.), up 48 percent from 1998. In addition, the personal net worth of Charles Schwab, the founder of Schwab, has grown about five times during this period and it now exceeds $6 billion (U.S.).

In 2005, Schwab had over 4 million online accounts—the grand total of online and offline accounts is over 6.6 million—with the majority of trades being executed on the Internet. Schwab has also been able to provide its customers with excellent service at fair prices, thanks largely to the low cost of providing this service due to the Internet. By building on its advantages—strong brand, excellent service, existing customer base, and superior technology—and with its "bricks-and-clicks" combination of human and online service, Schwab was the big winner in the fast-growing online brokerage industry during the 1990s.[1]

Introduction

As the Schwab story illustrates, the Internet is revolutionizing the way business is conducted and its use is becoming increasingly critical to the success of business firms. The **Internet** is a worldwide network of computers that allows users access to information and documents made available by commercial and non-commercial organizations. It has become such a pervasive tool that virtually every company uses it in some way or another and those that don't will be using it in a few years. The Internet is a powerful tool that a business can use to obtain a competitive advantage. It offers many opportunities for businesses to grow in sales and reduce costs. According to the business publisher American City Business Journal, small businesses that use the Internet have grown 46 percent faster than those that do not.[2]

But the Internet has brought with it some challenges. Many organizations will not survive Internet-induced changes unless they change the ways they conduct their business. Some of the major changes brought about by the Internet can be seen in the way we purchase products and services, obtain information, and conduct our banking. Customers can quickly find product and price information and obtain advice from a wide variety of sellers. Online visitors can check product availability, place an order, check the status of an order, and pay electronically. Companies no longer face competition just from local companies but from companies around the world that come together in this electronic marketplace. As a result of this increase in competition, customers can order from a local vendor or from anywhere in the world.

The Internet empowers customers because they can go on the Web and quickly find out where to get the lowest prices for a particular product or service. It reduces customers' search costs for products and product-related information, but many retailers are concerned that "e-tailing" will increase the number of competitors as national and international competitors are more easily accessible.[3] As a result, many retailers design their websites in a way that makes it difficult to compare their merchandise with merchandise sold on competitors' sites.

There has been a tremendous amount of hype about e-commerce. The truth is that despite the changes brought about by the Internet, e-commerce is based on the same fundamental principles that have governed businesses for thousands of years.[4] Yet a lot of businesspeople view it as something completely new that requires a new way of doing business. Success in the Internet age is gained by learning the new rules of business while not giving up on basic business principles. Many e-commerce firms failed because they ignored a very simple fact: that every business, e-commerce or otherwise, is subject to certain fundamental business principles. Many Internet-based companies fail because they were built on business models that had no chance of ever making a profit. These companies spend enormous amounts of money on technology, people, advertising, and brand building without ever obtaining the sales levels required to support these expenditures.[5]

As we discussed in the introductory chapter, the Internet has become an indispensable tool in marketing strategy. This chapter discusses the strategic advantages of the Internet, online market segments, and the role of the Internet in marketing strategy formulation and the marketing mix. It winds up with an attempt to integrate online and offline strategies.

> The **Internet** is a worldwide network of computers that allows users access to information and documents made available by commercial and non-commercial organizations.

The Strategic Advantages of the Internet

The number of Internet-based businesses and customers making purchases on the Internet is growing daily. The explosive growth of the Internet is widely viewed as the single most important development in information technology in the last decade. The Internet is important to managers because, when properly employed, it can help firms obtain several advantages:

- *Low-cost communication.* The Internet is a low-cost means of communication. As such it is used by managers to disseminate information to customers or obtain information about them, competitors, and the marketplace. In a study of the impact of the Internet on information searches for automobiles, it was found that the Internet provides efficiency gains to both consumers and dealers.[6] Dealers save in selling time when consumers visit a dealership with information obtained from the Internet. Efficiency gains by companies, however, may be offset by reduced margins that result from increased consumer bargaining power stemming from information obtained from the Internet.

- *More efficient distribution.* The Internet can help firms improve business processes, lower costs, and make distribution more efficient. Online shopping lowers the distribution cost of digital products such as software, music, and videos. Firms can use the Internet to engage in online transactions and mass-customize their products and messages to different online customers.[7] E-commerce allows firms to automate transactions, making the scheduling of the workforce much simpler. Order filling is also more efficient because orders can be gathered together over a period of time and then an employee can work on them continuously. By asking customers to enter the order information and answer their questions, companies reduce the amount of work required to be performed by employees.

- *Centralization of inventory.* Internet companies can obtain significant gains by centralizing inventory instead of keeping it scattered in various locations. One advantage of centralized inventory is that the company can deal more effectively with fluctuations in demand. It is also easier to manage inventory when it is concentrated in one place than when it is in several locations. Companies that sell only on the Internet can save significant amounts of money by not having to invest extensively in costly facilities designed to impress customers. Facilities for online companies don't have to be fancy or aesthetic but functional, and designed with efficiency in mind rather than customer convenience.[8]

- *Evening the playing field.* The Internet can be used by smaller firms to even the playing field, allowing them to compete more effectively against large organizations. Small companies do not enjoy the advantages of larger volume and economies of scale and must find other ways of competing, such as adding value to their goods and services or developing customer relationships. It has been found that small businesses with a website have higher revenues than those that do not.[9] E-business can also make a business more competitive by improving business operations, increasing revenues, and decreasing costs. In companies that introduced online operations, revenues increased by 7 percent and costs decreased 9.5 percent for cost of goods sold and 7.5 percent for selling and administrative expenses.[10]

Online Market Segments

The Internet has fundamentally changed the way people and businesses communicate, share information, and perform their business. This new technology is being rapidly adopted by more people and it is now used by a large percentage of the population. The worldwide number of Internet users was 445.9 million in 2002 and it was projected to grow to 709.1 million by 2004.[11] Developed nations hold 15 percent of the world's population but account for 88 percent of all Internet users.[12]

Who are the Internet users? Canadians spend more time online per capita than any other country.[13] In 2001, 60 percent of Canadian households were connected to the Internet, up from 51 percent in 2000.[14] It is predicted that 77 percent of Canadians will have access to the Internet by 2006.[15] Canadian businesses have also embraced the

Internet in earnest. Seventy-six percent of Canadian businesses used the Internet in 2002, up from 63 percent in 2000. In addition, 93 percent of Canadian businesses with 20 or more employees used the Internet in 2002.[16]

A recent study conducted by the Bristol Group in the United States and Canada found that 73 percent among those aged 18 to 24 were connected to the Internet, making them its heaviest users. The lightest users (36 percent) were those aged 55 and older. It was also found that the lowest percentage of Internet buyers was among those aged 18 to 24. The survey found that only 25 percent of them had purchased something online in the previous year. The group aged 45 to 54 made the most purchases over the Internet, at 43 percent. Among those aged 55 or older, 29 percent had purchased something online over the same period.[17]

Canada's Internet connectivity is higher than in the United States, where 58 percent of the population had access to the Internet in 2002.[18] Despite their higher Internet connectivity, Canadian consumers shop online less than their American counterparts—21 percent of Canadians shop online compared to 29 percent in the United States. This gap is predicted to widen somewhat in the future, to 36 percent of Canadians compared to 45 percent of Americans.[19]

Effective Internet marketing requires that site strategies fit the needs and behaviour of the online segments targeted. McKinsey, a management consulting firm, collaborated with Media Metrix, a leading Internet and digital media audience measurement company, and analyzed actual online behaviour of a U.S. panel of 50,000 Internet users.[20] They came up with six online segments as shown in Figure 13.1.

Figure 13.1	Online Market Segments

- Simplifiers
- Surfers
- Bargainers
- Connectors
- Routiners
- Sportsters

The six groups are different enough to warrant a different online marketing strategy for each one. Online marketers need to thoroughly study the six segments and target the ones most appropriate for their business to maximize the effectiveness of their marketing efforts. E-marketers who select and pursue all segments indiscriminately and fail to target the most promising ones will most likely experience an inferior level of profitability and suboptimal results.

Simplifiers

Simplifiers make up 29 percent of active online users. They are the second largest online group, spending little time on the Internet, but when they are online, the vast majority of them end up making a purchase—in fact, they account for about half of all online transactions. They are experienced Internet users and are looking for ease of access and information that is readily available and reliable. They use the Internet to make their lives easier—convenience is very important to them.

Simplifiers have specific goals that they want to accomplish with a minimum of effort. They want to complete an Internet transaction very quickly. They are attracted by site functionality and dislike sites that are too complicated or have pop-up windows designed to encourage impulse buying or unsolicited e-mails. Marketers must provide end-to-end convenience that includes ease of access and use, such as one-click ordering, reliable customer service, easy returns, and thorough product information.

Surfers

Surfers make up 8 percent of active online users but they spend the most time online of all groups. Surfers use the Internet for many purposes, including searching for information and purchasing products. Although they are one of the smallest segments of active Internet users, they account for a large percentage (32 percent) of time spent online, which is more than any other group. They access, by far, more sites than any other group, but they spend little time on each site. A large percentage of them end up making a purchase. The benefits sought by surfers are variety and novelty and finding good deals.

Surfers also use the Internet for finding information about entertainment and shopping. They are attracted by innovative sites that are continuously updated and by features such as chats rooms, games, and audio clips. Sites that satisfy these requirements have a better chance to get Surfers to visit them on an ongoing basis. The major challenge for online marketers is to get Surfers to stay when they visit a site, expose them to their online advertisements, and motivate them to make a purchase. A further task is to convert Surfers from one-time visitors to long-term ones by finding ways to make them come back to the site.

Bargainers

Bargainers make up 8 percent of active online users. They use the Internet for finding the best online deals and taking advantage of shopping and entertainment opportunities while they are doing so. They are typical bargain hunters looking for the best deal. The Bargainers, like Surfers, are a small group and while they spend a little less time than the average online user, a large percentage of them buy online but it is usually from places like eBay, priceline.com, and Quote.com; Bargainers generate 52 percent of all visits to eBay. The best way to appeal to Bargainers is through rational and emotional ways designed to satisfy their desire and the excitement of searching for an attractive deal.

Connectors

Connectors are the largest online group (36 percent) and are relatively new to the Internet. They primarily use the Internet as a means of communicating with others. Connectors are not experienced Internet users—40 percent of them have been using the Internet for less than two years. Only 42 percent of Connectors have purchased on the Internet compared with an overall average of 61 percent, making them the lowest-ranked group in this category. They are feeling their way around the Internet, trying to find out what the Internet has to offer them, and they haven't formed any Internet habits. Due to their inexperience with online shopping, the Connectors prefer established brands, giving the owners of such brands an advantage. The marketers' task is to convert Connectors into a more profitable group by earning their trust and teaching them various Internet skills, such as explaining how the Internet works and how to send e-mails.

Routiners

Routiners make up 15 percent of active online shoppers. They use the Internet more as a source of information and less as a means of online shopping. The Routiners visit the fewest sites of any of the six groups but they spend more time in each one relative to other groups. For example, Routiners spend over 80 percent of their time online with their ten most favoured sites. Individuals in this group spend a lot of time reading newspaper news and financial information.

Routiners are interested more in content than shopping. They do not use the Internet for buying as much as other groups; only 50 percent of them have ever bought something online and only 6 percent of them have made five or more online purchases. They are attracted by outstanding content and timely and exclusive information. Their favourite sites are newspapers such as the *Toronto Star* and the *Globe and Mail*. A major challenge for marketers is to convert these visitors from free to subscription status. Some sites allow access to some free content but they offer much more information to paid subscribers.

Sportsters

Sportsters use the Internet as a source of sports and entertainment information. They are the smallest among the six groups (4 percent of all active online consumers). Sportsters are very similar to the Routiners but they spend somewhat less time online than the Routiners and they visit more sites. Their favourite sites are mainly sports and entertainment sites, such as tsn.ca and Yahoo! Entertainment. Sportsters prefer sports and entertainment sites that are interactive and colourful and filled with game results, chats, news updates, and radio broadcasts.

The Internet and Marketing Strategy Formulation

The Internet provides the foundation of the information age. Its role is the same as that of roads, highways, waterways, and railways by providing companies with powerful technologies that can help them to carry out their strategy. It provides companies with new ways to serve customers and obtain competitive advantages.[21]

Marketing success depends on the extent of the business's market orientation. This principle applies equally to e-businesses. It is very important for companies to see the online business through the customer's eyes, whether it is with regard to designing the site, selling products, taking or processing orders, or just providing information. Companies that fail to take the customer's point of view in designing their Web strategy have only a slim chance of succeeding. Unfortunately, many firms use the Internet without considering how it fits within their marketing strategy. Developments in Web-based technologies make it necessary to rethink how firms should conduct their business and market their products as this new technology affects all aspects of marketing.[22]

The Internet has changed traditional marketing in three major ways:

- *It shifts power away from sellers to buyers.* Power is shifting away from sellers to buyers as individuals and businesses are becoming more demanding—they are just one click away from switching to a competitor. Some companies have realized this power shift and are looking for ways not only to attract online customers and get them to make a purchase, but to get them to come back and purchase from the site again.[23]
- *It changes consumer behaviour.* Consumer behaviour has changed in the era of the Internet as shoppers combine traditional shopping methods with e-commerce. Consumers' online shopping behaviour is fundamentally different from that in brick-and-mortar retail stores.[24] An important influence on online consumer behaviour is the degree and type of interactivity that is available. The interactive tools in online shopping greatly affect the consumer's search for product information and purchase decisions, making it easier for them to compare such things as features, prices, and warranties. To help in their research and decision-making, consumers can use a wide range of software tools such as general-purpose search engines (e.g., Google.ca, Altavista.ca, Excite.com) and more sophisticated interactive shopping agents (e.g., mySimon, Compare.net).
- *It revolutionizes marketing functions.* The Internet has revolutionized all traditional marketing functions. For example, marketing researchers can now reach large numbers of people worldwide in a cost-effective and timely manner. Information about consumers is easier and less expensive to gather, store, and analyze. Electronic marketers can use traditional marketing research techniques as well as more recent techniques, such as online surveys completed by visitors to the site using a variety of

software programs. Also, the formulation of marketing and communication strategy has changed through the process of marketing convergence, whereby managers integrate traditional marketing tools such as television, print, and direct marketing methods with the Internet.

Using the Internet has become necessary for most businesses and it is no longer a matter of choice. The key issue is how to use it, not whether to use it. However, the Internet should not replace a firm's business strategy, but it should be used by management to help implement it. The Internet should be viewed as part of the firm's long-term marketing strategy and, through the process of marketing convergence, it should be integrated with other means of formulating and implementing strategies in a way that conforms to the principles of a sound business strategy. Therefore, the role of the Internet varies depending on the particular situation as, for example, some companies use their websites as online brochures, while others such as eBay use the Internet as the foundation of their business model.[25] The Strategy in Action box illustrates the integration of traditional promotional methods with online strategies:[26]

Strategy in Action

MELITTA

In 2002, coffee products maker Melitta Canada spent just $46,000 on media advertising, all on radio. In early 2004, Melitta greatly increased its marketing budget by launching a $1.8-million advertising campaign that focused on making Melitta coffee an "everyday indulgence" with women ages 25 to 54. The campaign ran from March until May, and then from September to December. Additional campaigns during the summer months focused on new Melitta products. Radio ads aired in Vancouver, Calgary, Toronto, and Montreal on stations with weekly gross ratings points of at least 200. TV spots ran on networks including Prime, Deja View, Mystery, Cool TV, and W (The Women's Television Network). The campaign also included product placement on the W show *Me, My House*. Print ads appeared in 10 Southam newspapers, including the *National Post*, Vancouver's *Sun* and *Province*, the *Ottawa Citizen*, the Montreal *Gazette*, and the Regina *Leader-Post*. A three-month magazine campaign appeared in *Canadian Living* and *Coup de Pouce*. Ads in the trade publication *Canadian Grocer* also ran for one month. The company's campaign was complemented by an online component that included English and French microsites at MochaSofa/MokaSofa.com. These websites featured a viral messaging element and gift basket giveaways.

The next section considers the role of the Internet in creating customer relationships and product, brand, pricing, distribution, and promotion strategies.

Creating Internet Customer Relationships

A central problem facing electronic retailers is how to turn Web surfers or browsers into purchasers and eventually repeat customers. Similar to traditional businesses, customer retention is vital to the success of online retailers. Acquiring customers on the Internet can be very expensive, and unless the company retains these customers, it will be difficult to earn a profit. For example, in apparel e-tailing, finding new customers costs 20 percent to 40 percent more for Internet-only companies than for retailers with both physical and online stores.[27]

The popular notion has been that online customers are fickle and not loyal to a specific site, but it has been found that many of these customers develop loyalties toward sites that earn their trust, because they deliver a consistently first-rate performance and create a positive experience. Internet customers also tend to purchase from one primary supplier, especially in business-to-business settings.[28] Some ways to create and foster Internet customer relationships are discussed next.

Keep customers informed. Retaining valuable customers requires actions that help establish an ongoing relationship with such customers. An important aspect of relationship marketing is to establish a consistent and continuing communications program with desirable customers. Some companies carry out this communication task by building websites that focus on keeping customers informed and providing ways for them to communicate their opinions, thoughts, and questions to customer service and sales. The websites of such companies provide links to other sites for additional information and technical help as part of their service offering. Some of these sites obtain the visitor's name and use it to greet the visitor with new information related to his or her interests every time he or she returns to the site.

Establish interactivity. Another important feature of websites is interactivity. Interactive sites allow visitors to chat with company employees, provide feedback for improving the site, use chat rooms for engaging in conversation with other visitors or company employees, and let visitors sign up for a newsletter, free reports, and e-mails. Among the most successful customer relationship–oriented online businesses are banks whose website allows visitors to access their accounts, pay bills, transfer funds, check account balances, buy and sell stocks, check stock market indicators, find mortgage information, and a host of other services.

Offer exceptional value. Online companies must find ways to build long-term relationships with customers so they put down roots. The site design should attract and retain customers and encourage the development of longer relationships. Building online relationships involves more than monitoring click-through rates and page impressions.[29] Companies must offer exceptional value to have a chance of creating loyal customers who will visit the company's site again.

Offer a positive experience. Creating online relationships requires that companies offer customers a positive experience and that they are responsive to customers' attempts to communicate with them. Some companies encourage their customers to contact them but then fail to respond in a timely way. Many companies fail to respond in a timely fashion because they lack the resources or the systems to handle large volumes of customer requests. It is imperative for companies that want to create relationships with online customers to acquire the necessary systems and resources that will help them provide the appropriate level of service and response.[30]

Make contact personal. Another way to form online relationships is to make the contact as personal as possible. For example, Yahoo! allows people to personalize their MY Yahoo! Pages by choosing exactly the information they prefer. Users can choose from numerous information sources such as news, stock quotes, and e-mail, and organize them in desirable ways. Such personalized information could include local weather, and Yahoo! will add the weather forecast to the person's My Yahoo! Page. Other ways to personalize the My Yahoo! Page include using the person's birth date to provide him or her with a daily horoscope.

Create an online community. Companies such as eBay.com and MSN.ca have been very successful in creating **online communities,** which are groups of individuals who have something in common and communicate frequently among themselves and share ideas on topics that are of interest to all community members. Members of the online community often communicate with each other to help solve mutual problems. Companies can foster the development of an online community by offering chat rooms, e-mail, and personalized websites. An example of an online community is Harlequin, the publisher

> **Online communities** are groups of individuals who have something in common and communicate frequently among themselves and share ideas on topics that are of interest to all community members.

of romance novels which, as we saw in the opening vignette of Chapter 11, offers online book serials, newsletters, and interactive contests and chat rooms that allow members to connect with other readers, authors, and editors in online community discussions.

Internet Product Strategy

Effective marketing focuses on offering superior customer value. The Internet enables firms to increase the value of their products by offering certain services that lower costs or increase product benefits. For example, websites collect information and greet site visitors by name and suggest product offerings based on previous purchases. Internet companies also allow customers to get involved in the purchasing process. The ability to check the status of an order is an attractive feature for those Internet shoppers who prefer a greater degree of involvement when they purchase things on the Internet. E-tailers such as Amazon.ca and Chapters.ca allow buyers to check the status of an order at any time.

Internet-based technologies have significantly reduced the marginal cost of producing and distributing digital goods such as software, news stories, music, photographs, stock quotes, horoscopes, sports scores, and health tips. Some firms such as America Online are selling large bundles of digital goods for a low flat monthly fee. Such aggregation of so many products would be extremely expensive using traditional distribution media but this bundling offers **economies of aggregation** that favour large distributors of such bundles and make it difficult for smaller companies that sell unbundled products to compete effectively.[31]

Most websites log the pages that are viewed to determine which parts of the site are visited most often and also log which site the visitor came from. Some companies store a small file called a cookie on the visitor's computer. **Cookies** contain a personal identification code that is used to save the purchaser's shopping bag and retrieve it the next time the customer visits the site. They are also used to personalize the online experience by alerting the visitor to features and information that might be of interest to him or her.

The Internet has helped create new types of businesses such as search engines (e.g., Google.ca) and directories (e.g., sympatico.msn.ca) and interactive shopping agents such as priceline.com and mySimon that help online buyers find the best prices on the Internet. The Internet has also helped create **digital goods** such as music, software, videos, and pictures. It also enables customization of digital and non-digital products. For example, online customers can purchase personal computers on the Internet in a variety of combinations by choosing the appropriate features, or music retailers can create CDs containing songs ordered by customers.

A more recent Internet development is **recommendation systems,** which are a form of mass-customization.[32] Search engines such as AltaVista and Google use recommendation systems to recommend relevant sites for products or services on the basis of keywords supplied by users. Electronic book sellers such as Chapters.ca and Amazon.ca also use these systems, so when a customer is searching for a specific book, the site will recommend other books that the customer might also want to purchase on the basis of past purchases of similar customers.

It is important that online companies adopt physical and technological processes to keep customers' personal information safe and secure. Many Internet companies take measures to reassure customers that any information they provide will not be misused and that the company will maintain their privacy in order to convince them that the site is secure. Online businesses state their privacy policy on their websites, where they explain the type of information they do and do not gather when someone visits their site.

E-businesses also guarantee that if the customer's information is abused, they will be responsible for any financial losses that may occur. Usually, the personal information provided to the e-tailer when an order is placed or an account is opened is secured using Secure

Economies of aggregation involve selling large aggregations of digital goods for a low flat monthly fee.

Cookies contain a personal identification code that is used to save the purchaser's shopping bag and retrieve it the next time the customer visits the site.

Digital goods are downloadable products such as music, software, videos, and pictures.

Recommendation systems are a form of mass-customization to recommend products or services on the basis of keywords supplied by users.

Socket Layers (SSL) encryption technology. SSL technology prevents this information from being intercepted and read as it is transmitted over the Internet to the company's servers. This information is decrypted only when it reaches the company's servers and is then stored on restricted-access computers located at restricted-access sites.

Internet Brand Strategy

Online companies create strong e-brands and highly satisfied customers by providing them with a positive experience by using traditional advertising and promotional efforts. Many of the methods that lead to higher customer satisfaction and loyalty in traditional businesses also work in e-businesses. Delivering excellent service and value is equally important for customer satisfaction, customer loyalty, and retention in offline and online businesses. Companies hoping to attract and, most importantly, retain visitors to their website need to improve their service levels and offer online customers superlative value and satisfaction.

Branding is becoming important in Internet-based businesses because online consumers prefer to buy from well-known and reputable e-companies. Companies such as Amazon.com and Schwab are widely known, recognized, and trusted by online consumers. Many Canadian consumers avoid purchasing online because of trust and privacy issues. Even the 69 percent of those who shop online frequently are still concerned about security and privacy.[33] According to an Ipsos Reid survey, 59 percent of Canadians have Internet access but have not purchased anything online.[34] Gaining people's trust is a major challenge for Internet companies as many online visitors are reluctant to provide credit card information because they do not trust the site. Traditional retailers with established names such as Canadian Tire and Best Buy have an advantage over Internet-only companies because these names have been known for years and consumers have a higher degree of trust in them. In addition to leveraging their brand name, traditional organizations can also take advantage of existing infrastructure and facilities, as the Tesco example discussed in the Strategy in Action box illustrates. Tesco was able to leverage its name and existing network of stores and facilities to create its online business for a fraction of what it would cost to establish a pure-play (that is, only online) business.[35]

Strategy in Action

TESCO

When Tesco, the largest supermarket chain in Britain, launched its online shopping service, it focused on both offline and online customers. That gave it an advantage over pure-play competitors such as Webvan, an online supermarket retailer that targeted online customers by offering only online ordering for home delivery. Tesco had several advantages over pure-play competitors such as Webvan. It already had several warehouses in place and it could utilize its existing stores and supermarket experience.

In addition to capitalizing on its existing infrastructure, the company could leverage its brand name. Tesco's reputation provided its online business with instant recognition and trust while it minimized the perceived risk online visitors might experience about shopping online. Existing customers felt more comfortable buying from Tesco's online business than from another online business.

Thanks to its website, Tesco's customer acquisition costs for its traditional business are very low as its Web business attracts new customers who then migrate to its physical stores. Many online visitors began to visit Tesco's physical stores for the first time as a result of their online experience.

(continued)

Unlike pure-play competitors, Tesco doesn't have to invest in building new facilities. For example, it cost the company $1 million (U.S.) to launch its electrical products division. However, it cost its competition $50 million (U.S.) to launch a similar product line. These advantages enable Tesco and other hybrid companies to become profitable in a short period of time while their clicks-only competitors take much longer to become profitable.

Internet Pricing Strategy

As we've seen earlier, the Internet is affecting every aspect of a firm's marketing strategy. Among the marketing areas that have been affected the most is pricing. The Internet influences a firm's pricing strategy in several ways, including providing consumers with more information, increasing competition, increasing the number of suppliers, establishing various auction houses, and undertaking pricing research.

1. *Increased information.* One major effect of the Internet is the explosion of information that has resulted in more competition among firms and lower prices.[36] Many Internet-only companies offer substantially lower prices than other retail or even mail order firms. For example, Chapters.ca sells books considerably more cheaply than brick-and-mortar bookstores. Customers of Autobytel.com, an Internet referral service on automobile dealer pricing, pay less for a particular car than customers who don't use this referral service.[37] Online book and CD prices are 9 to 15 percent lower than prices in conventional retail stores.[38]

2. *Interactive Shopping Agents.* The Internet makes the search for the lowest price for products easy, quick, and inexpensive, especially with the various interactive shopping agents that provide one-click access to price and availability information about a relatively large number of online suppliers.[39] **Interactive shopping agents,** or shopbots, are designed to make online shopping easier by checking availability and company prices of the same item in different online stores. These agents only provide the information—the shopper still connects with the site and makes the transaction. The first interactive shopping agent developed by Andersen Consulting was called Bargain Hunter. Since then a number of interactive shopping agents have appeared, including mySimon and EvenBetter.com.

   Shopbots reduce the ability of online firms to charge higher prices by closing existing information gaps between buyers and sellers, providing online buyers with a variety of sites with product and pricing information, increasing both the buyer's ability to make informed decisions and his or her bargaining power.[40] Before the appearance of shopbots, e-businesses were able to maintain higher prices because consumers lacked pricing information about various products. Shopbots reduce search costs at least 30-fold in comparison to searching offline retail stores and making telephone calls.[41]

3. *Growth of Online Suppliers.* Other Internet-related factors that are putting downward pressure on prices include the growth of Internet users and the entry of large numbers of electronic retailers, which have provided online shoppers with a wide variety of choices, further enhancing their bargaining power. The number of suppliers has increased even more as distance has become less of a barrier—people can now purchase from online vendors located anywhere in the world. Another factor leading to lower prices has been the elimination of many traditional intermediaries, such as wholesalers and retailers, and the fact that online information intermediaries normally take a much smaller percentage of the final selling price for the information they provide to Internet buyers than traditional intermediaries.

4. *Auction houses.* The various Internet auction houses such as eBay.com also affect the prices of products sold on the Internet. Online auctions serve as powerful methods of

Interactive shopping agents are designed to make online shopping easier by checking availability and company prices of the same item in different online stores by tabulating the sites selling the product and the prices charged.

real-time pricing. These auctioneers enable buyers and sellers to buy or sell products through an online bidding process that usually results in products being sold at lower prices. The Internet is making it possible to auction many more products than has ever been possible previously. One of the biggest problems with auctions had been bringing enough bidders together in the same place at the same time. The Internet has solved this problem, as bidders no longer have to be physically present, decreasing the cost of participation in auctions and increasing the number of bidders. The larger number of participants often results in somewhat higher auction prices, making auctions more profitable to sellers in comparison with non-Web auctions.[42]

5. *Pricing research.* Another impact of the Internet on pricing practices is that it offers marketers excellent new capabilities in pricing research and testing. In contrast to traditional retailing, where pricing research is costly in time and money, the Internet allows marketers to research and test pricing decisions in real time and with low costs. By making it easier to track consumer responses to prices, e-tailers can set prices with far greater precision and make appropriate price adjustments when necessary.[43]

Online pricing research makes information available from many sources such as customers' buying history that is stored in databases or in cookies created in customers' computers or clickstream information. Such pricing information can help managers segment their markets in new ways and uncover profitable customer groups. For example, Zilliant, an electronics company, reduced the price of its four products by 7 percent. Revenues from three of the four products increased by 5 percent to 29 percent but the volume increase wasn't enough to offset the revenues lost due to the price reduction. However, sales of the fourth product more than doubled because the company had uncovered a new segment of latent demand made up of high school and university students. This finding led the company to create a special website for these segments and offer special prices not available to other segments.[44]

Despite some evidence that prices in electronic commerce are lower than in brick-and-mortar stores, there is skepticism about whether the Internet leads to lower prices across the board. Although price is an important factor in consumers' decision-making, it is not always the main criterion when people are making buying decisions. Other factors such as product quality, shipping and handling fees, ease of ordering, customer support, and timely delivery may be equally or even more important than price to online customers.

Also, as the number of electronic companies grows, search costs increase. One weakness of shopbots is that they do not provide online consumers with non-price information such as shipping and handling fees, customer support, delivery, and other types of information required to make a buying decision. Collecting such information requires time and increases search costs. As a result, many online consumers try to reduce search costs with decision shortcuts such as purchasing from a recognized and trusted electronic retailer, even if that company charges higher prices than the competition.[45] This explains why well-known electronic retailers charge higher prices than lesser-known competitors without experiencing a decline in sales. For example, even with the proliferation of shopbots, Amazon.com's market share increased from 64 to 72 percent and Barnes & Noble's from 12 to 15 percent between 1997 and 1999 even though they raised prices by 8 and 7 percent respectively while discount rival Book-A-Million lowered prices by 30 percent during this period.[46]

Consumers' preference for purchasing goods from well-known and reputable online stores often forces firms to spend considerable amounts of money on marketing and promoting their site. This, in turn, necessitates charging high prices to cover these expenditures and still earn a profit. Companies that sell their products through both online and offline channels do not lower their prices for fear of alienating traditional distribution channel members. For example, when Compaq began charging lower prices on products sold online, its dealers complained vigorously. This concern often forces electronic retailers to charge similar online and offline prices.

Studies suggest that online consumers are not as price sensitive as it was once thought and do not actively search for the best price available. A study of online shoppers found that 89 percent of book buyers, 84 percent of those buying toys, 81 percent of music buyers, and 76 percent of those buying electronic products do not actively search competing sites but purchase from the first site they visit.[47] Also, in a study of North American consumers, fewer than 10 percent of online customers were aggressively looking for bargain prices; the rest of them returned to the same site when making a purchase rather than searching for the best price.[48]

Internet Distribution Strategy

Electronic channels are any channels that involve the use of the Internet as a means of reaching end users.[49] The Internet is changing distribution like no other environmental force has since the industrial revolution because it breaks many of the assumptions on which channels are based, transforming or even obliterating channels themselves in many cases, while giving rise to new forms of channels of distribution.[50]

The Internet is in many respects both a retail store and a delivery medium. The customer first locates a product, such as computer software or airline tickets, and then makes a purchase online. Once credit card information is entered, the customer proceeds to download the software. For non-digital products, the seller must arrange with a shipping company to have them delivered to the customer's address. Online distribution has a number of characteristics that differentiate it from offline distribution. These online characteristics are discussed next (see Figure 13.2):

Figure 13.2	Characteristics of Online Distribution

- Greater convenience
- More time consuming
- Different cost structure
- Electronic data interchange
- Death of distance
- Time compression

- *Greater convenience.* Convenience of online shopping, by allowing consumers to shop at home, is one of the biggest advantages of electronic shopping.[51] The Internet makes shopping more convenient as consumers can search and compare products and prices, and place an order without visiting stores. People who prefer shopping online value the convenience of shopping anytime of the day and the fact that it takes less time to complete the purchase than when shopping offline. In a study of business-to-business companies, it was found that most purchasing managers buy online because it lowers transaction and search costs and because it automates purchasing information for tracking inventory.[52]

  Returning merchandise purchased online, however, may be more inconvenient than simply being able to take it back to a store. Some electronic retailers who also operate traditional stores allow online buyers to return merchandise to the brick-and-mortar store. Consumers who purchase from companies that operate only electronic stores experience the most inconvenience as they have to wrap the merchandise, take it to the post office or other designated location, and pay to send it back to the online merchant. Some e-tailers eliminate this inconvenience by picking up the merchandise from the customer's home.

- *More time consuming.* One disadvantage of e-commerce is the time it takes for delivery of the merchandise after the order is placed. This is not a problem for downloadable digital goods such as stock trading, music, online banking, movies, videos, and software. But non-digital goods such as books and DVDs must be shipped after the customer places an order and it can take a substantial amount of time for delivery of the merchandise. Consumer demands for faster delivery is putting pressure on e-tailers to increase the speed of product delivery and has enhanced the importance of quick-delivery companies such as UPS, Federal Express, and others. To alleviate this problem, some electronic retailers offer various shipping choices ranging from overnight express or Canada Post Xpresspost to slower shipping methods such as U.S. ground mail and Canada Post's Expedited Parcel service.

- *Different cost structure.* The Internet is a channel of distribution with a different cost structure.[53] The Internet does not necessarily imply lower distribution costs for customers because of costs associated with returned merchandise, difficulty in returning products, concerns about slow product delivery, and high shipping and handling fees. A report by Retail Forward discovered that 56 percent of Internet buyers decided to make a purchase because they were offered free shipping. In addition, 70 percent of Internet shoppers stated that they would shop online more if they didn't have to pay shipping and handling charges.[54] Recently Amazon.ca and Chapters.ca reduced the minimum purchase required for free shipping to $39. Two online superstores, Buy.com and J&R, offer free shipping on selected items.

- *Electronic data interchange.* The Internet offers firms the ability to use **electronic data interchange (EDI) systems,** which are used to integrate the computers of different companies. EDI consists of various electronic technologies that enable companies to share data on shipments, orders, and sales.[55] It commonly involves a computer platform that is proprietary to the buyer, making it necessary for suppliers serving many retailers to use a different computer for connecting with each customer.

  EDI is used by many business-to-business firms and most major retailers. EDI technology allows firms to improve sales forecasting and reduce the amount of inventory they carry along with the costs associated with high inventory levels such as pilfering, obsolescence, and tying up scarce capital. EDI also provides the supplier with a much better information flow about sales of specific items; the supplier then knows what to replenish and when. For example, when a customer buys a certain type of toothpaste in a retail store, the item sold is recorded when the store clerk scans the item's tag at the checkout counter. This information is transmitted back to the supplier who now knows exactly how much has been sold and how much needs to be restocked at a particular store. There is a trigger point, a minimum stock level, arrived at by a mutual agreement between the suppliers and the buyer, which when reached automatically calls for restocking. A well-known example of EDI in practice is Procter & Gamble's agreement with Wal-Mart, which has been widely credited as a major contributor to Wal-Mart's highly effective inventory management.

- *Death of distance.* A major consequence of the Internet is **death of distance.** Location for a traditional retail store matters a great deal. It needs to be in a high-traffic location with appropriate surroundings. However, location is not a key marketing decision for Internet-based firms since the Internet has made location irrelevant. Death of distance implies that geographic location is no longer a crucial factor in business as the Internet has made place irrelevant. However, the Internet minimizes the impact of distance only for goods that can be digitized such as pictures, words, videos, and software.[56] This also has contributed to the process of **disintermediation**—reducing the number of intermediaries in a channel of distribution.

- *Time compression.* Traditional distribution takes place within certain times during the day, or on certain days of the week. The Internet, on the other hand, is independent of time as sites are always open for business. Internet transactions take place on a real-time basis as customers can shop and place orders any time and sellers can also serve customers any time. **Time compression** refers to the fact that the Internet

Electronic data interchange (EDI) systems are used to integrate the computers of different companies.

Death of distance implies that geographic location is no longer a crucial factor in business as the Internet has made location irrelevant.

Disintermediation is a process of reducing the number of intermediaries in a channel of distribution.

Time compression refers to the fact that the Internet has made time less relevant for business transactions as online stores can be open 24 hours a day.

has made time less relevant for business transactions as online stores can be open 24 hours a day. This has triggered a process of homogenization of time across countries and continents, causing the restrictions of time zones to disappear.[57]

An important function of traditional distribution is to offer attractive assortments and a broad variety of merchandise to enable customers to compare different products and to provide the convenience of one-stop shopping. Some online retailers such as Indigo.ca also offer a wide assortment of merchandise to attract online shoppers looking for a variety of merchandise. Several electronic malls also exist that offer access to a large variety of sites. For example, 24Hour-Mall.com offers one-click access to hundreds of electronic stores such as Bose.com, BestBuy.com, CircuitCity.com, and Handspring.com.

E-businesses should consider using more than one type of distribution. Using several channels enables Internet companies to exploit alternative ways of obtaining greater market coverage. Companies that combine a physical presence with an effective online strategy often have an advantage over companies that employ either strategy but not both. For example, many people prefer to obtain information about a company's products online and then make a purchase in the actual store. Or they first visit the store to personally inspect the merchandise and then place an order online to benefit from lower Internet prices. Some retailers, including Chapters.ca, have computer facilities in their stores so customers can order books online. Many online retailers also offer customers the flexibility to return unwanted merchandise purchased online to the store, adding an extra layer of convenience and flexibility to the purchasing process.

The Internet is not about to replace traditional shopping methods, however. Many people either have no access to the Internet or are not willing to use it for making purchases. Many people also prefer the personal contact and service that can only be provided in a store environment. The best strategy is often combining both offline and online approaches because, as it was noted earlier, it provides customers with the option of buying either offline, online, or both. In these cases, firms must design an integrated strategy that maintains the relationships developed offline and transfers them to the online environment. For example, as Future Shop customers are switching to Future Shop online, the company must focus its efforts on offering the same kind of offline experience to online visitors. The Kinnikinnick Foods case discussed in the Strategy in Action box illustrates some of these issues.[58]

Strategy in Action

KINNIKINNICK FOODS

Edmonton-based Kinnikinnick Foods was one of the few companies that made any money with Internet marketing during the Internet bust of the late 1990s. Its use of the Internet has transformed the company from a one-man bakery selling gluten-free bread and buns at a local farmers' market in 1991 to a company with 70 employees that produces 100 different gluten-free products that it sells to main Canadian grocery chains, food stores in 20 U.S. states, and individual customers throughout North America.

The company targeted people suffering from celiac disease, an inability to digest food in the presence of gluten. Since the company initially had a tiny marketing budget, it created brand recognition by sending samples of its products to celiac organizations around North America for use at special events, such as children's camps and annual meetings. Kinnikinnick also advertised in the 7,000-plus celiac association newsletters, a move that cost the company a fraction of the cost of advertising in magazines and daily newspapers.

Celiacs live throughout North America but they are not sufficiently concentrated in large numbers in any one area to justify building a plant. The Internet was the right solution for this diverse market. Jay Bigam, who joined Kinnikinnick Foods in 1996 as a CEO, designed the company's first website. Internet customers began to visit their local stores asking for Kinnikinnick products. Its name—an Algonquin word for a mixture made from bearberry fruit—gave the company a branding advantage. According to CEO Bigam, "Most people can't pronounce it, but they do remember it." Profits from Canadian Internet sales enabled the company to increase its plant capacity and meet the new retail demand; the company expanded its outlets by selling through health food stores in Canada and the United States. In addition, money from U.S. Internet sales was used to facilitate the expansion into U.S. retail stores.

Between 1999 and 2001, Internet sales increased from 10 percent to 40 percent of the company's business and 80 percent of the total year-over-year sales increase. The company avoided the problem plaguing other high-growth Internet companies by ensuring that invoicing, ordering systems, and production control accounting systems were in place. Increased awareness of its products in Europe created by the Internet has convinced the company to begin shipping its products overseas.

As we have seen in earlier chapters, there is potential for conflict when a firm sells the same product through both traditional stores and the Internet. This type of distribution arrangement tends to alienate intermediaries as their prices are usually higher than Internet prices. For example, Hewlett-Packard faced this problem for years and it made it difficult to compete against Dell Computer, which was selling its products direct. This fear of distributor backlash often forces companies to charge the same prices in both channels.

Internet Promotion Strategy

The Internet has become an important component of a firm's promotion strategy as it provides a new way to reach people and deliver the company's message. Marketers who use the Internet as part of an integrated marketing communications mix must assess its role as an advertising medium and its position in a firm's marketing communication mix.[59] Firms must ensure that their online messages and employees' e-mails convey an image that is consistent with all other communication efforts.

Internet advertising can be thought of as equivalent to print advertising delivered in a new way that is potentially more effective in getting people to process the information.[60] The primary role of the Internet as a communication tool is evidenced by a study by Schmid and Trollinger (1999), who found that 88 percent of Direct Marketing Association members use their websites primarily for providing marketing information, 60 percent for lead generation, and 51 percent for selling products and services.[61]

A website can be seen as a mix between direct selling (as it can engage the visitor in a dialogue) and advertising because it can generate awareness, provide information, and demonstrate the product. A website may be viewed as complementary to the personal selling effort by business-to-business suppliers and advertisers of consumer products. The Internet may also be viewed as a cross between an electronic trade show and a community flea market.[62] As an electronic trade show, it can be considered a huge exhibition hall where potential customers can enter any time of the day or night and visit prospective sellers. It resembles a community flea market because it is open, informal, and interactive—characteristics that are often associated with flea markets.

Many companies use their websites as a way to provide product information to potential customers who then call a toll-free number to place an order or visit the store. Holt Renfrew uses its website as an electronic brochure to encourage online visitors to subscribe to the company's newsletter and receive updates on fashion trends, new designers, and special events. Large-ticket items such as automobiles, furniture, or appliances are commonly purchased in actual stores but many customers gather product-related data from the company's website before visiting the store. For example, a car dealership's website such as Autobytel can help generate sales leads. Customers visit the dealership armed with information and "having kicked tires" on the Internet.[63]

In addition to their role as a product information source, websites are created to inform and to create a favourable image in the eyes of visitors. They provide quick access to information about the company. Such websites commonly emphasize a firm's mission, stock market success, or industry leadership. The main objective of such sites is to impress investors, stock market analysts, shareholders, and customers. They serve mostly as public relations and positioning tools. Corporate identity sites play the same role as corporate annual reports—they promote the company's philosophy and history. Many Canadian companies, including Petro-Canada, Alcan, and BCE Inc., have such websites.

However, although the website can provide visitors with product and price information, customers must not only know about it, but also return to it for future purchases. Thus, an important task for an online company is to make its site popular with potential customers who will hopefully put it on the list of their favourite sites in order to use it on a regular basis.[64] Firms spend substantial amounts of money promoting their websites to potential users in an attempt to make people more familiar with them.

Electronic retailers are also discovering that with the number of websites proliferating, it takes an enormous amount of spending to convince online customers to visit their site, let alone to get them to make a purchase and subsequently retain them.[65] Many online retailers spend between $100 and $500 or even higher amounts in some cases to acquire a new customer. Internet companies also use banner advertising that promotes a firm's website and provides links to it. Many companies promote their site by registering it with several search engines and directories such as Google, Yahoo!, and AltaVista.

A necessary requirement for e-business success is to establish two-way communication with online customers. Effective two-way communication involves communicating with customers and allowing them to easily contact the company. Company-initiated communication may be activities such as e-mailing customers with information about items they could be interested in purchasing. Many such efforts are rejected by people as a nuisance if they realize that they are automatically created through some database technology lacking a personal touch. On the other hand, information that is valuable to customers, such as upcoming events or new products, special offers, and personalized information, could be of more interest to people and probably will not be rejected.

Making it easy for customers to communicate with the company is an important aspect of the communication effort. Providing an e-mail address is often what is needed for customers to get in touch with the company. Other companies provide toll-free telephone numbers for customers to call when they have questions or face problems. Some sites include a toll-free phone number for people who prefer to shop by phone. Others provide online chat rooms where customers can exchange information with company employees. Some online companies customize their sites based on customer preferences. For example, customers provide their preferences and companies use them to communicate interesting information or design banner advertisements that take into account the product preferences of targeted customers.

Integrating Offline and Online Strategies

The process of marketing convergence discussed in an earlier chapter suggests that many companies are integrating the Internet with traditional marketing methods into a holistic view of consumers and business. This process implies a fusion of offline and online approaches into a new business model and value proposition. The exact nature of the new entity will depend on the particular business.[66] Every organization must strike the right balance between its offline and online business to meet the needs of its customers.

The company needs to understand the type of business, its existing infrastructure, and the needs and motivations of its customers before it designs its e-commerce strategy. In some cases, companies such as Boston Pizza and Zellers use the Internet as a complement to their existing business. For pure-play businesses such as Priceline.ca or Expedia.ca, the Internet is the entire business. However, combining traditional with e-commerce businesses is not an easy task as firms involved in such efforts are faced with numerous challenges. In designing an integrated offline/online strategy, companies should consider the following factors:[67]

Develop the right brand or set of brands. The company needs to decide whether it will use the brand name of the existing business or a different one. Some companies use the brick-and-mortar name such as canadiantire.ca and futureshop.ca. Other businesses use a different name, as was the case with Kmart, which initially used the name BlueLight.com to separate it from the established brand. BlueLight.com was eventually dropped and the company adopted Kmart.com as its only online name. Other companies such as Procter & Gamble and *Sports Illustrated* initially used separate online names but most of them eventually brought them in line with their better-known offline names.

Leverage the assets of the existing business. Brick-and-mortar firms can leverage their existing capabilities to create an online business at a much lower cost than the pure-play business. For example, Chapters can capitalize on its existing facilities and brand name to compete effectively against online bookstores.

Manage offline/online channel conflict. Establishing an online business may result in a conflict with existing distributors. As we discussed earlier, intermediaries react negatively when a company establishes an online business and sells its products at lower prices. The company must find ways to resolve such conflicts.

Use partnerships and alliances. Brick-and-mortar companies should seek partnerships with companies that have online experience to complement areas of weaknesses. For example, Toys R Us formed an alliance with Amazon.com, which had extensive experience selling on the Internet.

Create the right degree of separation. Companies must decide whether to create the online business as a standalone entity or integrate it with the existing business. For example, Procter & Gamble established its Reform.com online business as a separate business entity. This move is often necessary if the offline executives lack the experience to run the new online business. Forming a separate business is also necessary if existing organizational structure rules and procedures could stifle the online initiative.

Create integrated information systems. Firms need to harmonize the flow of information by integrating their databases of both offline and online businesses. This ensures that all customers, regardless of whether they are offline and/or online shoppers, are recognized in order to create an integrated customer experience. For example, people who hold a Chapters/Indigo membership card receive a discount whether they shop at a Chapters store or at Chapters online.

Create integrated supply chain and logistics. In designing effective supply chains, firms need to reevaluate their supply chain and logistics from customer ordering to delivery. Some companies allow customers to place orders in a store, online, through catalogues, or over the telephone. Then the item can be home delivered, purchased in the store, or even downloaded digitally. Also, as noted earlier, some offline/online businesses allow merchandise to be purchased online and returned in one of the company stores.

Manage the path to evolution. The relationship between offline and online businesses changes over time. Some companies evolve from a product or technological orientation to having more of a marketing focus as they build up their customer and competitive skills. These companies eventually realize that they need to focus their technical competences on serving customers' needs.

- The Internet is revolutionizing the way companies conduct their business and it is becoming an increasingly critical tool for marketing success. The Internet enables companies to obtain several competitive advantages over the competition.

- Some of the changes brought about by the Internet can be seen in the way we purchase goods and services, find information about products and services, and do our banking. The Internet has significantly reduced the cost of producing and distributing digital goods such as software, news, music, stock quotes, and pictures.

- The strategic advantages of the Internet include low-cost communication, more efficient distribution, centralized inventory, and a more even playing field.

- A McKinsey/Metrix study came up with six online consumer segments: Simplifiers, Surfers, Bargainers, Connectors, Routiners, and Sportsters.

- Marketing managers must assess the role of the Internet in their marketing strategy. The Internet has changed the way marketing strategy is formulated and executed in a number of ways. All aspects of marketing, including marketing research, consumer behaviour, segmentation, relationship marketing, product management, pricing, distribution, and promotion, are affected by the Internet.

- Today many companies are integrating the Internet with traditional marketing methods into a holistic view of consumers and business. This process implies a fusion of offline and online approaches into a new business model and value proposition. The exact nature of the new entity will depend on the particular business. Every organization must strike the right balance between its offline and online business to meet the needs of its customers.

Review and Discussion Questions

1. Describe the strategic advantages of the Internet.

2. Identify and describe the various online consumer segments.

3. Discuss, in general, the role of the Internet in marketing strategy.

4. Describe the role of the Internet in creating customer relationships.

5. Discuss the role of the Internet in a company's product, brand, pricing, distribution, and promotion strategy.

6. Discuss strategies for integrating offline and online strategies.

Critical Thinking and Application Questions

1. An Internet-based company positioned its business as follows: "We offer state-of-the art Java-based e-commerce solutions for mission critical enterprise applications on cross-platform architectures." In the meantime, the customers in this market were looking for a reliable Internet connection for their employees. What do you think of the positioning statement of this company?

2. Select a local retailer and assess its Internet marketing strategy. What changes would you make to this retailer's Internet strategy, if any?

3. Ace Electrics is a manufacturer of industrial lubricants that traditionally distributed its products directly through its own salespeople. Following the advice of e-commerce consultants, Ace recently changed its sales model by emphasizing the selling of its products through its newly built website, call centres, and e-portals. Despite making a large investment in establishing its e-commerce facilities, Ace's sales declined. In your opinion, what happened?

4. Visit the websites of Canadian Tire and The Bay. What do you think is the role of these sites in the two companies' marketing strategy?

1. Bill Davidson, *Breakthrough* (Hoboken, N.J.: Wiley, 2004), 97–100; Gerald J. Tellis and Peter N. Golder, *Will and Vision* (New York: McGraw-Hill, 2002), 218–223.
2. Caroline Howard, *Winning the Net Game* (Irvine, Calif.: Entrepreneur Press, 2002), xv.
3. John Quelch and Lisa Klein, "The Internet and International Marketing," *Sloan Management Review,* Spring 1996, 60–75.
4. Howard, 46.
5. Howard, xv.
6. Brian T. Ratchford, Myung-Soo Lee, and Debabrata Talukdar, "The Impact of the Internet on Information Search for Automobiles," *Journal of Marketing Research* 40 (May 2003), 193–209.
7. Eric T. Bradlow and David C. Schmittlein, "The Little Engines That Could: Modelling the Performance of World Wide Web Search Engines," *Marketing Science* 19, No. 1 (Winter, 2000), 43–62.
8. Kenneth K. Boyer, "E-Operations: A Guide to Streamlining with the Internet," *Business Horizons*, January-February, 2001, 47–54.
9. Howard, xviii.
10. Net Impact Study Canada, "The SME Experience," November 2002, www.cebi.ca, retrieved on November 23, 2003.
11. Kent B. Monroe, *Pricing: Making Profitable Decisions* (Boston, Mass.: McGraw-Hill Irwin, 2003), 596.
12. Judy Strauss, Adel El-Ansary, and Raymond Frost, *E-Marketing*, 3rd ed. (Upper Saddle River, N.J.: Prentice Hall, 2003), 3.
13. INSEAD, Information E-Economy Benchmarking Report, November 2002.
14. Statistics Canada, *Household Internet Use Survey 2001*, Ottawa, August, 2002.
15. IDC, *Internet Commerce Market Model V8.3*, 2002.
16. Statistics Canada, *Survey of Electronic Commerce and Technology 2002*, Ottawa, April 2, 2003.
17. James G. Barnes, *Secrets of Customer Relationship Management* (New York: McGraw-Hill, 2001), 231.
18. IDC.
19. Ipsos Reid, *The Canadian Interactive Reid Report*, March 2002.
20. *McKinsey Marketing Practice*, 2003.
21. Michel E. Porter, "Strategy and the Internet," *Harvard Business Review*, March 2001, 63–78.
22. Donna L. Hoffman, "The Revolution Will Not Be Televised: Introduction to the Special Issue on Marketing and the Internet," *Marketing Science* 19, No. 1, Winter, 2000, 1–3.
23. Strauss, El-Ansary, and Frost, 9.
24. Gerald Haubl and Valerie Trifts, "Consumer Decision Making in Online Shopping Environments," *Marketing Science* 19, No. 1, Winter 2000, 4–21.
25. Noel Capon and James M. Hulbert, *Marketing Management in the 21st Century* (Upper Saddle River, N.J.: Prentice Hall, 2001), 562.
26. Paul-Mark Rendon, "Melitta brews national promotions," *Marketing Magazine*, March 8, 2004, 4.
27. Frederick F. Reichheld and Phil Schefter, "E-Loyalty: Your Secret Weapon on the Web," *Harvard Business Review*, July–August 2000, 105–113.
28. Reichheld and Schefter.
29. Barnes, 239.
30. Barnes, 245.
31. Yannis Bakos and Erik Brynjolfsson, "Bundling and Competition on the Internet," *Marketing Science* 19, No. 1, Winter 2000, 63–82.
32. Asim Ansari, Skander Essegaier, Rajeev Kohli, "Internet Recommendation Systems," *Journal of Marketing Research* 37 (August 2000), 363–375.
33. Ipsos Reid.
34. Ipsos Reid.
35. Yoram Wind, Vijay Mahajan with Robert E. Gunther, *Convergence Marketing: Strategies for Reaching the New Hybrid Consumer* (Upper Saddle River, N.J.: Prentice Hall, 2002), 54.
36. Florian Zettelmeyer, "Expanding to the Internet: Pricing and Communications Strategy When Firms Compete on Multiple Channels," *Journal of Marketing Research* 37 (August 2000), 292–308.
37. Fiona Scott Morton, Florian Zettelmeyer, and Jorge Silva Risso, "Internet Car Retailing," *Journal of Industrial Economics*, 49(4), 2001, 501–519.
38. Karen Clay, Ramayya Krishan, and Eric Wolff, "Prices and Price Dispersion on the Web: Evidence From the Online Book Industry," *Journal of Industrial Economics* 46 (December 2001), 521–539.
39. Ganesh Iyer and Amit Pazgal, "Internet Shopping Agents: Virtual Co-Location and Competition," *Marketing Science* 22, No. 1 (Winter 2003), 85–106.
40. Monroe, 599.
41. Erik Brynjolfsson and Michael D. Smith, "Frictionless Commerce? A Comparison of Internet and Conventional Retailers," *Management Science* 46 (April 2000), 563–585.
42. Ward Hanson, *Principles of Internet Marketing* (Cincinnati, Ohio: South-Western College Publishing, 2000), 340.
43. Walter Baker, Mike Marn, and Craig Zawada, "Pricing Smarter on the Net," *Harvard Business Review*, February 2001, 122–127.
44. Baker, Marn, and Zawada.
45. Rajneesh Suri, Mary Long, and Kent B. Monroe, "The Impact of the Internet and Consumer Motivation on the Evaluation of Prices," *Journal of Business Research* 55 (2001), 1–12.
46. McKinsey Marketing Practice, "Internet Pricing," www.mckinsey.com, retrieved on November 20, 2003.
47. Baker, Marn, and Zawada.
48. Baker, Marn, and Zawada.
49. Anne T. Coughlan, Erin Anderson, Louis W. Stern, and Adel I. El-Ansary, *Marketing Channels*, 6th ed. (Upper Saddle River, N.J.: Prentice Hall, 2001), 447.
50. Leyland Pitt, Pierre Berthon, and Jean-Paul Berthon, "Changing Channels: The Impact of the Internet on the Distribution Strategy," *Business Horizons*, March-April 1999, 19–25.
51. Coughlan, Anderson, Stern, and El-Ansary, 454.
52. Baker, Marn, and Zawada.
53. Rajiv Lal and Miklos Sarvary, "When and How Is the Internet Likely to Decrease Price Competition," *Marketing Science* 18, No. 4, 1999, 485–503.
54. "Free Shipping Is Still the Most Powerful Lure for Shoppers," *Internet Retailer*, June 27, 2002.
55. Coughlan, Anderson, Stern, and El-Ansary, 458.
56. Pitt, Berthon, and Berthon.
57. Pitt, Berthon, and Berthon.
58. Norma Ramage, "Making Dough on the Net," *Marketing Magazine*, June 7, 2004, 11.
59. Pierre Berthon, Leyland F. Pitt, and Richard T. Watson, "The World Wide Web as an Advertising Medium: Toward an Understanding of Conversion Efficiency," *Journal of Advertising Research*, January/February 1996, 43–54.
60. Larry Percy, John R. Rossiter, and Richard Elliott, *Strategic Advertising Management* (New York: Oxford University Press, 2001), 11.
61. J. Schmid and S. Trollinger, "Who's Making the Net Work?" *Target Marketing*, 22 (6) (1999), 72–75.
62. Berthon, Pitt, and Watson.
63. Fahri Karakaya, D. Steven White, "E-Commerce and Marketing Strategy," *Academy of Business Administration*, 2000, 353–358.
64. Donna L. Hoffman and Thomas P. Novak, "How to Acquire Customers on the Web," *Harvard Business Review*, May-June 2000, 179–188.
65. Hoffman and Novak.
66. Wind, Mahajan with Gunther, 56.
67. Wind, Mahajan, with Gunther, 132.

Chapter Fourteen

Defensive and Offensive Marketing Strategies

The whole art of war consists of a well-reasoned and extremely circumspect defensive, followed by rapid and audacious attack.

Napoleon

Learning Objectives

After studying this chapter, you should be able to:

1. Describe several pre-entry defensive marketing strategies

2. Describe several post-entry defensive marketing strategies

3. Discuss the factors that affect the decision by established firms to respond to competitors' attacks

4. Explain the principles of offensive marketing warfare and their role in formulating offensive marketing strategies

5. Discuss several offensive marketing strategies

Air Canada's and Richmond Savings Credit Union's Successful Defensive and Offensive Strategies

Companies constantly engage in defensive and offensive marketing strategies. The following two stories illustrate this business reality. In September 2001, Air Canada started Zip Air, a low-cost, no-frills, low-fare, western-based airline. Zip Air operated on short-haul routes, serving Edmonton, Vancouver, Calgary, and Winnipeg. Zip Air started with six Boeing 737–200 aircraft with the goal of eventually growing to twenty 737–200 aircraft. Air Canada introduced Zip Air to counter the growing threat of western-based WestJet, which was modelled after Southwest Airlines, a successful no-frills, discount airline that serves short-haul routes in the United States.

On November 1, 2001, shortly after Zip Air was started, Air Canada introduced Tango, another no-frills airline. Tango flew its planes longer distances than Zip Air, charged for in-flight services, had more seats within the same space than other airlines, and allowed online bookings; in addition, Tango, like other Air Canada airlines, was part of a closed network—it could connect only to other Air Canada planes. Tango was intended to fight other airlines that were offering discounted fares, such as Canada 3000, which had become Canada's second-largest airline following the merger of Air Canada with Canadian Airlines. When Canada 3000 failed, the introduction of Tango, along with the decline in air travel, was cited as a factor in its demise. Following the failure of Canada 3000, Air Canada was preparing to launch another discount carrier, LowCostCo, to support Zip Air in its head-to-head rivalry with its last major competitor, WestJet Airlines.

Other major airlines have attempted to launch similar airlines but failed. These airlines include Continental with Cal Lite, USAir with Metro Jet, British Airways with Go, and KLM with Buzz. Although data on Zip Air are not available, Tango was hailed a success with 81.4 percent capacity utilization and accounting for 19.2 percent of Air Canada's domestic revenue.[1] Tango helped Air Canada to retain air travellers despite a weak air travel market and stiff competition from other full-service and discount airlines.

In another field, a similar battle also broke out. In 1992, Richmond Savings Credit Union of Vancouver was perceived as just another stodgy credit union. To break out of this mould, it adopted non-traditional media to deliver its message and attacked big banks in ways that struck a nerve with the public. Richmond Savings' promotional campaign included advertising on the side of a bus, something no other bank had done This promotional campaign used pictures of a fat cat or a dead dinosaur with the copy saying, "Tired of dealing with the big banks?" and "Have the big banks had their day?" The intention was to poke fun at the big banks' attitude toward customers.

Richmond Savings' radio ads focused on two characters: the hapless customer and the snarly teller. The slogan was "We're not a bank—we're better." Richmond Savings also ran more ads based on the fictional Humongous Bank with the slogan "Your money is our money," and the worst jingles imaginable. Big banks were so offended by the slogan that they took Richmond Savings to court. News of the lawsuit

(continued)

immediately reached the national media, and it reinforced the image of big banks trying to squash a small flea. As a result, Richmond Savings received free publicity worth thousands of dollars.

Richmond Savings' underdog campaign worked well because the people of British Columbia were not happy with the big banks, while Richmond Savings had an excellent record for service and for not making claims it couldn't keep. Richmond Savings was extremely satisfied with the results of its campaign. By 1997, the number of members had increased by 50 percent, its asset base had grown by 100 percent, and the awareness level had gone up to 16 percent compared to just 5 percent in 1991.[2]

Introduction

As the Air Canada and Richmond Savings Credit Union stories illustrate in the opening vignette, rivalry forces companies to constantly engage in offensive and defensive marketing strategies. Rivalry occurs because one or more competitors either feels the pressure or sees an opportunity to enter an industry or to improve its position within an industry. In most cases, competitive moves by one firm have noticeable effects on its competitors and, thus, may invite retaliation or efforts to counter the move.[3] Companies respond to competitors' challenges by counterattacking with increasing advertising expenditures, cutting prices, increasing innovation, and introducing new products, or even accommodating the entrant by doing nothing or decreasing the level of marketing effort.[4]

Firms become market leaders by creating new markets or by taking market share from rivals. Successful incumbents need to be prepared for attacks by new entrants and existing firms seeking to expand their business. The incumbents' objective then is to defend their market share and strengthen their position by making it harder for companies to enter or for existing firms to challenge them.

Incumbent firms may also attack in an attempt to enter a new market, reposition themselves, or improve their market position. Markets are dynamic arenas where firms try to expand into their industries or reposition themselves in other segments within the industry. As firms attempt to improve their position, they engage in competitive battles and adopt offensive strategies. Successfully using offensive strategies can help a firm, as the Richmond Savings story suggests, improve its competitive position, gain market share, and increase profits.

This chapter examines both defensive and offensive marketing strategies. It discusses the pre-entry and post-entry defensive marketing strategies, the factors that affect the decision by established firms to respond to competitors' attacks, the principles of offensive marketing warfare and their role in formulating offensive marketing strategies, and the different offensive marketing strategies.

Defensive Marketing Strategies

Because of ongoing rivalry, established firms need to engage in defensive strategies to fend off various challengers. The primary purpose of defensive strategy is to make a possible attack unattractive and discourage potential challengers from attacking a firm. Incumbents try to shape the challenger's expectations about the industry's profitability and convince them that the return on their investment will be so low that it does not warrant making an investment in that industry.

Defensive strategies work better when they take place before the challenger makes an investment in the industry, or if the challenger enters the industry before exit barriers are raised, making it difficult for it to leave the industry. For this reason, an incumbent needs to take timely action to discourage a challenger from making any substantial commitment, because once the commitment is made, it is more difficult to dissuade the challenger from following through with the attack, especially if exit barriers are high.

If an attack has already begun, a defending firm may attempt to lower its intensity and potential for harm by directing the attack to areas where the firm is less vulnerable or to areas that are less desirable to the attacker.[5] Or they could initiate actions designed to make the entrant's life difficult after entry has occurred. This may convince the entrant that its calculations were too optimistic and its early experience in the industry is so negative that it does not warrant continuing the entry effort.

Factors Affecting Competitor Retaliation

How do firms respond to competitive attacks? Firms engaged in offensive marketing strategies need to understand how defending companies react when their market position is challenged. A response is a specific move by a rival prompted by a competitor's attack that is intended to defend its market position. Different firms tend to exhibit different response patterns to rival challenges. A crucial question for any offensive strategy is to ask whether and how defending companies will respond to the attack.

Firms are unique bundles of tangible and intangible resources and capabilities. They differ in the mix of these resources and capabilities and this makes each firm behave in a different way. Resources and capabilities are "sticky" (that is, they are not mobile or transferable to another industry) and they tend to constrain a firm's strategic choices and the way it responds to competitive challenges or potential opportunities. Firms also respond differently to competitors' initiatives because of differences in other areas such as their management systems and the cultural attitudes they have developed over the years.

The probability and extent of competitors' retaliation depends on a variety of factors. These factors include the following:

The extent of perceived threat by incumbent firms. The extent to which an incumbent perceives a competitor's moves as a threat to its market position and profitability affects its response. If the challenger attacks a firm's core business, it is highly likely that it will elicit a strong response. For example, Fido challenged Telus' residential business—its core markets—in British Columbia and that provoked an instant reaction by Telus, which attacked Fido in several of its markets across the country. If the challenge comes from a small competitor, however, it may not be noticed. If it comes from a large, well-known competitor, the move will probably elicit a retaliatory response.

Amount of resources and capabilities of the defending firm. The amount of resources and capabilities at the disposal of the established competitors will also be a factor. The more powerful the firm is, the more forceful its response is likely to be. For instance, it is well known that whenever a rival challenges Johnson & Johnson, the company quickly launches a powerful retaliation. Smaller firms may find it difficult to respond to competitive attacks by much larger firms. The Strategy in Action box describes Royal Crown Cola's inability to mount a credible response to attacks by larger competitors due to lack of resources.

> **Strategy in Action**
>
> ## ROYAL CROWN COLA
>
> Royal Crown Cola dominated the diet soft drink market through the mid-1960s. It initially challenged both Coke and Pepsi successfully with its sugar-free product, Diet Rite Cola. However, Royal Crown Cola had very limited resources with which to respond when both Coke and Pepsi attacked its Diet Rite Cola brand with their own brands, Tab and Diet Coke and Diet Pepsi respectively. Coca-Cola and Pepsi-Cola had greater financial and distribution resources, which resulted in Royal Crown Cola losing its leadership position in the diet soft drink market.[6]

The incumbent's willingness to respond. The probability of competitive reaction also depends on the incumbent's willingness to respond, which is, in turn, determined by its current strategy, image, profit margins, capacity utilization, and binding contracts with customers. A firm with a premium image, for instance, will be reluctant to respond to a smaller firm that engages in price-cutting, for fear of tarnishing its image and reputation as a premium brand. If a small firm cuts its price, a much larger firm may be reluctant to follow suit. Such reluctance is normal as the large firm stands to lose disproportionately more than the smaller firm due to its much larger size, as it will lose margins on many more product units than the smaller firm. A firm with full-capacity utilization or binding contracts may also be reluctant to follow suit with a price reduction because its sales will probably not be affected, at least in the short run.

Over the years, marketing managers and business strategists have developed a number of defensive marketing strategies to defend their position and maintain their sales and profitability. There are two types of defensive marketing strategies. Pre-entry strategies are actions taken by incumbents before they are attacked by challengers. Defensive marketing strategies may also take the form of post-entry actions that are initiated after the challenger has entered the market (see Figure 14.1).

Figure 14.1   Defensive Marketing Strategies

Pre-Entry Defensive Strategies

Pre-entry defensive strategies are actions taken by firms that are intended to persuade potential entrants to believe that market entry would be difficult or unprofitable. Such actions include signalling, fortifying and defending, covering all bases, continuous improvement, and capacity expansion.

Signalling

Companies often use signalling to announce their intention to take an action. Announcements can be made through interviews with the press, press releases, speeches, and other means. Such announcements may serve different objectives that are not necessarily mutually exclusive. They could signal a commitment to the industry and therefore try to preempt or deter competitors. A defending firm can effectively keep potential entrants out of the industry by using the threat of retaliation. The higher the perceived probability of retaliation and its degree of severity, the lower the probability of attack by a challenger. Firms enhance their reputation for rigorous retaliation by the way they responded to past attacks, which signals their commitment to defend their market share.

Other times, companies announce their intention to undersell their competitors. Future Shop, a large chain selling consumer electronics in Canada, has publicly stated that it will not be undercut by competitors and that it will meet their prices. Announcements may be used to issue a threat that action will be taken if a competitor makes a certain move. For example, firms can announce that they will match a rival's prices, rebates, credit, or any other terms offered.

Fortify and defend

This strategy attempts to build barriers to entry for competitors. The purpose of defensive marketing strategies is to lower the inducement to attack. Firms frequently enter an industry because existing firms are earning high profits. The higher the profits earned by incumbent firms, the higher the motivation to enter. Thus, the inducement to attack can be lowered by reducing the profit expectations of the entrant. This can be achieved by raising barriers to entry for new competitors.

Erecting barriers usually hinders entry by new competitors because they will have to incur costs not borne by existing competitors. The most common barriers to entry, as we have noted in earlier chapters, include economies of scale, product differentiation, capital requirements, switching costs, experience curve cost reductions, proprietary technology or patents, access to raw materials and other inputs, access to distribution channels, and location. Industries in which there are significant barriers to entry include the automobile, aerospace, and ship-building industries. Because of high barriers, entry is notoriously difficult in these industries.

Covering all bases

Covering all bases, also called product proliferation, entails introducing new products to ensure a full product line or to fill gaps in the market.

Covering all bases, also called product proliferation, entails introducing new products to ensure a full product line or to fill gaps in the market. Covering all bases may involve introducing several models or versions of a product. Many firms carry full product lines to block access to the industry by new entrants. For example, the leading ready-to-eat cereal companies compete with a full line of cereals that appeal to a range that includes adults, children, and dieters and that have different nutritional content, different flavours, and so forth, making it very difficult for other companies to enter and threaten their position. This strategy is also used by chain stores when they rush to expand rapidly and keep competitors out of the market.

A firm that floods the market avoids being outflanked by competitors. It is also a way to tie up distribution channels and shelf space. For example, Procter & Gamble, a master practitioner of this strategy, dominates retail shelf space with products such as Ivory Soap, Crest, Tide, Pantene Pro-V, and many others.

A firm that is trying to cover all bases may face one or more of the following difficulties. First, some firms, especially the small ones, may not have the resources to offer a full product line. Second, product proliferation may cause a firm to spread its resources too thinly, violating the principle of concentration of forces at the decisive point. Covering too many markets and overextending itself leaves a firm vulnerable to competitors' attacks, as it makes for an easy target. Third, this strategy cannot fully protect a company from attacks by other competitors who wish to enter the industry. Even if a firm was able to cover the major segments, it is impossible to cover every possible niche in the market. This allows small companies to enter the market and occupy these niches. These niches, although small and unattractive at the time, often explode into large segments, posing a threat to established firms.

Blocking brands are brands used by incumbent firms to block access to the market by potential entrants.

A special case of the cover-all-bases strategy is the introduction of a **blocking brand.** Blocking brands are brands used by incumbent firms to block access to the market by potential entrants. The firm introduces a brand designed to fill a niche in the market that could be used as a point of entry by a competitor. Often the intent of introducing a blocking brand is to protect an existing profitable brand by precluding competitors from entering the market and stealing market share by undercutting the price of the existing product.

Continuous improvement

A **continuous improvement strategy** calls for a relentless pursuit of improvements in costs, product quality, new product development, and manufacturing processes and distribution.

A **continuous improvement strategy** calls for a relentless pursuit of improvements in costs, product quality, new product development, and manufacturing processes and distribution. The choice of areas to improve depends on the value proposition of the organization. A low-cost competitor continuously tries to find ways of decreasing costs through economies of scale, cutting costs, and introducing new production methods. A differentiated company looks for ways to maintain its competitive advantage through innovation, quality improvements, and new features, among other possibilities.

The continuous improvement strategy also involves innovation and improvement in the firm's marketing mix. Product innovation may involve offering superior features or benefits. Price innovation could include offering better sales terms and other incentives. Distribution could become more effective by looking for new channels, making existing channels more effective, and seeking strategic alliances. Promotion can become more effective by improving positioning and execution, using different media, and increasing emphasis on public relations and publicity. The sales promotion function could be examined to see if improvements can be made in the way the firm uses free samples, coupons, bonus packs, frequent buyer programs, and refunds.

Through a continuous improvement strategy, firms try to stay one step ahead of their competitors and help protect their competitive position from hostile challengers. Firms following this strategy are often required to make their own products obsolete by replacing them with new versions. Intel is a prime example of a company that follows the continuous improvement strategy. Its strategy is to introduce new and more powerful generations of its microprocessors at regular intervals, a move intended to satisfy computer users' never-ending appetite for increases in processing power. Each successive version of its chip makes its existing version obsolete in the span of a few months.

Capacity expansion

Manufacturing firms may build excess capacity as an entry-deterrent strategy. When a potential entrant realizes that the industry has excess capacity and its own entry will only add to the volume of unutilized capacity, it will be reluctant to enter. Capacity expansion is a credible deterrent strategy if capacity costs are very high. Otherwise, if the cost of adding capacity is low or capacity can be utilized for other purposes, it would be relatively easy for rivals to enter.

DuPont used capacity expansion to increase its market share in the titanium dioxide market. In 1970, DuPont had been using ilmenite in the production of titanium dioxide. This proved advantageous since the price of rutile ore, the raw material used primarily by its competitors, sharply increased, giving DuPont a significant cost advantage over its competitors. In order to maximize this cost advantage, DuPont developed a growth strategy of rapidly expanding capacity to satisfy all the future increases in demand and deter entry or expansion by existing competitors. At the time DuPont adopted this strategy in 1972, its market share was 30 percent. By 1985, its market share was over 50 percent and five of its major rivals had exited the market.[7]

As a defensive strategy, capacity expansion is not as powerful as other entry deterrents such as barriers to entry. In general, a decision to use capacity expansion for entry-deterring reasons should take into account the size of barriers to entry. If entry barriers are high, then capacity expansion should not normally be used as a deterrent. On the other hand, if entry barriers are low, incumbents should consider using capacity expansion as an entry-deterring device, taking into account the cost of additional capacity and its reversibility.

Post-Entry Defensive Strategies

Post-entry defensive strategies are actions taken by firms intended to protect their market position from companies that have already entered the market or incumbents that are threatening to take away market share. Such actions include defending a firm's position before competitors become entrenched, fighting brands, and cross-parry strategies, as shown in Figure 14.1.

Defend position before entrant becomes entrenched

When a company enters an existing market, its objective usually is to get established first in its chosen market segment, consolidate its position, and then start expanding into other market segments. Upstarts are especially dangerous if they enter the market by breaking the rules of the game with radically new products or innovations in pricing, distribution, delivery, service, and positioning. New entrants entering markets with radically new products usually come from markets unrelated to the one they are invading.[8] For example, the personal computer industry was not invented by IBM but by companies such as Apple and Microsoft—unrelated to the existing mainframe or mini-computer business.

Established firms need to defend their position while their newly entered opponents are small and vulnerable rather than waiting until the new entrants become strong and a serious threat. Market leaders, by consistently and swiftly meeting any moves intended to challenge their position, send out a clear message to would-be challengers that aggressive behaviour, such as price-cutting or entering core segments, will not be tolerated and that these moves will be met with rigorous and painful retaliation. Therefore, such actions would not pay off and would probably make the challenger worse off. In an effort to limit losses, such counterattacks often are not broadly based, but involve only a market segment of the defending company. The Strategy in Action box illustrates how Monsanto was able to confine Holland Sweetener Company successfully to its home European market with a limited counterattack, dissuading it from entering its lucrative U.S. market.[9]

Strategy in Action

MONSANTO

Holland Sweetener Company (HSC) was formed in 1986 as a joint venture between a Japanese and a Dutch company. HSC was selling aspartame, a generic version of NutraSweet, in Europe. In response to HSC's entry, Monsanto, the owner of NutraSweet, dropped its price from $70 to $22–$30 (U.S.) per pound in the European market. To meet that price, HSC had to sell at a loss, while Monsanto saw its NutraSweet revenues cut drastically. Although this appeared as an overreaction to HSC's entry, it was a smart, strategic move by Monsanto. HSC's entry was limited to the European market, which is a small part of the world aspartame market. As a result, Monsanto protected its much larger U.S. market. By attacking HSC in a smaller market, Monsanto sent a signal to its rivals to not enter its other larger markets. Monsanto's counterattack forced HSC to delay expansion plans. HSC never became a threat to Monsanto's U.S. market, even after the aspartame patent expired.

Incumbents often defend themselves by embracing and improving on the intruder's technology, attacking the upstart's reputation as a reliable source of supply, and hiring some of the best people away from the attacking firm. The Strategy in Action box below describes how some of these tactics were used by Microsoft in 1995 in fighting the challenge of Borland Delphi, a rapid development visual computer language that was by far a superior alternative to Microsoft's Visual Basic language.

Strategy in Action

MICROSOFT VISUAL BASIC

When Borland International introduced its Delphi computer language, many people predicted the demise of Visual Basic, the language that had dominated the industry since it was introduced a few years earlier. Although

---

the clear superiority of the Delphi programming environment encouraged a large number of programmers, including some Visual Basic programmers, to switch, the prediction did not come true. By sensing the threat coming from the intruder, Microsoft went on the counterattack and hired some of Borland Delphi's best programmers and spent large amounts on upgrading and improving Visual Basic, including providing a faster compiler, thus neutralizing one of Delphi's major advantages. Microsoft also criticized Borland Delphi as a non-mainstream language and pointed out the lack of enough Delphi programmers. Visual Basic not only survived, but it increased its stranglehold on the market, forcing Borland Delphi into an also-ran status.

Fighting brands

Fighting brands are introduced by organizations to fight a competitor's brand that threatens one of their major brands. Competing brands are typically lower-priced versions of the firm's premium brands that claim equal quality at a much lower price. Introducing fighting brands can be an appealing strategy because they help fight off a price-cutting brand that is threatening the firm's core brand while preserving its premium image and profit margins.

> **Fighting brands** are introduced by organizations to fight a competitor's brand that threatens one of their major brands.

Heublein successfully used a fighting-brand strategy to defend its Smirnoff vodka brand. When a smaller rival attacked its Smirnoff vodka, a core brand, by offering its brand at a dollar less than Smirnoff, Heublein increased the price of Smirnoff by one dollar and introduced a new fighting brand at a price below the competitor's brand. This enabled Heublein to fight the intruder without jeopardizing its core brand's profitability and image.

Fighting brands can also take the form of a secret weapon that exists to wreak havoc against competitors. Like other fighting brands, their goal is to defend the premium brand and to prevent competitors from making inroads against it. Companies using fighting brands as secret weapons usually try to maintain their distance from them and conceal their connections to them. For this reason they often use names of defunct companies or companies that they purchase for the sole intent of producing fighting brands. The Strategy in Action box discusses Texsun, a relatively unknown canned juice brand sold in grocery stores, as an example of a fighting brand.[10]

Strategy in Action — TEXSUN CANNED JUICE

Texsun was purchased by Procter & Gamble along with several small brands when it acquired a small juice company named Sundor in 1989. Texsun had some name recognition since it had about a 10 percent share of the market for canned grapefruit juice. Procter & Gamble positioned Texsun Frozen Orange Juice as a direct competitor to generic brands with a low price and not against premium brands such as Citrus Hill, Tropicana, or Minute Maid. However, the real purpose of Texsun was to neutralize the effectiveness of other premium brands' promotional campaigns. Whenever other premium brands were featured in a store's advertising, Procter & Gamble would offer tremendous discounts on Texsun juice as an unadvertised special. As a result, consumers would often buy the heavily discounted Texsun instead of Tropicana or Minute Maid frozen juices at the point of purchase. When Texsun was heavily discounted, the other premium brands would fail to gain significantly against Procter & Gamble. This would allow P&G's Citrus Hill to stay away from price wars and maintain its premium image. Many stores also became increasingly reluctant to feature Tropicana or Minute Maid since promotions did not generate the expected sales volume.

Some risks are associated with fighting brands. There is the risk of cannibalization as the fighting brand may take sales away from other company brands. Also, the cost of producing and marketing the fighting brand may be too high, making it a losing proposition. For example, after British Airways lost about 10 percent of its market share to discount airlines, it launched its own discount carrier, Go, in an attempt to combat EasyJet and other discount carriers. Unfortunately, Go had higher operating costs than the other discount carriers because it recognized union contracts. Three years into its Go experiment, British Airways sold the discount carrier.

Cross-parry

Many companies compete with other companies in more than one market. The degree of multi-market contact between two firms affects the intensity of rivalry and the extent of retaliation among these firms. Competitors interacting in several markets are less motivated to compete aggressively because of the possibility of retaliation across various markets.[11] On the contrary, competitors have an incentive to cooperate since they stand to gain if they allow their rivals to dominate certain markets in exchange for similar treatment in the markets in which they are dominant.

If multi-market contact is low, firms have an incentive to enter the market segment of their rivals to gain the ability to engage in multi-market retaliation, should they come under attack.[12] For this reason, firms prefer to stay in certain markets to maintain the threat of multi-market retaliation. Also, as multi-market contact increases, firms may avoid entering new markets that are already occupied to avoid provoking any multi-market retaliation and to honour any tacit agreements that they have made with their competitors.[13]

Cross-parry is used when a firm that is challenged by a competitor in one area chooses to challenge this competitor in another area. For example, if a company is attacked in one of its core markets or products, instead of retaliating at the point of attack, it counterattacks in the challenger's area of strength. In a sense, the cross-parry strategy says, "If you hurt me, I will hurt you where it hurts most." By attacking the challenger in its core area, the defending firm diverts attention from its own core area and attacks the challenger where it hurts most.

The objective of a cross-parry strategy is often to avoid involving the core brand in a price war. A larger firm stands to lose more than a smaller firm. In addition, such a price war not only leads to lower profit margins but could permanently tarnish a premium brand's image. Cross-parrying may also be used to send a signal to the challenging firm that it will suffer more than the cross-parrying firm.

For instance, how should a company enjoying a large market share and profit margins respond when a competitor lowers its price in an effort to take market share away from the firm with the large market share? The natural response would be to go on the counterattack and attack the challenger with a similar or even greater price reduction. Such a move could be quite costly for the large-share firm since it would mean lower margins on a large volume just to recover the small market share lost to the challenger. If the challenger operates in another market segment that is important to its business but not to its competitor, a smarter move would be to attack the challenger by cutting the price in that segment. Goodyear's response to Michelin's challenge discussed in the Strategy in Action box illustrates the use of cross-parry as a defensive strategy.

> **Cross-parry** is used when a firm that is challenged by a competitor in one area chooses to challenge this competitor in another area.

Strategy in Action

MICHELIN VERSUS GOODYEAR

Several years ago Michelin, using its strong European base, decided to increase its market share of the North American tire market by significantly lowering the price of its tires. Michelin's managers thought that such a price move would attract mostly new customers. They also calculated that Michelin's chief rival, Goodyear, would be unlikely to respond due to the significant cost such a move would imply given Goodyear's dominant market share.

Michelin's calculations were only partly correct, however, because Goodyear didn't match Michelin's lower price. What Michelin failed to anticipate was that Goodyear could respond with a price cut in another market. Goodyear could fight back by reducing prices in North America or offering dealers better margins or increasing advertising spending. Such a strategy would fail because Michelin had only a small part of its worldwide business and it would lose very little by Goodyear's retaliation. Goodyear, on the other hand, stood to lose a lot because it would cut its margins in its largest market.

Goodyear's response was to lower its prices in Michelin's core European markets where Michelin makes large profits. Goodyear's price reduction in Europe caused significant losses and forced Michelin to restore prices to the previous levels in North America after it incurred a significant drop in profits without raising market share appreciably. Goodyear's move slowed the pace of Michelin's expansion and made it rethink the cost of gaining market share in North America.

Offensive Marketing Strategies

As we explained earlier in the chapter, firms engage in offensive marketing strategies to improve their own competitive position by taking market share away from rivals. Offensive strategies include direct and indirect attacks or moving into new markets to avoid powerful competitors. If a firm possesses great resources, a direct attack may be called for. However, if a firm faces superior rivals, indirect attacks are more appropriate than direct, frontal attacks. Direct attacks invite retaliatory responses especially if they pose a serious threat to the defending firm.[14] Indirect attacks are less likely to elicit a competitive response because they are difficult to detect, especially if they are targeted toward non-core segments or products. An extreme form of an indirect attack is to avoid competitors and undertake activities that are far removed from those of rivals.

Firms may choose from a multitude of different strategies to accomplish their offensive objectives. Before we begin discussing these strategies, we need to gain an understanding of the principles of offensive warfare. How a firm exploits these principles can greatly affect the outcome of an offensive strategy.

Principles of Offensive Warfare

Success in offensive marketing depends on many factors, such as resources and capabilities of competing firms, strategies chosen, and implementation. In addition, there are several principles of offensive warfare that have the potential to affect the outcome of aggressive competitive actions.

The superiority of defence. **The superiority of defence** contends that, all other things being equal, the defending force usually wins. This is one of the most enduring principles of warfare. As Clausewitz wrote, "The defensive form of warfare is in itself stronger than the offensive."[15] The superiority of the defensive war is reflected in the generally accepted view that an attacking force needs a superiority of three to one to overcome the advantage of the defending forces. This is equally true in business where existing firms can enjoy a tremendous advantage over new entrants in the form of brand loyalty, lower cost, and switching costs. For this reason, attacking another firm without a decisive competitive advantage or superiority can be disastrous to the challenger.

The superiority of defence contends that, all other things being equal, the defending force usually wins.

Concentration of force. Many firms have been able to overcome their numerical inferiority by using the principle of **concentration of force.** This principle allows even small companies to take on much larger competitors by concentrating on one particular segment of the market that they dominate while their much larger competitors are spreading themselves thinly across many segments or markets.

The element of surprise. Competing offensively requires the element of surprise, which reduces the ability of the opponent to react effectively. The military strategist Liddell Hart calls it **the line of least expectation.**[16] Offensive strategies have a better chance of being successful if they are designed to strike at a place, time, and in a manner not expected by the opponent. Many small firms have been able to grow by operating undetected for long periods of time. Firms involved in new product development or market testing should ensure that competitors are not aware of their product development plans.

The path of least resistance. The principle of the **path of least resistance** calls for attacking a competitor in areas where they are weak and that are difficult to defend.[17] The competitor's weakest point is the critical point of attack, what Clausewitz calls "the enemy's center of gravity."[18] Weak points take the form of high production costs, obsolete or lower quality products, poor service, inferior distribution systems, or narrow product lines. Finding the critical point of attack is not easy. However, concentrating all their resources and attacking competitors at their weakest point may enable even small firms that are seeking expansion but lacking superior resources to successfully challenge larger firms.

Creation of mixed motives for opponent. Creating mixed motives for competitors is a strategy firms use to attack their rivals by creating a situation that makes it very difficult for the rival to retaliate effectively. This principle is especially effective for smaller or newly entered firms that lack the resources to withstand a sustained retaliation by powerful defendants. For example, the Japanese carmakers' attack of U.S. carmakers in the small car segment was effective because the latter were reluctant to defend due to the lower margins they would earn in that segment. As we noted earlier in the chapter, some companies may be reluctant to retaliate by lowering their price for various reasons, including fear of tarnishing their upscale image, because they operate at full capacity, or they are afraid of experiencing lower profit margins.

Offensive Strategies

Like defensive strategies, offensive strategies take many forms, from flanking attacks or bypassing the competition to all-out frontal attacks intended to defeat the competition with all available means at the attacker's disposal (see Figure 14.2).

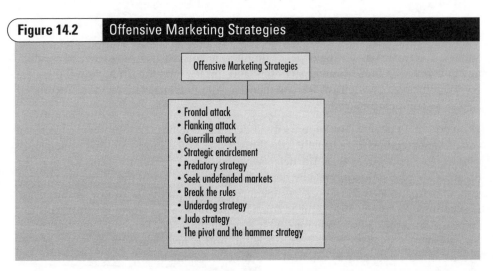

Figure 14.2   Offensive Marketing Strategies

Offensive Marketing Strategies

- Frontal attack
- Flanking attack
- Guerrilla attack
- Strategic encirclement
- Predatory strategy
- Seek undefended markets
- Break the rules
- Underdog strategy
- Judo strategy
- The pivot and the hammer strategy

Concentration of force allows even small companies to take on much larger competitors by concentrating on one particular segment of the market that they dominate while their much larger competitors are spreading themselves thinly across many segments or markets.

The **line of least expectation** calls for striking at a place, time, and in a manner not expected by the opponent.

The **path of least resistance** calls for attacking a competitor in areas where they are weak and that are difficult to defend.

Frontal attack

A **frontal attack** is an offensive strategy that involves attacking a competitor head-on. Frontal attacks can be pure frontal attacks by going after the customers of the attacked firm with similar products, prices, promotion, and distribution. Such attacks are very risky, however, because victory is never assured unless the aggressor has a clear competitive advantage over the defendant. For this reason, a modified frontal attack—a limited version of the pure frontal attack—may be a more appropriate choice. Modified frontal attacks can be price-based where the attacker matches the rival product's features and quality but offers a lower price. Modified frontal attacks may also be value- or quality-based, involving challenging rivals with products that offer greater value or quality at competitive prices. The Strategy in Action box describes Zoom Airlines' attack of Air Canada as an example of a modified frontal attack:

A **frontal attack** is an offensive strategy that involves attacking a competitor head-on.

Strategy in Action

ZOOM AIRLINES

Fledgling low-frills carrier Zoom Airlines, which began offering flights to England and Scotland in the spring of 2004, launched a multi-million-dollar advertising campaign aimed at stealing customers away from Air Canada. Owned by Scottish entrepreneur Hugh Boyle, Zoom began flying from six Canadian cities to Glasgow and London in May 2004 and had stirred up hype for the routes before that. Zoom launched television ads intended to highlight its low prices (one-way flights started at $199).

Zoom planned an annual advertising budget of $1 million to $5 million according to chief executive Kris Dolinski. Zoom's ads emphasize that it's a low-cost alternative to Air Canada. Flying a pair of used Boeing 767s it bought for $15 million apiece, Zoom offers low-frill flights from several Canadian cities—about once a week to Glasgow and London's Gatwick Airport, the city's second-largest airport after Heathrow. Air Canada's advantages included its ability to connect its flights with other airlines, let customers collect and redeem frequent flyer points, offer the use of a network of airport lounges to qualifying passengers, and fly to several cities in the United States. Since Zoom's successful entry into the Canadian airline market, it has increased its flight schedule by offering flights from more Canadian cities to more United Kingdom cities and Paris, France. The company also provides flights to a number of tour operators. Other recent Zoom activities include a partnership with GO Travel Direct, which specializes in direct-sell vacations to southern destinations departing from Halifax, Ottawa, and Montreal, and GG Tours, which serves a number of Caribbean destinations departing from Toronto.

Frontal attacks succeed better when the attacker concentrates its resources on its rivals' centre of gravity or weakest point. Once the centre of gravity is identified, the challenger needs to concentrate its resources, even diverting resources from other activities, at the point of attack. If such a point is not found, the attacker requires at least three times the resources of its rivals to have a better chance of winning the battle. In cases where the defending firm is well entrenched, the attacking firm needs even greater than three-to-one resources. Companies entrenched in their local markets are especially difficult to defeat as they hold the high ground due to years of serving their communities and having developed loyalties with their customers. For example, RCA, GE, Xerox, and Univac tried to frontally attack IBM in the past in its mainframe business and they failed because they lacked any competitive advantages or clear superiority over IBM.

The frontal attack also has a better chance to succeed if the incumbent is constrained in its ability to react to the attack for fear of antitrust prosecution, or for fear that a low price may damage its brand's image. An incumbent may be reluctant to reduce its price or increase advertising and promotion spending because of expectations for return on investment or profit by shareholders or stock market analysts. Incumbents are usually reluctant to retaliate if they operate at full capacity.

As we noted earlier, launching a frontal attack carries many risks and is not suitable for most firms. The most important risk is that if the attacking firm does not possess clearly superior resources it will invite a rigorous retaliation from those being threatened, which could result in substantial losses not only for the attacking firm but for the industry as a whole.

Flanking attack

A **flanking attack** is an offensive marketing strategy used to exploit an opponent's weaknesses while avoiding the risks associated with other offensive marketing strategies such as frontal attacks. Flank attacks are based on the principle of the path of least resistance, attacking competitors in areas that they are least capable of defending. For instance, some segments are not served well by major competitors because they do not see them as important enough to warrant more attention, or they are less profitable than other segments. If competitors offer poor service or inflexible terms to their customers, flanking firms could exploit this opportunity by improving service and offering better terms. If the incumbent's product is too expensive, a flanking firm could offer its product at lower prices. For example, President's Choice Financials, the financial arm of Loblaw Companies, Canada's largest food distributor, is challenging big banks in Canada where they are most vulnerable, their high service charges. By offering low mortgage rates and a variety of insurance and banking services with no service charges, President's Choice's tactics are attractive to those customers who are looking at low rates or despise the higher service charges imposed by the big banks.

Firms using the flanking attack strategy should try to escape detection by established competitors to avoid retaliation. The flanking firm should lie low and avoid showing up on the radar screen of established competitors by concealing its true intentions. It should try to appear as a specialist interested only in its niche and not in its competitors' markets. It should also give the impression that it is in a different line of business. The more different the entrant's product is, the better the chance it has of not being detected. For example, Amazon.com was not perceived by established booksellers as an immediate threat because it looked different from them and they didn't understand what it was trying to do until it was fully established in the bookselling market. Also, successful flank attackers differentiate their products in a way that appears to be in a different category to avoid direct confrontation with established competitors.[19] For example, if incumbents dominate the low end of the market, an entrant might offer a premium version of the product.

A flanking strategy involves a number of risks that may jeopardize the outcome of such a strategy. Competitors being flanked may retaliate by attacking the flanking firm in its niche. The flanking firm needs to assess the odds of such a counterattack and how it could best respond if this happens. Firms successfully pursuing flanking attacks eventually find themselves in direct competition with their larger rivals, making a confrontation inevitable. As explained earlier, this happens because as the flanking firm extends its product lines, it starts to encroach on the market segments occupied by the market leaders.

Guerrilla attack

Guerrilla attacks are used against market leaders by challengers who are small and have limited resources. Guerrilla strategy is less ambitious in scope than other offensive marketing strategies, and it often aims at harassing, demoralizing, and weakening an opponent through random attacks intended to keep it off-balance and continuously guessing about where the next attack will take place. Firms employing the guerrilla attack employ hit-and-run tactics by selectively attacking rivals whenever they can exploit the situation to their advantage.

A **flanking attack** is an offensive marketing strategy used to exploit an opponent's weaknesses while avoiding the risks associated with other offensive marketing strategies such as frontal attacks.

A **guerrilla strategy** often involves many small and surprise attacks on established competitors in areas where the attacked are not strong or entrenched.

A guerrilla strategy often involves many small and surprise attacks on established competitors in areas where the attacked are not strong or buyers have weak loyalty toward the rival's brand. A guerrilla strategy may be manifested in raiding competitors' sources of supplies and attacking specific products or segments with sales promotion initiatives, including coupons, rebates, and temporary price cuts or customer deals in selective geographic areas and then quickly retreating.

Guerrilla marketers often attack competitors in areas where they are overextended and vulnerable with short-duration and random raids using tactics such as lowballing on price to steal their customers. These attacks are carried out quickly and in a limited geographic area in order to have the element of surprise and not allow the leader enough time to react decisively. Leaders very often avoid responding to a guerrilla attack because their large market share would make such a response very costly.

Guerrilla attacks may take the form of legal action. Such legal actions by small firms can effectively slow down the leader and thwart its growth plans. Legal action may also be used by market leaders against upstarts perceived to be a serious threat, to divert their attention from important activities such as product development or entering new markets.

Guerrilla strategies are more appropriate for small firms prior to establishing a significant market position. They are also more successful when they cause a disproportionate drain on the attacked firm's resources by forcing them to spread their resources to deal with the attack or to commit more resources than necessary in certain markets. Companies using guerrilla strategies run the risk of provoking a swift and powerful retaliation that could have devastating consequences for the attacker. For this reason it is important to carefully assess the odds of a competitive retaliation and develop a contingency response plan should such retaliation occur.

Strategic encirclement

Strategic encirclement entails targeting and surrounding a competitor with the purpose of completely defeating it. The objective of encirclement strategies is long-term market dominance. Encirclement strategies are very similar to product proliferation strategies except that the former is an offensive strategy designed to suffocate a rival by not allowing it room to grow, while the latter is a defensive strategy designed to preempt shelf space and not allow rivals to gain entry to the market.

Strategic encirclement entails targeting and surrounding a competitor with the purpose of completely defeating it.

Encirclement essentially involves surrounding a competitor with several brands and forcing it to defend itself on many fronts at the same time. This way, the defender's attention and resources will be spread over many products and markets, making it harder to defend all of them successfully at the same time. Also, by attacking the rival with many products in many markets, the attacker is capable of blocking whichever moves the attacked firm is attempting to make. Strategic encirclement may take three forms: product, market, and distribution encirclement.

Product encirclement. Product encirclement involves encircling the opponent with many versions of the product, matching it in quality, features, and styles. Through product proliferation, the attacker hopes to swamp the opponent and leave very little room for manoeuvring.

Market encirclement. Market encirclement involves entering most market segments by appealing to different buyer needs and tastes. This ensures that there are no vacant niches in the market, making it difficult for the attacked firm to move to another segment in case it gets into trouble in its current segment.

Distribution encirclement. Distribution encirclement involves tying up most viable channels of distribution, making it difficult for the attacked firm to reach the market.

A firm pursuing a strategy of encirclement requires considerable financial resources and a willingness to commit them for extended periods of time. The encircling company also needs strong R&D and product development capabilities, and the power to influence channel intermediaries. It also requires continuous quality improvement, product proliferation, product line stretching and extension, and a large sales force.

Encirclement strategies are usually undertaken against smaller or weaker rivals, since to successfully encircle another company or group of companies the encircling firm requires far greater resources than its opponent. This strategy is often employed by a larger firm against a smaller firm that is perceived as a threat to the larger firm or to the whole industry. In every industry there are instances of certain firms, called **industry destroyers,** who attempt to buy market share through lower prices, hoping to increase prices later. The end result of such action by industry destroyers often is to weaken the industry and lower its profitability.

Encirclement strategies have been used extensively by Honda, which successfully encircled its Japanese rival Yamaha and its U.S. rival Harley-Davidson in the motorcycle industry, almost driving them into bankruptcy. Komatsu, one of the world's largest manufacturers of construction, mining, and utility equipment, had "Encircle Caterpillar" as its slogan for many years and attempted to surround Caterpillar with a variety of products. Encirclement was the strategy that led to the demise of many major U.S. and European industries at the hands of the Japanese, including the semiconductor, steel, and consumer electronics industries in the United States and the auto industry in the United Kingdom.

Predatory strategy

A **predatory strategy** typically entails accepting lower profits for the purpose of keeping new competitors out, or inflicting damage on existing rivals and forcing them to leave the market. This strategy often takes the form of predatory pricing—cutting prices below costs to eliminate a rival, with the expectation that prices will be raised again, after competitors have left the industry. A predator operating in many markets may cut prices selectively in markets with intense competition, and use profits from less competitive markets to finance the price cuts. If successful, low pricing by the predator can induce the rival to leave the market.

In order for predatory pricing to work, the opponent must be financially weak. Otherwise, charging low prices against financially strong competitors could elicit a rigorous response with disastrous results for both companies. It is also important that the predator has some sort of cost advantage through economies of scale, lower overhead, or lower cost of capital, and extra production capacity to accommodate the increased volume of sales. However, it may be difficult to use predatory pricing to eliminate and keep competitors out of an industry forever. Once prices are restored to profitable levels, many companies enter the industry, attracted by the higher profits. Exiting competitors are often purchased by powerful companies that provide the predator with more competition than they previously faced.

Large companies pricing aggressively to drive competition out of business also run the risk of inviting government intervention. Although predatory pricing is illegal, it is extremely difficult to distinguish between anti-competitive pricing behaviour and a genuine pricing strategy based on low margins. For example, low-cost companies may wish to sell at low margins as a signal of low cost, to establish a reputation of toughness, or to establish a critical mass early in the product's life cycle. Price predation in response to a new competitor's entry can be interpreted as a competitive response rather than as an attempt to drive the competitor out of business. Firms often leave the market as a result of increased competition and a reduction in the general level of prices and not necessarily because of predatory behaviour.

Many firms also price aggressively as a signal of low cost. Lowering prices signals that the incumbent's costs are low and the entrant will have difficulty competing in the market. By pricing aggressively, incumbents hope to acquire a reputation of being tough, thereby discouraging competitors from entering in the future.

Industry destroyers are companies that attempt to buy market share through lower prices, resulting in weakening the industry and lowering its profitability.

Predatory strategy entails accepting lower profits for the purpose of keeping new competitors out, or inflicting damage on existing rivals and forcing them to leave the market.

Predatory strategies can take other forms besides predatory pricing. Firms use various exclusionary practices to deter entry by new firms or squeeze existing firms out of the market. One non-price predatory technique is to impose contractual terms on the users of the company's products. For example, Microsoft entered into contractual agreements with computer manufacturers to pay Microsoft per computer sold, not per copy of MS-DOS shipped. Microsoft would be paid a fee regardless of whether the computer shipped had MS-DOS installed or not. Rivals like IBM were effectively kept out of the market for DOS operating systems and Microsoft was able to establish its operating system as the de facto standard in the market for personal computers. Other forms of exclusionary practices include tying or bundling. For example, a customer buying a mainframe from IBM would be forced to buy its software as well.

Some companies may attempt to cut their rivals' lines of supplies. For example, large companies can sometimes affect the availability of supplies for the smaller competitors because the larger companies are given priority by their suppliers. By forming alliances or obtaining contracts with parts manufacturers, suppliers, and distributors, a firm may be able to stifle its competitors by denying them access to markets or materials. If this happens, the smaller firm's survival may be placed at risk. Companies—particularly small ones—with limited purchasing power and market clout that depend on a few key suppliers for vital raw materials are especially vulnerable to such actions.

A firm seeking ways to cut an opponent's line of supply should look at products or businesses that are a major source of revenues or profits for the rival. For example, businesses identified as cash cows can be a rival's vulnerable point. Cash cows are high-share businesses in low-growth markets. Companies earn high margins on these businesses and they use them to support other businesses. Cash cows are vulnerable to challengers offering products of superior value or quality. A successful attack on a competitor's cash cow can cut off the competitor's source of cash and may hamper its efforts to finance new product development or enter new markets.

Seeking undefended markets

Seeking undefended markets entails avoiding head-on confrontations with entrenched rivals that often lead to aggressive price-cutting, advertising wars, or costly efforts to outspend or outdifferentiate their products. Its aim is to bypass competitors altogether and be the first to move into markets that are not currently served by existing suppliers, or to develop radically new technologies to leapfrog the competition, making existing products obsolete and creating new markets.

Seeking undefended markets entails avoiding head-on confrontations with entrenched rivals that often lead to aggressive price-cutting, advertising wars, or costly efforts to outspend or outdifferentiate their products.

Seeking undefended markets is a strategy often undertaken by firms that do not have the resources for successfully competing against industry leaders. It is a strategy also used in highly competitive conditions that make it very difficult to compete effectively. 3M is a company that uses this strategy by continuously looking for new products and withdrawing from markets with crowded competitive conditions. 3M claims that 30 percent of its sales come from products that didn't exist fours years ago. Another company that follows this strategy is Pepsi-Cola, as discussed in the Strategy in Action box.

Strategy in Action

PEPSICO

When Roger Enrico became CEO of PepsiCo, he realized that going head-to-head with Coca-Cola in every market, especially in those markets that Coca-Cola dominates, was a self-defeating strategy. Instead, he concentrated on emerging uncontested markets. Pepsi-Cola shed restaurants, spun off bottling

(continued)

Chapter 14 / Defensive and Offensive Marketing Strategies

operations, and developed a strategy that centred on the supermarket, a battleground where it had triumphed in the past. As a result of the change in focus, soft drinks accounted for a much smaller percentage of Pepsi's market share in 2000. Frito-Lay, a PepsiCo subsidiary, which controls two-fifths of the world market for salty snacks, generated more than 71 percent of PepsiCo's profits in the fourth quarter of 2000. The addition of Tropicana orange juice helped strengthen Pepsi-Cola's position with retailers because of that brand's huge importance. But the move had already proven to be wise—as early as late January 2002, Tropicana, the nation's top-selling orange juice, surpassed Campbell's soup as the third-largest grocery brand, behind Coca-Cola Classic and Pepsi-Cola. During the same period, Pepsi's Aquafina was the number one brand in the fast-growing bottled water category, while PepsiCo's Mountain Dew edged out Diet Coke for third place in the soft drink category.

The strategy of seeking undefended territories is not without risks. First, firms using this strategy need to make sure that they have the skills and resources to successfully develop new products and enter new markets. Second, by entering new product markets, a firm may in fact end up conceding part of its existing business to competitors. By concentrating its efforts on developing the new business, the firm may take its eyes off the ball and allow its competitors to strengthen their position in the firm's core business and then use that strength to attack the bypassing firm.

Breaking the rules

In every industry there are certain assumptions about customers, competitors, and how to be successful in that industry. These assumptions exert an influence over the behaviour of managers without their even realizing it. The more successful a business becomes, the more deeply held these assumptions are until they become widely accepted truths not to be challenged or questioned.

The **break-the-rules strategy** entails breaking the traditional rules of competition in an industry by introducing truly innovative products or unusual and even outrageous programs and actions. Such strategies are often pursued by smaller firms or new entrants that enter an industry without being hamstrung by existing strategies so they are free to pursue strategies that have been rejected by incumbents. Large, established market leaders, on the other hand, are content to play by the same old rules because these rules clearly favour them and not the smaller niche players. Many of today's market leaders, including broadcaster CNN and technology firm Research in Motion, became established by breaking the rules of competition in their industries.

Market leaders have difficulty becoming innovators compared with new entrants or niche players because they suffer from certain pathologies, including complacency or satisfaction with the status quo, fear of destroying existing competencies, cultural inertia, fear of cannibalizing their existing products, and internal politics. For this reason it is very difficult for large, established firms to pursue a different course of action than the current one.

Most market leaders are doing a good job at improving their operations and are having little difficulty competing with firms that play by the same rules. However, as they get better at playing their own game, it becomes more difficult for them to compete against firms that change the rules of the game. For example, IBM had little difficulty competing against GE and RCA in the mainframe computer market, but had a terrible time competing against Digital Equipment Corporation, which had changed the rules of competition by making mini computers, a product very different from mainframes. The advantages of the mini computer—its power, flexibility, and price—made it very difficult for IBM to compete against

The **break-the-rules strategy** entails breaking the traditional rules of competition in an industry by introducing truly innovative products or unusual and even outrageous programs and actions.

the Digital Equipment Corporation. Xerox successfully met the challenges of IBM and Kodak but, as we've discussed in Chapter 2, it had no answer for Canon's flanking attack.

Existing firms frequently find it difficult to exploit new marketing opportunities because of existing relationships with suppliers and distributors, organizational structure, and corporate culture. For instance, despite the existence of the Internet as a potent selling tool, many traditional firms, including computer manufacturers such as Hewlett-Packard and traditional bookstores such as Barnes & Nobles, found it extremely difficult to take advantage of this new technology. Firms such as Amazon.com, however, not being tied to any outside arrangements or organizational culture, fully capitalized on this opportunity and experienced tremendous rates of growth.

Underdog strategy

An **underdog strategy** involves a small and, usually, young firm taking on a much larger competitor. It is, in many respects, similar to the classic battle between David and Goliath. It is often employed by an upstart company that doesn't hesitate to get into a fight with much bigger opponents in order to break their monopoly and offer the market better products, lower prices, or both. The underdog enters a market dominated by established players that are portrayed as being somewhat bureaucratic, complacent, and unresponsive to customer needs. Firms following this strategy promise to offer an attractive alternative to what customers have been buying. The Strategy in Action box portrays Southwest Airlines as an example of a company that successfully used the underdog strategy against its much larger rivals.

The **underdog strategy** involves a small and, usually, young firm taking on a much larger competitor.

Strategy in Action

SOUTHWEST AIRLINES

The early years of Southwest Airlines provide an example of a company that became an underdog in its fight against established competitors, as it offered the travelling public highly attractive prices and superior value. Southwest was ready to begin operations in 1967 but could not do so until 1971 due to fighting time-consuming court battles initiated by Braniff and Texas International Airlines, two established competitors that are no longer in business. These two competitors, in an attempt to keep Southwest out of their market, argued in court that there was not enough demand to support three airlines in the Texas interstate market. Southwest won the case. After Southwest began operations, these same competitors initiated a price war against Southwest, causing airfares to plummet to record-low levels. Southwest managed to survive these competitive wars and it acquired the image of a gutsy fighter and an underdog in the eyes of the public and its own employees.[20]

The Virgin Group is a company that has also used the underdog strategy very successfully by creating the perception of being an underdog willing to attack the establishment, always doing a good job, and having high product and service standards. Virgin is a company that enters industries dominated by large firms such as British Airways, Bell Canada, and Levi Strauss. Virgin's strategy is to be perceived as the underdog who fights for the consumer with good quality, excellent value, and friendliness. An event that helped solidify this perception occurred when British Airlines made an effort to prevent Virgin Airlines from gaining access to certain routes. In response, Virgin portrayed British Airways as a bully standing in the way of a young company that promised to offer better value and service. With this stance, Virgin positioned itself as a friend of the little guy.

Judo strategy

Judo strategy is an offensive marketing strategy suitable for small companies willing to take on larger opponents.

Judo strategy is an offensive marketing strategy suitable for small companies willing to take on larger opponents. It is similar to the martial art of judo, in which the smaller opponent uses the weight and strength of the larger opponent to its advantage. Judo strategy combines elements of other offensive strategies. The principles of a successful judo strategy are to attack weakness with strength, be flexible, and use leveraging.[21]

1. *Attack weakness with strength.* The principle of attacking weakness with strength calls for avoiding frontal attacks and attacking the competitor in markets where the challenger has an advantage, where the competitor is ill prepared to fight, or where it is most uncomfortable about defending. For example, WestJet attacked Air Canada in western Canada with low fares using a low-cost operating structure based on short-haul flights and minimum in-flight service. Air Canada had difficulty defending itself against WestJet because of its higher cost structure and as a result it experienced market share losses.

2. *Be flexible.* The principle of flexibility requires yielding when attacked by a superior competitor to avoid being crushed. Firms should never fight a war that cannot be won and should know when to engage in a tactical retreat when it is up against dominant rivals. For example, a hardware store in an area where Home Depot has recently entered should not declare a price war on Home Depot but it should adapt its business and strategy to the new reality and make the necessary adjustments in the merchandise carried by the store in order not to compete directly with the market leader.

   A tactical retreat may also involve embracing and extending an opponent's successful moves. Sam Walton, the founder of Wal-Mart, used this tactic by visiting rival stores such as Kmart and copying their best ideas. Microsoft used the same method when it attacked Netscape Navigator by accepting the main features of the opponent's product and improving on them, offering CD-quality sound and the ability to use the browser with Microsoft Word.

3. *Use leveraging.* The principle of leverage is about finding ways to turn the strength and strategy of an opponent against him. The judo strategist must find the factors that make it hard for the larger competitor to react and use them as leverage to launch his attack. A company can implement the principle of leverage by looking for the opponent's strategic commitments and investments and turn them to its advantage by creating a situation in which it would be very difficult for the larger firm to retaliate effectively. Many companies find it difficult to react to new entrants and reposition themselves because of their established image. Attacking a premium-priced brand with a lower-priced brand may not elicit a response, because lowering the price may harm the image of the premium-priced brand. Also, commitments to distributors may prevent a company from adopting a different distribution system. As we discussed in an earlier chapter, Hewlett-Packard found it extremely difficult to imitate Dell's Internet business model for fear of alienating their existing dealers. This allowed Dell to gain market share at the expense of these two companies.

Having a large market share may in fact be a handicap to a company. Larger competitors frequently avoid retaliating against smaller price-cutting firms for fear of incurring significant losses due to their much larger market shares. For example, Maxwell House had difficulty matching Folgers Coffee's price cuts because of the former's large market share and the enormous impact on margins and profitability. Large firms may also avoid attacking a smaller firm if the smaller firm enters a segment where margins are low. In addition, large firms avoid retaliating against smaller firms when they operate with high capacity utilization.

A small firm can also use the principle of leverage to challenge larger competitors by turning the large companies' marketing strategy to its favour. Drypers, a disposable diaper maker, was able to neutralize Procter & Gamble's aggressive couponing campaign. Specifically, Drypers issued "converter coupons" that holders of P&G's Pampers coupons could use to receive $2 off on a bag of Drypers. This helped neutralize a large number of P&G's coupons and it reduced the overall effectiveness of the P&G campaign. Another advantage of this strategy for Drypers was that retailers, mistakenly, sent the Pampers coupons to P&G for redemption instead of to Drypers.

The pivot and the hammer strategy

The **pivot and the hammer strategy** combines defensive and offensive strategies; it is associated with Evan Dudik, a business strategist.[22] According to Dudik, every business strategy should have a pivot and a hammer. The **pivot** represents a firm's efforts to hold its market position, defend itself against competitors, and retain customers. The pivot includes distinctive competencies—such as a strong brand name, low cost, or superior innovation skills—to defend its position. For example, a firm such as Canadian Tire may use its well-recognized name to fend off any attacks and protect its current position, or to retain customers and maintain its share of the market. Other firms may rely on their most profitable products as cash cows to finance any expansion opportunities.

Each pivot contains one or more bearings. A **bearing** can be certain key competencies, assets, skills, or people that the company relies on to perform its defensive action. A bearing could be a highly skilled employee, a very effective purchasing manager, or a very specialized asset. For example, Microsoft's pivot may be its Windows operating system and its bearing is, arguably, Bill Gates, as it is very questionable that Microsoft would be where it is today without the hard-driven and motivated Gates.

The **hammer** is the central offensive force of the company and the cutting edge of the attack. It is where the company concentrates its offensive forces and pushes to exploit its advantages. It is where the company tries to attract new customers, attacks competitors for capturing their customers, or pushes for expansion into new markets. While the pivot is trying to maintain the current market position and defend against competitor attacks, the hammer is where the firm tries to grow and expand its sales and market share. Without a hammer, a company is, in effect, pursuing a harvest strategy, which will inevitably cause the firm to decline. A firm needs a pivot to survive, but it needs a hammer to grow and win new business. The success of the hammer depends on the effectiveness of the pivot. If the pivot is doing a good job in defending the firm's current business and profitability, more resources can be channelled into the hammer to enable it to do its job.

Like the bearing of the pivot, the hammer has a **hammerhead,** where the power of the hammer is concentrated. It is the strongest part of the hammer, and it carries the entire force of the company's offensive effort. Hammerheads can be the firm's sales force, advertising prowess, financial resources, or whatever is used to accomplish the objectives of the offensive drive of the firm.

A very important consideration is that a firm using its existing assets, brand names, business functions, or business units to support its expansion activities must ensure that these expansion activities are not undertaken at the expense of existing assets. For instance, introducing a new brand using the name of a well-known existing brand should not tarnish the image of the existing brand. If a firm uses the cash flow from an existing business unit to finance the growth of a new brand, the existing business unit should receive enough investment support to maintain its viability.

The **pivot and the hammer strategy** combines defensive and offensive strategies.

The **pivot** represents a firm's efforts to hold its market position, defend itself against competitors, and retain customers.

A **bearing** can be certain key competencies, assets, skills, or people that the company relies on to perform its defensive action.

The **hammer** is the central offensive force of the company and the cutting edge of the attack.

A **hammerhead** is where the power of the hammer is concentrated.

- Firms are constantly engaged in offensive and defensive marketing strategies. Established firms continuously face attacks by new entrants and incumbents trying to reposition themselves or improve their competitive position. Defensive strategies work better if they take place before the challenger commits to the industry by making investments or other types of commitments, or before exit barriers are raised, making it difficult for a challenger to leave the industry.

- It is easier to defend a position because it requires fewer resources than offensive strategies. Incumbents enjoy several advantages relative to new entrants, including economies of scale, capital requirements, switching costs, brand loyalties, and brand recognition. Attacking firms need three times more resources than defending firms for launching a successful attack. In some circumstances, the resource requirements can be higher, if the incumbent is deeply entrenched in its market.

- The probability and extent of competitive retaliation depends on the extent to which a firm perceives competitors as a threat to its market position and profitability, the amount of resources at the disposal of the incumbent, and the incumbent's willingness to respond.

- Pre-entry defensive strategies include signalling, fortifying and defending, covering all bases, continuously improving, and expanding capacity. Post-entry defensive strategies include defending the position before an entrant becomes entrenched, introducing fighting brands, and using the tactic of cross-parrying.

- Markets are dynamic arenas in which firms try to expand into their industries or position themselves in other segments within their industry. Firms need to engage in offensive strategies to accomplish their growth objectives.

- There are five principles managers must be familiar with to enhance the chances of a successful offensive marketing strategy: the principle of superiority of defence, the principle of concentration of force, the principle of surprise, the principle of the path of least resistance, and the principle of creating mixed motives for competitors.

- Offensive marketing strategies include frontal attacks, flanking attacks, guerrilla attacks, strategic encirclement, predatory strategy, seeking undefended markets, break-the-rules strategy, underdog strategy, judo strategy, and the pivot and hammer strategy.

Review and Discussion Questions

1. Discuss the various pre-entry defensive strategies.

2. Discuss the various post-entry defensive strategies.

3. Discuss the factors that determine whether an established firm will respond to an attack by a rival.

4. Why do attacking firms need far superior resources to overcome the resistance of entrenched competitors?

5. Describe the various principles of offensive warfare.

6. Why would a firm pursue a flanking attack instead of a frontal or an encirclement attack?

7. Discuss the logic of the seek-undefended-markets strategy. Why would a firm adopt this strategy instead of a frontal attack or an encirclement attack?

8. Why would a firm adopt an underdog strategy? What are the differences between an underdog strategy and a guerrilla attack?

9. What are the differences between the judo strategy and the flank attack strategy?

10. What are the elements of the pivot and hammer strategy? What is the role of the pivot, the hammer, the bearing, and the hammerhead?

1. Despite their limited resources, most premium beer manufacturers are able to successfully survive side-by-side with their much larger competitors. Explain how the principle of concentration of forces can help a small firm overcome its inferior resource disadvantage and compete on equal or even better terms with a larger firm.

2. Molson Coors is one of Canada's largest beer manufacturers. Molson Coors has come under attack by low-cost competitors who have stolen market share from its flagship brands. Molson Coors' CEO Dan O'Neil has acknowledged this problem and stated that his company would fight back against the challengers in an effort to regain its market share. Your task is to help Molson Coors develop strategies to defend and regain its market share.

3. In the summer of 2004, Sony announced the launch of a Walkman digital player dubbed the Network Walkman NW-HD1. Sony said its new digital music player would take direct aim at Apple's market-leading iPod brand. The 20-gigabyte device would sell at $400 and store 13,000 songs compared with iPod, which was sold at $499 and stored 10,000 songs. Sony claimed the battery of NW-HD1 would last 30 hours, at least three times longer than iPod's. How would you characterize Sony's offensive strategy? Using appropriate pre- and post-entry strategies, outline several actions that Apple could take to defend its iPod brand.

Notes

1. Allan Swift, "Tango Puts Spark into Air Canada," *Financial Post*, October, 28, 2002, FP3.
2. Ian Portsmouth (ed.), *Marketing Masters* (New York: Wiley, 1998), pp. 53–54.
3. Michael E. Porter, *Competitive Strategy* (New York: The Free Press, 1980), 88.
4. F. M. Scherer, *Industrial Market Structure and Economic Performance* (Chicago: Rand McNally, 1980), 244.
5. Michael Porter, *Competitive Advantage* (New York: Free Press, 1985), 483–498.
6. Steven P. Schnaars, *Managing Imitation Strategies: How Late Entrants Seize Markets from Pioneers* (New York: The Free Press, 1994), 87–92.
7. Luis M.B. Cabral, *Introduction to Industrial Organization* (Cambridge: The MIT Press, 2000), 261.
8. Constantinos C. Markides, *All the Right Moves: A Guide to Crafting Breakthrough Strategy* (Boston, Mass.: Harvard Business School Press, 2000), 13.
9. Adam M. Brandenburger and Barry J. Nalebuff, *Co-opetition* (Boston: Harvard Business School Press, 1996), 73–74.
10. Eric Schulz, *The Marketing Game* (Holbrook, Mass.: Adams Media Corporation, 1999), 98–99.
11. D. Edwards, "Conglomerate Bigness as a Source of Power," in *Business Concentration and Price Policy*, The National Bureau of Economics Research Conference Report (Princeton: Princeton University Press, 1955), 331–352.
12. A. Karnani and B. Wernerfelt, "Multiple Point Competition," *Strategic Management Journal* 6 (1985), 87–96.
13. Joel A.C. Baum and Helaine J. Korn, "Competitive Dynamics of Interfirm Rivalry," *Academy of Management Journal* 39, No. 2, 1996, 255–291.
14. Michael E. Porter, *Competitive Advantage* (New York: The Free Press, 1985), 514.
15. Carl von Clausewitz, *On War*, edited and with an introduction by Anatol Rapoport. This edition is based on the J.J. Graham translation (Harmondsworth: Penguin, 1968).
16. B.H. Liddell Hart, *Strategy*, 2nd ed. (New York: Meridian, 1991).
17. Daniel F. Spulber, *The Market Makers* (New York: McGraw-Hill, 1998), 252.
18. von Clausewitz.
19. Spulber, 253.
20. *Southwest Airlines: 1993 (A)* (Boston, MA: Harvard Business School Publishing, 1993).
21. David B. Yoffie and Mary Kwak, *Judo Strategy* (Boston, Mass.: Harvard Business School Press, 2001), 10.
22. Evan M. Dudik, *Strategic Renaissance* (New York: Amacom, 2000), 36.

Chapter Fifteen

Marketing Implementation and Control

The strategic plan is a beautiful twelve-meter America's Cup hull; the implementation plan is the sails and the crew. One doesn't get very far without the other.

C. Davis Fogg, Implementing Your Strategic Plan

Learning Objectives

After studying this chapter, you should be able to:

1. Describe the relationship between marketing strategy and implementation

2. Assess the effectiveness of marketing strategies and understand the common problems of strategic marketing planning

3. Explain the different implementation levels and the requirements for successful implementation

4. Describe the concept of fit and its relationship to implementation and organizational change

5. Discuss David Nadler's Congruence Model

6. Explain the role of control in marketing implementation and the importance of the balanced scorecard framework

Dell's Superior Execution Is Key to Its Success

In 1984, Michael Dell, working from his University of Texas dorm room, started Dell Computer (it was initially registered as PC's Limited) with $1,000 in seed money. Today, Dell is the largest personal computer manufacturer in the world. Dell views its mission as providing computing technology in a much more efficient way than other computer companies.

Dell's success is the result of a strategy that is based on direct sales, building to order, keeping a close eye on costs, and first-class execution at every stage in its manufacturing system. When Dell began operations, all the major computer manufacturers, including IBM, Compaq, and Apple, were building computers and selling them through computer interme- diaries, who then sold them to individual consumers and businesses. Dell, on the other hand, sought to answer the question: How can one make the process of buying a computer better? The answer was to sell computers directly to the end customers, eliminate the dealer's markup, and pass the savings on to the customer.

Building to order entails producing a personal computer to specifications after the customer's order is placed and transmitted to the factory. Parts suppliers receive the order information at the time Dell receives the customer order via electronic links that connect Dell with its suppliers. Suppliers then deliver the components to Dell and production starts immediately.

Allowing consumers to order by telephone and the Internet and receive personal computers directly from the manufacturer has certain benefits. This interaction results in obtaining a real-time input from customers about their product needs. It also enables the company to build products that customers want. So instead of guessing which product configuration customers want, Dell listens to consumers and builds the computer to the exact customer specifications. Another benefit is that it helps build a direct relationship between the company and its customers.

Dell's model also allows it to minimize inventory levels because it manufactures only what customers order so it doesn't have to carry a lot of inventory. By minimizing inventory, Dell eliminates problems such as obsolescence, pilferage, and tying up capital. Holding large amounts of unsold inventory is especially costly in industries in which the value of inventory declines rapidly.

Lower levels of inventory help improve inventory turnover—the ratio of net sales to inventory. A higher inventory turnover reduces working capital, improves cash flow and profit margins, reduces costs, and helps achieve a higher return on investment. Dell turns its inventory more than 80 times a year while its competitors achieve an inventory turnover ratio of under 20.

Dell's direct model can be seen in action in the Topfer Manufacturing Center, located a few miles south of its headquarters in Round Rock, Texas. This plant is the newest of seven Dell plants worldwide and is larger than five and a half football fields. The average time it takes to produce a computer in this plant is three to five minutes for a total of more than 25,000 systems a day.

What is remarkable about the Topfer manufacturing plant is that it rarely needs more than two hours' worth of inventory, equivalent to the storage space of a regular bedroom. This makes Dell, by far, the most efficient computer manufacturer in the world. Operating costs were 10 percent of Dell's $35-billion revenue in 2002. By comparison, Hewlett- Packard's and Gateway's operating costs were 21 percent and 25 percent of revenues respectively. Dell spends 1.3 percent of its revenues in research and development, compared

(continued)

with 15 percent at Intel and Microsoft. Given the low amount spent on research and development, it is no surprise that Dell owns very little proprietary technology.

Dell's highly efficient system allows it to keep prices low and continue gaining market share from its competitors. The strength of Dell's model was evident in 2001 when the PC industry slipped into its worst slump in its history. During this time, while its competitors were losing hundred of millions of dollars, Dell's revenues increased by 14 percent.

The direct business model is today recognized as an effective way of doing business. Dell's main competitors, Hewlett-Packard and IBM, have also implemented direct sales models similar to Dell's. The performance of these companies so far shows they are far from mastering a system that Dell has perfected over the years. Hewlett-Packard's acquisition of Compaq did little to prevent Dell from making additional market share gains. Further, Dell is trying to replicate its success in the PC industry in other markets, such as servers and storage systems. The outcome of these moves will prove whether Dell's direct model is applicable to markets other than the PC market.[1]

Introduction

An effective marketing plan includes the firm's marketing strategy and the performance objectives to be met. But the existence of a marketing plan does not guarantee that the marketing objectives will be achieved. Good marketing strategies often fail because of poor implementation. **Marketing implementation** is the part of strategic market planning where the chosen marketing strategy is put into practice through specific actions taken by management. It provides the link between the strategy and results.[2] Implementation involves linking strategy to operations, assigning responsibility, linking rewards to outcomes, creating a mechanism for making adjustments to the strategy as the environment changes, and upgrading the company's capabilities to meet the requirements of the strategy. Dell's success, as we have seen in the opening vignette, owes its success, largely, to its superior implementation.

Organizations need a culture of execution in which things get done and people meet their commitments. Some companies emphasize the creation of a high-level strategy and a process of intellectualizing and philosophizing about the strategy but do not pay enough attention to implementation.[3] Also, in organizations that fail to execute, the strategic plan sometimes is full of numbers but little attention is paid to the action plan. Effective implementation requires that marketing plans have specific action plans and programs to deliver the desired outcomes.

Implementation needs an appropriate marketing strategy as implementing an incorrect marketing strategy will lead to failure. In addition, the marketing strategy must be flexible enough to allow a company to make adjustments when there are unexpected changes in its environment.[4] Execution-oriented companies go through organizational changes faster than other companies because they are closer to the market and are more familiar with the real situation.

Companies that excel at implementation always try to spot problems early and fix them quickly before they grow into enormous dimensions. For example, companies with a high-growth strategy need to upgrade their infrastructure to support the high growth. As a company grows at high rates, it outgrows its existing system—factory system, capacity, accounting system, inventory system, support system, telephone system, or pool of employees with the experience to run a larger company. Firms need to build the infrastructure as they grow to accommodate the additional demands growth places on their capacity and systems instead of allowing them to reach a point where demands are impossible to meet, causing a crisis.

Everyone must understand the strategy and be committed to its implementation. For this reason, the people involved in implementing the plan should also be involved in shaping the plan. The right people must be in charge of the implementation task. In addition, implementation requires accountability for results, rewarding the best performers, and following through.

Implementation often fails because the organization lacks the resources and capabilities needed to implement the strategy.[5] Some managers fail to understand reality and they get ahead of their firm's capacity to execute. When top managers plan their strategy, they must take into account the organization's ability to implement it. This can be best achieved if the implementation plan is an integral part of the strategic planning process and steps are taken to ensure that the plan is implementable.

This chapter examines the relationship between marketing strategies and implementation. First, it looks at the Marketing Strategy–Implementation Matrix and its implications for implementation. Given the importance of implementing the correct marketing strategy, we discuss a number of criteria that firms could use to evaluate their marketing strategies prior to implementation. Subsequently, common strategic planning problems, the different implementation levels, the requirements for successful

> **Marketing implementation** is the part of strategic market planning where the chosen marketing strategy is put into practice through specific actions taken by management.

implementation, and the reasons that change programs fail are discussed. The concept of fit and its role in implementation and organizational change are also covered. Finally, the role and importance of control in implementation is examined with a view toward making the task of monitoring implementation more effective.

Marketing Strategy and Implementation

Successful firms need an effective strategy. Having an effective strategy means occupying a unique and viable position in the marketplace.[6] Failure to occupy a unique and viable position may lead to poor performance if there is not enough business to sustain the firm or because of tough competitive conditions. In addition to a successful strategy, firms need an effective implementation that entails taking appropriate actions to put the marketing strategy in place.

The relationship between marketing strategy and implementation is an iterative one. Marketing strategy affects implementation but implementation also affects the marketing strategy. Marketing strategy affects implementation because different marketing strategies require different implementation. For example, a company that introduces a low-cost, low-price new product will require a different implementation from a company that introduces a high-quality, high-price product. Implementation affects the marketing strategy because, by implementing the marketing strategy, managers learn what works and what doesn't work and they can revise the marketing strategy to make it more in line with market realities.

Marketing managers also need to know that marketing success requires a superior marketing strategy and a superior implementation. Having a superior marketing strategy but inferior implementation or having a superior implementation but a poor marketing strategy is not enough to win the marketing war. All the effort and resources that went into the formulation and implementation of the marketing strategy will be wasted unless the marketing plan is properly implemented.

Some managers believe that what is needed is a good strategy, and implementation will take care of itself. This can be a serious mistake as even the most brilliant marketing strategy will fail if care is not taken to properly implement it. In fact, in cases in which a firm is fighting a competitor who has equal capabilities, superior implementation may be the only factor that differentiates one firm from another. The example of Dell discussed in the opening vignette illustrates the benefits of successful implementation.

The quality of a firm's marketing strategy and implementation may be combined into the Marketing Strategy–Implementation Matrix that is shown in Figure 15.1. The four quadrants of this matrix are discussed below:

1. *Effective marketing strategy—Superior implementation.* Firms that have a solid and properly implemented marketing strategy are in the best possible position to achieve market success and meet their objectives. Firms in this quadrant should spend the resources required to maintain the quality of their marketing strategy and its implementation.
2. *Ineffective marketing strategy—Superior implementation.* If the implementation is excellent but the marketing strategy is incorrect, it will hasten failure as the firm is trying to implement an inappropriate strategy. For instance, investing resources in products that customers do not want can spell trouble for any company. This happened to Motorola, which wasted a lot of resources improving its analogue cellular telephone when its competitors were developing cellular telephones using the much better digital technology. Motorola suffered serious problems as a result of its misplaced strategy.
3. *Effective marketing strategy—Inferior implementation.* An appropriate marketing strategy with an inferior execution leads to disappointing results as a poor execution

Figure 15.1	The Marketing Strategy-Implementation Matrix

		Marketing Strategy	
		Effective	Ineffective
Implementation	Superior	1. Best position — keep up the good work	2. Quickest way to fail — change strategy
	Inferior	3. Keep strategy, but improve execution	4. High likelihood of failure

SOURCE: From Thomas V. Bonoma, *Managing Marketing* (New York: The Free Press, 1984), 13. Adapted with the permission of The Free Press, a Division of Simon and Schuster Adult Publishing Group, from *Managing Marketing* by Thomas V. Bonoma. Copyright © 1984 by The Free Press. All rights reserved.

hampers a good strategy. Companies often have difficulty tracing the problem to implementation, and they frequently assume that the problem is due to poor strategy and then compound the problem by tinkering with a good strategy.

4. *Ineffective marketing strategy—Inferior implementation.* When both marketing strategy and implementation are poor, failure is the most likely result. It is very important to trace the problem to the incorrect marketing strategy. Firms often attribute the poor performance to implementation, and they make things worse by trying to come up with a better way to implement a poor strategy.

What Is an Effective Marketing Strategy?

Once a marketing strategy is created, it needs to be implemented. However, as we discussed in the previous section, not all strategies are equally effective; some marketing strategies are more effective than others. For this reason, before a marketing strategy is implemented, it must be assessed to ensure that the correct strategy is used. Marketing managers can use the following criteria to assess the effectiveness of their marketing strategy:

- *Feasibility.* Is the marketing strategy feasible? Are the required resources and capabilities (such as financial resources, technological know-how, strong distribution system for access to the market, servicing capabilities, sales force coverage, and an adequate advertising effort to implement the strategy) all available?
- *Internal consistency.* The various elements of the marketing strategy must fit together well. For example, a growth strategy is normally inconsistent with a reduction in advertising spending and sales force size; a strategy of high product quality is not compatible with a low pricing policy.
- *Sustainable competitive advantage.* Will the marketing strategy help gain a sustainable competitive advantage? Positions of leadership do not last forever so market leaders need to continuously search for new sources of advantage to maintain their market position.
- *How it deals with strengths, weaknesses, opportunities, and threats.* Does the marketing strategy help exploit opportunities, neutralize threats, build on strengths or help create new strengths and avoid their weaknesses? A proper analysis of the external

Chapter 15 / Marketing Implementation and Control

and internal environmental factors and a classification into strengths, weaknesses, opportunities, and threats can greatly help a firm accomplish this objective.

- *Degree of difficulty for competitors to respond and match or offset the competitive advantages.* Marketing strategies should make it as difficult as possible for competitors to respond and neutralize the strategy by exploiting competitors' complacency, short-term focus, inability, or unwillingness to react.
- *Lower risks.* What are the risks of the marketing strategy? A strategy that involves lower risks is superior to other strategies, everything else being equal. For example, diversifying into a new market with a new product poses greater risks than introducing a line extension into an existing market. Risks include the market not accepting the product, competitor retaliation, failing to build the necessary product technology, or not finding the resources and capabilities needed to implement the marketing strategy.

Common Strategic Marketing Planning Problems

Developing effective marketing strategies hinges on a proper use of a firm's strategic marketing planning. However, many firms are ineffective in their strategic marketing planning efforts. These firms fail to properly monitor their environment and respond to emerging trends and developments. As a result, they do not capitalize on opportunities or react to threats on a timely basis and are often overwhelmed by changes that are realized too late to allow time for proper action to be taken. Such failure also makes firms vulnerable to nimble competitors who quickly capitalize on these opportunities.

Ineffective strategic marketing planning occurs because any of a number of problems exist, and these problems prevent organizations from thoroughly scanning their environment or considering all alternatives in their strategy formulation process. The most common problems in strategic marketing planning are discussed next.

Complacency

All too often, successful firms acquire an internal focus. As a result of their achievements, they begin to treat competitors as irrelevant. Managers of these companies become overconfident and often exhibit signs of arrogance, which leads to complacency. As a result of winning the competitive battle in the past, they come to believe that they are superior to competitors and tend to ignore them. Complacency can lead to decreased market focus, and it may cause companies to fail to track changes in the external environment with respect to both competitive actions and customers' preferences. Over time, there is a danger that the firm will miss important external trends that seriously affect the organization. For example, the success of its instant camera made Polaroid oblivious to technological changes that were occurring in the photography industry. As a result of its complacency and internal focus, Polaroid failed to respond to customers' demands for digital cameras and the company eventually declared bankruptcy as its business suffered.

Conservatism

For many successful companies, the longer they are successful the more they become risk averse. Reluctance to take risks and try new things or learn from successes or failures sets in. Failure becomes unacceptable. As a result, many people in these organizations stop experimenting with risky new ideas and merely implement minor modifications of existing products. Maintaining the status quo becomes the ultimate objective, as there is little incentive to deviate from the tried and true. Large firms commonly pursue opportunities that are mostly extensions of current initiatives and are reluctant to pursue truly new opportunities and to create new markets.[7]

Incomplete Analysis

The result of the strategic planning process should be a clear, consistent course of action and a marketing plan. The foundation of a strong marketing plan is a detailed analysis of the internal situation and the external environment. Frequently, feeling pressure to take quick action to address new environmental developments, firms may prematurely move to the stage of generating strategies before fully understanding the complex nature of the changing environment. Firms sometimes fail to adequately consider competitors' and customers' responses to their actions. For example, a decision to cut prices may have the intended effect of increasing sales volume if there were to be no competitive response. However, competitors are not likely to sit idly by and watch another firm steal their market share. Rather, they will attempt to counteract the actions of the firm.

An effective marketing plan is one that not only generates strategies to be employed, but also outlines the anticipated customer and competitive response and necessary future actions. Moving too hastily from the analysis stage of planning to the generation of strategies may result in an inadequate account of all important environmental factors and customers' and competitors' responses. This can, in turn, lead to an ineffective or flawed marketing plan.

Prior Hypothesis

A common problem for marketers engaging in the planning process is that, even before beginning the planning process, they have already formulated strategies for the firm to pursue. Consequently, the focus during the planning process becomes a search for evidence to validate their ideas. This is particularly troublesome during the analysis stage. Factors that point to inherent dangers in the proposed strategy are readily dismissed. As a result, the marketing plan fails to adequately account for internal weaknesses or external threats that may negatively affect the desired result of the strategies. While admittedly difficult to do, postponing the generation of strategies until the marketers have developed a clear picture of the present and future situation is the best course.

Escalating Commitment

One of the toughest choices facing a marketer is the decision to discontinue the pursuit of a previous strategy. Often, considerable resources and time have been invested in the strategy. Thus, deciding to abandon that particular course of action might be viewed as a waste of the resources previously invested. As more and more resources are dedicated to a particular project, the firm becomes increasingly committed to seeing it succeed. It may, however, be more advantageous for the firm to cut its losses and abandon the initiative. This can be especially difficult for marketers who have become personally committed to the project as a result of their investment of time and energy. Firms must focus on the expected future returns of strategic alternatives, rather than past investments, when undertaking the strategic marketing planning process.

Cannibalization

Incumbent firms have less of an incentive to innovate if the gain from the innovation is reduced by the cannibalization that may occur if the new product takes sales away from the existing products.[8] Thus, if the potential for cannibalization is high, the incumbent's incentive to innovate is low. Also, the higher the profit from the existing business, the lower the incumbent's incentive to innovate. For example, a telephone company that sells high-end telephones at $90, a price at which it earns a large profit margin, would be reluctant to aggressively compete in the $30 telephone segment in which it would earn a much lower profit margin.

This cannibalization effect could be used by a competitor to his or her advantage and launch a direct attack on a profitable incumbent as the latter firm will be reluctant to respond to the entrant's attack.[9] Examples of the cannibalization problem abound. According to Lou Gestner Jr., former chairman of IBM, one of the reasons for IBM's decline in the early 1990s was its reluctance to bring its scientific discoveries and new technologies into the marketplace and commercialize them. IBM invented the relational database, network hardware, network software, and UNIX processors among others. Oracle, Sun, Seagate, and Sipco, however, have exploited these discoveries more successfully. The reason for IBM's inability to capitalize on its discoveries and technologies was the fear of cannibalizing existing IBM products.[10]

Complexity

Frequently, the success of an organization in its early stages can be traced, in part, to the informal systems and structures it employs. As the company grows larger, it may attempt to adopt these systems and structures in a more formalized manner. Consequently, inflexible policies and procedures are developed. As companies begin to codify and formalize many of their policies and procedures, they become increasingly complex and, in many cases, excessively bureaucratic. Increased complexity necessitates even more formalized procedures for handling regular business operations. For example, at IBM, the useful practice of using overhead slides during presentations, which began on an informal basis, eventually turned into a formal procedure with presenters spending an excessive amount of time arguing about the right way of using the slides instead of spending their time on issues of more substance.[11]

Implementation Levels

A marketing strategy that is judged to be appropriate on the basis of the qualitative criteria discussed in the previous section is ready to be implemented. Implementation is a complex marketing activity that can be described in four levels: actions, programs, systems, and policies.[12]

Actions involve low-level activities that take place in the various marketing subfunctions, such as marketing research, sales promotions, personal selling, channel-related activities, product development, developing promotional materials, and price-setting. A firm needs to develop excellent skills in these subfunctions. In fact, firms that do not develop these skills but instead farm them out to outside suppliers often run into difficulty: if their relationship with these outside contractors turns sour, the firm itself has not developed these skills to the level necessary to compete effectively.

The **program** level involves bringing together various marketing actions such as product development, branding, pricing, advertising, and marketing research. Examples of programs include new product development, relationship marketing, and account management programs. New product development programs require collaboration between several functions such as design, engineering, and manufacturing. Relationship marketing programs include various functions such as marketing, manufacturing, accounting, and design. Account management programs often involve input from engineering, sales, and finance.

Systems are designed to organize, allocate skills, and monitor the many tasks required for marketing implementation. They include financial, budgeting, and accounting systems; human resource practices such as performance evaluation and reward systems; and systems designed for intelligence gathering. Many firms suffer from inadequacies in these areas, and existing systems, if they are not capable of handling the implementation task, frequently negatively affect the marketing effort. For example, as organizations grow, many of its systems such as accounting and inventory are not capable of handling the increased volume—such shortcomings may even cause the company to fail.

Actions involve low-level activities that take place in the various marketing subfunctions, such as marketing research, sales promotions, personal selling, channel-related activities, product development, developing promotional materials, and price-setting.

The **program** level involves bringing together various marketing actions such as product development, branding, pricing, advertising, and marketing research.

Systems are designed to organize, allocate skills, and monitor the many tasks required for marketing implementation.

Policies are guidelines shaping management actions in areas such as recruiting, hiring, compensation, promotion, purchasing, and pricing. These marketing policies may aid or hamper the proper implementation of the marketing strategy if they are not consistent with the implementation requirements. For example, the implementation of a new product development program may require hiring specialized personnel. However, compensation policies may prevent the company from spending the amount required to hire the skilled labour needed to carry out the program.

Requirements for Successful Implementation

Since implementation is so important, why do so many firms fail to successfully implement their carefully designed marketing strategies and plans? Implementation efforts do not succeed because marketing managers fail to meet the basic requirements for effective implementation.

Top management support. Top management support is important for successful implementation. The higher the commitment and support of top management to the implementation effort, the more committed middle-level managers and other employees are. Middle-level managers and personnel at lower levels want to see that top managers are fully behind the implementation effort and doing all they can to see the process succeed.

Top management can help the implementation process by communicating the marketing plan to the entire company. Top managers need to clearly spell out the changes needed to implement the plan, the likely impact of these changes on the various departments, and the expected results from implementing the marketing plan. Employees need a shared understanding of the organization's marketing strategy, objectives, and expected results. If employees have different views about these matters, organizational problems could arise. For example, some employees may view the firm as trying to increase its sales and market share and doing everything it takes to make the sale while others may believe the focus is on more controlled growth through superior quality and service. The result of these divergent views will lead to confusion and poor implementation.

Employees associate top management's support of the strategy with allocation of necessary resources. Management must allocate the resources needed to carry out the marketing plan. For example, if the plan calls for an increase in the advertising budget, top management must ensure that the necessary funds are made available. Also, management must help resolve conflicts among various departments and managers. The involvement of top management is crucial as differences among departments can derail the implementation process. Turf wars among different departments are quite common, especially when implementation requires a significant organizational change.

Commitment to the strategy. The extent to which management understands and supports the marketing strategy is an important determinant of marketing implementation. The higher the shared commitment to the strategy, the higher the chances of a successful implementation. Firms often formulate strategies without the participation of key executives. The job of developing a strategic plan in these cases is left up to consultants and strategic planners. Key executives who are excluded from the strategy formulation process feel no commitment to a strategic plan that does not include their own input. The development of strategy should involve the widest possible participation by people who really know the business and will be actively involved in its implementation. Highly committed managers are continuously thinking of different ways to make the strategy work.

Managers' commitment to the strategy is affected by the perceived fit between organizational vision and strategy. The better the fit between the firm's strategy and its broad strategic direction, the greater the commitment to the strategy, and the higher the likelihood of successful implementation. The importance of the strategy also affects the commitment to the implementation effort. The more important the strategy, the keener people are to support the implementation process. Many managers know that "bet the company" strategies make employees more committed due to the high stakes involved.[13]

Availability of resources and capabilities. Successful implementation rests on the firm having the necessary resources and capabilities to execute the marketing strategy. There must be a strong alignment between the capabilities of a company and the execution requirements of the strategy. Managers need to check whether the necessary financial, physical, and human resources are available. For example, products frequently fail because the company lacks access to markets through the best channels of distribution, lacks appropriate technological know-how or service capabilities, or lacks an adequate sales force or advertising funds.

Correct information for making crucial decisions. Top managers often make important strategic decisions on the basis of information that is incorrect or on the basis of opinions and not facts. Decisions based on incorrect information lead to the implementation of the wrong strategy. Quality expert W. Edwards Deming always advised managers to base their decisions on facts, and he advocated the use of consumer research for collecting market information.

Existence of a schedule and target completion date. Top management should monitor compliance with schedules and target dates. For example, if a new product is to be developed in a year, top management must ensure that the new product is indeed ready to be marketed in 12 months. Dedication to the established strategy is also required in order to avoid a knee-jerk decision to allocate resources to other markets, products, or projects.

Willingness to change. Implementation of a new marketing plan frequently necessitates change. Strategy implementation often fails because companies fail to change. Change is a comprehensive process that involves every part of the organization. **Change** entails changing people's perception, expectations, and performance in ways that are focused and consistent with the new reality.[14]

Change entails changing people's perception, expectations, and performance in ways that are focused and consistent with the new reality.

People resist change for many reasons. They are generally afraid of change because of the fear of the unknown. There are several ways to allay people's fears and make them more cooperative. One of the most powerful ways to get people to accept change is through participation and getting them involved in the marketing planning process from its early stages.[15] Inclusion in the planning process enhances the self-esteem of those who are involved and they feel important. Participating in the planning process makes people more familiar with the plan and better prepared to implement it. They also better understand why change is needed and in which ways the new plan is better than the existing plan. By participating in the planning process, people take ownership of the new plan and are more committed to seeing it implemented.

Other reasons for failure to change include lack of a vision to help focus the change effort on the projects required to bring about change. The vision helps align the activities of organizational members in a desired direction. Top management needs to communicate the vision to all members of the organization. Communicating the vision effectively helps people understand what is involved in the change, and this can help bring people on side.[16]

People often resist change because they resent a disruption of their routine or they fear losing their position or budgets or even being demoted as a result of the change. Managers often have difficulty implementing a marketing strategy that is different from the one they are used to. For example, a firm with a long history of producing large quantities of the product that was sold at low margins to obtain the volume needed to cover overhead costs and keep the plants at capacity will have difficulty selling premium-quality, high-price products. Top managers and the sales force will likely lack the discipline to implement the necessary marketing program and will probably revert to the volume-oriented logic that made the firm successful. Such a "commodity culture" is often encouraged by a reward system that promotes volume at low prices. As a result, plant managers' performance is based on volume and the sales force often resorts to price reductions to increase sales volume.

Aligning the Marketing Strategy with Organizational Actions

Firms often perform poorly because they fail to align processes, work, people, formal and informal organization, and marketing strategy.[17] Firms need a system that aligns actions throughout the organization with the strategy and the external and internal environment. Alignment ensures that people, the work performed in the organization, and formal and informal systems support the strategy and that strategic and operating plans are aligned. The better the alignment, the more effective the implementation and the more energy available to propel the organization in the right direction. Aligning an organization is an ongoing balancing act that involves constant adjustments as the various variables continuously change or efforts are made to improve the alignment among these variables.

David Nadler proposed a model called the Congruence Model, an input-output model, to help organizations remain aligned as they struggle to deal with the challenges of implementation and organizational change and to achieve superior performance.[18] The Congruence Model is shown in Figure 15.2.

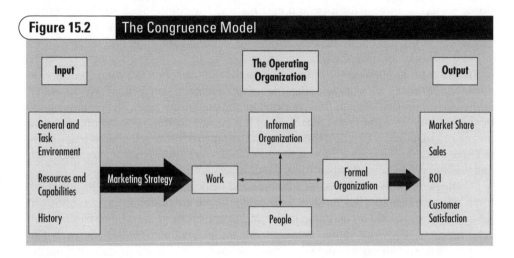

Figure 15.2   The Congruence Model

SOURCE: Adapted from David A. Nadler, *Champions of Change* (San Francisco: Jossey-Bass Publishers, 1998), 41. Reprinted with permission of John Wiley & Sons, Inc.

Input

Input includes the organization's environment, its resources and capabilities, and its history. The environment, as we discussed in Chapter 3, consists of the general and task environment. The environment exerts a powerful influence on an organization, and it is the source of major changes in the industry. Environments create threats and opportunities to which firms must respond by avoiding threats and exploiting opportunities.

Resources and capabilities, as we defined them in previous chapters, include capital, facilities, plants, equipment, and customer and channel relationships. A comparison of a firm's resources with competitors' resources gives rise to strengths and weaknesses, which, in turn, determine the actions that a firm can successfully pursue. A firm should pursue strategies that build on its strengths and de-emphasize its weaknesses.

History entails past events, activities, decisions, and successes and failures that influence the way the organization operates. An organization's history exerts a great deal of influence on its future decisions and strategies. Highly successful firms sometimes become complacent and fail to respond to environmental challenges on a timely basis. Successful past decisions and strategies tend to loom large in a firm's future decisions and strategies.

Input includes the organization's environment, its resources and capabilities, and its history.

History entails past events, activities, decisions, and successes and failures that influence the way the organization operates.

Marketing Strategy

Marketing strategy consists of the target market, positioning, and the marketing mix. Target markets include customers and their needs, which the organization will attempt to satisfy. For instance, Pontiac Grand Am targets those customers who are looking for a high-performance automobile at an affordable price.

Positioning refers to how the organization is going to compete in its chosen market. Will it compete on the basis of low cost, high quality, better design, or convenience? Finally, objectives are the desired outcomes of a successful implementation of the marketing strategy. The marketing mix consists of the product that the organization will offer to its target market in order to satisfy its needs, the price, channels of distribution, and the communications plan.

The Operating Organization

The operating organization is the main mechanism by which the input is transformed into output. Input, as has already been discussed, consists of the environment, organizational resources and capabilities, and past history. The components of the operating organization include work, people, and the formal and informal organizational arrangements. The better the alignment between the operating organization and the marketing strategy, the more effective the implementation.

The first task in aligning the operating organization and the marketing strategy is to align the organization's work with the marketing strategy requirements.[19] Work consists of the basic tasks that need to be performed by the organization, and it is often defined by the industry or category the organization has chosen to serve. For example, work at Magna International might be defined as production and marketing of auto parts. Work at Ottawa-based Corel could be described as developing and marketing graphics, Web and desktop publishing, photo-editing, and business software.

People perform the work in organizations, and work is the reason for which they are hired. Alignment occurs when the most capable people are placed in appropriate positions and they are held accountable for results. Compensation must be consistent with achieving objectives and should reinforce aligned behaviour.[20] Nadler argues that in order to diagnose an organizational system, the following characteristics of the people must be analyzed: the level of knowledge, skills, and capabilities of the people who work in the organization; the benefits people expect to receive by working for the organization; the expectations and perceptions they develop over time about the nature of their work; and the demographics of the workforce measured by age, gender, and ethnicity and how these demographics relate to the work that needs to be done.[21]

The **formal organization** consists of the structure, systems, and processes—such as accounting and management systems—that are in place to help the organization perform the work and achieve its objectives. The **informal organization** includes the informal arrangements and interaction patterns that exist in parallel to the formal organization. These informal organizational arrangements include the **organizational culture,** which includes the values, norms, and beliefs shared by members of the organization. Culture refers to the unwritten rules shaping behaviour in an organization. One of the most powerful manifestations of culture is reflected in the way things get done in an organization. Culture is also reflected in who is considered an effective or ineffective employee. In some organizations, a good employee may be one who is capable of working independently while in a different organization an effective employee may be one who excels in teamwork. Other informal arrangements include rules and work practices that have been developed over the years in an informal manner, the communication patterns among members of the organization, and the day-to-day behaviour of the organization's leaders and managers.

The **formal organization** consists of the structure, systems, and processes—such as accounting and management systems—that are in place to help the organization perform the work and achieve its objectives.

The **informal organization** includes the informal arrangements and interaction patterns that exist in parallel to the formal organization.

Organizational culture includes the values, norms, and beliefs shared by members of the organization.

Output

Output represents the performance of the firm measured by market share, sales, ROI, customer satisfaction, and other performance measures. Performance depends on variables such as the external environment, resources and capabilities, history, marketing strategy, people, work, the formal and informal organization, and how these variables interact with one another.

In order to understand how an organization operates and why different organizations vary in their effectiveness, it is very important to understand the concept of fit or alignment. **Fit** refers to how well the various components of the Congruence Model interact with one another. The tighter the fit among the components, the higher the organizational effectiveness.

The significance of the Congruence Model is that the better the fit or congruence among the components of the model, the more effective the organization will be in implementing its strategy and the better its performance. Managers need to identify the areas of poor fit among the components of the congruence model and find ways of improving them. The Congruence Model produces a better fit when the following occur:

There is consistency between the marketing strategy and resources and capabilities. For instance, a marketing strategy that requires intensive new product development will probably fail if the organization lacks new product development capabilities. On the other hand, a cost leadership strategy will benefit if the firm has strong engineering skills to design the product for ease of manufacturing, an efficient manufacturing process, and strong distribution capabilities.

The marketing strategy is consistent with the formal structure, systems, and resources of the organization. If the strategy calls for large-scale decentralized decision-making but the organizational structure is highly hierarchical, the strategy has only a slim chance of succeeding.

The marketing strategy fits the culture and informal processes that dominate the organization. For instance, a culture that values cost-cutting will clash with a strategy that calls for a high degree of creativity and product quality.

There is a high degree of fit among all components of the Congruence Model. All components of the Congruence Model, including the marketing strategy, the people, the work, and the formal and informal organization, must demonstrate a high degree of fit among themselves. Lack of fit among the components can cause problems for the organization. Some of the questions managers need to ask are the following: Do employees of the organization have the skills to perform the required tasks? Is the organizational structure appropriate to meet the demands of the required tasks? Is the reward structure adequate to motivate workers to perform their work? Are the informal organizational arrangements, such as culture and communication, consistent with the tasks to be performed? Are individual employee requirements met by the formal organizational requirements?

> **Output** represents the performance of the firm measured by market share, sales, ROI, customer satisfaction, and other performance measures.

> **Fit** refers to how well the various components of the Congruence Model interract with one another.

Marketing Control

Marketing plan implementation requires appropriate controls to monitor progress and to ensure that the company is achieving its marketing objectives. **Control** is the process of measuring actual performance against desirable performance and taking action to ensure that the actual results match the desired results. Effective control systems enable the marketing manager to achieve the following: (1) detect when actual results differ from planned results; (2) determine why actual results differ from planned results; and (3) recommend ways to correct the situation and bring actual results closer to planned results.

> **Control** is the process of measuring actual performance against desirable performance and taking action to ensure that the actual results match the desired results.

Many firms use financial reporting for control purposes. Financial reports for purposes of control are necessary but not sufficient as there are many other areas that should be controlled. From a marketing point of view, marketing managers need information about areas such as how the firm performs in its market share and customer satisfaction, and about the effectiveness of its advertising, distribution, and pricing strategies. Firms need controls for all important marketing objectives in the marketing plan for the purpose of evaluating progress in meeting these objectives. As part of these controls, marketers need to put in place mechanisms to monitor progress so if actual performance is different from desired performance the firm can initiate action to change the company's direction.

The Control Process

Marketing managers must establish control processes to ensure that organizational performance is monitored and that all important marketing objectives are met. The process of control involves the following steps (see Figure 15.3).

Figure 15.3	The Control Process

- Choose control variables and establish baseline measures
- Develop measurement procedures
- Measure actual performance
- Interpret actual differences
- Act on the difference

Choose control variables and establish baseline measures

Creating an effective control system involves choosing appropriate control variables and establishing baseline measures. **Control variables** are important aspects of an organization whose performance is monitored. **Baseline measures** are derived from control variables and are benchmarks against which actual performance is compared. For example, if a company has an objective to increase brand awareness by 10 percent, this could become a baseline measure. Baseline measures are compared with actual results to detect negative deviations so that appropriate action can be taken to correct the problem.

The number of control variables can be fairly large because they are used in all areas of marketing, including market share, sales performance, customer satisfaction, brand equity, segmentation, positioning, image, product, price, distribution, and promotion. However, because it is not possible to measure and control every possible action taken to implement the plan, only the key variables should be monitored.

Some firms use the balanced scorecard method to evaluate their firm's performance. The **balanced scorecard** is a framework for measuring organizational performance.[22] It provides a means to describe, communicate, and manage the marketing strategy in a consistent and understandable way.[23] Managers who use the balanced scorecard realize that no single measure can provide a comprehensive view of the business performance. For example, an exclusive reliance on financial measures encourages short-term performance at the expense of long-term performance.

The balanced scorecard offers a balanced representation of a firm's performance. While the balanced scorecard retains financial performance measures, it also incorporates other equally important performance measures. It allows companies to look beyond financial measures and focus on factors that create future economic value. Financial indicators, on the other hand, are lag indicators as they report on the consequences of past actions.

The balanced scorecard provides a framework for looking at the marketing strategy from all critical perspectives. It enables managers to evaluate their firm's performance by

Control variables are important aspects of an organization whose performance is monitored.

Baseline measures are derived from control variables and are benchmarks against which actual performance is compared.

Balanced scorecard is a framework for measuring organizational performance.

checking activities across four areas: customer, financial, internal business processes, and learning and growth (see Figure 15.4).

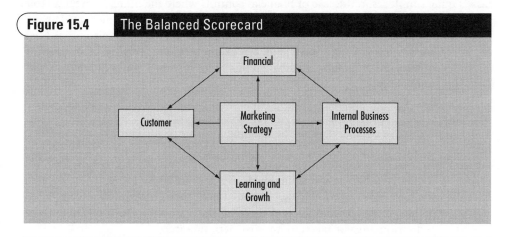

Figure 15.4	The Balanced Scorecard

Customer. The strategy is viewed from the point of view of the customer. This perspective involves the ways in which the company will create value for customers. It defines the value proposition that differentiates the company from the competition. Customer-related measures include customer loyalty, customer retention, customer satisfaction, market share, number of customers, and sales growth.

Financial. The strategy is viewed from the point of view of the shareholder. It specifies the financial objectives for growth and productivity. They include traditional measures of financial control, including return on investment, earnings-per-share, profit margin, cash flow, cost reduction, and financial ratios.

Internal business processes. The strategy is viewed from the point of view of internal operations. This perspective measures the performance of key organizational processes. Such measures include cycle time, unit cost yield, number of defects, order processing time, on-time delivery, and inventory turnover.

Learning and growth. The strategy is viewed from the point of view of the long term and the survival of the organization. These measures include the number of new products, percentage of sales from new products, new product development, and research and development expenses.

Once the control variables are selected, baseline measures are established. Control variables and corresponding baselines are determined within the context of the marketing plan, and they reflect the firm's marketing strategy and objectives, unique competitive strengths and weaknesses, and resources relative to competitors. Each baseline measure should be linked to a marketing objective. For example, a firm with a marketing strategy of growth through new product development might establish baselines that involve dates for completing pilot testing, revenue trends by quarter, when designs are to be released, engineering capacity to avoid overloading engineering staff, and number of line extensions versus truly new products.

Develop measurement procedures

Once the baseline measures have been established, the marketing manager develops procedures for obtaining measurements of the control variables and sets up a feedback system to provide timely reports on results. These reports could be based on market research data and financial or personnel reporting forms. In some cases the measurement task is quite simple, as in the case of financial controls where the numbers are available from the financial statements. In other cases, such as measuring customer satisfaction, brand awareness, or customer loyalty, the marketing manager must establish procedures for obtaining the necessary measurements. For example, many firms establish ongoing customer monitoring programs that involve surveying customers on a quarterly, semi-annual, or annual basis.

Measure actual performance

The firm must make comparisons of the baseline measures with actual results to assess performance and take action when performance falls short of marketing objectives. Figure 15.5 shows several control variables, their baseline measures, and actual performance. A comparison between baseline measures and actual performance shows that with the exception of brand awareness, the actual performance of the firm in question falls short of the planned performance. In this case, the reasons for the shortfall must be examined and action must be taken to improve performance.

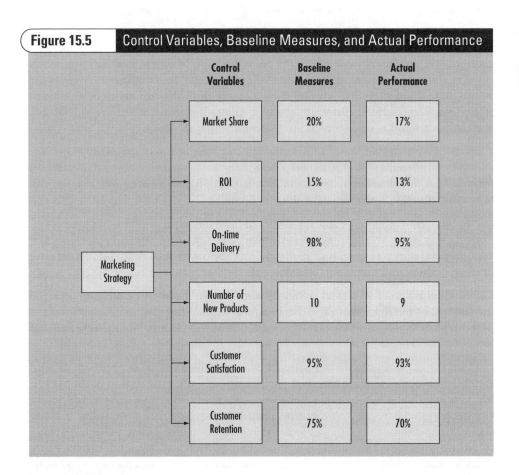

Figure 15.5 Control Variables, Baseline Measures, and Actual Performance

Control Variables	Baseline Measures	Actual Performance
Market Share	20%	17%
ROI	15%	13%
On-time Delivery	98%	95%
Number of New Products	10	9
Customer Satisfaction	95%	93%
Customer Retention	75%	70%

Marketing Strategy

Interpret differences

The marketing manager should closely examine those cases where performance falls short of what was desired in order to diagnose the cause of the problem and determine an appropriate course of action. For example, if the company's goal is to increase market share by 5 percent but this goal is not being achieved, the marketing manager must examine possible reasons for the shortfall. Possible reasons might be competitive action, lack of better-quality products, ineffective pricing, or insufficient advertising spending.

Act on the difference

Once the reasons for the company's failure to achieve its desired performance are determined, proper action is initiated. For example, if the firm has decided that it needs a better-quality product, a quality-improvement program needs to be established. Xerox discovered in the early 1980s that the major reason for its loss of market share relative to Canon and other competitors was the poor quality and high cost of its products. This led Xerox to introduce a far-reaching quality-improvement program that reduced product development costs and increased the quality of its products. As a result of this effort, Xerox's market share increased and its competitive position improved.

Requirements for Effective Control Systems

Effective control systems are necessary for the proper implementation of a marketing strategy. Yet most firms lack effective control systems. This lack makes it difficult for a firm to obtain accurate and timely information to know whether its implementation effort is working. Setting up an effective control system requires the following:

- *Measurement procedures are implementable and accurate.* Measurement procedures can sometimes be difficult to implement and they lack accuracy. Concepts such as brand equity or image are hard to measure or their measurement may not be valid or reliable. Fortunately, advances in marketing and survey research have made it possible to measure many of these control variables with a great deal of accuracy. Many firms have measurement systems, such as accounting or sales management systems, already in place for many of the key control areas.
- *All key result areas are included.* It is important that baseline measures include all key result areas. As was discussed earlier, these key areas are derived from objectives included in the marketing plan. For example, if a firm considers a certain percentage of sales from new products to be an important objective, that objective should be one of the baseline measures to be used by the firm.
- *Objectives and goals have desirable characteristics.* It is important that all objectives and goals are appropriate and have the desirable characteristics as explained in Chapter 3. Effective objectives should be measurable, feasible, consistent, acceptable, and understandable. Aiming, for example, at increasing return on investment by 10 percent is a more effective objective than a general objective of just increasing return on investment. Setting overly ambitious objectives that will be difficult to reach may discourage those company employees who have responsibility for achieving them. If management sets more than one objective, the objectives should be consistent among themselves. Managers who disagree with objectives because they were imposed by top management without their consent may not be very cooperative or exert the effort required to achieve the objectives. In addition, objectives must be clear to avoid misunderstanding or confusion among those with responsibility for implementing the strategy.
- *Reward system is linked to objectives and goals.* The firm's reward system must be linked to objectives and goals and must influence individual behaviour in the intended ways—individuals are rewarded on the basis of ability to meet the goals and objectives. For example, if an objective is to increase customer satisfaction, the company's reward system should be designed to reward increases in customer satisfaction. If, on the other hand, the objective is to increase sales or market share, the company should reward efforts consistent with these objectives.

- The existence of an effective marketing plan does not guarantee marketing success. Appropriate implementation is also required. Organizations need a culture of execution in which people meet their commitments and things get done.

- The relationship between marketing strategy and implementation is an iterative one. Marketing strategy affects implementation but implementation affects the marketing strategy. Marketing success requires a superior marketing strategy and a superior implementation.

- The quality of a firm's marketing strategy and implementation may be combined into the Marketing Strategy–Implementation Matrix, which provides firms with useful guidelines depending on their placement on the matrix.

- The effectiveness of marketing strategy depends on the following criteria: top management commitment; feasibility; a sustainable competitive advantage; a way of dealing effectively with strengths, weaknesses, opportunities, and threats; and ability to make it difficult for competitors to respond and match or offset the firm's competitive advantages.

- Not all firms are equally capable of using the strategic marketing planning process effectively. Managers often face a number of commonly occurring problems that limit their ability to develop sound marketing strategies. These problems include complacency, conservatism, incomplete analysis, prior hypothesis, escalating commitment, cannibalization, and complexity.

- Implementation is a complex marketing activity and may be described with four levels: actions, programs, systems, and policies.

- The requirements for a successful implementation include management support, commitment to the strategy, availability of resources and capabilities, crucial decisions being made on the basis of correct information, existence of a schedule and target date to be completed, and willingness to change.

- Firms often perform poorly because they fail to align processes, work, people, organization, customers, and strategies. Firms need a system that aligns actions throughout the organization with the marketing strategy and the external and internal environment. Alignment ensures that people, the work performed in the organization, and the formal and informal systems support the marketing strategy and that strategic and operational plans are aligned. The better the alignment, the more effective the organization.

- A useful model that can help companies remain aligned is the Congruence Model developed by David Nadler. This model is an input-output model in which inputs are aligned with the marketing strategy. The operating organization, which includes work, people, and the formal and informal organization, must be aligned with the marketing strategy. The output expresses the performance of the firm measured by market share, sales, ROI, customer satisfaction, and other measures.

- Marketing plan implementation requires appropriate controls to monitor progress and to ensure the company is achieving its marketing objectives. Some marketing managers use the balanced scorecard approach to measure and evaluate their marketing strategies. The balanced scorecard enables managers to evaluate their firm's performance by checking activities across four areas: customer, financial, internal business processes, and learning and growth. Effective control systems must satisfy the following criteria: measurement procedures are implemented and accurate; all key result areas are included; objectives and goals have desirable characteristics; and an appropriate reward system exists.

Review and Discussion Questions

1. Discuss the relationship between marketing strategy and implementation. Explain why the existence of an effective marketing strategy does not guarantee marketing success.

2. Describe the Marketing Strategy–Implementation Matrix using a diagram.

3. Discuss the criteria for evaluating marketing strategies. How does the quality of a marketing strategy affect the effectiveness of implementation?

4. Discuss the various common problems that affect a firm's ability to use the strategic marketing planning effectively.

5. Describe the four levels of implementation. What is the importance of the implementation levels for effective implementation?

6. Discus the requirements for successful implementation of marketing strategy.

7. Discuss the Congruence Model using a diagram. How could a company use this model to improve its implementation efforts and performance?

8. What is control? What is the role of control in implementation? Discuss the process of establishing controls. What are the requirements for effective control systems?

9. Describe the use of the balanced scorecard approach in strategy implementation and control.

Critical Thinking and Application Questions

1. Gemini Technologies is a high-technology company that specializes in the field of robotics. Gemini has developed a new robot that performs a number of household tasks, including cooking, cleaning, dusting, and doing the dishes. The new product has been on the market for over a year but sales have been disappointing. Bob Stanfield, marketing manager of Gemini, believes that Gemini's marketing strategy is appropriate and that a major problem is lack of effective implementation of its robotics marketing strategy. What could have gone wrong with Gemini's implementation of its marketing strategy?

2. Discuss the following statement: "Companies that spread themselves thinly over a large number of products have difficulty implementing their strategy."

3. Select a local company and assess its implementation capabilities. Propose a program designed to improve this company's implementation performance.

4. Design the marketing strategy for a company of your choice. Using the balanced scorecard, propose several measures for measuring and evaluating the performance of this company.

Notes

1. This material is drawn from the following sources: Larry Bossidy and Ram Charan, *Execution: The Discipline of Getting Things Done* (New York: Crown Business, 2002); Michael Dell, *Direct from Dell* (New York: HarperBusiness, 1999); Kathryn Jones, "The Dell Way," *Business 2.0*, February 2003, 63–64.
2. Bossidy and Charan, 19.
3. Bossidy and Charan, 6.
4. Bossidy and Charan, 7.
5. John Kay, *Why Companies Succeed* (New York: Oxford University Press, 1995), 3.
6. Constantinos C. Markides, *All the Right Moves: A Guide to Crafting Breakthrough Strategies* (Boston, Mass.: Harvard Business School Press, 2000), 1.
7. Markides, 13; Richard Rumelt, "Theory, Strategy, and Entrepreneurship," in *The Competitive Challenge*, ed. David J. Teece (Cambridge, Mass.: Ballinger Pub. Co., 1987), 151.
8. Rumelt, 150.
9. Rumelt, 150.
10. Louis V. Gerstner Jr., *Who Says Elephants Can't Dance?* (New York: HarperBusiness, 2002), 148–149.
11. David A. Nadler, *Champions of Change* (San Francisco: Jossey-Bass Publishers, 1998), 69.
12. Thomas V. Bonoma, *Managing Marketing* (New York: The Free Press, 1984), 6.
13. Charles H. Noble and Michael P. Mokwa, "Implementing Marketing Strategies: Developing and Testing a Managerial Theory," *Journal of Marketing* 63 (October 1999), 57–73.
14. Nadler, 4.
15. Robert J. Hamper and L. Sue Baugh, *Strategic Market Planning* (Lincolnwood, Ill.: NTC Business Books, 1990), 175.
16. John P. Kotter, *Leading Change* (Boston, Mass.: Harvard Business School Press, 1996), 16.
17. George Labovitz and Victor Rosansky, *The Power of Alignment* (New York: Wiley, 1997), 22.
18. Nadler, 41.
19. C. Davis Fogg, *Implementing Your Strategic Plan: How to Turn "Intent" Into Effective Action for Sustainable Advantage* (New York: Amacom, 1999), 11.
20. Fogg, 274.
21. Nadler, 35.
22. Robert S. Kaplan and David P. Norton, "The Balanced Scorecard—Measures That Drive Performance," *Harvard Business Review*, January–February, 1992, 71–79.
23. Robert S. Kaplan and David P. Norton, *The Strategy Focused Organization* (Boston, Mass.: Harvard Business School Press, 2001), 6.

Appendix

A Marketing Plan Example: A Marketing Plan for National Depot Inc.

Executive Summary

This marketing plan has been developed for National Depot, a chain of retail stores carrying home, leisure, and sporting goods. National Depot needs to respond to socio-economic changes taking place in the Canadian economy. At the same time, National Depot should strive to increase the quality of the products offered while remaining price competitive. National Depot should increase the depth of its product line by offering higher-quality products. National Depot will maintain consumer awareness through mass media promotion and increase its appeal to individual users by offering a greater depth of products and one-stop convenience. National Depot's new message will be carried through television and radio media, on its website, and through print media and an enhanced in-store design.

Marketing Objectives

National Depot's marketing objectives include annual same-store sales increases of 5 percent and earnings per share growth of 10 percent. It intends to increase the number of stores from 250 to 300 by 2007. The company also intends to aggressively pursue new business growth opportunities that leverage its core capabilities and unique assets.

Situational Analysis

Review of Current Marketing Program

Target market
National Depot's market targeting strategy is very broad with regard to the segment targeted. It targets adult males in a slightly higher-income group than its competitors Wal-Mart, Home Depot, and Canadian Tire.

Merchandise
National Depot offers customers a large selection of brands. National Depot stores stock over 65,000 home, leisure, and sporting goods. Its products are widely recognized for their value and quality.

Price
National Depot keeps its prices as low as possible through the use of mass merchandising and a constant control of distribution and operating costs. National Depot aims to keep prices slightly higher in an effort to associate its products with higher quality.

NOTE: This sample marketing plan was written by Professor Peter Yannopoulos solely to provide material for class discussion and it is not intended to illustrate either effective or ineffective handling of a managerial situation.

Stores/location

Location is crucial to the National Depot success. National Depot utilizes centralized warehouses that process dealer orders and deliver merchandise to its stores. Products are shipped from the manufacturer directly to National Depot warehouses. Merchandise is then transported to individual stores where it is bought by customers. In 1997, National Depot launched an online version of its "brick and mortar business," which has become an additional vehicle for selling the company's products.

Promotion

National Depot uses a marketing program that reaches its customers using print, broadcast, and online media. The company participates in local community events and supports several charities. It also utilizes frequent sales promotions.

Performance

The market share of National Depot in 2004 was 10.5 percent. National Depot reported a net income of $57.8 million for the last quarter of 2004, up 12 percent from 2003. This gain represented an increase in earnings per share of 9.4 percent over the same period in the previous year.

Internal Analysis

Finance

National Depot has been building strong relationships with banking institutions and suppliers. This has earned the company credibility as a reliable and trusted business partner. National Depot always pursues sales increase strategies through innovation and the pursuit of growth opportunities. National Depot regards financial flexibility, strong working capital, and capital management as a top priority along with improvements in cost efficiencies.

Management

National Depot follows a policy of employee empowerment and rewards employees through profit-sharing programs in order to create a participative and accountable workforce. By using the franchising system, National Depot is involved in community relationship building. Recruitment of franchisees involves aggressively seeking the best candidates, followed by quantifiable assessments, and a store internship program. This method assures the company that only the best and most likely to succeed are chosen and trained. However, some frontline employees lack in-depth product knowledge, usage, and location of products within the store.

Marketing

National Depot uses print media such as flyers and annual catalogues, broadcast media, as well as online media for its marketing. National Depot's franchising system enables the company to tap into local demand and adapt the marketing mix components to better exploit regional demand differences.

Technology

National Depot stores are all connected, allowing them to look at inventory supplies across different stores, better enabling the company to satisfy consumers' needs. Furthermore, National Depot stores are directly linked with distributors for ease of ordering. In 2000, National Depot invested $75 million in new technology to streamline its stores, with the goal of better inventory management and lower operating costs.

External Analysis

Social factors

The increasing percentage of women in the workforce, the deterioration of the nuclear family structure, the changing roles of men and women, and the increasing diversity of Canada are also significant social trends. These trends have the potential to affect National Depot. Canada has also seen an increase in the average age of its population. As baby boomers move to the later part of their lifespan, National Depot could benefit by taking advantage of the increased leisure time held by these individuals.

Competition

National Depot is in a fiercely competitive industry, facing pressure from other large and small retailers. Although pressures do exist from small companies, the most serious threats come from three major competitors in the industry: Home Depot, Wal-Mart, and Canadian Tire.

Home Depot. Home Depot is the world's largest home improvement retailer and operates in the United States, Canada, Mexico, and Puerto Rico. Having a broader scope allows Home Depot greater economies of scale, letting the company offer lower prices. But Home Depot only carries about 45,000 products whereas National Depot averages 65,000. It also lags behind National Depot on promotions that draw consumers to the store. The interior design and attractiveness of National Depot is superior to that of Home Depot's stores.

Wal-Mart. Wal-Mart is the largest retailer in the world with superior logistics skills as well as economies of scale. Wal-Mart was given the Award of Corporate Leadership in 2002 for outstanding achievement in employee and community relations. Its involvement in community affairs is diverse, ranging from college scholarships to fundraising for local seniors' centres. In Canada, Wal-Mart also offers leadership in recycling initiatives, environmental protection, and its commitment to its "Buy Canadian program" according to which a large percentage of the products sold at Canadian Wal-Mart stores are produced by Canadian companies. Wal-Mart also attempts to bolster community economic development by providing guidance and grants for industrial facilities. Wal-Mart's product lines coupled with its "everyday low price" guarantee places enormous pressure on National Depot to be price competitive.

Canadian Tire. Canadian Tire has more than 450 Canadian retail stores across Canada. A Canadian Tire store is within 15 minutes' driving distance of 95 percent of the Canadian population. This increases the availability, awareness, and convenience of Canadian Tire stores to target customers. Canadian Tire is aiming at strengthening and accelerating its growth and performance with the goal of being among the top performers in North America.

Canadian Tire is positioned as the store for Canadians to start a new season, small project, sport, or life event. Canadian Tire differentiates its stores from competitors by offering Canadian Tire "money"—the most recognized customer loyalty program in Canada and one that has been in existence for many years. Canadian Tire also uses its comprehensive automotive product line and automotive expertise as a technique to gain competitive differentiation over its major competitors. A Canadian Tire store stocks over 100,000 products and carries the label MasterCraft, which is exclusive to Canadian Tire.

Economy

In recent years we have experienced a decrease in the interest rates that chartered banks charge consumers to borrow funds. The lower interest rate motivates consumers to spend their money instead of keeping it in the bank. The lower interest rate and the predicted increased consumer spending are beneficial to National Depot and its competitors.

Figure A.1	SWOT Matrix

I Strengths	**II** Weaknesses
1. Strong name recognition 2. Convenient store locations 3. Extensive community involvement 4. Strong distribution system	1. Somewhat higher prices 2. Limited financial resources 3. Lower market share
III Opportunities	**IV** Threats
1. Canadians have more leisure time 2. Number of dwellings increase 3. Low interest rates 4. Large untapped female segment	1. Highly competitive industry 2. Low margins

Development of Marketing Program

Based on our situational analysis and National Depot's performance, the following marketing program is proposed.

Target market

Currently, National Depot's market targeting strategy is very broad with regard to the segment targeted. New merchandise should be added to appeal to men but also to women. National Depot should continue to compete as a retailer that provides a one-stop shop for all individuals interested in its products. This will be reinforced with a guarantee of value-added services for time-constrained people seeking value and convenience.

Positioning strategy

National Depot's positioning strategy needs to change to exploit current marketing opportunities and avoid threats. In such a fiercely competitive environment it is essential that National Depot clearly differentiates itself from its competitors with respect to the products and services it offers. Currently, National Depot is positioned as having moderately high quality and moderately high pricing. The company should reposition itself by increasing its perceived quality while keeping its perceived price relatively the same. This strategic move will also bring National Depot above Home Depot with respect to both quality and price. National Depot will further enhance its differentiation through exclusive labels offered only at National Depot.

Marketing Mix

Product strategy

In order to attract different segments, the home products line will be expanded with respect to quality and price depth of the merchandise. Specifically, it will include brand names with high awareness for those in a higher income bracket while offering more realistic price point products for others. Carrying more home products, footwear, and apparel would attract more female customers.

The sporting and leisure product line needs a revitalization to better meet the needs of the customers. Given that income is positively related to sporting and leisure activities, National Depot will add highly recognizable brand names, while keeping a limited stock of lower price point merchandise. Emphasis will also be placed on developing other leisure activities that target an aging population, such as gardening.

Great emphasis will be placed on designing the entire store to more effectively promote each product line. Clearly planned product zones, signage, creative and eye-catching product displays, better lighting, and improved cash register location are all top priorities. Sound store layout that categorizes similar products and products that are complementary will be undertaken by National Depot. Catchy merchandising displays will be of primary importance, and sale items will be prominently displayed.

Pricing strategy

National Depot is in a very competitive industry and being price competitive is essential. The company will leverage its purchasing power to offer relatively lower prices over its smaller competitors. However, larger competitors have greater purchasing power over smaller competitors. Thus, a low-price strategy is not suitable for National Depot. Hence, first-class merchandising is crucial for National Depot to offer a better selection than competitors with the goal of one-stop shopping for all home, leisure, and sports product needs.

Offering excellent value is also very important. National Depot will use value-based pricing to entice shoppers into its stores. In summary, the positioning of National Depot calls for an increase in merchandise quality and service without a substantial increase in price to enhance the perceived value of its offerings.

Store/location strategy

National Depot will continue to build strong relationships with suppliers to help improve its market performance. National Depot has centralized warehouses, systematically located across Canada to minimize transportation costs. Its stores are linked with warehouses via an ordering database. This system controls levels of inventory for each store and allows communication to flow instantly, reducing the lead time required for orders. This vertical integration allows for product assortment to be tailored to each store and improves coordination across channels. In-store warehousing space will be reduced by 10 percent. This will increase functional merchandise square footage on the sales floor, decrease inventory costs, decrease slow-moving merchandise, and increase product turnover.

Promotion strategy

National Depot will continue to provide a clear message of its intention to be the most valuable source for customer needs for home, leisure, and sporting goods. Factual and emotional messages will continue to be the basis of National Depot's integrated communications strategy. The main message to customers is that National Depot offers more than what customers expect, thus signifying superior customer value.

Given the seasonal nature of many of the products carried by National Depot, the media needs to follow the flighting approach whereby advertising is run only during the high season. In order to ensure that the company's marketing media mix reaches all the targeted segments, television ads will be aired during different days of the week and times of the day. National Depot will also sponsor local events in order to reach targeted customers at local events.

National Depot will continually update its signage in order to present products in the most pleasing way to customers. Their trademark will be displayed around the store so that it is associated with everything that National Depot sells. Merchandising displays will be more inviting, and the in-store changes mentioned above will allow for more shopping space and a convenient shopping experience for the customer by emphasizing clear store layouts and illumination.

Advertising strategy

National Depot must have a well-balanced public advertising media mix, including radio and television promotion. Since each method is very costly, National Depot will take care to develop the most appealing visual and audio stimuli. Television advertising will be used to maximize awareness of new product assortment, brands, and existing value-added services. Television advertisements will be broadly targeted to reach the various target segments. National Depot will also employ radio advertising to target niche markets via short radio announcements. This will allow National Depot to target those customers interested in specific new and existing products and services.

National Depot will also use print media and in-store signage to promote sales. Print media will be in the form of weekly flyers distributed to local community members. Each flyer will outline feature products and those products that are currently on sale. Furthermore, flyers will be tailored to fluctuations in demand caused by seasonality, holidays, and social events. In-store merchandising, signage, and location of sales items will also be emphasized. Information signage located at the ends of aisles will ensure that customers are easily directed to the appropriate areas, while creating opportunities for impulse purchases.

Publicity and community events

National Depot will benefit from publicity sparked from its community involvement. Being visible is essential for market success. National Depot will continue to associate itself with environmental sustainability, educational sponsorship, charity involvement, sport sponsorship, and participation in community events. Store managers will continue to build strong relationships with local businesses and nonprofit charities in an effort to enhance the company's stature in its local markets.

Implementation

The implementation of the above marketing program will take place in several steps:

Step 1. Management of National Depot recognizes the need for strategic change as outlined and will seek to take appropriate steps to bring about successful change and strategy implementation. Management will search the organization for a person with extensive experience in both marketing and franchise operations to head a task force designed to issue strategy changes.

Step 2. The chosen candidate will create a change team by appointing members of each functional department: Marketing, Purchasing, Finance, Logistics, and Franchise Operations. Each of the members will be highly respected within each department and capable of instituting large-scale change. The task force will be completed by February 28, 2005.

Step 3. Each member of the task force will be briefed via memorandum about the goals of the team, including each department's role in implementing change. A meeting will take place, headed by the project manager and attended by all team members. The meeting will include a detailed description of reporting relationships, goals and objectives, and an intense question and answer period where each member can clarify, object, or state opinions. This meeting will take place by March 3, 2005.

Step 4. Marketing will begin work on segmenting the market based on the aforementioned variables, and building precise profiles of target segments. Purchasing will compose a complete breakdown of products offered in each product line for later evaluation and modification. The deadline for these two tasks is March 31, 2005. Logistics and Franchise Operations will simultaneously be working on designing a space-reduction strategy to be completed by June 31, 2005. E-commerce will begin to improve the website to make navigation easy and begin to think about how to design the site for optimal use by target customers by June 31, 2005.

Step 5. Information regarding new customer profiles will flow from Marketing to Purchasing. Purchasing will then use its product expertise to compile a list of new products designed to meet new customer needs. This task will be completed by May 20, 2005.

Step 6. The newly proposed product assortment will flow back to Marketing in order to determine its fit with the proposed merchandising strategy. Here emphasis will be put on understanding National Depot's image and positioning in relation to new products. Some products will be eliminated. This task will be completed by May 30, 2005.

Step 7. Once customer and product decisions have been finalized, Logistics will receive the information and seek availability and feasibility of suppliers. Consideration will also be given to warehousing space and transportation requirements, and lead-time requirements. This is to be completed by June 10, 2005.

Step 8. The final goal is to determine the merchandising fit. The goal is to include products with existing high awareness that do not directly compete with or violate any other ongoing product contracts. Shelf space and product saturation within the store will also be considered. Franchise Operations and Marketing will eliminate products that do not fit and come up with a final list of products that are appropriate given the new strategic direction. This task is to be completed by June 24, 2005.

Step 9. Marketing will generate a complete report outlining new products. A meeting with the team members to finalize product development strategy will commence June 30, 2005, and will include a presentation of the final space reduction plan and e-commerce strategy for improved navigation of the existing website. All modification resulting from the meeting will be completed by July 14, 2005.

Step 10. The space reduction strategy will begin to be implemented in the design of new concept stores. E-commerce will begin to redesign the newly improved website for the installation of new product offerings and work closely with Marketing in order to illustrate a consistent message. Logistics will place orders for new products to be delivered to warehouses by August 21, 2005. Dealer Operations will inform associate dealers of new products and create an ordering guideline for new products by July 20, 2005.

Step 11. With the information on product development formalized, the next step is to develop a promotion strategy for market penetration. Marketing must work closely with Franchise Operations, who will convey messages to store managers in order to fine-tune store layout for optimal promotional capability, while simultaneously working with Finance for cost analysis and budgetary resources. This step will be completed by July 14, 2005.

Step 12. Marketing will conduct a research of target markets' viewing and listening preferences to aid in the promotional campaign. This research will be completed by July 31, 2005. Marketing will seek out available options for promotions, including sales promotions, television ads, radio ads, and community events. This preliminary analysis will be completed by July 31, 2005.

Step 13. The advertising research information will be presented to Marketing via a presentation and written documentation. Marketing will then use this information to choose the best media to reach the target audience. Marketing will contact available media to ensure placement of promotional ads and design promotional messages and advertisements. The complete promotional campaign and store layout changes will be completed by August 31, 2005, and presented to the team.

Step 14. Any discrepancies with the promotional campaign will be cleared up by September 21, 2005, and the promotional campaign will launch on September 31, 2005, in order to get optimal customer traffic from back-to-school shoppers, the beginning of the hockey season, and early Christmas shoppers.

Step 15. The first evaluation of the campaign will be held on November 14, 2005. Marketing will report sales results. Logistics will report inventory figures and turnover, Franchise Operations will report store sales, and E-commerce will report online shopping statistics. The team will discuss improvements to be made that will be carried out and put into place by November 25, 2005.

Spectrum Consulting International

Peter Yannopoulos

This case was written by Professor Peter Yannopoulos, Faculty of Business, Brock University, St. Catharines, Ontario, Canada, L2S 3A1 as a basis for classroom discussion. This case study is meant as a portrayal of a real-life business situation and it is not intended to illustrate effective or ineffective business management. Certain names have been disguised to preserve the anonymity of the companies involved.

It was early April 2004. The management team of Spectrum Consulting International was holding its regular Friday afternoon meeting to discuss clients and projects that were new to the company. Spectrum was a Vancouver-based management consulting firm specializing in helping client firms become more market oriented. In the past week, Spectrum had signed two new projects. One project, with West Coast Packaging, was to be headed by Tina Conway. The second project, with Econo Component Enterprises, was to be headed by Tim Chui. Both Tina and Tim were asked to summarize information they had gathered on their respective projects. The two presentations follow.

West Coast Packaging

West Coast Packaging (WCP) is a $1.2-billion manufacturer of custom plastic packaging. It specializes in heat-sealed flexible vinyl as well as heat-bent rigid PVC. It offers expertise in pressure-sensitive pouches of all sizes, sheet protectors, computer diskette holders, vinyl file folders, passbook jackets and other vinyl sleeves, as well as custom worksheet holders. With over 20 years of experience, WCP has earned a reputation by providing customers with the highest-quality products, meeting all custom specifications, delivered on time, with competitive pricing. It was prepared to create and manufacture practically any custom shape or design of sign holders, plastic packaging, or any related product that customers might require.

It is in a very competitive industry, which is making it increasingly difficult for WCP to maintain its market position. Barriers to entry are crumbling and the market is fragmenting and splintering. Thanks to opportunities for global alliances and technologies that allow real-time worldwide linkups, everyone can become a significant player in any market segment.

The company focuses on moving ahead of the pack by offering products that exceed customers' expectations. Managers are fanatics when it comes to serving customers. WCP is not led by customers but leads them. It is obsessed with leading the market, not just responding to it. Top managers believe that to be successful in business, the company must go in the opposite direction from everyone else.

The company has the courage to deliberately make products obsolete regardless of what competitors are doing. It continually creates new products and new markets. Its key to competitive advantage is to gear all organizational activities to being first to market with exceptional products. Anything that smacks of commonplace and mundane is rejected as uninteresting. In this organization, there are no sacred cows other than the corporate mission and values. Everyone tries to continually challenge the status quo.

Everyone embraces change wholeheartedly and thrives on change. Management is organized in such a way that it can capitalize on change. Thinking about the future is a daily routine in this company. Top executives manage with both a view to dealing with today's market realities and at the same time trying to anticipate and prepare for tomorrow's environment. Senior management spends approximately 50 percent of their time planning for the future, thinking about how to tap new marketing opportunities, and concentrating on the total imaginable market of tomorrow.

WCP is externally focused, constantly scanning its marketing environment to identify emerging trends in technology, competition, consumer preferences, social trends, and demographics. It uses but does not rely exclusively on strategic planning, competitive analysis, and market research because they reflect today's realities. It feels that traditional tools such as marketing research are sometimes inadequate in today's fast-moving economy. It also hires outside consultants for market analysis and interpretation of marketing research studies, with little company involvement.

At company planning sessions, they discuss such things as their unique strengths, the meaning of world-class products, how to serve customers in ways competitors can't, how to become a market leader, whether there are any possible alliances or partnerships they should investigate. People are hired based on their specific technical skills and experiences and they are expected to contribute within the narrow scope of their job definition. Ideas that might be developed outside their particular jobs are not welcome.

WCP makes extensive investments in information technology and training that enable it to support its salespeople, to learn a lot about customers, and to help build relationships with customers. It believes that the most successful organizations are those that are knowledge-based. WCP, therefore, accumulates knowledge and makes sure that this knowledge is disseminated throughout the organization. It also believes that information technology is an essential tool for everyone, including top management, middle management, and factory workers. It does not overwhelm people with data but ensures that they have access to the information they need when they need it.

Sharing and exploiting knowledge and information are vital for success. Actually, all incoming mail is scanned and anyone can access anyone else's mail. WCP has created an organization without boundaries where the different functions and divisions encourage the sharing of ideas, resources, and people. Top managers strive to create an environment in which people indepen-dently work in teams and where they identify and solve problems.

WCP is afraid of the complacency that usually accompanies success. It continually perfects its products. At the same time, it continually makes obsolete and abandons products to create the next generation of products before they become commodities and become more suitable to low-cost competitors. Management feels that focusing on improving products that are becoming low-cost commodities would be a waste of resources.

Everyone at WCP strives to outperform its competitors. They know a lot about direct competitors but very little about substitutes. Performance is measured in financial terms such as profits, market share, and return on investment. WCP constantly seeks feedback from customers and employees to monitor progress toward achieving company objectives. It tailors products to individual customer needs. It offers personalized service, customized products, and solution-based efforts. It also strives to build long-term relationships with all customers. Key accounts receive special treatment and are targeted for loyalty-building programs.

Customers view WCP as a hungry vendor who needs their business rather than an arrogant supplier entitled to their business. WCP watches for hints that its products may be difficult or confusing for customers and attempts to make them easier to use. It constantly tries to anticipate the need for change and initiate proactive moves on its own terms, not as a response to competition. The company CEO was an hour late during his first board meeting because he had to deal with a customer problem.

Econo Component Enterprises

Econo Component Enterprises (ECE) is a manufacturer and supplier of high-quality fibre-optic components. With over 30 years of manufacturing experience, the company has the commitment and capacity to meet customers' requirements for performance, reliability, and service. Sales last year exceeded $250 million.

In this organization, profit and shareholder value are the primary goals and the raison d'être of the business. Senior management conducts a strategy review annually, with a focus on financial projections and budget requests. The planning process usually yields a list of generalized strengths, weaknesses, opportunities, and threats. Also, the planning process is mainly routinized and is a prelude to the annual budget. The top leaders spend more than 90 percent of their time solving current problems and crises and the rest of their time on planning for the future. Internal concerns have priority, leaving little time for customer visits.

ECE has a mission and corporate strategy but I am not sure that everybody in the organization knows and understands them. The managers are emotionally and analytically detached from the business. Managers are obsessed with cost-cutting. Managing costs, assets, cash flow, and profits are the primary objectives. Success is defined as sales performance compared to last year.

ECE holds several two-day trips each year in resort hotels which the CEO, the president, and the entire management team attend. It hires a consultant to facilitate the discussions. The topics include competition, emerging technologies, and the future of the business. Objectives are set, and strategies are developed to achieve these objectives. At the last session, a goal of doubling revenues in five years was established.

The firm is a technology-driven firm with an engineering-driven culture. Technological leadership is a necessary condition for success. The company has outstanding engineers, salespeople, and some of the most advanced factories in the world. It has an excellent sales force whose job is to sell to the target market, and marketing's job is to help the sales force. Salespeople understand customers and their needs for the purpose of putting together persuasive presentations. In this organization, understanding and responding to customers' requirements is marketing's job.

ECE often ignores marketing input because it often reflects what competitors are doing. Marketing lacks technical expertise and is not aware of the latest technological developments. Due to time constraints, and time-to-market pressures, the team must make decisions quickly.

Another reason ECE ignores customers when it develops new products is because it believes customers are unable to come up with breakthrough products. Using marketing research through focus groups and surveys leads to new products that are very similar to existing products. Customers do not know what they want. Customers can tell you what they like about products that are already on the market but cannot tell you what new products to make.

Although most other firms in the industry begin their product development efforts with known customer needs, ECE starts with brilliant science and finds unique uses for it. Its scientific effort is aided by collaborative efforts with colleges and universities to identify new scientific research. So the product development efforts start with the technologies it has discovered, which, in turn, determine the product requirements to be met.

The emphasis of the concept and product testing is on technical feasibility and acceptance. ECE does not collect extensive market information before proceeding with the product. Customer benefits are dictated by the technology and customer input is often obtained as the development process proceeds. ECE listens to customers through its customer relations department. The sales force's job is to placate customers at the least cost.

The company invests extensively in identifying segments and tracks emerging opportunities. It sells to whoever will buy. It is reluctant to discourage unprofitable customers from buying. Its slogan, "The customer is at the top of the organizational chart," is used as a rallying point in speeches and wallet cards.

ECE is intensely competitive. It watches rivals closely and benchmarks its performance against their performance, and celebrates wins over competitors. It tries to anticipate competitor moves and their reaction to ECE moves. The behaviour of competitors can be anticipated and influenced with signalling strategies that include announcements. ECE sends signals to competitors to discourage them from attacking its core markets or uses capacity announcements to dissuade them from adding capacity. However, in the past year—during the peak buying period—its major rival surprised ECE with a price reduction that stole 25 percent of its market share in some markets. This could have been predicted and pre-emptive actions could have been taken, since the rival had just hired an aggressive CEO and it was able to improve its cost structure in recent years.

ECE tries to beat competitors at all costs. This sometimes results in expensive price wars. ECE believes in what Jack Welsh, former CEO of General Electric, used to advise his managers: "Hit your competitors before they are big enough for it to be a fair fight." Sometimes ECE underestimates the challenge from rivals. It knows very little about competitors' strategy and tactics, and this understanding is based more on rumour and reputation than on facts. For this reason, it is sometimes slow responding to competitors.

ECE is structured around functions while most of its competitors have moved to a customer-based structure. Functions have different and conflicting assumptions and lack a common understanding of marketing strategy. In addition, functions are largely isolated with very little interaction. Each function is empowered to get its own inputs and insights from customers and then tries to act separately on the information so the product development people talk to their contacts, marketing managers talk to those they know, and engineering people approach their counterparts in the customer's organization, and then they make a decision.

The company culture is internally focused. Emphasis is on conforming to internal standards while quality is defined as performance to internal standards. The focus is on attracting customers and one-time transactions. It sometimes misses signals from customers and competitors. Channel partners are looked at as expensive entities to be bypassed if the opportunity arises. Market monitoring involves tracing sales and market share. ECE has invested extensively in databases but some of them are incompatible and ECE is having software difficulties with outside suppliers.

The reward system is designed to reward short-term and long-term results consistent with strategic priorities. Executives are rewarded for being safe, careful, and avoiding taking risks. The planning process focuses on next year's profit and fast payback. Primary goals are to grow with the industry, establish product leadership across its entire product line, and, by excelling in technology and quality, to be the most efficient in everything it does and to sustain its profitability.

ECE constantly seeks partnerships whenever it can find allies because it believes that its partners have unique resources and capabilities of which it can take advantage. It views partners as an extension of its organization. Its views itself as part of a network or cluster of interlinked companies, where information is freely shared. These alliances are becoming increasingly virtual and they stay together on the basis of trust.

Discussion Questions

1. Assess the market orientation of each of the two client companies.
2. As part of the Spectrum Consulting International management team, what recommendations would you provide to Tina and Tim that might help them with their projects?

Mobile Knowledge Inc.

Peter Yannopoulos

In May 2005, Mobile Knowledge was a provider of advanced location-tracking systems for taxis, limousines, and other similar fleet-type applications. The company was working with different technologies to offer products such as global positioning tracking systems, on-board computers, navigational aids, credit card swiping machines, and in-vehicle advertising. Mobile Knowledge's principal operating office and research facilities were located in Kanata, near Ottawa, with additional sales and marketing personnel in the United States and Europe. Most of the company's sales were derived from North America, followed by the United Kingdom and the rest of the world.

After a period of phenomenal growth, the company had gone into receivership in early 2003. It successfully emerged from receivership later in the same year and, after a thorough restructuring and some new financing was able to turn its fortunes around and become a viable competitor once again. Mobile Knowledge was led by Mick Chawner, who was the president and chief executive officer of the company. Chawner was one of the architects of Mobile Knowledge's turnaround. He was currently thinking about the company's new challenges as he had to decide about the future direction of Mobile Knowledge.

Company Background

Mobile Knowledge Inc. was founded in 1997 in Kanata as a provider of location-tracking systems that link cars, on-board computers and high-flying satellites. It was initially called SiGEM Microsystems Inc., and it was a spinoff from SiGE Microsystems Inc. Its mission originally was to develop and commercialize specialized technology for high-speed semiconductors. After having little success, the company decided to turn to the global positioning systems (GPS) market and secured a GPS microchip design from Bristol University, England. Armed with the GPS technology, the company focused on becoming a world leader in the design of wireless location-tracking technology.

SiGEM bought a number of companies in order to acquire the expertise needed to establish itself as a credible competitor in its industry. John Roberts, who became the president and CEO of the company, successfully attracted investments of approximately $500,000 and brought in another $1 million after a reverse takeover. Roberts used this money to acquire Cygnus Satellite Systems Inc., which added a strong engineering team and expertise in satellite systems and antennas, to complement SiGEM's existing knowledge base. Roberts also used shares and cash from a $14-million private placement to acquire GMSI Inc. Through this acquisition, SiGEM was able to add both fleet management and online mapping services to its core products, allowing it to provide total end-to-end products for its location-tracking systems. In early 2001 the company also acquired Auriga Communications, a profitable fleet management company, in order to add more revenue to SiGEM and help it penetrate the U.K. fleet management market.

More recently, the company acquired Cantech International, a leading provider of transportation solutions that specialized in developing and implementing Intelligent Dispatching Systems in North and South America, Europe, and the Middle East. The XDS, XCS, and DRS applications developed by Cantech had been well received for their ease of deployment, ease of use, and extensive functionality.

But SiGEM went through two painful years. As a start-up it was the favourite of investors in 2000 and 2001. It was named the fastest-growing start-up in 2000 by *Profit* magazine based on revenue growth of 20,000 percent in 24 months. But despite the high growth, the company was losing money. For example, although the company had $13.7 million in revenues in 2000, it ended up losing money. The company had overextended itself by going in many different directions just as the venture capital market was shrinking. In March 2003, Mobile Knowledge went into receivership and it surrendered its public trading status.

Emergence from Bankruptcy

Latitude Partners, the venture capital firm that was SiGEM's principal investor, acquired the assets of SiGEM after it had gone into receivership. It then formed a new privately held company with the Mobile Knowledge name and provided it with new seed investment. In August 2003, Mobile Knowledge successfully emerged from the interim receivership as a new private company, with a healthy balance sheet and a significantly reduced cost structure. The new privately owned Mobile Knowledge completed a $2.6-million financing that gave the company a new life and would allow it to execute a renewed marketing strategy that focused on taxi, limousine, and other fleet management applications.

The corporate restructuring and privatization of Mobile Knowledge allowed the company to conduct a complete overhaul of the business to deliver strong service and a sense of accountability to its current and prospective customers. Part of the effort included the development, with input from customers, of new service agreements, the implementation of a new enterprise resource planning system, the addition of a new contract manufacturing partner to the Mobile Knowledge team, and an enhanced delivery process for customer service. The company also undertook various cost-cutting measures. One of them was to reduce overhead expenses by approximately 70 percent and total expenses by 50 percent.

The company was run by David Levy and Mick Chawner, who managed to revive Mobile Knowledge and make it a viable concern. The company became profitable, unlike its previous years when Mobile Knowledge never made a profit. But it required a lot of work on the part of Mick Chawner, its new president and chief operating officer, and the company as a whole. It took more than 12 months to get Mobile Knowledge back on its feet. Now the company paid more attention to customers. Previous customers had to be reassured the business was viable this time. As a result of its efforts, 95 percent of its customers signed new agreements with the company.

Current Operations

Mobile Knowledge developed and marketed hardware and services for a variety of wireless location-tracking applications including taxi, limousines, shuttle, courier, and transit. Its products utilized global positioning systems and wireless communications technology for cost-effective, energy-efficient, two-way location tracking and messaging. Its long-term mission was to become the world leader in the design of wireless location-tracking technology.

Its professional services included project management to facilitate the acquisition and installation of its systems and updated hardware and software. Training programs helped clients develop their own in-house professionals who could do everything from in-vehicle installations to system operations hosting. Software for the Cabmate host dispatch system could be customized. The company could add new features, enhance existing features, and customize the interface to suit the customer's needs. Installation services were offered to ensure the host system and in-vehicle installation were executed according to the project plan. A service called performance optimization was offered to ensure that clients got the most out of their system. And radio compatibility testing was performed to develop the proper settings to ensure compatibility between the mobile radio and the in-vehicle technology.

The main benefits these customers received were enhancing personal safety, increasing asset utilization, and reducing insurance. In one instance, Mobile Knowledge products improved the efficiency of a cab company by 25 percent. Many considered the display system, a crucial part of its products, as being very important to cab drivers. When the dispatcher transmits an address or instructions by voice, there is often misinterpretation or misunderstandings because frequently the voice message is not clear. But with a data message on the screen, the problem no longer exists.

Mobile Knowledge contracted out to third parties for the manufacturing, packaging and testing of its products.

The company used a three-tiered approach to meet its manufacturing needs. In-house facilities provided a number of functions, including the design and engineering of prototypes, early-introduction marketing samples, product qualification and quality assurance of production units, and limited pilot production runs. Pre-production volumes were provided by internal facilities with support from external board assembly facilities. High-volume manufacturing was provided by external manufacturing facilities. Mobile Knowledge used building on consignment and turnkey manufacturing when approaching third parties to manufacture its products.

The Industry

Mobile Knowledge operated in the telematics industry, which was the result of the convergence of wireless communications, location technology, and motor vehicles. Telematics technology made use of the Internet, wireless data networks, and GPS technology and involved the real-time delivery of critical information about location, vehicle status, and diagnostics to both the drivers of the vehicles and fleet managers. This merging of technology promised to revolutionize the taxicab industry. For example, location-tracking systems would link vehicles via on-board computers, and satellites would allow taxi dispatchers to pinpoint the location of vehicles. Then, instead of sending the first car available, it would send the one closest to the pickup point.

The telematics industry represented a significant opportunity in overall market potential. The industry as a whole was expected to grow at a high rate over the next few years. Industry analysts predicted that 84 percent of new cars in the United States would come with optional or standard GPS by 2002 compared with only 17 percent in 2000. The number of U.S. telematics subscribers was also expected to rise from approximately 1 million in 2000 to 4 million in 2002 and more than 17 million in 2005. The market potential of the telematics-based commercial fleet management systems in North America alone was estimated at 20 million vehicles, including taxi fleets, leased fleets, heavy trucks and equipment, transit fleets, corporate fleets, and emergency vehicles. This market was expected to grow from under $2 billion in 2001 to nearly $6 billion by year-end 2007.

Current Marketing Strategies

Mobile Knowledge was positioning itself as both a hardware supplier and a service provider to the telematics industry. Although currently lagging, it expected that in a few years service sales would be higher than equipment sales. One of their more important core competences was being able to provide a complete package that included the equipment and location tracking technology.

Mobile Knowledge had tried to expand its revenue mix through expanding its product, technology, and customer base. It selectively acquired complementary companies and technologies to increase its market share and its ability to offer more products to its customers looking for complete solutions. By investing an estimated 11 percent of its sales on R&D, Mobile Knowledge had continually tried to satisfy customers' needs better by advancing its technology and quality of services and introducing new products. In an effort to maintain its growth, Mobile Knowledge formed strong relationships with electronic suppliers and engaged in R&D on web tracking and hosting services. It had immediately deployable technologies and experience that enabled it to serve customers in a highly effective way and develop partnerships with customers.

Mobile Knowledge had implemented marketing and communications programs that were designed to increase the company's recognition in the wireless location-tracking industry. The company believed that industry recognition and understanding of its offerings was crucial to support sales. Part of Mobile Knowledge's communications strategy had been the change in its name to Mobile Knowledge and the change in the name of its products to Mobile Knowledge products. This name change was undertaken because the company felt that customers did not know what SiGEM, its former name, stood for and, the company believed a name change would increase its sales and change its image. It was felt that the new name better reflected what the company was selling. The focus of its new communications strategy was to create a strong brand image in its market segment.

A significant aspect of its market strategy was product bundling that included the sale of both hardware and services. A good example of this strategy was the GPS systems put in the taxicabs in Singapore. These systems told dispatchers where the cab driver was and where the next fare was and kept track of the total number of fares for that shift.

One of the initiatives launched by Mobile Knowledge in recent years was targeted advertising, in which MDTs (mobile data terminals) were installed in the passenger section of a cab and were intended to screen ads. The idea was that when a cab was in the vicinity of a restaurant, for instance, its ad would appear on the screen. The company had estimated that it would require 4,000 installed units and 18 months to receive adequate ad revenues in order to make a profit.

Another initiative focused on the paper taxi chit that corporations give to employees to use on company business. The chit system had existed for years. Companies knew it was widely abused but it was virtually impossible to know if a chit truly was used for company business or to get home after a night on the town. Mobile Knowledge introduced a card-swipe system that would bill a company's business office instantly, show the cost, and authenticate the journey. This new technology was a paperless trail for monitoring the taxi expenses of corporations, some of which spent millions of dollars a year on taxis for their employees.

The Challenges Ahead

The successful emergence of the company from receivership and its subsequent performance that resulted in the company becoming profitable for the first time had placed the company on a solid footing. However, Mick Chawner, the company's president and chief executive officer, was aware of the many challenges his company was facing. The telematics market was an emerging market, and it was fraught with many uncertainties. As with all emerging new markets, it was highly fragmented. Currently, there were approximately 200 firms providing wireless location-tracking devices. It was expected that as the industry continued to grow, there would be consolidation as many competitors would be forced to exit, merge, or be acquired by more efficient competitors. Differentiation, product quality, and price competition would also play major roles as the industry reached maturity.

Technological change within the telematics industry was also expected to affect Mobile Knowledge in the future. Technology was constantly changing and rapidly improving within the industry. The success of a firm in this industry would depend on the market accepting the technology itself and the firm's ability to keep pace with the technological change in the industry. It was essential that companies both monitor their technological environment and invest a significant percentage of their revenues in research and development to maintain their position in the industry.

Currently, the company was experimenting with a card-swipe system for bus companies. Other possibilities included cabs being able to print out airline boarding passes while they were on their way to the airport by entering the plane ticket and flight number, or cabs being able to print out tickets to the Toronto Symphony Orchestra or the National Arts Centre in Ottawa so the customer didn't have to wait in line.

But above all, Mobile Knowledge had to decide what kind of company it was and what it should be. Which major markets should it compete in? Should it stay within its currently served markets consisting of mainly taxis and limousine fleets and other fleet-type operations or should it compete across the entire telematics market by supplying new cars with GPS systems? A number of other companies were supplying this market, including OnStar, a mobile data service developed by General Motors that it currently deploys in many of its passenger vehicles and also sells to other automakers for use in their vehicles. The OnStar package included services such as unlocking the car doors when they are locked and no key is available, roadside assistance, or notifying emergency personnel—all with the push of a dash-mounted button (or a phone call if the driver is locked out). Other basic services include airbag deployment notification and remote diagnostics.

Discussion Questions

1. What are the threats facing the telematics industry?
2. Assess the current marketing strategy of Mobile Knowledge.
3. Should Mobile Knowledge expand its strategic market to include the entire telematics industry?
4. Should Mobile Knowledge enter the consumer global positioning system market or stay within its commercial-fleet telematics markets?

Sources

Company annual reports; Keith Woolhouse, "Back-seat screens air ads for taxi passengers," *Ottawa Citizen*, October 7, 2003; Bert Hill, "Back from the Brink," *Ottawa Citizen*, July 20, 2004; Emily Westhafer, "Mobile Knowledge Acquires Cantech Intl.," *Venture Wire*, July 13, 2004; "Mobile Knowledge Successfully Emerges as a Private Company with New Customer Contracts and New Financing," Company press release, August 19, 2003; "About Mobile Knowledge," retrieved from http://www.mobile-knowledge.com/corporate/about.asp, on May 4, 2005; "Mobile Knowledge Delivers Data Dispatch and Mobile Media to Chicago Carriage Cab Co.," Company press release, July 31, 2003; "Mobile Knowledge launches 'Mobile Media,' New Revenue Source for Taxi/Limo/Paratransit Operators," Canada NewsWire, October 15, 2002; "Mobile Knowledge Continues Winning Streak, Signs Key Order in California," Canada NewsWire, September 24, 2002; "Mobile Knowledge Accelerates Winning Pace, Gains Another New Taxi Customer in California," Canada NewsWire, October 29, 2002.

Steinhouse Knitting Mills (Canada) Ltd.

Mark Haber and Christopher A. Ross

This case was written by Mark Haber and Christopher A. Ross of Concordia University as a basis for classroom discussion. It is not designed to illustrate either effective or ineffective handling of administrative issues. Some of the information in this case may have been disguised but the essential relationships remain.

In the fall of 1999, Abraham (Abe) Steinhouse, 64, and his son Mark, 36, were wondering what action they should take regarding their knitting business. Steinhouse Knitting specialized in the manufacture and sale of men's sweaters. In 1998, annual sales were $2.7 million. In 1999, with overheads at about $100,000 per month, excluding management salaries, estimated annual sales were approximately $2.4 million (U.S. sales excluded). This latter figure was approximately 30 percent of their 1988 peak sales figure of $7.5 million. Since 1988, sales had been declining steadily. In 1993, for example, annual sales were $3.5 million. Both Abe and Mark felt that changes had to be made to the operations of the business in order to reverse this downward trend and ensure the survival of the business.

History of the Company

Abe's father, who had been trained as a knitter, founded Steinhouse Knitting in 1929. He began operations making babies' wear—romper sets—in the back of a store, with 12 square metres of space. He had a great sense of quality, though, according to Abe, he did not have a great sense of fashion. He manufactured babies' wear because he liked it. He also felt that the babies' wear industry was not as competitive as the ladies' or men's wear industries. While he made the outfits at the back, his wife sold at the front.

Abe was still in high school when he started in the business in 1952. He took care of invoicing, the payroll, and some of the bookkeeping. As he became familiar with the business, he realized that there was a low upper limit to price in the children's sweater business. For example, while price points for children's sweaters were $3.95 to $4.95 at retail, the price points for men's sweaters were $10.95 to $12.95. As a result, he started making increasing quantities of men's sweaters.

By the time Abe was 17, the company had a staff of 20 employees working in 279 square metres of space. At this time too, Abe began working as a salesperson, going from door to door, selling to independent stores. In 1957, Abe graduated from university. By 1958, the physical space for the business had grown to 1,115 square metres and it was located on St. Lawrence Street, Montreal. In 1960, annual sales were $500,000. By 1967, Abe had started visiting Europe looking for new styles and had also started to buy sophisticated computerized knitting machines.

By 1986, the business was well established, profitable, and successful. There was enough money for the family to live comfortably. In August of that year, Mark Steinhouse, Abe's son, joined the business. Mike had graduated in Industrial Psychology from McGill University in Montreal. He entered the business immediately after graduating and has never worked in any other business. His cousin was in charge of production, and Mark worked in shipping, cutting, and sewing. After gaining experience and knowledge of the inner workings of the business, Mark went out to sell. He sold to independent men's wear stores for three years, a total of six selling seasons in all.

In 1988, with sales at $7.5 million, including imports, and approximately 50 employees, the owners made the decision to move from the rented premises on St. Lawrence Street, where they had been for 30 years, to an owned location. They built their own plant and moved, in May 1989, to Chabanel Street, still in Montreal. In that same year, the company made a brief and unsuccessful foray into the U.S. market. The company hired two sales representatives, one in New York and the other in New Jersey. These two salespeople were successful in bringing in new business but one of them was caught in fraudulent activities. Steinhouse Knitting lost about $65,000 (U.S.). After this event, the company left the U.S. market in 1991.

In 1990, Abe bought his sister's share of the business, and she and her son left the company. Steinhouse Knitting continued as usual with Abe's father, with Abe and Mark as the management team. Steinhouse Knitting re-entered the U.S. market in 1996 and by 1998 sales in that market were $250,000 (U.S.).

In December 1997, the management of Steinhouse Knitting invited a family friend, Jacob Lieberman, to use part of their facilities as the head office of his sport-shirt manufacturing business, Styles JMD. The motivation behind this move was symbiotic: Styles JMD would benefit from economies of scale and Steinhouse Knitting would have a modern brand name that also generated financial benefits. Steinhouse's executives owned 50 percent of JMD and financed the complete operation. The two businesses operated separately although the owners shared ideas and overheads, such as secretarial help, salespeople, and computing facilities. Styles JMD paid Steinhouse 5 percent of sales in lieu of rent and overhead. All manufacturing for the shirt business, however, was subcontracted out. In 1998, the year that Abe's father passed away, annual Canadian sales for Steinhouse Knitting was $2.7 million. By 1999, the sales of JMD shirts was about equal to the sales of Steinhouse's sweaters. Styles JMD also imported a small quantity of sweaters from Asia. Like Steinhouse Knitting, the customers of Styles JMD were independent men's clothing stores in Canada and the United States.

Product

Steinhouse Knitting manufactures and sells high-quality men's sweaters. The company produces three different brands: Steinhouse, Etcetera, and España. Customers perceive España as having the highest quality and price. However, for the three brands, the company does not differentiate on the basis of style, price, or fabrication.

Currently 80 percent of the yarn used in making the sweaters is sourced from one supplier in Toronto. Because all the yarn is NAFTA-approved, Steinhouse Knitting does not pay any duties on sweaters shipped to the United States. When the yarn arrives at the factory door, it is knitted, washed, and finished. Fabric softener

is then added. It is also pressed flat, even, and smooth. Employees cut the sweaters from the fabric one at a time. The sweaters are then sewn, cleaned, and tagged prior to shipping. In total there are 27 operations in making a sweater. Mark commented on the process, "[Our sweaters are] cut piece by piece as opposed to cutting in piles. That is one of the differences between a quality sweater and a so-so sweater. There are lots of differences among brands apart from the yarn. For example, an inexpensive manufacturer will not finish the sweater properly, then when you buy the sweater it will shrink 10 percent to 15 percent. We take out the shrinkage, we tumble it with softener, so it is treated. We cut them one by one, so that each line will fall where it is supposed to fall. An inexpensive manufacturer will pile the material to cut and then when the sweaters are cut, the top one and the bottom one are off centre."

Steinhouse Knitting has not changed its raw material inputs for the sweaters in the last ten years. All sweaters for the fall line are 70 percent acrylic and 30 percent wool. The fall line contributes 85 percent to annual sales. In the spring, the sweaters are 50 percent cotton and 50 percent acrylic. Management believed that their product quality was very good. There was a problem, however, in people's perception of acrylic. Most people cannot tell the difference between acrylic and wool, but when they read the manufacturer's label on a sweater and see "Acrylic," they perceive a cheaper garment. However, the sweaters of Steinhouse Knitting are in the upper price ranges. There appears, therefore, to be an inconsistency between what customers perceive and the price points at which the sweaters are sold. Adding more wool is a possible solution to this problem. Even 5 percent angora, alpaca or linen could make a difference, according to Mark. Abe pointed out, however, that European manufacturers used the same type of yarn as Steinhouse Knitting, and that in the United States, the image of acrylic was improving.

Steinhouse Knitting produces most of its sweaters to order. During the selling season, the salespeople visit the customers and book orders. All the orders are then entered into a computer, yarn is bought, and the orders are produced. Sometimes the company may have yarn in inventory ahead of time because from experience they may know what is popular. For example, there may be black sweaters in 20 different styles, so they may order 10,000 pounds (4,536 kilograms) of black yarn. However, when the salesperson deposits the order with the company, Steinhouse begins production with inventoried raw material and does not wait until the yarn arrives. Thus, the company may purchase yarns ahead of time when they believe the risk is minimal. It takes six to eight weeks to receive the yarn once the company places the order.

Steinhouse Knitting normally finishes the fall line at the beginning of January. From January to March, the factory is practically at a standstill. Only the principal employees are retained. The company may knit a few styles that they are confident will sell in the next period. Consequently, they will have some styles in stock, ahead of time. In past years, 10 percent to 15 percent of sweaters were knitted in advance.

The company makes about 30 different styles a season. Each style might be made in a polo, a cardigan, a crew, and a V neck, and each might have four different colours in four sizes. If the style is sized in "bigs and talls," this adds eight more sizes. As a consequence, the company has many Stock Keeping Units (SKUs). The large number of SKUs sometimes results in inefficiencies, especially if the demand is only for a small quantity. About 10 percent of the SKUs are responsible for 50 percent of the annual sales. In a few cases, only 100 sweaters may be made of one style. The company makes to order, but the order is rounded up to the closest dozen. Thus, if an order is for 7.5 dozen, the company will make 8 dozen. If, subsequently, a retailer calls and requests additional sweaters and they are in stock, Steinhouse will ship, but they will not make only one or two sweaters for a retailer. Retailers are therefore taking a chance that their order can be filled if they call for just one or two sweaters.

Like many other manufacturers in this industry, Steinhouse Knitting does not have an in-house designer. Prior to 1967, the company borrowed ideas for different styles of sweaters from competitors, from store displays, or from magazines. After a while, Steinhouse's management began making annual trips to Europe to look at the fashions and to examine different styles of sweaters. All the fashion in sweaters originate in Europe, according to Abe and Mark. Abe and Mark usually visit different European countries, shop at different stores, meet at some agreed point, and compare purchases. For the fall season of 1999, for example, they purchased upwards of 50 sweaters in Europe. Upon returning to Canada, they incorporate the best fashion ideas and colours into their own products while keeping their customers in mind. Because the equipment and machinery in Steinhouse Knitting is different from what is available in Europe, the products they make do not look exactly like the samples purchased.

Abe believes that the fashion business is like no other and that many factors determine the different trends. Men's sweaters are not as fashionable as they were even five years ago. The fact that yarn is still at the same price it was 15 years ago indicates the market. The weather also determines the level of sweater sales. For the last three years in Western Canada, for example, the winters were unseasonably warm. On the upside, in Europe, men's sweaters are becoming popular. It is also seems that the

name brand concept may be weakening. This may be of benefit to Steinhouse.

Customers

Steinhouse's customers are largely independent clothing stores. They also sell to some stores with four or five outlets and to private brands Ernest with 34 stores and Bovet with 22 stores. Ernest and Bovet account for 20 percent of Steinhouse's annual sales. Quebec and Ontario account for 30 percent of sales each, 5 percent of sales occur in the Maritimes, 10 percent in Alberta and the rest in Manitoba, Saskatchewan, and British Columbia. The typical order size is $1,500 but a few customers may buy $10,000 and a few may buy $800. Retailers will sometimes call for one or two sweaters if a client is asking for a special size or colour and they are out of stock.

Management believes that the independent stores are fast disappearing (Exhibit 1). In Mark's experience there is almost a constant stream of bankruptcies among these stores. Mark believes that their customers are disappearing because of competition from category killers like Wal-Mart and Price-Costco and the strong established brand names such as Hilfiger, Polo, Nautica, and Point Zero. Very little effort has been made to sell to other types of customers. Steinhouse Knitting did try to win Simons as a customer, but their efforts did not bear fruit. Simons imports most of its sweaters from low-wage countries. "We cannot compete against Chinese and Bangladeshi prices, and these and similar countries are the major source for stores such as Simons. We are the suppliers of last resort," Abe said.

Exhibit 1	Men's Clothing Store Sales[1]
Year	Sales (000,000)
1999	1,536.4
1998	1,581.7
1997	1,569.5
1996	1,516.0
1995	1,623.0
1994	1,848.1
1993	1,756.3
1992	1,622.5
1991	1,703.2
1990	2,202.0

[1] SOURCE: Statistics Canada, CANSIM database, Matrix 2400

Steinhouse Knitting does not do any market studies. Customers are not consulted before Steinhouse's management makes the annual trip to Europe. From experience, the company believes that a major influence on the purchasing behaviour of the retailers, their customers, is the previous year's sales. Retailers examine what was popular last year and tend to buy similar styles. Another influence on purchasing behaviour is the business climate at the time the sales representative makes a sales call. The company believes that, in general, the sales representative who calls on the retailer first gets most of the business. The company has some sense of the kind of people who purchase sweaters from the independents. Again, because of long experience in the industry and good communication with their retailers, the management of Steinhouse Knitting believes that women purchase most of the men's sweaters, for their husbands or boyfriends. Women probably purchase 75 percent of all men's sweaters. "We believe that most of the women are over 40 years old because at our retail prices, they must have income levels that are moderate to better," Abe said.

A recent trend among customers is the growing popularity of the "big and tall" sizes. About 20 percent of Steinhouse's sales in 1999 was "bigs and talls." The cause of this popularity is not known for sure—customers may be getting bigger. Another problem is the trend of "dressing down" in business or what is sometimes called "casual days." Because of increasing informality at work, customers are buying fewer suits, and suits are what brought many customers into a men's wear store. For many stores, suits accounted for 40 percent or 50 percent of sales. Accessories like sweaters, shirts, ties, handkerchiefs, and socks accounted for the other 50 percent. Because men buy fewer suits, they visit men's wear stores less frequently and therefore they also buy fewer accessories such as sweaters. Furthermore, casual days result in men buying fewer dressy sweaters. The weather over the last few years has also hurt business.

Both Abe and Mark observed that customers were increasingly demanding higher-gauge, lighter sweaters made of natural fibres such as wool and cotton. Sweaters can be made in different gauges such as eight, ten, or twelve. The higher the gauge, the finer the knitting and the lighter the sweater. This move to higher-gauge sweaters by customers is believed to be suitable for today's fashions. Fashion dictates change and thus other-gauge sweaters eventually appear. While Steinhouse's current machinery can knit natural fibres, the machines cannot produce higher gauges of knit. Thus, substantial retooling would be necessary and new machinery would be required if Steinhouse Knitting was to take advantage of this new demand. To convert all their machinery is a major investment. One of the biggest changes taking place in the industry is in the area of technology. Steinhouse's machinery can be programmed in a matter of hours, not a week as in the past, for example. New machines can be programmed to make the whole garment. They can also put in the V neck in sweaters and the button holes. These machines are very slow and costly, however. The yarn has to be perfect. The price of this kind of yarn is high and it is not always available in North America. Abe believes that at the present time none of these machines are running in North America. The last time the company put money into machinery was about six years ago when they bought two new knitting machines. The capital cost for modern knitting machines is about $250,000 to $300,000 each. Steinhouse needs about 20 machines but is hesitant to purchase them in this market. Compounding the problem is Steinhouse's large inventory of acrylic-wool fibres, which cannot just be disposed of although they expect to reduce their stockpile to a reasonable level.

Promotion

Steinhouse Knitting depends largely on commission salespeople to promote its products. Salespeople in Montreal are provided with an office and are paid a straight commission. The company has salespeople all across the country: one in the Maritimes, three in Quebec, three in Ontario, one in the Prairies, one in Alberta, and one in British Columbia. They pay their own expenses and the company pays them commissions upon delivery of goods to the customer. The average commission rate is 7.5 percent, which is standard in the men's wear industry. If the salespeople discount prices to any customer, their commission is reduced on a sliding scale. For example, a discount of 10 percent reduces the commission to 3 percent.

The salespeople visit the customers twice a year—once for the fall line and once for the spring line. They do not do any servicing of customers between those two selling seasons. In the opinion of the salespeople, it does not pay to visit customers at any other time. A sales booking season lasts from about four to six weeks, so the salespeople work for about three months of the year. For the rest of the year they are free to do whatever they wish.

Mark concluded, "I don't believe that our declining sales is because of our sales force. I believe that we have very good salespeople. In general, I am happy with our sales reps. I can't really blame it on them. They are pretty much stuck with the stores they have. Our reps sell to independent stores. Each one of those guys is losing market share—whether it is in British Columbia, Northern Ontario, Toronto, Alberta, the Prairie provinces, or wherever. It is no secret that they are getting hurt by the same people we are getting hurt by."

The principal salesperson in Montreal recruited the salespeople in the United States. He called the U.S. accounts with which Steinhouse Knitting was doing business and obtained references about possible candidates for the job. As in Canada, commission salespeople are standard in the United States except that a national sales manager might be hired. According to Mark, the hardest part about selling in the United States is finding good sales representatives. Current sales for the company in the United States are $250,000, and one person is responsible for about 85 percent of that. This sales representative covers the New Jersey/New York area. Because Steinhouse's U.S. customers are also independent men's stores, the company entered the U.S. market with more or less the same marketing mix, aiming at the higher end of the market with products exported from the Montreal plant. In the United States, while the compensation system is the same as in Canada, straight commission at 7.5 percent of sales, the salespeople may also receive "draws" of approximately $1,000 to $2,000 per month.

The company has never spent money on advertising except for 1998 when they created a colour catalogue, at a cost of $25,000, and mailed it to their existing customers. The company participates in a number of trade shows. They supported their re-entry into the United States in 1996, for example, by participating in trade shows. At the trade shows they often succeeded in winning some accounts. They participated for five years, two seasons per year. Each year cost about $60,000, which is expensive in Mark's opinion, but the government subsidized each year by about $20,000.

Pricing

Retailers pay anywhere from $22 to $70 for Steinhouse's sweaters. However, the average price is approximately $40. Steinhouse's average gross margin is approximately 40 percent of sales and their receivable-days is about 95. Customers of the retail stores pay an average of $80 to $100 for a Steinhouse sweater. In contrast, the average retail price for an imported sweater is $40 or lower. In 1998, 67 percent of all sweaters sold in Canada were imported. These were mostly women's and children's. The major source of imports in 1996 was Hong Kong (transshipped from China), the United States, China, Italy, and Taiwan. Today in Canada, retailers have difficulty if they merely sell the sweater at double the price they paid for it. A typical retail store must have a gross profit of 50 percent after markdowns.

Competition

In Canada, the major sweater manufacturers are located in Ontario, Quebec, and Manitoba. In 1996, the total sales of sweaters in Canada, from both domestic production and imports, equalled $0.5 billion dollars. According to the management of Steinhouse Knitting, a number of plants that specialized in men's sweaters have closed in recent years (Exhibit 2). Current competition includes Cooper Knitting and San Remo Knitting in Montreal. Cooper Knitting has approximately 50 employees and San Remo Knitting has over 100 employees. In Toronto, Straton Knitting has over 100 employees and Standard Knitting, in Winnipeg, has over 100 employees. Competitive profiles are shown in Exhibit 2.

In the view of Steinhouse management, competition is surviving because they are concentrating on the U.S. market. Others survive by reorienting their production to suit the demands of Wal-Mart and Zellers. Consequently, they operate more down-market than Steinhouse Knitting does. They sell to the discount stores at $12 and $13 a sweater, made from 100 percent acrylic or 100 percent cotton. While the material and the machinery might be the same, the sewing and cutting of lower-quality sweaters is inferior to that of a Steinhouse product. Furthermore, these down-market competitors do not finish their sweaters the same way Steinhouse does.

In fact, there has been a polarization in the marketplace. Steinhouse's products are too expensive for Costco, Wal-Mart, and Zellers. These stores buy directly from Asian manufacturers who require letters of credit. Steinhouse is at a big disadvantage with regard to financing as well as labour. Steinhouse sells in the fall for delivery in March and is paid an average of 95 days after that. The high end of the market, on the other hand, sells the Italian brands—sweaters that sell for $200 or more. The large department stores focus on the name brands such as Nautica, Polo, Tommy Hilfiger, and Point Zero at slightly lower prices. So with their customers, the independent boutiques and small chains, disappearing, Steinhouse Knitting is in a precarious position.

Exhibit 2	Competitive Profiles

Name	Location	Age	Emp'yees	Sales: (000,000)	Exp'ting	Main Product
Boutique Knitting Mills[a]	Montreal	24 yrs	175	≤$25	Yes–U.S., Europe, Aus ≤$500,000	Ladies' sweaters
Grace Knitting[b]	Montreal	15 yrs	39	≥$25	Yes–U.S. <$100K	Ladies' sweaters
Niagara Knitting[c]	St Catharines	8 yrs	45	<$5	No	Uniforms and school sweaters
Standard Knitting Ltd.[d]	Winnipeg	23 yrs	100	≤$25	Yes–U.S., Europe, Latin Amer.	Men's sweaters
Straton Knitting Mills Ltd.[e]	Toronto	57 yrs	175	≤$25	Yes–U.S., Japan, Asia ≤$1,000,000	Men's sweaters
San Remo[f]	Montreal	–	100	≤$10	–	Men's sweaters
Cooper Knitting[g]	Montreal	70 yrs	50	≤$10	Yes–U.S.	Men's sweaters

[a] This company produces sweaters for men, boys, women, and girls in acrylic, wool, nylon, polyester, and cotton.

[b] This company produces sweaters for men and women, boys and girls, in wool, acrylic, and cotton.

[c] This company produces primarily sweaters. Occupational clothing is secondary. They use standard materials for the RCMP, Canada Customs, Correctional Services, and different police forces. They specialize in windproof, lined sweaters.

[d] This company produces primarily sweaters but also operates in the sporting goods industry. They use cotton, wool, cashmere, silk, linen, and various blends. Their brand is Tundra.

[e] This company manufactures largely sweaters; they also produce some shirts. They use the standard materials.

[f] This company was owned by Dylex. Over 86 percent of their sales went to Tip Top, which was also owned by Dylex. Dylex sold Tip Top to Graft & Fraser and San Remo is now for sale.

[g] This company manufactures sweaters, with some private branding. They use standard materials.

The Company: Current Perspectives

Management believes that they have a financially sound company. The firm has no long-term debt. Finance is therefore not a constraint on decision-making. If they had to, they could buy new technology or different kinds of raw material. They also believe that they have tremendous experience in manufacturing and selling men's sweaters.

The Future

Both Abe and Mark feel that producing ladies' sweaters is not a viable option. The ladies' business is very competitive, and they will have to compete against extremely competent businesses. In any event it is a very different business, in the view of management, as different as marketing is to finance.

The management of Steinhouse Knitting also feels that getting into department stores is not feasible.

Department stores in Canada have, in fact, disappeared. Only The Bay and Sears remain and they sell mostly imported sweaters or name brands. The discounters such as Wal-Mart and Costco buy in such large quantities that they do not need wholesalers and purchase directly from manufacturers in low-wage countries. Steinhouse Knitting is of the opinion that they cannot match the prices of the imported sweaters.

One possibility is changing the mix of yarn in the sweaters. Some customers, particularly in the United States, have made such demands. By adding a bit of cashmere to the sweaters, for example, it is possible that Steinhouse's established brands may be perceived differently. But they cannot compete with the Chinese, who produce cashmere. Cashmere yarn costs $50 per pound and it takes 1.5 pounds to make a sweater.

Another possible route for survival and prosperity is to make a bigger push into the U.S. market since the company can export to the United States virtually duty free.

The clothing industry is labour intensive and can function with a limited number of special skills; clothing is therefore manufactured in almost every country of the world. Low-wage developing countries with an abundant supply of labour provide tough competition to countries such as Canada.

Statistics Canada classifies Clothing (SIC 24) into four sub-groups: Men's and Boy's Clothing (SIC 243), Women's Clothing (SIC 244), Children's Clothing (245), and Other Clothing (SIC 249), which includes sweaters, hosiery, fur, and occupational clothing.

In 1997, men's and women's clothing accounted for 68.1 percent of manufacturing output of this industry. Other clothing accounted for 25.8 percent and children for 6.1 percent.

Clothing is manufactured in all regions of Canada except the territories. Fully 62 percent of establishments were located in Quebec in 1997, accounting for an equal percentage of the industry's shipments and 57.1 percent of employment. Ontario was home to 22.5 percent of establishments and produced 25.2 percent of the shipments.

Shipments originating in Quebec rose by 5.4 percent over the past decade, despite a decline of 42.5 percent in the number of establishments, indicating that there has been some consolidation of apparel production and efficiency gains.

The industry as a whole has been slow to adopt advanced manufacturing technology, although some sub-sectors such as knitting (which is more capital intensive than other sub-sectors) and men's wear (which is less susceptible to style changes) have been quicker to embrace technological advancement.

The clothing industry consists of many small establishments. Of the 1,665 establishments in 1997, 74.5 percent employed fewer than 50 people and contributed only 28.1 percent to the value of total shipments.

Canadian households in 1988 spent 6 percent of their personal disposable income on clothing and footwear, but that amount came down to 4.7 percent in 1998. The demand for apparel has been affected by other competing priorities, such as the purchase of computers and electronics, by a trend toward shopping in discount stores and by consumers' increased insistence on good value for the price paid.

Since 1989, domestic shipments of clothing have decreased persistently, except for 1995. Manufacturers have been able to maintain the present level of production only as a result of phenomenal growth in exports. While imports doubled, exports in 1998 were five times the value of 1988.

SOURCE: Sheikh, Yasmin, "Has the clothing industry adapted to the changing economic environment?" Statistics Canada site, December 1999 www.statcan.ca/english/freepub/34-252-XIE/1999/34-252.htm, accessed November 9, 2002. Yasmin Sheikh is a Statistics Canada economist in the Manufacturing, Constructions, and Energy Division of Statistics Canada.

The independents are also disappearing in the United States but it is such a big market that it is still possible to get 100 or 150 stores as customers, enough to be profitable. In addition, the low value of the Canadian dollar relative to that of the United States is a big advantage. But the United States is a difficult market to break into. Management believes that to succeed they will have to modify their product but modify it in a way that makes it different from American styles. Continuing to focus on the European styles is the answer, they believe. Right now they are crawling along but the goal is to double U.S. sales in the next two years. That target will depend on producing a lot more "big and tall" sizes.

A final alternative is to continue supplying customers who would like to have Steinhouse's traditional products in their stores. At the same time, they can also import the type of sweaters that Steinhouse does not produce, from low-wage countries, and sell these to a different market segment. Sweaters imported from Asia, Italy or Turkey would also yield a 35 percent to 40 percent gross margin. One consequence obviously is that the plant will continue to operate below capacity.

Both Abe and Mark were wondering what they should do. They are very comfortable financially and can afford to close the business. They want to stay in business, however. They also know that cycles change. Sweaters will be in fashion again, and Abe is committed to be more demanding on his customers when it becomes a seller's market. The biggest fear is that when the market changes, there will be nobody to sell to. Exhibit 3 provides some salient characteristics of the clothing industry in general, of which the sweater industry is a part.

WestJet Airlines

Peter Yannopoulos

In May 2004, WestJet was a regularly scheduled passenger and cargo services airline serving the Canadian domestic market. It also provided charter services on a contract basis to third parties. It was built on the Southwest Airlines model, offering low fares within a low-cost organizational structure. As was the case with Southwest Airlines, WestJet's low fares stimulated air travel among people who would have used other transportation means or would not have travelled at all. Among low-fare competitors, WestJet had systematically captured the largest portion of the additional volume of passengers on the routes it chose to enter, becoming in the process the largest discount airline in Canada.

WestJet had recently embarked on an aggressive expansion program by serving various Canadian cities in Central and Eastern Canada. Bill Lamberton, WestJet's vice-president of marketing and sales, stated that his company was interested in offering "greater connections to our Eastern Canada network." This effort led to WestJet serving 24 Canadian cities coast to coast from Victoria to St. John's, by early 2004. Also, in an effort to increase the utilization of its airplanes, WestJet entered into an agreement with Air Transat, the leading Canadian charter airline, to rent its airplanes during the off-season winter months. WestJet also sublet its hangar space in Hamilton and Calgary, it did maintenance work

for other airlines, and it rented out its three Calgary-based flight simulators.

In light of WestJet's aggressive expansion plans and recent developments in the Canadian airline industry, Clive Beddoe and the rest of his management team needed to evaluate the various opportunities available and make a decision on WestJet's future strategic direction. Should WestJet focus on consolidating its position as the leading Canadian low-cost, low-fare airline? If so, how? Should it enter the airline charter segment in a bigger way now that it had aircraft with greater long-range capabilities? Or should it set its eyes on the transborder segment, where margins are much higher than the domestic discount segment? Another possibility was the Central and South American market where Air Canada was planning to expand in mid-2004. Answers to these questions had some degree of urgency in light of recent Air Canada and Jetsgo aggressive expansion moves. Air Canada was expected to emerge from its restructuring effort a leaner and more formidable competitor. Many industry observers expected that WestJet would continue its expansion farther in the near future and some of them believed that it would begin regularly scheduled flights to the United States within the coming year.

The Southwest Airlines Business Model

On February 29, 1996, WestJet Airlines began operations to five Canadian cities with 220 employees and three aircraft. At the end of 2003, WestJet had become Canada's second-largest airline behind industry leader Air Canada, employing 3,610 people and with a fleet of only 44 aircraft—one-seventh the size of its main rival. In 2000, WestJet's four founders were honoured as "The Ernst & Young Entrepreneur of the Year" for Canada, in recognition of their success. Also, in 2003, WestJet was chosen Canada's second most respected company in the 9th Annual Survey of Canada's Most Respected Corporations, which was conducted by Ipsos-Reid and involved a randomly selected sample of 255 CEOs in Canada.

A major reason for WestJet's success was that it was based on the wildly successful Southwest Airlines business model, which focused on keeping costs low, empowering employees, sharing profits, and maintaining a well-motivated labour force within a happy culture. According to chief executive officer Clive Beddoe, "WestJet studied Southwest very closely because it is one of the most successful corporations in recent North American history." In addition to Southwest Airlines, WestJet's founders had studied other low-fare, no-frills airlines, such as JetBlue, ValuJet, and Ryanair.

Southwest's business model was designed to offer price-sensitive passengers low-cost, convenient service on the routes it chose to serve. A key aspect of Southwest's business model was to bypass large cities, such as New York and Chicago, and operate out of small airports not served by the major carriers. This allowed Southwest to avoid direct confrontation with the major full-service airlines, which operated out of large airports using the hub-and-spoke system that enabled them to serve a large number of customers and destinations.

Southwest used a standardized fleet of 737 aircraft that helped increase the efficiency of aircraft maintenance. The turnaround of its planes was 15 minutes, enabling the airline to keep its planes flying longer than its rivals and achieve a high frequency of departures with fewer aircraft. It did not assign seats and did not offer meals, premium classes of service, and interlink baggage checking. Through automated ticketing at the gate, passengers were encouraged to bypass travel agents and avoid paying their commission. Large U.S. airlines, on the other hand, offered a variety of services, including checking and transferring baggage to accommodate customers who change planes and coordinated passenger schedules.

By lowering costs and raising the level of service, Southwest made it difficult for full-service airlines to compete effectively against it. Certain large airlines attempted unsuccessfully to replicate Southwest's model. For example, Continental established Continental Light, a Southwest clone, but it failed to compete successfully against Southwest and it was discontinued.

WestJet's Business Model

Commenting on WestJet's business model, Beddoe said, "If there is one defining lesson to be drawn from WestJet, it's this: Put your employees first." According to Beddoe,

this relationship is more important than the airline's relationships with its customers because "if we have good relations with our employees, then the employees create good relationships with their customers." WestJet empowered its employees to make decisions and solve customer problems right away. Empowering employees reduced the number of customer complaints because problems were solved on the spot. Employees often went to great lengths to correct a customer service problem. For example, once the company lost a wedding dress on a flight. In order to rectify the problem, WestJet employees went out and bought a new wedding dress for the customer. WestJet management believes that it is actions like these that create an intense satisfaction and loyalty among customers.

One of WestJet's distinctive capabilities was its low-cost structure. WestJet and other small airlines enjoyed lower costs relative to larger airlines because they operated fewer planes, employed fewer employees, and cherry-picked only the most profitable routes. WestJet had developed a low-cost culture, and it seized every opportunity to cut costs and make the airline more efficient. For example, in 2003, it installed vertical-blended winglets on the wingtips of its planes. Each of these winglets cost $635,000 per plane; however, they were expected to drive costs down in the long run by reducing fuel consumption by 3.4 percent to 7 percent for an average of $122,500 in annual savings per plane. At this rate, the company should recover the cost of winglets in five years and enjoy additional savings for the rest of their useful life, which was about 20 years.

In addition to lower costs, WestJet maintained an excellent level of service through friendly, highly motivated people and hassle-free booking. WestJet also invested in training and technology in order to enhance customer service and safety, cut costs, and improve profitability, such as installing the winglets.

WestJet strived to recruit people with the right attitude and align their interests with those of the organization. Flight attendants and call-centre staff participated in group interviews for new hires. The company didn't hesitate to terminate the employment of those employees who didn't fit the company culture or had a bad attitude. According to April Shand, a former WestJet human resources manager, "Getting a person with a bad attitude, well, that's toxic. And in an environment in which you have a lot of entry-level people—and many of these people can be impressionable—the last thing you want is some toxic individual coming in and planting seeds in their head. All of a sudden, you can end up with turnover because of this one person." Recognizing that reinforcing company values is important, WestJet launched its

CARE (Create a Remarkable Experience) initiative in 1999 as a means of promoting its corporate culture and helping employees in turning company values into everyday experiences.

The company's profit-sharing program had also been credited for its employee loyalty and productivity. It was also a means of aligning employee and organizational goals. Although base salaries may have been lower than competitors' salaries, the total take-home pay was higher thanks to WestJet's profit-sharing plan. The profit-sharing plan involved distributing to employees a percentage of the company's pre-tax profit that was equal to the profit margin for the year. For example, if the company earned a 12 percent pre-tax profit margin, it distributed 12 percent of that profit to its employees twice a year. Payments were weighted proportionally to reflect the base wage of employees. WestJet also ran an employees' share purchase plan, whereby it matched every dollar employees invested in the company's stock, to a maximum of 20 percent of the employee's annual salary. According to Beddoe, "We want them to think like filthy capitalists, think like owners, think like shareholders and then drive the company to success."

WestJet departed from the Southwest model in important ways. The cornerstone of Southwest's model was serving short-haul routes, which were not served by major carriers. However, WestJet realized that such a strategy wouldn't work in Canada. In recent years, short-haul and small markets in Canada had become uneconomical to serve due to a number of factors exacerbated by the terrorist events of September 11. In Canada, the cost of flying had been driven higher through government policies that off-loaded costs on the industry or imposed user charges that were passed on to airline customers. Also, nonprofit airport authorities had embarked on ambitious expansion plans that were funded by current airline customers through the imposition of flat-rate airport improvement fees. All these extra charges on airline customers have had a greater impact on short-haul, low-cost airlines, leading people to seek alternative modes of transportation.

WestJet also deviated from Southwest's no-frills service strategy by offering passengers a number of amenities. In addition to offering snacks, WestJet ordered all new aircraft to be equipped with leather seats and enhanced legroom. WestJet was also seeking regulatory approval to equip all its new aircraft with live on-board television. In December 2003, it finalized a contract with Bell ExpressVu for 24 channels of live television with a broad range of programming, making WestJet the first airline in Canada to offer live, satellite television. This feature would be free of charge initially, but the company might eventually charge a nominal fee for the service.

WestJet's Marketing Strategy

WestJet was positioned as Canada's national low-fare airline. Its low-cost, low-fare strategy was well timed as the Canadian airline industry was undergoing a major change as more customers were becoming price sensitive and looking for reduced airfares while resisting paying for traditionally high ticket prices. Its marketing strategy focused on low airfares that stimulated demand for air travel by price-sensitive travellers, while improving efficiency to keep costs and prices low.

WestJet emphasized simplified everyday low fares with non-stay-over requirements, convenient schedules, and a completely ticketless reservation system. On average, WestJet's fares were 55 percent lower than fares charged by Air Canada. In addition to its affordable airfare and simplified structure, WestJest focused on the delivery of excellent customer service and passenger satisfaction as a core component of its marketing strategy.

WestJet had formed its Advertising and New Media division of the marketing and sales department to produce advertising that reflected its image and positioning. The majority of WestJet's advertising was done in magazines, in newspapers, on radio, on television, through outdoor advertising, in transit messaging, and on Web advertising. The airline sold package deals to some of its destinations and it offered special fares for groups of 10 or more people. In 2002, WestJet offered a "Prime Ministers Day" special, when people with the first and last name of any Canadian prime minister, past or present, could fly for free on a particular day on select routes. In 2002, WestJet donated more than 10,000 flights for two to people and organizations across the country. Many of these flights went to nonprofit organizations to be used as prizes in draws and raffles for fundraising purposes.

One of the major trends in the airline industry was the use of the Internet for purchasing airline tickets. The Internet allowed people to book flights on their own time with relative ease. As people felt more comfortable with its capabilities, the Internet was becoming more widely used. WestJet's online booking ability enabled the company to sell its product quickly and efficiently. In 2002, WestJet's Internet bookings exceeded 50 percent of total sales. The ticketless nature of Internet sales eliminated the high cost associated with the printing, distribution, and tracking of tickets. It also allowed quick and efficient check-in procedures at airports.

WestJet also sold tickets directly through its Sales Super Centre and through travel agents via the Sabre and Galileo distribution system. Travel agency bookings accounted for approximately 38 percent of total sales. Of WestJet's bookings through travel agents, Sabre and Galileo bookings accounted for approximately

16 percent, 57 percent of bookings were generated through the Internet, and sales through the call centre accounted for 27 percent. Travel agents received a 9 percent commission when booking a flight through westjet.com. Travel agents booking through call centres or Sabre and Galileo earned a 7 percent commission.

WestJet's Performance

WestJet had carved out a profitable presence in a tough industry. In the eight years since WestJet was established, it had posted 28 consecutive profitable quarters in an industry where very few companies were profitable. WestJet's revenues and profits had increased constantly since it started operations. In 2002, its net sales were $680 million, up from $478 million a year earlier. This produced a healthy annual compound growth rate of net sales of 42.1 percent.

In November 2003, WestJet announced higher traffic figures for November, a typically slow month. Its Revenue Passenger Miles (RPM) were 3,407 million in 2002, up from 2,236 million in 2001. Revenue Passenger Miles are the number of paid-for seats times the distance the passengers flew. The company's Available Seat Miles (ASM), which measure the company's seating capacity, grew by 43.8 percent on a year-over-year basis, following the company's recent expansion to 28 Canadian cities. Its Available Seat Miles in billions were 4,651 in 2002, up from 2,996 a year earlier. Its load factor (the percentage of an airplane's capacity that is filled) was 73.2 percent in 2002, slightly down from 74.7 percent in 2001.

WestJet had only 20 complaints of the 1,756 complaints made to the national airline ombudsman in 2002. During the same period, WestJet had flown 4,334,789 passengers. In 2002, WestJet was ranked number two for being on time among North American carriers—behind Skywest—beating out heavyweights such as Southwest, JetBlue, United, American, and Delta.

With regard to financial performance, WestJet's current ratio at .82 : 1 and its quick ratio at 0.69 : 1, in 2002, were somewhat lower than the standard benchmark of 2 : 1 and 1 : 1 respectively, which many financial experts felt was needed to meet the airline's short-term financial obligations. Its ratio for total liabilities to shareholders at 1.2 : 1 was higher than the standard benchmark ratio of 1 : 1 needed to remain solvent. During the same period, total debt relative to shareholders' equity increased from 22 percent to 65 percent, indicating a sharp increase in WestJet's total debt relative to shareholders' equity. These financial ratios were indicative of a tight cash flow and the possible need for seeking external financing.

Rival Moves and Countermoves

In March 2004, Air Canada was WestJet's largest competitor, controlling in excess of 90 percent of the Canadian airline industry. It had superior resources and it operated many more airplanes than WestJet. Air Canada had been ranked "the world's safest airline" from more than 500 airlines, and its frequent flyer program, Aeroplan, was Canada's most popular such program, having over 6 million members worldwide.

In December 1999, Air Canada acquired the insolvent Canadian Airlines, a move that enabled it to obtain a dominant share (over 90 percent) of the Canadian domestic, U.S. trans-border, and international markets. The decreased competition following the amalgamation of Air Canada and Canadian Airlines presented WestJet with an opportunity to expand beyond its base in Western Canada to eastern destinations, a move that was facilitated by establishing a hub in Hamilton, Ontario.

Soon after WestJet announced its decision to expand eastward, and in view of Air Canada's mounting operating losses, Air Canada announced that it would shut down its unprofitable routes and redirect its planes to trans-border flights that were historically more profitable than domestic flights.

Following the dramatic events of September 11, 2001, and the demise of Canada 3000, Canada's second-largest airline at the time, a number of low-cost, low-fare airlines had been launched that included Jetsgo, CanJet, HMY Airways, and Zoom Airlines. Air Canada, having already launched its first low-fare, no-frills airlines, Tango and Jazz, started its third low-cost airline-within-an-airline, Zip Air, in September 2002. It also launched Air Canada Jetz, a charter airline offering premium business service catering to the needs of corporate clients and professional sports teams.

In 2002, Air Canada's revenues were $9.83 billion, yet it experienced a net loss of $428 million, while WestJet earned a net profit of $52 million on revenues of $680 million. In light of its continued losses over the past 15 years since the deregulation of the Canadian airline industry, Air Canada filed under the Companies' Creditors Arrangement Act on April 1, 2003, seeking protection from creditors while attempting to restructure the airline to make it profitable again.

While Air Canada was trying to restructure its operations under the protection of bankruptcy laws, other discount airlines announced plans to expand their operations. In June 2004, Zoom Airlines was beginning twice-a-week flights to Paris from Toronto and Montreal. David Clements, Zoom's director of sales and marketing, said that the company expected 15,000 to 20,000 passengers to fly to Paris annually at $199 before taxes for a one-way trip. Management of Zoom felt that the Paris route would complement the year-round route to London that would start in May 2004. According to Clements, 80,000 to 100,000 passengers were expected to fly to the United Kingdom with Zoom Airlines in its first year of flying there.

In March 2004, Jetsgo, another upstart discount airline, announced that it had obtained $25 million in financing to increase its fleet from 14 to 32 aircraft, by purchasing 18 used Fokker F-100s. Jetsgo also announced plans to boost the number of its flights. Jestgo had been criticized by industry observers for its aggressive pricing tactics that aimed at buying market share by selling airfares at deeply discounted levels.

Industry leader Air Canada was planning to use its subsidiary Jazz to compete more aggressively in the low-cost air travel segment and had placed an order for 30 new regional jets to be used in this market. Air Canada would also start to offer nonstop flights from Toronto to Caracas, and Bogotá, Colombia, in June 2004. According to Bill Bredt, the company's vice-president of network and revenue management, Air Canada was "seeing an increase in travel demand to and from South America as a result of a strengthening economy as well as the convenience of Air Canada's services for travellers impacted by U.S. government visa requirements when transiting via the United States."

WestJet's Expansion Drive

By early 2002, WestJet had begun twice-daily flights between Toronto and Winnipeg and increased service to several other cities that included nonstop flights between Edmonton and Ottawa, between Halifax and Montreal, between Toronto and Thunder Bay, and between Hamilton and St. John's and Gander, Newfoundland. It also switched from weekend to daily service between Windsor and Calgary. New initiatives announced on December 22, 2003, were to aggressively ramp up its schedule in 2004, adding several new routes and increasing frequency across Canada. This expansion would involve increasing the number of flights between Toronto and Ottawa to 40 a week, between Vancouver and Toronto to 27, one daily nonstop flight between Toronto and Victoria, and 46 weekly flights between Toronto and Montreal. In order to better serve these new markets, WestJet announced that it was redeploying its capacity from Hamilton to Toronto in the new Terminal 1 of Pearson International Airport.

Other initiatives included deliveries of eleven 737–700 aircraft in 2004 and twelve more in 2005. At the end of 2005, WestJet expected to have a total of 63 aircraft in its fleet after the delivery of the new aircraft and the retirement of some of its existing aircraft. These next-generation aircraft would allow WestJet to fly nonstop between various cities in Canada.

WestJet's strategy in expanding in Central and Eastern Canada entailed moving into the largest cities first, and then building up its network by increasing the number of flights. The company's strategic objective was to expand rapidly to preempt the large Canadian markets before other low-fare airlines such as Jetsgo, Tango, and Jazz fully ramped up service in those places.

In 2003, WestJet entered the charter flight business by announcing plans to team up with Montreal-based Air Transat to fly charter flights from several Canadian cities to winter holiday destinations such as Mexico and the Dominican Republic. The two-year deal was worth $29 million in the first year. This deal would enable WestJet to earn revenues from its unutilized planes, especially during the slow winter months. According to WestJet management, winter charter flights generated better margins than scheduled flights.

The Future

In early 2004, the total Canadian airline market excluding the international segment was approximately $8.5 billion—$4.5 billion and $4 billion for the domestic and trans-border markets respectively. Since its annual revenues in 2002 were $860 million, WestJet's market share was 10 percent of its potential market. This represented a significant opportunity to WestJet for further expansion.

The two-year deal with Air Transat presented WestJet with another opportunity to find new uses for existing assets and increase revenues from otherwise idle assets. The replacement of its older 737-200s with the newer 737-700s, which were capable of flying triple distances and at a speed of 150 kilometres per hour faster than the older models, allowed WestJet to fly to farther destinations, such as the southern Caribbean, Mexico, and even Hawaii. According to Tim Morgan, co-COO, the Air Transat deal had only scratched the surface of a number of other opportunities available to WestJet such as, for instance, flying from Kelowna, B.C., to Honolulu nonstop. The lucrative $5.5-billion trans-border market also looked quite appealing as a future growth opportunity although competition was higher than domestic routes because it included Canadian and U.S. airlines.

Discussion Questions

1. What factors contributed to the success of WestJet Airlines?

2. In what significant ways has the WestJet model deviated from the Southwest Airlines model? What do you think of these differences?
3. Describe WestJet's marketing strategy.
4. Which of the alternatives discussed in the case would you recommend to WestJet's management in order to help the airline continue on its growth path? Justify your answer.

Sources

James Stevenson, "WestJet begins Toronto-Winnipeg, Halifax-Montreal as part of expended service," The Canadian Press, 2003, http:// www.ibrowsetravel.com/ newsstories/westjet.htm, retrieved on March 23, 2004; John Partdridge, "WestJet plans stock split for third time in 4 years," *Toronto Star*, March 24, 2004, B3; WestJet, Renewal Annual Information Form, 2002; Anthony A. Davis, "Sky High—How WestJet got there—and how you can, too," *Profit*, March 2004, 20–26; "WestJet—On Time Performance," http://c0dsp.westjet.com/ internet/sky/about/otpTemplate.jsp, retrieved on March 23, 2004 Susan Pigg, "Zip, WestJet in fare war that could hurt them both," *Toronto Star*, January 22, 2003, C1; Rick Westhead, "Newest discount airline launches ad campaign," *Toronto Star*, November 4, 2003, D6; James Stevenson, "WestJet eyes openings in Air Canada schedule," *Toronto Star*, April 29, 2004, D3; "WestJet says expansion on track," *Toronto Star*, February 25, 2004, C3; Paul Vieira, "Jetsgo to buy 18 planes to protect Eastern turf," *Financial Post*, February 6, 2004, FP4; Paul Vieira, "Jetsgo big bet," *Financial Post*, February 9, 2004, FP1; Paul Vieira, "Jetsgo to announce expansion in flights, more destinations," *Financial Post*, March 30, 2004, FP5.

Green Acres Seed Company

Thomas Funk

This case was written by Thomas Funk of the Ontario Agricultural College at the University of Guelph, Guelph, Ontario, Canada. It is intended as a basis for classroom discussion and is not designed to present either correct or incorrect handling of management issues. Some of the information in this case has been disguised to protect confidentiality.

Tom Simmons, marketing manager for Green Acres Seed Company, was faced with the problem of increasing his company's sales and profits in the highly competitive Ontario seed corn market. One option under active consideration was a strategy to increase the company's share of the market for silage corn seed. Although this was a small market compared to the grain corn seed market, Tom believed the silage market offered good potential. This option would be a major strategic move for Green Acres, and Tom would have to build a strong case to gain top management's approval.

Background

The Ontario seed corn industry was very competitive: seven companies competed for a total market estimated to be worth approximately $80 million per year. Pioneer, the leading company, was estimated to have more than 50 percent of the market. Novartis and Dekalb each had approximately 13 percent, while Green Acres' share was about 11 percent. Green Acres' management believed that Pioneer would continue to dominate the market for the foreseeable future and that the market shares of the smaller companies would change only as a result of mergers.

Farmers can grow corn for two very distinct purposes. Grain corn has only the ear or grain harvested and is either stored on the farm in bins and subsequently fed to livestock or sold after harvest to local grain elevators.

Silage corn is harvested by cutting the entire plant and is stored in silos and fed directly to livestock on the farm. Silage corn does not enter commercial markets. In the past, with the exception of lower-priced silage blends, seed companies have not sold separate silage varieties; the same varieties are used by farmers for both grain and silage corn.

Currently in Ontario, slightly over 2 million acres of corn are harvested as grain corn compared with less than 600,000 acres harvested for silage. Over the past several years, both the acreage of grain corn and the acreage of silage corn had experienced very low growth. It was not known whether this trend would continue. All major seed companies concentrate their research and marketing efforts on grain corn because of the larger size of the market.

Two types of dealers distributed seed corn to customers: store dealers and farmer dealers. Store dealers were farm supply outlets that sold crop supplies such as fertilizer and agricultural chemicals. Many of these retailers wanted a complete line of crop supplies so they also carry seeds from one or two seed companies. Farmer dealers are farmers who supplemented their income by also selling seeds.

Green Acres had approximately 175 dealers of the total (500) in Ontario. Most of the dealers sold several brands of seeds. While approximately 20 percent of Green Acres dealers were large-volume outlets, most were relatively small and served a limited number of customers. Most Ontario farmers would be no farther than 16 kilometres from a Green Acres dealer. Green Acres' sales force of seven people coordinated the selling activities of dealers. Dealers received a 10 to 15 percent commission (based on the selling price to farmers) on the seed they sold, depending on the volume.

The average price of seed corn to farmers was $90 per unit and ranged from $75 per unit to $125 per unit. Higher prices were charged for better-performing varieties while lower prices were charged for poorer-performing or discontinued varieties. In general, varieties mainly used for silage sold at the low end of the price range ($75 to $80), while varieties mainly used as seed for grain corn sold at various prices within the entire range. Each unit of seed planted approximately three acres. For all the companies, including Green Acres, direct production costs for seed averaged 55 percent of the average selling price to dealers, leaving a contribution margin of roughly 45 percent to cover all fixed costs and profits.

Silage Production

Farmers who were in the beef or dairy business often found it advantageous to raise silage corn for feeding to their livestock. In many cases, they would raise both grain and silage corn on their farms. Generally, they would follow the same management and cultural practices for each crop, including using the same seed varieties. A very common attitude among farmers and seed companies has been that if a variety was good for grain production, it was also good for silage production. As a result, farmers often spent considerable time selecting a grain corn variety and then used the same variety for their silage corn.

The performance of a grain corn variety is relatively simple to assess. Basically, farmers are concerned with yield, normally measured in bushels or tonnes per acre. After harvesting the crop, a farmer simply measures the amount of grain sold or put into a bin to determine yield. Measuring the performance of silage varieties is not as straightforward. As in the case of grain corn, many farmers estimate yield by observing how full the silo is after harvest. Although this gives a measure of volume, it does not measure protein or energy, the two factors important in subsequent feeding. These can be measured only by taking samples of the silage to a laboratory for feed analysis. Relatively few farmers take the time to have this sort of analysis carried out. Instead, they fall back on the guideline stated earlier that a good grain corn variety is also a good silage corn variety.

For many years the Ontario Ministry of Agriculture, Food and Rural Affairs has operated a variety-testing program in which they scientifically measure corn variety yields and publish the information for farmers to use in making purchase decisions. At the present time, the only measures of performance assessed in this program are related to grain corn production. Several scientists, as well as some farmers, were advocating the incorporation of a silage performance measure in this program, but to date this has not been done. The yield information generated through this program was published in a booklet and circulated to most corn growers in Ontario. It was widely used by farmers in making decisions about which variety to select.

Silage Strategy

Tom Simmons felt that Pioneer's current dominance of the total seed corn market would make it very difficult for Green Acres to increase its market share if the company continued to concentrate on seed for grain production. He reasoned that it might be much easier to gain share by targeting the silage producer with hybrids having high silage performance attributes and therefore avoiding direct competition with the market leader. Several facts seemed to support this strategy:

- No market leader existed in the silage market.
- A silage strategy would allow Green Acres to differentiate itself from competition.
- Recent field data indicated that some Green Acres' varieties had better silage performance characteristics than competitors' varieties.

There appeared to be a substantial product-use overlap in the sense that many farmers grew both grain and silage corn. As a result, the silage strategy might allow the company to gain new customers initially by selling them silage varieties, and then later, trying to sell them Green Acres' grain varieties. Such a "back door" approach would avoid head-to-head competition with Pioneer, Novartis, and Dekalb in attempting to get new customers. While Tom felt he would pick up some new grain customers with the silage strategy, the primary goal was to sell more silage seed.

The primary measure of silage performance the company decided to use was harvestable energy, or TDN (total digestible nutrients). Crop scientists at many universities supported this approach. Their research has proven that grain yield is not the most suitable measure of silage performance because it has been consistently found that the highest-yielding varieties often have lower levels of energy.

The research department at Green Acres had been developing and testing silage varieties for some time. The company had six varieties that produced a significantly higher level of TDN than most competitive varieties tested. Two varieties in particular yielded over 8,000 pounds of TDN per acre. The selling price for any of the six varieties that Green Acres had developed would reflect the level of TDN. That is, the higher the level of TDN, the higher the price.

Under the so-called silage strategy, the company would attempt to maintain current sales in the grain corn segment, while directing growth efforts at the silage segment. Implementation of the strategy would require additional resources for promotion, field-testing, and program coordination. Tom estimated that he would need an additional $150,000 per year for promotion and one full-time person to coordinate the strategy at approximately $75,000 per year. Field-testing expenses were hard to estimate, but probably would be in the neighbourhood of $100,000.

Market Research

To provide information to help decide whether to pursue the silage strategy, Tom commissioned a market research study of silage growers in Ontario. The study involved interviewing a random sample of 400 farmers from all areas of the province. The sample was geographically balanced to insure that the major silage-producing regions were represented in the proper proportion. All interviews were conducted over the telephone.

The basic purpose of the marketing research was to assess the viability of the silage seed strategy. In addition, the research was designed to provide information to further develop the strategy if it was determined to be sound. Specific objectives of the research were the following:

- Determine the size of the corn silage seed market measured by number of buyers and number of acres.
- Determine the decision-making process used by farmers in buying silage seed.
- Determine basic attitudes farmers have about corn silage seed.
- Determine possible segments that exist in the corn silage seed market.

The major findings of the study are shown below:

- Current market shares for grain corn and silage corn seed were estimated to be the following:

Grain Corn	Silage Corn	
Pioneer	53%	54%
Novartis	13%	13%
Dekalb	14%	12%
Green Acres	12%	11%
All others	8%	10%

- Approximately 70 percent of the farmers growing silage corn in any year also grow grain corn in the same year.
- The total number of Ontario farmers growing silage corn is 11,800. The average farmer grows 49 acres of silage.
- Farmers tend to make their decision concerning which varieties to plant in the fall and early winter months. Orders are placed with seed dealers in the early winter.
- High yield of feed per acre is the most important reason cited by farmers for feeding corn silage. Other reasons given were source of energy and source of protein.
- Most farmers indicated that they planned to grow the same amount of silage corn in the future as at the present time. A small percentage said they planned to grow less silage corn in the future compared to the present time.
- Approximately 35 percent of all silage growers change seed varieties from one year to the next. Beef producers are more likely to switch than dairy producers. Many farmers who switch varieties stay with products produced by the same company.
- More than 60 percent of farmers who grow both grain corn and silage reported using the same varieties for both.
- Approximately one-third of all silage growers reported having their silage analyzed for its feeding value. More dairy farmers than beef farmers have this type of analysis done. Almost all farmers who have feed analysis done use the information to balance rations. Less than 5 percent use the results to aid in silage variety selection.
- The information sources used by farmers in selecting a silage variety together with the percentage of farmers rating each as either useful or very useful is shown below:

Source as Useful	Percent Rating
Own experience	93%
Other farmers	92%
Seed company information	84%
OMAFRA trial results	84%
Seed dealers	82%
Silage test plots	80%
OMAFRA extension	74%
Farm magazine ads	66%
Television ads	25%
Radio ads	24%

- Farmers hold a variety of attitudes concerning silage seed. Some of these attitudes, and the percentage of farmers agreeing with each, are shown below:

With Each Statement	Percent Agreeing
When I plant my corn I know which fields will be harvested for silage	83%
The energy of corn silage comes mainly from the grain	81%
I think I could do a better job evaluating my silage corn	78%
If there were more silage testing, I would use it to choose my silage variety	76%
I would use performance information on silage varieties if it were available	65%
Different varieties have different levels of protein	59%
There is quite a bit of difference among varieties in the energy they produce	54%
The best grain variety makes the best silage variety	50%
Total tonnage per acre is the only reliable method to evaluate silage varieties	45%
Currently no seed company has reliable silage performance information	40%
A tall corn variety usually makes the best silage variety	39%
Most lower-price varieties perform as well for silage as higher-price varieties	34%

- The study also generated some interesting results about market segmentation. Based on cluster analysis of the results, four segments emerged. These segments were named performance, potential performance, dual purpose, and price. The distinguishing characteristics of each segment are outlined below:
  - The *performance* segment consists of those farmers who are concerned with performance characteristics of silage varieties. This concern has been demonstrated by the fact that these farmers carefully evaluate silage variety performance by using performance evaluation methods such as setting up silage test plots, using feed analysis to evaluate varieties, and/or weighing off of silage varieties to accurately determine yield.
  - The *potential performance* segment consists of those farmers who do not currently use performance evaluation methods for selecting silage varieties, but have favourable attitudes toward using this type of information in the future.
  - The *dual purpose* segment consists of those farmers who grow both grain corn and silage and consistently use the same variety for both.
  - The *price* segment consists of those farmers who consistently purchase lower-price varieties for silage compared to grain corn.

Exhibit 1 shows a detailed profile of the four segments organized by demographics, buying behaviour, and attitudes.

Exhibit 1   Silage Segment Profiles

	Performance	Potential Performance	Dual Purpose	Price
Demographics				
Age	Youngest	Middle Age	Oldest	Middle Age
Farm size	Larger than average	Average	Smaller than average	Smaller than average
Silage acres	Larger than average	Slightly less than average	Average	Slightly less than average
Grain acres	Larger than average	Average	Smaller than average	Smaller than average
Size of dairy operation	Above average	Average	Smaller than average	Smaller than average
Size of beef operation	Large	Average	Medium	Small
Buying Behaviour				
Green Acres share	15%	10%	5%	25%
Brand loyalty	Lowest level	Low level	Highest level	Average
Timing of purchase	Latest	Early	Earliest	Early
Source of information	Government testing	Government testing	Farm magazines	Seed dealers
Measure of performance	Performance indicators	Visual estimates of volume	Visual estimates of volume	Visual estimates of volume
Attitudes				
There are differences among hybrids in protein and energy	Strong agreement	Agreement	Neutral	Neutral
If there were more testing for silage varieties I would use it to choose varieties	Strong agreement	Agreement	Neutral	Neutral
The best grain variety makes the best silage variety	Neutral	Neutral	Strong agreement	Agreement
When I plant my corn I know which will be harvested for silage	Agreement	Strong agreement	Neutral	Strong Disagreement
Segment Size				
Percent of all silage growers	10%	50%	20%	20%
Average silage acres	72	46	43	46

The Workabout: Developing and Introducing a New Product

Nicolas Papadopoulos

This case was developed by Dr. Nicolas Papadopoulos, Professor of Marketing and International Business at the Sprott School of Business, Carleton University, Ottawa, Canada. It is designed solely for use as a basis for education and training and is not intended to illustrate appropriate or inappropriate handling of any aspect of business management. The situation described is real but names, locations, and some dates are disguised to protect confidential information and/or improve the learning experience.

In late 2002, the executives at Souliers Aniel Ltd. of Lachine, Quebec, felt they at last had a new product idea that would work. The idea was to produce a complete line of high-quality, fashionable shoes for people whose work required them to stand for several hours or to walk extensively while on the job. They felt that this idea, code-named the Workabout, had the potential to help Souliers Aniel do two things at the same time.

First, it would help boost their sales and provide much-needed revenue that would enable the company to upgrade its plant equipment and increase its profitability. Second, it would help them to break free from contract manufacturing. Since its beginnings in the 1950s, the company's founder and present major shareholder, Raymond Aniel, had opted for the safety of producing shoes for others to market. Contract manufacturing for Canada's major shoe retailers accounted for 90 percent of the business, the rest coming from occasional exports. Since the new product line would be branded, Souliers Aniel would be able to have more control over marketing activities and thus realize higher margins on the products it sold.

The Footwear Industry

This product idea had arisen out of top management's concern for the company's long-term future. It seemed that, without some sort of new and substantial activity,

Souliers Aniel would be condemned to an unexciting future at best, or even to what some managers called "a slow and agonizing death." This pessimistic assessment reflected more the unique characteristics of the footwear industry than any shortcomings or problems of the company itself. After all, the company's annual sales of about $50 million were certainly not negligible, its reputation in the market for making quality products was solid, and its financial position was, at least for the time being, strong—the company had no long-term debt and enjoyed an excellent working relationship with its bankers.

Canada's footwear industry as a whole, however, faced several problems. One was the nature of the product itself. To most analysts, the market for shoes was a typical example of complete saturation. People have two feet, the reasoning went, and the number of pairs of shoes that consumers are willing to buy to dress these feet is limited. Therefore, for a particular company to grow, the only way was to improve its market share within this saturated market by displacing competitors.

Gaining market share is not easy, since the market is highly competitive. Traditionally, shoes had been an unbranded shopping good. Consumers seemed to make their choices based on who sold them rather than who made them. That is, the retailer was seen as more important than the manufacturer. The typical consumer would walk around a shopping centre and compare the styles carried and prices charged by various shoe retailers. This made a retailer's selection of merchandise very important. In turn, to be able to carry a wide selection, retailers developed the practice of buying from several different manufacturers, just as most apparel retailers have always done.

With the emergence of several major retail chains in the footwear sector, the retailer's importance increased even further. Buying in much larger volumes than before,

Case 6 / The Workabout: Developing and Introducing a New Product

these chains were able to contract their selection requirements to a variety of manufacturers and then give their own brand name to the shoes they sold. Conversely, some shoe manufacturers integrated forward by establishing their own retail chain operations. As a result of these trends, shoe retailing is dominated by such giants as Bally of Switzerland, Bata of Canada, Florsheim, Armstrong and Richardson, Aldo's and Pegabo, and others.

Another problem faced by Canada's footwear industry is foreign competition. Footwear manufacturing is labour intensive and does not (at least not yet) involve much advanced technology. This means that producers in several foreign countries, where labour costs are low, can compete against manufacturers in industrialized countries on the basis of price. Brazil is one example of a country with a thriving footwear industry. It specializes in making low-cost, medium-quality shoes on contract for large retailers in countries like Canada. The footwear industries in Greece, France, and mainly Italy, having lost part of their price advantage because of higher labour costs, have switched to producing higher-quality, higher-priced, and often branded footwear.

Canada had tried to keep all these competitors at bay through quotas on footwear imports. The quotas had the effect of increasing the cost of imported shoes in Canada, but foreign producers, through lower manufacturing costs or better-styled shoes, managed to at least maintain their strength. So, in spite of the quotas (and perhaps even because of them—some analysts had observed that the quota protection made Canadian producers lazy and unwilling to work hard to become more competitive), Canadian footwear production suffered and things became steadily worse as worldwide tariffs declined and Canada joined the NAFTA.

It was mainly for these reasons that Souliers Aniel's executives felt that future prospects were dim unless something was done soon. Continuing to work as a contract manufacturer would mean a continuation of the company's present predicament: doing what the contracting retailer wanted, having little or no control over the way Aniel's products were marketed, and having to live with low profit margins, since retailers (drawing strength from the fact that it was they who controlled brand loyalty) could always threaten to take their business elsewhere.

Some New Trends

The idea for the Workabout had come as a result of observations by some forward-thinking company executives about the changing nature of the shoe industry. One was that competition was increasing as the federal government gradually liberalized shoe imports to satisfy the demands of its external trading partners. Another was that several manufacturer-branded shoes had been introduced to the market successfully.

In addition to the early success of Hush Puppies and Kickers in the children's market, there now seemed to be a near-infinite variety of shoe brands—such as Walkabouts, Timberland, Sea and City, Buster Brown, Cougar, Sebago, Lucchese, Gucci, Dr. Martens—covering essentially all tastes and wallet sizes. Some of these brands were for hiking; other manufacturers specialized in boots, while still others produced shoes only for children; many were upscale and expensive brands addressed to high-income consumers. They all, however, seemed to share one characteristic: they were designed for very clearly defined sub-segments of the broader market for shoes. Sea and City and Timberland, for example, specialized in "deck" shoes, while Gucci and Lucchese specialized in shoes and boots, respectively, for the very rich.

It had also been observed that a new and huge market had been created in sport and athletic shoes. Jogging, running, tennis, squash, aerobic running, yachting, boardsailing, and many other varieties of shoes were made by producers ranging from Nike, Adidas, and other brands to several "no-name" contract manufacturers, selling for as little as $30 at a discount store to as much as $300 or more at specialty shops.

The Workabout

These trends made Souliers Aniel executives think that the way to a bright future was through a well-focused market-niche strategy. They had generated and screened several ideas and finally settled on the Workabout. The basic concept for it was simple: a broad selection of well-styled shoes for people whose work required them to stand or walk for several hours.

This strategy, the executives felt, would enable them to drive a wedge between the three main types of offerings that were currently available: working shoes, such as NurseMate, which were comfortable but basically bland and colourless; regular casual shoes, which were stylish but not as comfortable; and athletic shoes, which could be comfortable (depending on what they were designed for) but were too casual for many work environments.

Current market offerings did not really give workers much choice. Nurses, for example, must wear white shoes as part of their uniform, but, short of extravagant styles, there is virtually no limitation on the style of shoes they could wear. Yet they have little real choice when it comes to styles, since white professional shoes are produced by a few specialized manufacturers who offer only a handful of style varieties. In other occupations, where there isn't even a colour restriction, workers normally choose the shoes they wear from the available selection of regular casual footwear. So what they gain in style they lose in comfort, since these shoes are not specially designed for long standing or walking periods, or what they may gain in comfort by wearing sneakers they might lose in "appropriateness" for the environment in which they work.

From a technical perspective, the Workabout was to incorporate features from two types of footwear. The engineering would utilize the high-technology advances that have enhanced "comfort" in the sport and athletic shoe industry. These would include features such as special cushioning materials as part of the insole; hard rubber or other "grip" materials for the outsole; "breathing" leather, suede, or artificial leather compounds for the shoe's upper part; and "natural formatting" so that the shoe follows the shape of ("cups") the human foot. The Workabout's appearance would be modern and stylish. In other words, it would not be possible to distinguish it outwardly from regular casual shoes. This would be a classic case where the product's technology is very much there ("After all, why should only Nike have the air bubble?" a company executive had joked) but hidden from outward view.

Souliers Aniel executives had made a preliminary effort at listing occupations that might become targets for the Workabout, to obtain a feeling of whether a market existed for the shoe. The list convinced them that the potential was indeed great. It included nurses, doctors, dentists, surgeons, and many other occupations in the health care field; bank tellers; retail store cashiers and salespersons; messengers working for courier services; street vendors and door-to-door salespeople; postal workers, both "inside" (e.g., sorters) and "outside" (mail carriers); teachers, from pre-school to college and university; business consultants in the training sector, a new and booming business employing thousands; floor traders at the stock exchange; and so on.

It was felt that many of these workers would be particularly interested in style, many others would place more emphasis on price, but all of them would be willing to buy shoes that looked like normal ones and yet offered extra comfort. It was also decided to exclude from consideration, at least for the time being, some specialty markets that were already being supplied by well-entrenched producers (e.g., coaches and referees in sports, who typically bought sport shoes, or construction workers, who need safety-toe boots).

Preliminary Marketing Plan

Souliers Aniel executives felt that their plans were progressing reasonably well. They already had a strategy and a targeted market niche, and they had generated and considered a number of new product ideas, settling on one that looked promising. They also recognized, however, that a lot remained to be done.

To begin, they would have to get a better estimate of potential market segments—it was good to list various occupations, but how many people worked in each? Next was the matter of brand name. The "Workabout" had a certain nice ring to it and it did reflect the product's main benefit, but was it the "best" name available? Also, there was the question of "Walkabouts," Goodyear's entry in the hiking shoe market—could the similarity between the two names bring about a lawsuit?

Another consideration was the size of the product line and its implications for branding. Business consultants and stockbrokers, for example, would be more interested in fashion and less in price. Mail carriers would probably emphasize price more than style. Schoolteachers might be somewhere between those two occupations. Aniel executives were not sure whether it would be proper to market to all these targets under one brand name.

Related to this problem was the question of price. Two schools of thought seemed to exist within the company. One, supported by the marketing and production people, held that the Workabout would offer a special benefit to consumers and should therefore be priced to reflect that—perhaps a 10 to 20 percent premium over going prices for similar casual shoes could be justified. The other line of reasoning, supported mainly by the financial people and by the company's founder (who still held the position of chief executive officer), was that it would be extremely difficult to make consumers switch their loyalties from whatever they bought now to a new and untried product. These executives felt that the new product line should be sold competitively, perhaps at a level of 10 to 20 percent *below* competitors' brands.

Of course, they all realized that the success or failure of the Workabout (or whatever else it might be called in the end) depended largely on Souliers Aniel's ability to sell the concept to the retailers. They felt that for this to be accomplished, several things had to be done as a minimum. First, the company should plan to market aggressively directly to the ultimate consumer, both to create a product "pull" and to convince retailers that the brand would be well-supported by the manufacturer. Second, an extensive personal selling effort, aimed at the retailers themselves, would have to be undertaken. And third, retailers would have to be offered attractive profit margins on the product if they were to carry it.

Raymond Aniel, and practically everyone else in the company, shivered at the thought of what might happen if a few large retailers didn't buy the idea. After all, the new shoe would be competing in some cases against the shoes Souliers Aniel already sold unbranded to the same retailers. The only apparent alternative in such an eventuality, they felt, would be to start up their own retail chain. The founder's low risk-taking threshold had already been stretched to the limit by the mere thought of having to market a branded shoe directly to consumers. Getting into retailing was an idea that he considered to be totally and irrevocably out-of-bounds.

Discussion Questions

1. Assess Souliers Aniel's new product development practices to date. Do company executives seem to be going about it the right way, in your opinion?
2. Assume you have been retained as a marketing consultant to advise the company. Conduct a preliminary feasibility analysis to determine whether the concept is viable.
3. Develop a program that would take the idea from its present stage to national introduction, specifying the actions that must be taken, the relevant time frames, and any other information you feel is pertinent.

Front 54

Bryan Clancy

This case was written by Bryan Clancy under the supervision of Professor Peter Yannopoulos. The author may have disguised certain names and other identifying information to protect confidentiality. This case was written solely to provide material for class discussion and it is not intended to illustrate either effective or ineffective handling of a managerial situation.

Copyright © 2004 by Dr. Peter Yannopoulos, Faculty of Business, Brock University, St. Catharines, Ontario, Canada L2S 3A1.

Introduction

"Should we agree it is time for a drastic change? Front has been red hot for a good six years, but business has been tapering away for the last four years and we have reported a loss for the last two." It was May 1, 2003, the end of a second unsuccessful year for Front 54. Paul Dedivitiis had decided with his brothers Hector, Michael, and Serge, owners of Front 54, that it was time for a change in the marketing strategy of the business. He concluded, "Before we expand to our new downtown opportunity, we need to fix our problems here. We've tried a bunch of little adjustments to rejuvenate this bar, I think it's time for a serious change."

The History of Front 54

The Dedivitiis family opened Front 54 in 1988, on 54 Front Street, in Thorold, Ontario. The building itself had been a strip club with motel rooms above it. The family had purchased the building and closed it for six months' renovations, while working with the City of Thorold to set up a bylaw prohibiting strip joints in Thorold. The Dedivitiis family wanted to prove to the Thorold community of 16,000 people that they were socially responsible and ready to help clean up Front Street from the existing strip businesses.

Front 54 had three floors—the top floor was the living residence of the family and had a few motel rooms, the main floor was a restaurant and bar, and the lower basement floor was used as a banquet floor. The restaurant was not very successful, as the potential customers were more of a lunch-pail crowd. However, Front 54 became very successful at attracting university students on its Bar Nights. It was the first bar in the area to play dance music, and it also developed partnerships with the top radio stations to play live to air with the radio station broadcasting out of the bar. These moves attracted large numbers of university students on Wednesday, Friday, and Saturday nights, leading Front 54 to focus on university customers as its primary target market and discontinue its restaurant operations to capitalize on the club potential. Having over a thousand students on the main floor made it difficult to rent out the banquet hall, though. As a result, in 2000 the banquet hall was converted into another level of the bar to handle the large numbers of students coming to the club.

Business for Front 54 was cyclical, very busy during the school semesters from September to May, and empty for the summer months, when the university students headed home. This prompted the Dedivitiis family to open another bar, Arizona's, to reach the summer crowd with a large outdoor patio, which had a capacity of over 2,000 people. Arizona's became very successful as it attracted large numbers of patrons on weekends during the summer and became a sort of cash cow for the Dedivitiis family.

The Decline

Front 54 was extremely successful from 1993 to 2000. However, in 2000, business at Front 54 began to decline, as customers started to visit other locations, especially in downtown St. Catharines. The Dedivitiis brothers attempted to revitalize the business by attracting new types of customers. The downstairs section was given its own unique style, a separate access, and different types of music on different nights to attempt to reach new types of clientele. Unfortunately, in 2002 the downstairs section was shut down because it was so large, the customers were spread out over a large area, which often made the bar look empty, hurting its image. Paul knew that students were attracted to bars that were "hot." For a place to be perceived by students as "hot," it had to be packed solid with all their friends; if the place didn't have an image of being packed, students would look somewhere else for the next big hangout. From September 2001 to April 2003, Front recorded financial losses, as the number of students declined from a high of 1,000 customers a night to struggling to attract 100 customers a night.

The Causes of the Decline

One of the main reasons for the decline in Front 54's business was the entry of new competitors that fragmented the market and gave customers a wider choice than before. Downtown St. Catharines became the new battleground as a large number of bars opened during this period catering to the needs of the many different types of students. A bar called Big Bucks had emerged as a serious competitor as it had become the main competition for Front 54 on weekends.

Another reason for the decline in Front 54 was the change in the tastes and behaviours of its primary target market. During the "hot" period, Front 54 had started an "all ages" night on Fridays. "All ages" was very successful at the time, but it had an after-effect. The 16- to 18-year-old segment of adolescents who frequented Front 54 on "all ages" nights became of age. As these adolescents became university students, sales began to drop. This happened because as they grew out of their underage hangout, they started looking for a new place to visit that would suit their new self-image. Front 54 became their kiddy bar, which they had gone to during their high school years. The new bars in downtown St. Catharines, which they had never visited before, became their favourite hangout places.

A third reason for the decline in the sales of Front 54 was that, around this time, the rap music it featured heavily attracted patrons who wore clothing that made them look like thugs, which portrayed an unsafe gang image at Front 54. This thug-like image affected the student market, as students began to avoid Front 54 and started visiting safer-looking bars.

After two bad years, the downward spiral continued, as students had the perception that Front 54 was always empty. They would avoid visiting it and were instead attracted by downtown bars that they knew would be busy. Since Front 54 had become so dependent on the university student population, its business was in trouble. Management realized they had put too many eggs in one basket.

The Purchase of a Third Location

While running Front 54, the Dedivitiis brothers had purchased an old factory in downtown St. Catharines. Renovations had begun to convert the place to a bar that would be named Stella's. The bar would reach a segment of age 25 and older with a dress code and a more prestigious higher-income image. Management would try through Stella's to recapture the market segment that had aged out of the Front and Arizona's target. Stella's was also established as a restaurant for downtown employees who would stop in for lunch or 5 o'clock happy hour. Stella's presented the owners of Front 54 with a great opportunity to fight back their downtown competition, but the brothers wanted a strong solution to their Front 54 crisis before embarking on a new business. Their concern was that this bar and restaurant could not be started until the other two businesses were stabilized.

The Options

The four brothers started looking at several options in an attempt to find a solution to the decline of sales at Front 54. Closing the business was not an option, and there was a growing pressure to make the location profitable again as they had purchased the property downtown and were prepared to create a new bar and restaurant there as soon as their two current bars could once again be self-maintaining. The first possibility was to begin advertising for different nights as band nights. Front 54 had been well known for bringing in big-name bands in the past and they could use this popularity to begin band nights to reach alternative segments.

Another option was to re-establish the restaurant to capitalize on a number of recent trends. The brothers felt that due to the increasing trend in families eating out, there could be a newfound potential market in Thorold for a family restaurant. However, the main concern was that Front 54 had the perception of being a bar, and it would be very hard to change that perception.

A third option was to make better use of the upstairs motel area. Paul had begun looking into the possibility of creating 30 hotel units above the bar. The money brought in from their rental would cover the overhead costs of the location, with or without the performance of the bar. This option was attractive because housing had become a major concern in the area due to the influx of students caused by the double cohort in Ontario—two graduating years descended on Ontario universities and colleges—including nearby Brock University—in the 2003 academic year.

The final and most drastic option considered by the Dedivitiis brothers was the possibility of changing the name of the bar and its perception among local patrons. Paul felt that the business could become a successful restaurant but not with the name Front 54 as past events had hurt its brand image. The new branding strategy would involve a great deal of change. It would mean closing down the bar to give the perception of new ownership and spending six months renovating the decor inside and outside the bar to give a more casual atmosphere. The brothers had created the name "Moose and Goose," and they liked its "Canadiana" feel. They felt that with such a name and the new restaurant perception, they could sponsor sports teams and reach out to many other segments of the local market that the Front 54 club image could not reach. Sponsorship was never very attractive with the Front 54 name because no one wanted to be sponsored by a club, but a new sporty name such as Moose and Goose had many more sponsorship options. This new restaurant would attract a wider section of the local population, and it would provide a more stable revenue source instead of relying on one segment two nights of the week. The disadvantage of this alternative was that it would mean the demise of the brand Front 54, which had become so well established over the years.

Decision

"This one-dimensional brand strategy worked very well for the last decade, we were hot and the students were a great customer base, but I think it's time we were involved with more diverse segments of customers, so that we aren't so dependent on one group of customers." Paul was confident that his brothers would agree, and he also knew that whatever decision was made, it would have to be implemented immediately.

Discussion Questions

1. What factors contributed to the decline of Front 54?
2. Which alternative would you recommend to the Dedivitiis brothers?
3. What actions would you initiate in order to build a strong brand, given your recommendations?

Bombardier Inc.

Peter Yannopoulos

In May 2004, Montreal-based Bombardier Inc. was in the process of deciding whether to launch a new class of commercial airplanes in the 110- to 150-seat range, in addition to its existing family of 50-seat to 86-seat planes. Bombardier had formed a team of 200 experts who worked on an $18-million study to assess the merit of building the new aircraft. The new jet initiative was viewed by many industry observers as a make-or-break project for Bombardier. Its outcome would determine to a large degree whether Bombardier would continue to be the world's third-largest manufacturer of commercial aircraft and a continuing player in the aerospace industry.

The new jet represented Bombardier's bid to overtake Brazilian rival Embraer SA, which already had a 100-seat jet coming into the market. It would also provide the company with a growth opportunity, especially in light of sagging sales growth in its existing commercial aircraft product line.

It is noteworthy that in 2000, Bombardier had abandoned plans to build a similar 100-seat jet. But the company had to reconsider its earlier decision in light of the positive response to rival Embraer's new family of 70- to 110-seat jets. For example, Air Canada had announced a $1.3-billion order for EMB-190 jets and had options to buy another 45 aircraft from Embraer. Air Canada had originally planned to order some of these airplanes from

Bombardier but it subsequently switched to Embraer. In addition, U.S. discount airline JetBlue Airways had already ordered 100 Embraer ERJ-190s with options for 100 more.

Bombardier's new jet program was spearheaded by Gary Scott, who had recently joined the company. Scott had worked for Boeing Co. for 28 years where he was in charge of the highly successful 737/757 commercial aircraft division. Scott had joined Bombardier after he had worked for 19 months at CAE Inc., maker of the flight simulator.

The new aircraft would cost about $2 billion to bring to the market. It would take five years to develop, and it would typically sell for 20 to 30 years. The cost would be shared between the company, its suppliers, and the Canadian government.

The proposed aircraft had already been technically defined. It would have five seats across (two seats on one side and three seats on the other). It would be a long-range aircraft, and unlike other aircraft of that size (including the new Embraer jet), it would be capable of flying from New York to Los Angeles, nonstop. The program would consist of two types of aircraft: 110- to 115- and 130- to 135-seat jets.

The new Bombardier plane had several advantages over its much-touted Embraer rival and aircrafts of other makers. Embraer planes were limited in their performance capabilities while the Bombardier aircraft would be more efficient and technologically advanced. The new jet would be 15 percent more efficient than aging DC-9s, 737s, and Fokker F100s. Also, it was 20 percent more efficient than introduction planes, such as the new Embraer 100-seat plane. Bombardier's new plane would have the capability for long-range flights such as New York to Los Angeles while Embraer's new plane could only fly half that distance.

Demand for smaller jets was driven by airlines seeking to cut costs and economically reconfigure their business model. U.S. airlines were also gradually moving away from the traditional hub-and-spoke system of connecting flights at major cities. The post–9/11 trend in the airline industry was to favour larger regional jets that were closer to mid- and full-sized jet liners.

According to analysts, the market potential of the 100- to 150-seat aircraft was about 5,600 planes over 20 years, worth $259 billion (U.S.). Although Scott didn't say how many planes Bombardier expected to sell, he indicated that for the program to succeed, the company needed to get a minimum 25 percent of that market.

However, there were several complicating factors. At the time of the announcement, the airline industry was still reeling from the effects of two years of economic downturn, following the devastating terrorist attacks of September 11, 2001. The world's major airlines were in a fragile state. As a result, it was extremely difficult for airlines to obtain financing for new planes.

Some analysts were concerned that even if the company decided to enter this market, the entry would be too late by as much as five years. However, although it would take about five years to commercialize its all-new-from-scratch jet, Bombardier was confident of its success. According to Gary Scott, there was a lot of customer interest in the new aircraft. He expected that major airlines, including discount carriers such as WestJet and Southwest, would appreciate the flexibility of offering both shorter- and longer-haul routes and would be willing to wait five years for the new Bombardier plane.

Another concern was that the introduction of the new jet would put Bombardier in direct competition not only with Embraer but also industry giants Boeing and Airbus Industrie, which both made planes in the 100-plus-seat range. But, according to Gary Scott, the new plane did not compete directly with Embraer's new aircraft, which was targeting the under-100-seat segment; Bombardier was targeting the 100-plus-seat market, a much bigger market. Similarly, according to Scott, the new aircraft would not compete with Bombardier's smaller regional planes of 50-, 70-, and 90-seat or the smaller jets made by industry giants Boeing and Airbus Industrie of Europe.

Also, some analysts thought that entering the transcontinental market might provoke the much larger aircraft manufacturers, Boeing and Airbus Industrie, since they would be attacked in one of their core markets.

Another issue was finding suppliers who would be willing to enter into partnerships with Bombardier into such a high-risk project. Bombardier management felt it would have no difficulty finding suppliers who would be willing to share the risks involved in the project. Bombardier already had similar risky deals with various suppliers such as Mitsubishi, which manufactured the wings for its Global Express business jet.

In mid-2004, Bombardier was in the midst of a major restructuring of its rail division. The company had recently announced it was closing a railway car factory in Ammendorf, Germany, as part of a plan announced earlier in the year to reduce its labour force by 6,600 jobs and to shut seven plants in Europe. Also, for the three months ended April 30, Bombardier reported a loss of $35.7 million, compared with a loss of $16.5 million in the same period in the previous year. As a result, the company would cut 500 jobs and it would adjust some contracts in the transportation division. At the same time, an upcoming election in Canada could mean a Conservative government, which was of concern to Bombardier as the Conservative party had announced that it would cut back on corporate subsidies.

Deciding on the project was a major product decision for Bombardier. Paul Tellier, Bombardier's chief executive officer, had given Scott's team until the end of January 2005 to submit a proposal to the board of directors with a recommendation either to go ahead with the project or cancel it. Among the advantages of going ahead with the project was that it offered operating and cost savings to airlines. Another key aspect of Bombardier's evaluation process was finding an airline willing to take the role of the launch customer by placing a large initial order.

Some analysts also felt that going ahead with the project would be an enormous challenge for Bombardier, a company not particularly known as a hothouse of product innovation. A commitment to such a project would entail a dramatic change in the company's approach to innovation. Also, because it would be a latecomer in this segment, it would have to rely on an aggressive marketing campaign that played up the uniqueness of the product and the company's track record for reliability.

If the project were to go ahead, Bombardier would use the new aircraft to expand beyond the North American regional market into the much broader European, Asian, and South American markets. On the other hand, if Bombardier decided not to invest in the project, the company would have to rely on its 50- to 86-seat jets, which were much smaller and cramped compared with the much larger Embraer jets.

Discussion Questions

1. What are the advantages of the new aircraft over competing aircraft?

2. What are the benefits and risks Bombardier would face if it proceeded with the production of the new aircraft?

3. Should Bombardier proceed with the development of the new aircraft? Explain your recommendation.

Sources

Bertrand Marotte, "Bombardier recreational loss deepens," *Globe and Mail*, June 30, 2004, B4; Allan Swift, "Money-losing Bombardier cuts 500 jobs in Montreal," *Toronto Star*, May 28, 2004, E2; Bertrand Marotte, "Bombardier shares shaken by huge loss in first quarter," *Globe and Mail*, May 28, 2004, B1; Konrad Yakabuski, "Bombardier as a division of Boeing?" *Globe and Mail*, March 5, 2004, B2; John Partridge, "Bombardier may see jet order shrink," *Globe and Mail*, March 10, 2004, B4; "Bombardier builds case for new aircraft," *Toronto Star*, June 20, 2004, D2; Bertrand Marotte, "Bombardier exudes confidence in plans for new jet," *Globe and Mail*, June 6, 2004, B1; Sean Silcoff, "Bombardier hires leader for jet project," *Financial Post*, February 27, 2004, FP5; "Suppliers like new plane: Tellier," *Toronto Star*, July 21, 2004, E5; Bruce Stanley, "Air travel rebound boosts new jet orders," *Globe and Mail*, July 20, 2004, B9.

CASE 9

Atlas Chemical Company

Thomas Funk

This case was prepared by Thomas Funk of the Ontario Agricultural College, University of Guelph, Guelph, Ontario, Canada. It is intended as a basis for classroom discussion and is not designed to present either correct or incorrect handling of administrative problems.

Bob Aitken's mood matched the dreary November day as he guided his car along the Gardiner Expressway. The morning sportscaster droned on about the pathetic Maple Leafs. Undoubtedly, this would be another losing season. Why did he continue to cheer for them? Bob reached over and turned off the radio, putting his thoughts to the day that lay ahead. Today was it. If Atlas was going to launch its new line of micronutrient fertilizers on the Ontario and Quebec markets this spring, a decision would have to be made today. These decisions always made Aitken somewhat nervous. As manager of new product development he was responsible for initiating the launch of new and, presumably, profitable products for the company. Initially he was very excited and enthusiastic about the micronutrient line, but lately he had become less sure. Was the product really profitable enough to go with? At what price level should they enter the market?

The Opportunity

Atlas was a wholly owned subsidiary of its U.S. parent. Although the U.S. company had long been involved in agriculture through its complete line of dry and liquid fertilizers, the Canadian company had not yet entered this sector. Micronutrients would be the first agricultural product sold by Atlas in Canada and could pave the way for other products in future.

Fertilizers are commonly used by farmers to provide essential plant nutrients to promote growth and higher yields. The most common major nutrients are nitrogen, phosphorus, and potash (N-P-K). Virtually all fertilizers contain one or more of these ingredients in significant volume. Micronutrients include magnesium, manganese, zinc, iron, copper, molybdenum, boron, calcium, and sulphur. Micronutrients are not used as often, or in the same volume, as nitrogen, phosphorus, and potash.

Atlas was proposing to enter the micronutrient market with three products imported from the U.S. company: Supergrow-M (magnesium), Supergrow-Z (zinc), and Supergrow-I (iron). Although farmers could use up to 12 different micronutrients, the Atlas line currently consisted of only three. The three Atlas products were in liquid form and designed for foliar application at that point in a plant's growth when lack of these nutrients could limit the full development of grain or fruit. In addition to the micronutrients, each Atlas product contained small amounts of nitrogen. This was included to give the crop an added boost at a critical stage in its development, as well as to promote a rich, green colour. It was felt that the added greenness would be an indication to farmers that the product was really working. With the added nitrogen, however, it became important that the product be applied in precisely the right manner to avoid burning the crop. When using the foliar method of application, conventional soil tests for micronutrient deficiencies were of limited value in gauging the extent to which micronutrients were needed. Visual signs such as colour changes in leaves were considered to be the best indicator of certain deficiencies, although these were far from being accurate.

Aitken felt the micronutrient market was questionable. Considerable debate had arisen recently as to the value of micronutrient fertilizer applications. While there was some industry evidence that the use of micronutrients could increase yields, most farmers had a very low awareness of micronutrient deficiencies and

Exhibit 1　　　No Substitutes for Rotation*

Recently there has been a lot of interest in Ontario about micronutrients. There are numerous plots out this year with different formulations and mixes and ways of application on a variety of different crops. I am sure there will be a lot of discussion this winter about the subject.

Some things are becoming evident about micronutrients; at least I think they are. The first is that you cannot expect dramatic yield increases with individual micronutrients on small areas.

Secondly, none of the micronutrient sales staff have been able to explain the problem of over-applying micronutrients. They suggest if you put on too much potash you may tie up magnesium. If you put on too much phosphorus, you may need to put on more zinc and manganese. I believe, with our variable soils, in some fields you can put on too much zinc and manganese.

Finally, these micronutrients seem to be most attractive to growers with poor crop rotations. Some of your neighbors have gone to poor crop rotations and their yields have dropped. (You know they are the ones that think Pioneer corn followed by Dekalb corn is crop rotation.) Now they are searching for something to pull their yield back to former highs. Micronutrients appear to them to be an answer.

What puzzles me is why some of you are willing to spend large sums of money on products you are not sure will work: shotgun micro-nutrients. We both know what the problem is. You have to get more crops into the rotation, especially perennial forages. I suppose the bottom line is when you hear your neighbor talking about all the micronutrients he is using. That's just a polite way for him to tell you he has a terrible crop rotation.

---

* This article was written by a soils and crops specialist with the Ontario Ministry of Agriculture, Food and Rural Affairs. The article appeared in an issue of *Cash Crop Farming*, a publication widely read by Ontario farmers.

---

products. What information was available to farmers from provincial departments of agriculture and Agriculture Canada did not support the use of micronutrients (see Exhibit 1). As well, the University of Guelph, which farmers looked to for technical information, was not promoting or recommending the use of micronutrients. Two major soil-testing labs in Eastern Canada had recently added both soil and tissue micronutrient testing to their line of services. These tests were relatively expensive and not widely used by farmers at this time.

However, some of the more progressive farmers were anxious to use micronutrients and considered the University of Guelph to be too conservative in its approach. They noted that many universities and farm publications in the United States were recommending the use of micronutrients.

Bob commissioned some marketing research among farmers and fertilizer dealers to provide additional information. Some key findings of this research were the following:

- Farmers and fertilizer dealers had a number of positive and negative attitudes concerning micronutrients. On the positive side, the most common attitude was that a lack of micronutrients could be a limiting factor that, when corrected, could dramatically increase yield potential.

- On the negative side, the most common attitudes were these: micronutrients are not as important as other management practices; it is very difficult to know when real deficiencies exist; some fertilizer companies are pushing micronutrients without adequate research data; foliar application of micronutrients may cause some burning of plants in hot weather and does not result in lasting benefits. Foliar application was not widely used by farmers in Ontario and Quebec.

- Ten percent of all farmers in Ontario and Quebec had used micronutrients at one time or another during the past five years.

- The total long-run market potential for magnesium, zinc, and iron in Ontario and Quebec was conservatively estimated to be 7.5 million litres. (Market potential in this case was defined as the total litres of product that could be sold if every deficient acre of every crop was treated with the recommended application rate.)

- The potential for magnesium sales was much larger than for zinc or iron.

- It was estimated that only 10 percent of the long-run market potential for magnesium and zinc had been developed at the current time, and that 50 percent of the long-run market potential for both these products would be reached within a five-year period.

- On average, farmers required a 5:1 benefit-to-cost ratio in deciding whether to use new chemical and fertilizer products.

All micronutrients in Ontario and Quebec were sold to farmers through local retail fertilizer dealers. Many of these dealers were directly controlled by large chain organizations such as Terra, Cargill, and the Co-op, while others were independently owned and operated. There were approximately 300 retail outlets serving farmers in Ontario and Quebec. At least 200 of these were branch operations of major chains. Micronutrient sales were a relatively small but growing part of overall dealer sales. There was considerable variation among retail outlets, even within the same chain, in their interest in and knowledge of micronutrients. Large chain organizations made their decisions to add new products at both the head office and branch levels. The major factors considered in assessing a new product were margins, performance, testing, information, and technical backup.

Competition

Aitken managed to gain considerable intelligence about the current competition. Two companies were selling micronutrients in Ontario and Quebec: Stoller Chemical Company with about 60 percent of the market, and Frit Industries with the remaining 40 percent.

Bob knew that Stoller, one of the leading suppliers of micronutrients in the United States, had developed a very good reputation in Canada. They distributed a full line of dry and liquid micronutrients for all crop segments in Eastern Canada. They were widely recognized for selling quality products using well-conceived marketing plans.

Stoller sold two types of products: ingredients and packaged micronutrients. The ingredients were sold to fertilizer dealers for mixing with bulk fertilizers. Fertilizer dealers would add micronutrients to their fertilizer products (N-P-K blends) based on their own recommendations or at the request of customers. Customers' requests were usually based on soil tests that would indicate a need for a certain level of one or more micronutrients. Micronutrients supplied in this manner would almost always be applied to the soil in the spring and, therefore, be available to the plant throughout the growing season.

The packaged products sold by Stoller were not intended to be mixed with other fertilizer ingredients. Instead, they were designed for separate soil or foliar application during the growing season. Most Stoller products in this category were designed for foliar application (directly on the leaves of the plant). All products in this category were attractively and conveniently packaged to meet the needs of specific growers. (As an example, Stoller sold "Apple-Grow," which was a pre-mix of the common micronutrients that were often needed for apple production. The micronutrients in this product included magnesium, zinc, manganese, copper, boron, and sulphur.)

All Stoller products were well supported with technical backup, product literature, salespeople, and effective advertising. Their packaged products sold to farmers for $9 per litre.[1] Canadian prices were substantially above current U.S. prices for the same products. Stoller was headquartered in Indiana and sold its products in Canada through a major agricultural chemical distributor. The distributor, in turn, sold to local fertilizer dealers who then sold to farmers. The distributor operated on a 10 percent margin.

Frit Industries also distributed a full line of micronutrients, but their product line was limited to ingredients sold to fertilizer dealers for mixing with bulk fertilizers. As such, Frit had a very low profile with farmers. Their products were sold on the basis of price, with little or no technical backup or marketing support. When expressed in comparable terms with Stoller and Atlas, Frit products would sell to farmers for $6 per litre and were used almost entirely on field crops such as corn and wheat.

Of the two major companies selling micronutrients in Canada, Stoller clearly had the most similar products and therefore was considered by Bob to be the main competitor.

Launch Strategy

Bob's tentative plan was to enter the market in the six crop segments they felt had the greatest short-run potential for the company's line of micronutrients. These were apples, tomatoes, potatoes, soybeans, tobacco, and vegetables. The segments were selected on the basis of potential volume, anticipated willingness of farmers to try new products, and concentration of production in small areas to facilitate initial distribution. According to the market research conducted by Atlas, the total long-run market potential in the above segments was 1,413,000 litres of magnesium per year and 162,000 litres of zinc per year. The potential for iron in all segments was too small to be of any consequence. The details of market potential in the six crop segments are shown in Exhibit 2.

Aitken was aware that the ability to penetrate these markets would depend to some extent on price. A recent Atlas study on the economics of micronutrients for

---

[1] A product such as Apple-Grow actually sold for more than $9 a litre because it contained several other micronutrients. The Stoller prices referred to in the case are comparable in value to Atlas products.

Exhibit 2

Specialty Crop Segment	Supergrow-M (litres)	Supergrow-Z (litres)
Apples	378,000	1,500
Potatoes	186,000	6,000
Tomatoes	36,000	3,000
Soybeans	399,000	150,000
Tobacco	408,000	0
Vegetables	6,000	1,500
Total	1,413,000	162,000

Exhibit 2 — Long-Run Market Potential for Micronutrients by Segment

various crops revealed a considerable difference in the marginal value of the product among the six target crops. The details of the study results are shown in Exhibit 3 for magnesium and Exhibit 4 for zinc. Opinions concerning the ability of Atlas to penetrate these markets over the next five years were varied. Bob believed Atlas would have no difficulty gaining 10 per-

cent market share for the six target crops in the first year if they were priced in line with Stoller. He hoped that within five years they would be able to capture 50 percent of the target market. This would depend, to some extent, on the pricing strategy they decided to use. Atlas was considering three possible price levels for the micronutrients: $6, $9, and $12 per litre.

Exhibit 3 — Economics of Using Magnesium

Crops	Recommended Application Rates (litres/acre)	Gross Revenue Per Acre Without Micronutrients	Gross Revenue Per Acre With Micronutrients	Other Benefits to Farmer
Apples	7.0	$4,791	$5,257	Improved Appearance
Potatoes	3.0	$1,029	$1,192	Improved Appearance
Tomatoes	2.5	$1,707	$1,835	Improved Colour
Soybeans	2.0	$361	$430	Improved Uniformity
Tobacco	4.0	$2,047	$2,402	Improved Quality
Vegetables	2.0	$1,468	$1,593	Improved Quality

Exhibit 4 — Economics of Using Zinc

Crops	Recommended Application Rates (litres/acre)	Gross Revenue Per Acre Without Micronutrients	Gross Revenue Per Acre With Micronutrients	Other Benefits to Farmer
Apples	1.0	$4,791	$4,824	Improved Appearance
Potatoes	0.75	$1,029	$1,066	Improved Appearance
Tomatoes	0.6	$1,707	$1,737	Improved Colour
Soybeans	0.5	$361	$376	Improved Uniformity
Tobacco	1.0	$2,047	$2,069	Improved Quality
Vegetables	0.5	$1,468	$1,501	Improved Quality

Bob felt that Atlas had three distribution options available: follow Stoller and sell through a chemical distributor, sell direct to fertilizer dealers in key market areas, or sell direct to farmers. Of the three, Bob favoured the second alternative of working directly with local dealers. He estimated that 50 key dealers would provide good coverage in the six crop areas selected as initial targets.

Bob estimated various costs associated with entering the market. He knew dealers would require a 25 percent margin. On top of this he would need to put up $80,000 a year for a sales representative's salary and expenses to handle the product line, another $100,000 a year on advertising and promotion ($50,000 in Ontario and $50,000 in Quebec), and $50,000 a year on product testing. To date, he had invested $40,000 in market research for the product line. In addition, Atlas would have to refit part of a Canadian manufacturing facility into a product formulation and packaging plant. Atlas would purchase the chemicals in bulk from its U.S. parent and then mix and package them into retail lots. This would cost approximately $300,000 and could be depreciated for taxation purposes at 10 percent per year.

Atlas's product costs were $1.90 a litre for Supergrow-M and $2 a litre for Supergrow-Z. These costs included raw materials, transportation, and the direct costs of mixing and packaging. Aitken knew that Atlas expected new products to break even within three years of launch. He also knew that Atlas was interested in agriculture as an area for future investment and needed a line of products to break into this market.

CASE 10

Hannas Seeds

Thomas Funk and Patricia Hannas

This case was prepared by Thomas Funk of the University of Guelph and Patricia Hannas of Hannas Seeds. It is intended as a basis for classroom discussion and is not designed to illustrate either effective or ineffective handling of administrative problems. Some of the information in the case has been disguised to protect confidentiality.

© 2001 Thomas Funk. Reprinted with permission.

Patricia Hannas and Warren Stowkoski were engaged in a heated debate concerning the future direction of distribution at Hannas Seeds. Patricia, daughter of the founder, Nicholas Hannas, and current president of the company, was a strong supporter of further development of the company's dealer distribution, while Warren, sales manager, was more inclined to favour direct distribution. As they sat in the company's head office in Lacombe, Alberta, Patricia commented, "Warren, I appreciate that direct distribution has a place in our company, but I can't see building our long-term plans around this method of distribution. It's just too limiting in scope and would require hiring more people and incurring more marketing costs. In addition, it would take years to reach the volume objectives we have for the company." Warren replied, "I appreciate your point of view, Patricia, but further development of our dealer system will require more people too. And, of course, it means we have to compensate our dealers for selling our product. This is a costly activity. And our dealers are always complaining about something. Just last week, a couple of dealers mentioned again that they were not adequately trained to provide technical advice to customers. And we're getting more and more complaints about not protecting dealer territories. It just isn't worth the hassle." And so the debate continued as Patricia and Warren argued the pros and cons of dealer versus direct distribution.

Company Background

In 1956, Nicholas Hannas purchased Lacombe Seeds, which was a retail store selling forage seed (alfalfas, clovers, and grasses) for use as hay or pasture to area farmers. Shortly after buying the company, Nicholas changed the name to Hannas Seeds and continued to operate in Lacombe. For the next 15 years, the company consisted of both a garden centre that supplied packaged seeds, bulbs, tools, and chemicals to local customers, and a warehouse for forage seeds that were sold to central Alberta farmers. The marketing program during this period consisted of the distribution of forage seed price lists by mail or by customer pickup up at the store. Advertisements were placed in the local newspaper during the busy spring season. Sales came from repeat customers, referrals, walk-in traffic, and telephone inquiries. Little or no effort was devoted to aggressively generating new business. The company did not own a delivery truck so all sales were picked up by customers.

The 1970s were a time of significant growth for Hannas Seeds. Sale revenues and volumes increased substantially as a result of the well-established presence of Hannas Seeds in Lacombe, the continually expanding client base, and the absence of significant competition in the area. In 1973, the company purchased a grain cleaning and processing facility in the Peace River region of northwestern Alberta and converted it into a processing facility for creeping red fescue seed. Creeping red fescue was a primary component in packaged lawn grass mixtures sold for residential lawns, playgrounds, golf courses, and parks. The demand for creeping red fescue was substantial, so the purchase of this facility provided Hannas Seeds with the ability to produce and market a product that could be sold into world markets. During this period, only a handful of companies were in the creeping red fescue market. Export sales were generated through the use of commodity brokers so there was no need to market one's own product. Brokers would approach a seller of creeping red fescue with a bid from a prospective buyer. If interested in selling one or more loads of seed, the seller would agree or counter the bid. Conversely, the seller could approach the broker first with an offer and the broker would then search for an interested buyer. The identities of both the buyer and seller remained undisclosed until a transaction was completed. As there were only a small number of fescue processors and exporters, demand tended to be greater than supply, and the sellers could be assured that they would attain very attractive margins.

The successful entry of Hannas Seeds into the export market was accompanied by similar rapid growth in the domestic market. In the early 1980s, the company began developing a dealer network to complement retail sales. Despite this growth, marketing and sales efforts remained more or less the same as in earlier years with the exception of targeting golf courses, oil and construction companies, and parks and recreation departments, as well as the traditional farm customers. Occasionally an employee would be assigned the task of contacting potential customers by telephone, but this was never a sustained activity.

The retail side of the business continued to develop in the early 1980s although not at the same pace as in earlier years. Several new seed companies sprang up in Alberta, and large eastern Canadian seed companies also sought to establish a presence in the province. Many of these companies entered the lucrative fescue market attracted by the possibility of attaining very high margins. Consequently, it was not long before the fescue market became saturated and margins declined accordingly.

Even with the entrance of new competition, Hannas Seeds did not alter its low-key approach to marketing. More advertising vehicles were used, such as radio, local newspapers, and telephone Yellow Pages, but there was no formal marketing program nor was any individual hired or assigned to concentrate exclusively on marketing. The company continued to rely on its spring mailing campaign to generate direct sales, and there was a small dealer network. Hannas Seeds dealers generally sold forage seed as a sideline to their existing farm or business operations and tended to order seed as they received orders from customers. Only a few dealers inventoried Hannas Seed products and attempted to sell them aggressively.

In the early 1990s, it became apparent that more effort should be devoted to marketing. In 1990, a customer appreciation day was created, when customers were offered discounts on their forage seed purchases. That same year the company purchased a custom-designed display booth for use at various farm, turf, seed industry, and horticultural trade shows. Most competing seed companies had been attending such shows for years and

it was felt that Hannas Seeds should establish its own presence at these shows in order to reach more prospective customers. More efforts were made to visit existing dealers in person as well as approach potential dealers. However, this was not formalized into a job function and therefore not done on a regular basis.

An individual with a strong sales background was hired in the mid-1990s to focus on sales and marketing. In the last half of the 1990s, the company still was achieving some success in recruiting new dealers, especially in the eastern part of the province. At the same time, the number of customers who purchased directly from Hannas Seeds was increasing, although not as rapidly as dealer sales. In 2000, direct sales declined for the first time in many years.

Forage Seed Business

Forage crops were mainly used by farmers to produce hay and pasture for feed to livestock. The most common forage crops were alfalfa, clover, bromegrass, fescue, ryegrass, and timothy. Most of these crops were perennials, which meant that, once seeded, they would grow year after year. Even though this was the case, farmers usually reseeded every three or four years because after this period of time the forage crops started to loose vigour and production declined. Although Patricia was not sure how many pounds of forage seed were sold in Alberta each year, her best guess was approximately 8,500,000 pounds (1 pound = 0.45 kilograms), and that this had remained relatively stable for many years. The industry was hoping that the Canadian Seed Trade Association would start to collect and publish this type of information.

Although some seed companies developed their own proprietary lines of forage seeds, most accessed products from either public or private seed-breeding organizations. Public seed breeders included universities and government agencies. The University of Alberta, for example, had an active forage seed-breeding program. When they developed a new forage variety, they provided information about this variety to a number of seed companies and solicited bids from these companies. The company with the winning bid was then allowed to grow and distribute the variety and paid the developing organization a royalty. In addition to public institutions, a number of private seed breeders developed varieties and provided them to seed companies on a similar royalty basis.

Most seed companies did not own seed production facilities. Instead, they contracted with farmers (seed growers) to produce seed on their behalf. The seed companies supplied seed growers with a small amount of the seed they wanted produced and then the growers multiplied this seed for the seed company under a contract. After the seed had been multiplied, it was transported to the seed company for cleaning and packaging under the company's brand name. In cases where more than one company had access to the same variety, seed companies often "traded" with each other. For example, if Hannas Seed had an excess supply of Alsike clover, they might sell some of this to a competitor who was short of this variety.

There were a number of seed companies in the Alberta forage market. The most active were these:

- Agricore, formerly the Alberta Wheat Pool, distributed forage seeds in all regions of Alberta through their system of grain elevators and local farm supply outlets located in most communities in the province. Agricore was estimated to have a market share of approximately 10 percent.
- Western Seeds of Manitoba operated in central and southern Alberta, mainly through a dealer organization. Western Seeds had one sales rep in Alberta who spent most of his time managing the existing dealer organization and obtaining new dealers. The company experienced some growth in recent years by increasing the number of dealers. Hannas Seed recently lost some dealer accounts to Western Seeds. Western Seeds was thought to have a 15 percent share of the forage market in Alberta.
- Peace Seeds was located in the Peace River region in Alberta and had its head office in Grande Prairie. Although primarily an exporter of creeping red fescue, Peace Seeds had a small dealer organization in northwestern Alberta and northeastern British Columbia. They did not have sales reps on the road, relying instead on telephone contact with their dealers. Their current share was thought to be about 5 percent.
- International Seeds was a Saskatchewan seed company that had developed some business in eastern Alberta. They were a division of a very large European seed-breeding organization. Recently they created a division called Performance Seeds to set up a dealer organization in Alberta. Their estimated share of the market was 10 percent, but many thought it was likely to grow in future.
- North American Seeds was an eastern-Canadian-based business with a division in Alberta. The Alberta division had a number of dealers, but also four sales reps who did a lot of direct business with larger farming operations. They were probably the largest forage seed company in the province with an estimated share of 20 percent.
- Alberta Seed Company of Edmonton sold in central Alberta. They sold only through a dealer organization and had approximately 10 percent of the market.

- Canada West Seed was owned by Continental Grain of Manitoba. They sold through independent dealers as well as through their comprehensive network of grain elevators in many Alberta communities. In addition, they had five sales reps selling a complete line of seeds directly to large farm accounts. They currently had a market share of about 15 percent.

Current Operations

By the end of the 1990s, three distinct divisions made up the operations of Hannas Seeds: the garden centre, international forage seed sales, and domestic forage seed sales.

The garden centre provided a wide assortment of competitively priced gardening products and accessories to Lacombe and area gardeners. Products included vegetable and garden seed, lawn grass seed, bird feed, horticultural supplies, ornamental concrete products, bedding plants, and nursery stock in a 167-square-metre retail store and a 93-square-metre greenhouse situated in downtown Lacombe. The garden centre accounted for approximately 5 percent of total company sales in fiscal year 1999–2000.

The international forage seed division exported high-quality creeping red fescue seed to the United States, Japan, and eastern and western Europe. This division accounted for approximately 65 percent of total sales in fiscal year 1999–2000.

The domestic forage seed operation provided a wide selection of competitively priced, high-yielding seeds to western Canadian farmers for use in the production of annual and perennial legumes and grasses. Although these products were sold throughout western Canada, the primary market was central Alberta. Domestic forage seed sales accounted for approximately 30 percent of total company sales in fiscal year 1999–2000. Exhibit 1 provides a list of all products sold by Hannas Seeds in the domestic market and their prices as of March 2000.[1] Patricia felt the real growth opportunities for Hannas Seeds were in this area of the business. Although the size of the forage seed market in Alberta was not growing, Patricia felt the company could increase its current 15 percent share of the market.

All the forage seed products sold by Hannas Seeds were non-proprietary varieties of annual and perennial legumes and grasses. These varieties were developed in public institutions such as agricultural universities and

---

[1] The average retail price of a pound of forage seed was approximately $2. Direct costs of producing and processing the seed were about $1.25 per pound.

provincial and federal government research departments. Hannas Seeds acquired the rights to sell these products and contracted with Alberta seed growers to produce certain quantities of seeds that were cleaned and shipped to Hannas' facilities for packaging and distribution.

Marketing and sales were under the direction of Warren Stowkoski. Warren had been with the company for six years but had extensive prior experience as a sales rep for BMW Canada. Although Warren's responsibilities were to manage both the company's direct and dealer sales of domestic forage seeds, time pressures meant that he spent most of his time working in the direct sales area of the company. Warren also attended a number of trade shows in western Canada as well as industry meetings in both Canada and the United States. Patricia managed the company's modest advertising program, which averaged 2 percent of sales and was mainly spent on local newspaper and Yellow Page ads.

Exhibit 2 shows the operating statement for the domestic forage division for the fiscal year ending July 31, 2000.

Direct Distribution

Hannas Seeds had been involved in the direct distribution of forage seeds in the Alberta market since its inception. At first, distribution was through the retail store in Lacombe. Local farmers visited the store to purchase forage seeds, usually prior to or during the spring, summer, or fall planting seasons. This was an excellent method of reaching local farmers, but as Hannas Seeds wanted to expand outside the local area, other activities became necessary. In the early 1980s, the company started to advertise in community newspapers in areas up to 200 kilometres from Lacombe. The ads included a 1-800 phone number that prospective customers could use to obtain more information and place orders. Hannas Seeds also obtained a number of farmers' lists they used for direct mail.

In 1989, the company purchased a custom-designed display booth for use in various farm, turf, seed industry, and horticultural trade shows. Most competing seed companies had been attending such shows for years and it was felt that it was time for Hannas Seeds to establish its own presence at these shows and reach more prospective customers.

Exhibit 1	Hannas Seeds Retail Price List — March 1, 2000

Alfalfas	$/lb	Wild Rye	$/lb
Alfalfa, Common No. 1	1.70	Altai wild rye, Common No. 1	6.75
AC Blue J	2.75	Altai wild rye, Prairieland	7.75
Algonquin	1.95	Dahurian wild rye, Common No. 1	2.15
Beaver	1.95	Dahurian wild rye, James	2.25
Hannas High Tech Brand	2.25	Russian wild rye, Common No. 1	2.50
Proleaf	2.50	Russian wild rye, Swift	ask
Rambler	2.20		
Rangelander	2.20	Wheatgrass	
		Crested wheat, Common No. 1	2.25
Clovers		Crested wheat, Fairway	2.75
Alsike clover, Common No. 1	3.10	Crested wheat, Kirk	2.75
Red clover, Common No. 1	0.90	Intermediate wheat, Common No. 1	1.90
Red clover, double cut	1.95	Intermediate wheat, Chief	1.95
Sweet clover, Common No. 1	0.70	Northern wheat, Common No. 1	17.95
Sweet clover, Norgold	1.25	Pubescent wheat, Greenleaf	2.50
White clover, Common No. 1	2.50	Slender wheat, Common No. 1	2.10
		Slender wheat, Revenue	2.25
Special Legumes		Streambank wheat, Common No. 1	11.00
Birdsfoot Trefoil, Common No. 1	2.50	Streambank wheat, Sodar	11.50
Birdsfoot Trefoil, Leo	2.75	Tall wheatgrass	2.75
Cicer Milk Vetch, Common No. 1	2.40	Western wheat, Common No. 1	8.95
Cicer Milk Vetch, Oxley	2.45	Western wheat, Rosanna	9.95
			(continued)

Bromegrass	$/lb		Special Grasses	$/lb
Meadow brome, Common No. 1	3.25		Canada bluegrass, Common No. 1	2.95
Meadow brome, Fleet	3.95		Creeping foxtail, Common No. 1	2.70
Smooth brome, Common No. 1	0.90		Kentucky bluegrass, Common No. 1	1.95
Smooth brome, Carlton	1.30		Meadow foxtail, Common No. 1	2.70
Smooth brome, Manchar	1.95		Orchardgrass, Common No. 1	1.20
			Orchardgrass, Potomac	1.35
Fescue			Reed canarygrass, Common No. 1	3.50
Creeping red fescue, Common No. 1	1.70		Reed canarygrass, Palaton	3.75
Creeping red fescue, Boreal	1.75		Reed canarygrass, Rival	3.80
Hard fescue, Common No. 1	1.95			
Sheeps fescue, Common No. 1	4.25		Timothy	
Tall fescue, Common No. 1	1.25		Timothy, Common No. 1	1.25
			Timothy, Basho	1.75
Ryegrass			Timothy, Carola	1.75
Annual ryegrass, Common No. 1	0.60		Timothy, Champ	1.75
Italian ryegrass, Common No. 1	1.10		Timothy, Climax	1.75
Perennial ryegrass, Common No. 1	1.25			
			Special Seed	
* Prices subject to change without notice *			Fall rye, Prima	0.22
			Field peas	0.19

Hannas Seeds

*5039–49 St * Lacombe, Alberta * T4L 1Y2

Exhibit 2   Domestic Forage Seed Division Operating Statement For the Period Ending July 31, 2000

Gross sales	$2,462,000
Less: Discounts	$55,440
Net sales	$2,406,560
Less: Cost of Goods	$1,625,000
Less: Delivery	$65,480
Gross Margin	$716,080
Expenses	
Marketing manager	$75,000
Office staff	$90,000
Bad debts	$13,000
Advertising and promotion	$52,000
Direct marketing	$60,000
Customer Appreciation Day	$15.000
Travel	$30,000
Division overhead	$200,000
Division Profit	$181,080

In 1990, an annual customer appreciation day was created when customers and prospects on the mailing list were invited to Lacombe for a one-day event where they could purchase forage seeds at a 10 percent discount. The day, usually scheduled for mid-March, also featured live entertainment, product seminars, and a great meal. Attendance at this event grew every year, reaching a peak of 250 in 2000. Company records indicated that approximately 33 percent of direct sales were made on this day. The event took a lot of staff time to organize and cost Hannas approximately $15,000 in out-of-pocket costs.

All these efforts allowed Hannas Seeds to develop a direct marketing list of approximately 6,000 customers and prospects by the year 2000. This list was used extensively: in 2000 they spent approximately $60,000 on direct marketing activities, mainly direct mail. The direct distribution activities were carried out by Warren with the assistance of three women in the office who were all capable of assisting forage seed customers in person or on the phone.[2] These women would pass a "difficult" customer on to Warren when that customer required

---

[2] Each of the office staff was paid $30,000 in salary and benefits. Warren's salary and benefits totalled $75,000 in 2000.

more technical information, had a complaint, or specifically asked to talk to "a man." Hannas Seed also had a production manager who was responsible for all shipping and receiving. The office staff was responsible for maintaining the customer and prospects database. Warren enjoyed this part of his job, especially the customer contact.

Once an order was obtained, Hannas Seeds shipped the product to the customer. Because of the small volume purchased by each customer, shipping costs were relatively high at $0.10 per pound. Hannas Seeds paid the full cost of distribution to all direct customers except those who purchased and took delivery at Customer Appreciation Day.

Direct sales of forage seeds in 1999–2000 were approximately 840,000 pounds. This was down about 50,000 pounds from the previous year.

Dealer Distribution

In the early 1980s, Hannas Seeds began to dabble in dealer distribution as well as direct distribution. Patricia felt this was an important step for the company to achieve significant sales growth.

Four types of dealers were available for seed distribution in western Canada: independent farm supply dealers, branches of large distribution companies, co-ops, and farmer dealers. Farm supply dealers varied in the type of product lines they carried. Some dealers carried a very narrow line such as fertilizer, seed, or feed whereas others carried a broad product line, including most of the items a farmer would need to purchase for his or her farm. Seed-cleaning plants often carried branded forage seeds to supplement their main business of cleaning grain for local farmers. In addition to the agricultural dealers, a few highly specialized dealers served the oilfield and land reclamation markets.

Independent dealers were locally owned businesses that normally had one or two retail outlets. Although the number of independent dealers had been declining in Alberta, it was estimated that there were approximately 100 businesses in this category.

A growing percentage of farm supplies were sold by branches of large distribution companies such as Agricore, Continental Grain, and United Farmers of Alberta. With the exception of United Farmers of Alberta, the other large distribution companies had their own lines of forage seeds, making it difficult, but not impossible, for a company like Hannas to establish distribution in this channel. Each of the three major distribution companies in Alberta had approximately 50 retail outlets serving the province. Most of their retail outlets carried a full line of farm supplies.

Co-ops were farmer-owned retail outlets that operated much like independent dealers. Most co-ops had one or two retail outlets serving local farmers. Patricia and Warren felt there were probably 50 co-ops in their market area.

In an attempt to develop new sources of income, some farmers would become dealers for seed companies. Although some farmer dealers were very active in attempting to develop business, most were fairly passive, waiting for customers to contact them.

All forage seed dealers performed similar activities. They ordered supplies of forage seeds based on their sales forecast. Once received, these supplies were put in a warehouse for storage until purchased. This usually was done in the winter months as dealers prepared for the busy spring selling season. To the extent possible, they trained their inside and outside salespeople on forage seeds so they were able to advise customers on which varieties to purchase. If seed companies supplied them with point-of-purchase material, this was normally displayed in the retail store. With the exception of specialized seed dealers, most retailers did not make a special effort to push forage seeds; they simply attempted to answer questions and took orders.

Patricia took major responsibility for recruiting new dealers for the company and then Warren worked with the dealers once they were established. To date, Patricia had set up 37 dealers that carried Hannas Seeds products. Exhibit 3 shows a listing of all Hannas dealers. Exhibit 4 shows the sales of these dealers over the past four years. Based on this information, Patricia was able to estimate the average size of different types of dealers in pounds sold per year. The average sizes were the following:

Type of Dealer	Pounds/year
Farmer dealers	45,500
Feed dealers	14,500
Fertilizer dealers	50,000
General farm supply dealers	37,000
Oilfield supply dealers	91,000
Reclamation supply dealers	98,500
Seed-cleaning plants	31,000
Seed dealers	116,000

Contact with dealers was minimal and irregular. Warren made it a point to personally visit each dealer at least once a year and supplemented this with phone calls, letters, faxes, and e-mails. The sales reps of most competing companies would call on dealers much more frequently.

Hannas dealers were allowed the industry standard 15 percent margin on all seed products they sold. So, for example, if a dealer purchased 1,000 pounds of Climax

Exhibit 3 | Hannas Seeds Dealers

Name	Product Line	Ownership	Other Brands Carried	Years a Dealer
Agri Farm Supplies	General farm supplies	Independent	0	5 to 9
Alberta Agro Services	Fertilizer dealer	Independent	2	Less than 5
Alberta Ranch & Farm	General farm supplies	Independent	2	Less than 5
Alberta Seed Cleaning	Seed-cleaning plant	Independent	2	10 or more
Aylmer UFA	Feed dealer	Branch	0	Less than 5
Bruce Seeds	Seed dealer	Independent	2	5 to 9
Cedarview Co-op	General farm supplies	Co-op	1	10 or more
Clarence Seed Cleaning	Seed-cleaning plant	Independent	1	10 or more
Dartmouth Supplies	General farm supplies	Independent	0	10 or more
Drumbo Co-op	General farm supplies	Co-op	1	Less than 5
Eccles Co-op	General farm supplies	Co-op	2	10 or more
Eyckville Fertilizer	Fertilizer dealer	Independent	0	10 or more
Fowler Farm & Ranch	General farm supplies	Independent	0	10 or more
Francesville Agri Supplies	General farm supplies	Independent	1	Less than 5
Grimsby UFA	General farm supplies	Branch	1	Less than 5
Harry Krabbe	Farmer	Independent	0	Less than 5
Harvard Fertilizer	Fertilizer dealer	Independent	1	10 or more
Hi Tech Agro	Fertilizer dealer	Independent	1	10 or more
John Krug	Farmer	Independent	0	5 to 9
Laroche County Supply	General farm supplies	Independent	1	5 to 9
Lawrence Seed Cleaning	Seed-cleaning plant	Independent	1	10 or more
Len's Feed Store	Feed dealer	Independent	0	10 or more
Lloyd's Seed Cleaning	Seed-cleaning plant	Independent	1	5 to 9
Muller Feed Mill	Feed dealer	Independent	0	10 or more
Parkview Fertilizer	Fertilizer dealer	Independent	0	5 to 9
Philip Reynolds	Farmer	Independent	0	5 to 9
Purvis Seeds	Seed dealer	Independent	1	Less than 5
Richardson Supplies	Oilfield supplies	Independent	0	5 to 9
Riverside Supplies	General farm supplies	Independent	1	5 to 9
Sagamore Livestock Supplies	Feed dealer	Independent	0	5 to 9
Smith Feeds	Feed dealer	Independent	0	5 to 9
Smithville Co-op	General farm supplies	Co-op	2	5 to 9
Sunshine Seeds	Seed dealer	Independent	2	5 to 9
Valley UFA	General farm supplies	Branch	2	Less than 5
Western Farm Supplies	General farm supplies	Co-op	1	Less than 5
Western Forest Supplies	Reclamation supplies	Independent	0	5 to 9
William Torsten	Farmer	Independent	0	5 to 9

Timothy, which had a retail price of $1.75 per pound, he or she would be invoiced for $1,487.50.[3] Hannas Seed paid all freight on dealer sales except in cases where dealers would place an order for a couple of bags they needed in a hurry. This was usually shipped via courier and paid for by the dealer. If a dealer wanted to pick up an order from the Hannas warehouse, the invoice would show the cost of shipping deducted. Because of larger volumes, shipping costs to dealers averaged only $0.02 per pound. All accounts were expected to be settled in 30 days. In the case of a few very large dealers, Hannas would rent a large truck trailer, load it with seed, and drop the truck off at

---

[3] The difference between the retail value of $1,750 and the purchase price of $1,487.50 is the margin the retailer earns.

Exhibit 4   Hannas Seeds Dealer Sales

Name	lbs Sold 96–97	lbs Sold 97–98	lbs Sold 98–99	lbs Sold 99–00	Total
Agri Farm Supplies	4,460	3,430	4,230	7,735	19,855
Alberta Agro Services	0	950	750	9,060	10,760
Alberta Ranch & Farm	0	0	265	0	265
Alberta Seed Cleaning	9,655	165	1,895	165	11,880
Aylmer UFA	0	0	280	1,795	2,075
Bruce Seeds	5,150	14,467	9,290	22,055	50,962
Cedarview Co-op	8,712	9,870	18,604	165	37,351
Clarence Seed Cleaning	1,495	16,150	19,625	10,965	48,235
Dartmouth Supplies	47,370	36,525	42,663	34,305	160,863
Drumbo Co-op	0	3,525	15,497	11,256	30,278
Eccles Co-op	31,969	33,985	45,192	23,050	134,196
Eyckville Fertilizer	8,430	11,905	13,710	1,660	35,705
Fowler Farm & Ranch	12,930	29,335	12,139	18,515	72,919
Francesville Agri Supplies	3,765	0	0	535	4,300
Grimsby UFA	0	200	1,924	2,635	4,759
Harry Krabbe	0	875	1,750	55	2,680
Harvard Fertilizer	15,684	11,265	13,657	1,485	42,091
Hi Tech Agro	8,870	0	11,350	14,640	34,860
John Krug	29,060	36,265	25,370	33,545	124,240
Laroche County Supply	975	2,900	2,860	2,575	9,310
Lawrence Seed Cleaning	18,787	17,295	13,615	1,000	50,697
Len's Feed Store	2,098	1,510	2,885	1,500	7,993
Lloyd's Seed Cleaning	705	2,360	4,960	4,870	12,895
Muller Feed Mill	0	100	50	0	150
Parkview Fertilizer	12,898	17,475	46,261	50,674	127,308
Philip Reynolds	3,190	2,275	6,517	14,085	26,067
Purvis Seeds	51,533	81,010	61,808	49,465	243,816
Richardson Supplies	13,701	22,335	7,455	47,515	91,006
Riverside Supplies	2,745	2,695	630	2,355	8,425
Sagamore Livestock Supplies	15,385	10,770	15,288	9,341	50,784
Smith Feeds	350	1,760	5,655	3,715	11,480
Smithville Co-op	4,165	0	100	0	4,265
Sunshine Seeds	2,550	10,135	25,691	14,978	53,354
Valley UFA	0	1,200	6,710	5,250	13,160
Western Farm Supplies	0	700	6,111	11,745	18,556
Western Forest Supplies	26,850	19,085	15,218	37,395	98,548
William Torsten	10,640	6,045	2,868	9,245	28,798
	354,122	408,562	462,873	459,329	

their yard. At the end of the season, Hannas would pick up the truck trailer and invoice them for what was sold.

Other than margin, payment terms, and shipping, Hannas had not developed any dealer policies in areas such as sales incentives, training, exclusivity, or territory protection. Although Patricia was pleased with the growth of dealer sales over the last ten years, she was sure this aspect of the business could be improved by expanding the number of dealers and by getting existing dealers to increase sales.

Many of the current Hannas dealers had been recruited in the early 1990s when this was a priority task for Patricia. Lately, growth in dealer numbers had declined because Patricia was not able to devote as much time to this activity. In fact, recruiting dealers was a very time-consuming process. The first step was to identify prospects, and then it was necessary to contact these businesses and sell them on the benefits of carrying Hannas products. If a prospect did not carry forage seeds, it was much easier for Patricia to convince them to add this product line than it was to persuade a dealer currently carrying forage seeds to change brands or add a second brand. Patricia had no idea how many potential Alberta farm supply dealers currently did not carry any forage seed products, but estimated it might be 20 percent. The data in Exhibit 3 shows Patricia's estimate of the number of competing brands of forage seed carried by existing Hannas dealers.

In addition to recruiting new dealers, Patricia felt there was a lot of opportunity in working with existing dealers to help them increase sales of Hannas products. In reviewing sales by dealer (Exhibit 4), she noted that there was a lot of variability from dealer to dealer and, for any dealer, from year to year. Only a few dealers had shown a steady increase in sales over the past five years. She was not sure why this was the case, but speculated that it might be due to dealers starting to carry more than one line of forage seeds or dealer dissatisfaction or apathy. In an effort to understand the perspectives of dealers more fully, Patricia interviewed a number of dealers on a fairly wide range of topics. These interviews revealed a number of issues:

- Some dealers were unhappy with the fact that Hannas sold seed direct as well as through a dealer system. They felt that some customers would come to their dealership to obtain information on forage seeds and then go to the Hannas Customer Appreciation Day to purchase their needs at a 10 percent discount.
- Other dealers expressed some concern over the fact that Hannas had established two or more dealers in close proximity to each other, leading to some local competition for sales. In a few cases these dealers said there was occasional price-cutting at the local level to secure sales.

- There was fairly general concern over the fact that Hannas did not provide sales support for their dealers. Although Hannas did provide brochures listing their products and some technical information on each product, this was the only thing they did.
- A number of dealers mentioned that the financial rewards for carrying Hannas products were not adequate.
- Some dealers mentioned that they could not afford the time and expense to aggressively sell forage seeds. This line represented such a small portion of their business that it was not worth it to devote much effort to selling it. If farmers asked for a forage seed, they would take the order and fill it, but that was the extent of their involvement.
- A few dealers expressed concern over occasional delays in receiving orders.

Future Direction

Patricia and Warren were at odds about how to expand sales of forage seeds in the Alberta market. Warren was strongly in favour of gradually phasing out dealer sales and putting a major effort into direct sales. He felt it would not be possible to get a consistently strong effort from dealers to provide the sales growth Hannas Seeds required to meet company objectives. In his mind, using the margin currently allowed dealers to fund other marketing efforts would have greater payoff. Some of the activities he had in mind included the use of company salespeople to call on large accounts, greater use of advertising and direct mail, the possibility of having Customer Appreciation Days at other locations in Alberta, and the use of the Internet. He also noted that a substantial increase in direct sales would require hiring at least one more person in the office since the three current employees were operating at maximum capacity.

Patricia, on the other hand, had serious concerns about direct distribution. She felt that some face-to-face contact with customers was required to sell forage seeds and that it would simply be too costly for Hannas to do this themselves. Having dealers allowed for this face-to-face contact at a reasonable cost. She was, however, concerned about the ability of the company to attract good new dealers and motivate existing dealers to sell larger volumes of seed. She realized the company needed to review its distribution policies, particularly those policies related to compensating and motivating dealers. She also wondered whether it was possible to operate a system of direct distribution along with dealer sales.

A New Spirit for the New Age

Nicolas Papadopoulos

This case was developed by Dr. Nicolas Papadopoulos, Professor of Marketing and International Business at the Sprott School of Business, Carleton University, Ottawa, Canada. The case is designed solely for use as a basis for education and training and is not intended to illustrate appropriate or inappropriate handling of any aspect of business management. The situation described is real but names, locations, and some dates are disguised to protect confidential information and/or improve the learning experience.

What will the "spirit of the new century" be like? Beer producers would probably like to think that more and more consumers will opt for light beers and special brews. Many wine producers prefer to place their bets on light wines, coolers, and specialty wines (like Canada's ice wine) thinking that this is the direction in which the "new upper class," and many female drinkers, are moving. But producers of liquors, which are more technically called distilled spirits, would like to see a revival of a "spirit" that favours the "real thing"—alcoholic beverages such as scotch, bourbon, rye whisky, vodka, gin, or rum.

After all, spirits producers argue, the emphasis on "light" is largely misplaced. They claim that the calorie content of a 12-ounce bottle of regular beer is about 40 percent higher than that of a bottle of most light beers, a 5-ounce glass of wine, or a 1.5-ounce shot of liquor, all three of which have about the same number of calories. The percentage of alcohol in standard wine and liquor is the same as that of regular beer. So, individually or collectively, the distillers and their association from time to time undertake publicity campaigns to let weight-watching and fitness-minded consumers know the relevant facts; they support the publicity with paid advertising in magazines such as *Maclean's* or *Time*.

For example, under the umbrella of their association, Canada's distillers sponsored joint magazine ads for this purpose some 15 years ago using the headline "It's time to learn the facts of light." The ad's main visual was a photo of a slim female, dressed to convey an upper-class image, replicated three times with the only difference being the drink held by the model—a mixed liquor drink, a beer mug, and a glass of wine. To make sure consumers wouldn't miss the point, the photo was accompanied by a graphic of stylized typical glasses of the drinks being compared with "equals" signs between them. At about the same time, Bacardi ran a print ad asking which of a 5-ounce glass of white wine and a 5-ounce drink of rum and Diet Coke had the fewer calories, with the answer obviously being in the rum's favour (66 compared to 121).

These promotional efforts reflect the distillers' worries over a general long-term downward trend in the market for spirits, and their realization that they were perhaps slow in catching on to the changing mood and preferences of consumers in recent decades. During some periods over the past 20 years or so, some individual distillers have seen year-to-year declining sales of as much as 30 percent. Several factors seem to have been responsible for this situation:

- rising health-and-fitness consciousness among Canadians (as well as Americans and consumers in most other industrialized countries), which has made consumers more careful about what they eat and drink;
- rising concern about drinking and driving;
- intense competition among brewers and wineries for a shrinking market that resulted, as a side effect, in reduced interest in spirits;
- the shifting habits of consumers who grow up in a "light"-oriented culture, in everything from coffee to milk and colas, which turned them more toward wine and light beers and away from "hard" liquor;
- the high taxes imposed on distilled spirits by government, which has traditionally seen this product

as an easy source of revenue but which leads to higher prices; and

- restrictions on television and some other forms of mass advertising, which do not affect their beer and wine competitors.

Coupled with these external environmental factors, however, is the relative absence of a planned reaction by the distillers themselves. They did not jump onto the "lifestyle bandwagon" in promoting their products and do not seem to have made any concerted attempt at upgrading and modernizing their marketing approaches. A case in point is that campaigns such as those described above to "explain the facts of light" have been run only sporadically and in an ad hoc fashion rather than as part of a long-term plan. The combination of such factors means that they have ended up looking somewhat old-fashioned in comparison to their average competitor in the beer or wine sectors. For example,

- Many liquor brands are advertised simply in four-colour magazine ads featuring static pictures of a bottle and/or a glass containing the product. Some observers have wryly commented that many liquor ads do little more than "list their appointments to royal courts of old." This contrasts sharply with a small handful of brands, such as Absolut vodka, which have adopted more modern and exciting approaches, with obvious success.
- Many liquor brand advertisements seem to have fallen into the trap of talking mostly, or even exclusively, about the product, rather than focusing on how the consumer may benefit from it and using its characteristics only as a "reason why" behind its benefits. For example, an ad for a Black Label scotch shows the brand's external package (carton), the bottle, and a half-full glass, with the slogan "The really great statements are made in black." This seems to violate the cardinal marketing rule that a "try my product" emphasis is more suitable to the growth stage of the life cycle, as compared to the "buy my brand" promotion that would be called for in the case of a mature product of this type. More importantly, this type of advertising does not appear to provide the strong consumer-benefit product associations offered by, for example, lifestyle beer commercials.

Recently some things, at least, seem to be changing. The distillers appear to be more prepared to take a proactive role in protecting their consumer franchise, and some companies are engaging in efforts aimed specifically at revitalizing their brands, introducing new products to the market, and branching out into new areas through diversification. Some of these distillers are so large (e.g.,

Seagram, Hiram Walker) that they seem to be able to apply the necessary marketing expertise and financial muscle to accomplish their objectives. For example,

- An advertising campaign for Canadian Club rye whisky was based on the lifestyle approach and reflects the realities of the new marketplace. One of the magazine ads in the campaign showed a man preparing dinner in a modern kitchen. A woman, apparently having just returned from work and holding a glass with CC rye in her hand, leans over his shoulder and says, "So, what's for dinner?" The ad's slogan was "Be A Part Of It," and the words "Light. Crisp. Versatile. Enjoy." appeared beneath the brand's name. The brand's bottle itself can only be seen in the ad's background, on the countertop behind where the man is cooking.
- Another campaign conducted on television for Baileys Original Irish Cream features a lifestyle situation in a crowded bar that suggests flirting between a man and woman—not much unlike many beer commercials.

Just as distillers appear to be awakening from their long, self-induced lethargy, recent developments on the health-and-fitness front are presenting a new set of challenges—or, in the minds of some, of opportunities. Growing attention to health issues and the obesity problem has helped to catapult to the forefront a host of low-carb dieting methods such as the Atkins approach, which dominated the news in the early years of the 21st century. Beers like Michelob Ultra and Guinness, which are much lower in carbohydrates than such standard brands as Budweiser or Coors, were quick off the mark promoting themselves as diet friendly, and distillers took notice of the positive effect of such campaigns on the promoters' market shares.

Building on the fact that such standard liquors as rum, tequila, whisky, gin, and vodka are low on, or free of, carbohydrates or fat, many distillers are now engaging in promotional campaigns to stress their fit with contemporary approaches to dieting. Bacardi, for example, was preparing in late 2003 to re-run its 1980s campaign on the equality of calorie content between wine and a mixed rum drink.

In addition, distillers are going to greater lengths to explain to consumers that a drink's carbohydrate or calorie content may be largely due to the mixer rather than the liquor itself: a "skinny" White Russian, for example, using skim milk with Kahlúa, has about two-thirds the carbohydrates and only one-half the calories of the same drink made with regular milk. Since much of the overall consumption of liquors takes place in bars and restaurants, a large part of this promotional effort consists of educating bartenders on the use of more diet-friendly mixers in the drinks they serve. For instance, UV vodka is promoting to bartenders the use of sugar-free rather than regular lemonade as a mixer.

Another recent development that is also presenting the distillers with a new challenge is the lobbying by consumer groups in Canada and the United States to persuade the respective governments to legislate "full disclosure" through nutrition labelling requirements for all alcoholic beverages. Like most businesses, producers of alcoholic beverages are opposed to such legislation— but at the same time it is they themselves who are promoting heavily the nutritional advantages of their products. This places them in a complex conundrum, since they appear to be resisting attempts to legislate something that they need to, and do, promote, since not doing so risks losing them more of their clientele.

Discussion Questions

1. Analyze the complex environment for promotion of distilled spirits today, focusing on changes in the socio-cultural and legal environment.

2. Assume the position of an individual distiller or brand and develop an advertising or broader promotional campaign that would address the concerns outlined in the case.

3. Assume the position of the distillers' association and develop an advertising campaign that would address the concerns outlined in the case from the standpoint of a variety of distilled spirit products.

4. Apart from advertising, what other forms of promotion might individual distillers, or their association, use to enhance their relative position over beers and wines, if they were to utilize the full spectrum of potential activities offered by the concept of the "promotion mix"?

5. Apart from promotion, what other elements of the marketing mix can individual distillers use to help upgrade and modernize their outdated image?

Source

"Hard stuff's hard times," *Canadian Business*, June 1985, 219–220, and "New liquor pitch: How to drink on a diet," *Wall Street Journal* and *Ottawa Citizen*, December 12, 2003.

CASE 12

Tim Hortons

Peter Yannopoulos

In 1964, Tim Horton, the legendary national hockey player, opened Tim Hortons' first store in Hamilton, Ontario, serving coffee and doughnuts. Soon after, Tim Horton entered into a partnership with Ron Joyce, who was also the first Tim Hortons franchisee. Following Tim Horton's tragic death in a car accident in February 1974, Ron Joyce became the sole owner of the rapidly expanding franchise.

Years later, on December 29, 1995, the Tim Donut Ltd. (TDL Group Ltd.) signed an official merger with U.S.–based Wendy's International, Inc. This merger benefited Tim Hortons in two ways: First, financially, because it provided TDL with 13.5 percent of Wendy's stock, and second, by making it easier to expand into the U.S. market. Since the merger with Wendy's, Tim Hortons has opened stores in New York, Michigan, Ohio, Kentucky, Maine, and West Virginia.

Over the years, Tim Hortons had experienced a dramatic increase in market share. For example, each year since 1991, Tim Hortons enjoyed a growth rate of at least 7 percent. Tim Hortons had grown to over 2,300 restaurants in Canada and another 180 in the United States. According to 2001 statistics, Tim Hortons was one of the largest coffee and fresh baked goods chains in Canada by holding over 22 percent of the quick-service restaurant market and 70 percent of the coffee and baked goods market in Canada. In 2004, the chain reported a 6.1 percent rise in same-store sales in Canada in May and a 9.3 percent increase in U.S. same-store sales. Despite its impressive achievements, Tim Hortons planned to continue its ambitious growth program as its corporate objectives called "for further expansion and continued renovation plans across Canada and into the U.S. over the next several years." In March 2004, the question for Tim Hortons' management was to decide which of the many opportunities available to it was the most attractive.

Company Background

Tim Hortons' primary target market was working male and female consumers with low to medium incomes. The company was positioned as having "always fresh" products and outstanding service. Its positioning strategy was based on three attributes: fast, fresh, and friendly (the 3F's formula). The chain's focus on superior product quality, fresh products, and friendly and efficient customer service was largely responsible for Tim Hortons' success.

Much of Tim Hortons' marketing efforts were focused on convincing customers that the food it served was just what they would serve in their own home, and to make customers feel like its restaurants were a home away from home. Each year, Tim Hortons implemented a variety of marketing and advertising programs, including "Roll up the Rim to Win," "True Stories" TV commercials, and "New!—Hockey Day in Canada." The company has had the most success with the "Roll up the Rim to Win" promotion, which offered customers the chance to instantly win a variety of prizes ranging from fresh baked goods to cars.

Over the years, Tim Hortons extended its menu beyond freshly brewed coffee and fresh baked goods. Starting in 1976, the Timbit variety was introduced. Next, items such as muffins, bagels, cakes, pies, croissants, soups, and chilli were added to the menu to offer customers a greater variety of meal choices. In the summer months, cooler drinks such as iced cappuccinos and iced coffee beverages were offered to appeal to younger customers and to compensate for slow sales. Other additions to the menu included fruit-filled muffins and baguette sandwiches. The company also sold coffee beans as well as collectable items such as coffee mugs, coffeemakers, and coffee canisters with hockey scenes depicted on them.

Tim Hortons had policies that ensured its products were kept fresh at all times. Coffee not used within 20 minutes was discarded, and its doughnuts had a shelf life of between six and eight hours before being discarded as well. All the freshly baked goods served at Tim Hortons were baked daily on the premises of each restaurant. However, if no adequate baking facilities existed, then a nearby Tim Hortons would supply the needed goods. This policy had changed in recent months so that Tim Hortons stores reheated previously frozen products instead of cooking them on-site.

Toward the late 1990s, the growing demand for lunch meals and a preference for healthier foods led to Tim Hortons merging with Cuisine de France to help with the preparation of soups and baguette sandwiches. In 2002, Tim Hortons invested over $35 million in a bakery plant in Brantford to produce baguettes to be supplied fresh daily to its restaurants across Canada.

However, not all choices were available at all locations, resulting in loss of customers who would go elsewhere if Tim Hortons did not carry the product they wanted. Also, unlike many of its competitors, Tim Hortons accepted only cash and not other payment methods such as debit or credit card, in order to speed up the payment process at the cash register. In addition, the introduction of new product lines such as sandwiches or soups had slowed down the service. People who visited Tim Hortons to grab a quick coffee were often held up in line behind someone trying to decide what he or she wanted on a sandwich. Tim Hortons had attempted to offset the impact of such delays by adding more staff during peak hours.

Tim Hortons stores were located across Canada at major high-traffic areas, ranging from full standard stores to combo units with Wendy's, to carts and kiosks found in shopping malls, universities, colleges, and hospitals. Most of these locations provided a 24-hour drive-through service. On March 26, 2002, Esso and Tim Hortons announced that they had reached a ten-year agreement to open Tim Hortons stores at the various Esso outlets across Canada.

Five different warehouse distribution centres serviced Tim Hortons restaurants across Canada and the United States. These centres were strategically set up to maximize efficiency and minimize transportation time. Each distribution centre monitored the volume activity of each restaurant to ensure that each one is supplied with enough products to meet its daily demands. In addition, Tim Hortons used a fleet of decorated trucks that delivered supplies from these distribution centres to individual stores.

Following the merger in 1995 between Wendy's and Tim Hortons, the company developed an innovative "combo" restaurant format that provided a unique approach to food service convenience and customer appeal. Combo buildings were freestanding with a shared dining room and separate food preparation areas, storage areas, and staffs. The Tim Hortons and Wendy's combination benefited both restaurants because it took advantage of each other's customers, helping increase the sales of both establishments.

The Food Service Industry in Canada

The Canadian food service industry was one of the largest industries in the country. In 2002, there were almost 64,000 food service establishments in Canada that included restaurants, caterers, and taverns, as well as sales at hotels, sports stadiums, vending machines, and department stores. The industry employed 1,020,700 Canadians or 6.6 percent of the country's labour force. More than 42 percent of the employees were under 25 years of age.

With annual sales of more than $41 billion, food service represented 4 percent of Canada's gross domestic product. In 2002, the food service industry accounted for 40.5 cents of the total food dollar spent by consumers, with the remaining 59.5 cents spent at grocery and convenience stores. In 2000, according to Statistics Canada, the average household spent $1,951 on food and alcohol in restaurants. This amount was about 30 percent of the average household food budget.

Several major trends were taking place in the Canadian fast food industry. As Canadians became busier with everyday life and had less time for preparing meals, it was expected that the fast food industry would continue to grow. The trend toward working extra hours caused customers to require faster services and to seek the convenience of a fast food restaurant. A large number of Canadians were also concerned with healthier meal options, especially those customers with allergies or dietary needs.

Other trends affecting the food service industry included the practice by an increasing number of rival restaurants of offering consumers the convenience of paying by debit or credit. Other restaurants were moving toward selling their products in other places such as grocery stores or hotel restaurants to increase overall retail sales. Some restaurants were disclosing nutritional information, such as ingredient lists, to provide consumers with additional information about what they were consuming.

The Competition

In March 2004, competition in the quick-service food industry was intensive, with several companies vying for a share of this industry. Tim Hortons fell in the lower end of the coffee and sandwich market along with Krispy Kreme, Dunkin' Donuts, and Subway. In the higher end of the market were Second Cup and Starbucks.

Dunkin' Donuts. Dunkin' Donuts was a subsidiary of Allied Domecq International. It had a strong presence internationally with stores in 35 countries. Its annual company-wide sales volume was $1.4 billion (U.S.). It had recently embarked on a brand rejuvenation and expansion program in Canada, especially in Quebec, its stronghold in Canada. In 2002, it was planning to open 170 new stores in Canada over the next five years. Most of its locations were freestanding units in detached buildings situated next to busy roads. Its stores had good visibility, limited seating, and some drive-through facilities. Some of its stores followed an "end-cap strategy"—locating in a corner position on the outside of shopping centres.

Krispy Kreme. Krispy Kreme Donuts was well established in the United States before it opened a number of stores in Canada. In 2002, it had 250 stores in the United States and Ontario. It had differentiated its products with an "old-fashioned secret recipe," offering the doughnuts warm and having an illuminated sign to let customers know when the doughnuts were ready. Its stores are specially designed to let customers watch the doughnuts being cooked. Krispy Kreme had a narrow menu consisting mainly of doughnuts. For this reason, it did not provide much competition to Tim Hortons, which also offered coffee and sandwiches.

Second Cup. Second Cup was Canada's largest retailer of specialty coffee with close to 400 stores across Canada. Its stores were located in malls, street fronts, office towers, libraries, colleges, universities, and hospitals. It served Air Canada flights and sold its coffee in restaurants at Delta Hotels. Its owner, Cara Foods, was Canada's largest integrated restaurant company, owning several restaurants in Canada. Second Cup positioned itself as the "ultimate coffee experience." Second Cup's focus on convenience was demonstrated by offering a drive-through and take-out service as well as a retail section in many of its cafés.

Starbucks. Starbucks was the largest specialty coffee retailer in the world with more than 7,500 retail locations in North America, Europe, the Middle East, and the Pacific Rim. Starbucks specialized in gourmet coffee and appealed to young urban professionals, 25 to 40 years of age, with a higher level of education, and earning more than $35,000 a year. The chain differentiated itself from the competition with high-quality coffee and an exciting retail atmosphere. In addition to selling coffee, drinks, and pastries, Starbucks offered mugs, coffeemakers, coffee grinders, and storage containers. The company also sold its coffee beans to airlines, restaurants, hotels, online, and through catalogues.

Subway. Subway was the largest sandwich franchise in the world with over 20,000 restaurants in 74 countries, 1,564 of which were in Canada, in 2003. It held 58 percent of the sandwich segment market share. Subway outlets could be found in airports, business centres, amusement parks, stadiums, colleges, universities, convenience stores, hospitals, military bases, recreational facilities, elementary and secondary schools, and supermarkets. Subway competed by offering "fresh made," tasty, and healthy and low-fat sandwiches. Its restaurants were completely franchised, and it provided a variety of services, such as store design and local marketing assistance to its franchisees.

The Future

Tim Hortons intended to expand aggressively through the pursuit of attractive growth opportunities. One of the opportunities available to Tim Hortons was further expansion into the Canadian and U.S. markets by opening additional combo units or opening more single Tim Hortons locations. There was room to open new Tim Hortons stores in the United States, especially in combo format with Wendy's. The success of its existing combos suggested a high probability of success for any new openings. However, this option became less plausible, since Wendy's announced on July 29, 2005, that it was planning to sell a portion (15 to 18 percent) of Tim Hortons by March 2006. Wendy's chairman and chief executive officer, Jack Schuessler, said the company eventually planned to spin off Tim Hortons entirely and could do so within two years. According to Schuessler, with Tim Hortons moving into the lunch business and Wendy's moving into the cold-sandwich business, Wendy's and Tim's would become competitors in the future.

Tim Hortons could also expand its current product line to include hot sandwiches such as meatball, roast beef, and cheese, for customers interested in a hot, healthy, and fresh meal. Offering hot sandwiches would further satisfy its target market as many consumers desiring a warm meal could have something other than chilli and cold sandwiches. Adding a "homemade"-style meatball and pot-roast beef sandwich to its menu would increase its menu variety and strengthen its "home away from home" image—a place where one can go to get a fresh, healthy, and hot meal.

A third opportunity for Tim Hortons was to follow the lead of other fast food restaurants such as KFC, Subway, Pizza Hut, and McDonald's by expanding into Europe and Asia. The Chinese market was a particularly attractive one for Tim Hortons because China was the world's most populous nation at approximately 1.3 billion people, and the largest market for consumer goods. The Chinese fast-service restaurant industry was experiencing a dramatic growth approximating 20 percent per year while its total worth was about 200 billion Yuan ($24.39 billion U.S.) in 2002.

The Chinese opportunity was especially attractive because of its improved stability, as well as the nation's entry into the World Trade Organization (WTO). The share of Chinese-style fast food was 78.9 percent while Western-style was 21.1 percent of the market. The share of Western-style food companies was growing as many Chinese consumers were abandoning traditional Chinese food restaurants and were turning to Western-style fast food establishments. Chinese consumers did not particularly like coffee but green tea was very popular in China.

Tim Hortons could enter the Chinese market through a joint venture. Such a business strategy would solve many logistics problems, split the risk, and ease the entry process. Entering through a franchising strategy would not be feasible due to Chinese regulatory laws and strict foreign investment rules. Making a direct investment would involve no risk sharing, a high commitment with little flexibility, and possible difficulties due to lack of knowledge of the Chinese business environment.

Discussion Questions

1. Assess Tim Hortons' competitive advantages over its competitors.
2. Explain Tim Hortons' segmentation and positioning strategy.
3. Evaluate Tim Hortons' customer relationship management efforts.
4. Which alternative growth options do you recommend to Tim Hortons? Explain your answer.

Sources

History of Tim Hortons, www.timhortons.com/english/images/mediakit.pdf, retrieved on March 26, 2004; Wendy's International Inc., www.wendys.com, retrieved on November 30, 2003; Tim Hortons, www.timhortons.com, retrieved on November 30, 2003; 411 Canada Directory Information, www.statscanada.com, retrieved on November 30, 2003; www.aftonfood.com, retrieved on November 30, 2002; collections.ic.gc.a/wentworth/timhorto.htm, cultural landmarks of Hamilton-Wentworth, Tim Hortons, retrieved on November 30, 2002; www.krispykreme.com/investorrelations.html, retrieved on November 29, 2002; www.newswire.ca/release/sep2000/27/c7617.html, retrieved on November 29, 2002; www.newswire.ca/release/November2001/19/c8717.html, retrieved on November 28, 2002; www.subway.com, retrieved on November 29, 2002; www.timhortons.com, retrieved on November 29, 2002, mwww.wendys-invest.com/library/annual/ 01/wen01annsec3.pdf, "Building on Our Foundation, Tim Hortons Long Term Strategic Marketing Plan," retrieved on November 29, 2002; Jonathan Drew, "Wendy's Int'l to Spin Off Tim Hortons," Associated Press, http://abcnews.go .com/Business/wireStory?id=990742, retrieved on August 2, 2005; "Wendy's to sell part of Tim Hortons," http://money.cnn.com/2005/07/ 29/markets/ipo/ wendy_horton.reut/, retrieved on August 2, 2005.

CASE 13

AutoPlus Ltd.

Nicolas Papadopoulos

This case was developed by Dr. Nicolas Papadopoulos, Professor of Marketing and International Business at the Sprott School of Business, Carleton University, Ottawa, Canada. It is designed solely for use as a basis for education and training and is not intended to illustrate appropriate or inappropriate handling of any aspect of business management. The situation described is real but names, locations, and some dates are disguised to protect confidential information and/or improve the learning experience.

© N. Papadopoulos 2004. Reprinted with permission.

"This is a fail-safe business idea, if I ever saw one!" exclaimed David Simon, when Gill Ladouceur had finished her presentation. "I think we should pursue the concept further. The idea of a total car-care centre goes way beyond what we have in Canada now—for that matter, I don't know of any place in the world where this has been tried before. Now, as you know, I like to move quickly. I'm prepared to take this up with my partners at the earliest possible date. We meet every Thursday to consider new ventures, so time is not a problem as far as we're concerned. I will, however, need some more information from you before I can push your proposal through. Here's what you can do. . . ."

As Mr. Simon listed the information he would need, and as Jim Quain, her partner, took notes, Gill could hardly contain the feeling of enthusiasm that was building inside her. What had started as a miserable experience three years ago, when she tried to sell her used car, now seemed ready to be turning into a business that could well make her rich. The business concept was simple yet complex: a chain of car-care outlets specializing in selling automobile accessories and car-cleaning services to consumers, coupled with a line of specialized car-care services addressed to industrial customers. She let her mind wander back to how it had all begun.

Background

In 1995, Gill Ladouceur had tried to sell her old Toyota, a 1984 Camry. Thinking she could get a better price for the car if it looked immaculate, she set out to "upgrade" it. After several hundred dollars spent on repairs, all that remained was to clean up the car's interior, take it to a car wash, and place an ad in the local paper. Gill had felt the best thing to do was to take it to a service station and give it the full treatment—have the floor vacuumed, the upholstery cleaned, and the exterior washed and waxed carefully by hand, so that the whole car would be truly spotless.

It had taken a while to find a station that offered this kind of service in Calgary, where Gill lived, since most outlets had automatic car washes. When she did find one that would do the job, the price was too high. The man asked for $150! So she decided to take the only "reasonable" alternative—clean up the car by herself. And this is where her troubles began. There just didn't seem to be any part of the car that could be brought to, or kept in, "like new" condition—what Gill, being a perfectionist, defined as "perfectly clean." After two hours of vacuuming and polishing the interior, she could still find dust and other kinds of dirt under the carpets, around the dashboard, on the bottom side of the steering wheel, or in little crevices around the rear window. Using a special cleaner bought from Canadian Tire, she had sprayed and washed down the entire engine compartment, yet she could still find numerous spots of baked-on grease, corrosion around the battery poles, and oil mixed with dust and caked on at difficult-to-reach parts underneath the engine.

Worse yet, it seemed impossible to keep the car in good shape, inside or outside, during the eight long weeks between the time she had first tried to clean it and when it was finally sold. Every time she drove to work or to a store, the car got new mud spots or a new layer of dust. And there seemed to be no way to avoid bringing in dried leaves, broken twigs, and other dirt particles every time she or a passenger got in the car. After several more exterior washes and interior cleanups, a frustrated Gill Ladouceur sold her car for $600 less than she had hoped for.

One year later, while visiting her parents who lived in France, Gill noticed a store in Paris that brought back memories of her frustrating experience with her car. The store carried an amazing variety of automobile accessories and was named, quite appropriately although somewhat unimaginatively, Accessoires d'Auto. It sold interior and exterior mirrors, what seemed like an infinite variety of decorative self-adhesive stripes and decals, mag wheels, tachometers, front and back seat consoles, coffee-cup holders, add-on clocks, radio aerials, emergency kits (containing flares, candles, fuses, and reflector triangles), complete first-aid boxes, picture frames (for hanging from the rear-view mirror), battery-operated vacuums, radios, hood ornaments, mudguards, spoilers, roof racks, seat covers, map-reading lights, and, of course, a complete line of do-it-yourself cleaners, waxes, and the like.

While thinking how much more her car might have fetched had she dressed it up with a few racy stripes outside and an add-on tachometer or spoiler, Gill realized that most of these products were, of course, available in Canada. What seemed to make a difference here was that they were all displayed within a single but large specialty store that carried nothing but auto accessories. Unlike Canada, where such products are just part of a hardware or even department store's offerings, or are sold by car dealers who limit their selection to products that fit the brands of cars they sell, this store seemed to be a one-stop supermarket for any accessory, for any type of car, for any taste.

The Business Concept

The business concept slowly evolved in Gill's mind out of her two experiences in Calgary and in Paris, and then gathered steam after she decided to invite Jim Quain to join her as a partner. Jim was managing a large auto dealership at the time. Gill felt he could bring to the business what she lacked—technical knowledge about the automobile industry—and Jim was more than glad to consider quitting his nine-to-five job and trying his hand at being an entrepreneur. Gill, having a business degree and considerable marketing experience, felt comfortable with the knowledge she herself had about developing a marketing program.

After several revisions and changes, here's what Gill and Jim's plan looked like.

Product. AutoPlus would be involved in three main lines of business. First would be a "car detailing" service line.

This term is used to describe the type of service involving personalized, non-automated car washing, cleaning, and polishing. Detailers typically spend from half an hour to over eight hours on a car, depending on what the customer wants. A half-hour job includes hand-washing and then drying a car's exterior, using special non-abrasive rubbing compounds that protect its paint, and ensuring that no dirt or dust spots are left on any surface. The more detailed job (hence the term "detailing") includes the same exterior service but also a meticulous cleaning of a car's interior (complete with carpet cleaning and upholstery shampooing), as well as of its engine and trunk compartments and the car's underside, where all grease is removed, battery poles are cleaned, and so on.

As far as the two partners could judge, demand for this type of service was increasing in Canada. There were two or three major franchise chains in this area and, on a trip to Toronto, Jim had noticed an outlet called Presidential Car Care—apparently a thriving business judging by the numerous (and expensive) cars waiting for service on its parking lot. This type of service seemed to draw clientele from among three segments: people preparing to sell their used cars; owners of antique or expensive cars who don't want to see their valued possessions subjected to the rough treatment of automated car washes; and "perfectionist" consumers wanting to keep their vehicles spotlessly clean.

The second AutoPlus line would consist of selling a variety of auto accessories, along the lines of the selection Gill had seen in Paris. The partners reasoned that if some consumers were willing to spend extra money to give their cars such personalized care, they would also be interested in add-on items that could further enhance a vehicle's value or appearance. Unlike hardware stores, AutoPlus would carry a specialized and complete selection of accessories, enabling consumers to shop while their car was being serviced.

The third line, the partners felt, was the true masterstroke. From the beginning, they had felt uneasy investing in a venture that, great as it sounded, could always fail if its success depended only on one type of customer. What the business needed, they decided, was a "cash cow." From this, the concept of industrial services emerged. AutoPlus would offer its specialized car-care services to car-rental companies, corporate headquarters, government offices, and any other organization that maintained a small or large fleet of vehicles whose appearance had to be spotless. This would include, for example, executive limousines, salespersons' cars, rental vehicles, and even odd-shaped vehicles such as vans or small trucks that could not go through some automated car wash set-ups.

This industrial service would be offered on a contract basis. One or two major contracts, the two partners felt, would provide enough cash flow to help the consumer side of the business weather any hard times. What seemed particularly appealing about this idea was the assumption that industrial customers' vehicles would probably be serviced at different times than consumers' cars—say, after 6:00 p.m. or on weekends. AutoPlus could therefore maintain two or even three shifts per 24-hour period, thus utilizing its plant better and spreading its overhead costs.

Distribution. Another ingenious idea occurred to the two partners regarding distribution. AutoPlus outlets would be located at one of two kinds of places—either free-standing locations within a five-minute radius of major shopping centres or locations within modern high-traffic power centres featuring big-box stores.

At free-standing locations, each outlet would have a minivan offering free shuttle transport to its customers between the outlet and the shopping centre. Consumers could thus do their shopping while their cars were being taken care of. By locating near, but not right next to, a shopping centre, Gill and Jim felt they could find buildings whose rental rates would not be too high. On the other hand, big-box stores at power centres might be handled somewhat differently, perhaps even by excluding the detailing line and focusing on the merchandise side only. After all, the partners reasoned, there seemed to be a big-box chain for every type of product these days, from Michaels crafts to Danier leather and Mikasa housewares—why not a store specializing in car accessories? Whether or not the detailing line was excluded, the set-up at power centres would probably make it less necessary to offer the shuttle service.

Promotion. AutoPlus would undertake a variety of promotion activities. To obtain organizational customers for long-term contracts, Gill and Jim were prepared to do some personal selling. This would involve visiting selected corporate headquarters, government offices, and businesses that maintained fleets of vehicles, to explain the new service and offer (at first) a trial three-month contract. The industrial promotion effort would also include direct mailings to potential customers.

For consumers, AutoPlus would advertise in the local newspapers and later, perhaps, on radio and television, especially for its free-standing outlets (those in power centres might not need as much promotion since each centre has its own traffic that benefits all its retailers). An attempt would also be made to identify owners of antique or expensive cars and then to approach them by direct mail. Sales promotion could also be undertaken by combining AutoPlus offerings. For example, customers buying the complete car detailing package might be offered a discount on buying accessories, and vice versa.

Pricing and Demand. The entrepreneurs felt less certain about pricing than they did about the other marketing mix elements. This was mainly because of the difficulty in estimating demand and its elasticity to price. After considerable discussion and some research, the following price schedule was decided upon:

1. Three main car-care options would be offered to consumers: (a) an exterior hand-wash and drying, estimated to take about one half-hour, for about $25; (b) option (a) plus a complete interior cleaning (upwards of two hours of personal labour) for about $90; and (c) a complete package, including option (b) plus cleaning the engine and trunk compartments, as well as the underside, for about $200 (upwards of three hours of labour). Special add-on options would be available, such as option (a) plus hand-waxing and polishing. Gill and Jim felt they could afford to price their services competitively, since their overhead would be spread over a wider variety of offerings. Rates for special cases, such as antique cars, would be negotiable.

2. A cost-plus policy would be implemented concerning accessories. AutoPlus would add a 35 percent markup on its purchase costs from wholesalers and manufacturers. This, the partners felt, would bring their retail prices to just about the same level as those charged at hardware stores, but to lower levels than those of specialty competitors (e.g., car dealerships), whose markups on accessories were higher.

3. The industrial car-care service would be priced along the same lines as the consumer service, but with quantity discounts to reflect the long-term contracts and larger number of vehicles involved. The partners had not yet worked out the details, but they felt that three types of factors should influence the value of the final contract: the frequency of service (for example, a specification for a minimum of one service per two weeks for regular washes, and two per year for complete jobs, would be necessary for the customer to get a discount); the length of the contract (the longer the term, the greater the discount) and the number of vehicles involved (the greater the number, the greater the discount).

Estimating demand at such (or any) rates seemed difficult. The partners had observed the traffic at a busy local automated car wash, charging $8 for a wash or $5 with a gas fill-up. Taking both slack and busy times into account, one car went through every 15 minutes or so. Assuming a seven-day-per-week, 12-hour-per-day operation, and assuming that 80 percent of the drivers paid the discount price, that outlet would have revenues of almost $100,000 in a year—not bad, considering that the operation required virtually no labour and that its revenue could help cover part of the service station's overhead.

For their business, Gill and Jim found it virtually impossible to estimate demand, given the confusing array of combinations among types of customers, services, and rates. When they had last talked about it, Jim had given up.

"Look," he had said. "There's just no way to make an accurate forecast. But there's also no way we can go wrong in terms of profit. Consider it this way: That automated car wash we checked out does more than 17,000 car washes in a year. Even if we did only 2,000 low-end jobs at $25 and only 500 fuller ones at the lower level of $90 each, our annual revenue would just about match theirs. And this comes to only 38 regular washes and 10 complete jobs per week! Let alone that this doesn't account for accessory sales and business contracts. I tell you, it'll all add up."

Business Plan. In the end, Gill and Jim decided to be "cautiously optimistic." Their final plan consisted of both "floor" and "sky-is-the-limit" projections. On the floor side, they would start their business by opening two outlets at opposite ends of the city. They felt that one outlet would not be enough to give AutoPlus the credibility and prestige it needed to get off on the right start. Their first effort would be toward securing business contracts worth about $50,000, to ensure some revenue would be coming in, and toward making the Calgary public aware of the new service. The accessory line would be limited, and to keep costs down, they would hire only one person per outlet to wash cars in the beginning. Each partner would manage one of the outlets, acting as manager, retail salesperson, and occasional car-wash helper if the need arose. If the venture proved successful, accessory products and personnel would be added gradually and promotion would be expanded. This approach, they felt, was a "test market" of sorts.

If the venture proved to be very successful, as they were sure it would, they were prepared to franchise the concept. Since they felt that the idea might be relatively easy to copy, they resolved to have a complete franchise plan ready before opening the Calgary outlets. Assuming they could tell how the business was doing by the end of the first six months, they could thus be first-to-market with a franchise offering. The plan would include a training manual and instructions and guidelines on where and how to choose a location and acquire equipment and merchandise (e.g., minivan, washing and cleaning supplies, accessories). It might be possible eventually, Gill and Jim felt, to become the suppliers of all these products for their franchisees, thereby enlarging the scope of the business and its revenue potential.

Mr. Simon's Request

The point of no return had almost been reached. They were now presenting their idea to a venture capital group, asking for an initial investment of $200,000 and willing to put up a total of $50,000 of their own money to get AutoPlus started.

". . . so, let me summarize," Mr. Simon said. "What we need is more complete information on profit potential. You must make a better estimate of demand, and furnish me with details on plant costs, labour rates, utility costs such as water and power, and the like. I think the idea will pan out anyway, but it's good to have this kind of information just in case."

Discussion Questions

1. Evaluate the AutoPlus plan. Does it seem like a viable venture, in view of target market and marketing mix considerations?
2. Assess AutoPlus's pricing policies. Which pricing concepts have the two partners focused on? What other policies and/or concepts might have been considered?
3. Have the partners taken into account all necessary elements in making up their basic revenue forecasts? How realistic do you think Mr. Quain's assumption is, that the revenue potential is such that they can't go wrong?
4. Construct a price list for AutoPlus industrial customers, using the consumers' prices and the factors affecting the business discount structure discussed in the case. You can do this by making up one grid for each of the types of detailing jobs being contemplated, listing contract-length options across the top and number-of-vehicles options along the side. Having constructed the price list, assess its attractiveness to potential buyers.
5. Assume AutoPlus was to operate in a large Canadian city of your choice (Calgary, your city, or any other). Gather appropriate information from local sources to make as accurate a profit-and-loss forecast as you can. You can concentrate on operating costs (e.g., utilities, labour, supplies, depreciation of minivan—do not worry about the capital costs themselves for acquiring assets) and on marketing research to estimate demand (e.g., observation at local car-wash outlets). Having developed a P&L statement, assess the survival potential of this venture.

Centre for the Arts

H. F. MacKenzie

Debbie Slade, managing director for the Centre for the Arts (www.arts.brocku.ca), was preparing for a meeting with Erin White, the marketing coordinator. Debbie had called the meeting to discuss what to do concerning the Centre's theatrical programming. It was Monday, October 27, 2003, two days before the Centre was scheduled to present *Halo*. This would be the first theatrical performance for the 2003–2004 professional entertainment season, and ticket sales were disappointingly low. Early indications were that sales for the other two theatrical performances were likely to be similar. Debbie was concerned in the short term with what to do to increase sales for this performance, but also for the other two theatrical performances that were scheduled for the current season. More importantly, she had to decide the longer-term issue of what role live theatre should have within the Centre's programming; that is, what she should do for the 2004–2005 season and beyond.

The Venue

The Centre for the Arts is an integral part of Brock University. The Departments of Dramatic Arts and Music are given scheduling priority as the Centre's facilities are needed for the practical components of their studies. The Centre is mandated to stimulate cultural interest in the arts within the Niagara Region. See Exhibit 1 for a statement of the Centre's vision, mission, and values and beliefs. The Centre provides hands-on experience for Brock students, as well as for high school students and community users. Through its live performances and educational programs, the Centre has been successful in attracting thousands of visitors annually to Brock University.

The Centre for the Arts is intended primarily as an educational and cultural resource for Brock University. Therefore, there are clear priorities when it comes to determining usage for its facilities:

1. Department of Dramatic Arts, for rehearsals, performances, and exhibitions (required 700 hours over 18 weeks during the 2003–2004 season; expected to increase needs by 30 percent beginning the following year)
2. Department of Music, for performance classes and concerts (required 300 hours during the 2003–2004 season for lunch-hour concerts, the Encore Concert Series, and pedagogical examinations)
3. Niagara Symphony Orchestra
4. Faculty of Education
5. University departments/groups for performances, lectures, speakers, etc.
6. Community groups
7. Centre for the Arts professional entertainment events

The Centre for the Arts employs 10 full-time staff members. The managing director, Debbie Slade, is responsible for directly managing the other nine employees and for indirectly managing 60 part-time student workers and 25 volunteers. The marketing coordinator, Erin White, is responsible for managing the advertising and promotion budget; media releases; magazine, radio, and newspaper advertising; and hospitality for guest artists. She is also responsible for selling advertising space in promotional programs distributed by the Centre and media and other kinds of sponsorship and in-kind gifts. A production manager is responsible for all the technical operations of the Centre; to directly

Vision

To be Niagara's *best* Cultural Centre, to foster excellence in the performing arts, and to be a leader in the arts community by providing access to all citizens to the live performing arts.

Mission

To stimulate cultural interest in the performing arts within the University and the Niagara Community.

Values and Beliefs

1. To provide leadership for the arts and live entertainment in the community.
2. To program local, national, and international artists to reflect community needs by offering a balanced performing arts program that is shared by educational, community, and professional use on an equitable and flexible basis.
3. To provide a facility that is accessible to all citizens through a variety of programming and culturally diverse programs based on availability, market demand, and fair pricing.
4. To maintain and enhance the Centre's facilities and operations at the highest possible standard in order for the Centre for the Arts to continue to be a valuable community and national asset.

manage three technicians responsible for sound equipment, lighting, and computers; to enforce fire regulations; and to act as assistant managing director when Debbie Slade is absent. An audience services supervisor is responsible to select, train, and supervise part-time staff and to manage concession inventory and bar supplies. There is also an administrative assistant, a box office manager, and a box office assistant. The number of staff has not increased since 1987, although the scope of operations has more than doubled. See Table 1 for a list of scheduled performance for the 2003–2004 professional entertainment season.

Table 1	Season Schedule 2003–2004
Tower of Power	October 4
Remy Shand	October 9
Zucchero	October 22
Two Planks and a Passion Theatre: *Halo*	October 29
Chantal Kreviazuk	October 30
Harlem Gospel Choir	October 31
The Royal Winnipeg Ballet: *The Magic Flute*	November 15
The Second City National Touring Company: *The Puck Stops Here!*	November 26
Brass Rings: *A Time for Christmas*	December 4
Natalie MacMaster	December 5
Cantabile	December 10
Ron Rexsmith *with Mad Violet*	December 16
Holly McNarland *with Shaye*	January 15
The Heillig Manoeuvre	January 17
The Flaming Idiots	January 18
Motus O: *A Midsummer Night's Dream*	January 24

(Continued)

Table 1	Season Schedule 2003–2004 (*Continued*)	
The Musical Box:		
Genesis: Selling England by the Pound		January 28
Dave Coulier		January 29
Smythe and Saucier		February 8
Kiran Ahluwalia		February 19
Nearly Neil and the Solitary Band		February 21
Sampradaya Dance: *Revealed by Fire*		February 28
Gregg Lawless and the Acoustic Orchestra		March 3
Jory Nash and Aengus Finnan		March 6
One Acre Productions: *Fingers and Toes*		March 11
John McDermott		March 12 & 13
Roger Whittaker		March 14
The Cottars		March 19
Jane Bunnett and the Spirits of Havana		March 25
Sinha Danse: *Loha/Thok*		March 27
Cleo Laine & the John Dankworth Group		April 1
Catalyst Theatre: *The Blue Orphan*		April 7
Nnenna Freelon		April 16
David Usher		April 17
Shona Rppe Puppets: Cinderella		April 18
Rik Emmett		April 21
Buddy Wasisname and the Other Fellers		April 28
The Big Band Broadcast		April 30

The Act

Halo, a compassionate and funny play written by actor and playwright Josh MacDonald tells the story of the sighting of an image of Jesus that appeared in small-town Nova Scotia. The play is based on a true story, the Christ-like apparition having appeared under the floodlights on the outside wall of a Tim Hortons in Bras D'Or, Cape Breton, and first noticed by staff at the Lick-A-Chick restaurant across the road. The apparition appeared for several days, resulting in nightly traffic jams around the doughnut shop when as many as 4,000 people came to view it.

The main character in the play is Casey Quinn, a high school dropout who has taken a full-time job at the local Tim Hortons. Casey, who resents the rigidity of her local community, has become an outcast. She ridicules the faith of her boyfriend and boss, while she befriends the new priest in the community. Following the appearance of the apparition, the community becomes a "faith circus" where everyone, including Casey, has something to learn. While this is happening, a local Christmas tree farmer and

devout Catholic, Donald McMullen, has been sitting at the bedside of his daughter who has been in a coma for the past two years. Donald's faith is tested and his motivations examined when his older daughter, Lizzie, joins him at the bedside. The two stories come together to provide a powerful and hilarious look at modern faith and community.

The play was being performed by a cast of seven members of Two Planks and a Passion Theatre (www. twoplanks.ca), founded in 1992 in rural Kings County, Nova Scotia. The company's mission is "to commission, develop, and produce challenging Canadian drama with strong roles for women that is reflective of the lives of the audiences for whom they perform, and to disseminate this work to communities large and small nationwide." Other works that it created and produced included *Westray: The Long Way Home* and *Hockey Mom Hockey Dad*.

The touring performers had booked numerous performances across eastern Canada, beginning with the Confederation Centre, in Charlottetown, P.E.I., on October 16 and ending on November 8 at the Markham Theatre in Markham, Ontario. The St. Catharines performance was booked for October 29, 2003, at the 538-seat Sean O'Sullivan Theatre, Centre for the Arts, Brock University. One of the main advantages that the Centre had was its membership in an organization that allowed it to procure the services of a number of performing artists through a network of block booking with other members, thereby getting reduced artistic fees because of "volume" booking. The artistic fees charged to the Centre for *Halo* amounted to $4,000. Artistic fees varied depending on the venue, and the Centre simply adjusted box office prices to reflect the fees it paid.

Costing *Halo*

When Debbie reviewed the other costs associated with *Halo*, she noted that she would have to spend $600 for hotel accommodations for the performers. The promotional costs that were either spent or committed at that time included $950 for flyers, brochures, and posters; $475 for print advertising (newspapers), and $450 for radio advertising. Projected costs also included three local crew members to unload and set up stage props and equipment for two hours each ($27 per hour); four local crew members to take down the stage props and equipment and load them for shipment for one hour each ($27 per hour); one spot operator for 2.5 hours ($27 per hour); one house manager for four hours ($15 per hour); two catering staff for five hours each ($8.50 per hour), and eight ushers for 3.5 hours each ($9.85 per hour). The only other actual cost that would be involved would be to service the credit card administration as credit card companies charged a small percentage for a handling fee. Debbie's best guess was that it would be somewhere between $150 and $200. Debbie included a cost of $915 for theatre rental, although this was not actually paid to the university as a rental fee. It was included because it was an opportunity cost since that is what would be received if the theatre were rented for another purpose. When all costs are finally known, including this opportunity cost for theatre rental, the Centre could make up to 10 percent profit. Any revenue above this amount was then split 80/20 between the artist or artists and the promoter. This arrangement had become increasingly popular over the past few years and was now being demanded by almost all performers.

Sales to October 27, 2003

Prior to the meeting, Debbie Slade asked for an up-to-date summary of sales. With two days remaining before the performance was scheduled, there were only 225 paid seats. Table 2 shows a breakdown of sales. Historically, there were very few, if any, seats sold in the last few days before a theatrical performance.

Seat prices varied depending on the particular performance. Prices for musical performances varied from $55 per single seat for John McDermott or Natalie MacMaster, to $49.50 for Chantal Kreviazuk or Remy Shand, to $32.00 for the Cottars or Buddy Wasisname and the Other Fellers, to $28.50 for Ron Sexsmith or Holly McNarland. Theatrical performances were priced at the lower end of the range. All three performances scheduled for the 2003–2004 season were priced at $28.50 for single seats, with a 10 percent discount for groups of 10 or more, or for Brock University staff and faculty; $23.50 for Gold Members; and $20.50 for Platinum Members. Brock University had 490 faculty members and 16 librarians in its Faculty Association, and 654 staff. The Centre sold approximately 600 memberships annually, mostly outside the university. Memberships were almost equally divided between Gold memberships and Platinum memberships. Gold members paid $50 annually. For this, they got advance notice of upcoming performances and special events, plus an opportunity to purchase tickets prior to their being offered to the general public. They also got reduced prices of up to 20 percent and could buy

Table 2	Sales to October 27, 2003			
Buyer Type	Seats	Revenue	GST	CRF
Advance (Ticket Office)	57	1624.50	106.02	57.00
Advance (Internet)	16	456.00	29.76	16.00
Group Tickets	36	923.40	60.48	36.00
Brock Staff/Faculty	2	51.30	3.36	2.00
Gold Members	45	1057.50	69.30	45.00
Platinum Members	69	1414.50	92.46	69.00
	225	5527.20	361.38	225.00

as many as six discounted tickets per show. Membership also entitled them to three complimentary parking vouchers valued at $3 each, an invitation to a special Member's Night sneak preview, and complimentary tickets to selected shows. Platinum members paid $100 annually and received all the benefits of Gold members, but got discounts of up to 25 percent and five complimentary parking vouchers, and they could buy up to 10 discounted tickets per show. Platinum members also got advance purchase privileges prior to Member's Night.

From total revenue, the Centre for the Arts had to pay GST to Revenue Canada, and a $1 per seat charge that was to contribute to a capital reserve fund (CRF) that was used to repair and renovate the facilities when needed. One of the main marketing objectives for the 2003–2004 season was to have an average 80 percent capacity paid attendance, with 50 percent of all tickets sold through membership. While the Centre was not specifically focused on generating a profit, Debbie was certainly aware that generating some positive financial contribution would position the Centre better within the university hierarchy, and this would make it easier to negotiate for things that it might need in the future.

Marketing

Erin White is the marketing coordinator for the Centre for the Arts. Erin received a B.A. in Media Communications from Brock University in 1998 before being hired by a small theatre company in Fort Erie, not far from St. Catharines. The job was very much "trial by fire." The position was supported by a grant from Human Resources Development Canada. Otherwise, the company had limited resources and no understanding of business. Taking an opportunity for a more stable position, Erin joined Conference Services at Brock University, where she worked for two years and where she gained some marketing and promotion experience. Then she moved to the Centre for the Arts, with responsibility for marketing and promotion.

The major promotional item for the Centre was a full-colour, 12-by-16.5-cm glossy brochure with a page dedicated to each of the scheduled performances. The brochure was distributed at the start of the season to all Gold and Platinum members and to 17,000 people registered in the Centre's database. It was also distributed throughout Brock University via its internal mail system and to local hotels and libraries, and then it continued to be distributed at the box office throughout the performing season. Direct mail was commonly used to promote a specific item or series. For example, to promote the three theatrical performances scheduled for the

2003–2004 season, the Centre made a series of mailings in late September: 404 letters were sent to people in the database who had bought theatre tickets within the previous two years, 284 letters were sent to church and seniors' groups, and 24 letters were sent to "theatre educators" at local high schools. For the latter group, the Centre made a special offer for secondary school students of $11.75 per ticket for a group of 10 or more, plus one free ticket for every 10 tickets purchased.

The Centre received some free radio publicity on local radio stations that aired "A Brock Minute" each day, a short description for the local community of what was happening throughout Brock University. Aside from this, radio was a regular medium for promoting the Centre. For *Halo*, for example, four radio ads per day were booked on each of three local radio stations, 105.7 Easy Rock FM, 97.7 Hits FM, and 610 CKTB AM Talk Radio, for the six days before the scheduled performance.

Print advertisements were placed locally each week during the program season from early September through late April. These quarter-page print ads usually featured a particular performance, and sometimes more than one if there were several performances scheduled within a particular week. The St. Catharines *Standard* gave the Centre a 25 percent discount based on its seasonal volume. *Pulse Niagara*, a regional paper that was distributed throughout the Niagara Region promoting upcoming events, gave a one-for-one promotional deal, "buy one and get one free." *Halo* was advertised in both papers each of the two weeks prior to its scheduled performance.

Other promotional media included e-mail newsletters to select patrons who had agreed to receive them, occasional letters to Brock University staff and faculty, and large, 28-by-43.25-cm posters. Exhibit 2 shows the promotional poster for *Halo*. Volunteers distributed several hundred of them to businesses around town and throughout Brock University. Students at Brock were encouraged to buy "walk-up" tickets on the night of performances. The price to students was just $6 per seat. For popular performances, of course, there were never walk-up seats available. For some comedy or musical performances a dozen or so students might decide to see if seats were available at the last minute. For theatrical performances, it was highly unlikely that there would be any additional seats sold the last few days before a performance, including student walk-up purchases.

The Meeting

Debbie Slade had asked to meet with Erin to discuss the upcoming performance of *Halo* when it became apparent that the performance would likely not generate enough box-office revenue to cover its costs. Together they reviewed the promotion for the show and what could possibly be done.

The two women agreed that cancelling the performance was not an option, and spending any additional money at this time would most likely be ineffective. Several alternatives were discussed, however. One alternative was to contact the 300 Gold and 300 Platinum members who had not purchased tickets for the performance and make them a special "buy one and get one free" offer. If this were successful, it might create some interest and gain additional sales for the later theatre performances as well. Unfortunately, given the sales that had already been made, there was also the possibility that it would create dissatisfaction among those who had booked and paid for their seats early. A similar option was to make the same offer to Brock University staff and faculty as they could be reached on short notice through the Brock University e-mail system. There were only two tickets sold so far to staff and faculty, and that was most likely a single sale for two tickets. If the staff or faculty member became aware of this and was disappointed, it would be easy to provide him or her with two additional tickets to the performance or to another performance.

Another option that was discussed was to provide free tickets for local radio stations to give away to listeners. One issue was whether single tickets or pairs of tickets should be given away. Another issue was what paying patrons might feel if they found that too many people in the audience were attending without having paid for their admission. This type of promotion would not generate much revenue immediately but would help build awareness around the local community and might encourage new potential patrons to attend and they might possibly then purchase tickets for other performances or even purchase a membership. Some additional revenue might be received through concession sales. The average patron spent approximately $4 for food and beverage items. Providing promotional tickets also could generate a few immediate sales if ticket winners decided to buy additional tickets for friends or family, but Debbie and Erin both agreed that this was really not likely to generate many additional sales.

As they discussed this option, Debbie also suggested they could give some free tickets to other people who had recently made some contribution to the Brock University community. One example would be volunteers who had helped with the university's United Way campaign. Giving them free tickets would help recognize their volunteer work, might also encourage some of them to attend other theatrical performances, and, at the very least, would help fill the theatre. If paying patrons viewed the theatrical performances as popular, it would encourage them to purchase tickets to other shows in advance to ensure that they were available. Either alternative would at least fill seats and this was important for the performers, for other patrons, and for reviewers who often tended to write poor reviews of poorly attended performances.

As the meeting neared its end, Debbie turned to Erin. "I guess, for your part, I would appreciate if you could look over the revenue and cost projections and see if there is anything we can do immediately or for the other two scheduled theatrical performances. While we do not have to generate a profit on every performance we book, there will be increasing pressure on us to increase revenue, particularly as demand increases within the university for the facilities. We may have to book fewer performances in future years, and we may have to become more concerned about which ones help us generate sales. Once I have your ideas, I will be better able to decide what to do about the larger programming issue. It could be that theatre is better left to other venues around the community."

Exhibit 2 *Halo* Promotional Poster

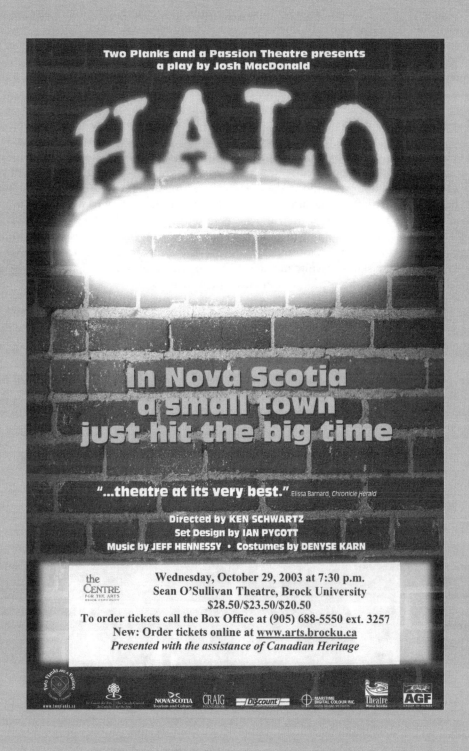

Organ Transplant Centre

Nicolas Papadopoulos

This case was developed by Dr. Nicolas Papadopoulos, Professor of Marketing and International Business at the Sprott School of Business, Carleton University, Ottawa, Canada. It is designed solely for use as a basis for education and training and is not intended to illustrate appropriate or inappropriate handling of any aspect of business management. The situation described is real but names, locations, and some dates are disguised to protect confidential information and/or improve the learning experience.

By October 2003, the committee knew the problem was more serious than they had thought when it all began. The committee had been appointed a couple of years earlier by the chief administrator of the Winnipeg-based Organ Transplant Centre (OTC), which was housed in a major local hospital and was co-funded by the federal, provincial, and local governments. The OTC's task is to act as a clearing-house for human organs that can be used in transplants, to actively promote the concept of donorship, and to "actively help Canadian health institutions to identify and obtain organs to meet their patients' needs." In other words, although some emphasis is given to the local market and needs, the centre's mandate has a national scope.

The committee's mandate was to study the availability of human organs and the need for organ transplants in Canada, and to recommend ways to improve the organ donation rate. "Look, if we really want to remain *the* organ transplant centre in the country, I think we should at least have a good idea of what's going on and where we should be going," the chief administrator had said to the committee members at a recent meeting. "After all, we don't get all these grants for nothing; I'm telling you, I can feel the pressure mounting every time I talk to Ottawa or the province. The supply of organs hasn't changed much in the last few years, but the demand, as you very well know, keeps going up. I want you to find out what's going on, and tell us what to do."

The original six-month period given the committee to prepare its report had been extended to a year, yet its members still felt at a loss as to what to conclude and recommend. Things were simply bad—too many patients, too few donors, no obvious solutions. Worse yet, as time passed it seemed that the world was closing in on the committee's members. Maybe it had been a mistake to tout the formation of this mini–"task force" across the country as the body that would find ways to solve the problem once and for all—that had seemed like good publicity for the OTC at the time, but it had also raised expectations. Now the federal government was demanding to see some progress, and the province was threatening to cut back the centre's grant unless some action was forthcoming. Physicians and hospital administrators from many cities and towns were getting increasingly impatient with the centre's inability to supply them with needed organs.

The organ transplant situation in Canada represents a paradox. On the one hand, Canada is an advanced country with excellent and sophisticated technology and well-trained doctors for transplants, 28 hospitals country-wide that are equipped for them, and a successful history with, for example, over 2,000 heart transplants over the past 20 years, some 2,600 corneal transplants performed in the year 2000 alone, and a survival rate ranging from a low of 65 percent for heart to a high of over 95 percent for kidney transplants.

Furthermore, it seems that just about everyone agrees with the concept of donating the organs of deceased persons. An Ontario poll of 1,000 people had found that 88 percent would agree to donate the organs of relatives in case of accident or terminal illness, and in a national poll 78 percent of respondents indicated they "believe there is a great need for organs," with 71 percent noting a willingness to donate any organs and only about 15 percent outright preferring to not donate (the remainder are willing to donate only certain organs or did not respond).

On the other hand, and although Canadians are generally known for their generosity, this trait does not seem to be reflected in organ donation rates. Only 26 percent of the respondents in the Ontario survey said they have signed the donor cards on their provincial driver's licences. The national donor rate remains at a low of 14 for every million inhabitants as of 2001, which translates to about 420 donors in total that year. As a result, in the year 2000 almost 4,000 patients were on waiting lists for organs, and almost 150 died while in the queue. By comparison, the nationwide Canadian Blood Services boasted 800,000 blood donations by 450,000 donors in 2002, and Spain's organ donor rate stands at 31 per million, or twice Canada's level.

In the United States, some states have mandatory "recorded consideration" rules whereby physicians must check whether the dying person has signed the donor form, and if not, to check with the next-of-kin of the deceased for a possible donation. The doctor must then report on the outcome in writing. When it implemented this procedure, an American hospital saw the number of donors increase four-fold. In Canada, recorded consideration is practised at several hospitals voluntarily. More generally, the demand for human organs for transplants is so much larger than the supply that there is increasing pressure on governments worldwide to permit the legal sale of organs, notwithstanding the broader negative implications that such a practice would entail.

By early fall 2003, the committee had identified a handful of old and new solutions, such as recorded consideration and the long-standing donor cards on drivers' licences, as steps in the right direction. However, the problem was still there (not enough organs), some potential ideas were seen as beyond the committee's mandate and at any rate in the far horizon timewise (e.g., lobbying the federal and provincial legislatures for recorded consideration legislation), and no new ideas seemed to be forthcoming on how to fix it in the foreseeable future. In despair, the committee called a meeting of senior personnel at the hospital. Besides its own members (two physicians and the director of personnel), others invited to the meeting included the chief administrator, the directors of finance and of planning, the chiefs of cardiology and of surgery, and the OTC's director of public relations.

Having outlined the problem, Dr. McInnock, the physician chairing the committee, concluded by saying, "So, the reason why we called you all here is, quite honestly, to ask for help. We just don't know which way to go.

We've toured the country and talked to every senior person in this field, and all we know is that there is a problem—a big problem indeed."

McInnock was interrupted by Dr. Mikoloyuk, the chief of surgery: "You know, I'm not even sure we're talking about the right problem. Sure, we're supposed to be a clearing-house—but don't we all work in a hospital, too? My problem is the pain I go through each time I have to tell the parents, 'Sorry, folks, we just can't find a kidney for your kid.' Frankly, my interests are right here. Instead of travelling around the country finding out what we already know, I think we should be focusing on finding organs for our own patients."

"Well, now, wait a minute," said Janice Stewart, the chief administrator. "I don't think this is fair. The centre was funded to do work for the country, not just this province, let alone this hospital. You know as well as I do that if we spent all or even most of our energies within the Manitoba borders, someone up there wouldn't be very pleased." The argument over the centre's responsibilities dragged on for several minutes.

The public relations director, Jim Fowles, sat listening. At a pause, he managed to change the subject. "Tell me, has your committee considered advertising? After all, what we have here is a clear-cut case: you said the polls show that most people agree to donate, but few actually sign their cards. Well, maybe all they need is some persuasion—perhaps some promotion telling them that they may be at the receiving end themselves one day."

This is where Pierre Laflamme, the director of finance, spoke for the first time: "On the face of it, this actually makes quite a bit of sense. However . . . I'm not sure. We don't have enough money to replace the staff's old computers, let alone get into promotion. Of course, we could always ask for additional funds from the feds. But then again—is this the right way to spend public money? You know, when you get your renewed driver's licence, it says it right there—sign the donor card. Yet people just don't do it. Maybe they're afraid. . . ."

"I guess they are," interjected the chief of cardiology. "Unfortunately. But this is human nature; signing the card has something final about it—even I hesitate just before signing it. And have you looked at the Health Canada website lately? My goodness gracious, it talks about 'cadaveric' transplants and 'brain-dead' patients—that's enough to spook anyone!"

"You know what?" the chief administrator said with a smile. "Maybe we should do it like the Book-of-the-Month Club! You know how you have to sign and return the card if you *don't* want the month's selection? Well, there! You'll sign only if you *don't* want to be a donor. How many people will have the nerve to do that?"

"I wonder why we didn't think of that earlier," said McInnock. "What do you think, Jim?"

"Actually," Pierre Laflamme cut in before Jim Fowles had a chance to respond, "I've been wondering all along if we're right talking about persuasion and book clubs and so on. After all, buying a book is not the same as donating your heart. Is it ethical, Jim, to force people to do something they don't want?"

"Let me say something before you answer that, if you don't mind, Jim," interrupted the planning director. "You know, I just don't think we have enough information here to talk about this thing. Sure, we know only a minority of the population sign their cards. But who are these people? Why did they sign it and others didn't? Are they young, maybe, too young to worry about dying? Are they older, having come to terms with the prospect of dying or thinking their organs are too old to be of value for transplants? Another thing—you said most agree with donating. Sure they do, but maybe they agree to donate their *relatives'* organs, not their own. How many agree in principle to give their own, let alone sign the card? Oh yeah, I had jotted another question here too: We've been here for almost an hour now, and you guys have been at it with the committee for a year, but all I hear is drivers' licences and hospitals. Isn't there anybody else that can help in some way? Whom do people listen to when it comes to this type of thing? Their family physician? Their priest? I mean, I'm sorry for dragging on, but it seems to me we've been looking for answers—but have we even asked the right questions? Tell me this, Jim: what did Participaction do a couple of decades ago when they managed to get half the country out jogging five miles a day?"

After the planning director had finished, there was a rather lengthy pause in the room. Somehow, it seemed like a nerve had been hit: Was it possible they had been asking the wrong questions all along? To Jim Fowles, this all sounded like marketing—but to the others, it just felt like the problem had just become even more complex than before.

Discussion Questions

1. Analyze the operating context of the OTC and the committee. Where are they located? What is the background of the participants? How do such factors influence the way each participant, and the committee and centre overall, approaches the problem?
2. Research the background for organ transplants in Canada and identify key statistics that may help to shed light on the problem faced by the committee.
3. Outline a marketing research study designed to address the sorts of questions that seem to confound the committee's attempts to solve the problem.
4. Develop a complete marketing plan for the committee and the OTC.

Sources

"I am, therefore I sell," *Ottawa Citizen*, January 7, 2004, p. A15; www.hc-sc.gc.ca/english/media/releases/2001/2001_93ebk2.htm; www.hc-sc.gc.ca/english/organandtissue/; www.bloodservices.ca.

CASE 16

Boston Pizza International Inc.

Peter Yannopoulos

Boston Pizza was established in 1963 by Gus Agioritis as a pizza and spaghetti restaurant in Edmonton, Alberta, known as Boston Pizza and Spaghetti House. In 1968, Boston Pizza began franchising. By 1978, the company had expanded from a single restaurant to a chain of 42 outlets. Gus wanted to spend more time with his family, so he sold the franchise rights for 31 Boston Pizza restaurants in British Columbia, Alberta, and Ontario to his long-time friend Ron Coyle. Gus's brothers, who operated them under separate names, kept the other 11 restaurants. Ron Coyle changed the name of the restaurants to Boston Pizza International Ltd.

In 1983, Jim Treliving and his accountant and business partner, George Melville, purchased Boston Pizza International Ltd. from Coyle for $3.5 million. At that time there were 38 stores in the chain. In 1992, Boston Pizza's headquarters were moved to Richmond, B.C., to manage the chain's growth and expansion into Eastern Canada and the United States. It also opened management units in Dallas, Montreal, and Mississauga. In 1998, the business began expanding into the United States. There were a few changes made between Canadian and American restaurants such as changing the name of the U.S. restaurants to "Boston's: The Gourmet Pizza," introducing different menu items and changing the pricing strategy.

It was late March of 2005, and Jim Treliving and George Melville were evaluating the firm's advertising plans. The company was doing well as it had grown to over 400 outlets with an average annual growth rate of 15 percent. However, the two partners were considering changes in the company's advertising strategy in an effort to increase its impact on the company sales and market share.

Company Performance and Franchise Policies

Boston Pizza had expanded over the last 15 years by an average growth rate of 15 percent. Its growth strategy was built on steady, carefully managed expansion, as the company had focused on building same-store sales while adding new outlets. This expansion strategy had worked to its advantage as it ensured that Boston Pizza's market share was achieved profitably at the unit level.

Boston Pizza's annual sales for 2004 exceeded $400 million. Boston Pizza operated over 190 franchisees across Canada, 24 in the United States, and one in Mexico. The company planned to have a minimum of 73 restaurants open in Eastern Canada by the end of 2005, many of them in the province of Quebec. Boston Pizza's U.S. concept known as "Boston's: The Gourmet Pizza" also planned to expand the number of locations to a total of 43 by the end of 2005.

Boston Pizza had developed a rigorous and systematic approach to franchisee selection. A potential franchisee went through a series of interviews with people in each of the functional areas as well as a series of financial and background checks. Once a franchisee was selected, training began. Owners and managers underwent a six-week training program at one of the fully operational corporate training restaurants. Each franchisee then completed an intensive 10-day business management program at Boston Pizza's corporate office.

Individual franchisees did not have to pay a standard up-front franchise fee but they paid a royalty of 7 percent of revenues. Of this, 4 percent went into the Boston Pizza Income Fund. This fee was monitored carefully through the networked Boston Pizza computer system. At the franchise level, each of the decisions made by the franchisee must be within the guidelines set by the corporation. For example, if the franchisee decided to sell pizza slices in order to compete more effectively and increase revenues for its location, it would be frowned upon because it did not support the image Boston Pizza was trying to convey.

Marketing Strategy and Operations

Boston Pizza targeted people of all ages, but it was mostly families that visited its stores (52 percent of the restaurant's customers were families). While its daytime customers were mostly families, its late-night clientele consisted mostly of customers in their 20s. Boston Pizza positioned itself as a medium-price, high-quality restaurant. The company differentiated itself from the competition in several other ways. For example, Boston Pizza offered two experiences under one roof (casual dining and a sports bar), a combination that was not offered by any of its competitors. The "two experiences under one roof" concept was viewed as one of Boston Pizza's core competencies. Its sports bar featured a sports theme with sports memorabilia, big-screen TVs, and games in a contemporary, energized setting. All Boston Pizza locations were easily accessible from main routes and had excellent parking facilities. The company was seeking triple-A locations, such as pads on movie theatres or shopping mall properties.

Boston Pizza offered an extensive menu, consisting of over 100 items. Its menu was made up of pizza, pasta, appetizers, chicken, desserts, and ribs and some unique menu items, such as perogy pizza. Although the restaurant's menu selection was large, it had not compromised the integrity of its selection. According to George Melville, "We've been very conscious of maintaining our product. When we have expanded the menu, we have expanded within our menu group. That's why you won't find hamburgers on our menu. We don't do burgers." However, by not offering hamburgers, the company might be losing potential customers interested in hamburgers, although the company had attempted to remedy this problem by introducing a Cheeseburger Pizza.

Boston Pizza offered excellent service. Employees were trained to be friendly to all guests in the restaurant, to be knowledgeable about the menu items, to be prompt, and to know that the customer is always right. Servers were required to know the ingredients of menu items in case a guest had a food allergy. Special preparation procedures were taken if a guest had an allergy. The company has implemented the G.E.M. (Guest Enjoyment Meter), which measured customers' satisfaction and gave the restaurant's staff feedback on how the restaurant was performing on key performance indicators. The G.E.M. ratings were based on silent shoppers, focus groups, phone surveys, and visits by quality-control personnel. If a store won, each employee received a cheque and recognition of his or her excellence at a cake-and-champagne ceremony. Also, the company rewarded its employees and franchises for exceptional performance using its S.T.A.R.S (Standards + Training + Action = Results in Sales) program and featured the winning employees' names in the Boston Pizza magazine.

Each Boston Pizza location operated under strict corporate guidelines that meant customers could visit any Boston Pizza restaurant yet still receive the same quality of food and service. When a group of guests walked into a Boston Pizza restaurant, they were greeted by a host/or hostess. If there was a table available for them to be seated at, they were shown to the table by the host or hostess. However, if all tables were occupied, the guests were given a pager and asked to wait for an approximate waiting period, either in the waiting area or in the bar area. By allowing patrons to wait in the bar area, their wait seemed shorter (because they could watch TV, order drinks, play games, etc.), and as a result they remained satisfied. When the pager vibrated, the customers approached the host or hostess who seated them. A few minutes after they were seated, the server approached the table, distributed the menus to all the guests, and took the beverage order. After the beverages were delivered to the patrons, the server asked for the meal order, relayed the order to the kitchen, and served the food after it was prepared.

Boston Pizza had created its innovative inventory management system in a way that allowed it to be prepared for any unexpected increases in lunchtime or dinnertime demand. Each store had a very detailed output system that forecast how much pizza, pasta, and other foods would need to be ready and prepared for a typical day. These forecasts were so detailed that they could determine the actual amounts of cheese used in pizza from day to day as well as the amounts of mushrooms, pepperoni, and other toppings. This allowed Boston Pizza to minimize its inventory costs by monitoring food amounts put on pizza, which gave the company a large advantage over its competitors.

Boston Pizza's Promotion Program

Boston Pizza's promotion program consisted of advertising, sales promotions, and public relations. These promotional activities are discussed below.

Advertising

The main goal of advertising is to bring about mutually satisfying exchanges with target markets by informing, persuading, reminding, and educating customers of the benefits of an organization or a product. A potential customer of Boston Pizza could find out about the restaurant through its website, through TV ads that aired during selected sports telecasts, and through word of mouth from their friends and family. Boston Pizza was always searching for ways to introduce itself to the community. The company spent three-quarters of its 2.5 percent advertising royalty on advertising campaigns and direct media. Its "Spaghetti Western" promotion received the Award for Best Media Campaign.

Boston Pizza had a set of TV ads featuring stand-up comic Howie Mandel that run during late-evening sports broadcasts. There were four versions of the Boston Pizza television commercials. Each relayed a different message: (1) "You're among friends at Boston Pizza," (2) "Eat great, even late," (3) "Rib Rageous Special," and (4) "Spaghetti Western Special." These ads were funny and energetic, and tried to portray the restaurant as having a great, relaxed atmosphere where friends could come and hang out, have a drink, or grab a bite to eat. The ads informed potential patrons about the chain's hours of operations, the fun and exciting atmosphere, special promotions, and the types of food available, and promoted the restaurant as a good place for families.

Another form of advertising utilized by Boston Pizza was the company websites: www.bostonpizza.com (Canada) and www.bostonsgourmet.com (U.S.). These websites contained information about Boston Pizza (history, locations, menu items, franchising, etc.) as well as provided visitors with the ability to rate Boston Pizza's service. In addition to print media in the form of magazine and flyers, it produced an eight- to ten-page magazine called *The Slice* that was distributed at each restaurant.

Sales Promotions

Boston Pizza made extensive use of sales promotions to attract guests. For example, customers received one Air Mile for every $12 spent at Boston Pizza. Boston Pizza also offered certificates available in $10, $20, and $25 denominations. Along with every purchase of a gift certificate of $25 or more, the purchaser received a Boston Pizza glass in a gift box.

Boston Pizza employees visited local area businesses and gave away empty pizza boxes with the promise that once it was returned to Boston Pizza, it would be filled with a pizza free of charge. This helped the company increase awareness and sales, as some of the people who came into the restaurant because of the promotion became regular customers.

Boston Pizza employees were urged to suggest ideas to promote sales. Some of the ideas suggested in the past included the following: develop relationships with partners such as tanning salons, amusement parks, water parks, and miniature-golf courses; become a registration site, meeting point, or wrap-up-party destination for sports tournaments, festival volunteers, parades, and walk-a-thons; use banners to promote Boston Pizza as the weekend vacation place; create a special atmosphere by featuring special drinks, desserts, etc.; host summer events to drive traffic to the restaurant; offer a bike safety check clinic; host a kids' safety fair.

Public Relations

As part of Boston Pizza's integrated marketing communications effort, the company relied heavily on public relations. It supported local sports teams and events—its name was rink-side at some major league hockey arenas. The company also raised money for various charities. As an example, on February 14, 2000, Boston Pizza raised $130,000 for the Heart & Stroke Foundation by donating $1 from each heart-shaped pizza and all the money from the sale of paper hearts on that day. The chain also donated funds to many other beneficiaries, including the Kids Help Phone. In 2001, Boston Pizza raised over $500,000 through such efforts.

Issues

In Western Canada, Boston Pizza had well-established roots. In small towns across British Columbia and Alberta the chain was a main social point. Teenagers would go to Boston Pizza to hang out with friends and families and order a meal during the outing. But the company did not enjoy the same recognition in Eastern Canada, where locals were often confused as to what Boston Pizza really was. Many new customers coming into the stores had misconceptions about the restaurant. Some thought it was a lower-scale pizzeria or some other type of restaurant. They had no knowledge of the restaurant's set-up. Only when they came in did they realize that there was a dual set-up, consisting of a sports bar and a family restaurant section.

The name Boston Pizza itself did suggest an American-style restaurant, something that may not always play to the chain's favour. In fact, founder Gus Agioritis is reputed to have said that Boston Pizza was "a Canadian company, with an American name, operated by Greeks, selling Italian food."

There was a concern that the current advertising campaign was not effective in promoting the fact that Boston Pizza restaurants specialized in much more than pizza. For example, while Boston Pizza heavily promoted its pizza and pasta, its grade-A steaks got little promotion. Using advertising to inform potential customers of the variety of its menu could result in higher sales. Boston Pizza also wanted to position its stores as high-end restaurants. This type of image needed to be reflected in its advertisements.

The company's large markets were highly diverse, consisting of people from different ethnic backgrounds. The chain could address the diversity of the population in its advertising campaign. For example, it could advertise in different languages: Chinese, Indian, Italian, and others.

The National Hockey League lockout in 2004–2005 reduced revenues for the franchise since a lot of people used to go to a Boston Pizza outlet just to watch their favourite teams play. To reduce the risk, the company could plan for a more diverse showcase of sports shows in the bar. For example, given the recent surge in the popularity of soccer and cricket, the company could show soccer and cricket games to attract fans of those sports who do not have access to satellite TV to watch the games.

Decision

In early 2005, Boston Pizza was assessing its marketing communications campaign. The company's advertising effort could become more effective if it aired its commercials more often. For example, by airing them during prime time (6:00 p.m. to 10:00 p.m.), families that watch television during those times could see the advertisements, increasing overall awareness of the chain. If management decided that a change in its advertising strategy was desirable, it would have to decide which was the most appropriate time to air the Boston Pizza commercials, the exact message, media plan, and advertising reach and frequency. Additional questions included what to feature in its advertising campaigns. Should the company emphasize promotions such as "pasta Tuesdays" or try something different? What about the ethnic diversity of the chain's major markets? Should they become part of the company's advertising campaigns?

Additionally, it might be beneficial for the company to run at least one or two billboard campaigns. These billboards would help establish their company name in the eyes of the public and would be paired up with the rest of its advertising campaign for one of its menu items.

For example, to increase the sales of its trademark pizza, which currently only made up a small percentage of its total sales, they could initiate an aggressive nationwide billboard campaign telling the public all about their pizza special.

The restaurant chain could further capitalize on Howie Mandel's celebrity power by featuring him in radio commercials that could be aired at any time during the day or night. Boston Pizza currently used many catchphrases such as "Eat great, even late," and "You're among friends at Boston Pizza." Management was also wondering if its advertising campaign would be more effective if it used only one jingle or slogan that would be nationally recognized as Boston Pizza's slogan. For example, "Eat great, even late, among friends, at Boston Pizza." If such a decision was made, management would have to decide on the most appropriate radio station in each area.

Another option for management's consideration was the use of coupons. Boston Pizza had never distributed coupons or other types of discounts in an effort to maintain its reputation as a high-quality restaurant chain. However, they might consider such an option when they were opening a new location. If people living in the area surrounding a new location were not aware of the Boston Pizza outlet, management could utilize a one-time sales promotion such as a newspaper coupon appearing on opening day only.

Discussion Questions

1. What factors account for Boston Pizza's strong performance to date?
2. Critically evaluate Boston Pizza's current marketing strategy.
3. Evaluate Boston Pizza's proposed integrated communication changes. What changes, if any, do you recommend?

Sources

Dan Ovsey, "Scrambling for a bigger piece: But pizza shop owners disagree on who's the Big Cheese," *Edmonton Journal*, June 15, 2002; Mark Hamstra, "Successful casual chains from Canada seek fortunes in the U.S.," *Nation's Restaurant News*, New York, January 18,1999, 5; http://www.bostonsgourmet.com/about_us/history.cfm, retrieved on January 12, 2005; Boston Pizza Franchise Profile Booklet, November/December 2000, p. 3; http://www.bostonpizza.com/home/index.cfm, retrieved on January 12, 2005; "Heart and Stroke Foundation Gets $130,000," *Alaska Highway News*, March 4, 2002; Patricia Chisholm, "Chasing Pizza Profits," *Maclean's*, August 8, 1998; National Trivia Network Information, www.NTN.com.

Nature-Plus Limited—U.S. Expansion?

Joseph J. Schiele

Joseph J. Schiele prepared this case for the Direct Selling Education Foundation of Canada, solely to provide material for class discussion. The author did not intend to illustrate either effective or ineffective handling of a managerial situation. The author may have disguised certain names and other identifying information to protect confidentiality.

The Direct Selling Education Foundation of Canada prohibits any form of reproduction, storage or transmittal of this material without its written permission. To order copies or request permission to reproduce materials, contact the Direct Selling Education Foundation of Canada, 190 Attwell Drive, Unit 630, Etobicoke, Ontario, Canada, M9W 6H8, Tel: (416) 679-8555, Fax: (416) 670-1568.

On August 1, 1998, Brian Reis, president of Nature-Plus, a network marketing company, located in Toronto, Ontario, faced the following problem. The number of new distributors that were joining the company each month had been steadily declining. After reviewing a proposal to expand Canadian operations into the United States, Brian wondered what action he should take next.

Industry Overview

In 1996, U.S. and Canadian sales by direct selling sources amounted to $20.84 billion (U.S.), according to an estimate by the Direct Selling Association. The percentage of sales by major product groups was as follows: home and family care products (cleaning, cookware, and cutlery etc.), 33.6 percent; personal care products (cosmetics, jewellery, and skin care, etc.), 29.2 percent; services and miscellaneous, 18.3 percent; wellness products (weight loss, vitamins and nutritional supplements, etc.), 13.1 percent; and leisure items (books, toys and games, etc.), 5.8 percent.

The total North American market for wellness products was highly fragmented and rapidly growing. For the U.S. market, 1996 sales were $6.5 billion (U.S.) compared to $5 billion (U.S.) in 1994. This rapid growth was due to a number of factors, including increased interest in healthier lifestyles, the publication of research findings supporting the positive effects of certain nutritional supplements, and the aging of the baby boom generation combined with the tendency of consumers to purchase more wellness products as they age.

Nature-Plus: General Company Background

Nature-Plus was established in June 1995 by Brian Reis and his wife, to pursue the expanding market for wellness products in North America and internationally. After examining the nutritional requirements of the human body, Mr. Reis had developed products that would help improve people's health and quality of life. The products that Nature-Plus developed, packaged, and marketed included nutritional supplements, antioxidants, and weight management products. The company was a privately held organization incorporated under the laws of the Province of Ontario. The registered office of the company was located in Toronto.

Canadian and U.S. Operations

Nature-Plus had an established network of distributors who actively marketed and sold the company's products directly to individuals across ten provinces. (Company sales presence throughout Canada is shown in Exhibit 1.)

The company had only recently expanded activities into the United States. In order to do this, Brian recruited Alex Harkins to act as a national sales manager and start up a network marketing organization in the United States, with a small office and distribution warehouse in

Exhibit 1	Company Sales Force Presence in Canada	
Province	Approximate Number of Distributors	Approximate Percentage of Overall Revenue
Maritimes	500	8
Quebec	200	5
Ontario	3,000	55
Manitoba	500	10
Saskatchewan	250	10
Alberta	250	5
British Columbia	300	7

SOURCE: Internal Company Documents

southern California. Additionally, Canadian distributors saw the U.S. market as a golden opportunity for new business. Consequently, many Canadian distributors had begun developing their own down-line sales organizations into the United States.

Products and New Product Development

Existing Products

The line of Nature-Plus products consisted primarily of consumable products that were designed to target the growing consumer demand for natural health alternatives for nutrition and wellness. In developing its product line, the company had emphasized quality, purity, potency, and safety.

Nature-Plus created a four-step system for better health: Step 1—cleanse and detoxify; Step 2—restore and protect; Step 3—nourish; and Step 4—balance. Included within this system was Revive, a product that helped the body maintain normal regularity and rid itself of accumulated digestive waste, which had been found to contribute to fatigue and sickness; Renew, a product that helped the body eliminate unwanted parasites, which had been found to cause symptoms including stress, fatigue, and general poor health; Repel, a product that helped protect the body from free radicals, which had been shown to contribute to cancer, stroke, and Alzheimer's and Parkinson's disease; Exfat, a product that helped the body control body fat by breaking down existing fat, reducing the formation of new fat, and reducing food cravings; and Essentials Plus, a natural vitamin and mineral dietary supplement.

New Product Development

Nature-Plus expanded its product line through the development of new products. New product ideas were derived from a number of sources, including trade publications, scientific and health journals, the company's management and consultants, and outside partners. Nature-Plus did not maintain its own product research and development staff but relied on independent research, vendor research, research consultants, and others for such services. When the company, one of its consultants, or another party identified a new product or concept or when an existing product had to be reformulated for another market, the product or concept was generally submitted to one of the company's suppliers for development. The company did, however, own the proprietary rights to most of the product formulations.

Manufacturing and Raw Materials

Nature-Plus purchased its vitamins, nutritional supplements, and all of its other products from third parties that manufactured these products to the company's specifications and standards. Nature-Plus did not have any long-term supply agreements with any single vendor. The company believed that it could establish alternative sources for most of its products and that any delay in locating and establishing relationships with alternative sources would not result in significant product shortages and back orders.

Raw materials were purchased from reliable sources, and backup sources were available. Most of the suppliers of raw materials were large, well-established North American companies. Raw materials represented approximately 50 percent of the cost of goods sold for the company.

The company sought the highest-quality ingredients from competitive sources. These products were encapsulated and packaged by licensed pharmaceutical companies. All nutritional supplements, raw materials, and final products were subject to sample testing, weight testing, and purity testing by independent laboratories.

Company Structure

General Workforce

As of December 31, 1997, the company employed six people. There were no collective bargaining agreements in effect at that time. The company enjoyed good relations with employees. Employees received competitive benefit and compensation packages.

General Management

Nature-Plus was managed by Brian Reis, president; Christine Cook, vice-president, marketing; and Alex Harkins, national sales manager.

Brian Reis, President

Brian Reis had been with Nature-Plus as a co-founder since its inception. His primary responsibilities included the regular administration of the company's operations, oversight and negotiation of sales and purchasing for the company, and the development of the company's business. Mr. Reis had over 11 years of related industry experience and had run several large network marketing organizations, including the Canadian operations for Body Wise from 1991 to 1994. He was a director of the Multi-level Marketing International Association and a member of the Direct Sales Association's Strategic Committee that dealt directly with Health Canada. Mr. Reis had received his Honours Business Administration degree from the University of Western Ontario in 1986.

Christine Cook, Vice-President, Marketing

As co-founder of Nature-Plus, Ms. Cook had over eight years of network marketing experience on two continents. From 1989 to 1993 she was the marketing manager for Vita-Max Inc. of Carlsbad, California, where she oversaw the advertising and marketing activities for this international nutrition company. Her duties included the coordination of advertising efforts on behalf of the company, the development of advertising strategies, consumer research, management of the advertising budget, and acting as liaison with divisions in China, the United Kingdom, and Canada. Ms. Cook received her Honours Bachelor of Science degree from the University of Loughborough in England in 1989.

Alex Harkins, National Sales Manager

Prior to his appointment at Nature-Plus, Mr. Harkins had been an independent marketing and advertising consultant responsible for projects that included marketing director for Endless Health Products Inc., where his responsibilities included the design and creation of advertising materials and direct response programs, the development of special training programs, and the creation of product sales efforts for Links Golf Company. From 1994 to 1996 Mr. Harkins was the director of marketing for Nu-Ideas In Travel of Irvine, California. From 1993 to 1994 he was the national marketing director for Mega-Merger Bancorp, a financial services company in Irvine, California. Mr. Harkins received his Bachelor of Arts degree from the University of California, Irvine, in 1983.

Company Advisory Council

In order to assist in the implementation of its marketing strategy, Nature-Plus created a six-person advisory council. Members of the advisory council were available to provide the company with ongoing support with their views on new products, potential development plans, and trends within the industry. Members of the advisory council were selected according to their knowledge of and experience within the nutrition industry.

Sales and Marketing

Nature-Plus established three primary marketing objectives for its company:

1. To produce a strong distribution network for the sale of its products.
2. To develop a comprehensive and regular customer base.
3. To establish an expanding network of distributors across North America.

Distribution

The company's products were distributed through a network marketing system consisting of approximately 5,000 distributors who serviced about 20,000 customers. Distributors were independent contractors who purchased products directly from the company for their own use and resale to retail consumers.

Nature-Plus created an environment that valued people and that brought health and opportunity to all people through a network marketing system that enabled distributors to become involved on a part- or full-time basis. Nature-Plus concentrated its efforts on encouraging individuals to develop their own business, at their own pace, without the costly expense inherent in franchise operations or other start-up enterprises. Network marketing gave individuals the opportunity to go into business without significant risk, yet offered them significant potential, albeit wholly dependent upon their own efforts.

Network marketing used word-of-mouth advertising to grow and capture market share. The network was made up of people talking to other people, sharing something they believed in. In addition, network marketing allowed an individual to use his or her time, talent, and energy to earn commissions from sales to all the people that were introduced to the business.

There were three major marketing plans that were common to network distribution organizations: (1) stair step, (2) uni-level/matrix, and (3) binary system. Management believed, that because the binary system, which was employed at Nature-Plus, provided greater contact between the company and the consumer, this system would dominate the network marketing industry in the future.

These marketing networks were most commonly developed through word of mouth. Classified advertising was also used. Most of the distribution occurred through home-based distributors. These organization methods had proven to be a simple and effective distribution model.

The compensation plan developed at Nature-Plus for its distributors provided several opportunities for distributors to earn money. Each distributor was required to purchase and sell products in order to earn any compensation. Therefore, the distributor could not simply develop a down-line sales organization or receive payment for recruiting new distributors.

The first method of earning a commission was through retail markup on product sales. Distributors purchased product from the company and resold the product at retail prices to consumers. The difference between the price paid by the distributor and the retail price was a distributor's profit or compensation.

The second method of earning money through the distribution of the company's products was by receiving commissions on sales volumes generated by the distributor's sales organization, which consisted of as few as two additional distributors introduced to the company by the distributor, and by meeting certain personal sales volumes.

The company's ability to increase sales was significantly dependent on its ability to attract, motivate, and retain distributors. The company utilized a marketing program that it believed was superior to programs offered by other network marketing companies. The program provided financial incentives, distributor training and support, a low-priced starter kit, no inventory requirements, and low monthly purchase requirements. Management attempted to reach new distributors through various advertising initiatives, the company's website, teleconferencing, and regional sales meetings.

In an effort to continue to motivate distributors, Nature-Plus developed several programs. Some of these programs included the Car Advantage Program, which made car payments of up to $3,000 per month for qualifying distributors; the Personal Recruiting and Sales Campaigns, which were developed to assist distributors in developing their down-line distribution networks and increasing sales; and 24-Hour Teleconference and Voicemail, which provided access to a weekly recorded teleconference call to its distributors including interviews with successful distributors, up-to-date product information, announcements, and current product specials offered by the company. Other supports were *Health and Wealth Trends* and *Living Well* magazines, which provided information on network marketing and the company. The magazines were developed to recruit new distributors by answering the questions most commonly asked by potential new distributors. Product literature was produced for its distributors, including comprehensive and attractive catalogues and brochures that displayed and described the company's products. Distributors also could contact the company toll free to place orders, get customer service assistance, and fax orders and inquiries.

Competition

Nature-Plus competed with many companies marketing products similar to those it sold and marketed. It also competed directly with other network marketing companies in the recruitment of distributors.

Not all competitors sold all the types of products marketed by Nature-Plus. Some competitors marketed products and services in addition to those offered by Nature-Plus. For example, some competitors were known for and were identified with sales of herbal formulations, others with household cleaning and personal care products, while others were known for and identified with sales of nutritional and dietary supplements.

Another source of competition in the sale and distribution of health and nutrition products was from direct retail establishments such as large retailers, independents, and non-category stores (e.g., drugstores). The most prominent retailer was the General Nutrition Center (GNC), which had a number of retail stores located in the United States and Canada.

Many network marketing companies also competed with Nature-Plus for distributors. Some of the largest of these were Amway, Herbalife International Inc., Rexall Sundown Inc., Market America Inc., and Relive International Inc. These companies were substantially larger than Nature-Plus and had access to far greater resources. The company competed for these distributors through its marketing program that included its commission structure, training and support services, and other benefits.

Management Information Systems

The company maintained a computerized system for processing distributors' orders and calculating commissions and bonus payments that enabled it to remit such payments promptly to distributors. The company believed that prompt remittance of commissions and bonuses to distributors was critical to maintaining a motivated network of distributors.

The company's computer system made available to its distributors a detailed monthly accounting of sales and recruiting activity. These statements eliminated the need for substantial record keeping on behalf of the distributor. The computer system was also integrated with the company's reporting system that generated monthly reports, invoices, and payroll.

The company's objective was to handle service inquiries made by distributors and customers immediately. However, only about 50 percent of all telephone inquiries were being handled in this manner. The current system was reaching capacity limits and would require upgrading as sales from business increased. Brian estimated that these upgrades would cost approximately $50,000 for additional hardware and software. An effective information system had a direct impact on the company's profitability. Communication between the company and its distributors was central to the growth and development of the company's business.

Company Financials

Overview

The financial performance of the company showed steady improvement despite its short history and a significant increase in net income from 1995 to 1997. (Comparative financial statements for 1995 to 1997 can be found in Exhibit 2.)

Exhibit 2	Comparative Financial Results from 1995 to 1997		
(Canadian Dollars)	Year Ended 1997	Year Ended 1996	Year Ended 1995
Income Statement			
Sales	$1,559,055	$1,207,462	$173,539
Less Cost of Sales	993,728	775,911	111,817
Gross Margin	565,327	431,551	61,722
Gross Margin %	36.2%	35.6%	35.5%
Less Expenses	455,211	408,314	103,373
Net Income/(Loss) before tax	$110,116	$23,237	($41,651)
Balance Sheet			
Total Assets	$240,839	$194,794	$113,887
Working Capital	59,698	(44,171)	(69,270)
Shareholder's Equity	105,371	(18,288)	(41,524)

SOURCE: Internal Company Documents

Inflation

Inflation could affect the cost of raw materials and goods and services purchased by the company. The competitive environment limited the extent to which the company could raise prices to recover costs. Generally, overall product prices had been stable and the company expected to recover increased costs through improved productivity and cost containment programs. The company had not been subject to material price increases by its suppliers, and inflation was not expected to have a significant effect on operations in the next 12 months.

Outlook

The company believed that its success to date was due to its reputation and commitment to providing a wide range of premium-quality, innovative health and nutritional products, and an appealing business opportunity for persons interested in establishing a direct sales business.

The company's primary objective for the future was to capitalize on its operating strengths in order to become a leading distributor of consumer products in each of its markets. The company intended to do this by introducing new products, opening new markets, attracting new distributors, and increasing brand awareness and loyalty.

Situation

New Distributors

During the last six months, the number of new distributors joining the firm each month had been declining.

Canadian Dollars Income Statement	Year Ended 1998	Year Ended 1999	Year Ended 2000
Sales			
Existing Products	$1,700,000	$4,900,000	$16,000,000
New Products	300,000	5,100,000	4,000,000
Product Literature	80,000	400,000	800,000
Other Income (net)*	48,000	249,000	480,000
Less Cost of Sales			
Products and Literature	314,000	1,568,000	3,140,000
Commissions & Other	910,000	4,660,000	9,320,000
Gross Margin	$904,000	$4,421,000	$8,820,000
Less Expenses			
Operating (net wages)	483,000	1,636,000	2,283,000
Wages	220,000	1,425,000	2,000,000
Net Income/(Loss) before tax	$201,000	$1,360,000	$4,537,000

* Other Income (net) includes freight and miscellaneous less returns.
SOURCE: Internal Company Documents

This indicated that business in Canada was slowing down. Because the network marketing industry was essentially a cash business, where money was received when products were sold, as the number of new distributors declined, so did the cash flow for the business. New distributors and renewed distributors were critical to the success of any network marketing operation. This was a key indicator of the overall health of a network marketing company. Essentially, if distributor growth declined or levelled off, something had to be done.

Payments to Suppliers

As a result of this decline and subsequent slowdown in cash flow, Brian found himself behind on some of his payables. Suppliers had been expressing concern over the timing of late payments and Brian knew that if this continued, they could ultimately cut off his supply of products. This would have very serious implications and could result in the cessation of the business. Brian owed suppliers approximately $100,000 in past due payables.

U.S. Expansion

Rationale for Expansion

Brian felt that the United States would provide access to the new distributors needed to sustain his business for the long term. Expansion into the United States seemed to represent a logical progression since the company had successfully demonstrated its viability and the quality of its products in the Canadian market. The company believed that it had refined its marketing strategies and procedures to be able to capture a profitable portion of the U.S. market. Past experience within the market had achieved some success and, therefore, indicated the possibility for greater opportunity. (Financial forecasts for 1998 to 2000 for the United States and Canada can be found in Exhibit 3.)

Strategic Plan

Management developed a strategic plan, whereby the company intended to establish an effective distribution network for the sale of its products in the United States. As a result, the company would be concentrating on marketing all its products, as well as developing and expanding its market penetration, in these markets.

The expansion plan also included a comprehensive training and educational program designed to teach distributors the specific methods and procedures for the marketing and distribution of its product line.

The company intended to expand its distribution network through the use of increased distributors. Southern California was selected as the base of American operations for several reasons. This area represented one of the largest markets for health and nutritional products. Network marketing systems were generally more accepted in California. In addition, the company believed that a number of positive marketing features for distributors were inherent to southern California, such as rallies, seminars, and incentive plans, all of which could be administered through the company's U.S. office.

Additional Resources Required

At this point, the company had leased approximately 1,200 square feet of office and warehouse space. However, Brian believed that he would need an additional 1,800 square feet of space if he were to commit to the U.S. expansion. Brian had estimated that this additional space would cost Nature-Plus an additional $1,000 (U.S.) per month.

Management also anticipated that its facility in the United States would require a contemporary and attractive design and decor. The company was contemplating retaining an interior design consultant to assist in the layout of these offices, which would include a well-appointed reception area. This feature was essential since this area would convey the first impression to prospective distributors. Two meeting rooms would also be included. Remodelling costs were estimated between $30,000 and $40,000 (U.S.).

Existing information systems in Canada would be insufficient to meet the needs of the U.S. market. In order to develop an integrated operation, the U.S. office would require computer upgrades in hardware to link the company's offices and their operations. These hardware costs were estimated at $25,000 (U.S.).

In addition to hardware upgrades, Brian would have to purchase more software to effectively handle the dramatic increase in business that was expected. This software would cost approximately $100,000 (U.S.).

In order to run the U.S. operations effectively, additional personnel would be required. Similar to the Canadian operations, two administrative staff and a sales manager would be required. The cost for these additional personnel annually would be approximately $40,000 (U.S.) and $50,000 (U.S.), respectively. These costs would include base pay and basic benefits but not performance bonuses. Brian was not sure if he could manage both the Canadian and U.S. operations at the same time. He estimated that a general manager for the U.S. operation would cost approximately $60,000 (U.S.) annually.

To effectively launch Nature-Plus products and attract new distributors to the company, Brian had estimated that he would need approximately $100,000 (U.S.) as an annual budget for advertising and promotion in the United States.

Opportunities for Fundraising

In order to meet anticipated funding requirements for expansion into the United States, Brian identified six sources for funds:

1. He had calculated that for a $2-million (Cdn) public offering, he would be able to raise approximately $1.7 million (Cdn) net of fees and charges. In order to complete the public offering, Brian would have to undergo an extensive audit going back three years. This audit would cost approximately $20,000 (Cdn). He would also have to prepare a detailed business plan for potential investors and arrange for an investment banker. It could take anywhere from six to twelve months to complete the offering. The offering would require Brian to give up 49 percent ownership of his company. Also, there was no guarantee that the offering would be successfully completed since it ultimately depended on the public's interest in the company as a viable investment. However, taking the company public could raise the credibility and public's awareness of the company, thereby stimulating more growth in new distributors.

2. Brian could also raise funds through a private offering. Similar to the public offering, he would have to undergo an extensive audit, develop a business plan, and arrange for an investment banker to handle the private offering. Brian would offer potential investors a 50 percent discount on the share price identified for the public offering. Brian believed that he could raise approximately $150,000 to $200,000 (Cdn) this way. The offering could take anywhere from one to six months to complete, depending on investors' interest.

3. Brian could go to the Canadian Business Development Bank (CBDB) where he would get a loan of $250,000 (Cdn) secured (against the company and Brian's personal assets) loan at 15 percent interest. This loan would be repayable over a five-year period. It would take approximately one to two months to secure the loan from the CBDB.

4. In one to two weeks' time, Brian could obtain a personal bank loan for $50,000 (Cdn) at 12 percent interest over five years.

5. Various members of Brian's family had offered to invest $75,000 (Cdn) in Nature-Plus. They would have the money for him in two to three weeks. However, he was not sure what they would expect as a return on their investment, or when they would expect repayment.

6. As a last resort, Brian believed that in about one week he could come up with $50,000 (Cdn) of his own money. This represented the bulk of Brian's net worth, and he was not really sure that he wanted to risk the investment.

U.S. Regulation

Although the company confined its activities to marketing and distribution, the manufacturing, processing, formulation, packaging, labelling, and advertising of the company's products in the United States were subject to regulation by federal agencies. The company's network marketing system was subject to governmental laws and regulations generally directed at ensuring that product sales were made to consumers of the products and that compensation and advancement within the organization were based on sales of the products rather than investment in the organization by distributors.

However, the company did not believe that these laws or regulations would have a material effect on its products or operations. Nutritional and dietary supplements such as those sold by Nature-Plus, for which no therapeutic claim was made, were not subject to Federal Drug Administration approval prior to sale. Also, the company did not anticipate developing any new products that would fall under this regulation in the future.

Decision

Having gathered the key information that he felt relevant, Brian wondered what action he should take next.

Assumptions

1. Gross Margin was expected to improve because of larger production runs and greater cost savings due to volume purchasing.
2. Commissions for 1998 were expected to be lower than 1997 because of adjustments to the compensation plan.
3. The geographical breakdown for revenues was estimated to be 70/30 between Canada and the United States in 1998 and 40/60 for 1999–2000.

CASE 18

Research in Motion Limited

Peter Yannopoulos

On June 1, 2005, Mike Lazaridis and Jim Balsillie, co-CEOs of the mobile-communications firm Research in Motion (RIM), were considering what would be the most effective response to several threats that had been gathering on the horizon. One serious threat was coming from competitors who were working on alternative versions to their popular device, the BlackBerry. In addition, one of the major wireless carriers with whom RIM had a partnership agreement had introduced a competing device. One of the decisions the two were considering was whether to introduce less expensive versions of their wireless technology to tap the consumer and small business market. If such a decision were taken, RIM might have to change its distribution strategy to reach these segments by introducing new methods of distribution such as using the Internet, opening their own stores, or selling through office supplies stores such as Staples/Business Depot.

Company Background

Research in Motion Ltd., founded in 1984 in Waterloo, Ontario, was a designer, manufacturer, and marketer of innovative wireless products and services for the worldwide mobile-communications market. Through the development of integrated hardware, software, and services that supported many wireless network standards, RIM provided a platform and solutions for seamless access to time-sensitive information, including e-mail, phone, SMS messaging, Internet, and intranet-based applications. RIM technology also enabled a broad array of third-party developers and manufacturers to enhance their products and services with wireless connectivity to data. By April 2005, the company was four times bigger than it had been two years ago (company financial information for years 2000 through 2004 are presented in Exhibits 1 and 2).

RIM's agreements with wireless carriers was considered its biggest advantage over its competitors. RIM had about 100 carrier partnerships around the world so far. By April 2005, RIM had more than 2.5 million BlackBerry subscribers worldwide, up from less than 1 million at the beginning of 2004. RIM was ahead of its target to sign agreements with an additional 100 carriers by the end of 2005. But analysts thought that RIM had barely scratched the surface of the market it had launched. They expected 2.1 million additional subscribers would be signed on in 2006, bringing the total number of BlackBerry users to 4.6 million. That number could even be conservative as demand for RIM's new 7100 series of "smart phones" kicked in, particularly in Europe, where subscriber growth hadn't been as strong as recently, largely because earlier BlackBerrys did not have adequate talk capabilities.

According to industry analysts, the industry was still in its infancy stage with regard to market potential. The mobile e-mail market was forecast to reach $11 billion (U.S.) by 2007, while corporate enterprise users—RIM's primary market—was expected to reach 58 million by that year. But in addition to the corporate enterprise market there were the consumer and small business markets for mobile e-mail. These two segments had been underserved by RIM and were expected to be the next frontier

Exhibit 1 | Income Statements

As of February 5, 2000 through 2004
Financial data in U.S. dollars

	2/2004	2/2003	2/2002	2/2001	2/2000
Sales	594.6	306.7	294.1	221.3	85.0
Cost of Sales	296.9	178.5	195.2	133.4	48.6
Gross Operating Profit	297.7	128.2	98.9	87.9	36.4
Selling, General & Admin. Expense	173.9	160.9	139.8	83.5	21.6
Other Taxes	0.0	0.0	0.0	0.0	0.0
EBITDA	123.8	−32.7	−40.9	4.4	14.8
Depreciation & Amortization	55.9	31.1	17.7	9.1	4.7
EBIT	67.9	−63.8	−58.6	−4.7	10.1
Other Income, Net	10.6	11.4	25.7	22.9	6.0
Total Income Avail. for Interest Exp.	43.3	−117.2	−38.3	3.4	16.1
Interest Expense	0.0	0.0	0.0	0.0	0.0
Minority Interest	0.0	0.0	0.0	0.0	0.0
Pre-tax Income	43.3	−117.2	−38.3	3.4	16.1
Income Taxes	−4.2	31.8	−9.9	9.7	5.5
Special Income/Charges	−35.2	−64.8	−5.4	−14.8	0.0
Net Income from Cont. Operations	47.5	−148.9	−28.5	−6.2	10.5
Net Income from Discont. Opers.	0.0	0.0	0.0	0.0	0.0
Net Income from Total Operations	47.5	−148.9	−28.5	−6.2	10.5
Normalized Income	82.7	−84.1	−23.1	8.6	10.5
Extraordinary Income	0.0	0.0	0.0	0.0	0.0
Income from Cum. Eff. of Acct. Chg.	0.0	0.0	0.0	0.0	0.0
Income from Tax Loss Carryforward	0.0	0.0	0.0	0.0	0.0
Other Gains (Losses)	0.0	0.0	0.0	0.0	0.0
Total Net Income	47.5	−148.9	−28.5	−6.2	10.5

for wireless e-mail carriers. RIM was selling its products through the various wireless carriers with whom it had signed agreements. More than 100 wireless carriers around the world were essentially acting as a global sales force for Research in Motion's BlackBerry device. In Canada, BlackBerries were sold though Bell Mobility, Rogers Communications, and electronics stores such as Best Buy, as well as various online electronics stores based in the United States. Wireless carriers such as Rogers Wireless in Canada and Circular in the United States had become the focus of RIM's distribution strategy. RIM was trying to keep carriers happy by not posing a threat to their business and not putting the interests of one carrier over another.

By 2005, the idea of the mobile phone being the central communication device for both voice and data had caught on. RIM's strength was that it was capable of making phone and messaging functions work together without any of them losing strength. At the same time, RIM's rapid expansion had attracted a large number of competitors. Telecom carriers, software companies, cellphone makers, and consumer electronics firms were all looking at the best way to capitalize on the market that RIM had created for wireless e-mail and other mobile applications. These players continued to partner with each other while competing for a leadership position. To compete effectively with such global corporations, RIM would need more resources to expand its hardware and software

Exhibit 2   Balance Sheets

As of February 5, 2000 through 2004
Financial data in U.S. dollars

Annual Balance Sheet (Values in Millions)	2/2004	2/2003	2/2002	2/2001	2/2000
Assets					
Current Assets					
Cash and Equivalents	1,156.4	340.7	340.5	508.8	0.1
Receivables	107.4	45.3	48.6	64.2	33.3
Inventories	42.8	31.3	37.5	68.0	36.9
Other Current Assets	43.4	11.1	310.8	216.0	224.1
Total Current Assets	1,350.0	428.4	737.3	857.1	294.4
Non-Current Assets					
Property, Plant & Equipment, Gross	246.9	225.3	187.1	114.0	49.0
Accum. Depreciation & Depletion	99.2	64.1	35.3	18.8	9.7
Property, Plant & Equipment, Net	147.7	161.2	151.8	95.2	39.3
Intangibles	94.4	82.1	30.4	0.0	0.0
Other Non-Current Assets	333.3	190.0	28.6	17.8	3.5
Total Non-Current Assets	575.4	433.3	210.8	113.0	42.8
Total Assets	1,925.3	861.7	948.2	970.1	337.2
Liabilities & Shareholder's Equity					
Current Liabilities					
Accounts Payable	35.6	18.6	46.9	45.9	11.0
Short-Term Debt	0.2	6.1	0.4	0.2	0.2
Other Current Liabilities	173.1	124.3	12.2	14.7	8.1
Total Current Liabilities	208.9	149.1	59.5	60.8	19.3
Non-Current Liabilities					
Long-Term Debt	6.2	5.8	11.9	6.3	6.5
Deferred Income Taxes	0.0	0.0	0.0	0.0	0.0
Other Non-Current Liabilities	0.0	0.0	0.0	0.0	0.0
Minority Interest	0.0	0.0	0.0	0.0	0.0
Total Non-Current Liabilities	6.2	5.8	11.9	6.3	6.5
Total Liabilities	215.1	154.8	71.4	67.1	25.8
Shareholder's Equity					
Preferred Stock Equity	0.0	0.0	0.0	0.0	0.0
Common Stock Equity	1,710.2	706.8	876.7	902.9	311.4
Total Equity	1,710.2	706.8	876.7	902.9	311.4
Total Liabilities & Stock Equity	1,925.3	861.6	948.1	970.0	337.2

offerings. RIM's success had led to speculation that the company would be a takeover target. One of the reasons for these acquisitions rumours was that RIM didn't have the resources to fight this battle. But few companies were currently considering buying RIM, given its $14.1-billion market capitalization. Also, if a major wireless carrier were to buy RIM, RIM's relationship with other major carriers would be jeopardized. Another reason analysts doubted that RIM would be acquired any time soon was that Mike Lazaridis and Jim Balsillie believed they could still bring more value to RIM as it continued on its growth path.

Competitive Threats

RIM's technology was currently considered to be the best, making wireless carriers license its technology rather than develop their own. But while wireless carriers liked the benefits of BlackBerries, they didn't like sharing so much of the revenue with RIM and were looking for alternative data services. So some RIM rivals were working on alternatives to BlackBerry e-mail technology, as well as new, more powerful multimedia technologies and services that could make consumers and corporate executives switch from wireless e-mail technologies to other technologies.

One such example was Rogers Communications, Canada's largest wireless company and RIM's longest and closest partner. The two companies had worked together on wireless e-mail since the early 1990s. Rogers was the first company to include BlackBerry in its wireless service. It was also the first to offer BlackBerry when it had no mobile telephone component and it was the first company to launch a BlackBerry that handled both wireless e-mail and mobile phone service. It has consistently been the first to offer updated versions of the device.

But in April 2005, Rogers Wireless launched its own mobile push e-mail service called MyMail through an agreement with Visto Inc., based in California and one of several companies working on wireless e-mail technologies that competed with BlackBerry. Visto's push technology provided two-way access to e-mail, calendars, and contact information through a number of different wireless devices. It was not tied to a particular product, which is the case with BlackBerry. According to Jim Balsillie, initiatives such as the Rogers one represented "a cheap down market thing" and he did not think they posed a threat to RIM, which offered a richer stream of wireless data.

Visto was one of several companies working on less expensive alternatives to BlackBerry. According to Sanjay Kamble, vice-president of marketing at Visto, the company enabled wireless operators to package it differently to different user segments. Carriers can completely brand their service as their own, and it would cost them $1 to $2 less per subscriber than the estimated $10 that RIM collected from carriers for each Blackberry user who signed up. Some wireless carriers preferred the Visto approach because it offered more flexibility and choice for the consumer. Visto was hoping to beat RIM by supporting not only e-mail, but also cellphone-style text messaging and at a lower cost than RIM.

Rogers Wireless, Bell Mobility, Telus Mobility, and a division of Sasktel and Manitoba Telecom Services all offered Visto's basic e-mail product, which gave people access to their corporate e-mail but only when people requested it as the device didn't push the e-mail on its own. Rogers would be the first service provider in Canada to offer the enhanced push version of Visto's technology, but it was expected that Bell, Telus, and other wireless carriers would follow suit with Visto or someone else. Visto was already working with wireless service providers to support 30 of the top mobile devices such as Motorola, Palm, Sony, and Kyocera, and aiming to expand that selection to 50 within the next six months. Visto was hoping to get to millions of users faster than RIM. Currently, it boasted more than 250,000 subscribers and aimed to reach 10 million by 2007, a growth rate that would be difficult even for RIM to match.

Visto and other competitors were better than RIM at relaying users' calendar and contact information. But they were options only for companies with servers running Microsoft's Exchange Software, while RIM also connected to the IBM's Lotus e-mail platform. According to RIM, that was an important selling point in overseas markets where there was a lot of resistance to Microsoft. But another mobile e-mail rival began to compete with lower costs than RIM—Seven Networks, Inc. connected low-end users to Lotus and pledged to do it for all customers soon.

A big threat came from cellphones and personal digital assistants that were merging into "smart phones" with text-messaging capabilities. This led Palm to acquire Handspring, the maker of Treo smart phones in 2003. The Palm device could incorporate powerful calendar and address book functionality with the ability to run the thousands of other programs that run on the Palm platform. Treo offered the functionality of a "smart phone" with a handheld device. Treo was already distributed through wireless carriers Bell Mobility and Rogers Communications and various electronic stores such as Best Buy and Staples/Business Depot, and various online electronics stores based in the United States. Palm was also selling Treos through its own website.

Microsoft was testing wireless communications software that it planned to incorporate into the next version of its Exchange Server, a product companies use to store and send e-mail to their desktop machines. In a sense, this product could offer the same e-mail function that is offered by BlackBerry. Symbian Ltd., a consortium of wireless firms formed by Nokia to try to keep Microsoft in check, agreed to license part of Microsoft's Exchange Server software. That meant that more than 20 million handheld devices using Symbian software could receive e-mails from networks using Exchange Server software.

Microsoft was also trying to make smart phones work more like BlackBerries using its own operating systems or to partner with someone with better technology. It hoped that by getting onto more handsets and smart phones, in addition to selling more copies of its Windows mobile operating system, it would ensure demand for its other products, such as software for delivering Web-based services including banking and shopping.

But many questioned carriers' willingness to adopt Microsoft technology for fear that, much like the personal computer market, Microsoft might expand its own brand at the expense of other industry players. The carriers saw what had happened in the personal computer market and they didn't want to be commoditized in the same way.

Some of RIM's customers had already deserted to the competition. For instance, Keesal, Young & Logan, a California-based law firm, switched to Good Technology Inc. because it offered better user interface and less set-up time. Good offered e-mail services that were used in handspring devices and others, even BlackBerries. Dell was selling a BlackBerry-like messaging device powered by Good Technology.

RIM critics said that this stage of the industry resembled the competitive landscape of the personal computer market in its earlier stage, when high-end companies such as Sun Microsystems and Apple saw their markets become standardized and commoditized. RIM executives, on the other hand, argued that there was still room for companies to distinguish themselves with superior technology.

In the meantime, other companies continued to develop alternatives to BlackBerry's e-mail technology to attract customers away from BlackBerry-like devices and toward other technologies such as mobiles phones that allowed instant, face-to-face conversations.

Other RIM Initiatives

One of RIM's other initiatives was to license its software to rival handset makers, such as Nokia, Sony, Ericsson, and Motorola, which have direct licensing deals with RIM. Also, its e-mail software could be incorporated into

digital assistants running Microsoft's Pocket PC operating system. The initiative, which the company announced in 2003, met with limited success, as very few devices using RIM software had been sold at the time. But industry observers thought that could change, especially after RIM had settled a patent dispute with U.S.–based NTP Inc.

On April 4, 2005, RIM announced plans to introduce a new wireless application development framework for BlackBerry customers and developers for later that year. The BlackBerry Mobile Data System (MDS) v4.1 was the next generation of RIM's MDS technology that would build on the existing features of BlackBerry Enterprise Server and provide an easy-to-use and integrated system for organizing data and optimizing wireless applications.

BlackBerry MDS v4.1 would make it easier for developers to create and deploy business applications for mobile employees, providing a comprehensive framework for building wireless applications and reducing the amount of time and resources spent on in-house development. Through the use of Web Services, BlackBerry MDS v4.1 would allow BlackBerry customers to mobilize applications in a variety of environments, including Microsoft.NET and J2EE.

The introduction of BlackBerry Mobile Data System v4.1 would provide an integrated system with added services and tools to simplify wireless application development by leveraging Web Services, industry standards, and the proven technology of BlackBerry. The new device would have several user-friendly features that would make it easy to use, including a powerful visual application design and assembly tool that would allow developers to quickly assemble wireless applications.

Among other plans RIM was currently working on were efforts to roll out the BlackBerry service in Russian, Arabic, and Chinese. It was a challenging project, however, because each new language must not only be worked into the BlackBerry, but also throughout the infrastructure that delivers the data. RIM had no plans to add digital cameras, music players, or detachable memory to the BlackBerry.

The Task Ahead

A major issue for RIM's management team was how to respond to the increasing threat coming from various competitors currently offering competing wireless technologies. Rogers's adoption of the Visto technology was a crucial wake-up call for RIM management. Soon other wireless carriers were expected to follow Rogers' lead and adopt Visto's or a similar technology. Visto's aggressive expansion plans were also of concern to RIM management. The introduction of Treo through retail chains such as Staples/Business Depot was another threat. Palm was selling its Treo handheld device through a variety of electronic stores and directly over the Internet. Microsoft's entry into the smart phone market was posing a serious threat to all players in the industry. The critical issue for RIM's management was whether to target individuals and small business. Also, what additional method should RIM use to reach its target markets? Should RIM utilize the Internet as Palm was doing? Another option would be to sell BlackBerries through office supplies stores such as Staples/Business Depot. Or should it sell its products directly to the public by opening its own stores as other high-tech companies such as Apple had done in recent years?

Discussion Questions

1. What factors have accounted for RIM's success?
2. Evaluate the various threats facing RIM. Which of these threats are most serious for RIM?
3. Should RIM be concerned about not being in the low end of the market? If yes, what should RIM do about it?
4. Develop a distribution strategy for RIM to capitalize on all available distribution opportunities.

Sources

David Padon, "RIM shares fall 7% on patent verdict," *Toronto Star*, November 23, 2002; Paul Roberts, "BlackBerries vs. terrorism," IDG News Service, August 17, 2004; Paul Roberts, "Logan Airport using BlackBerries for background checks," IDG News Service, June 22, 2004; Phil Hochmuth, "Nortel to support converged apps on Wi-Fi," *Network World Fusion*, February 8, 2005; Nick Baker, "PalmOne's Treo takes on BlackBerry," *Financial Post*, April 14, 2004, IN 3; Tyler Hamilton, "RIM's sudden rise is no fluke, analysts insist," *Toronto Star*, December 29, 2003, C1; Tyler Hamilton, "Rogers jabs at RIM," *Toronto Star*, April 18, 2005, C1; Tyler Hamilton, "BlackBerry: Ripe for the Picking?" *Toronto Star*, February 14, 2005, D1; Simon Avery, "BlackBerry sticks to what it does best," *Globe and Mail*, July 22, 2004, B1; Simon Avery, "RIM hits a major crossroad," *Globe and Mail*, September 18, 2004, B5; Simon Avery, "When it comes to BlackBerry, RIM feels the sky's the limit," *Globe and Mail*, April 19, 2005, B6; Simon Avery, "RIM's booming sales spur rivals," *Globe and Mail*, April 4, 2005, B3; M. Corey Goldman, "RIM still at cutting edge," *Toronto Star*, April 4, 2005, C4; Brian Bergstein, "RIM's struggle to keep its edge," *Toronto Star*, November 17, 2003, D1; Kevin Restivo, "RIM bites bullet to avoid future royalties," *Financial Post*, March 17, 2005, FP1; "RIM plans to launch Chinese-language BlackBerry," *Toronto Star*, July 7, 2004, C1; Rachel Ross, "RIM misses analysts' forecast," *Toronto Star*, April 6, 2005, C1.

Zeneca Ag Products

Thomas Funk and Colin Steen

This case was prepared by Thomas Funk of the University of Guelph and Colin Steen of Syngenta Crop Protection. It is intended as a basis for classroom discussion and not designed to show either effective or ineffective handling of administrative issues. Some of the data in the case have been disguised to protect confidentiality.

"We may be behind some other companies in biotechnology, but our new precision agriculture technology should be a huge help to us in selling our more traditional products. In addition, it should be a profitable product in itself." So thought Colin Steen, manager of pulse and oilseed products for Zeneca Ag Products, as he began thinking about his upcoming presentation to management on the introduction of some exciting new precision agriculture technology Zeneca had developed for disease detection in Saskatchewan lentils (peas).

Agriculture in western Canada and the world had undergone a significant shift over the past five years. The crop protection industry that once relied on traditional chemistry as a source for sales and profits now used biotechnology to develop crops that contained traits never before seen. A good example of this was herbicide tolerance as exemplified by Monsanto's Roundup Ready technology. Using genetic engineering, Monsanto was able to develop new crop varieties that were resistant to Roundup, their popular non-selective herbicide. After planting these varieties, farmers could spray a field with Roundup and kill all vegetation except the crop they wanted to produce. This industry shift occurred very quickly and left Zeneca trying to catch up to other companies leading the biotechnology movement. Though Zeneca was investing significant research dollars in biotechnology, the company was at least five years behind the industry in this area. Colin was sure that the new precision agriculture approaches would

help Zeneca maintain the perception of technological leadership until other, new high-tech products were developed.

Zeneca Ag Products

Zeneca, created from a de-merger of ICI, the large British chemical manufacturer, was a leading global supplier of crop protection products. The company's products included herbicides, insecticides, and fungicides for a broad range of crops. In Canada, Zeneca was a major supplier of crop protection products.

Zeneca had substantial strength in fungicides, which were chemical products designed to control diseases in plants. Zeneca brands in this category included Bravo, Quadris, Amistar, Heritage, and Abound. According to market research, Zeneca was the world leader in fungicide sales in 1999 with products registered for use in over 43 crops in 46 countries. Key crops requiring fungicides were potatoes, rice, and turf in the United States, and canola and lentils in Canada. The fungicide portfolio was among the fastest-growing line of products manufactured by Zeneca, and sustaining this growth was very important to the future of the company.

Precision Agriculture Technology

Zeneca Ag Products had invested significant resources in developing a broad range of precision agriculture technology over the last five years. To date, the most promising technology was photo imagery that allowed farmers to identify disease symptoms that may not be apparent to the naked eye. Using high-resolution images from orbiting satellites or fixed-wing aircraft, Zeneca could determine the presence of disease symptoms long

Exhibit 1   Example of Field Map

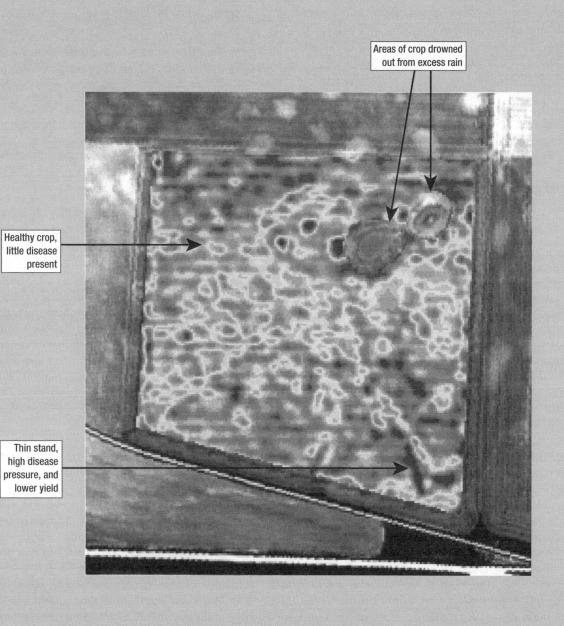

Areas of crop drowned out from excess rain

Healthy crop, little disease present

Thin stand, high disease pressure, and lower yield

before those symptoms were visible. Based on the premise that unhealthy plants reflect a different band of colour than healthy plants, this technology had the potential to save farmers thousands of dollars in lost yields due to disease. Zeneca also felt it could boost fungicide sales and be a profitable service they could provide customers.

Zeneca had some initial success with this technology in tomato and turf crops in the United States, identifying disease in advance of symptoms and preventing yield and profit reductions. By being able to identify diseased plants before visual symptoms occurred, farmers would be able to apply a fungicide to control the disease and, therefore, avoid the economic losses associated with the disease. In addition, this breakthrough technology had the potential of giving Zeneca the perception of technological leadership, even in the absence of a line of biotech crops and products.

Zeneca expected that when the process was in operation, they could provide reports to farmers within 24 hours of an initial request. The report generated for the farmer consisted of a series of field maps that outlined the relative health of crops. An example of a field map is shown in Exhibit 1. The map measures relative crop vigour. The lighter areas are healthy crops while the darker areas are unhealthy crops. Moving from northwest to southeast, the crop worsens and disease increases.

Initial estimates placed the cost of providing a photo at approximately $2.50 per acre (1 acre = 0.4 hectare).

Lentil Production in Western Canada

Lentil production in western Canada was very important to the success of Zeneca. Acreage in Saskatchewan had increased dramatically over the past five years, reaching 1.6 million acres in 2000. The lentil acreage was divided into three markets: large-seeded green, small-seeded green, and red. The Crop Development Centre, based at the University of Saskatchewan, had been responsible for the influx of lentil varieties well suited to the Saskatchewan climate. Exhibit 2 illustrates the growth in lentil acres in Saskatchewan since 1978.

Lentil growers in Saskatchewan faced plant diseases that potentially could affect yield and quality. Depending on when the farmer detected the disease, the financial impact could vary from minimal to severe. The main diseases that affected lentil production were ascochyta and anthracnose.

Ascochyta (*Ascochyta lentis*) was a stubble- and seed-borne disease primarily affecting seed quality, and in severe cases, it also affected yield. Primarily spread by rain-splash throughout the growing season, ascochyta was prevalent in most areas of Saskatchewan. An application of

Exhibit 2	Lentil Production in Saskatchewan 1980 to 2000
Year	Acres (000)*
1980	50,000
1982	100,000
1984	100,000
1986	100,000
1988	400,000
1990	300,000
1992	400,000
1994	700,000
1996	1,000,000
1998	1,300,000
2000	1,600,000

* 1 acre = 0.4 hectare

Bravo at 0.8 litres/ per acre, which cost a farmer approximately $10.25 per acre, stopped the spread of infectious spores in the crop by preventing new infection from forming. A second application of Bravo was sometimes necessary if weather conditions continued to be moist. The lesions that developed from ascochyta were cream-coloured with a tan margin and black spores in the centre. Under severe disease conditions, ascochyta blight seeds became partly or wholly brownish in colour, resulting in economic losses due to poor quality. The losses from poor-quality lentils due to ascochyta could range from 5 percent to 70 percent of the value of the lentil. Ascochyta also could reduce the yield of lentil in cases of severe infection in a range of 10 percent to 50 percent.

Severe anthracnose (*Colletotrichum truncatum*) resulted in a significant impact on yield. Anthracnose lesions developed on the leaves and stem, causing plants to turn golden brown when they coalesced, resulting in plant death. Anthracnose was primarily stubble-borne and spread from leaf to leaf via rainsplash throughout the growing season. Bravo was the only product registered for the prevention and control of this disease. An application of Bravo at 0.8 litres per acre prevented the formation of new lesions on what was already a healthy crop. A second application was sometimes necessary later in the growing season to protect new crop growth from developing lesions. As anthracnose attacked the lower part of the stem, it was important to apply Bravo early in the growth stage, preferably just before flowering. Bravo served only as a protectant and did not cure disease already present. This underscored the importance of the early detection of lentil disease.

Farmers were limited in the ways they could deal with disease problems in lentils. The most satisfactory method was to use Bravo. Zeneca estimated that 40 percent of lentil acres in 2000 were treated with this fungicide. Some farmers felt they could not justify the use of a fungicide based on likely economic returns. Other farmers felt that once they saw visible signs of disease, it was too late for a fungicide to do any good.

Over the past several years, researchers at the University of Saskatchewan had developed several varieties that were resistant to lentil diseases. Although resistant to disease, most of these varieties had a 10 to 15 percent lower yield potential than non-resistant varieties.[1] This made them less attractive to farmers, resulting in relatively low adoption. In 2000, disease-resistant varieties were seeded on less than 20 percent of the acreage given over to lentils in Saskatchewan.

In addition to Bravo, Zeneca also offered three other products for lentil production: Touchdown (glyphosate), Venture (grass herbicide), and Reglone (desiccant). This broad product line, and the visibility of Zeneca among growers, made lentils a very important crop for the success of Zeneca in Saskatchewan.

Marketing the Imagery Technology

Although Colin was excited about the new imagery technology and the impact it could have on Bravo sales, he had little idea how farmers might react to the product. To gain additional insight, he decided to retain the services of Agri Studies, a Calgary-based marketing research firm, to determine farmer reaction to the new technology. Appendix 1 contains a summary of the key results of this research.

Colin felt the research supported the introduction of the new technology. Even at the highest price level tested, the research showed a high proportion of farmers that said they would try the imagery. Colin knew, however, that to say they would try it in a research study, and to actually try it, were two different things. He also knew that trying the technology was only half the battle; the other half was making sure they were satisfied with the results and would use it again in subsequent years. To achieve a high level of trial and repeat buying required a solid marketing plan.

In developing the marketing plan, Colin first considered the target market. Obviously, the broad target was the 5,000 lentil growers in Saskatchewan. Colin wondered whether there were smaller groups that would be better prospects for the new product.

The product itself was very simple—a colour satellite photo of a field with an accompanying legend indicating the degree of disease infestation. Colin felt he should stop short of including a recommendation for Bravo use, although he was not sure of this. He also wondered how he should position the new technology. Should it be positioned as a tool that would help farmers better manage fungicide use? Or a tool that could help farmers maximize returns per acre from lentils? Or was there some other positioning that should be used?

The price of the service was also something that was not determined. In the marketing research, three price levels were tested: $6 per acre, $8 per acre, and $10 per acre. Although the $6 per acre would undoubtedly promote faster adoption of the technology, higher prices would increase the contribution margin on the imagery product significantly.

Distribution was a real dilemma because there were different ways to approach this. The first was to distribute the images through the same dealers that sold Bravo. Under this plan, farmers would place orders for an image with a chemicals dealer. The dealer would forward the request to Zeneca, who would then arrange to have the photo taken and couriered or sent electronically to the dealer. The dealer would then deliver it to the farmer. Under this system the dealer would receive a margin on the sale. Colin was not sure what margin was appropriate but felt something in the range of 20 percent (the same margin they received on the sale of Bravo) was reasonable.

In Saskatchewan, there were approximately 100 dealers that sold fungicides for use on lentils. Of these dealers, 25 sold approximately 75 percent of the total fungicide used. Colin felt there might be some merit in restricting distribution to the top dealers.

A second distribution approach was for Zeneca to sell the product directly to farmers. Colin thought this could be done by sending the farmers information on the imagery product and having farmers order by calling a 1-800 number or by going to the Zeneca website. The photos would be delivered by courier or electronically if the farmer had the appropriate computer technology to receive them.

The final area Colin needed to address was promotion. Here, of course, there were many options available. Some of the main options were these:

- Farmers' meetings where groups of 25 to 50 farmers could be assembled and introduced to the technology. These meetings usually featured an information session followed by a meal. To do a session in the right way would probably cost approximately $20 per farmer.
- Advertising in publications specifically oriented to lentil growers. The most obvious choice here was the

---

[1] Many scientists believed that the "yield drag" associated with disease-resistant varieties would become smaller as additional plant breeding work was undertaken.

magazine *Lentils in Canada*, which was published quarterly. A full-page colour ad in this publication costs $6,500.

- Direct mail targeted at all lentil growers. To produce and distribute a high-quality direct mail piece would cost about $20 per farmer.
- Personal sales calls could also be used. Since the existing Zeneca rep was fully committed to current activities, any personal selling would have to be done through part-time reps hired specifically for this purpose. Colin felt that summer students might be a great choice. The total cost for a personal sales call was estimated to be $50.

A final area Colin wondered about was the possibility of bundling the imagery technology with sales of Bravo.[2] He was not sure if this was a good idea or how to put together such a program. One possibility was to offer a discount on Bravo purchases if a farmer had already purchased images.

Colin wondered what impact the imagery technology might have on Bravo sales. On the one hand, he felt it could boost Bravo sales because more farmers would be aware of disease problems and want to use Bravo to solve these problems. On the other hand, some farmers who in the past had sprayed Bravo to prevent disease might now discover that they did not have a problem at all, or only a problem in certain parts of fields that might be dealt with using a spot treatment.

The Decision

As Colin pondered his decision, he was very aware of the fact that the imagery technology was new and seemed to meet a real need for farmers. He was almost sure it would have a positive impact on the brand image of Bravo both in lentils and other crops. The likely introduction of competitive products into the fungicide category made the establishment of a strong brand position all the more important.

Zeneca management felt the introduction of the imagery technology in lentils should cover additional overhead costs of $200,000 a year. They expected the new product might lose $100,000 in the first year, earn a contribution of $500,000 in the second year, and earn a contribution of $1,000,000 in the third year.[3] They

---

[2] The contribution margin on Bravo was approximately 60 percent.

[3] These contribution values include gains or losses from changes in Bravo sales.

would view the imagery product in a much more favourable light if it resulted in higher Bravo sales in lentils.

Appendix 1: Results of Marketing Research

In order to assess the potential of the new imagery technology, Zeneca carried out some marketing research in the summer of 1999 with a random sample of 100 Saskatchewan lentil producers. The sample was selected from a database maintained by Zeneca. Data were collected using personal interviews. Personal interviews were used because it was necessary to show farmers images of their own fields and explain the technology prior to asking questions. A brief summary of research findings follows.

After explaining the technology, each farmer was asked to indicate what he or she saw as the primary benefits of this approach. The most frequently mentioned benefits were these:

- Save money on fungicides—don't need to spray if the results show no disease is present.
- Facilitate spot treatment of a fungicide—only treat areas of a field where there is evidence of disease.
- Monitor disease-susceptible varieties of lentils—allows for better selection of disease-resistant varieties in future.

Respondents were also asked to indicate potential concerns with the technology. The most frequently mentioned concerns were the following:

- Accuracy of the imagery.
- Possible misinterpretation of fertility problems for disease problems.
- Amount of time it might take to get images.
- Cost of the technology.

Three price points were tested in the research: $6 an acre, $8 an acre, and $10 an acre. One-third of the sample was asked their willingness to try the new technology at each of these prices. Results are shown below:

	$6	$8	$10
Definitely would try it	26%	14%	11%
Probably would try it	56%	36%	23%
May or may not try it	18%	44%	45%
Probably would not try it	0%	4%	11%
Definitely would not try it	0%	0%	0%

Regardless of the price, respondents who indicated they would try the technology indicated they would use it on 20 percent of their lentil acres in year 1 and, if successful, they would use it on 50 percent of their lentil acres in year 2 and 100 percent of their lentil acres in year 3.

When asked how they currently used fungicides, the following responses were given:

- 20 percent said they used a disease-resistant variety so they didn't need to worry about spraying.
- 40 percent said they used a fungicide if disease was detected in a field after carefully examining the crop.
- 20 percent said they always used a fungicide as a preventative measure.

- 10 percent said they used a fungicide when weather conditions appeared to favour a disease problem.
- 10 % percent said they would only use a fungicide if they saw a neighbour using one.

Lentil growers indicated varying degrees of disease problems in the past:

- 30 percent indicated they had past disease problems, but the associated economic losses have been small.
- 50 percent indicated they had past disease problems that resulted in significant economic losses.
- 20 percent indicated they had past disease problems that resulted in severe economic losses.

CASE 20

Wal-Mart

Peter Yannopoulos

In early 2004, Wal-Mart was the largest U.S. corporation. Its 2003 revenues totalled $259 billion (U.S.), topping the list of the largest U.S. publicly traded companies for the third straight year. Since Sam Walton, Wal-Mart's founder, opened his first store in Arkansas, the upstart company had experienced a solid growth over the years, overtaking its main competitors Sears and Kmart in 1991 and becoming in the process the largest U.S. company ahead of industrial giants such as Exxon and General Motors.

Sam Walton had little intention of expanding his company into foreign markets. According to his son John, Sam Walton thought more of serving domestic markets and pursuing domestic opportunities than expanding into other countries. The only store Sam Walton ever opened in a country other than the United States was in 1991 when he opened a Sam's Club store in Mexico City, after he and his son Rob visited Mexico.

After Sam Walton died, Wal-Mart's new management team broadened its strategic market vision and began an aggressive expansion overseas. In January 2004, after years of following an aggressive international expansion strategy, John Menzer, president of Wal-Mart International, was facing some difficulties in Germany, and he was considering his options regarding the future of Wal-Mart in that country. A related issue was whether, in view of the German experience, Wal-Mart should continue its aggressive international strategy or slow down to absorb the lessons learned from its international experience and formulate a foreign marketing strategy based on these lessons.

Company Background

On July 2, 1962, Sam Walton and his younger brother Bud Walton established the first Wal-Mart store in Rogers, Arkansas. Sam Walton realized soon enough that he was too small and too poor to take on JCPenney and Woolworth head-on. So he focused on rural towns in the southwestern United States with populations under 10,000 people, where his only competition was local independent stores. At that time, customers had to travel long distances to find discount stores in order to pay lower prices because small-town merchants charged higher prices due to high distribution costs and low purchasing power.

Wal-Mart took advantage of the unwillingness of the large retail chains at the time to serve small communities. By locating in small towns Wal-Mart avoided challenging the major retailers Sears, Woolworth, and Kmart, which operated primarily in large cities. Wal-Mart was ignored by its large competitors for a long time. In fact, very few people outside its geographical territory knew about Wal-Mart until much later when it was large enough to take on its large competitors. It wasn't until the late 1980s that its large competitors paid serious attention to Wal-Mart. In 1991, Wal-Mart overtook Sears and Kmart to become the largest U.S. retailer.

Wal-Mart exploited the lack of competition by methodically expanding the number of its stores and improving the efficiency of its operations. New information technology was introduced that allowed data to be beamed from stores through satellites to suppliers and warehouses to ensure that inbound and outbound trucks were full and store shelves fully stocked.

Wal-Mart forced suppliers to deliver shipments exactly when they were told. If suppliers failed to deliver at the specified time, shipments were returned until the next available time or they might even be rejected altogether.

In the 1970s, Wal-Mart established a network of cross-docking warehouses. In this system, deliveries from suppliers were accepted only in full truckload quantities. Delivered goods were then moved across the dock and onto trucks that departed fully loaded for the stores. Cross-docking led to a dramatic reduction in transportation costs.

In 1983, the first Sam's Club appeared in Midwest City, Oklahoma. Sam's Club consisted of no-frills, cash-and-carry discount warehouses targeting small businesses. It is noteworthy that over the years many people advised Sam Walton to enter other fields such as manufacturing or financial services but he would quickly reject the idea because he knew that his company's strengths were in discount retailing and not in manufacturing or financial services.

Wal-Mart's International Expansion

In 1993, Bob Martin, Wal-Mart's chief information officer, executive vice-president and senior vice-president, became president and CEO of Wal-Mart's International Division. At that time, Wal-Mart had no international presence other than a Sam's Club in Mexico. Martin's mandate was to make Wal-Mart's international division one of the company's main growth engines, which would contribute one-third of the company's growth over the next five years. Wal-Mart's overall corporate plan called for deriving its sales growth half from its food, one-third from its international, and the rest from its U.S. stores.

Martin's initial plan was to build Wal-Mart into North American's dominant retailer and establish a firm foothold in several other counties. His plans included expanding into Central and Latin America, Europe, and Asia, where he intended to use China and Indonesia as the entry point for the Asian continent.

Under Bob Martin's leadership, Wal-Mart embarked on an ambitious international expansion program throughout the mid and late 1990s and early 2000s. By April 2002, Wal-Mart International had 1,186 stores in nine countries: Canada, Mexico, Argentina, Brazil, the United Kingdom, Germany, China, South Korea, and Japan. Those countries were chosen largely because they had a large population base and a large and growing middle class. Overseas sales in 2001 were $35 billion (U.S.), representing almost 16 percent of Wal-Mart's revenue and an operating profit of $1.4 billion (U.S.).

In just a few years, Wal-Mart had become the largest retailer in Canada and the third largest retailer in the United Kingdom. In 1998, Wal-Mart acquired a controlling interest in Mexico's largest retailer, Cifra, which operated various stores throughout the country, including the largest chain of sit-down restaurants and department stores. Following this acquisition, Wal-Mart became Mexico's largest retailer.

Wal-Mart's culture included everyday low prices, a strong customer focus, greeters, cheers, and Sam Walton quotations and pictures; this culture had become one of the company's distinctive competencies that were largely responsible for its domestic and international success. Wal-Mart's everyday low prices strategy—whereby all products are discounted instead of only some—had been embraced in the various countries it had entered. According to senior vice-president Don Soderquist, Wal-Mart's customers were the same no matter where they lived and shopped: "Over the years many said that we would not be able to serve customers west of the Mississippi, outside of the South, in metropolitan areas or outside of the United States. Frankly, we find the customers want the same things. Regardless of where we are, customers want to be treated well, want to have a good assortment of products to choose from, and they want the merchandise at a great price. The most amazing fact is that our associates around the world embrace and protect the culture that they have built over the last 30 years."

Wal-Mart's Entry in Canada

Wal-Mart entered Canada in 1994 by purchasing all 122 Canadian Woolco discount stores and converting them into Wal-Mart stores. Wal-Mart Canada incurred losses in 1995, its first year of operations, but it showed an operating profit in 1996 and it was well on its way to becoming Canada's largest-volume discount retailer, as its profits and market share continued to grow in subsequent years. By 1999, Wal-Mart Canada had captured 30 percent of the Canadian department store market while its main rivals, Zellers, Eaton's, Sears, and The Bay were rapidly losing market share. Eaton's, one of Canada's oldest department stores, declared bankruptcy and some of its stores were acquired by Sears.

Wal-Mart's entry shook up the Canadian retail environment and it forced many companies to change their way of doing business in order to become more competitive. For example, suppliers to Wal-Mart distribution centres had to arrive within 15 to 30 minutes of schedule, otherwise they faced fines. These suppliers had to initiate programs to improve their operations or risk losing Wal-Mart's business. Wal-Mart also took advantage of its enormous power to obtain concessions from its suppliers.

The Challenges Abroad

However, expansion into some foreign markets didn't go smoothly. For example, Wal-Mart shut down operations in Indonesia because of disagreements with its domestic partner and the anticipation of political unrest. Wal-Mart faced some challenges in Japan, where its unique retail market was evident in consumer tastes, packaging, the supplier-retailer relationships, and logistics systems.

In Argentina, the aisles were too narrow for the large number of customers that visited its stores. In Mexico, after it built large parking lots, the company learned that most shoppers travelled to the stores by bus. It also sold tennis balls that did not bounce properly because of the high altitude. Wal-Mart ran into trouble in Mexico when its Mexican managers decided not to adopt its everyday low prices strategy. They introduced their own strategy of putting only certain items on sale. As soon as Wal-Mart learned of this pricing policy, it closed the store for a day and converted all prices to conform to the everyday low prices strategy.

By the end of 2002, with the exception of the United Kingdom, Wal-Mart had yet to establish a strong presence in Europe. Wal-Mart's management felt that the reasons for the mixed results in Europe were high labour costs, tough regulations, and powerful unions. In Europe, Wal-Mart also faced several challenges that included logistics and transportation difficulties, and lack of retail locations and local partners because Wal-Mart was still too young and unproven to them. Of special interest was Wal-Mart's experience in Germany, which is detailed next.

The German Experience

Although Wal-Mart invariably faced difficulties in almost every country it entered, its experience in Germany has been so far the most difficult one. In December 1997, Wal-Mart purchased 21 Wertkauf stores and a year later 74 Interspar hypermarkets, which were very similar to Wal-Mart supercentres. The company spent money remodelling the newly acquired stores by improving the lighting, widening aisles, adding checkout counters, hiring additional staff, and inculcating them with its corporate culture. In August 1999, it opened its flagship supercentre in Dortmund. During 2002, Wal-Mart opened two new stores and planned to open a new supercentre in Berlin and a new distribution centre in Bingen the following year.

German shoppers first appeared to welcome Wal-Mart's lower prices, friendly employees, less cramped stores, and fast checkout service. However, profit margins were very low due to higher labour costs, stronger competition than expected, and small, uneconomical stores. Specifically, while its operating margin was 6 to 8 percent on average in its British stores, it was only 1 percent or less in Germany. According to *Newsweek* magazine, some analysts felt that Wal-Mart was losing $100 million (U.S.) a year in Germany in 2002. Competition was more intense in Germany than in other countries, with several discounters among the competition, including Aldi, a large chain of no-frills and no-service stores that targeted price-sensitive consumers. Wal-Mart's labour costs were higher than in other countries due to German labour laws and tough unions that made wage reductions difficult.

German shopping hours differed from the U.S. ones, as stores closed on Saturday afternoon and reopened on Monday morning. Unlike Germany, a large percentage of Wal-Mart's sales in the United States were made on Sundays. Another problem that hampered Wal-Mart's effort to improve the productivity of its stores was that German customers were used to bagging their own groceries, slowing down the checkout lines. German shoppers had also been alarmed by greeters talking to them when they entered the stores. In addition, there was some evidence that, despite the initial impression, German shoppers did not respond positively to the company's everyday low prices strategy, adding to its woes.

The tough zoning laws in Germany made it almost impossible for Wal-Mart to build new stores. As a result, it was not until 2001 that Wal-Mart opened two brand-new stores. Adding to the difficulties was German red tape, which slowed down efforts to enlarge existing stores.

In 1999, Bob Martin stepped down and was replaced by John Menzer as head of Wal-Mart's international division. Menzer adopted a more disciplined approach than the more opportunistic approach of his predecessor by being more cautious and taking more time to do proper research before opening a new store. John Menzer acknowledged that Wal-Mart faced difficulties in Germany and attributed it to "trying to put in our distribution, technology, and operating expenses in a market that is slow to change—slow to adapt to technology and distribution."

Chief executive officer Lee Scott, appearing on CNBC in March 2002, admitted Wal-Mart's difficulties in Germany and blamed it on Wal-Mart's strategy. Lee stated, "We got confused on what's important, and so we went out and we remodelled stores—and spent a lot of money doing things that weren't what the customers wanted from us." He also added in the future "we'll be successful because we reprioritized what our efforts are and understanding that market, understanding the German consumer, and understanding Wal-Mart stores."

Among the changes made by Wal-Mart during this period, in an effort to adapt to local customer requirements, were to offer baked soft pretzels and wurstbrot (open-faced sandwiches with sausage and butter). Customers were given the option of doing their own packing while greeters spoke more quietly and they learned not to approach customers but simply wait on the side. Another change was made to its hours of operation—its stores opened at seven o'clock, two hours earlier than the usual nine o'clock opening hours.

Decision

In 2002, in view of the challenges facing Wal-Mart in Germany and elsewhere, Wal-Mart revised its initial growth estimates of how much the international division would contribute to the company's overall growth. According to Rob Walton, over the next five years, 60 percent of Wal-Mart's growth would come from domestic Wal-Mart stores and supercentres, another 10 percent from Sam's Clubs, and the remaining 30 percent from Wal-Mart International.

In January 2004, John Menzer had to decide how to handle the situation in Germany. Should Wal-Mart remain in Germany or should it pull out and focus its time and efforts on pursuing opportunities in other countries? If it stayed in Germany, should Wal-Mart abandon its everyday low prices policy in favour of keeping prices higher and offering periodic price reductions? John Menzer was optimistic that with time Wal-Mart would smooth out all remaining problems in Germany and it would eventually enjoy the same degree of success as other countries. Another urgent question was whether, after several years of frenetic growth, to maintain Wal-Mart's explosive growth rate or slow down while developing a foreign growth strategy on the basis of what had been learned so far from Wal-Mart's international experience.

Discussion Questions

1. Discuss the reasons for Wal-Mart's success in the United States.
2. What were the problems facing Wal-Mart International? What were the causes of these problems?
3. Should Wal-Mart continue operations in Germany given the many problems it is facing in that country?
4. Should Wal-Mart continue to expand at the same frenetic speed or should it slow down and develop a growth strategy based on the lessons learned from its international experience?

Sources

Robert Slater, *The Wal-Mart Decade* (New York: Portfolio, 2003); Jeffery Rubin, "Wal-Mart's impact far-reaching," *Globe and Mail*, March 8, 2004; Hollie Shaw, "Loblaw to fend off Wal-Mart 'invasion' with cheap labour," *Financial Post*, June 20, 2003, FP1; Sean Silcoff, "Quebec business adapts to a Wal-Mart world," February 20, 2004, FP8; Ginny Parker, "Will Japan buy Wal-Mart's style?" *Globe and Mail*, April 21, 2004, 11; Steve Match, "'Wal-Mart effect' has officially arrived in Canada," *Financial Post*, April 27, 2004; Marcel Michelson, "Ahold sells chain in Brazil to Wal-Mart," *Financial Post*, March 2, 2004, FP16; Sue Fleming, "Historical society targets Wal-Mart," *Toronto Star*, May 25, 2004, E2; Ann Zimmerman, "Wal-Mart builds up legal team to fight sex discrimination suit," *Globe and Mail*, July 1, 2004, B7; Jerry Langton, "Wal-Mart tests alternative to bar code," *Globe and Mail,* June 3, 2004, B18; Dana Flavelle, "Sam's Club coming to Canada," *Toronto Star*, November 23, 2002, E1.

Index